"After decades of rhetorical criticism of the Gospel of John, here is a serious study of the origins of the Johannine writings, including the three Letters. The author, a recognized Johannine scholar, presents a hypothesis of three literary layers in the Gospel of John which he attributes to three successive authors. Von Wahlde's contribution differs from earlier literary analyses of the Johannine writings by refining the criteria for the distinction of layers. His work can be recommended to all readers interested in the history of Johannine Christianity."

— JOHANNES BEUTLER, SJ
Hochschule St. Georgen,
Frankfurt am Main, Germany

"No one has analysed the composition history of the Gospel and Letters of John with such consistency and thoroughness as von Wahlde. The clarity of his exposition, as he lays bare the criteria that must be used to identify the traditions, his respectful use of other scholarship, and his lucid commentary on each of the strata make this work a milestone in Johannine scholarship."

— FRANCIS J. MOLONEY, SDB
Australian Catholic University

THE EERDMANS CRITICAL COMMENTARY

†David Noel Freedman, *General Editor*

Astrid B. Beck, *Associate Editor*

THE EERDMANS CRITICAL COMMENTARY offers the best of contemporary Old and New Testament scholarship, seeking to give modern readers clear insight into the biblical text, including its background, its interpretation, and its application.

Contributors to the ECC series are among the foremost authorities in biblical scholarship worldwide. Representing a broad range of confessional backgrounds, authors are charged to remain sensitive to the original meaning of the text and to bring alive its relevance for today. Each volume includes the author's own translation, critical notes, and commentary on literary, historical, cultural, and theological aspects of the text.

Accessible to serious general readers and scholars alike, these commentaries reflect the contributions of recent textual, philological, literary, historical, and archaeological inquiry, benefiting as well from newer methodological approaches. ECC volumes are "critical" in terms of their detailed, systematic explanation of the biblical text. Although exposition is based on the original and cognate languages, English translations provide complete access to the discussion and interpretation of these primary sources.

THE GOSPEL AND LETTERS
OF JOHN

VOLUME 3

Commentary on the Three Johannine Letters

Urban C. von Wahlde

WILLIAM B. EERDMANS PUBLISHING COMPANY
GRAND RAPIDS, MICHIGAN / CAMBRIDGE, U.K.

Published 2010 by
Wm. B. Eerdmans Publishing Co.
2140 Oak Industrial Drive N.E., Grand Rapids, Michigan 49505 /
P.O. Box 163, Cambridge CB3 9PU U.K.

Printed in the United States of America

16 15 14 13 12 11 10   7 6 5 4 3 2 1

Library of Congress Cataloging-in-Publication Data

Von Wahlde, Urban C.
The Gospel and Letters of John / Urban C. von Wahlde.
p.   cm.   — (The Eerdmans critical commentary)
Includes bibliographical references and index.
ISBN 978-0-8028-0991-9 (Introduction) (pbk: alk. paper)
ISBN 978-0-8028-2217-8 (Gospel) (pbk: alk. paper)
ISBN 978-0-8028-2218-5 (Epistles) (pbk: alk. paper)
1. Bible. N.T. John — Commentaries.
2. Bible. N.T. Epistles of John — Commentaries.
I. Title.

BS2601.V66   2010
226.5′07 — dc22

2008044624

www.eerdmans.com

Contents

Contents

Contents

Contents

THE SECOND LETTER OF JOHN

Contents

Contents

General Introduction to the Letters

This general introduction will concern issues pertinent to all three of the Johannine Letters. This will include issues of authorship, place, date of composition as well as the order of composition. It will also include a brief discussion of the various rhetorical techniques used by the author in his writings. However, the most important issue pertinent to the discussion of the Letters is the nature of the crisis that divided the community. Here, in the Introduction, I will summarize my view of the crisis, and the evidence for that view will be argued in detail in Appendix 4 (The Crisis That Divided the Johannine Community) below.

The Commentary will dialogue primarily with the watershed commentary of R. E. Brown in 1982 and with those commentaries, monographs and articles that have been written since then. But it will regularly take advantage of the insights of earlier literature also.

A. THE GREEK TEXT OF THE LETTERS

The Greek text of the Letters is less fully attested than is the text of the Gospel. Only two papyri of the Letters remain. The earliest comes from the third century and is designated P^9.[1] The other, P^{74}, is from the seventh century.[2] As a result, the first complete texts are those of the great uncials (Sinaiticus, Alexandrinus and Vaticanus). The critical texts used as the basis for this analy-

---

1. The fragment contains 1 John 4:11-12, 14-17. The text is published in Grenfell and Hunt, *Oxyrhynchus Papyri* 1:4-7.

2. This manuscript is also fragmentary but contains parts of all three Letters: 1 John 1:1, 6; 2:1-2, 7, 13-14, 18-19, 25-26; 3:1-2, 8, 14, 19-20; 4:1, 6-7, 12, 18-19; 5:3-4, 9-10, 17; 2 John 1, 6-7, 13; 3 John 6, 12. The text is published in Kasser, *Papyrus Bodmer XVII*.

sis are the Nestle[27] and UBS[4]. The view of the text of the Letters conducted in this Commentary varies only minimally from these critical editions. The most significant change is perhaps that suggested in 1 John 4:3 to choose *lyei* rather than *mē homologei*. This will be discussed at the appropriate place.

B. A COMMENT ON THE TRANSLATION

In the Introduction to the Commentary on the Gospel, I made several observations about principles employed in the translation of the Greek text of the Gospel. While those principles are also applied here, the Johannine Letters exhibit a number of rhetorical features not found in the Gospel. There are a number of passages in 1 John in which the rhetorical design is quite marked and modestly impressive. The attempt has been made to reproduce these even at the cost of some fluidity in the translation.

At the same time, 1 John is replete with ambiguous antecedents and obscure grammar. This gives rise to considerable frustration and inevitably has its effect on the translation. Two examples may be given from the first four verses of the First Epistle. In those verses, the conjunction *kai* ("and") appears twelve times. Most of these have been retained in order to reproduce the cadence of the original. In addition, in the same four verses the reader meets repeated interruptions that result in half sentences as well as interjections that all but destroy the sequence. The translation will preserve the awkwardness of the original. Where the original is repetitive, the translation will tend to be also. Where the original is awkward, the translation may be also. In this way, I hope that the translation serves as something of a window into the Greek text even at the cost of some readability in its English form.

C. THE CRISIS THAT DIVIDED THE COMMUNITY AT THE TIME OF 1 JOHN

At the time of the Johannine Letters, the Johannine community was experiencing an internal theological crisis. That is clear from the pages of the Letter. However, there is extraordinary diversity of opinion among scholars regarding the nature of that crisis. The problem is that the crisis is not described systematically. Rather, the author has chosen to comment on various aspects of the crisis in a way that is seemingly random. Consequently, in order to determine the nature of this crisis, it is necessary to comb the pages of 1 John for statements that relate to the views of the opponents and for those espoused by the author himself. By combining these various comments, it becomes apparent that the views of each group do in fact constitute an integrated "system" of beliefs. Furthermore, it becomes apparent that the opponents of the author of 1 John based their views on the second edition of the Gospel and mirror the theology of that edition quite closely. At the same time, the views espoused by the author of 1 John are represented within the Gospel by those of the third author.

As a result, not only does the analysis of 1 John itself reveal evidence for the nature of the crisis, but, in the light of the identification of the stages in the development of the Gospel itself, it becomes apparent that these same two views are reflected, respectively, in the second and in the third editions of the Gospel! This provides an additional level of confirmation, not only of the nature of the crisis, but also of the correctness of the identification of the second and third editions of the Gospel.[3]

1. An Overview of the Crisis

By the time 1 John was written, the Johannine community constituted a community independent of the synagogue but one that was undergoing its own internal theological crisis resulting from differing interpretations of the community traditions. One group (the "opponents") takes a strict interpretation of the theology of the second edition of the Gospel regarding the outpouring of the eschatological Spirit and the implications of that outpouring. The group has drawn conclusions that the author of 1 John holds to be inadequate. Consequently, the author writes 1 John to explain the errors of the opponents and to put forward his own understanding of the tradition.

The differences between the author and his opponents are discussed in some detail in Appendix 4 (The Crisis That Divided the Community) in this volume and in more detail in Volume 1, Part 4, which deals with the development of Johannine theology. Here I will provide only a brief overview of the positions of each group and the way these positions relate to the eleven major areas of theology discussed in Volume 1, Part 4.

a. The Views of the Opponents

For the opponents, the ministry of Jesus was focused primarily on the promise that God would give the Spirit, which would be given in its eschatological fullness and would be the source of eternal life, to all who believed in Jesus. Belief

3. It will be mentioned again and again that, although the third edition reflects the views of the author of 1 John, the third edition should not simply be equated with those views. The third edition seeks to incorporate the views of the author of 1 John but at the same time, the third edition goes beyond the thought of 1 John in several respects. These differences will be treated where appropriate.

for the opponents centered on the person of Jesus: those who believed in him would receive the Spirit.

Implicit in this overall view of the ministry were a number of other beliefs that they understood to be based on the second edition of the Gospel. The opponents had their own distinctive understanding of Jesus (#1 Christology). While they agreed that Jesus was all that he claimed to be, they saw this to be the result primarily of his having received the Spirit at his baptism. He was anointed and he was Son of God. His ministry consisted of announcing that God was about to bestow the Spirit in its eschatological manifestation on all those who believed in him (#3 Pneumatology). When the believer received the Spirit, that person too was reborn and became a son (daughter) of God and could be said to be anointed — and to possess the (#4 Eternal) life of God, just as Jesus did. Moreover, because of the transforming effect of the Spirit, the believer would no longer sin and so had no need of ethical directions such as the essential commandment to love (#8 Ethics). The believer had already passed over from death to life (#5 [realized] Eschatology). In all these respects, according to the opponents, the believer was similar to Jesus (#9 Anthropology). Yet another effect of the transformation by the Spirit was that the individual would now know God fully (#6 Knowledge) and would have no need of the "historical" words of Jesus (#2 Belief). The Spirit would provide all the direction that was needed.

The opponents also believed, in accordance with numerous texts in their Scriptures, that the eschatological Spirit would wash them clean from their sins. Thus, although they believed in Jesus, he was considered important because he announced God's gift of the Spirit. However, his death was not an atonement for sin but his means of departure to the Father (#7 Soteriology). Because the believer's guidance came from the Spirit, there was no need or place for human authority. All were united through the Spirit (#10 Ecclesiology). Because the reception of the Spirit was all-important, ritual or anything dealing with the material aspects of religion was simply unnecessary and ineffectual (#11 Attitude toward the material aspects of religion).

b. The Views of the Author

When the author of 1 John corrects his opponents, he does so in what might be called a "both/and" manner. The author was a member of the same community and accepted the same traditions as the opponents although he understood many of those traditions differently. Thus, the task that confronted the author was not one of confirming belief in Jesus versus unbelief, as it had been at the time of the second edition. Rather, the author must now confirm correct belief versus incorrect belief (#2 Belief).

Like the opponents, the author believed that Jesus was anointed and was Son of God, but he believed that Jesus' sonship was unique and one of the aspects of this uniqueness was that Jesus had existed before coming into the world. Jesus was not simply human; he was also divine. Thus, as exalted as the Christology of the second edition was, the third edition makes it even more exalted and brings the identity of Jesus closer to that of God the Father (#1 Christology).

Moreover, although the believer had received an anointing, had been born again, had received eternal life and was now a child of God, the transforming effect of the Spirit was not yet total and complete (#3 Pneumatology; #9 Anthropology). The believer had eternal life but needed to continue to work to bring that life to completion (#4 Eternal life). It was possible for the believer to lose eternal life, and a future judgment would decide one's final destiny (#5 Eschatology). Although the believer was radically sinless, the believer could still sin and so needed ethical directives such as the love commandment (#8 Ethics). Although the believer had knowledge of God and of what was right, the individual still needed to have the external guidance provided by the actual words of Jesus and so needed the commandment to keep the words of Jesus (#6 Knowledge).

Even though the Spirit was the principle of life, it was the atoning death of Jesus which took away sin (#7 Soteriology). Moreover, for the author of 1 John the ongoing religious life was not a purely spiritual undertaking but had a human and material element to it (#11 Attitude toward the material aspects of religion). Not only should the believer keep to the historical words of Jesus (rather than just the inspiration of the Spirit), the believer also had need of ritual actions such as Baptism and the Eucharist. Finally, the believer had need of human intermediaries who would provide leadership and authority within the community (#10 Ecclesiology).

But the most important aspect of the author's thought was the introduction of an apocalyptic worldview as the framework within which the overall ministry of Jesus was to be understood. Thus, although there is no indication that the conflict between the author and his opponents involved the issue of worldview in itself, clearly there *is* a new worldview introduced at the time of 1 John.

2. 1 John as a "Handbook" for Understanding and Dealing with the Community Crisis

In the earliest period of Christianity, it was said that 1 John functioned as a kind of handbook for explaining the Gospel of John and that the interpretation this afforded enabled the acceptance of the Gospel into the canon.[4] The view of the

---

4. This view of the function of 1 John is not confined to early Christianity. Scholars such as C. Köster, Grayston, and Smalley still refer to it in these terms.

role of 1 John presented here confirms that. For the community at the time, the author of 1 John presented the views of the opponents and then explained why they were erroneous. At the same time, he explained the correct interpretation of the tradition.

For the modern reader, 1 John has something of a different function. Once the material of the second and third editions of the Gospel has been identified, we are able to recognize certain features as distinctive of the material. In a number of cases, however, the particular significance of those features is not fully intelligible until we read 1 John. For example, we have noticed the absence of any attention to ethics in the second edition. While we may speculate about the significance of this feature, it is only when we read in 1 John that the opponents held to a theory of ethical perfectionism that we see the full meaning of the absence of ethical material in the second edition. At the same time, it is only when we realize that the author of 1 John argued that ethical instruction is still necessary that we can understand the importance of the love commandment for 1 John and for the third edition of the Gospel.

When we understand 1 John's insistence on keeping the word of Jesus and on remaining faithful to what was "from the beginning," we are able to see that this is a reaction to the lack of attention to the "historical" words of Jesus (the so-called revealer without a revelation) in the second edition. In addition, once we see that the second edition had a one-sided understanding of the role of the Spirit, we are able to see the significance of the description of the Paraclete as "not speaking on his own" but only reminding the believer what Jesus had said. Thus, 1 John confirms not only the understanding of the crisis put forward here but also indirectly confirms the editorial analysis of each edition of the Gospel.

D. THE AUTHORSHIP OF THE THREE LETTERS[5]

1. A Statement of the View Put Forward in This Commentary

The author of 1 John is the same as the author of 2 and 3 John. He is the person who identifies himself in those Letters as "the Elder." He is an eyewitness to the ministry and the foundation of the community's traditions. He is the person

---

5. What can be known of the authors of the three editions of the Gospel is given in the Introduction to each of the editions in Vol. 1. The discussion of the authorship of each of the Letters is given in the General Introduction to the Letters as well as in the Introductions to 2 and 3 John. John the son of Zebedee as well as the Beloved Disciple and the Elder are discussed in individual Appendices.

identified by the author of the third edition as "the Beloved Disciple." The reasons for proposing this view are explained in detail in the paragraphs that follow.

2. Is the Author of 1 John Also the Author of 2 and 3 John?

Brown quotes statistics showing that 70 percent of the "significant words" of 3 John are found in either 1 John or the Gospel. Also 86 percent of the significant words in 2 John are likewise found in either 1 John or the Gospel.[6] These similarities are impressive — so impressive that some scholars have argued that they are due to imitation. One cannot completely disprove such a theory but the fact of variations in wording suggests that the similarities are probably not due to imitation since an imitator would have sought to achieve even greater similarity.

However, some more substantive differences do appear.[7] First is the obvious fact that the author identifies himself in 2 and 3 John but not in 1 John. However, 1 John is not a true letter as are 2 and 3 John. This may explain why the author does not identify himself in the first of these documents.

In 1 John, *tekna* refers to the "children" of God or of the devil, whereas in 2 John it refers to the members of the community as children "of the Elect Lady" rather than children of God. Moreover, in 1 John other terms (such as *teknia* and *paidia*) are used besides *tekna*.

The fact that the title "the Elect Lady" appears only in 2 John is striking but this is the only Johannine letter to a group. The Third Letter of John is a letter to an individual and, as has been said repeatedly, 1 John is not a letter at all.

Some have argued that 2 and 3 John do not manifest the apocalyptic dualism of 1 John.[8] However, the lack of explicit development of this dualism in the Letters is due precisely to the fact that they are occasional letters rather than a tract like 1 John. At the same time, while apocalyptic dualism is less overt in the Letters, the language used is that which was used apocalyptically in 1 John, and the context of the Letter presumes that worldview. This will be discussed in the Introductions to those Letters.

Only in 2 John 2 is truth said to "abide." The next verse (2 John 3) speaks of "Jesus Christ, son of the Father." This latter phrase is unique in the New Testament. The combination "Jesus Christ" does not appear in the first or second editions of the Gospel but appears frequently in 1 John and several times in the

---

6. Brown lists many of these in Appendix I, Charts One and Two (*Epistles* 755-59). The argument of this section follows closely that put forward by Brown, *Epistles* 16-19. See also Schnackenburg, *Epistles* 268-73.

7. The listing of all but the last of the problems comes from Brown, *Epistles* 17-19.

8. See, for example, Bergmeier, "Verfasserproblem" 96-100, esp. 96-97; Lieu, *Second and Third* 69, 84, 87. Strecker (*Epistles* 226) argues that the dualism manifests an earlier stage of development than that of 1 John and the Gospel.

third edition. Its appearance here is an indication of the similarity between the writings. The awkwardness of "the Son of the Father" is a grammatical peculiarity rather than a theological one. Theologically, Jesus is repeatedly said to be Son in relation to God as Father. Since this was an issue in the community at the time of 1 John, it is not surprising that the Elder attempts to emphasize it here with the resulting awkwardness.

Only in 2 John 3 does "in truth and love" appear joined. Again, this would seem to be a matter of grammatical peculiarity rather than of theological difference since it was the hope of the author of 1 John as well as of the author of 2 John that both faithfulness to the word of Jesus (truth) and mutual love were the commandments given to the community by God. The close relation of these two concepts is also apparent in 3 John where the brothers are said to witness to Gaius' truth (v. 3) and his love (v. 6).

The phrase "walk in truth" appears in 2 John 4 and in 3 John 3, but nowhere else. Yet there is an instance of "walking in light" (1 John 1:7). Bergmeier argues that the identification of "truth" with a body of teaching in 2 John is distinctive of that letter.[9] However, the obligation to walk in truth is said to be the object of a commandment, and this commandment is expressed in 1 John as keeping the word of Jesus. Thus, the tradition found in 1 John and 2 John is consistent in focusing on the necessity of remaining faithful to the tradition and not giving in to an unfettered inspiration of the Spirit. Thus, the theology here is consistent.

Finally, in 2 John 9 Jesus is referred to as "the Christ" (rather than the more common "the Son" or "Jesus Christ"). This is the only instance in the Johannine literature of such a use. The use of "teaching" (noun) in the same verse is also unusual but does appear in the Gospel (7:17; 18:19) and in 2 John 10.

In 3 John, a number of theologically significant words appear that appear only there.[10] In v. 2, the Elder expresses the hope that Gaius will "do well" *(euodousthai)* both physically and spiritually. While this is a new term, it is warranted by its presence in the part of a letter known as the "health wish." In v. 7, it is said that the brothers have gone forth "for the sake of the Name." This expression is not found earlier in the Johannine literature. It does reflect a development in ecclesiological language but not in theology. The same may be said of the term "assembly" *(ekklēsia)* (vv. 6, 9, 10). The reference to "imitating" good (v. 11) is unique to the Johannine literature but does not indicate a change of authorship in itself. The two dualistically opposed statements in v. 11 "doing good"/"doing evil" *(agathopoiōn/kakopoiōn* v. 11de) represent a change in lan-

---

9. Bergmeier, "Verfasserproblem" 96.

10. I do not include words such as *philoprōteuō* ("to wish to be first," v. 9) and *synergoi* ("coworkers," v. 8) or the language associated with the reception and support of the missionaries. Although these words may appear only here, they are required by the specific context of the Letter and do not indicate distinct authors.

guage. But the theological framework remains the same. At the same time typically Johannine expressions occur throughout which would seem to balance out the changes.

There is a shift in language, but most of these can be attributed to the context of letter writing as opposed to the more formal context of either Gospel or "tract" (1 John). As a result, it seems best to conclude that, in spite of differences of language and terminology, the author of 1 John is the same as that of 2 and 3 John.[11]

3. Is the Author an Eyewitness to the Ministry of Jesus?

The author of 1 John begins with an emphatic assurance that he is one of a group that has had personal experience of the ministry of Jesus. Strecker argues that this is not possible because the author is too far removed in time from the events themselves.[12] Schnackenburg says the author belonged to a group of eyewitnesses but was not one himself. Schnackenburg further suggests that the author may be a disciple of an original disciple and so feel qualified to represent his witness as that of an eyewitness. While this theory is attractive, there is no way to prove or disprove it.[13]

Another possible explanation is that the author speaks as a representative of the Johannine "school," that group of authoritative authors responsible for the second edition of the Gospel, for 1, 2, 3 John and for the third edition of the Gospel.[14] In this view, the "we" could be said to have been eyewitnesses even if the time had come when no specific individual still alive had been an eyewitness.

However, I am of the opinion that the author of 1 John and the author of the third edition put too much emphasis on the fact that the testimony being given is that of an eyewitness for this to be anything other than factual. The Second and

---

11. Strecker (*Epistles* xl) is one of the few who would dissent from this view. Although he would see 2 and 3 John as coming from the same author, for Strecker "the differences in form and content make an identical authorship unlikely" for the three Letters. In addition, he points to "unique features . . . in the realms of theology and church discipline." Among these is what he sees as a more primitive development in the realm of apocalyptic dualism, as I noted above. In my view, Strecker seems to base his decision on too rigid an understanding of what "could" happen. That is, I see no reason why an individual could not write in different genres ("tract" and "letter"), writing anonymously in the one and identifying himself by the title of Elder in the other. Moreover, the differences in the presentation of apocalyptic are certainly explainable on the basis of the differences of genre, as I suggest above.

12. Strecker, *Epistles* 13-15.

13. Schnackenburg, *Epistles* 55.

14. This is the view of Brown, *Epistles* 158-61. Whether the first edition of the Gospel was a product of the Johannine school is difficult to say given the fact that its theology reflects so little of the later viewpoints.

Third Letters of John were written to communities where the author was known. If the author were not truly an eyewitness, the community would have known that the claim was false. Moreover, the author identifies himself as "the Elder," a seeming recognition of the fact that he was of an unusually advanced age. The chief reason for skepticism in this regard is that the commonly proposed date for the composition of the Gospel and the Letters (ca. 90-100) is so late.

I have proposed that the Letters had been composed before the year 70 and the death of the BD/Elder had taken place by the year 90. If the Elder had been one of the younger disciples of Jesus and if he did live to an old age (a proposal based primarily on evidence in the Gospel and the Letters, not on external tradition), then it is possible to think of the Elder as dying at perhaps the age of 80. This is hardly an unreasonable age for a long-lived person in the first century, even if such age was not the average.

4. Is the Author the Same as the Author of the Second Edition of the Gospel?

There are considerable theological differences between the second and third editions as we have seen.[15] One of the most striking of these differences is the introduction of an apocalyptic perspective. Moreover, the author of the Letters repeatedly supplements the perspective of the second edition. We do not know if the viewpoints of the second author and those of the third were the same and thus the opponents simply *misunderstood* the tradition, or whether the viewpoints of the two authors were different and so the author of 1 John saw his work as a *correction* and *nuancing* not only of the opponents' views but also of the tradition itself (as it appeared in the second edition). Brown argues that the Gospel was written at the time of the crisis with the synagogue and, because of the desire to emphasize certain elements of the tradition, other elements were neglected.[16] Thus, it would be neglect rather than deliberate difference of opinion that would explain how certain elements of the tradition that were "from the beginning" could be neglected by the opponents.

If the position of the opponents was a consistent one, derived from their understanding of prerogatives of the eschatological Spirit, it is more difficult to say that their view was simply one of misunderstanding. If this is the case, then the second edition would seem to be the product of a segment of the community that later was nuanced by the Elder, who shared many of the insights of the opponents but who at the same time witnessed to other dimensions of those in-

---

15. For a discussion of whether the author of the Letters was the same as the author of the third edition, see the Introduction to the Third Edition.

16. Brown, *Epistles* 34-35.

sights and insisted on their essential importance for the tradition. In short, there is no substantial evidence for identifying the author of the second edition with the author of 1 John.

5. The Author of 1 John, the Elder of 2 and 3 John and the Beloved Disciple

We saw above that the anonymous author of 1 John is the same as the person who refers to himself as "the Elder" in 2 and 3 John. It was this person who was an eyewitness to the ministry, who was the disciple whose witness to the tradition was recognized as "true," and who lived to an old age. It is argued in detail in Appendix 9 (The Beloved Disciple) in this volume that this is the same person upon whom the third author bestows the title "the disciple whom Jesus loved." That argument will not be repeated here.

E. DATE OF COMPOSITION

1. The Order of the Letters

Most scholars agree that the canonical order of the Letters also represents the chronological order of their composition.[17] It is tempting to argue that ideas developed in 1 John are reflected in 2 and 3 John. However, this is not a foolproof argument, for we must acknowledge the possibility that what is assumed in 2 and 3 John is based not on 1 John itself but either on oral communications that took place face-to-face or even on the basis of other lost documents.

In 2 and 3 John, there are a number of theologically significant terms that are *hapax legomena* (or nearly so) in the Johannine tradition. For example, in 2 John, we find "reward" *(misthos)* (v. 8);[18] "teaching" *(didachē)* (v. 9 [twice], 10);[19] the title "the Christ" *(ho Christos)* (as an independent substantive referring to Jesus) (v. 9). Yet it must be said that, while the particular terms are new, they all have a related meaning elsewhere in the tradition. In 3 John, such terms as "assembly" *(ekklēsia)* (v. 6, 9, 10), "for the sake of the name" *(hyper tou*

---

17. Strecker (*Epistles* xlii) is one of the few who hold a different position. In keeping with his view that 2 and 3 John reflect a more primitive form of the apocalyptic worldview, Strecker holds that 2 and 3 John were written near the turn of the first century and that 1 John and the Gospel were written near mid-2nd century. His student Schnelle holds the same view (*Antidocetic* 235).

18. This is not precisely a *hapax legomenon* since it appears in John 4:36, referring to the harvest.

19. It appears in John 7:16, 17; 18:19 referring to the teaching of Jesus.

11

onomatos) (v. 7); and "coworkers" *(synergoi)* (v. 8) appear. These terms particularly are distanced further from the ordinary Johannine vocabulary. In 3 John, "soul" *(psychē)* is used to refer to the spiritual part of the person while in the Gospel it is used to refer to physical life.

In both 2 and 3 John, these terms reflect a later stage of language rather than an earlier one. In addition, the church situation in 3 John whereby Demetrius assumes a role of authority over the community appears to reflect a later, rather than an earlier, period in the community's development. This is consistent with seeing the canonical order as chronological.

2. The Date of the Letters in Relation to the Gospel

Elsewhere in this Commentary, I have provided detailed arguments for seeing 1 John as having been completed prior to the third edition of the Gospel.[20] I would also argue that 2 and 3 John were also completed prior to the third edition of the Gospel. If the title of BD is an honorific title given to the Elder after his death, then clearly 2 and 3 John were completed before the completion of the third edition.

Although 2 and 3 John reflect a vocabulary that is different from that of 1 John or the third edition of the Gospel, I would attribute that to the differences in genre. Clearly, 2 and 3 John are occasional letters, which allude to most matters rather than discussing them in detail. Because they deal directly with matters of the community, they employ terms that would not be used in the kind of "glossing" that takes place in the third edition of the Gospel. Nor would these terms be used in 1 John, which is written as a "tract" that lays out the differences between the author and his opponents in a much more detailed way than either 2 or 3 John.

However, the view of the role of human authority in the third edition is more advanced than in any of the Letters. There is no recourse in 1 John except to "witness" to "what was from the beginning." In 2 and 3 John, the primary authority is that of "the Elder" who in his actions and words shows no sign of having an authoritative office. At the same time, he is in confrontation with Diotrephes who also claims an authority but one that is not linked to any defined "office." The most that is said is that Diotrephes "likes to act as leader." Yet in the third edition, the community has recognized the role of Peter as a human authority given care of the sheep. As I explained in the Interpretation of that passage in the Commentary, this reflects a situation in which the role of the BD is related to (and subordinated to) the role of Peter as shepherd. Thus, we can be reasonably certain that the third edition was composed after all three of the Letters.

---

20. See "The Date of the Third Edition" (Vol. 1, Part 3, Section 3.10).

3. Assigning a Specific Date to the Composition of the Letters

Scholars have varied widely in their estimates of the date for the Letters.[21] Brown provides no argumentation but simply speculates that "(m)ost probably 1 John was written not only after GJohn but after an interval long enough for a debate to have arisen about the implications of GJohn and for a schism to have taken place."[22] Then starting from his proposal that the Gospel was written ca. 90, he proposes that 1 John "may feasibly be dated to *ca.* 100." He further suggests that 2 John was written about the same time and 3 John about ten years later.[23]

While the assignment of specific dates to the various stages in the development of the Johannine tradition continues to be speculative, both internal and external evidence provide some sense of the time before which the Gospel (and therefore the three Letters) must have been written.

If we review the composition process proposed in this commentary, several elements of the dating process can be reasonably assured. First, the sequence of the three editions is quite certain, given the way each edition relates to the previous one. Second, the dating of 1 John relative to the second and third editions of the Gospel is quite certain, given the number of features in both 1 John and in the third edition of the Gospel.

Third, the period of time between the second edition and 1 John, and between 1 John and the third edition cannot have been great. The author of 1 John makes it clear that the intra-community dispute resulted in defections from the community. He would not have waited long to compose his refutation of their beliefs. Fourth, it is very unlikely that the community would have waited long to incorporate within the text of the Gospel the modifications and clarifications contained in the material of the third edition. Again, the attestation of these matters within the text of the Gospel would have been too important for the author's community to postpone it for an extended period. Fifth, it is clear that the BD/Elder had died before the completion of the third edition. Finally, although we do not have direct evidence of the death of the BD/Elder, it does not seem likely that the BD/Elder would have lived as late as A.D. 90. Therefore the closer we get to A.D. 90, the more likely we are to be approaching the date of his death, if we have not already passed it. Consequently, it seems reasonable to conclude that the final edition of the Gospel was almost certainly completed before A.D. 90 and that the Letters were completed perhaps a year earlier. Just how much before

21. Opinion ranges from A.D. 60-65 (J. R. Robinson) to A.D. 170-180 (Baur). Brown (*Epistles* 101) and Klauck (*Erste Johannesbrief* 49) provide surveys.

22. Brown, *Epistles* 101.

23. Brown, *Epistles* 101. Klauck (*Erste Johannesbrief* 48-49) proposes a date between 100 and 110.

A.D. 90 the writing of the Letters and the death of the BD/Elder occurred is impossible to say, but a date several years before that is not impossible.

If we turn to look at the external evidence, evidence concerning the first attestation of the Letters, we have an independent way of approximating the time before the Letters were probably written.

There is evidence of knowledge of 1 and 2 John by Polycarp in his *Letter to the Philippians*.[24] Although the date of Polycarp's *Letter* is difficult to determine, it is clear from *Phil.* 13.2 that, at the time when that letter was written, Ignatius of Antioch was still alive. Ignatius' death can be dated to the reign of Trajan (A.D. 98-117). Thus, the date of A.D. 108 for Ignatius' death, as proposed by Eusebius *(Chronicon),* is not unreasonable and, if we were to assume that the Letter of Polycarp was written even a short time before Ignatius' death, we would arrive at a date of A.D. 100-105 for the *Letter of Polycarp* and, once again assuming that Polycarp had known of 1 and 2 John some time before writing his letter, we would arrive at a date of about A.D. 95 for Polycarp's awareness of those Letters. Allowing additional time between their composition and Polycarp's awareness of them, we come to a period of A.D. 85-90 for the actual composition. This is a date not far from the date proposed on the basis of internal evidence.

But even this date is acknowledged to be speculative, but at the same time, it does lie within the commonly accepted range of dates for the composition of the Gospel (although the dating proposed here lies at the lower end of that range).

F. PLACE OF COMPOSITION OF THE THREE LETTERS

Nothing internal to the three Letters gives any indication of where they were composed. There is, however, some slight external evidence, particularly with respect to 1 John, that should be considered.

In discussing the provenance of the third edition of the Gospel, it was suggested that a number of features tended to locate the final stage of the Johannine tradition at Ephesus. In fact, some of those features relate to the Letters rather than the Gospel as such. For example, the first reference to the Johannine Letters comes from the *Letter to the Philippians* of Polycarp. Polycarp was from Smyrna, a city about twenty miles from Ephesus. Moreover, the "heresy" combated by Polycarp bears a marked similarity to that confronted by 1 John and the third edition of the Gospel.[25] Together these factors suggest

---

24. See the discussion in Appendix 4 (The Crisis That Divided the Johannine Community) in this volume.

25. These similarities are also discussed in Appendix 4 (The Crisis That Divided the Johannine Community) in this volume.

that the Letters were also written either in Ephesus or in the area around Ephesus. Furthermore, if it could be established that Papias' John the Elder is to be identified with the Elder of the Johannine Letters, we would have one more indication that the Letters may have come from Ephesus, since some traditions identify John the Elder with that city and his grave was said to be there. Meager as these indications are, there are no others.

G. THE FORMAT OF THE COMMENTARY

The Commentary will be arranged according to the following pattern. First, there will be my translation of the Text. This will be followed by detailed Notes on the Text. Finally, there will be the Interpretation of the Text. The Interpretation will often include subdivisions dealing with the structure or with literary techniques present in the passage followed by the Interpretation proper.

Introduction to 1 John

The First Letter of John represents a stage in the history of the Johannine tradition subsequent to the Gospel's second edition, but prior to its third. This conclusion is reached on the basis of a detailed comparison of features in 1 John with similar features in the third edition. In all cases, the third edition either represents a development of ideas found in 1 John or presumes ideas expressed in that Letter. The detailed arguments for this view are given in the Analysis of the Third Edition in the section entitled "The Dating of the Third Edition Relative to 1 John" and will not be repeated here. We have discussed the arguments for the actual date of the Letters in the General Introduction to the Letters.

A. AN OVERVIEW OF THE PURPOSE OF COMPOSITION

At the time 1 John was written, there was an internal theological crisis dividing the Johannine community. This crisis was caused by two divergent interpretations of the community's traditions. The crisis had gotten to the point that some in the community had left, evidently to form their own community guided by their own beliefs.

It is clear that 1 John was written to deal with this crisis. However, the Letter is not aimed primarily at the opponents but at the author's own followers. The author speaks to those who have remained faithful to him and faithful to the tradition as he understood it. The author is not in direct dialogue with his opponents. Consequently, the majority of his Letter explains how his views differ from those of the opponents and why the opponents have no right to make their claims.

While the author is concerned primarily with the refutation of the opponents' views, at times he exhorts the faithful to live out the ideals that they hold (e.g., 2:15-17; 3:3, 9, 16-18). At still other times, he seems intent on encouraging his readers by speaking to them of the hope and confidence they should have (e.g., 3:3, 19-21; 4:17-18; 5:13-14) and the reward that awaits them (e.g., 3:2). Occasionally these three aspects of the author's purpose can be identified and isolated from one another, but most often his refutation, exhortation and encouragement are woven together in a way that does not allow them to be separated easily.

B. THE GENRE OF 1 JOHN

There have been numerous attempts to define the genre of 1 John. Although it is traditionally called a "letter," it lacks the characteristic formal aspects of ancient letters in that it has no identification of the sender or the addressee, or any of the concluding formulas found in ancient letters.[1] Moreover, although it has many of the characteristics of a tract, it certainly is not an impersonal one. It is addressed to the members of the author's community (not to the adversaries) and there is a regular use of the first and second person in direct address. There is also exhortation and there are homiletic elements. If we attempt to describe its genre in terms of its internal characteristics rather than by association with other known examples, I would describe it as "exhortatory exposition." That is, it attempts to explain the differences between the views of the opponents and those of the author and his followers. In this sense, it is "exposition." At the same time, the author regularly exhorts his readers/hearers to continue in their faithfulness to the viewpoint he expounds in the Letter. This may help us recall the true nature of the document more than any more formal designation. Nevertheless, for the sake of convenience, I will regularly refer to 1 John by its more traditional designation as "letter."

C. WORLDVIEW

The worldview is that of apocalyptic dualism similar to that of the SDQ and the *T12P*.[2] It is the worldview that also characterizes the third edition of the Gospel.

In the Analysis of the third edition, we provided a detailed discussion of the characteristics of apocalyptic; here we need call attention to only some of

1. A brief survey of these features is given in Appendix 6 (Formal Elements in Greek Letter Writing) in this volume.

2. That this is commonly recognized can be seen from the surveys of parallels in the SDQ and in the *T12P* in, for example, Brown, *Epistles* 487; Klauck, *Erste Johannesbrief* 242-43; Strecker, *Epistles* 140-41.

the features of apocalyptic that appear in 1 John. The modified dualism of apocalyptic is evident in the contrast between the Spirit of Truth and the Spirit of Deception (4:1-6), between being children of God and being children of the devil (3:10), between being "of" God (3:10) and "of" the devil (3:8, 12), between walking in the light (1:7) and walking in the darkness (1:6; 2:9-11), between being "of the world" (4:5) or "going out into the world" (2 John 7) and not being of the world (implicit in 1 John 4:2d) and "conquering" the world (5:4).

But this dualism is "ethical," in that one's status is determined by one's actions (e.g., 2:9-11). The dualism is also "modified" (that is, God is ultimately superior to the spirit of evil) as is evident from 4:4, where it is said that "he who is in you is greater than he who is in the world."

As is typical of apocalyptic, there are references to a final hour of judgment (2:18e; 4:17), a figure associated with that hour, that is, the Antichrist (2:18cd, 22c; 4:3b ["whom you have heard is coming"[3]]; 2 John 7); "the Evil One" (1 John 5:19), "the Liar" (2:22a); "false prophets" (4:1) and also reference to a Second Coming of Jesus (2:28; 3:2). Moreover, the notion of possession by evil spirits is implicit in 5:18-19 (where it is said that "the Evil One does not touch" the believer, but "the world lies in the grasp of the Evil One"). Like the *T12P,* 1 John speaks of mutual love that is extended only to other members of the community (2:10; 3:10, 14, 16-18, 23; 4:11-12; 5:2, etc.) reflecting the conviction that love of those who are "of" the devil is to take part in their evil deeds (2 John 10-11; cf. 3 John 5-8).

D. THE STRUCTURE OF THE LETTER

In his commentary, Brown surveys a large number of theories prior to his own regarding the structure of 1 John. That survey will not be repeated here. From a review of the commentaries appearing since that of Brown, it is evident that the variety of opinion has not been erased by the appearance of Brown's work. Although there is unanimity about the existence of a Prologue and a Conclusion, a variety of other theories exist with respect to the body of the letter. Some (e.g., Smith) see the letter as consisting of two major parts as does Brown. Others (e.g., Smalley) see two major parts but different ones from those suggested by Brown. Still others hold that the letter consists of three major parts (e.g., Beutler, Culpepper, Klauck, Painter, Schnackenburg), or six (e.g., Grayston, or seven (e.g., Strecker).

My own view is that the observations first made by Feuillet and adapted by Brown are the most helpful.[4] They both divide the Letter into two parts, each

---

3. See Brown (*Epistles* 365) regarding "this bold use of apocalyptic imagery in 1 John."
4. Feuillet, "Structure."

dominated by the themes of "light" and "love" and initiated by the recollection of the "proclamation" that God is love and that we are to love one another. I would see those two themes as dominating the two halves of the Letter. As we will see in the discussion of the third edition of the Gospel, the author of that edition has imposed his own overarching structure upon the Gospel, and that thematic structure follows the themes of "Jesus as light" and "the need for mutual love."[5] The fact that these themes also appear in the Gospel in material identified on literary grounds as coming from the third edition is a strong indication that the author of the third edition recognized those themes as central to the Letter and so intended to provide the final edition of the Gospel with a similar perspective.

Within the two halves of the Letter, I think it is possible to identify sections much as Brown does, although I would disagree with some of his decisions about where those divisions occur. At times, the structure would seem to contain a logical development; at other times, it seems to be based simply on the occurrence of catchwords that chain various sections together.

In short, I have not found any but the most general of structures to be satisfying. The more detail that is claimed for the outline, the greater the number of features that can be found that are not consistent with the proposal. As a result, I will occasionally comment on elements of overarching structure but will focus primarily on the smaller, individual units of the Letter, attempting to understand the internal structure and thought of the unit itself as well as the relation of the unit to its immediate context.

E. HOW THE AUTHOR REFUTES HIS OPPONENTS

The opponents denied a permanent role for Jesus in the attainment of eternal life. However, these opponents claimed to believe in God the Father and in the eschatological outpouring of the Spirit. Consequently, in order to refute the views of the opponents, the author of 1 John couches his overall argument in a framework in which his primary reference is to God the Father rather than to Jesus. This is a major shift from the orientation of the first and second editions of the Gospel.

As evidence of this shift in focus from Jesus to the Father, we see that the features that are attributed to Jesus in the second and in the third editions of the Gospel are attributed to God the Father in 1 John. Thus, in 1 John, God is "the

---

5. Both Feuillet and Brown see the Gospel as having been written before 1 John and so would argue that the Letter reflects the structure of the Gospel. However, I would argue that the author of 1 John employed these themes first, to structure his Letter, and that the author of the third edition then adopted them as structuring elements for his own work.

light" (1:5); but, in the Gospel, Jesus is "the light" (1:4 [3E]; 8:12 [3E]; 9:5 [3E]; 11:9 [3E]; 12:35-36 [3E]). In 1 John, "life" comes from the Father (2:25; 5:11-12, 16) rather than from Jesus, as is the case in the Gospel (1:4 [3E]; 3:36 [3E]; 4:10-15 [2E]; 6:54 [3E]; 11:25 [3E]; 14:6 [3E], etc.).[6] In 1 John, "the commandments" are the commandments of God (2:3, 4; 3:22-24; 4:21; 5:2-3; 2 John 4, 6), rather than the commandments of Jesus (13:34; 14:15, 21; 15:10, 12 [all 3E]) as they are in the Gospel. In 1 John, "the word" is the word of God (1:10; 2:5, 7, 14) rather than Jesus' word (John 4:41 [3E]; 5:24 [3E]; 8:31 [3E], 37 [2E], 43, 51, 52 [all 3E]; 14:23-24 [3E]; 15:3 [2E]).[7]

By taking this approach, the author argues from the "common ground" he shares with his opponents and so hopes to refute the opponents' views on the basis of what they themselves would claim as their prerogatives as believers.

Within this general orientation of his argument, the author uses several other types of distinctive arguments. He appeals to the witness of those who saw, touched, etc. He reminds his readers that what he is saying is what they themselves had direct contact with. He also appeals to the fact that what he is witnessing to them is what was from the beginning. His words are not "new" but "old." The author uses the principle that was later articulated by Tertullian (*Adv. Prax.* 2): "what is earlier is true and what is later is counterfeit." He appeals to the commandments given by God. These commandments are twofold: to base their belief on what was given them by Jesus and to love one another.

But the most extensive means of refuting the opponents is by providing tests and ways to know if the claims are true and actual. Specifically the author insists that every prerogative claimed by the opponents (see Chart E-6, pp. 367-69) has to be tested in terms of both correct belief and ethics.

F. STYLE

The style of the author of 1 John is one of the most difficult in the New Testament. One of the major problems is the repeated ambiguity of pronouns and

---

6. It is also instructive to note that with respect to being "begotten," in 3:5 [2E], the believer is to be born "of the Spirit" whereas in 1 John the believer is born "of God" (2:29; 3:9 [twice]; 4:7; 5:1 [twice], 4, 18 [twice]). Both are theologically correct in the sense that the one is the immediate and the other the ultimate source of being begotten. At the same time, the consistent use of God the Father as the primary reference point in 1 John was undoubtedly chosen because of the author's desire to base his argument on theological convictions his opponents shared.

7. Yet, in each case, what is claimed for Jesus is related to a similar claim made for the Father. Thus, the Father gave to Jesus to have life in himself (John 5:26). The commandments given the disciples by Jesus are correlated to the two commandments given to Jesus by the Father (cf. 10:18; 12:49). The word that Jesus speaks is given him by the Father (for example, 5:38; 8:55; 12:49; 17:6, 14, 17).

their antecedents. Two of the most notorious ambiguities are the antecedents of "just" in 2:29 and of "that one" in 3:7. But many of the pronouns throughout 2:28–3:10 are also ambiguous. The same is true for 5:14 and 5:16. The antecedent of *"autēi"* in 2 John 6 is of considerable significance but is difficult to determine.

Another feature of the author's style is that at times transitions from one theme to the other are so sudden and abrupt that they could easily be called interruptions or interjections. Among the more striking examples are the following: (1) the introduction of the discussion of how the blood of Jesus cleanses us from sin in 1:7c is so abrupt that scholars such as Bultmann and O'Neil have proposed that it is a redactional insertion; (2) both the purpose of 2:12-14 and its relation to the previous (and subsequent) context are difficult, if not impossible, to determine; (3) 2:25 is abrupt and unexpected in its context; (4) the introduction of the Spirit in 3:24c is unexpected and poorly related to the earlier context and would appear to be intended only as an introduction to the discussion of the Spirits in 4:1-6. At times the author even fails to complete a sentence before beginning another theme. The most prominent example of this is in the first two verses of the Letter.

It would be easy to argue that these features indicate that the Letter is simply haphazard in its construction. But other features suggest not. Elsewhere in the Commentary I have shown that every claim made by the opponents is tested in terms of correct belief and in terms of mutual love somewhere within 1 John.[8] The consistency and thoroughness of this are remarkable, yet they are scattered so thoroughly that it is difficult at first to believe the process is deliberate.

Another feature of the Letter is that the author seems to speak often by allusion, using elliptical language that was well known to the community but difficult for a reader unfamiliar with this language.[9] For example, he introduces into the (written) Johannine vocabulary the term "anointing" *(chrisma)* (2:20, 27), the figure of the Antichrist (2:18, 22; 4:3), the designation of Jesus as a Paraclete (2:1), the mention of God's "seed" (3:9), and the reference to "idols" (5:21) in a way that seems to indicate the terms were known to the community. The cryptic designations of groups within the community as "Fathers" and "Young People" were undoubtedly classifications familiar to the readers. He speaks of "coming in the flesh" (4:2; 2 John 7) and of "coming in water" and "in blood" (5:6-7) in a way that indicates these were not new expressions but ones

---

8. See Chart E-6, pp. 367-69.

9. Nida (*Style* 49) comments: "When participants in a communication know one another well, it is not necessary to spell out all the details in complete sentences. Accordingly, omissions are not only appropriate, but they also serve to signal the degree of interpersonal identification." This is noted by de Boer (*Perspectives* 257, who also refers to de Jonge, *Brieven* 11). See also de Boer, "Death" 326-46, esp. 330-31.

familiar to his readers. Perhaps this was a kind of theological jargon developed during the debate regarding the meaning of the tradition. Most important of all are the statements that are understood to be the object of one's confession. We hear of the need to confess that "Jesus is the Christ" (2:22); "Jesus Christ come in the flesh" (4:2); "Jesus is the Son of God" (4:15; cf. 5:5); "Jesus Christ coming in the flesh" (2 John 7). All of these were certainly slogans employed in the debate and carried a content that supersedes the simple formulations that are found in the text.

All of this supports the view that 1 John was composed in a time of crisis and of great emotion. The author is intent on making his point and he does so with such intensity that he is unable to compose with the organization and clarity that one would normally expect. One important thought leads to another, and so the units are chained together rather than organized by some larger principle.

G. LITERARY TECHNIQUES OF THE AUTHOR

As we attempt to understand 1 John, we need to come to grips with the way the author writes. The author of the Letters has a distinct style, quite different from that of the authors of the Gospel. It is a style that to many has seemed a lack of style. Houlden has spoken of this as the author's predilection for combining "favorite words in all directions."[10] Brown has noted the frustratingly ambiguous use of pronouns that at times brings reading to a halt. This expresses well the first impression of the Letters on the reader. However, underlying this seeming randomness are several literary and rhetorical techniques that, while not of the first rank, are nevertheless noteworthy. Eight of these are listed here and described briefly.

1. Poetic Identification

It is common in the Johannine tradition for the authors to identify certain characteristics with the person. This is done typically with regard to Jesus and to the Spirit. Thus, in 1:2 "And the life was revealed" is not to be taken literally but intends to say that Jesus (who is the source or the embodiment of life) was revealed. In 5:6, it is said that "the Spirit is the truth." But in 4:6 we hear of "the Spirit *of* Truth." Here again the identification of the Spirit with Truth is poetic and indicates the close association of the Spirit with truth and the Spirit as the source and guarantor of truth.[11]

---

10. Houlden, *Epistles* 145.
11. This occurs frequently in the Gospel also. See at John 6:63.

2. Catchword (or "Chaining") Technique

Catchword technique is the device by which a word appearing at the end of one unit also appears at the beginning of another unit and introduces a new topic there. When this is used throughout a passage, it can be referred to as "chaining." There are two extensive instances of chaining within passages at the beginning of 1 John. The first appears within 1 John 1:3–2:2. In v. 3, there was mention of "proclaiming." This is linked to "proclamation" in v. 5 that leads to the discussion of "darkness" (in v. 5e), which links with "darkness" (in 6a), which then leads to a discussion of "sin" (in v. 7c) which in turn links with "sin" (in v. 8a) and continues as the catchword through 2:2. The second instance of extended chaining appears in 1 John 2:3-11.[12]

In addition, the author uses catchwords to join larger sections of his composition. In these instances, the first instance of the catchword is often somewhat awkward in its context but more appropriate to the second, related context. This technique appears in the last phrase of 2:27, which is awkward in relation to its context but establishes a catchword connection with the beginning of 2:28; in 3:10, which is awkward in relation to its context but establishes a catchword connection with the beginning of 3:11; in the last clause of 3:24, which is awkward in relation to what precedes it but provides a catchword connection with what follows in 4:1; in the way the second-last phrase in 4:12 ("God abides in us") is awkward in its context but provides a catchword to 4:13; in the way the theme of love in 4:19 provides a catchword connection to 4:20 where the theme of love is taken up again. There is also something of a catchword established between the confession of Jesus as Son of God in 5:5 and the mention of him in 5:6 as "Jesus Christ."[13] And a final, clearer example of the connection appears in the conclusion of 5:12, which speaks of Jesus as "Son of God," and prepares for the reintroduction of the term at the beginning of the next section in 5:13.

3. Chiasm

While chiasm is used only minimally in the Gospel, it is a favorite technique of the author of the three Letters.[14] Sometimes these chiasms function simply as

---

12. Because of the complexity, the reader is referred to the Commentary on these verses for a detailed description.

13. The mention of "Son of God" appears in 5:5 as the conclusion of a chiasm that began with the confession of Jesus as "the Christ." It may be that the author thinks of this combined confession as somehow providing the catchword to the following section.

14. Chiasms will be identified in the translation by indentation and by the presence of a "+" before each element of the chiasm. The classic study of chiasm is that of Lund, *Chiasmus*. While failing to recognize chiasms neglects an important element of style and arrangement of thought and thus fails to do full justice to the author, it is equally important to recognize the danger of pro-

stylistic devices. But more generally they are structural means of indicating similarities and contrasts between ideas. As such they can be helpful in clarifying the meaning of words, phrases or a passage in cases where the parallelism between features is clear but where the meaning of one element may be ambiguous.[15] They are also useful for determining the extent of material considered by the author to belong to a given "unit."[16]

The following are some of the more significant chiasms:[17] 1 John 2:20-27*;[18] 3:11-13*; 3:22b-24; 4:17-18*; 5:1-5*, 17*. Among the more minor ones are: 1 John 2:18, 19,[19] 24*; 3:9*; 4:1-3,[20] 7-8*,[21] 19, 20a, 20b; 5:16a-f*.

4. Definition

The author of the Letters regularly uses definitions as a means of furthering his argument. The most prominent examples of this occur in 1 John 1:5 ("This is the proclamation . . . that God is light . . .") and 3:11 ("This is the proclamation . . . that we love one another"), where the definitions serve to mark off the two major divisions of 1 John. Definitions of the commandment to believe and to love are also given in 3:23b-24. Another type of definition is the use of the formula "Everyone who . . ." (or "The one who . . .") with a participle. Instances of this abound in 2:28–3:10 (cf. 2:29; 3:4, 6 [twice], 7, 8, 9, 10).

5. Reciprocity and Interrelatedness of Topics

The author of the Letters is fond of testing and demonstrating the truth of a statement by exploring it from all angles. One remarkably complex example of this occurs in 1 John 2:28–3:10.[22] This is also evident in the first part of 1 John 5:1-5 (vv. 1-3). The passage begins with belief ("everyone believing that Jesus is

---

jecting chiastic arrangements onto material where the similarities and parallels are insufficient to be able to indicate with any assurance that they were, in fact, intended to be chiasms.

15. See, for example, 2 John 6e, where the nominalized adjective "it" is ambiguous but clarified by its position in what is identified on other grounds as a chiasm.

16. See, for example, 4:17-18. Here the presence of a chiasm helps confirm that these two verses were considered a unit by the author.

17. All of these are based on the Greek text of the Letters. At times, the translation appears to reveal a chiasm in the text but this can be erroneous (for example, at 4:15bc, 16de).

18. An asterisk indicates that the chiasm has not, to my knowledge, been noted in the literature previously.

19. Smalley, *Epistles* 103.

20. Noticed by, among others, Smalley and R. E. Brown.

21. So also Klauck, *Erste Johannesbrief* 246.

22. Because of the complexity of the argument there, the reader is referred to the Commentary on the verses.

the Christ") and concludes with "this one is born of God." Then it is said that the one who loves the begetter (God) should also love the begotten (one's fellow believer). Next we are told that we know that we love our fellow believer if we love God — and obey his commandments. Thus, the commandments are interrelated and each requires the presence of the other: if we love God, we love our brother; if we love our brother, we love God.

6. Parallelism

The author also makes considerable use of parallelism, particularly in 1 John. The parallelism gives a certain unity to a section but also tends to connote thoroughness of argumentation. Major examples of parallelism occur in 1 John 1:6-10 where the expression "But if we say . . ." appears three times (vv. 6, 8, 10) and then a contrasting position expressed by "But if . . ." (vv. 7, 9, 2:1b). A second example appears in 2:3-11, where the clause "The one claiming . . ." appears three times (vv. 4, 6, 9). A third example follows in 2:12-17 where "I write to you . . ." appears six times (vv. 12, 13a, 13c, 14a, 14b, 14c). Moreover, the addressees are mentioned in two parallel sets of three (children, fathers, young people) in vv. 12-14. Parallelism is also evident in the arrangement of 2:29–3:10 where "everyone who . . ." appears six times (2:29b; 3:4, 6a, 6b, 9a, 10b) and "the one who . . ." appears twice (3:7a, 8a). Brief examples also occur throughout, for example, 1 John 2:16. These will be noted in the Commentary.

7. Predilection for Groups of Three

Klauck points out that the author exhibits a fondness for expressing ideas in groups of three.[23] As examples of this Klauck notes: a listing of three claims (1:6-10 and 2:3-11); the threefold repetition of "I write" (2:12-13) and "I wrote" (2:14); three groups of people (Dear Children, Fathers, Young People) (2:12-14); three characteristics of the world (2:16); three witnesses (5:6-8). To this list could also be added the threefold parallel of "you," "they," and "we" with a statement regarding their origin (4:4-6c), repetition of the statement concerning reciprocal abiding (3:13-17), and the threefold repetition of the relationship between love of God and love of one's brother (4:20-21).

8. Combination of Techniques

At times these various techniques are combined. For example, in 3:22b-4:1, there is a combination of chaining, definition and chiasm. The same is true of

---

23. Klauck, *Erste Johannesbrief* 27-28.

1 John 5:1-5 where we see another extensive instance: the one "believing" has been "born," the one who "loves the begetter loves the begotten," we know if we "love the children," if "we love God" and "keep his commandments," and this is "the love" that we keep "his commandments," and commandments are not burdensome because the one "born of God"/"conquers" the world, and this is the "conquest" that "conquered," and who is the one "conquering except the one believing."

H. THE AUTHOR OF 1 JOHN

The authorship of 1 John was discussed in the General Introduction and will not be repeated here.

I. THE DATE OF COMPOSITION

The date of composition of 1 John was discussed in the General Introduction and will not be repeated here.

J. THE PLACE OF COMPOSITION

The place of composition of 1 John was discussed in the General Introduction and will not be repeated here.

Commentary and Notes on 1 John

1:1-4

Witness and Fellowship

1 That which was from the beginning,[1]
  which we have heard,
  which we have looked at with our eyes,
  which we have seen and
  our hands have touched,
    that which concerns the word of life —
2 and the life was revealed,
  and we have seen
  and we bear witness
  and we proclaim to you the life
    that is eternal and
    that was in the presence of the Father and
      was revealed to us! —

3 whatever we have seen
and we have heard,
  we proclaim to you also
    so that you also may be in fellowship with us.

1. Throughout the Letters, I will arrange the text in sense lines in order to aid in noticing parallels and other features. Chiasms will be arranged in such a way that each element of the first half of the chiasm is indented further than the one before. The process will be reversed in the second half of the chiasm. Each element of the chiasm will also be identified by the presence of a "+" at the beginning of the element.

And our fellowship is
   with the Father and
   with his Son, Jesus Christ.

4 And we write these things so that our joy may be brought to fulfillment.

NOTES TO 1:1-4

V. 1 That which was from the beginning "Beginning" is used in two primary senses in the Johannine literature. The first meaning refers to the beginning of the community's experience or the beginning of the tradition. It appears with this meaning in 1 John 2:7, 24 [twice]; 3:11; 2 John 5, 6. The second meaning is that which appears in the Prologue of the Gospel, namely, the cosmic beginning. For a discussion of this meaning, see 2:13. (In 1 John 3:8 the word is also used to indicate that the devil was a sinner "from the beginning," but this is distinct from the two uses mentioned above.)

Here the term refers to the beginning of the community's experience, as is clear from the fact that it is linked with the community's sensory experience of the earthly Jesus. These opening words of the Letter express one of the central convictions to which the author witnesses, namely that what he witnesses to stems from the very beginning of the tradition. Implicit throughout the Letter is the conviction that his opponents do not remain with what was from the beginning. This becomes explicit in 2 John 9 where he contrasts his views with those who became "progressive" and who "do not remain in the teaching of the Christ." (See also at 2:6, 24; 3:11.)

Nevertheless, given the mention of preexistence in v. 2e, it is evident that "beginning" in v. 1 also is intended to refer to the primordial beginning as in the Prologue of the Gospel. In this sense, the verse would be calling attention to the fact that what had existed before was recently able to be touched, felt, seen and heard — in the person of Jesus.

Scholars disagree about which meaning is primary. Schnackenburg thinks the term refers primarily to the cosmic beginning while R. E. Brown holds that it refers mainly to the beginning of Jesus' ministry. Both aspects will be important to the author's thought throughout the Letter.

and (Gk: *kai*) The word appears twelve times in these four verses. Because the translation has been designed to be literal and to make the reader aware of the cadence of the Greek text, this monotony has been retained. However, it is translated "also" in v. 3c, d. Moreover, for reasons given below, "and" is inserted in v. 2e.

heard, looked at, seen In the Gospel, Jesus is said to have spoken what he had heard (e.g., 8:26, 40) and seen (e.g., 8:38). Unbelievers are said not to be able to hear his word (8:43).

that which concerns In Greek this is a single preposition *peri* with the genitive. Some take this as an interjection interrupting the surrounding sequence. However, the overall context makes more sense if it is taken as the antecedent of the relative clauses that begin the verse. The author wishes to proclaim everything that was from the beginning and that they have seen, which concerns the word of life.

the word of life The exact phrase "word of life" does not occur in the Gospel or elsewhere in the Letters. The closest parallel in the Gospel is in 5:24 where Jesus says that the one "hearing my word . . . has eternal life."

In the Prologue of the Gospel, Jesus is "the Word" (1:1). That simple usage does not appear in the Letters of John. Generally, in the Gospel and 1 John, "word" refers to the totality of the message of Jesus. However, two factors suggest that the phrase here and the word "life" are intended to refer functionally to the person of Jesus himself rather than to his message. First, the "word of life" is functionally a physical being that can be seen, heard, and touched (not an idea). So also in v. 2, the "life" is "revealed" and said to be "seen." Again these are actions directed to sense perception of a physical being rather than to a nonphysical reality. The phrase "in the presence of the Father" certainly would seem to imply a being rather than "a message."

Secondly, when we compare the usage in these verses with that in the Prologue of the Gospel, we find the same functions being ascribed to the Word (who is conceived of there as personal): he is "in the presence" of God (vv. 1, 2) and "life" was "in him." In John 1:14, the word "became flesh and dwelled among us." This is the functional equivalent of being "revealed" in 1 John. And, in the Prologue, that Jesus is the object of seeing is implied in the statement: "No one has seen God, but the only begotten God, the one at the breast of the Father, has made him known" (1:18).

It is also noteworthy that in the Gospel Jesus is described as the "Word" only in the Prologue while in 1 John he is described as "the word of life" and "the life" only in these introductory verses.

Finally, it seems unlikely that the author of 1 John would begin his tract by speaking about an *abstract reality* (either a "message" or "life," even divine life) rather than about the *person* of either the Father or the Son. Consequently, since 1 John was written before the final edition of the Gospel, it may be that we see in this expression (or at least the community's theology that lies behind this expression) the catalyst for the full development of the notion of the Logos, as it will appear in the Prologue of the Gospel.

V. 2 revealed (Gk: *ephanerōthē*) This verb occurs two times here and a total of nine times in 1 John. Twice, it refers to life being revealed (here); once the opponents are revealed not to have been part of us (2:19); once the love of God is said to have been revealed (4:9). The five other instances appear in 2:28–3:10 (2:28b; 3:2b, d, 5a, 8c). Of these, four instances clearly refer to Jesus (2:28b; 3:2d, 5a, 8c). Of these, two refer to the future (2:28b; 3:2d); two refer to the past (3:5a, 8c). One does not refer to Jesus (3:2b) but to the future status of the believer.

In 1 John, this is the favored term for implying that Jesus existed before his life in the human world. As such, this is the first reference to Jesus' preexistence within the Johannine literature. Although the notion of preexistence is common in the third edition, this verb is not used to express the concept. (For a full discussion, see Vol. 1, Part 4, Section 1.4.)

This term appears in the Gospel several times but refers to Jesus only in the words of John the Baptist (1:31), in the urging of Jesus' brothers (7:4), and in the Resurrection appearances (21:1 [two times], 14). None of these is quite the same as the instances in 1 John.

witness This is the first appearance of this verb in 1 John. It had occupied a central role in the theology of the second edition and continues to be important both for the author of 1 John and also for the author of the third edition.

proclaim This verb does not appear in the Gospel but is important for 1 John, where it introduces the themes that dominate the two halves of this work.

that is eternal In the Greek, this is a single adjective *aiōnion*. However, its presence after the noun puts an emphasis on it that can best be captured in English by a clause.

Eternal life is the primary object of the Johannine promise to believers in both the Gospel and the Letters of John. It is the life of God himself as contrasted with human life. See the full discussion of Eternal Life in Volume 1, Part 4, Section 4.3.

V. 3 fellowship The Greek is *koinōnia* and the term appears only here and in 1:6, 7 in the Johannine literature. It describes the unity that the author experiences with those who hold his interpretation of Jesus' ministry.

V. 4 our joy Many manuscripts have "your." However, it is generally agreed that "our" is more likely to be original. Not only is it supported by the best manuscript witnesses, but it is also the more difficult reading and the one most likely to have been changed. The reading does make good sense in that the author and his community will experience great joy in sharing all that they have experienced concerning the word of life with the readers so that they may join the fellowship of the community — and that will bring joy to the author and his community.

brought to fulfillment This is the only occurrence of the verb *plēroō* in 1 John. It also appears in a similar phrase (with "your") in 2 John 12. The author of 1 John also uses *teleioō* ("bring to perfection") four times with a similar meaning (cf. 2:5).

OVERVIEW OF 1:1-4

The author of 1 John is writing a "letter" to confirm for the members of his community the nature of correct belief and to encourage them to persevere in that belief. He evidently writes with great urgency and apparently in turmoil — and in some haste. This is indicated by the disjunctures, rapid shifts in topic, and grammatical ambiguities evident throughout the Letter.

The author begins by *proclaiming* to his readers and *witnessing* to them concerning the life that had been in the presence of the Father and that was revealed to the community. He reminds them in the most emphatic way that what he proclaims and witnesses to is what was from the beginning and is also the object of hearing, vision and touch. He does so that they might be in fellowship with one another and with both the Father and the Son. And the hope is that this writing will bring the community's joy to fulfillment.

THE STRUCTURE OF 1:1-4

The Letter begins with what is commonly referred to as a Prologue similar in some respects to that of the Prologue of the Gospel. But the Prologue here is marked by legendary awkwardness. The sudden breaks of sequence and shifts in thought seem intended to communicate the enthusiasm and emotion of the author. It is as if he is captured by the greatness and urgency of his topic.

The essential idea of these verses is that the author wishes to proclaim to his readers all that "we" (he and his fellows in community with him) know about Jesus, the word of life, so that the readers may join in their fellowship. However, v. 2 interrupts the overall flow of ideas to exclaim the wondrousness of the fact that this life (which was in the presence of the Father) was revealed to them. The author then seems to lose sense of the sequence of his thought and refers to the hearing and seeing and the proclamation — ideas that are part of what has preceded and that will follow in vv. 3-4.

In addition, the word "and" appears twelve times in the four verses creating considerable monotony. The translation has retained these various irregularities while at the same time attempting to express the sudden emphasis given to various ideas by the author throughout.

THE INTERPRETATION OF 1:1-4

The author begins (v. 1) by recalling that what he is speaking about is what has been from the beginning. This refers not primarily to what was at the beginning of time but to what they had heard, seen and touched from the beginning of the revelation of the word of life.[2] This fact anchors all else that the author has to communicate in the Letter. His message is not new but one that is grounded in the earliest experience of the community — in the earthly ministry of Jesus. It is this Jesus (the word of life) whom they have heard and seen with their eyes and looked at and whom their hands have touched. All of this is sensory language and reminds the reader of the physical reality of their experience. There can be no doubt that the author speaks about what was part of the ministry of Jesus. As we have seen, the author's opponents tended to neglect the earthly ministry in favor of knowledge given by the Spirit. Thus, from the beginning, he establishes the correct basis of the tradition over against that of the opponents.

Yet (v. 2) this word of life was not just an auditory word but present in a person, the person of Jesus, and the author now focuses on the personal source of that life. This life is eternal life, the very life of God, and is embodied in Jesus. This person who embodied this life was present with the Father and so existed before being revealed. But in spite of this exalted origin, the author affirms again that the word of life is something that they have seen and heard.

And now (v. 3) his purpose is to announce it to his readers, to share it with them so that they may share the fellowship with his own group. And this fellowship is not only with the author and his community but also with the Father and with his Son Jesus Christ.

The term fellowship is a new one in the Johannine vocabulary. It had not

2. It is common for scholars to observe that this phrase verbally echoes the beginning of the Gospel (1:1). However, in the light of the evidence that the Prologue of the Gospel represents a later stage than that of 1 John, it is more likely (and more reasonable) that the Prologue of the Gospel represents the later (and more polished) development and extends the "beginning" of 1 John back to the time before even the cosmic beginning.

appeared in the earlier editions of the Gospel and in fact appears only here and in vv. 6-7 within the Letters. It describes the harmonious association of those who believe as the author does but it also includes such association with the Father and with his Son Jesus. Although, for a modern Christian, this last statement might well seem to be somewhat perfunctory, within the context of the community dispute it has a specific polemical intent, for the author will explicitly argue later (2:22-24) that unless one believes properly in the Son one cannot be said to believe properly in the Father. Consequently, for the author to say that their fellowship is with the Father and the Son is in fact to make a polemical statement that will distinguish them from the opponents, who would claim to believe only in the Father.[3]

Finally, (v. 4) the author expects that writing this Letter will bring his own joy and that of the remainder of the community to fulfillment.

*   *   *

Much of the vocabulary in these verses is not particularly striking in its formulation, and its role in confronting the opponents may not be immediately evident. When these verses are read in another context, one might describe them as "useful" or "helpful" in terms of general Christian exhortation. Yet when read within the context of the crisis affecting the community at the time, it becomes clear that the author's words are carefully chosen and what would in another context seem quite innocuous is in fact intended to constantly assert the author's own views over against those of the opponents. At times the contrast is implicit, at other times explicit. But it is always present.

Thus, his references to "the beginning" are important for the author because, in his view, the opponents fail to remain faithful to what they have known "from the beginning." Instead they introduce "new" teachings, not from Jesus or from the Spirit of Truth. Likewise, the author's emphasis on sensory verbs stresses the importance of the community's historical experience of Jesus. Their faith is based on Jesus' historical ministry and not on Spirit inspiration unrelated to, and deviating from, the historical ministry of Jesus.

The author speaks of "life," the life that was the promise of Jesus in the Gospel. But now the author will emphasize that this life, which was revealed to them, had previously been in the presence of the Father. The person who embodies this life is preexistent, an aspect of Jesus' existence that the reader meets here for the first time in the Johannine literature. Thus, the author subtly affirms the uniqueness of the person and status of Jesus in a way that was unacceptable to the opponents. Even though the believer is like Jesus and is to imi-

---

3. For a full discussion of this, see the Interpretation of 2:22-24 below.

tate him and become like him, the believer's status will never equal that of Jesus, as the opponents would claim.

It is also significant that life is here identified with Jesus and not with the Spirit. There is ample evidence for associating eternal life with the Spirit in the tradition; here the author wishes to emphasize that life is not the prerogative only of the Spirit but also of Jesus.

Another of the author's themes throughout the Letter will be that if one claims a relationship with the Father (as the opponents would do), the person must also understand the person and mission of Jesus as the author does. If a person does not "have" Jesus, that person will not "have" the Father. As a result, the opponents who claim to have the Father but deny the continuing importance of Jesus are said not to have the Father either. Thus, the Prologue is a positive, constructive description of the foundation of the community's faith. But it is worded in such a way as to deny the false claims of the opponents and to stress aspects of correct faith right from the start.

The Proclamation That God Is Light

5 And this is the proclamation
   that we have heard from him [Jesus] and
   that we proclaim to you,
      that God is light and
      there is not any darkness in him [God].

6 If we say that we have fellowship with him [God] and we walk in the darkness,
   we lie and do not do the truth.
7 But if we walk in the light as he [God] is in the light,
   we have fellowship with one another and
   the blood of Jesus his Son cleanses us from all sin.

8 If we say that we do not have sin,
   we deceive ourselves and
   the truth is not in us.

9 But if we confess our sins,
   he [God] is faithful and just
      and so forgives our sins and
      cleanses us from all injustice.

10 If we say that we have not sinned,
   we make him [God] a liar and
   his [God's] word is not in us.

2:1 (My Dear Children, I write these things to you so that you will not sin.)
But if someone sins,
   we have a Paraclete before the Father, Jesus Christ, the Just One.

2 And he [Jesus] is an atonement for our sins
and not only for ours but also for those of the entire world.

NOTES TO 1:5-2:2

V. 5 from him The antecedent is uncertain but three features suggest that it refers to Jesus. The last mentioned person is Jesus (v. 3). The author speaks of the proclamation "that we heard" — which had been identified in vv. 1-4 as from Jesus. Finally, since the proclamation is about God, the proclamation would presumably be from the Son.

God is light Just as the similar statement in 4:8 that "God is love," this statement identifies the being of God with "light," an image known from apocalyptic and non-apocalyptic Judaism that symbolized truth and justice (see the following Note on the symbolism). The point here is that the very being of God is identified with light!

light (Gk: *phōs*); **darkness** (Gk: *skotia*) This pair of terms forms an important symbolic framework for the Letter. The pair also appears in the Gospel and is one of the linguistic and ideological characteristics that identify the material of the third edition.

In the Old Testament "light" is associated with truth and with righteousness while "darkness" is associated with error and sin (e.g., Pss 27:1; 119:130; Isa 5:20; Mic 7:8). It is also found throughout the Johannine literature and less often elsewhere in the New Testament (e.g., Rom 13:11-14; 2 Pet 1:19).

However, the background of the usage here is to be found more specifically in the modified (ethical) dualism typical of apocalyptic. This is most evident in the SDQ and the *T12P*. For example, 1QH 4:23 speaks of God as "perfect light." As Charlesworth ("Scrolls," 75) points out, this statement is "the functional equivalent" of the description of God in 1 John 1:5. Although God is here identified with light, the term appears (in addition to the present use) only five times (1 John 1:7 [twice]; 2:8, 9, 10) in the Letters. Its correlative "darkness" (*skotia*) appears only four times (1 John 1:5; 2:8, 9, 11) within the Letters and once in the variant form *skotos* (1 John 1:6). For an excellent treatment (with numerous citations), see Böcher, *Dualismus* 96-108.

in him The antecedent of "him" here is God. This is evident from the remainder of the verse, where it is said that it is God who is light and there is no darkness *in him.*

37

V. 6 with him The pronoun "him" refers to God the Father, the last person mentioned (v. 5d).

walk in darkness "To walk" denotes one's behavior. "To walk" in this metaphorical sense appears in a variety of ways in the Johannine writings: with "in the darkness" (John 8:12; 12:35; 1 John 1:6; 2:11); "in the light" (1 John 1:7); and "in the truth" (2 John 4; 3 John 3, 4). It is also used without a modifier (1 John 2:6) and with "according to the commandments" (2 John 6).

we lie This introduces the second of the dualistic Johannine sets: falsehood/lying and truth. Words associated with falsehood and lying (from the Greek root *pseud-*) — e.g., lie (verb *pseudomai*): 1:6; lie (noun *pseudos*): 2:21, 27; false prophet *(pseudoprophētēs)*: 4:1; liar *(pseustēs)*: 1:10; 2:4, 22; 4:20; 5:10 — are common in John because they represent the opposite of truth. The author addresses the issue of lying in relation to Jesus in 1:10 where he says that the opponents make Jesus a liar. In 2:27, the author assures his readers that the Spirit is not a liar. In 5:10, the author says that the one not believing properly makes God the Father a liar. The author identifies "the Liar" in 2:22 with the one who denies that Jesus is the Christ.

In the third edition of the Gospel, there is no explicit contrast between "lying" and "speaking the truth," except in 8:44.

do the truth (Gk: *poioumen*) The phrase, "to do the truth," appears only in the Johannine literature in the New Testament. Within the Johannine literature it appears only here in 1 John and in the third edition (John 3:21). It has been studied extensively by I. de la Potterie (*Vérité* 2:480-520). The expression is not found in Greek or Hellenistic texts, but is found in the Old Testament in Neh 9:33 and 2 Chr 31:20, where it is predicated of God and Hezekiah, respectively. In the LXX, it appears, without the article, predicated of God (e.g., Gen 32:11; 2 Sam 2:6; 15:20) and predicated of humans (e.g., Gen 47:29; Jos 2:14; Isa 26:10, etc.). It appears in *Jub.* 20:9; 36:3 and frequently in the *T12P* (*TReu* 6:9; *TBen* 10:3; *TIss* 7:5, etc.) and in the SDQ (1QS 1:5; 5:3; 8:2; 1QGenApoc 6:2; 19:25).

The issue here is a contrast between what a person claims and what the person actually does. To "not live out the truth" is synonymous with "walking in darkness" in v. 6b. In its context in the SDQ, the *T12P* and the Johannine literature, it reflects the worldview of modified dualism. See also at John 3:21, the other place where the term appears. For references and further discussion, see de la Potterie, *Vérité* 2:480-83.

the truth This is the first mention of truth in the Letter. The concept of truth becomes a major theological category for the author and contrasts with lying and falsehood as mentioned above. God is the "True One" (5:20). Those who do not believe make "him" (God or Jesus? 1:10b) a liar (1:10; 5:10b). Every liar is not of the truth (2:21). The person who makes claims but does not live them out is a liar and the truth is not in him (2:4). The person who claims to be in fellowship with God but walks in darkness is lying (1:6), as is the one who claims to love God but hates his brother (4:20). One who says he/she has not sinned is a liar (1:10). Further, the one who denies that Jesus is the Christ (2:22) is "the" Liar; and, moreover, false prophets do not confess Jesus properly (4:1-2).

In 2 John, the notion of truth plays an even more important role given the brevity of that Letter. Believers are said to know the truth (v. 1), to have the truth abiding in them (v. 2), grace, mercy and peace are wished "in truth" (v. 3). Members of the community "walk in truth" (v. 4). Those who have gone out into the world are "deceivers" and do not properly confess Jesus (v. 7).

In 3 John truth plays a lesser role but still forms the conceptual background of the author's thought. The author rejoices when he hears that members of the community "walk in truth" (vv. 3, 4) and says that Demetrius is witnessed to "by the truth" (v. 12). The most extensive treatment of this concept in the Johannine tradition is that of de la Potterie, *Vérité* (see above).

V. 7 he Brown (*Epistles* 200) argues that "he" here is God and says that this expression (rather than the expression that Jesus *is* light) has better biblical parallels. Yet it cannot be denied that the expression is awkward given the identification of God *as* light in v. 5. Also in favor of reading God as the antecedent is the reference to "his" in v. 7c where it refers to God (see below).

in the light The statement that God is "in the light" is unexpected after the statement of v. 5 that God *is* light. When speaking of darkness, the author had said that there was not any darkness "in him." Now he speaks of God as being "in the light." Brown is probably right that the change in phrasing is determined by the intended parallelism between we who walk "in" the light and he who is "in" the light (*Epistles* 201).

fellowship with one another We would expect the author to confirm that, if we walk in the light, we will have fellowship with *God;* but the author chooses to emphasize the other dimension of fellowship, the relationship with others in the community.

the blood of Jesus In the Gospel, the blood of Jesus is mentioned only in the Eucharistic section of the Bread of Life discourse (6:53, 54, 55, 56) and in the statement that blood and water flowed from the side of Jesus (19:34). Elsewhere in the Letters of John it is found only in 1 John 5:6 (twice), 8. This reference is a clear statement of the sacrificial interpretation of Jesus' death.

cleanses This verb appears only here and in v. 9 in the Johannine writings. But the adjective *katharos* appears in John 13:10, 11; 15:3.

Being cleansed from sin by the blood of Christ has as its primary background the Jewish understanding of sacrifice, particularly as described on the Day of Atonement. The primary focus is not on the death of the animal but on the blood that is the medium of atonement. See particularly Lev 17:11 (LXX): "For the life of all flesh is its blood, and I have given it to you to atone for your life upon the altar. For its blood will atone in place of your life." On the general notion of God forgiving sin, see Jer 40:8 (LXX): "And I will cleanse them from all their injustices *(adikiōn)* which they sinned against me, and I will not remember their sins *(hamartiōn)* which they sinned against me and rebelled against me." The New Testament Letter to the Hebrews 9:22 ("Indeed, under the Law all things are purified with blood, and without the shedding of blood there is no forgiveness of sin") is also often quoted as evidence of this notion. Although the primary background here is undoubtedly the notion of atoning sacrifice, in the third edition of the Gospel there are clear indications of the death of Jesus being paralleled with the Passover lamb. By the time of Jesus, the death of martyrs could also be viewed as having an atoning value (cf. 2 Macc 6:18-31; 7:1-23; 4 Macc 5-7; 8-18). See de Jonge, "Jesus' Death" 142-51, esp. 147-51. See also de Boer, *Perspectives* 272-76.

from all sin In the second edition of the Gospel, the only sin is that of unbelief. This is true throughout chapter 8 (vv. 21, 24 [twice], 34, 46), in chapter 15 (vv. 22, 24), and in chapter 16 (vv. 8, 9). Throughout 1 John, the word refers to moral failing (1:7, 8, 9 [twice]; 2:2, 12; 3:4 [twice], 5 [twice], 8, 9; 4:10; 5:16 [twice], 17 [twice]), although the author of 1 John frequently links the incorrect belief of the opponents with the failure to love and vice versa. In the third edition of the Gospel, it refers to moral failing as it does in 1 John (cf. 1:29; 9:34; and 19:11).

Klauck (*Erste Johannesbrief* 92) points to a parallel in 1QS 3:7-8 concerning the necessity of freedom from sin for dwelling in community. It is particularly significant that at Qumran (as was the case for the community at the time of the second edition) the purification from sin came through the imparting of the Spirit whereas, for 1 John and the third edition of the Gospel, it came through the blood of Jesus.

V. 8 If we say we do not have sin The expression "have sin" appears only here in 1 John but four times in the Gospel (9:41; 15:22, 24; 19:11). In 1 John, the verb "have" appears with other objects such as communion, confidence, hope, life, love, joy and peace (texts in Brown, *Epistles* 205). Schnackenburg (*Epistles* 80) understands this in its most radical form and takes it as a reflection of "the gnostic conviction that pneumatics could not be defiled by the material world and its impurities." Brown (*Epistles* 205-6) understands this as a reference to the present guilt of past sin.

Smalley (*Epistles* 29) comments, "To 'have sin' is the equivalent of possessing a sinful character or disposition." He refers to Brooke (*Epistles* 17) who remarks similarly, "'Sin' is the principle of which sinful acts are the several manifestations. . . . The latter, sinful *acts* are distinguished as such in v. 10 . . ." (italics in original).

It seems unlikely that the opponents (whom I would not classify as gnostics) would have claimed never to have sinned. The tradition of sin within the Jewish tradition is too pervasive for that. Rather, it is likely that they argue, on the basis of a considerable number of Old Testament texts, that they were cleansed of all sin by the reception of the Holy Spirit in its eschatological fullness (e.g., Ezek 36:25-28; Isa 32:15; Zech 12:10; 13:1). See also 1QS 3:7. As a result, I would hold a view very similar to that of Smalley and Brooke, as will be seen in the Interpretation.

V. 9 confess (Gk: *homologōmen*) This is the first appearance of "confess" in 1 John. It also appears in 2:23; 4:2, 3, 15; 2 John 7. In all other cases, it pertains to confession of proper belief. Whether "confessing sins" here refers to a ritual ceremony will be discussed in the Interpretation.

he is faithful and just "He" refers to God as it has throughout this section. Even when Jesus' saving activity is spoken of, the role of Jesus is tied to the relationship between the Father and the believer.

from all injustice This is the first of two uses of "injustice" (*adikia*) in the Letter (cf. 5:17). Given the synonymity of sin and injustice in 1:7 and 1:9, it would be wrong to look for a special meaning for one or the other. It is also used in the LXX of Jer 40:8 (see above) as a synonym for sin.

V. 10 If we say that we have not sinned This statement contains an implicit rejection of a claim on the part of the opponents. Many scholars have argued that there is no difference between this expression and that of v. 8 (e.g., Schnackenburg, *Epistles* 84). However, there does seem to be a shift in emphasis between the two statements. In the first, the issue is admission of the need for forgiveness, while in the present instance the emphasis is on handling sin "in the present and the future." That is, the author speaks of trying to avoid sin (2:1) but also recognizes that in fact there will be times when the believer sins.

Thus, the opponents' claim referred to here is that they have not sinned since becoming believers. This is true "perfectionism." But at the same time, there is no indication in the Letter that the author thought of the opponents as libertines who were given to wanton behavior. Rather, their view would seem to be more a matter of theory regarding the believer's status.

The author holds to what might be called a "realistic perfectionism" in that being born of God gives one the Spirit and consequently the life of God. Thus the one born of God possesses the roots of perfectionism. It is then characteristic of the one born of God not to sin. Yet sin is possible in the future as can be seen from the discussion of prayer for the one sinning (5:16-17).

Smith (*Epistles* 44-45) describes this as "an unresolved tension in 1 John." He goes on to comment: "Yet exist it [sin] does, even in the Christian, as 1:8 and 9 would seem to acknowledge (cf. 2:1). Nevertheless, in principle sin is conquered and must be rooted out." My only reservation is that the tension is not "unresolved" but simply "unarticulated." That is to say, rather than articulate the distinction precisely, the author states the two polarities.

we make him . . . and his word "Him" and "his" here refer to God the Father for it is God's word that would be shown not to be in the person. The primacy of the Father continues throughout these verses.

liar On the role of words associated with "lying," see comment on 1:6. In 1:6, the author spoke of the one making the false claim as being a liar. Here the author speaks of those who make a false claim as making *God* a liar, a charge that is far more serious (cf. also 5:10).

2:1 My Dear Children (Gk: *teknia*) This is the diminutive of *teknon* (child) and appears here for the first time in 1 John. From this point, it is used with some regularity to address the members of the author's community (2:12, 28; 3:7, 18; 4:4; 5:21). (But the author also uses "Beloved" [*agapētoi*]; see at 2:7.) The diminutive here is used to express the intimacy of the relationship and so will be translated "dear children." The author uses this term (rather than *teknon*) regularly in direct address to express his relationship with the readers. He uses "children" *(tekna)* consistently to describe the relation between God and the believer (1 John 3:1, 2, 10; 5:2) and to refer to believers as children of a community (2 John 1, 4, 13). The one exception to this pattern is in 3 John 4, where the author speaks of "my children" *(ta ema tekna)*.

For more detail on the use of the terms in the Johannine literature, see at John 1:12 and 3E-5.

Paraclete The figure of the Paraclete appears only in the Johannine literature within the New Testament (1 John 2:1; John 14:16-17, 26; 15:26-27; 16:7-11, 12-15). Here in its first appearance, the term is applied to Jesus. In the third edition of the Gospel, it is applied to the Spirit. We will discuss the general meaning of the term (as it applies to both Jesus and the Spirit) here and say something of its function as it is evident in 1 John. In an Addendum on the Commentary on John 14:15-31, we discuss its function within the third edition of the Gospel.

Attempts to understand the term "Paraclete" can be grouped in three categories: those that have an etymological basis, a history of religions basis, and a "functional" basis. Etymologically, the word "paraclete" *(paraklētos)* is a derivative of the verb *parakaleō,* which means literally "to call alongside." Therefore, a paraclete may be understood as an advocate in a legal sense. That is, the Paraclete is a kind of defense attorney. Yet, as we shall see this type of explanation is not fully satisfactory inasmuch as the Paraclete in John functions also as a prosecutor (cf. 16:8-11).

Other scholars have attempted to understand the term within the context of uses elsewhere in ancient literature. Such investigations often focus entirely on *the Spirit* as Paraclete and ignore the application of the same term to Jesus. This is perhaps understandable if the occurrence in 1 John is looked upon as secondary to the use in the Gospel. However, we gain a new perspective if we first examine its application to Jesus and then examine the application to the Spirit as secondary.

One of the earliest attempts to discover parallels to the Paraclete sayings was that of Johansson *(Paraclētoi),* who understood it against the variety of Old Testament intercessor figures. Betz *(Paraklet)* examined the Scrolls and found parallels with the figure of Michael. Boring ("Influence" 113-23) proposed that the Paraclete was a symbol for prophets within the Johannine community. Kremer ("Verheissung") saw similarities to the Johannine Paraclete in the Synoptic Gospels. Yet none of these has gained wide acceptance.

The term is intended to point to a function of Jesus that is at least distantly related to the apocalyptic concepts found in Q (Luke 12:8-9; Matt 10:32-33) where Jesus, as Son of Man, will confess *(homologeō)* those who confess him before men and will deny *(arneomai)* those who deny him before men. In this saying, a context of eschatological judgment is envisaged in which Jesus serves as both advocate and accuser for humanity. In the present verse, we see only the positive side of this function but in the third edition both positive and negative elements are evident. The term "Paraclete" is not used in the Q-saying but the similarity in function is noteworthy as is the language of "confessing" and "denying" — two verbs that have significant roles in the context (see "confess" 2:23 [cf. 1:9; 4:2, 3, 15; 2 John 7]; and "deny" 2:22 [twice], 23).

V. 2 atonement for our sins (Gk: *hilasmos . . . peri tōn hamartiōn hēmōn*) The same phrase appears also in 1 John 4:10 but nowhere else in the Johannine writings. The term *hilasmos* is translated in a variety of ways by scholars. R. E. Brown, Strecker, and Beutler translate it as "atonement"; Smalley as "atoning sacrifice"; Grayston, Painter as "expiation"; earlier Brooke used "propitiation." By separating the shades of difference between the various English terms used to translate *hilasmos,* we may be able to understand the Johannine author's thought more precisely. The Funk and Wagnall's Dictionary notes the similarity in the terms and provides helpful distinctions between them (see under "propitiation"). Expiation is "the enduring of the full penalty of a wrong or crime." Thus, in expiation, the focus is on the process by which the relationship is restored. Propitiation is concerned with an action that appeases or placates the one offended. Biblical texts that connote propitiation generally contain some reference to "the wrath of God" being taken away by the action. In this, the focus is on the change wrought in the attitude of the one offended. Atonement, which originally had the meaning of reconciliation ("at-one-ment"), now generally refers to an "offering, sacrifice, or suffering sufficient to win forgiveness." Thus, the focus is on what is offered and is, in this sense, similar to expiation. Brown (*Epistles* 219) distinguishes expiation/atonement from propitiation by asking: "Is there an angry God who is placated by having sacrifices offered to him by the offender (propitiation), or is the offender made pleasing in God's eyes by the wiping away of the sin and impurity that had made him offensive (expiation)?" In the LXX the term *hilasmos* has chiefly to do with "cleansing something from sin or impurity."

From studies of the general background to *hilasmos,* many scholars see in the term a reference to an activity that is intended to remove sin and reconcile man to God. However, perhaps the most satisfying background is that found in the rite that is performed on what Lev 25:9 calls "the Day of Atonement" (LXX: *hē hēmera tou hilasmou*). The rite, according to Lev 16, was performed by the high priest who sacrificed both a bull and a goat "for the sins of the people" and took the blood into the Holy of Holies and poured it on the gold covering of the Ark of the Covenant. According to Lev 16:16, this pouring of the blood would (using a verb from the same stem as *hilasmos*) the Holy Place from the uncleannesses of the sons of Israel and all their injustices concerning their sins. In this case, as Brown points out, the meaning of the verb must be "to cleanse" or "to purify."

Thus, if we read the text of 1:7 together with 2:2, we find that there are several elements that echo those of the Day of Atonement: in both, there is a *hilasmos,* and a reference to *blood;* and, moreover, the blood is said to *cleanse,* and to cleanse *from sin.* In the case of the Day of Atonement, the blood cleansed the sins of the whole nation; in the case of Jesus, the blood cleanses the sins of the whole world. There seems to be little doubt that this is the background against which the author of 1 John intended the text to be read.

for those of the entire world "World" occurs here for the first time in 1 John. It appears a total of twenty-three times (2:2, 15 [three times], 16 [twice], 17; 3:1, 13, 17; 4:1, 3, 4, 5 [three times], 9, 14, 17; 5:4 [twice], 5, 19) and in 2 John 7. In 1 John, it can describe (as here) the world as the ultimate object of God's saving love. It is the place to which God sent his unique son (4:9) to be the Savior of the world (4:14) the sins of which he took away (2:2).

However, it is most frequently a term that describes the arena of unbelief, the Evil One, and the author's opponents. The believer is not to love the world (2:15) or the things in the world (2:15). That which is in the world is "not of the Father" (2:16). The world will perish (2:17). The world does not know God (3:1) nor "us" (3:1). The world hates believers (3:13). The whole world lies in the grasp of the Evil One (5:19).

The opponents (false prophets) departed from the community and went into the world (4:1; 2 John 7); they are "of the world" (4:5); they speak of the world (4:5) and the world listens to them (4:5). The world is the place of the Antichrist (2:18, 22; 4:3). Yet there is confident hope for the believer: the one (spirit) that is in the world is not as great as the one that is in the believer (4:4) and the one born of God conquers the world (5:4, 5).

"The world" is one of the most characteristic terms of the Gospel (2E and 3E) and its range is as great as it is in the Letters (for a discussion of the use in the Gospel, see at John 1:9).

OVERVIEW OF 1:5–2:2

The author now clarifies the proclamation to which he referred previously: God is light and there is not any darkness in him. Consequently, if someone walks in darkness, the person cannot be in fellowship with God. But, if we walk in the light, we have fellowship with one another — and the blood of Jesus cleanses us from sin.

With this sudden introduction of a statement about the cleansing value of the blood of Jesus, the author turns from the topic of fellowship to plunge into what was obviously an important and pressing topic for him: sin and the role of Jesus in the forgiveness of sin. Consequently, the remainder of the section will deal in various ways with sin.

The author stresses the importance of admitting sin, because not to do so is to deceive oneself and to make God a liar. At the same time, the author exhorts his readers not to sin, but if they do Jesus is a Paraclete and an atonement for their sin and that of the entire world.

THE STRUCTURE OF 1:5–2:2

In v. 5, the author begins the first major part of the Letter.[1] The second part of the Letter will begin in 3:11.

Within the section that stretches from 1:5 to 2:2, the author arranges his material by means of chaining (catchword) and parallelism. There are three instances of chaining. In v. 3, the author had explained that the ultimate purpose of his "proclamation" was that the readers would have "fellowship" with him and his followers. Then, in v. 5, he makes a programmatic statement about what that "proclamation" is. In v. 6, "fellowship" appears for the second time and so is chained to its counterpart in v. 3. Also in v. 6, "darkness" appears again and is chained to its earlier counterpart in v. 5. Both "fellowship" and "darkness" in v. 6 then become the topics on which the author's comments are based.

After the programmatic proclamation in v. 5, the author begins an extensive set of parallel statements. Each set consists of a protasis ("If we say . . .") (v. 6a, v. 8a, v. 10a) with which the author does not agree. Each is then followed by a double apodosis (v. 6b, v. 8bc, v. 10bc) stating the negative consequences of the false statements.

The author then follows each set with a contrary protasis ("But if we/someone . . .") (v. 7a, v. 9a, 2:1b) and each is also followed in turn by a double apodosis (v. 7bc, v. 9bcd, 2:1c-2c), stating the consequences as the author sees them but this time in a positive sense.

Finally, it should be noted that the apodoses of which the author does approve all deal with Jesus' role in the forgiveness of sin.

THE INTERPRETATION OF 1:5–2:2

The author now (v. 5) begins the body of his Letter. The Prologue spoke of proclamation in general. Now, in the body of the Letter, the author provides a detailed statement of the content: "And this is the proclamation: . . ."[2] This is what the author and his community have heard from Jesus and what they in

1. Throughout, I will use "Part" to describe the two major subdivisions of the Letter. The next level of division will be labeled "Section" and I will speak of "Units" as subdivisions of Sections.

2. In the Introduction, I have argued that the structure of 1 John became the model for the structure of the Gospel in the third edition. Thus, just as there is a Prologue here that speaks of proclamation and then the first major part of the Letter begins with a specification of the proclamation, so the third edition will begin with a Prologue that speaks of witness and the body of the Gospel will then begin with: "And this is the witness" (1:19). However, the editorial process by which this is accomplished in the Gospel is more complex. See the discussion in the Introduction to 1 John.

turn are proclaiming to the readers, namely that God is light and there is not any darkness in him.[3]

After this programmatic statement, the author reveals his intention to refute the views of the opponents. The author begins by commenting on a series of paired hypothetical statements.

What is striking and yet very subtle is the way the author couches his message in a context that speaks primarily of God rather than of Jesus. Although he will soon speak of Jesus and his role (v. 7), the author begins by establishing an overall theological framework for his Letter, and that framework begins, not with Jesus whose identity and role are in dispute, but with God the Father, in whom both the author and his opponents claim to believe and about whom there is no disagreement. By doing this, the author establishes a common ground from which he will formulate his argument and refute his opponents. Consequently, when he challenges the propriety of their belief, he will do so by arguing that unless they properly understand Jesus and unless they exhibit behavior that is appropriate, they cannot be said to have proper belief in, or love of, *God the Father.*

Although there was a massive concentration on Christology in the second edition of the Gospel, the second author understood all of Jesus' claims to derive solely from the Father. Here the author of 1 John makes that perspective all the clearer by his decision to focus on God the Father and to relate everything to him as the ultimate object of belief. What had been background in the second edition becomes foreground in 1 John.

In v. 6 what is a claim on the part of the opponents and the author, namely to have "fellowship" with God, is shown to be false if it is not accompanied by appropriate actions: "If we say that we have fellowship with him and we walk in the darkness, we lie and do not do the truth." This statement affirms the necessity of a congruence between the believer's words and actions. To claim fellowship while walking in darkness is simply to lie and not to "do" the truth (that is, not to put the truth into action). To this point, the opponents would have no difficulty with what the author says.

---

3. Between this verse and 2:11, the themes of light and darkness will appear regularly but then will not appear again in the Letter. Strecker (*Epistles* 26-28) argues that the Qumran scrolls do not provide a sufficient background for this concept, pointing out that nowhere in the SDQ is God identified with the light nor is there "a revealer who mediates access to God." Strecker then argues that we "may not assert any dependence . . . on the Qumran literature." While we certainly should not attempt to claim dependence on the SDQ, these documents do represent the closest parallels in worldview and in language. To use a similar worldview and language is not to use the theology of the SDQ. We must allow for the unique development of Johannine theology within this worldview.

Moreover, an author need not refer explicitly to both parts of a dualistic pair to be dualistic. For example, references to "the Spirit of Truth" in the Gospel are apocalyptic even though there is no explicit reference to "the Spirit of Deception" as there had been in 1 John.

Verse 7 then takes up the implicit reverse of v. 6, namely walking in light. "Walking in the light" is both contrasted with walking in the darkness, as was mentioned in the previous statement, and shown to be how "he" (God the Father) acts. The author then explains two consequences of walking in the light. First, if we walk in the light, we will truly have fellowship with one another. This is the fellowship mentioned above in v. 3 and effectively chains this verse to v. 3. Moreover, it implicitly contrasts with those who claim to have fellowship but do not walk in the light (v. 6a). Again, the opponents would have no problem with what the author has to say so far.

Second, the author explains that, if we walk in the light, the blood of Jesus, his Son, cleanses us from all sin. The introduction of being "cleansed from all sin" is sudden and unexpected. When we turn to v. 8, however, we will notice that the notion of sin and its forgiveness appears again, and this indicates that the author has introduced the topic of forgiveness of sin here as part of his chaining (or "catchword") technique whereby the ending of this statement becomes the topic of the next claim.[4]

Third, although the statement itself that "the blood of Jesus cleanses us from all sin" is familiar throughout the Christian world and hardly controversial, within the context of the Johannine community's dispute, the statement would inevitably have had a polemical tone to it.[5] The opponents considered themselves to have received God's Spirit in its eschatological fullness and, consequently, they believed that they had been purged of past sin by the action of this Spirit (a view they would have shared with the Old Testament and with the community at Qumran). Because of this, the opponents would have rejected the notion of any role *for Jesus* in such forgiveness. His death was not a sacrifice for sin. Although he announced the outpouring of the Spirit, he was not an effective agent of forgiveness himself.

In v. 8, the author introduces the second claim: "If we say that we do not have sin. . . ." As is so often the case, the author is less than clear about the meaning of this statement, particularly when it is compared with the similar statement in v. 10. In the present statement ("If we say that we do not have sin . . ."), "having sin" is spoken of in the present tense. In v. 10, it is spoken of in the perfect tense: "If we say we have not sinned. . . ."

We have seen the various proposals regarding the meaning of this verse in

4. The chaining had been interrupted by vv. 4-5, but it is evident that the appearance of the topic in v. 6 is intended to clarify the basis for true fellowship.

5. In this discussion of sinfulness, the author touches on the issue of perfectionism for the first time. It is a complex topic and one that he will return to again. For further detail, see Vol. 1, Part 4, Section 7.3: Soteriology in 1 John (for Jesus' role in the forgiveness of sin) and Vol. 1, Part 4, Section 8.3: Ethics in 1 John (for a discussion of the views of the author and his opponents regarding ethical perfectionism).

the Note. Here, I would suggest that the difference in meaning between v. 8 and v. 10 can best be determined by understanding "sin" in the larger context of 1 John. From the Letter as a whole, it is evident that both the author and his opponents hold to a view of perfectionism (that is, the freedom from past sin and freedom from the ability to commit future sin) although they understand this perfectionism differently. Just what the difference is between the two views is evident from the "both/and" position the author takes toward the subject. On the one hand, he expresses the conviction that the believer is capable of future sin. On the other hand, he expresses the view that the believer "does not sin." These two positions are reconciled in the conviction that the believer has the roots of sinlessness but full perfection can only be the result of effort. Yet even in that effort, the believer does sin but can be forgiven.

The author holds that the believer is capable of sin (2:1b) even though he hopes that the believer will not sin (v. 2:1a). That future sin is a possibility is also evident from the author's statements about the coming judgment (2:28) and the necessity of the believer "making himself holy as that one [Jesus] is holy" (3:3). In 5:16, the author speaks of praying for the one who sins "and [that] God will give life to him." The inchoative nature of the believer's perfectionism is also evident in the author's assertion that the believer is now a child of God (3:2) but that there will also be a future status of the believer different from the present one (3:2b). Yet, at times, the author makes statements that are difficult to distinguish from those of his opponents. For example, he says: "Everyone abiding in him [Jesus] does not sin. Everyone sinning has neither seen him [Jesus] nor known him [Jesus]" (3:6). Once again, in 3:9 the author makes another statement that is difficult to distinguish from the view of the opponents: "Everyone born of God does not commit sin because God's seed abides in him, and is not able to sin because he has been born of God."

Thus, for the author, the believer is "both" perfect "and" sinful, and it is to these two states that he is referring in 1:8-10. In v. 8, the author argues that, if we refuse to acknowledge that we "have sin" (that is, have the inclination to sin), "we deceive ourselves and the truth is not in us." This is the view of the opponents. It is derived from their belief that their reception of the eschatological Spirit has so transformed them that they are free from all inclination to future sin.

Against this view, the author argues (in v. 9) that, if we confess our sins (here the author seems to talk not about the inclination to sin but about actual sins), God who is faithful and just will forgive our sins and cleanse us from all injustice. Again the author speaks about one's overall belief and so uses his customary word *(homologeō)* for public "confession" of such belief. Not only do we have to admit the inclination to sin, but we also have to acknowledge the actuality of sins.

Thus, v. 8 and v. 9 address different topics. In v. 8, the author argues that, if we fail to recognize that we continue to have an inclination to sin even after we have received the eschatological Spirit, we deceive ourselves and are not being realistic ("the truth is not in us"). Then, in v. 9, the author argues that (furthermore) if we acknowledge that we have *actually* sinned, God, who is faithful and just, will forgive our sins.

In all of this, the fact that God will forgive sin is based on the conviction that God himself is both "faithful" and "just," two attributes of Yahweh known from the Old Testament. Perhaps the prime example of the Old Testament's designation of Yahweh as "faithful and just" comes from Deut 32:4, where Moses, in his Farewell Discourse, says of Yahweh:

LXX	English
Deut 32:4	Deut 32:4
theos pistos,	A faithful God,
kai ouk estin adikia,	and there is no injustice,
dikaios kai hosios kyrios	just and hallowed is the Lord.

These attributes are the basis of God's constant readiness to forgive sin and to cleanse the believer from injustice, as in Exod 34:6-7:

LXX	English
Exod 34:6-7	Exod 34:6-7
alēthinos kai dikaiosynēn diatērōn	truthful and keeping justice
kai poiōn eleos eis chiliadas,	and being merciful to the thousandth generation,
aphairōn anomias kai adikias kai hamartias	removing lawlessness and injustice and sins.

Thus, the forgiveness of sins is available, if only the believer acknowledge his sins.[6]

Then in v. 10, the author addresses the issue of those who claim that they have not actually sinned (that is, sins committed after receiving the eschatological Spirit). If we claim that we have not actually sinned, then we make God a liar because God has indicated (through his word [v. 10c]) that he will forgive our sins and, if we claim we have no sins, then there is no need for the forgiveness that God has promised. Therefore, we have made God a liar!

Again the issue is an important point of conflict between the author and his opponents. Because they believed that they had received the eschatological

6. See also Mic 7:18-20.

Spirit in its fullness, the opponents believed that they were totally transformed and neither had guilt of sin nor would they sin again in the future. While the author also believes that the eschatological outpouring of the Spirit has occurred, he does not hold to a totally realized eschatology but one in which we are inchoatively "perfect" and thus still capable of sin.[7]

In 2:1a, the author interrupts his carefully arranged parallels and addresses his readers directly, earnestly expressing his hope that they will not sin in the future. That is, in spite of the past sins (which it would be wrong to deny), the author hopes that the believer will not sin in the future. But again (2:1b), the author recognizes the possibility of sin and affirms that even if the believer does sin in the future, Jesus, the Just One, will act as a Paraclete before the Father. Earlier the author had described God the Father as "just." Now he says the same thing of Jesus who is the Paraclete before the Father. The author then (v. 2) reaffirms that Jesus is an atonement not only for "our" sins (that is, the sins of the community) but for those of the entire world.

Addendum: Are There References to Sacraments in 1:5–2:2?

(1) Confession of Sin

Given the reference to "confessing our sins" in 1:9, it is not surprising that the question has arisen whether this implies a reference to a ritual confession of sin. There have been a considerable variety of responses to this question.

Schnackenburg argues that it is unlikely that 1:9 is intended as a reference to a kind of ritual confession of sin such as is found in the sacraments.[8] He understands the words against the background of the confession of sins within Judaism but not involving any human intermediaries as are envisioned in John 20:23. After examining the texts from James and the *Didache* and the related text in 1 John 5:16, Schnackenburg concludes: "The context in each case is quite different and presupposes a concrete situation quite unlike that in 1 John 1:9."

Brown rejects Schnackenburg's view (that, because the confession is to God, the reference is not to a public ritual) on the grounds that throughout 1:5–2:2 one's relation to God is understood to exist within a community context.[9] Brown also argues that everywhere "confess" is used in the context of belief, it involves a *public* declaration and so such a public acknowledgment is implied here. Although, in his Note on 1:9a, Brown does not say explicitly that 1:9 refers to a public ritual, he does say that "the confession would have been seen as related to Jesus' promise [in John

---

7. That the believer is still capable of sin is also clear from 2:28; 3:3, 19-21; 5:16.
8. Schnackenburg, *Epistles* 82-83.
9. Brown, *Epistles* 208.

20:23]." Later, in his comment on v. 9, we can deduce that this is his view when he states that the opponents' claim to freedom from sin "is matched with the idea of publicly confessing sins." Although he later discusses the life setting of 1:5–2:2 in some detail, Brown does not address the specific meaning of confession of sins again. Consequently, the most we can conclude is that, in Brown's view, v. 9a refers to some sort of public confession regarding sins.

Smalley's treatment is briefer.[10] While he recognizes that some public action is referred to, he claims that "the manner of the acknowledgment is not specified." Yet Smalley, citing Wescott, does not exclude the possibility that there is an allusion to a public confession of sins. He goes on to suggest that the plural "sins" "probably indicates that the confession of particular acts of sin is meant. . . ."

Klauck calls attention to the lack of normal terminology for the confession of sin and to the fact that the verb *homologeō* is commonly used in confession regarding matters of faith.[11] Klauck also notes that practice of public (ritual) confession of sins was common in the first century as is evident in the ministry of John the Baptist (Mark 1:5 and parallels) and in the statements of Jas 5:16 and the *Did.* 4:14. Moreover, John 20:23 refers to an adjudicatory power over sin being given to the disciples. On the basis of the evidence within the larger context of early Christianity and within the Gospel of John, Klauck concludes that it is likely that 1:9 also refers to a ritual action regarding the confession of sin.

Painter treats the text as referring to ritual confession of sin without argument.[12] Beutler thinks of the process as public confession of sin but associates it with the initiation process into the community, thus not thinking of it as recognition of ongoing sinfulness but of sinfulness before conversion. Strecker admits to uncertainty in the matter: "Whether such a confession is meant to be public and refers to the congregation's penitential practice, or whether it refers exclusively to a confession of sins before God, must remain an open question at this point."[13]

From this survey, it should be evident that, while most see a reference to some sort of public action, the nature of that action remains uncertain. Yet there can scarcely be said to be strong support for a sacramental understanding of the verse.

My own view, which has been presented in the Interpretation, is that, while there is clear evidence of ritual of the confession of sins in other sectors of early Christianity and, indeed, in the third edition of the Gospel, there is not sufficient support *from the pages of 1 John itself* to claim the existence of such a ritual at the time of 1 John. Rather, in keeping with the author's overall purpose in 1 John, he counters the opponents' conviction that the believer is incapable of sin with the conviction that he/she is and that, in fact, the believer must also acknowledge the

10. Smalley, *Epistles* 30-31.
11. Klauck, *Erste Johannesbrief* 94-95.
12. Painter, *Epistles* 145, 155.
13. Strecker, *Epistles* 32.

actuality of personal sins. In this sense, "confess" does not refer to a ritual act. It is a public acknowledgment of one's overall attitude and conviction regarding the possibility/reality of sin.

(2) Baptism/Initiation Rite

One of the foremost proponents of a sacramental view of 1 John was Nauck. In 1957, after a study of parallels to the language and thought of 1 John 1:5–2:2, Nauck proposed that there was a source underlying several parts of 1 John which consisted of a series of antitheses prepared for use in the community's Baptismal ceremony.[14] While the differentiation of this proposed source from the author's own additions has not been generally accepted, his study of the comparative materials has recently been taken up by Brown.

In his 1981 commentary, Brown provides an extended discussion of "The Life-Setting of the Material in 1:5–2:2."[15] From his survey of the ritual of admission for the community at Qumran (1QS 1:18–2:25; 3:17-22), the scattered evidence for a Christian initiation ceremony in various New Testament documents (Acts 26:18; Col 1:13-14; Eph 5:6-11; Heb 10:19-21; 1 Pet 1–2) as well as in *Did.* 7 and the *Epistle of Barnabas* 18, Brown concludes succinctly: "The similarities between the ideas common to these various forms of conversion/initiation/baptism and the ideas in 1 John 1:5–2:2 are striking. . . . I do not suggest that 1 John gives us in whole or part a homily for an initiation ceremony or for baptism. . . . But I do think that, in this unit of 1 John, the association of ideas is not accidentally similar to that found elsewhere in contemporary Jewish and Christian initiation practice."[16]

While there are recognizable similarities between the material of 1:5–2:2 and 1QS and to other references to conversion experiences in the New Testament, I would suggest that we need to be careful to recognize what we have discovered. It is clear from 1QS that the discussion of belief and forgiveness takes place in a context of community initiation. This is explicit in the text. When we look at the material of 1 John 1:5–2:2, we do not find any explicit references to an initiation ceremony. What we do find is material that *could* perhaps fit such a life setting. That is, it is *compatible* with such a setting. Imagery of light and darkness, which appears in the initiation ceremony at Qumran, also appears in some references to the conversion

---

14. Nauck, *Tradition*.

15. Brown, *Epistles* 242-45.

16. Brown also proposes that the complex of ideas underlying a number of other passages in 1 John can be associated with a "Covenant/Initiation/Baptism Background," among them 2:12-14, 20-23, 2:28–3:10; 4:7-10; 5:13-17. With regard to 2:28–3:10, Brown (*Epistles* 432-34) suggests that similarities in those verses to materials in 1 Peter 1–2 and Titus "represent exhortations drawn from a common body of ideas." Brown argues that the author is "reminding his readers of the Johannine theology proclaimed to them and accepted by them when they became Christians."

experience (not necessarily a ceremony) in Acts, Ephesians, Colossians, Hebrews and 1 Peter. In the preparation for Baptism, as it is described in the *Didache,* there is an instruction on two ways. In both the *Didache* and *Barnabas,* there is forgiveness of sins.

But there is also another explanation for the material and its configuration in 1 John. As we see throughout, the author is trying to articulate the important ways in which his opponents are "walking in darkness." He explains his own view of the tradition and refutes the views of his opponents. As a result, it should not be surprising that some similarity exists between this document and other documents that treated similar matters, though for different purposes and in different circumstances.

Further, there is an essential difference between the manner of argumentation in 1 John and that in the proposed parallels. While there is a general rejection of evil in the other documents that speak of the conversion experience, this is hardly the same as the detailed refutation of opponents such as we find in 1 John. If the material in 1 John 1:5–2:2 did not have such a clear, polemical thrust, it would be easier to argue for the more specific setting of an initiation rite. However, the material is not concerned with general issues but with refutation of specific claims and with the establishment of others. Thus, the overall purpose of 1 John is quite different from these other documents — and from the initiation process. Again, this is not to deny that elements of the Johannine material could function in the setting of a conversion process, but there is *no positive evidence* that the setting of the material within 1 John is either sacramental or connected with an initiation rite.[17]

In comparing 1 John with the Qumran materials, we find another striking similarity between the two, which suggests that the Qumran material had a broader application than an initiation process. As I have pointed out elsewhere,[18] the members of the Qumran community underwent an examination not just during the process of initial application but during the longer period leading to full membership in the Community and then, after the person was a full member, the individual continued to be examined annually.

In 1QS 6:13-23, we find a description of this entire process. The prospective member was first examined "concerning his understanding and his deeds" by the Guardian who was the head of the community. After the person was instructed in the rules of the Community, his case was deliberated by the Community. If he was allowed to enter the community, he began a series of steps involving progressive admission to the Meal of the Community, the enrollment of his property with the Community, his admission to the Sacred Drink of the Community, and eventually the merging of his property with that of the Community. At each stage, the person was examined by the Priests and the multitude of the men of their Covenant "with respect to his understanding and observance of the Law." Thus, within 1QS 6:13-18,

---

17. We have no knowledge of the process by which a person became a member of the Johannine community. Presumably, it involved some sort of public confession at the very least.

18. von Wahlde, *Commandments* 245-54.

there are three explicit references to examination "concerning one's understanding and one's deeds."

In 1QS 5:20-24, it is said that each person was inscribed in the community in a rank determined "with respect to his understanding and practice of the Law." Each year, the community examined the members regarding "their spirit and deeds" so that each might be advanced "in accordance with his understanding and perfection of way" or moved down in accordance with his offenses.

From the pages of 1 John, we see that the two major concerns of the author are functionally identical to the two elements of the scrutiny performed at Qumran. First, the author is concerned with correct belief ("understanding") and also with correct action ("deeds"). Correct belief concerns correct confession regarding Jesus, regarding sinfulness, regarding future judgment, etc. Correct action concerns, above all, the practice of mutual love, but also the general practice of "just deeds." This double pattern of correct belief and correct action is so pervasive that the central "claims" of the community were said to be determined by them. These are detailed in Chart E-6 (pp. 367-69).

But even here, the parallel is not exact. There is no evidence that the author of 1 John was concerned with either initiation or with annual review. He addressed his "letter" to those who were already members of the community and perhaps to those who had been members and who had departed (his "opponents"). His concern is distinguishing correct belief from false belief and correct behavior from incorrect behavior. He seeks to have his readers follow the correct path and so, inevitably, his language will reflect the assertion of truth over falsehood and, because he speaks within an apocalyptic framework, he uses the imagery of light and darkness. Consequently, there would naturally be an emphasis on correct confessional formulas and explanation of the essential elements of the community's convictions. Thus, the articulation of ideas in 1 John could well be compatible with Baptismal exhortation, but I do not find anything in the exhortation that would indicate that such exhortation actually derived from a Baptismal context.

The New Commandment: To Keep the Word

₃And by this we are certain that we have come to know him [God]:
   if we keep his [God's] commandments.
₄The one claiming "I have come to know him [God]" but not keeping his
[God's] commandments
   is a liar and
   the truth is not present in him.

₅But the one who keeps his [God's] word —
   in this person the love of God has been truly brought to perfection.
   By this, we know that we are "in him [God]."

₆The one claiming to abide "in him" [God]
   must himself also walk as that one [Jesus] walked.

₇Loved Ones, I am not writing to you about a new commandment
   but an old one that you have had from the beginning.
      The "old" commandment is the word that you heard.
   ₈In another sense, I am writing to you about a new commandment.
      This is true
         in him [Jesus] and
         in you
            that the darkness is being taken away and
            the true light is already shining.

₉The one claiming to be "in the light" and hating his brother
   is still in darkness.

₁₀The one loving his brother
   abides in the light and
   there is no cause for stumbling in him.

11 But the one hating his brother
   is in the darkness and
   walks in the darkness and
   does not know where he is going
      because the darkness has blinded his eyes.

NOTES TO 2:3-11

V. 3 that we have come to know This is the first instance of "know" (Gk: *ginōskō*) in the Letter. It will appear a total of twenty-five times. Although it can be used to indicate common knowledge of something, in the Johannine tradition it is used more frequently to denote a knowledge that was a prerogative of one who had received the eschatological outpouring of the Spirit. Such a one "knows" God. This claim is made by both the author's followers and the opponents.

There was considerable emphasis on "knowing" as an eschatological prerogative in the second edition of the Gospel, and it has a rich background in the Old Testament. In the debates within the community, the author now isolates this prerogative and denies that it can be true of the opponents. Note, however, that the author's isolation of this prerogative from its larger Old Testament context was undoubtedly one of the features that eventually made the Johannine tradition attractive to various gnostic groups.

him Grammatically, one would expect this to refer to Jesus because he had been mentioned in the previous verse. However, the claims *of the opponents* always refer to God rather than to Jesus. Where the object is explicit, it is God the Father (cf. 2:14; 4:6, 7, 8). Other instances where the object is not explicit probably refer to God the Father also (2:13, 14; 3:1, 6; 5:20). Only twice does the author say that the believer "knows" the Spirit (4:2, 6), and in these instances it means "to distinguish" (the Spirit of Truth from the Spirit of Deception).

his commandments In 1 John, the commandments are always those of God (rather than of Jesus as will be the case in the third edition). The word appears here in the plural and then turns to the singular. The author thus begins with general exhortation and then switches to the discussion of a specific commandment. This pattern is consistent throughout the Johannine literature. While many scholars argue that there is only one commandment in the Johannine tradition, it is difficult for them to explain why the author uses the plural as he does.

V. 4 liar See at 1:6. This is the fourth time in the Letter that false claims are described as lying and failing the truth: "we lie and do not do the truth" (1:6); "we deceive ourselves and the truth is not in us" (1:8); "we make him a liar and his word is not in us" (1:10); and here "[the one making false claims] is a liar and the truth is not present in him" (2:4).

V. 5 keeps his word The meaning of this phrase is important for understanding the Johannine commandment tradition. There are two issues. First, there is the meaning of the term "word"; second, there is the meaning of the larger phrase "to keep the word of God."

References to "the word of God" and "his word" and "my word" are frequent in the Gospel (appearing over twenty-five times). In the three Letters, statements regarding "the word of God" appear only five times (1 John 1:1, 10; 2:5, 7, 14). Yet, from its discussion here in 2:5, 7, 14, it is evident that the term is an important one for the community.

In some of these instances its meaning is patently clear. In 1:1, although "the word" is not specified as "of God," there can be no doubt that it is. It refers to the message and the content that was handed down to the community and which they believed would lead to life. In 1:10, we can see how the author uses "word" to refer to the message that they have received. The author explains that "If we say we have not sinned, we make [God] a liar and his word is not in us." Thus, the believers have sinned and are in need of redemption. This is part of the message ("the word") that they have received.

According to 2:5, the one who keeps God's word is the one in whom the love of God is brought to perfection. In 2:14, we will hear that the word of God abides in the "young people" and that they are strong and have conquered the Evil One. In each of these cases, "the word of God" refers to the message that had been handed down to them.

But what about the one remaining instance: "This old commandment is the word that you heard" (2:7)? The operative part of the sentence is "the word that you heard." This instance would also seem to refer to the overall message handed down to the community. But the question then remains: Why is "the word" seemingly equated with commandment in v. 7c? The common explanation is that "word" in v. 7c is simply a synonym for commandment (e.g., Brown, *Epistles* 252; Painter, *Epistles* 176). That is, just as the Ten Commandments are called the ten "words" (*dᵉbarim*) in the Old Testament (cf. Exod 20:1; 34:28; Deut 4:13; 10:4), so here the author uses "word" as a synonym for "commandment." Thus, v. 7c means: "The old commandment is the commandment that you heard."

But there are problems with this explanation. The first is that, since the author has already said that the commandment is one they have had from the beginning (v. 7b), little would be added by v. 7c, since v. 7c would then mean "the commandment is the commandment that you heard." That is redundant and awkward. But the greater problem is that if we understand "word" in v. 7c to mean commandment, "word" would be taking on a meaning that it has nowhere else in the context — and indeed nowhere else in the Johannine tradition! As we have seen, "word" is a term used often in the tradition: it always refers to the totality of the message delivered to the believer by God (in the case of the Letter) or by Jesus (in the case of the Gospel). It is hard to imagine that in this verse the author would adopt an entirely different meaning for the term without some explanation.

Now we will turn to the use of the larger expression "keep the word" *(tēreō ton logon)*. In the Gospel, this expression appears eight times (8:51, 52, 55; 14:23, 24; 15:20 [twice]; 17:6). Two things are noteworthy here. First, in all of these instances, it is generally recognized to mean "keep the message" (that is, be faithful to the message) of Jesus. So, for example, in John 8:38-50, the entire focus is on listening to the words of Jesus that are the words of God the Father. The same is true of John 14, where (in v. 24) it is made explicit that the words of Jesus are indeed the words of the Father. Thus, even though the "word" is specified as the word of Jesus, it is consistently as ultimately the word of God the Father. This is precisely the notion that is found in 1 John.

Secondly, all of these instances come from the third edition of the Gospel. That is, they were added to the Gospel *after* the writing of 1 John and so were undoubtedly motivated by the author of 1 John's insistence on the importance of remaining faithful to the historical words of Jesus.

In 1 John itself, the Greek verb *tēreō* occurs seven times. It appears once with "word" (2:5), five times with "commandments" (2:3, 4; 3:22, 24; 5:3), and once with "himself" (in the sense of "protect"; 5:18). Of the instances in 1 John, most uses of *tēreō* occur with "commandments" rather than "word." This could be seen as support for the common view that the expression "keep the word" is simply a synonym for keeping the commandments. Yet several factors argue against this interpretation. First is the fact that, elsewhere in 1 John, "word" refers to the message of Jesus and not to "commandment" as we have seen above. Second, the expression has the meaning "to keep the word" (of Jesus) throughout the third edition of the Gospel. Third, a discussion in John 14:15-24 links commandment with "keeping the word of Jesus," indicating that the third author also understands the injunction to "keep the word" of Jesus as a commandment. Fourth, in the larger context of the Johannine Letters there are two texts that speak of a commandment referring to something other than mutual love. The same is true in the third edition, where, in 14:15-24, it is clear that the commandment being referred to is not that of mutual love.

Admittedly, the formulation of 1 John 2:5-7 is awkward. Why this is so is uncertain. We can only offer some suggestions. The Johannine commandments are articulated for the first time in 1 John. As we will see, each of the commandments is expressed in a variety of ways. In the third edition, the presentation of the commandments is much more concise. This is true particularly of the "first" commandment. In John 14, the commandment deals with keeping the word of Jesus. It may be that at the time of 1 John, the author recognized that the "first" commandment had to do with belief but had not yet reached a fixity of expression, as becomes apparent by the time of the third edition of the Gospel. Yet this expression will become the standard way of referring to the first commandment in the third edition.

love of God This phrase appears six times in 1 John (2:5, 15; 3:17; 4:9, 12; 5:3). Klauck (*Erste Johannesbrief* 116-17) thinks that it refers to the love that God exhibits while Strecker (*Epistles* 42) sees it as ambiguous, referring to either love for God or God's love for others. I would accept the first of the meanings proposed by Strecker as relevant here since the focus is on what the believer manifests by his/her actions. In this case, keeping the word of God demonstrates the believer's love for God.

V. 6 to abide The Greek word *menō* is literally translated "remain." It can also mean "abide" and connotes having a deep and lasting relationship. Thus, the believer may be said to abide in God (2:6; 3:24a); to abide in the Son and the Father (2:24); or to abide in Jesus (2:28; 3:6). In other cases, it does not have a personal dimension but emphasizes a permanent relation of some other kind. Thus, the believer is said to abide in the light (2:10) and in love (4:16). The one not loving abides in death (3:14).

There is another class of texts in which something is said to abide in the believer: the word of God (2:14); what the believer has heard from the beginning (2:24 [twice]); the anointing (2:27 [twice]); God's seed (3:9); and the love of God (3:17). Every murderer does not have eternal life abiding in him/her (3:15). The one who does the will of God is said simply "to abide (forever)" (2:17).

In yet another series of texts, "abide" describes *mutual* abiding. In these texts, God is said to abide in the believer (something not stated in any of the above) and then the believer is likewise said to abide in God. This appears first in 3:24a. Immediately following that verse, there is an explanation of how the believer knows that he/she abides. And then the topic is not addressed until 4:13-18 where it appears three times in succession (4:13bc; 15bc; 16de) and then not again in the Letter.

Finally, it is used of the relationships within the community. Thus, the opponents do not "remain with us" *(menein meth' hēmōn)* (2:19).

In 1 John, the true believer "abides in" both Jesus and the Father (2:24). However, as is the case with many aspects of their beliefs, the opponents do not dispute the importance of abiding in God the Father but only whether it is important to abide in Jesus. Consequently, in his exhortation, the author will focus on the necessity of abiding in Jesus (e.g., 2:28; 3:6). (In this exhortation, the believer is always the subject of the verb.) The benefits of this abiding in Jesus are also explained: the believer will have courage, will not shrink from Jesus at his coming (2:28), and will never sin (3:6).

But the author also explains that the opponents will fail even in their own claim (to abide in God the Father) unless they *believe and act correctly.* The believer will not abide in God, unless he/she walks as "that one" (Jesus) walked. Unless the believer obeys God's commandment to love one another, the believer will not abide in God (3:24). Unless one believes in Jesus, one will not abide in God (4:15c). The First Letter of John 4:13 also speaks of how we know that we abide in God — by the presence of the Spirit. Thus, the overall usage is clear. Here the series of claims are those of the opponents and all deal with claims regarding the Father (for the notion of indwelling typical of the second edition, see 2E-23; for the notion as it appears in the third edition, see 3E-41).

"in him" The pronoun here refers to the Father. This is likely since all the pronouns refer to God the Father in the preceding context, that is, "him" in v. 3a; "his" in v. 3b; "him" and "his" in v. 4a; "his" in v. 5; "in him" in v. 5c. Moreover, a parallelism ("The one claiming . . .") is present among v. 4a, 6a and 9a; and, in all cases, the claims are those of the opponents, which, as we have seen, only concern the Father.

that one walked Here the antecedent of the pronoun suddenly shifts to Jesus. That is, the model for behavior is Jesus. If one claims to abide in the Father, one must walk as Jesus walked. "Walking" is a metaphor for the behavior urged by the second Johannine commandment, to love one another. This was how Jesus walked. In 3:24, abiding in God will be tested the same way: by one's behavior manifested as love for other believers. Although the shift of antecedents for the pronouns in v. 6a and v. 6b is sudden and awkward, it makes good sense of the verse, is consistent with the usage elsewhere in 1 John and gives the clearest meaning of the present context. For further discussion, see the Interpretation below.

V. 7 Loved Ones This form of address appears six times in 1 John (2:7; 3:2, 21; 4:1, 7, 11) and four times in 3 John (1, 2, 5, 11). Although the expression itself is ambiguous and could indicate that the listener is beloved either of the author or of God, it is probably intended to reflect the author's caring attitude and so function in a way similar to the diminutive "little children" *(teknia, paidia)*. But the listener is beloved of the author because he/she is beloved of God so the two choices are closely related.

61

I am not writing to you about a new commandment This is often taken to refer to the commandment texts in the Gospel and so to be an indication that the Gospel was written before 1 John. However, the contrast between "new" and "old," within the context of 1 John, opposes the views of the opponents (which are "new") with those of the author (which go back to Jesus and to "the beginning" of the tradition). Thus, it was a commandment they had "from the beginning"; it is not "new" like the beliefs of the opponents, which go beyond the teaching of Jesus (2 John 9).

V. 8 In another sense The Greek word *palin* ("again") indicates the author is reflecting again on the theme of old and new.

This The sentence beginning with "this" in the translation is an appositive clause in the Greek. "This" translates the neuter relative pronoun *(ho)* and refers to the entire following clause: "that the darkness . . . and the true light . . . shining." Because it is neuter gender, it cannot refer to "commandment," nor can it be intended to introduce a different commandment from that mentioned previously. The purpose of the statement is to explain the "newness" mentioned in v. 8a: the darkness is beginning to pass away and the light is beginning to shine. This passing away of the darkness and the coming of the light is actualized both in Jesus (his ministry) and in the life of the believer. The actuality of the believers' presence in the light is contrasted with the opponents' continued existence in darkness, which will be mentioned in v. 9.

true in him In keeping with the immediate context, "him" refers to Jesus. It is in Jesus that the true light is manifest and then also in the believer who follows Jesus.

The darkness is being taken away and the true light is already shining It was said in 1:5 that God is light. But no "being" was identified with "darkness." Rather, darkness is conceived of as a state of existence. Here "the light" (which is said to be manifest in Jesus and in the life of the believer) seems to take on something of the same meaning and to refer also to the state of existence created by the ministry of Jesus. See also the instances in vv. 9-11 below. This usage has parallels, for example, in *TNaph* 2:10 ("You are not able to perform the works of light while you are in darkness").

V. 9 to be "in the light" As was the case in the previous verse, "the light" here seems to refer primarily to a state of being and then secondarily to God (who is light).

hating his brother With the theme of "hating," the author introduces a third dualistic pair: loving/hating. The verb is always used either of hating one's brother (2:9, 11; 3:15; 4:20) or the world hating the author's followers (3:13).

Because 1 John was written prior to the third edition of the Gospel, this constitutes the first discussion of love and hate in the Johannine tradition. The author points to the one who claims to be in the light but hates his brother. He then goes on to speak of "the one who loves his brother" in v. 10.

V. 10 the one loving his brother The nature and importance of this love will be discussed repeatedly in 1 John (2:15; 3:10, 11, 14 [twice], 18, 23; 4:7 [twice], 8, 11, 12, 20, 21; 5:1, 2). It appears also in 2 John 5 and implicitly in 2 John 11 and 3 John 5-8.

The Johannine love is defined as "love for one another," that is, a mutual love. This form of love is also found in the *T12P* and in the SDQ. It is not formally as extensive as the love of one's enemies expressed, for example, in Matt 5:43-48. However, the seeming narrowness of this love is determined by the apocalyptic context in which it occurs. This is evident in the Johannine literature in 2 John 10-11. In that text, the author urges his readers not to give hospitality to the opponents since to do so would be to take part in their evil deeds. Thus, one cannot extend love (understood in this way) to the opponents since it would have an evil effect. On the background of mutual love, see 3E-15.

The term "brother" is used frequently in the New Testament for one's coreligionist. Within the Johannine literature, it is found only in 1 John and in the third edition. It also occurs in the SDQ (e.g., 1QS 6:10, 22; CD 7:1, 2; 20:18).

there is no cause for stumbling in him The Greek *skandalon* refers to something that causes stumbling or falling. There are two problems here. First, the Greek *en autō* is ambiguous and could mean either that "in it" (that is, in the light) there is no stumbling or there is no (cause for) stumbling "in him," that is, in the one who loves one's brother. Brown (*Epistles* 274-75) discusses the options at length.

The second problem also regards *en autō*. Does this phrase refer to one who does not stumble, or does it refer to someone else for whom the believer could be a cause of stumbling? This second problem seems readily solved since the surrounding context speaks of the effect on the believer (even when the issue is brotherly love).

Once the second problem is settled, it becomes apparent that whichever alternative is taken regarding the first problem, the meaning is not seriously affected. The overall meaning of v. 10c is clear: in contrast to the person who does not love the brothers, the person who does love the brothers does not walk in darkness and is not blinded. Therefore, the individual will not trip or fall (that is, be affected by the *skandalon*).

V. 11 the one hating his brother is in the darkness There is a close parallel to this in *TNaph* 2:10 (quoted in the Note to v. 8 above) although the emphasis is a bit different. In 1 John, one's evil actions reveal that the person is in darkness, but then 1 John goes on to say that while the one is in darkness, the person does not know where she/he is going because the darkness has blinded the person. Thus, the failure to perform good actions is associated with darkness in both texts.

OVERVIEW OF 2:3-11

The author now changes the topic suddenly, introduces the theme of "knowing" God and "keeping his commandments." The author argues that claims to interior prerogatives such as "knowing" God, "abiding" in him and being "in the light" need to be tested by something external and observable — by one's behavior. Such behavior consists, first, of proper belief evident in external confession of that belief. And then he compares the true believer with the opponents. The one who keeps the word of God demonstrates perfect love for God, but the opponents are liars because they do not obey the commandment to keep the word of God. And the word about which the author speaks is not new but what they had heard from the beginning. In that sense the commandment is "old," but it is "new" in the sense that it is actualized in Jesus and in the believer.

The second type of behavior that is used to test claims is the love of one's fellow believer. Again the author compares the true believer with the opponents. The one who loves his brother is in the light; the one who does not is in darkness, is blinded, and stumbles.

THE STRUCTURE OF 2:3-11

The structure of this section is quite precise, readily recognizable and achieved (as in the previous section) by parallelism, chaining, contrast, and inclusion.

Parallelism

Parallelism is evident in the three sections, each of which begins with the words: "The one claiming . . ." (vv. 4-5, 6-8, 9-11). The parallelism continues in the phrasing of three claims: (v. 4) to "know" him; (v. 6) to "remain in him"; (v. 9) to be "in the light."[1]

---

1. The only interruption to an even greater parallelism is that, in the first and third claims, the behavior of the opponents is contrasted with their claims while in the second claim this is present only by implication.

Chaining

Chaining is evident in the way these parallel sections are joined to one another and to what precedes them. The first claim (v. 4) is linked to the introductory statement in v. 3 by the repetition of the catchwords "know" and "commandment." The discussion of the first claim ends with a consideration of the possibility of being "in him." The notion of being "in him" then becomes the topic of the second claim (v. 6) and is evaluated in terms of being "in the darkness" and "in the light." In turn, being "in the light" becomes the basis of the third claim (v. 9) and is discussed in terms of loving one's brother. This discussion then ends with a final parallel in vv. 10 and 11 that contrasts the one who loves his brother with the one who hates his brother.

Contrast

The author used contrasting pairs throughout the section. For example, "not keeping his commandments" in v. 4a is contrasted with "but the one who keeps his word" in v. 5a. In v. 4b, "is a liar" is reversed in v. 4c: "and the truth is not in him." In v. 7, a "new" commandment is contrasted with an "old" commandment.[2] In v. 8b, "the darkness is being taken away" is contrasted with "and the true light is already shining" in v. 8c. Through vv. 9-11 "darkness" is contrasted with "light"; and "the one who loves his brother" is contrasted with "the one who hates his brother." Thus, throughout the section the reader is presented with stark alternatives from which to choose.

Inclusion

By the time we get to vv. 9-11, we have returned to the themes of light and darkness, which had been introduced at the beginning of the section (1:5-7a); thus these motifs tie the section together into a unit.[3] But beyond this inclusion, the section as a whole is bound together by an intricate and extensive use of rhetorical devices, as we have seen.

THE INTERPRETATION OF 2:3-11

In this section the author addresses three claims of the opponents: to know God, to abide in him and to be in the light. These are legitimate claims made by

---

2. There is also a minor chiastic arrangement in vv. 7-8a, evident in the alternation of "new" (v. 7a) with "old" (v. 7b) paralleled with "old" (v. 7c) and then returning to "new" (v. 8a).

3. There is considerable similarity in structure between 2:4 and 1:6. Klauck (*Erste Johannesbrief* 110-12) treats 2:3-11 as a quasi-repetition of 1:5-2:2.

the Johannine community. They are criticized only insofar as they are made by the opponents who cannot hope for such status for themselves because their behavior is improper.

Vv. 3-5

Verse 3 introduces the claim "to know him [God]" suddenly and unexpectedly. This is apparent when v. 3 is read directly after v. 2 (and not broken apart as it is in the commentary form). Awareness of this break makes the unity of the following section more clear. The claim to know God was one of the prerogatives of the eschatological outpouring of the Spirit. But the author explains that there is a test to determine whether one genuinely knows God. That test is whether the person keeps God's commandments. In v. 4, the author explains that the one who claims to know God but does not keep his commandments is a liar and the truth is not present in him. Thus, the author argues that the claim to know God (in the eschatological sense of the term), a claim that is abstract and thus something anyone could make, can be verified only by something external. In this case, whether one keeps the commandments can be verified and so it can be determined if the person who made the claim to know God was speaking the truth or was a liar.

Up to this point there is no problem because the discussion of commandments has been general. A first reading of the next verse (v. 5) seems to be relatively straightforward also; but, when we examine it more closely, a deeper significance emerges.

In v. 5, the author presents a contrast with the person who makes the claim in v. 4 to know God.[4] In v. 5, we see that the one who keeps the word of God truly loves God. Here "keeping the word of God" refers to being faithful to the message of God, as was explained in the Note. The author then adds that this person is "in him [God]." However, the opponents could agree with what the author is saying since they would have claimed to have kept the word of God. And so the true point of contrast has not yet been reached.

4. Verse 5 closely parallels v. 4 in three specific ways: (1) In each, a certain kind of person is identified: in v. 4, it is the one who claimed to know God but did not keep his commandments; in v. 5, it is the one who keeps his word. (2) The one described is then evaluated: the person spoken of in v. 4 is a liar; the person spoken of in v. 5 demonstrates the love of God brought to perfection. (3) Finally, the relationship of this actuality to claims is described: in v. 4, the truth is not in the person; in v. 5, it is said that "from this" we know that we are "in him." Notice also that the third element of each verse is introduced by the same phrase *(en toutō)* ("in this"), although the meaning is different in each case.

Vv. 6-8

In v. 6, the author introduces the second claim and takes the argument one step further by saying that "abiding in God" requires that the person walk as Jesus walked. This will become the point of contention with the opponents since they do not take Jesus as a permanent model.

The author then makes it clear (v. 7) that what he had just referred to as the obligation to "walk as Jesus walked" is what is more properly described as a "commandment," and it is to this commandment that he is referring. Whereas he had spoken previously of the commandments (plural) in general, now he speaks of "commandment" in the singular and therefore has in mind a specific commandment.[5] The author then enters into a contrast between "new" and "old" and applies both of these adjectives to the notion of "commandment." They are important features but tend to interrupt the flow of the larger sequence of thought.

His first point about this commandment is that it is not "new" but an old one that they have had "from the beginning." By speaking this way the author contrasts what he is saying with the "new" teaching of the opponents who "are progressive and do not remain in the teaching of the Christ" (2 John 9).

He then identifies the content of the commandment as "the word that you heard." This expression, in its literal form, is at least awkward, if not confusing. Only the context enables us to understand its meaning. Several elements of the context are particularly important. The first is the mention of "commandment(s)." Commandments are a topic three times in the Letter: (1) 2:3-8; (2) 3:22-24; (3) 4:21–5:3. In every other instance, in both the Letter (and the Gospel), the general statement of the need to keep the commandments is followed by the mention of a specific commandment. As was argued in the Note, if "word" is taken to refer to *dabar*, this would be the only instance of that meaning in the entire Johannine corpus. Moreover, if this were the meaning, then the present verse would be the only instance in the corpus in which the pattern of general exhortation to keep the commandments (plural) is not followed by a specific commandment presented in the singular. Nor can the statement mean that "the commandment" is "the message." That would be nonsense.

Consequently, the best explanation is that the verse refers to *keeping* the word of God. Because *keeping* the word of God was the issue in v. 5, the most reasonable conclusion is that when the author speaks here (v. 7) of the commandment as the "word," he is referring elliptically to (keeping) the word of

---

5. The consistency of this pattern throughout 1 John and throughout the third edition of the Gospel is shown in Appendix 5 (The Johannine Commandments) in this volume.

God.[6] Third, the references to "old," to "what we have had from the beginning" and to "the word that you heard" all echo the language the author had used at the very beginning of his Letter (1:1-3), namely the message that *"they had heard and seen from the beginning"* (v. 3).

Thus, all the evidence points to the conclusion that a specific commandment is being referred to here (although it is obscured by the elliptical way it is expressed) and that in full 2:7c would read: "This old commandment is [to keep] the word that you heard." It is not at all unusual for the author to speak elliptically (e.g., 1 John 3:11; 4:3, 13; 5:6; 2 John 12; 3 John 5) and so such shortening may well account for this phrasing. Thus, although the description of the commandment is complicated by the chaining technique, the elliptical manner of expression as well as by the awkward introduction of the contrast between new and old, there is no reason to think that the author has spoken of anything other than the obligation to keep the message which they heard from the beginning.

The first point the author makes about the commandment is that it is one they have had from the beginning. Then he says (v. 8) that, in another sense, the commandment can be said to be "new" in that it has just recently come to reality in Jesus (and in the believer). Although this second element of the contrast is often seen as simply a clever reflection on the opposite of the "old-ness," it is much more than that. The author is adopting as his own what was probably a claim of the opponents ("to have a 'new' message").[7] But, for the author, it is not "new" because it goes beyond the teaching of Jesus. For him, this "newness" is important because this commandment has begun to be actualized in Jesus and also in the believer insofar as the believer accepts and lives out the commandment and in so doing can be said to "walk[s] as Jesus walked."

This actualizing of the commandment manifests the fact that the darkness is being taken away and that the true light is shining (v. 8c-d). Earlier the author had identified God as the light (1:5); now the author speaks of the true light "already" shining. In the Letter the author speaks of the "light" both with respect to its *source* (God) and with respect to its *manifestation*. Here the manifestation of the light is evident both in Jesus and in the believer. It is manifest in Jesus through his ministry and it is manifest in the believer through proper belief and action. Thus, the author retains his God-centered focus but points to the presence of light in Jesus and in the believer as related to its source in God.

---

6. This understanding of the "first" Johannine commandment is confirmed, in the clearest of ways, by the fact that the author of the third edition takes over the notion of the commandment to keep the word of God and expresses it in a double fashion in the third edition. There Jesus receives a commandment from the Father concerning "what to say" (12:49), and Jesus, in turn, gives the disciples the commandment to keep the word that he was bidden to speak (14:21-24).

7. Such "insider language" also appears in 1 John 5:6. See below.

Consequently, it can be said that the true light is manifest without simply taking over the perspective of the Gospel that the light *is* Jesus. By adding that the light is *already* manifest, the author indicates not only the reality of the ministry but also the partially realized dimension of eschatology.

The line of thought throughout vv. 6-8 has been difficult to follow. But, for the author, the importance of these verses is that the commandment of God is to keep the word of God, that is, to remain faithful in correct belief. The one who keeps the word of God and actualizes it in his/her life can be said to be truly "in the light." Now in the following verses (vv. 9-11), any claim to be "in the light" will be taken up and challenged by the second test, that of proper behavior.

Vv. 9-11

From his explanation of the actualization of the light, the author then passes on (v. 9) to a discussion of the third of the claims, the claim to be "in the light." Brown aptly observes that, in 1 John, while the light is God, being "in the light" means to make claim to the prerogatives of being transformed from the realm of darkness to the realm of light.[8]

If someone claims to be in the light but hates his brother, that person is still in darkness. In other words, the claim is false because being in the light entails loving one's brother. Here we come to the first mention of mutual love in 1 John (and, therefore, in the Johannine tradition). Its proximity to the discussion of the commandment to keep the word of Jesus has led many to think that the commandment spoken of previously is really the commandment to mutual love, but that is not the case. Rather, the author has been speaking of testing claims to spiritual prerogatives. In vv. 4-8, he has said that claims to spiritual prerogatives have to be tested by the criterion of correct belief (do they truly keep the word of God?). Now he argues that such claims should also be tested by the other essential category of correctness: correct behavior, which is encapsulated in mutual love.

Then (vv. 10-11), the author compares the one who loves with the one who does not. The one who loves his brother not only *is* in the light, but *abides* in it. Because he has the light, he will not trip and fall.[9] But the one who hates his brother is completely taken over by the darkness because he *is* in the darkness (v. 11a), *walks* in the darkness (v. 11b) and *is blinded by* the darkness (v. 11c). With this scathing condemnation of the one who hates his brother, the author brings to a close his use of the images of light and darkness as symbols of the alternative states of existence open to the reader.

8. Brown, *Epistles* 288.

9. Although the word *skandalon* does not appear, a very similar idea appears in John 11:9-11. There, Jesus relates a parable that the person who walks during the day will not fall, but that the one who walks at night will fall because the light of the world is not in him.

Exhortation to Children, Fathers, Young Men

12I write to you, Dear Children,
> that your sins are forgiven through his [Jesus'] name.
13I write to you, Fathers,
> that you have known the one [Jesus] from the beginning.
I write to you, Young People,
> that you have conquered the Evil One.

14I wrote to you, Dear Children,
> that you have known the Father.
I wrote to you, Fathers,
> that you have known the one [Jesus] from the beginning.
I wrote to you, Young People,
> that you are strong and
> the word of God abides in you and
> you have conquered the Evil One.

15Do not love
> the world nor
> the things in the world.
If a person loves the world,
> the love of the Father is not in that person,
> > 16because everything in the world —
> > > the desire of the flesh, and
> > > the desire of the eyes, and
> > > the arrogance regarding life —
> > > > is not from the Father
> > > > but is from the world.
17And the world is passing away

and its desire,
 but the one doing the will of God abides forever.

NOTES TO 2:12-17

V. 12 I write to you The verb is in the present tense here and in the two instances in v. 13. In v. 14, it is in the aorist. A wide variety of explanations have
been offered for this shift (summarized and evaluated in Brown, *Epistles* 294-
97). Most of these would explain the past tense as a reference to some previous
writing, variously thought to be the Gospel, 2 John or a lost letter. All of these
proposals have serious deficiencies. Curiously, prior to this section, the author
uses only the present tense of *graphō* (1:4; 2:1, 7, 8) whereas after v. 14, he uses
only the aorist (also three times: 2:21, 26; 5:13). This has led many scholars to
conclude that the shift in tenses should be looked upon simply as a stylistic
variation without a difference in meaning. This will be the position adopted
here.

Dear Children For the meaning of the term and the translation, see at 2:1. This
is the first of three groups to be mentioned (children, fathers, young people).
Most commentators see the reference to children as a general reference to the
entire community and the references to fathers and young people as reflecting
subdivisions of the community. On the one hand, there is no precedent in the
Johannine literature for seeing the designation "children" as being anything
other than a reference to the entire community; and, on the other, there is significant precedent for seeing the reference to "fathers" and "young people" as
reflecting just such a subdivision (see below).

that There is considerable discussion whether the meaning of *hoti* in each of
the following six statements is declarative ("that") or causative ("because"). *Hoti*
appears only one other time with *graphō* in the Letter and that instance is also
ambiguous and provides no help. Brown's approach here is convincing in that
he attempts to see how each usage would fit within the context. To say that the
author writes "because" their sins are forgiven or "because" they have known
him from the beginning does not match the confident tone found elsewhere.
However, to say that the author is reaffirming "that" their sins are forgiven, and
"that" they have known him from the beginning is much more likely. This is the
view that will be adopted in all six instances here.

your sins are forgiven It is sometimes noted that both statements associated
with "children" (the entire community) can be found in Jer 38:34 (LXX) ("All

shall know me from the least to the greatest of them, because I will be propitious to their wrongdoing and I will remember their sins no longer"). Thus, the community will know Jesus (v. 14) and their sins are forgiven (v. 12). In so doing they will be part of the new covenant that Jeremiah predicts. It is also striking that this passage makes reference to the community in two groups as does the epistolary text.

through his Although *autou* ("his") is ambiguous, there can be little doubt that here it refers to Jesus. The two other instances of doing something in someone's name in 1 John (3:23; 5:13) refer to Jesus. Moreover, the context here requires Jesus. Finally, since the role of God is not at issue but that of Jesus is, it is unlikely that the pronoun refers to anyone else.

name "Name" appears three times in 1 John (here, 3:23 ["in the name of his Son, Jesus Christ]; and 5:13 ["in the name of the Son of God"]). It appears two times in 3 John (vv. 7, 15) but not in the same usage as here.

The common approach to the understanding of "name" as it appears in statements of belief in 1 John is to point to the Semitic understanding of one's name as encapsulating one's identity ("to know the name is to know the person"). Certainly, in the Gospel this is a very important dimension of the use of "name" (cf. John 17:6, 26). However, in each of the three cases in 1 John, the subsequent construction is different. Here it is used in the accusative with *dia;* in 3:23, it appears in the dative; in 5:13 it is used in the accusative with *eis.* Although scholars have attempted to discover precise distinctions in the use of prepositions in John, instances such as the present suggest that, for the author, the variations are not significant. To say that sins are forgiven "through the name of Jesus" is to say that it is in the authority connected with him that God chooses to forgive them. (See also the Note on John 1:12.)

V. 13 Fathers The "fathers" are one of the two divisions of the community. There is considerable Old Testament precedent (Exod 10:9; Josh 6:21; Isa 20:4 and Ezek 9:6) for a division of the community into "Elders" *(presbyteroi)* and "Young People" *(neaniskoi).* The Johannine use of "fathers" and "children" is probably a variant of this usage.

the one [Jesus] from the beginning There are two issues of concern in these words. The first involves the antecedent of the pronoun *ton* ("the one"). The closest antecedent (in v. 12) is also a pronoun and refers to Christ. Moreover, in v. 14, it is said specifically that the children will know the Father. Together, these factors suggest that the author is speaking of Jesus in this verse.

The second issue concerns the meaning of "from the beginning." The usage in the present verse and the occurrence of the same phrase in v. 14d are the only instances of *ton* (accusative sing. masc. of the article *ho, hē, to*) with *ap' archēs* without an expressed verb. Does this refer to the preexistence of Christ or does it refer to the beginning of the revelation of the Christ (that is, the beginning of the ministry)?

Although it is possible to understand the phrase as referring to the cosmic beginning (so Marshall, *Epistles* 139; Strecker, *Epistles* 117), two factors suggest this is not the case here. First, elsewhere in 1 and 2 John "beginning" refers exclusively to the community's beginning. In 1:1, we find *ho* (neuter nominative singular of the relative *hos, hē, ho*) with *ap' archēs* with the verb *ēn*. In that instance, the fact that the "beginning" refers to the beginning of the ministry rather than to a cosmic beginning is indicated by the repeated references to sensory experience of "what was from the beginning." In three other instances (2:24 [twice]; 3:11), there are references to things that "you heard from the beginning." In the two instances in 2:24, the antecedent is the neuter *ho* (as in 1:1). In 3:11, the reference is to the proclamation *(angelia)* and so the relative adjective is feminine, but the remainder of the wording is the same, as is the overall idea. Thus, all three of these refer to the beginning of the community's experience of Jesus.

The one remaining instance pertinent to the issue at hand is 2:7, where the reference is to an "old" commandment "which you have had from the beginning." Here, the feminine relative pronoun is used and agrees with "commandment" *(entolē)*. The beginning referred to is once again the beginning of their experience. (It is also said in 3:8 that the devil was a sinner "from the beginning" but this is not relevant to the present discussion.)

From this review, it is apparent that, in all other relevant instances in 1 John, "beginning" refers to the beginning of the ministry and not a cosmic beginning. However, it must be admitted that, in those instances, the relative pronouns refer to the message or some part of it (e.g., a commandment). In the present instances, the pronominalized adjective is used and refers to a person, not the message.

In the above examples, we were able to tell that the reference was to the beginning of experience rather than a cosmic beginning because of other factors in the surrounding context. In the present context, there is a significant similarity to the use in 2:7. There, the commandment was called "old" because it was one they had "from the beginning." Here the addressees are called "fathers" and they are contrasted with "young people." Thus, the differences in age are significant and in the present case those who are older are being referred to. In light of this similarity and in light of the fact that elsewhere in 1 John the phrase refers exclusively to the beginning of the ministry, I would conclude that this is the meaning intended in 2:13, 14. Thus, we are faced with the choice of putting more weight on precision of expression in the grammar of 2:13b or putting more weight on the contextual factors mentioned above. In light of the fact that the author's grammar is frequently awkward and ambiguous, the decision to rely on the context here seems a reasonable one. (So also notably Brown, *Epistles* 303-4, following de la Potterie, "Commencement" 397-99.)

Recognizing that the grammar is awkward, I see the statement as saying something similar to: "Fathers, I write to you that you have known the one [who is the one we knew] from the beginning." Thus, the author stresses the continuity between the Jesus they knew now and the one whom they knew at the beginning of the ministry.

Young People (Gk: *neaniskoi*) Those who had become members of the community more recently.

that you have conquered "Conquering" (Gk: *nikaō*) appears six times in the Letter (2:13, 14; 4:4; 5:4 [twice], 5). In these six instances, the verb has three objects: "the Evil One" (2:13, 14); "them" (4:4); and "the world" (5:4 [twice], 5). As will be seen from the exegesis of the individual passages, these various objects are all closely related. The key to understanding this concept is to be found in 4:4c which says that "you have conquered 'them' because that which is in you is greater than that which is in the world." That which is in the "world" is "the Evil One." Consequently, since the believers have conquered "them" (4:4) and since "they" have gone out into the world (4:1d) and are "of the world" (4:5), the believers can be said to have also conquered "the world" and "the Evil One."

the Evil One (Gk: *ton ponēron*) See also 2:14; 3:12 [twice]; 5:18, 19. The use of this term to refer to the devil is not unique to the Johannine community (cf. Matt 13:19; Eph 6:16). This instance refers to personified evil, the one dualistically opposed to God. Elsewhere in 1 John, the word *ponēros* always refers to "the Evil One," except in the second instance of 1 John 3:12 in which it is used to describe the works of a person who is under the influence of the Evil One. The term also appears in 2 John 11 where it refers to "evil deeds" and in 3 John 10, where it refers to "evil words."

The relation between "the Evil One" and "evil works" is expressed paradigmatically in 3:12. Thus, Cain was "of the Evil One" *(ek tou ponērou)* and killed his brother "because his [Cain's] works were evil" *(hoti ta erga autou ponēra ēn)*. This paradigm is presumed and is implicit in all the other uses of the term in the Gospel and Letters. That is, it is implicit in the statements of 1 John 2:13, 14 that "the young people" "have conquered the Evil One" and, in the statement of 5:18, that "the one born of God protects himself and the Evil One does not touch him." In 5:19, the two groups are spelled out explicitly: "We

74

know that we are of God and the whole world lies in the grasp of the Evil One." The paradigm is a reflection of the apocalyptic worldview of 1 John and is another version of the common stereotyped form of polemic where one's actions reveal one's allegiance to one or the other of a dualistically opposed pair. (For other examples see particularly 1 John 2:28–3:10; 4:1-6 and John 8:38-47 [which comes from the third author].)

V. 14 I wrote to you On the use of the aorist tense here, see at v. 12.

Dear Children, that you have known the Father The Greek word here *(paidia)* is different from that used in v. 12 *(teknia)*. If a distinction is intended, the distinction is not evident.

The second event that identifies them as "children" is that they have known the Father. This is "knowing" in the theological sense of having the true deep knowledge given by the Spirit. For the reason they are said to know the Father see on v. 13 above.

V. 15 Do not love the world In the eyes of the author, the world is the epitome of everything distant from, and opposed to, God. Nothing in the world is from the Father (2:16), rather the world lies in the grip of the Evil One (5:19). It is now the Last Hour and the Antichrist is already manifest in the world (4:3) as are false prophets, who have gone out from the community (4:3). Although the believer is in the world (4:17), the believer is not to love the world or the things of the world (2:15). The author's opponents are of the world and speak in a way typical of the world (4:5) and the world listens to them (4:5).

God had sent his unique son into the world (4:9) as the savior of the world (4:14), and Jesus was an atonement for the sins of the whole world (2:2). But the world rejected God and does not know the believer but rather hates him/her (3:13; 4:5). But now it is the Last Hour and the world is passing away along with all that is typical of it (2:17). The believer is to have courage because the power that is in the believer is greater than the one in the world (4:4). The one born of God conquers the world (5:4) and faith is what conquers the world (4:4), namely the belief that Jesus is the Son of God.

the love of the Father Is this "the Father's love" or "love for the Father"? Brown *(Epistles* 306) argues that something of both is involved. The parallel with loving the world suggests that it refers primarily to the Christian's love for the Father.

V. 16 the desire of the flesh The Greek term *epithymia* ("desire") appears only in these verses within the Johannine Letters and elsewhere in the Johannine literature only at 8:44, where those opposed to Jesus are said to have the devil as their father and to do his "desires." Here, the full phrase is the same as that appearing in Paul (e.g., Rom 13:14; Gal 5:16-17, 24) always with negative connotations.

"Flesh" *(sarx)* appears here for the first of three times in the Johannine Letters. It certainly can have a positive connotation in 1 and 2 John. In the two other instances in the Letters (1 John 4:2; 2 John 7), it is used to describe the modality of Jesus' own coming!

But what of the meaning of the current expression? Within the Johannine Gospel, flesh can have both a negative (3:6; 6:63; 8:15) and a positive (1:14; 6:51, 52, 53, 54, 55, 56) meaning. This is due, as we have seen, to the different attitudes toward the material aspects of reality in the second and third editions of the Gospel (cf. Vol. 1, Part 4, Section 11). Scholarly interpretation of the current expression has tended to side with one or the other of these Johannine uses as can be seen in Brown's survey (*Epistles* 308-10).

In my opinion, however, it is wrong to approach the problem from this perspective. As described in the discussion of the Structure below, the threefold listing in v. 16b-d has the form of a stereotyped listing of vices. Because such stereotyped listings of temptations were common in the ancient world and because the overall formulation of the present one is non-Johannine, it seems best to interpret it from the perspective of such generalized catalogues of temptation rather than from the perspective of unique Johannine theology. Scholars have warned of interpreting the expression through Pauline eyes, but the fact that the expression occurs so frequently in Paul and here in a stereotyped collection may indicate that the Pauline occurrences also reflect the broader understanding of the expression. If this is true, then we may not be wrong to understand the expression in this more general sense as referring to basic sinful human tendencies and perhaps more specifically to sexual desire. More will be said about this following the Note on the third phrase.

the desire of the eyes This exact phrase does not appear elsewhere in the Old Testament or New Testament. However, similar phrases do appear and can have positive or negative connotations. If we approach the meaning from the perspective of stereotyped lists of evils, it seems that the phrase refers to excessive desire for material possessions. The eye is sometimes understood as the source of sexual temptation, as is evident in Mark 9:47; Matt 5:29; 18:8-9. In the context of the previous saying, however, this is unlikely. More will be said about this following the Note on the third phrase.

the arrogance regarding life The noun *alazoneia* ("arrogance") appears only here and in James 4:16 within the New Testament. (The adjective appears in Rom 1:30 and 2 Tim 3:2.) The word means "pride," "ostentation," "boastfulness." In the LXX, the word means "boastfulness" or "arrogance" (2 Macc 9:8; 15:6;

4 Macc 1:26; 2:15; 8:19; Wis 5:8; 17:7) and can be boastfulness about a variety of topics. However, in the Johannine text, the boastfulness is about *bios* ("life"). *Bios* ("life") is also infrequent in the New Testament, appearing twice in the Johannine writings (here and in 3:17) and only eight times elsewhere. In the Johannine writings the more common term is *zōē* but has no significant difference in meaning. The genitive is ambiguous and could refer to arrogance regarding life or arrogance that comes from one's particular life. In either case the meaning is substantially the same.

The phrase as a whole is probably intended to describe false security with respect to life, much as in James (so also R. E. Brown, Schnackenburg, and others). However, we must be careful not to impose a precise Johannine meaning on what may have been a stereotyped expression. Consequently, to say that, in John, the term *bios* ("life") should be contrasted with *zōē*, the characteristic Johannine term and the one regularly used for the (eternal) life that comes from God, may be to presume a precision that was not intended.

Now that we have discussed the individual elements of the three phrases, we can review them as a group and perhaps get a fuller view of their meaning. The three phrases are:

the desire of the flesh
the desire of the eyes
the arrogance regarding life.

From the perspective of the list as a whole, we are able to notice, first, that the first two items speak of desires. It is very likely that the term "desire" here refers to what is sometimes called disordered tendencies, that is, undisciplined wants and desires. These are desires that are not properly controlled or disciplined. What differentiates the first two is the source of the desires. The source of the first desire is the flesh and the source of the second is the eyes. Within this context, it seems very unlikely that "flesh" has either of its characteristic Johannine meanings. Rather, when contrasted with the desires of the eyes, it probably refers to sexual desires.

In the same context, when contrasted with desires of the flesh, the second vice, desire of the eyes, probably refers to various desires for material possessions, that is, those things that are seen and then wanted for oneself.

Finally, arrogance and boastfulness regarding life seems to refer to pretensions and unfounded claims of security regarding life. Thus, the person fails to see that real security comes from God but boasts of his own resources.

is not from the Father In the Greek, this part of the verse is a brief chiasm (Klauck) that reads literally: "is not from the Father, but from the world is."

OVERVIEW OF 2:12-17

This section consists of two parts, each of which is somewhat independent of the other. The first part consists of three statements all of which are repeated once with some variation. They appear to be a form of encouragement to the community, first in general ("children") and then with respect to the longer-standing members ("fathers") and then the more recent ones ("young people"). While the meaning of each statement appears straightforward in itself, the reasons for the arrangement and the choice of these statements for this section are more difficult to determine.

The general meaning of the second part is also straightforward but requires discussion of the details. The author exhorts his readers to love the Father and not to love the world with all its allures. He ends by reminding them that the world is passing away but the one who does the will of the Father will remain forever. His comment that the world "is passing away" will be taken up in the next section, where the initial theme will be the Last Hour.

If the general thought of the two subsections of this passage is clear, details of the verses as well as the reason for their placement at this point in the Letter are not. But the attempt to suggest some possibilities will be taken up in the detailed discussion below.

THE STRUCTURE OF 2:12-17

As was indicated above, these verses are easily divided into two sections: vv. 12-14 and vv. 15-17. The first section consists of two sets of verses, each containing three parallel statements. The first set (vv. 12-13) consists of "I write to you . . ." repeated three times, each time using the present tense (vv. 12, 13ab, 13cd) but with varying addressees ("Children, Fathers, Young People"). This is then paralleled by the second set of statements (v. 14) except that the verb is now in the aorist ("I *wrote* to you . . ."). Again the addressees are the same and are listed in the same order as those in vv. 12-13 except that the first group is now referred to as *paidia* rather than as *teknia*. Also parallel structurally is the *hoti*-clause in each, which expresses the content of the writing in all six cases. This structure is strikingly evident and repetitive.

In the next verses (vv. 15-17), there is a sudden shift in thought and also in structure. These verses are organized primarily by a series of contrasts. Love "of the world" is contrasted with love "of the Father" (v. 15bc); that which is "from the Father" is contrasted with what is "from the world" (v. 16e). The world is said to be "passing away," but the believer is said to "abide forever" (v. 17).

Stereotyped Catalogue of Vices

In v. 16b-d, there is a set of three expressions that contain (1) language that is unique *(alazoneia)* or rare *(epithymia* — elsewhere only at John 8:44) within the Johannine corpus and (2) concepts that are also unique — and undeveloped — elsewhere in the Johannine literature and (3) a list format. All of these features suggest that the grouping owes its origin to some stereotyped listing of vices similar to the larger catalogue of vices found in Mark 7:17-23 and Gal 5:19-21 and in later Christian literature such as *Did.* 5:1-2. Such lists of threes were not uncommon.[1] A similar threefold list also appears in 1QS 5:4-5: "No one shall walk in the stubbornness of his heart in order to go astray following his heart, his eyes and his evil inclination." In this passage, the heart appears as a source of inappropriate urging, along with the eyes (as in the Johannine list) and the more general "evil inclination." (See also CD 3.7-8, 11 where "the desire of their heart" is contrasted with listening to the voice of God and his covenant.)

THE INTERPRETATION OF 2:12-17

Vv. 12-14

The author now addresses his readers directly, in a formal and repetitive pattern. We will look first at his two addresses to the entire community (v. 12 and v. 14). In these verses, the author picks up and emphasizes two essential elements of the community's belief. In v. 12, the author affirms for the community that their sins are forgiven through Jesus' name. As was pointed out in the discussion of 1:7–2:2, the role of Jesus as effective agent of the forgiveness of sin was one of the major issues disputed at the time of 1 John. Here the author assures his readers once again not only that their sins are forgiven but that this is done through Jesus.

In his second exhortation to the entire community (v. 14), the author assures his readers that they do in fact "know" God. While the possibility of "knowing" God was not a matter of dispute between the author and his opponents, whether a person could legitimately make the claim was in dispute. But the author assures his readers that they (in contrast to the opponents) do in fact know God. The reader familiar with the Old Testament would recognize

1. For an extensive listing of such catalogues of vices in the NT, the OT, the deutero-canonical writings, and in Greek philosophical writings, see Fitzmyer, *Romans* 274-75. Fitzmyer notes that Paul tends to list the attitude of mind from which such vices come rather than the vices themselves. This seems to be true of the Johannine list also.

in these two general affirmations an echo of the words of Jeremiah 31:34 about the benefits that will be an important part of the end-times: the sins of the people will be forgiven and they will "know" me.[2] The members of the community saw themselves as in fact living in those end-times and as recipients of those blessings.

In both parts of his comment, after addressing the community as a whole, the author turns (v. 13 and v. 14c-h) to address two specific subdivisions of the community: "fathers" and "young people." While actual age may have played a factor in determining the membership of these two groups, it is much more likely that the designation is meant to reflect the length of time each group had been members of the community.

The author's exhortation to the "fathers" is the same in both cases (v. 13b, v. 14d): "You have known the one from the beginning." The author reminds these members that they have knowledge of Jesus, who has been the central figure of their faith from the beginning. This group serves as a model for the community because they continue to know the Christ who was the center of belief from the beginning of their experience. What makes them different from the young people is that their knowledge extends back to the beginning. The point here is the continuity in the identity of Jesus. There has been no change, and the fathers are able to testify to this.

The author's exhortation to the young people is somewhat more complex. In both statements (v. 13cd, v. 14e-h) he affirms that they "have conquered the Evil One." This is probably intended to reflect the fact of their relatively recent conversion. Their choice to believe (that is, to follow the author and to be a member of his community) is a more recent decision and is evidence that they have "conquered the Evil One." The fact of their victory is still "fresh" and is lauded. Also, the author's reference to "the Evil One" reflects his apocalyptic worldview. The young ones are not in danger of having the Evil One as their father, now that they have conquered him and will have God as their Father.

However, in the second exhortation to the young people (v. 14e-h), the author expands his praise by assuring them that they are "strong," that is, they give evidence of being able to resist the Evil One in the future. Then he says that the word of God abides in them. For the author, this is a great compliment. One of the opponents' chief errors is that they do not keep the word of God but "go beyond" (2 John 9). In 2:5, the author had said that the love of God is brought to perfection in the one who keeps the word of God!

---

2. R. E. Brown makes much of the similarity of such language to the initiation rites of early Christianity and at Qumran. However, I am inclined to think that the parallels are too general. There is greater similarity in the two commandments that speak specifically of belief and of behavior, both of which are clearly and specifically attested at Qumran.

Vv. 15-17

In the previous verses, the author had addressed various aspects of belief; now he turns to the issue of behavior and exhorts them not to allow themselves to be attracted to the things of the world. It is not possible (v. 15) to love both the world and the Father. If someone loves the world, the love of the Father is not in the person.

Then (v. 16), the author lists what he considers to be typical of "everything in the world." In doing so, he makes use of what must have been a stereotyped list of worldly vices. First, there is the desire of the flesh; that is, sexual desire. Second, there is the desire of the eyes; that is, excessive desire for material possessions. Third, there is the arrogance of life, which leads one to deny the need for God.

The list of these three characteristics of the world has attracted the attention of scholars because of their specificity, but once their similarity to the stereotyped lists of vices (and virtues) as well as other codes of conduct common in the ancient world is recognized, it becomes clear that their specific meaning is not of primary importance to the author. In fact, he does not return to any extended discussion of them.

The author's main focus is on the overriding framework within which these specific vices are to be understood. In keeping with his apocalyptic worldview, the author shows that there are really only two choices open to the community: to love God or to love the world. To recognize this and to make the right choice is essential. And so, the author reminds his readers that all of this is not from the Father but from the world. The world, with its desires, is passing away (v. 17), but the one who does the will of God abides forever. All of the attractions of the world will come to an end, but the one who chooses to do what God wants will live forever.

The Antichrists: Those Who Deny the Son

18 Dear Children,
　　+it is the Last Hour,
　　　　+and just as you heard that the Antichrist is coming,
　　　　+and even now many Antichrists have come to be,
　　+from this we know that it is the Last Hour.

19 +They went out from us but they were not of us.
　　+If they were of us, they would have abided among us —
+but that it might be made apparent that they are not of us.

+[A] 20 And you have an anointing from the Holy One
and you know all.

　+[B] 21 I did not write to you
　　　that you do not know the truth but that you know it and
　　　that every lie is not of the truth.

　　　+[C] 22 Who is the Liar if not
　　　　　the one denying that Jesus is the Christ?
　　　　　This is the Antichrist,
　　　　　the one denying the Father and the Son.

　　　　+[D] 23 Everyone denying the Son does not have the Father.
　　　　　The one confessing the Son has the Father also.

　　+[C'] 24 As for you —
　　　　+let what you heard from the beginning
　　　　　+abide in you.
　　　　　+If it abides in you

+(what you heard from the beginning),
+you abide in the Son and in the Father.

(25 And this is the promise that he [Jesus] promised us:
    eternal life.)

+[B'] 26 I wrote these things to you about those deceiving you.

+[A'] 27 And as for you — the anointing that you received from him [God] abides in you, and you do not have need that anyone teach you, but as his [God's] anointing teaches you about all and it is true and not false, and just as it taught you, you abide in him [Jesus].

NOTES TO 2:18-27

V. 18 Antichrist This term appears only in the Johannine Letters within the New Testament and is introduced here for the first time. It also occurs in 1 John 2:22; 4:3; 2 John 7. The statement "as you heard" seems to indicate that this figure was part of the community's traditional teaching.

Although the term is unique to Johannine literature and is never defined, it refers to a figure the author identifies as the embodiment of evil. Similar figures appearing in the time immediately before the final judgment are a regular feature of apocalyptic literature. Scholars regularly point to 2 Thess 2:3-10, which speaks of the "man of sin," and to Mark 13:22, which predicts "false Christs" and "false prophets" as examples of such conceptions elsewhere in the New Testament.

Although there are figures in late Second Temple Judaism that could serve as antecedents for the Antichrist, the extent to which they are true antecedents is debated. In Jewish apocalyptic, we see the conviction that the last times would be marked by the presence of great evil and the rise of an evil empire. It is possible that this expectation was first embodied in Antiochus IV Epiphanes and that the personal leader of such an empire was later raised to the status of a mythological figure. This is evident in Daniel 11, and there are indications that Daniel 11 has influenced the wording of both 2 Thess 2:5 and Mark 13. Some trace the origin of the myth to Babylonian legends. (For further details on the historical background see Brooke, *Epistles* 69-79; Schnackenburg, *Epistles* 135-39 and the literature referred to there.)

The first patristic reference to the Antichrist is in Polycarp 7:1, which reflects knowledge of 1 John 4:1-3. While, in 1 and 2 John, the Antichrist is a figure separate from Satan, in later literature they become identified (cf. *Sib. Or.* 3.64-74; *Asc. Isa.* 4:1-18).

The term Antichrist has become so common in Christian literature that it is perhaps difficult to understand in its primitive (Johannine) sense. In its original formulation, it was almost certainly a term coined by the community to describe the opponents at the time of the crisis of 1 John. The figure is introduced here, in a context where the issue at stake is precisely the failure to confess Jesus as "the Christ" (v. 22) and where "anointing" is also ascribed to the members of the community. Because it is used to describe the figure diametrically opposed to "the Christ," it is identified as "the Antichrist." Yet it is unlikely that it was intended to refer to a single figure with specific characteristics other than its opposition to Christ. Moreover, the context here indicates that there were many Antichrists, a fact that shows it does not intend to identify a single figure but rather to represent all opposition of this type. (See Ernst, *"Antichristos."*)

V. 19 from us The Greek here is *ex hēmōn,* which means, literally, "out from us."

were not of us This is the first instance of the dualistic usage of *einai ek* (literally, "to be of") in 1 John but see also at v. 19b, c. These are the only instances where this dualistic phrase appears with "us"; elsewhere it is typically "of the truth," "of God," or "of the Evil One" or "of the world." The expression is always used to associate an individual or a group with one or the other of two dualistically opposed groups. The expression is to be understood as rhetorical exaggeration: the secessionists were never *truly* of us because, if they had been, they would not have departed. For further discussion of this expression, see 3E-11.

V. 20 an anointing (Gk: *chrisma*) This term appears only here and in v. 27 in the Johannine literature and nowhere else in the New Testament. The way it is introduced suggests that it was a technical term within the community and one central to its theological convictions but, at the same time, unique within early Christianity. Perhaps the most striking feature of its use is that nowhere else in the New Testament does an author come so close to identifying a prerogative of the Christian with the central prerogative of Jesus who was, more than anything else, said to be *christos.*

From its use here and in v. 27, as well as from the use of the related term elsewhere in the Old Testament (e.g., Isa 61:1) and New Testament (e.g., Matt 11:5; Luke 4:18; 7:22; Acts 4:27; 10:38), it is clear that it refers to an anointing by the Spirit.

This anointing by the Spirit endows the believer with a power of insight that makes any teaching by others unnecessary (see Vol. 1, Part 4, Section 6.2 and 6.3). That the author would make such a statement here during a conflict in which excessive dependence upon the Spirit was precisely one of the central errors of the opponents indicates just how central this conviction was for the community. It also indicates how difficult it was to both refute the distortions by the opponents and at the same time preserve the unique insights of the tradition.

from the Holy One In the Johannine Gospel, the Holy One can refer to either God (17:11), the Son (6:69) or the Spirit (1:33; 14:26; 20:22). However, the word *hagios* is used only here in the Letters and so other epistolary instances cannot be a guide.

The problem is complicated further by uncertainty as to whether it refers to the one doing the anointing or the source of the power that comes through the anointing. Schnackenburg (*Epistles* 141) sees it as referring to the Spirit. Smith (*Epistles* 72) views it as referring to the Spirit (but see also vv. 27-28 where he associates it with Jesus). In 3:24, it is God the Father who "gave" the Spirit. This is also the case in 4:2-3. Consequently, I would conclude that the author holds that the anointing involving the gift of the Spirit is accomplished by God, the Holy One.

and you know all The textual evidence is divided whether the form is *pantes* or *panta*. The UBS gives considerably more weight to *pantes* in light of its appearance in both Sinaiticus and Vaticanus, as well as the fact that it is the more difficult reading. Yet even with this reading, the statement is ambiguous and can mean either "all of you know" or "you know all." *Pantes* had appeared near the end of the previous verse and referred to "all" of the opponents who had left the community. *Pantes* also appears in v. 27c where, again, it is ambiguous.

Brown (*Epistles* 348-49) opts for the reading *pantes* but sees it as referring to the faithful ("you all have knowledge"). So also Schnackenburg, *Epistles* 143. This is certainly possible. However, I am inclined to view it as the object ("you know all persons"). In the previous verse, the author referred to the opponents as "all of them." In v. 26, he says that he has been writing about "those deceiving you," indicating that he has been writing about people rather than things. Moreover, in v. 27b, he says that the anointing teaches them "about all." Here there is no doubt that "all" is not the subject, but the object of "teaching." The fact that this statement is parallel to "and you know all" within the chiasm (see below) is yet further indication that the author understood "all" of v. 20 to be the object of "know" rather than the subject. This fits well with the overall orientation of vv. 20-27 where, in the two halves of the chiasm, the author explains the characteristics of, respectively, the opponents and the faithful (see the Interpretation below). But presumably the intended emphasis is not so much on the numerical extent as on the thoroughness of the knowledge. Thus, the believers know all the opponents in the sense that they know them and their falsehoods thoroughly.

V. 21 I did not write A similar expression appears in v. 26. Some think that this refers to an earlier writing while the majority thinks that it simply refers to the contents of this Letter.

every lie On the role of words associated with "lying," see at 1:6.

of the truth See at 2:19.

V. 22 Who is the Liar *Pseustēs* appears seven times in the Johannine literature, but this is the only instance with the definite article. The purpose is to make the notion of falsehood concrete. Whether this was a set title is disputed. The use of the definite article together with its equation with the Antichrist suggests that it is. Yet the four other times it appears in 1 John (1:10; 2:4; 4:20; 5:10), it does not have the article and so it could simply refer to anyone who is "of" falsehood and who does not speak or know the truth. See also at 1:6.

Jesus is the Christ Twice in 1 John, what is surely a fixed Christological statement appears in the form of "Jesus is the Christ." It appears as something that is denied by the opponents in 2:22; it appears as a positive statement in 5:1. In its simple, literal meaning, the denial of such a statement refers to someone who denies the applicability of the title "anointed" to Jesus. This was the meaning within the Gospel as people repeatedly discussed whether Jesus was the Christ.

There are, at the present time, two main ways of understanding this confession. According to some, it is an anti-docetic statement, designed to affirm that the historical person Jesus is truly "the Christ." The identification between Jesus and the Christ is real and lasting (so, for example, Strecker, *Epistles* 69-76). The second view is that it is to be understood in relation to the disagreement about the Interpretation of the Johannine tradition (Brown, *Epistles* 352, 368-69; Beutler, *Johannesbriefe* 73-74). It is in this second manner that I view the issue.

The opponents in 1 John are not like the unbelievers of the Gospel who have never believed in Jesus. Rather, the opponents here have "departed from us" (2:19). Thus, they are people who have at one time believed that Jesus was the Christ, just as they certainly would have believed that Jesus was the Son.

What the opponents mean by their denial that Jesus is the Christ is understood by the author as unacceptable. In 2:23, he says that everyone denying the Son does not have the Father and that everyone confessing the Son has the Father. Thus, the denial that Jesus is the Christ is the denial of something essential; one cannot believe in God (as the opponents claim to do) without believing in Jesus. It is almost surely correct to conclude that this is another of the author's cryptic formulas that served as a kind of shorthand but that was fully understood by his opponents.

But what would they have understood by it? The confessional formula in 2:22 describes Jesus as the Christ but in referring to both in v. 22c and v. 23a, the author refers to Jesus simply as "the Son." Why does he not continue to use the term "Christ"? Does this mean that he really does not intend any specific content to the designation "Christ" versus "Son"? Klauck (*Erste Johannesbrief* 234) sees the second simply as a shortened form of the first.

In my view, the key to understanding the formula lies in the role of anointing within the Johannine theology. Three times in 1 John, the author claims that the believer has an anointing (2:20, 27 [twice]). Thus, the author affirms with regard to the believer something very similar to what is affirmed of Jesus; but, at the same time, although he says the believer has a *chrisma,* he never refers to the believer as *christos,* a term that is reserved for Jesus. Thus, he keeps the two anointings distinct. One can imagine, however, that, if the tradition claimed that both Jesus and the believer had an anointing, it would have been relatively easy to blur the distinction between Jesus and the believer and so confuse the status of Jesus with that of the believer. It is apparent from 2 John 9 that eventually the community referred to Jesus simply as "the Christ," thus reflecting the usage in this title.

If the anointing is a result of the gift of the Spirit, it is clear from 1 John that the believer does not have the Spirit fully but has been given "of/from" the Spirit (4:13). Although there is no explicit statement about the manner of Jesus' possession of the Spirit in 1 John, the third edition of the Gospel states that God has bestowed the Spirit on Jesus "not in a limited way" (3:34).

Thus, because the opponents do not accept a distinction between these two ways of possessing the Spirit, they are said to deny that "Jesus is the Christ" (in the sense of being uniquely "Christ"), while the author and his followers affirm it (so, for example, Grayston, *Epistles* 18-19).

V. 23 does not have the Father . . . has the Father These are the first instances of "have" in the sense of possessing proper belief. It also appears in 5:12 and in 2 John 9. According to Hanse (*Gott* 35) the expression does not have precise biblical parallels. The closest parallels are in 3 Macc 7:16 ("They possessed ['had'] God even to death"); *TDan* 5:2 ("You will be at peace, possessing ['having'] the God of peace"); *TIss* 7:7 ("You will have the God of heaven and earth with you"). The expression continues to be used in the second century.

The opponents believed in God the Father but did not properly acknowledge the Son. For the author of 1 John, one cannot claim to possess correct belief in the Father (or to stand in correct relation with the Father) if the person does not also believe properly in the Son (since the Father has sent the Son and intends that his proper role be recognized and affirmed). Thus, those who deny that Jesus is the Christ cannot be said to believe properly in either the Father or the Son. In 2:24e, the author speaks of the similar attribute of "abiding" in the Son and the Father, an expression designed to reflect the fellowship that results from belief.

V. 24 what you heard from the beginning This expression, which appears twice in this verse, describes the nature of the belief of the author and his followers. They affirm not something new or something that "goes beyond" (cf. 2 John 9) but that which was from the beginning. (See also at 1:1; 2:6; 3:11.)

you abide in This is the first of five instances of "abide" in this passage (also in vv. 24d, f; 27a, d). In each case, the basic meaning of abide, that is, "to remain permanently," is evident. For the use of "abide," see also at 2:6.

V. 25 And this is the promise This sentence seems to be unattached to anything in the context. Neither the word "promise" (*epangelia* appears only in this verse in the Johannine literature) nor "eternal life" appears elsewhere in the context, and neither seems to follow from what precedes or to lead into what follows.

that he promised "He" here could refer to either God or to Christ. However, as a number of scholars point out, the context has focused on the role of Christ and so it is more likely that the author is referring to a promise made by Christ. This would be consistent with the thought of the second edition of the Gospel and would be one of that edition's features with which the author would agree completely.

V. 27 from him As before, "his" refers to God. See the discussion of "Holy One" (v. 20a) above.

teach . . . taught The shift in tense from the present to the past parallels the shift from the present anointing to the "past" of what they heard from the beginning. It also seems to parallel the shift in tenses from the present of *graphō* to the past throughout 2:12-14.

you do not have need that anyone teach you The background of this statement comes from Jer 31:33-34 and is discussed in Volume 1, Part 4, Section 6.2 (Background). It has a parallel in 1 Thess 4:9 where ethical conduct (mutual charity) is said to be "taught by God" to those who are recipients of the Spirit (cf. 1 Thess 4:8).

his anointing "His" refers to God. See above and at v. 20a. For a contrary opinion, see Schnackenburg, *Epistles* 149.

about all "All" here refers to the opponents (that is, "about all of them"). See the discussion of "all" in v. 20.

you abide The verb form in the Greek can be either indicative or imperative. In 2:28, it is imperative. However, there is a division of opinion about the mood here. Whether it is intended to exhort the reader to "abide" or whether it is an observation that they do in fact abide matters little for the interpretation of the verse. It perhaps makes better sense in the context if it is taken as indicative, thus preparing for a contrasting imperative in v. 28.

in him The word that is translated "it" is (in Greek) *en autō*. Grammatically this can be either neuter and so refer to "anointing" or masculine and refer to "Jesus." While it appears at first (on the basis of the earlier context) to refer to the anointing, it is preferable to take it as referring to Jesus on the basis of v. 28 that follows. As we shall see in the discussion of v. 28 below, the same phrase, as it appears in v. 28, refers to Jesus and, given the propensity of the author to abruptly introduce a new topic at the end of a section as a catchword to prepare for the next topic, this is almost surely what occurs here.

OVERVIEW OF 2:18-27

The author now begins to describe the crisis in the most dramatic of apocalyptic language and addresses directly the secession that has taken place. His concern throughout will be correct belief; there will be no mention of love or its failure. For the author the situation is nothing less than the "Last Hour," as is evidenced by the coming of the Antichrist(s). These Antichrists are those who departed from the community.

The author then turns to identify the opponents and he begins by reminding his readers of the anointing that they possess. This anointing enables them to recognize both the Liar and the Antichrist. The author then says that the Liar denies that Jesus is the Christ and the Antichrist denies both Father and Son. He urges his readers to hold fast to what they heard from the beginning and so to possess both the Father and Son. After reminding his readers that the promise Christ made is about eternal life, he reminds them again that their anointing teaches them the truth and that they should pay no heed to the opponents who try to deceive them. He ends the section by reminding his readers that they remain in Jesus as the Spirit has taught them.

THE STRUCTURE OF 2:18-27

This section is related to the sections on either side of it by catchword chaining although the chaining to the previous section is thematic rather than verbal.[1] The theme of "the world passing away" appeared in v. 17. In v. 18a, this is taken up and made more precise by identifying the present time as the "last hour." This connection is quite clear even though it is not the typical verbal catchword.

The section is chained to the following one (2:28–3:10) by the words "remain in it," which end this section (v. 27f) and also begin the following (2:28a). The Greek in both cases is identical: *menete en autō*.

The section is organized internally by means of a series of three minor chiasms and one major one. While the minor chiasms are primarily stylistic, the major chiasm is of considerable importance for the way it illumines the thought of the section.

The first minor chiasm appears in v. 18. References to "the last hour" constitute the first and last members and references to the Antichrist(s) constitute the second and second-to-last members. This is illustrated in the arrangement of the verses in the translation.

Verse 19 is an obvious (but somewhat awkward) attempt at a second minor chiasm, involving not only the usual parallelism but also a contrast built on the words "going out"/"remaining" and "from us"/"among us." In the first and last elements, the parallelism is indicated by the mention that the opponents "are not of us." In the middle two elements, there is the statement that if the opponents "were of us," they would have "remained among us." Moreover, the first of these two central elements ends in "of us" *(ex hēmōn)* (v. 19b) and the second ends with "among us" *(meth' hēmōn)* (v. 19b).

In addition to the features mentioned above, the first comments that "they went out"; the second that "they would have remained"; the third "but (they went out) in order that they might be revealed."

The final minor chiasm occurs in v. 24. This relatively brief chiasm is evident in the Greek but awkward in English. Here, the first and last elements are related on the thematic level but only minimally on the verbal level. However, the second and the second-to-last elements are quite similar on the verbal level and speak of "that which you heard from the beginning." The two central elements are also quite similar verbally and speak of what "abides in you." The

---

1. For Strecker, 1 John 2:18-27 constitutes the second major section of the Letter. It is mainly dogmatic and is the first discussion of false teaching. For Schnackenburg (*Epistles* 129) and Klauck (*Erste Johannesbrief*), 2:18 begins a major division. But these scholars see the section extending to 3:24. Schnackenburg further subdivides at 2:18-27; 2:28–3:3; 3:4-24 while Klauck sees subdivisions at 2:18-27; 2:28–3:10; 3:11-24.

chiasm as a whole constitutes the fourth element of the major chiasm described below.

In vv. 20-27, there is a considerably more extended and developed chiasm. This chiasm is significant for what it reveals about the author's literary arrangement and also about his theological intentions.[2] The first element of the chiasm [A] consists of v. 20. At the beginning (v. 20) the author states that his followers have an anointing and that they know all.

In the second element [B], the author refers to his writing about his followers and their knowledge of the truth.[3]

In the third element of the chiasm [C], the author describes the Liar and the Antichrist (that is, the author's opponents). He describes the Liar as the one who denies that Jesus is the Christ and the Antichrist as the one denying the Father and the Son.

In the central element of the chiasm [D], he provides his central conviction regarding belief in Jesus, in the form of a double evaluation: the one *denying* the Son does not have the Father; the one *confessing* the Son has the Father also.

In his third-to-last element [C'], he then describes (and expresses his hope for) the believer in yet another minor chiasm. The believer is the one who has what was heard from the beginning abiding within. And if what was heard from the beginning abides within the person, then the person abides in both the Son and the Father.

In the second-to-last element of the chiasm [B'], the author reminds his readers that he has written to them about the deceivers.

Then in the final element [A'], he returns to the topic of anointing and uses this to conclude his exhortation.[4]

Within vv. 20-23, a further sort of unity is indicated by a number of instances of minor catchword chaining. Although this is clearer in the Greek, it is

2. Brown (*Epistles* 362-63) suggests a chiastic arrangement beginning in v. 18 and extending to v. 28. But, as Brown himself recognizes, his proposal is weak in several respects. It is quite general and requires the omission of several verses. Moreover, it does not result in an arrangement that is significantly useful in the understanding of the theology of the verses. The proposal presented here demonstrates striking verbal and thematic parallels as well as a central element, which truly functions as a "key" to the arrangement.

3. The first two elements of the chiasm are somewhat related. While there is a clear parallelism between the mention of anointing in the first and last elements of the chiasm and of having written, in the second and second-last elements, the larger discussion of anointing permeates both the first and the second elements.

4. There is some discussion about whether this unit ends with v. 27 or v. 28. Some say it ends with 2:28 and so forms an inclusion with v. 18. Others (cf. R. E. Brown, above) argue that there is a chiastic arrangement ending in v. 28. However, the inclusion between vv. 20 and 27 provides persuasive evidence for ending the section after v. 27.

also discernible in the English. Thus, "all" *(pantes)* in v. 19c is repeated in v. 20; *oidate* from v. 20 is repeated in v. 21; *tēn alētheian* from v. 21a is repeated in v. 21c; *pseudos* from 21c is repeated in v. 22a; and *ho arnoumenos* from 22a is repeated in v. 22c and v. 23a. Finally, there are three expressions in vv. 22c-23 that deal with "denying" (v. 22c), "having" (v. 23a) and "confessing" (v. 23b) the Father and the Son.

Finally, it is striking that the author crafts his exposition to the point of a careful cross-referencing in vv. 21 and 26. In v. 21 he refers to his writing about the faithful and does so immediately before he speaks about the opponents. Then in v. 26, he refers to his having written about the deceivers immediately after writing about the faithful. Given the careful balance of the remainder of the chiasm, it is unlikely that this final detail is simply accidental.

THE INTERPRETATION OF 2:18-27

Vv. 18-19

After the statement in v. 17 that "the world is passing away," the author now (v. 18) addresses the readers directly and describes the crisis in terms that define it as a manifestation of the final, climactic, apocalyptic hour. It is the Last Hour and we know this from the presence of the "Antichrist." This figure is a unique Johannine embodiment of the traditional apocalyptic figure of evil characteristic of the end-times. What is distinctive of the Johannine presentation, however, is that the author goes on to identify this figure with his opponents who have departed from the community. Thus, in true apocalyptic fashion, he relates the present crisis to the climax of world history and the struggle between good and evil.

Although he first speaks of an Antichrist as a single figure, he immediately makes it clear that he has the opponents in mind as the (plural) embodiment of this apocalyptic figure. He explains (v. 19) that those who are Antichrists were originally part of the community *(ex hēmōn)* but that they were not truly members. If they had been true members, they would have remained with us *(meth' hēmōn)*. Then the statement is reversed and repeated (v. 19ef): But their departure (that is, their actions) revealed that they had never truly been part of the community, for otherwise they would not have departed. The verse is obviously redundant but intended as a rhetorical device to emphasize the distance between the two groups. This is also the first example in the Letter of one's identity being revealed by one's actions. We know that these departed members were not really members because they are revealed by their actions. True members would not have left.

The identification of the Antichrist thus sets the scene for the discussion of the opponents' erroneous view of Jesus that follows, linking this error with the figures of the Antichrist and the Liar — and with falsehood and deception.

Vv. 20-27

Having identified the present time as the Last Hour and having done so because Antichrists have arisen, the author now describes the views of the opponents and contrasts them with the views of the faithful believers. In doing so, he shows what in the opponents has revealed them to be the manifestation of the Antichrist and the Liar. He presents his material in the form of a major chiasm that extends from v. 20 to v. 27.

In our comment on these verses we will follow the form exhibited by the chiasm, a form that helps considerably with the understanding of the verses.

V. 20 [A][5]

The author begins his discussion of the opponents by reminding his readers that they themselves are well equipped interiorly for the work of identifying the opponents because they have an anointing from the Holy One (that is, the Spirit).[6] This thought will dominate the first (vv. 20-21) and last (vv. 26-27) elements of the chiasm. This framing thus becomes a further indication of the important role of the believers' anointing. In v. 20, the author explains that the anointing from the Holy One makes it possible for the believers to know all persons, and so they are well equipped for seeing through the pretensions of the opponents.

V. 21 [B]

The author then (v. 21) refers to having written them that they know the truth. Their anointing not only makes it possible to know the truth but also, conversely, to recognize that every lie is not "of the truth." With this contrast between truth and lying, the author reflects once again his classification of his followers and his opponents in terms typical of apocalyptic.[7] Moreover, by

---

5. The uppercase letters in brackets cross-reference the corresponding elements of the chiasm as indicated in the translation.

6. This anointing is from the Holy One (v. 20) and "from him" (v. 27a, b). This is the author's distinctive way of referring to the Father's gift of the Spirit to those who believed.

7. When he states that no lie is "of the truth," the author is very close to the apocalyptic thought of 1 John 4:1-6, which identifies two spirits, one "of truth" and the other "of deception."

introducing the notion of lying here, he prepares for the introduction of the figure of the Liar in the next section of the chiasm.

V. 22 [C]

The third element of the chiasm is also the second step in the author's argument. He has said that the faithful believer has an anointing that makes it possible to recognize lies. Now (v. 22), he identifies the Liar and in so doing identifies the Antichrist with the Liar; they are the same figure. The Liar is then identified as the one who denies that "Jesus is the Christ." The author then goes on to identify the Antichrist with the Liar and to say that this is the one who denies both the Father and the Son.

In the Note, I have discussed in some detail the meaning of the opponents' statement that "Jesus is not the Christ." Here I will summarize. The two primary affirmations of the Johannine community (and in this they were no different from other sectors of early Christianity) were that Jesus was the Christ and that he was the Son of God. In the discussion of the development of anthropology in the Johannine tradition,[8] I argued that while the Christology of the community was "high" so also was their anthropology. Both groups held to a view that the gift of the Spirit transformed the believer, giving a rebirth to a new level of life while at the same time bestowing prerogatives that were otherwise associated only with Jesus.

However, the two groups differed about the precise way in which these prerogatives were understood of the believer. The opponents held that their reception of the Spirit was identical to that of Jesus and that, therefore, they had the same right to be called "anointed" as Jesus.[9] For them, although Jesus was sent by the Father to announce the gift of the Spirit, the exalted Christology was overshadowed by an equally exalted anthropology. For the author, this view was simply false and one who would make such a claim was "the Liar" — and was not of the truth.

But why was there this particular expression "Jesus is not the Christ"? The answer lies in the fact that the opponents also argued that "Jesus is not the Son of God." The opponents could not have argued these claims in their literal sense. To do so would mean that they never would have believed in the first place. Rather, these statements were elliptical and served as a kind of theological jargon, current in the community and understood by the members in a particular way. Given the ways in which the bestowal of the eschatological Spirit enabled the believer to say that he/she was "anointed" or "a child (son/daugh-

8. See Vol. 1, Part 4, Section 9.2.
9. So also Beutler, *Johannesbriefe* 73-74.

ter) of God," it is very likely that the opponents challenged the right of Jesus to claim these titles in a unique way. Here, the author mentions only the first of these titles, but he says that the one who denies Jesus' right to a unique claim regarding these titles is the Liar and the Antichrist. Because the opponents' claim is false, they are "the Liar"; because the specific title rejected is that of "Christ," they are truly the "anti-Christ."

The author then goes on to say (v. 22cd) that the Antichrist is the one who denies both the Father and the Son.

V. 23 [D]

In v. 23, the author reaches the center of his chiasm; and, in it, he contrasts the one who denies the Son with the one who confesses Him. The sole point of contrast is that the one denying the Son does not have the Father while the one confessing the Son has both the Father and the Son.[10] The opponents would have bristled at this statement and would have said that they were in no way denying the Father. In fact, they held a strong belief in both the Father and the Spirit; it was only a distinctive, permanent, and effective role for Jesus that they denied. But the author argued that, because the Father had sent the Son, to deny a proper role for the Son is to so distort what the Father has done that those who hold this view cannot be said to "have" the Father either. For the author of 1 John, there is no compromise: unless one believes in the Son one cannot be said to believe in the Father.[11] Here at the focal point of the chiasm, the double statement divides the group spoken of in v. 22 from the author's group, which will be identified and exhorted in v. 24.

V. 24 [C']

In the fifth element of the chiasm, the author now speaks about the faithful and does so by means of another brief embedded chiasm. In doing so he balances the earlier (parallel) element of the overall chiasm (v. 22) in which he had spo-

10. The author does not seem to make too much of the specificity of the denial (that Jesus is the Christ) since he equates this with denying "the Son." The same seems to be true of the statement in 4:2, which speaks of those who deny "Jesus come in the flesh" and which is then paralleled in 4:3 by "the one who does away with Jesus" (a more general statement). There are distinctions intended between denial of Jesus as "the Christ" (2:22) and the denial of Jesus as "the Son" (4:15), but the author is not always interested in focusing on them. At times, he is concerned primarily with the wholesale rejection of Jesus as an *effective* agent.

11. It is only in the context of the dispute, as it is described in these verses, that we are able to understand the full polemical intent of the author's seemingly innocuous statement in the Prologue (1:3) that "Our fellowship is with the Father and with his Son, Jesus Christ."

ken of the opponents. The author gains an immediacy by addressing them directly with the words "As for you . . . !" He then urges them to stand by what they heard from the beginning. If that "word," which they heard from the beginning, abides in them, then they will abide in both the Son and the Father.

While this much is relatively straightforward, once the verse is viewed within the context of the chiastic structure, we are able to see the overall section in a much clearer light. We have already seen (v. 23) that the central element differentiates those who deny the Son from those who confess the Son. Here (v. 24) we see that those who confess the Son are the ones who allow what they heard from the beginning to abide in them. Because this section is intended to contrast with the third element of the chiasm, we know that the author is referring to confession of Jesus as the Christ as the specific content of "what they heard from the beginning." Therefore, we also know that what the opponents are doing can be characterized as something that is *not* "from the beginning." The opponents, individuals who had previously believed in Jesus, now are adopting a *new* position in which they deny that Jesus is the Christ. This is not the unbelief that was attributed to "the Jews" in the second edition; this is a theological perspective that leads the opponents to (in the words of 2 John 9) "go beyond and . . . not remain in the teaching of the Christ." To hold the view that "Jesus is not the Christ" (in the specific sense in which this statement was understood by the community) is to reject the original teaching of the community and to "go beyond."

When the position of the opponents, as it is revealed here, is viewed in the context of the third edition, we get still further confirmation that what is at stake in the crisis is a view of the role of the Spirit. Although there were no qualifications regarding the role of the Spirit within the second edition, in the third edition it will be said that the Paraclete "will remind you of all the things that I have told you" (14:26) and "will witness about me" (15:26) and "will not speak on his own but will speak whatever he hears" (16:13) and "will glorify me because he will take from what is mine and will proclaim it to you" (16:14).

V. 25

Verse 25 is a puzzle. From the point of view of the overall chiastic structure, the sentence is an unexpected interruption. It comes out of nowhere and the language is unusual. "Promise" *(epangelia)* appears only here in the Johannine literature and "life" has not been mentioned since the Prologue of the Letter, where we heard of the word of life (1:1) and the "life that is eternal" (1:2). And, once again, there is ambiguity connected with the subject of the verb. Moreover, the verse neither follows closely anything before it nor leads into anything that follows it.

The best explanation of v. 25 is that the author interrupts his own planned arrangement to remind his readers forcefully that what is at stake in their belief in Jesus is nothing less than eternal life, the ultimate goal of all their striving.

V. 26 [B′]

Having completed his exposition, the author now (v. 26) reminds his readers that he has written "these things" about those who are deceiving them. In doing so, he provides a stylistic parallel to his earlier reference (in v. 21 [B]) to having also written about his followers that they know the truth.

V. 27 [A′]

The author now comes to the conclusion of his exhortation — and of the chiasm (v. 27). In it, the author returns to the topic with which he began his current exhortation. The members of the community have an anointing that they received from God and it remains on them. Because of this anointing, they have no need for anyone to teach them — neither the author nor the opponents. No human should claim the role of teacher, but only the Spirit that comes through their anointing. God's anointing will teach them about all things, and the anointing they have is true and not lying. He then ends with the most pointed of statements, a statement that reflects the heart of the problem he has just discussed: "Just as the anointing taught you to do, you remain in Jesus." This is the sum of the entire section. The faithful must abide in Jesus as their anointing teaches them.[12]

Addendum: The Importance of the Notion of *Chrisma*

Because of this passage's importance for understanding the Christological issues dividing the author from his opponents, the Interpretation here will conclude with some general observations on two important topics.

We have seen in the Notes that *chrisma* is a term unique to the Johannine tradition within the New Testament. We have also seen that it associates, in a particularly close way, this prerogative of the believer with a central prerogative of Jesus. From the way the notion functions in both the beginning and the ending elements

---

12. While this statement is linked thematically to what precedes it, nevertheless there is a certain abruptness in the way it appears here. This abruptness is due to the author's desire to provide a link to the material that follows. We will see similar abruptness in passages such as 3:10d, which makes the preceding discussion more specific but also introduces a catchword that will link this to the following.

of the chiasm, it is clear how important it is and how certainly it is to be understood in connection with the bestowal of the Spirit.

By using such a distinctive term, the author intended to associate the anointing that the faithful received with the anointing that Jesus himself received. This was reflected in his primary title, "Anointed" *(Christos)*. This is one of several indications in the Letter that the community understood the prerogatives of the believer to be similar to those of Jesus himself.[13]

At the same time, it is surprising that the author speaks about such anointing and the fact that it makes teachers unnecessary, in a context where claims of inspiration unrelated to the teaching of Christ form one of the central issues being proposed by the opponents. Thus, the author must walk a narrow line between failure to recognize the importance of this anointing and between articulating it in such a way that he would appear to be agreeing with his opponents.[14] Just how the author accomplishes this is discussed in the following paragraph.

Addendum: Belief as Founded on Both *Chrisma* and "What Has Been Heard from the Beginning"

If it is evident that the notion of *chrisma* is a central component of both the outer elements of the chiasm and so calls attention to the significance of *internal* inspiration, it is important to notice that the Johannine author balances this with an equal emphasis on the importance of the *external* tradition in his repeated references to "what you heard from the beginning" in v. 24.

The emphasis on tradition (v. 24) is "nested" within the inclusion dealing with the importance of their anointing (vv. 20-22; vv. 26-27), thus indicating structurally the complementary relationship between the two bases for belief. In this way, the author achieves the balance and the nuance necessary for a proper understanding of the roles of the Spirit and of Jesus within the tradition.

In 1 John, the author achieves this balance by a "both/and" approach in which he affirms the role of "both" the Spirit "and" of Jesus. This is a first formulation of the dialectic between inspiration by the Spirit and guidance from the words of Jesus that will be expressed later in the third edition of the Gospel in the Paraclete say-

---

13. On this, see the overview of the heresy that split the community. See also the discussion of Johannine anthropology at the time of the second edition of the Gospel (Vol. 1, Part 4, Section 9.2) and at the time of 1 John (Vol. 1, Part 4, Section 9.3), particularly the discussion of the designation of the believers as "children" and as "born of God" in relation to the designation of Jesus as "son."

14. This is just one of many fine distinctions that the author must make. See also the discussions of the correct and incorrect understanding of the believers' sinlessness ("perfectionism"), the correct and incorrect understanding of the believers' possession of the Spirit, and the correct and incorrect understanding of the relation between the Spirit and Jesus as givers of life.

ings. Twice the Paraclete sayings address and describe the community's view of this relationship. The first instance is in 14:26, where Jesus explains: "But the Paraclete, the Holy Spirit, whom the Father will send in my name, will teach you all things and will remind you of all that I have told you." The second is in 16:13-14, where he says: "But when that one comes, the Spirit of Truth, he will lead you in all truth. For he will not speak on his own but will speak whatever he hears and will proclaim to you what is to come. That one will glorify me because he will take from what is mine and will proclaim it to you."

Although the expression is different, the ideas of the third author will be very much the same as those first worked out by the author of 1 John. It is a tension that exists within Christianity throughout history. It is to the credit of the Johannine author to have been the first to address the issue and to have done it so carefully.

Addendum: Is There a Reference to Sacramental Anointing in 2:20-23?

A second passage that is often said to echo a ritual action of the community is 2:20-23. The striking feature of v. 20 is that the aorist "you received" seems to suggest a specific event. Was this a ritual event or does it refer to the reception simply as "punctiliar"?

Nauck has proposed that here and in 5:8 the author refers to a sacramental anointing that was part of the initiation into the community.[15] However, Schnackenburg rejects this, arguing that "anointing" is a metaphor for the bestowal of the Spirit in the sacrament of Baptism.[16]

Regarding 2:20-23, Brown comments: "Once again then the author seems to be involving the memories of the conversion/initiation/baptismal experience of his readers. Anointing with the Holy Spirit was surely associated with the 'anointing' of Jesus by the Spirit at his baptism (Acts 10:38)."[17] Brown also sees the confessional formulas in 2:22-23 as related to this conversion process.[18] He further speculates that the confession from John 20:31 was recited at the entrance ceremony as well.

Smalley takes a different tack. He concludes that the verses do not refer to Baptism but to a spiritual anointing. He concludes this on the grounds that there is no evidence of a ritual anointing in connection with Baptism in first-century Christianity.[19] Strecker holds much the same view as Smalley but does so on a different basis. He argues that the anointing is something that only the author's followers have. He comments: "What is meant is therefore the possession of the spirit of

---

15. Nauck, *Tradition* 94-95, 147-82.
16. Schnackenburg, *Epistles* 142.
17. Brown, *Epistles* 370.
18. Brown, *Epistles* 348.
19. Smalley, *Epistles* 106.

truth, which is not automatically bestowed in the sacramental action but is a gift of God requiring faith."[20]

In my opinion, there is insufficient evidence to suggest that the anointing in vv. 20-23 reflects a particular ritual action. To argue that the descent of the Spirit upon Jesus is associated with his baptism in John is weak at best since there is no actual mention of Jesus being baptized in the Gospel of John. Moreover, the scene of Jesus' conferral of the Spirit upon the disciples in John 20:22 makes no mention of a ritual action. Although I agree that the confession of 20:31 was central to the community, I would not conclude that therefore this was the precise wording used in any ceremony.[21] It is compatible with a number of life-settings. Finally, if the *chrisma* of the believer was associated with the Spirit, then both groups would have claimed it since both groups claimed possession of the Spirit, as is evident from the central thrust of the second edition and as is evident from the author's comparison of the spirit possessed by the faithful and by the opponents in 4:1-6.

While there is no doubt that the author is referring to the gift of the Spirit when he speaks of *chrisma*, it is not clear why he does not use the term "Spirit" in his exposition here. When the author needs to, he can make undisputed reference to the Spirit, as he does in 3:24; 5:6, 8 and throughout 4:1-6! We can only suggest that because the opponents so exaggerated the role of the Spirit, the author of 1 John chose to emphasize the role of Jesus and that of the Father.

---

20. Strecker, *Epistles* 64-65.

21. I find no evidence to suggest that, when the author refers to "what was from the beginning," he was thinking of the individual believer's "beginning" (that is, the person's conversion). The beginning he refers to is the corporate beginning, the beginning of the community's experience of Jesus and the original traditions about him.

Sin, the Children of God and the Children of the Devil

28 And now, Dear Children, abide in him [Jesus],
so that when he [Jesus] is revealed,
we may have confidence and
not shrink from him [Jesus] at his coming.

29 If you know that he [the Father] is just,
you know that everyone acting justly has been begotten from him [the Father].
3:1 Behold how great a love the Father has given us
that we may be called children of God; and we are.
Because of this the world does not know us —
because it did not know him [the Father].

2 Beloved, now we are children of God,
and it has not yet been revealed what we will be.
We know
that, when he [Jesus] is revealed,
we will be like him [Jesus] and
that we will see him [Jesus] as he is.
3 And everyone having this hope in him [Jesus]
makes himself holy as that one [Jesus] is holy.
4 Everyone committing sin
also commits lawlessness and sin is lawlessness.

5 And we know that that one [Jesus] was revealed to take away sins
and there is no sin in him [Jesus].
6 Everyone abiding in him [Jesus] does not sin.
Everyone sinning has neither seen him [Jesus] nor known him [Jesus].

7 Dear Children, let no one deceive you.
The one acting justly is just,
      as that one [the Father] is just.
8 The one committing sin is of the devil
      because from the beginning the devil sins.
      For this the Son of God was revealed,
      that he might do away with the works of the devil.
9 +Everyone begotten of God
    +does not commit sin
        +because his [God's] seed abides in him [the believer],
    +and he [the believer] is not able to sin
+because he has been begotten of God.

10 In this are the children of God and the children of the devil made manifest:
Everyone not acting justly is not of God
— and the one not loving his brother.

NOTES TO 2:28–3:10

V. 28 in him The gender of the pronoun here is ambiguous. It could refer to either Jesus or "the anointing." The subject of the following verse is Jesus and the two other uses of *autos* in the verse also refer to Jesus. Thus, the context suggests that the phrase "in him" (as in v. 27) also refers to Jesus. This view is confirmed by the overall orientation of the section.

when *Ean* can mean "when" (cf. BDAG 268). If there is a note of uncertainty in the expression, it is regarding when, not whether, Christ will be revealed.

revealed For a survey of the usage of this term in 1 John, see at 1:2.

we may have confidence In 3:21 and 5:14, confidence *(parrēsia)* is mentioned in relation to making requests of God. In 4:17, it is mentioned in relation to the Day of Judgment before God. The context here is close to that of 4:17.

at his coming The term "presence, coming" *(parousia)* appears twenty-four times in the New Testament but only here in the Johannine writings. The word itself has a use in which it referred to the solemn arrival of the king. It also has a more informal meaning where it simply refers to one's arrival (e.g., 1 Cor 16:17 where it speaks of the arrival of Stephanas). However, in the New Testament, it refers most often to the coming of Jesus at the end of time. In apocalyptic thought, the notions of a return of Jesus and a final judgment are connected with one another inasmuch as, since Christ will be the agent of God at judgment, such judgment will necessitate a Second Coming on the last day. In these verses we focus on the use of the term *Parousia* as an almost technical term referring to the "coming" of the Christ at the end of time. In the following section, we will discuss the apocalyptic character of the notion of final judgment.

V. 29 If you know "If" here is intended to emphasize that what follows is the starting point for a logical argument: If you know that he is just. . . .

he is just In 1:9, God is called just; in 2:1 Jesus is called just. However, here and in 3:7 the pronouns make the antecedents ambiguous. And, since both "God" and "Jesus" are elsewhere described as just, scholarship has been divided on which is intended here. R. E. Brown surveys opinion on the matter and finds the weight of argument favoring a reference to Jesus, but there are factors not mentioned by Brown (or others) that are significant.

As will be argued in detail (both in the Interpretation and in the Addendum), the form of the argument throughout this section follows a stereotypical pattern. Once this pattern is recognized, it is apparent that v. 29 is paraphrasing the principle that God is just and the one acting justly is begotten of him (God). This is the same principle as employed in John 8:39-44 where the author says that if his listeners were children of Abraham they would do the works of Abraham, but they are children of the devil and do his works. See also at 3:7.

has been begotten from him The antecedent of "him" here is God the Father. In 1 John, when the antecedent is stated, the believer is always begotten "of God" (3:9 [twice]; 4:7; 5:1 [twice], 4, 18 [twice]). Thus, there can be little doubt that this is the case here also. That the antecedent is God the Father is also confirmed by the presence of the stereotyped pattern of argument referred to immediately above. Nevertheless, it should be pointed out that, in the Gospel, the only statement that the believer is begotten "of God" is in the Prologue (1:13); elsewhere the believer is born "of the Spirit" (3:5, 6, 8) or "from above" (3:3, 7). This is undoubtedly another element of the pervasive tendency in 1 John to attribute to God the Father what is attributed to Jesus and the Spirit in the Gospel.

In his translation of the verb *gennaō*, Brown (*Epistles* 384) uses "begotten" (as by a male) rather than "born" (as from a female). He points out that the next verse speaks of male seed, thus giving further evidence that "begetting" is closer to the Johannine viewpoint. This seems to be an appropriate distinction and I have adopted it.

3:1 the Father has given us More so than in the Gospel, the Father is said to give directly to the believer. This is consistent with the pattern in 1 John where there is a greater focus on the Father as the source of action than there is in the Gospel. Here in 3:1, the Father is said to have given the love that results in our being called children of God. In 3:23, he is the one who gave the commandment to believe "in the name of" Jesus. He is also the one who has given of the Spirit (3:24; 4:13) and who has given eternal life (5:11) and the one who will give life to the one sinning a sin not unto death (5:16).

did not know him "Him" is almost certainly God the Father given the preceding context.

V. 2 There is discussion about the antecedent of the pronouns in v. 2c, d, e. Some (e.g., R. E. Brown, Strecker) claim that they all refer to God; others (e.g., Brooke, Schnackenburg, Hass et al.; Smalley) say they refer to Jesus. Klauck thinks that all refer to God except "that one" in v. 3 although he does not rule out the possibility of a sudden change of antecedent in v. 2e. The antecedents are certainly not clear and not good style by modern standards; but, given the stereotyped pattern of identifying supernatural parentage that structures the surrounding passage, there is good reason for seeing a sudden change. Thus, given the context of the stereotyped pattern of argument in v. 2e, as in 2:28, 3:2c-3, 5-6, 8cd, the antecedent probably refers to Jesus.

now we are children of God There is disagreement in some manuscripts about where the major break appears in v. 2a-c. Some have a major break after 2a and a minor after 2b; some have the reverse. The latter is the more likely as the UBS committee proposes.

Scholars (e.g., Schnackenburg, *Epistles* 156; Brown, *Epistles* 388; Smalley, *Epistles* 136, 141) regularly point out that the Johannine author's identification of the believer as a "child of God" is intended to reflect the ways in which the believer is similar to Jesus. Those same scholars note that the author uses the title "child" rather than "Son," which he reserves for Jesus. See, for example, Smalley (*Epistles* 259): "John may be implying here that the relationship of believers to God in the world can and should reflect that of Jesus to God. . . ."

it has not yet been revealed what we will be The distinction between the present and future status of the believer is typical of the author's conviction that there are both a present and a future dimension to eschatology.

when he [Jesus] is revealed The subject of the verb is not expressed. Some think the subject is Jesus; some think it is the same as in v. 2b ("what we will be"). In favor of an impersonal subject is that it could be an elliptical parallel to the clause in v. 2b. In favor of Jesus as subject is that he is the subject in the three other instances in the section (except v. 2b where another subject is expressed). The purpose of v. 2ab is to contrast the (already exalted) present status of the believer as a child of God with the hope regarding the believer's future status. The purpose of 2bc is that "we will be like him because we will see him as he is." In light of the stereotyped pattern of apocalyptic argument structuring this section and in view of the way the various statements about Jesus are interjected so abruptly, I see the subject as Jesus.

But in v. 3ab what has just been talked about in v. 2 is now described as a "hope," not as a foreordained reality. In fact, v. 3b says that everyone makes himself/herself holy "upon him" (that is, in imitation of him) just as that one (Jesus) is holy. Thus, v. 3b indicates that the statements "we will be like him" and "we will see him as he is" are not foregone conclusions. Rather, they reflect a hope, the fulfillment of which is something to be striven for. All of this takes place at some future time. Is this the time when it will be revealed "what we will be" or is it the time when Jesus will be revealed (as is spoken of in v. 28)?

It may well be that the discussion of the subject of *ephanerōthē* in v. 2c is of relatively minor consequence. If we take the subject of the verb to be impersonal ("if what we will be will be revealed") we may well ask when it will be revealed — and the answer is that it will be revealed at the Parousia of Christ. Consequently, we can say that vv. 2b-3b speak about the future and about the Parousia of Christ. But this is also true of 2:28. Thus, we can see that the first two comments in this section (2:28 and 3:2b-3b) speak of the future manifestation of Christ, and the second two (vv. 5-6 and v. 8cd) speak of the past manifestation of Christ. This provides the proper context for interpreting these verses.

The second issue is the nature of "what will be revealed." We are already like him in that we are children of God, but v. 2b and v. 2c speak of something additional. What this future element will be is a matter of hope (v. 3a) and a matter of effort (v. 3b). In other words what we will be revealed to be is not a foregone conclusion, but the revelation will be just that — it will reveal us "as we are."

we will be like him Just what the clause "we will be like him" means is unclear. The author has already indicated that we are like Jesus in that we are children of God (v. 2a). We also know that the future similarity will be a result of the effort that the believer puts forth. There is clear evidence of this conception elsewhere in the New Testament (Rom 8:17, 19, 29; 1 Cor 15:49; Col 3:3-4).

Brown (*Epistles* 394-95) thinks "him" refers to God the Father. In this view, the believer will see God (something not possible for Jews earlier in their history) and the believer will be like God (since we are already like Jesus [4:17bc]).

However, it is more likely that the author is indicating that there are a present experience of who Jesus is and also a future experience that will be more complete, just as there are an "already" and a "not yet" to the status of the Christian.

that we will see him as he is The word "that" translates *hoti*, which could also mean "because." In the present instance it is more likely that the clause "that we will see him as he is" parallels with the previous *hoti* (v. 2c). Thus, we know that we will be like him and that we will see him as he is. In the Johannine tradition, to have seen Jesus is to have seen the Father. Consequently, the notion of seeing the reality of God the Father is not excluded from this understanding.

V. 3 having this hope in him "Him" here is Jesus. Note also that this is the only instance of the term "hope" *(elpis)* in the Johannine writings.

makes himself holy The Greek is a single verb. This verb and the adjective later in the verse are the only uses of the term in reference to the believer in the Johannine writings. It appears in John 11:55 but in reference to Jewish pilgrims purifying themselves before Passover.

as that one "That one" *(ekeinos)* is Jesus. Jesus is the one in whom the faithful hope and whom they have as model. The effort to be made holy is similar to the conviction that the believer "must walk as he (Jesus) walked" (2:6).

holy The Greek here is *hagnos* (pure, holy, innocent) rather than *hagios*. Strecker (*Letters* 91-92) is correct when he says that, in spite of the cultic background of the term, its use here (and other places in the New Testament) is ethical. In 3:5, Jesus is said to have no sin in himself, which is tantamount to saying he is "holy."

V. 4 lawlessness (Gk: *anomia*) This term appears only here in the Johannine literature. In 2 Thess 2:3, it is said that in the end time the "man of lawlessness" *(ho anthrōpos tēs anomias)* will appear. In 2 Thess 2:9, this figure is identified with Satan.

V. 5 that one This refers to Jesus since he (not the Father) is the one who is "revealed" in 1 John (cf. 1:2; 2:28; 3:2, 5, 8).

in him This refers to the same person who was mentioned earlier in the verse: Jesus.

V. 6 abiding in him The antecedent of the pronoun here is Jesus. The previous section (2:27) had closed and this section opened (2:28) with the assurance and exhortation that the faithful "abide in Jesus."

seen him nor known him Two points deserve comment here. First, the concepts of "seeing" and "knowing" are central to Johannine theology as a whole. In 3:2e, it was said that the child of God will "see" Jesus "as he is" when Jesus is revealed. In 3:1d, it was said that the world did not "know" the Father. Yet in spite of these possibilities, the determining factor should be that all of the pronouns following "that one" in v. 5 must refer to the same individual since no other person is mentioned in the interval. On this basis, both instances of "him" in v. 6b refer to Jesus.

V. 7 as that one is just Once more the antecedent is unclear. Does "that one" in v. 7c refer to the Father or to Jesus? Almost all commentators take it as referring to Jesus, but, in light of the overriding stereotyped polemic evident here, this view is almost surely wrong.

Verse 29 above identified the Father as the just one. Verse 7b returns to 2:29c to develop that thought more fully. If this is correct, then there is all the more reason for seeing the reference to "that one" in v. 7c as God the Father.

In v. 8, it is said that the devil sins (that is his nature) and the one who sins is therefore "of the devil" (that is, the devil is his father). Thus, once more the principle that one acts like one's father is invoked and applied. Verse 7bc is contrasted with v. 8 in two ways. First, there is an explicit contrast between acting justly (v. 7b) and committing sin (v. 8); second there is an implicit contrast between "that one" (who is just) and the devil (who sins). This dual contrast may be seen from the following literal translation:

> The one doing justice is just *(and is of God)*
> as *(from the beginning)* that one (God) is just.
> The one doing sin is of the devil
> because from the beginning the devil sins.

In other words, the contrast throughout is that typical of the stereotyped pattern that describes how the two classes of people act and how such action reveals who their father is.

As was pointed out, the first phrase in italics is not explicit. If it is objected that such conjecture seems unjustified, one can point to the additional parallels between 7bc and v. 8 that argue for such a meaning. But, in addition, one need only look at v. 10c where almost the same statement appears, except in the negative: "Everyone not doing justice is not of God." The issue, then, is who is "of God" and who is "of the devil."

This continues in v. 10 where the contrast is again explicit between the children of God and the children of the devil. Given this extensive parallelism as well as the repeated use of the principle that one acts as one's father acts, it seems clear that "that one" refers to God the Father.

V. 8 is of the devil The expression to be "of" someone is the same as saying that one is "born" of another. See, for example, Keck, "Derivation."

For this the Son of God was revealed, that he might do away with the works of the devil This is perhaps the clearest statement of the purpose of Jesus' ministry in 1 John, expressed in apocalyptic terms. It is very close to the Synoptic view of the ministry as reasserting the Kingdom (kingly power) of God over against Satan. In overall orientation it is quite similar to Mark 1:24.

V. 9 his seed This is a curious expression and appears only here in the Johannine literature. Dodd ("First Epistle," 150-51) correctly observes that it seems to be a technical term within the community for whom the Letter was written because it is introduced in such a way that it was presumed the readers would understand it. Unfortunately, the meaning is not so clear to the modern reader. In gnostic thought, some humans were said to have a divine seed within them and salvation consisted of freeing this divine element from its material surroundings and returning to the realm of the divine. Dodd gives several examples of such usage in Philo, the Hermetic literature, and Valentinus. Schnackenburg (*Epistles* 175) comments: "'God's seed' can hardly mean anything other than the Holy Spirit (cf. 3:24; 4:13)." Despite the verbal similarities to elements of gnostic thought, it is more likely intended here in a more general sense.

Many scholars see it as referring to the word of God, but recent major commentators lean toward viewing it as a reference to the Spirit. (So, for example, Schnackenburg, *Epistles* 174-75; Brown, *Epistles* 411; Klauck, *Erste Johannesbrief* 194).

OVERVIEW OF 2:28–3:10

The previous section had spoken of the arrival of the Last Hour. This section continues the theme by focusing intensely on the Second Coming of Christ and the judgment that will take place then. While the previous section dealt with Christological error, the present clarifies the status of the believer as a child of God who is, and is not, fully prepared for the *Parousia* of Christ. The author does this by distinguishing between "realized" and "unrealized" elements in the status of the believer.

The believer is to have both confidence and hope at the prospect of Jesus' coming. He or she is to have confidence because the Father is just and because the believer is begotten of God and a child of God. The believer is to have hope that she/he will be shown to be like Jesus, but this requires that the believer make the effort to be holy as Jesus is holy. Jesus himself is holy and sinless but he was revealed to take away sin. The one remaining in him does not sin. In sum, the one who acts justly is just in the same way the Father is just. The one who sins is of the devil because it is the devil's nature to sin.

THE STRUCTURE OF 2:28–3:10

There are numerous stylistic features throughout this section.[1] Some are quite minor, but others serve to structure the presentation in significant ways.[2]

Verse 28, at the beginning of this section, is chained to the last verse of the previous section by the catchword phrase "remain in him." The very last statement of this section (3:10d) is also linked to what follows in 3:11 by the catchword of "(not) loving his brother."[3]

In the body of material, there are nine statements that are quite similar in structure and wording.

> A. Everyone acting justly has been begotten from him. (v. 29c)
>   [Everyone having this hope in him (v. 3a)]
>   Everyone committing sin (v. 4a)
> B. Everyone remaining in him (v. 6a)
>   Everyone sinning (v. 6b)
> C. The one acting justly (v. 7b)
>   The one committing sin (v. 8a)
> D. Everyone begotten of God (v. 9a)
>   Everyone not acting justly (v. 10c)

---

1. I have also discussed this passage in detail in "Polemic."

2. Brooke (*Epistles* xxxv) sees 2:28–4:6 as a major division with subdivisions at 2:28–3:24 and 4:1-6. Strecker (*Epistles* 78) views this as the beginning of a major paranetic section (following the dogmatic section of 2:18-27) that stretches to 3:24 with the following subdivisions: 2:28-29; 3:1-3, 4-10, 11-18, 19-24. Culpepper (*Epistles* 254, cf. 262) sees a major division beginning here and extending to 4:6 with subdivisions at 2:28–3:10; 3:11-24; 4:1-6.

3. Note that the specific theme of loving one's brother is introduced here somewhat awkwardly. This reveals the effort of the author to show the relation between the sections on a literary level. The same awkwardness is evident in 2:27.

If the second of these statements (the one in brackets above) is put aside, the remaining statements constitute four antithetical sets. In each set, the first statement speaks of the proper action or state ("acting justly" in A and C; "remaining in him" in B; and "begotten of God" in D) and the second statement in each set speaks of improper action or state ("sinning" in A, B, C; "not acting justly" in D).

These contrasting statements are part of a stereotyped pattern of argument in which the members of two dualistically opposed groups are identified as "children" of either God or Satan. In this form of argument, the debate regularly focuses on terms such as "father," "begotten of," and "children of." The identity of one's parent, and consequently whom the person is "begotten of" or is "child of," is both determined and revealed by one's actions.[4] This stereotyped argument pervades the section and forms the structural backbone of the material.[5]

As is typical in such stereotyped argument, the two alternatives presented to the individual are to be either "of" God or "of" the Evil One. In the case of the community crisis, both the author and his opponents claimed to be "of" God. However, the author of 1 John has woven into this stereotyped pattern a series of statements about Jesus and his role as they relate to the issue of parentage. These statements deal with his Second Coming, his role as a model for the believer, and his role in the forgiveness of sin and destruction of evil.[6] In order to show more clearly the relation of these verses to the overriding stereotyped pattern, the verses dealing with Jesus are the most fully indented in the translation. The recognition of the way the stereotyped polemic and the statements about Jesus are interwoven is essential to understanding the thought of the section as a whole. Not only does it help explain the overall pattern of composition, but it also explains the somewhat awkward way the role of Jesus relates to this pattern. Finally, it helps explain the antecedents of some of the most confusing pronouns in the Letter.[7]

4. Although gnostics understood such "birth" as ultimately determining one's nature (predestination), this is not the meaning of the Johannine text. The Johannine dualism is functionally similar to that of 1QS where there is a juxtaposition of texts that seem to speak of determinism with other texts that imply the ability to choose and to change. See the discussion in Klauck, *Erste Johannesbrief* 200.

5. The pattern and its parallels in other literature will be discussed further in the Addendum below.

6. 1 John 3:3, the only one of the "everyone"-statements that does not fit the pattern of contrasting pairs is also the only "everyone"-statement that deals with Jesus. Thus, the exception to the pattern confirms the accuracy of the observation that the passage as a whole is structured by a stereotypical pattern.

7. It is possible that the underlying pattern of stereotyped argument was originally a *"topos"* of argument familiar to the community as a whole and the author of 1 John has modified it to indicate that his understanding of being "of God" necessarily involves the role of God's Son, Jesus.

But there are also other minor rhetorical details worth observing. Within the material associated with the stereotyped argument, there is a clear verbal parallelism (more evident in the Greek than in English) between *poiein dikaiosynēn* (literally, "doing justice") and *poiein hamartian* (literally, "doing sin"). This parallelism appears throughout the section.

There are also a number of other verbal relationships that are noteworthy and that contribute to the sense of dualism. For example, there is a parallelism between "If you know that he is just, you know that everyone acting justly has been begotten from him" (v. 29) and "The one acting justly is just, as that one is just" (v. 7bc).

There is also parallelism between "The one committing sin is of the devil" (v. 8a) and "Everyone not acting justly is not of God" (v. 10c). In v. 10ab, there is the verbal contrast between "children of God" and "children of the devil." Finally, there is the general thematic contrast between being "begotten of," "children of," or simply being "of" God (v. 29c) or the devil (v. 8a).[8]

In v. 9, there is a minor chiasm that is illustrated in the text of the translation.

More importantly, the first and last statements are the reverse of one another ("Everyone acting justly has been begotten from him" [2:29c]; "Everyone not acting justly is not of God" [3:10c]). When this formal feature is combined with the fact that thematically the section revolves around the notion of acting justly (and its opposite), it is evident that this formal parallelism functions as an inclusion for the entire section.

This inclusion is "marred" only by the awkward appendage of "and the one not loving his brother" in v. 10d. But this appendage is actually a catchword intended to link this passage with the one that begins in 3:11. Thus, while the structure of the section may appear awkward to the modern reader, it is certainly not haphazard.[9]

THE INTERPRETATION OF 2:28–3:10

In keeping with the stereotyped pattern that structures the section, the overriding theme is the relationship between one's actions and one's parentage. But the focus falls on the importance of one's actions that are characterized as either "acting justly" or "committing sin." The basic principle behind this argument is that one acts like one's Father. Thus, v. 29 will state that one acting justly is be-

---

8. Some have proposed that these multiple parallels constitute a full chiastic arrangement but, in my opinion, the arrangement is not sufficiently balanced to allow that explanation.

9. More detail on the background of the stereotyped structure will be given in the Addendum below.

gotten of God because God is just. But throughout, the principle will be probed from three different perspectives as though to test its validity from all angles.[10]

2:28

The author begins by addressing his listeners as "children" and urges them to "remain in Jesus." This connects the current section verbally (catchword) and thematically to the previous one, which had ended with the statement that the readers do indeed "remain in him." That is, the believers continue steadfast in their belief regarding the importance of Jesus. Now the author turns to exhortation because remaining in Jesus will be the basis of the believer's courage at Jesus' (second) coming.[11] Thus, when Jesus is revealed, those who have remained in him will have courage and confidence and will not shrink from him.

Implicit in this is the assertion that, if they do not remain in Jesus as they should, they will have to face the error of their belief at the time of Jesus' Second Coming.

2:29–3:3

Verse 29 then begins by presenting a kind of syllogism: "If you do 'X,' then you will know 'Y.' That is, if you know that 'he' is just, you know that everyone acting justly is begotten from him." Scholars have puzzled over the identity of the subject of "is" in v. 29a (which is implicit in the Greek) and about the antecedent of "him" in v. 29b. However, recognizing the presence of the principle that one acts the way one's father acts, helps considerably in the interpretation. Here the author takes as established the justice of the Father and reminds the reader that, if the Father is just, then everyone acting justly is begotten from him. This will be the first of several appeals to this principle.

The author then (3:1) reflects on the love that is demonstrated by God in giving believers the ability to be children of God.[12] It is as if the author recognizes the general applicability of the principle he has just invoked, yet continues to be amazed that this is true even of God who allows humans to be his children. The author then interrupts himself and interjects that the world does not know the author's followers because it did not know the Father.

10. But, as we have seen in the discussion of the structure, the recognition of this development is complicated by overlay of the various rhetorical turns, the theological asides, and by the number of ambiguous pronouns and other antecedents throughout the section.

11. This reflects the author's belief that Jesus will be revealed in the future, a belief that was not shared by the opponents.

12. For Smalley (*Epistles* 138), the third major section of the Letter begins in 3:1 and consists of 3:1–5:13, with subdivisions at 3:1-3, 4-9, 10-24; 4:1-6; 4:7–5:4; 5:5-13.

Rather than continue describing the relationship between acting justly and being children of God, the author directs his comments (v. 2) to the fact that the full extent of this status as children of God is not yet revealed. The author then begins speaking of Jesus and expresses his conviction (hope) that when Jesus is revealed, the believer will be like Jesus and will see Jesus fully as he is.

But (v. 3) the believer's hope that Jesus will be revealed and that the believer will be like Jesus is also the motive for the believer to work to make himself (herself) holy just as Jesus is holy. Thus, there are both an "already" to the believer's sonship and also a "not-yet," since it will only be by one's effort that he/she is able to become holy "as Jesus is."[13] In terms of his refutation of the opponents, the author expresses an eschatology that is partially realized and partially future. At the same time he affirms that there is an essential similarity between the status of the believer and the status of Jesus. Finally, the author affirms that, while the believer acts justly, to act justly requires effort and direction and so requires ethics because it is still possible to sin. One's status is not a *fait accompli* but a work in progress.

3:4-5

In v. 4, the author turns from the discussion of the one acting justly to a discussion of the one who sins.[14] The equation the author makes is simple: the one who commits sin commits lawlessness and sin is lawlessness. Jesus was revealed to take away sins and there is no sin in him.

Thus, in this brief discussion the point of comparison is again Jesus. The believer, described previously, works to make him/herself holy as Jesus is holy. The one described here (who sins) is not like Jesus because (v. 5) Jesus was revealed to take away sin and there is no sin in him.

3:6a

The statement of v. 6a is very brief and returns to the exhortation of 2:28 in order to combine the topic there with the topic of sin that had just been discussed. Thus, the author states that the one who "remains" in Jesus does not sin. Consequently, we see that this second set of statements does not speak primarily of the Father but of Jesus.

13. "There is a tension between the now and the not yet. The full consummation of salvation belongs to the future." These words of Nickelsburg (*Resurrection* 154), which describe the context of 1QH 3:19-23, could apply equally to this text from 1 John.

14. Schnackenburg (*Epistles* 169) sees this as the beginning of the third major section of the Letter, which extends to 3:24. He further subdivides the material into vv. 4-10, 11-20, 21-24.

3:6b

The second part of this statement is also quite brief and simply affirms that if one sins, one has not truly seen or known Jesus.[15]

3:7-8

The author now begins a new subdivision by his exhortation to his "children" not to let anyone deceive them. He returns to the first part of the topic sentence in 2:29c and speaks again of "the one acting justly," developing it further. That person is just, as the Father is just. However, the one committing sin (now we see the third negative statement) is "of the devil," because "from the beginning" the devil sins.

To fully understand vv. 7-8, we must note their parallelism throughout. The first element of each contrasts with the other: "The one doing justice" (v. 7b) with "the one doing sin" (v. 8a). The second element contrasts "is just" (v. 7c) with "is of the devil" (v. 8b). Finally, the third element of each contrasts: "as that one is just" (v. 7d) contrasts with "because from the beginning the devil sins" (v. 8c).

Thus, (v. 7) the one who acts justly is like God the Father and (v. 8) the one who commits sin is like the devil because the devil has been a sinner since the beginning. That the second element here is intended to refer to one's father is clear from v. 8b though it is elliptical (see the Note to v. 7 above). The reason the one who acts justly does so is that the person's father is just. Although there is no explicit mention of "being begotten" in v. 7, this is implicit as can be seen from its parallel in v. 8b, where the one who sins is said to be "of the devil." Then, in each, this justice and this sinfulness are directly related to the justice of the Father and the sinfulness of the devil.

Two elements of this interpretation should be specially noted. First, this parallelism clarifies the antecedent of "that one" in v. 7 in a way that is consistent with the interpretation of the parallel instance in v. 29. To see the antecedent here as "Jesus," as many commentators do, makes no sense of the context once the parallelism and the presence of the principle that one acts like one's father are recognized.

But the author reminds (v. 8cd) his reader that Jesus was revealed precisely so that he might "do away with" the works of the devil. That is, the actions of Jesus are meant to lead the believer away from sin to justice.

---

15. Brown (*Epistles* 428) makes the interesting observation that there is considerable similarity between the discussion of "sin," "justice," and "judgment" here and the power attributed to the Paraclete in John 16:8 where the Paraclete "will show the world its error with regard to sin, to righteousness, and to judgment." However, in the present passage, the theme of judgment is not explicit.

3:9-10

The notion that the sinner is "of the devil" (v. 8b) leads into a discussion of the second part of 2:29c, namely the phrase "begotten of God." The one who is truly "begotten of God" is not "of the devil" and so does not commit sin. Here (v. 9), the author invokes the principle a third time, but approaches it from a different perspective. This time, the author starts from the premise that the person is begotten of God. If this is true, then the believer will not sin because God's seed remains in the believer. Having the seed of God means that the person is not able to sin because he or she is truly "begotten" of God.

In v. 10 we reach the conclusion of the section and find a final explicit comparison between the children of God and the children of the devil. Previously the author has tested and applied the principle that one acts like one's father from three different perspectives. In 2:29b, he began from the premise that the Father is just; in 3:7b, he began from the premise that the person is acting justly; and in 3:9a, from the premise that one is begotten from God. Now he returns to the original formulation (cf. 2:29d) but phrases the principle negatively: everyone not acting justly is not "of God." Thus, not only does he end with an explicit contrast, but his last statement forms an inclusion with the first articulation of the principle in 2:29d.

Thus, in the major development within these verses, the author has laid out criteria by which one is able to determine whether he/she is a child of God or a child of the devil. In a similar way in 4:1-6, the author will present a concise discussion of how to distinguish the Spirit of Truth from the Spirit of Deception. The parallelism between these two discussions is reinforced by the fact that the two sets of verses also end with the same type of concluding and summarizing statements. Thus, in 3:10 we read: "In this are the children of God and the children of the devil made manifest" *(en toutō phanera estin ta tekna tou theou kai ta tekna tou diabolou)*, and in 4:6 we read: "From this we know the Spirit of Truth and the Spirit of Deception" *(ek toutou ginōskomen to pneuma tēs alētheias kai to pneuma tēs planēs)*.

Up to this point, the author has discussed proper action almost entirely in the abstract (that is, "acting justly"/"unjustly"). It is only here at the end that the author becomes specific, equating unjust actions with the failure to love the brothers. The mention of the failure of mutual love here at the end is awkward and unexpected, but it also functions to make the discussion of acting justly concrete: one demonstrates just actions in loving one's brother. And this is precisely what the opponents do not do. But the more immediate purpose of its introduction here is to provide a catchword-connection between this section and the next, where the notion of loving one's brother will be developed in much greater detail. There the argument will shift entirely from the abstract to the concrete and will focus on brotherly love as the specification of correct behavior.

*   *   *

Throughout this section the author has brought together a remarkable number of elements on which he and the opponents disagree, but he has done this all under the aegis of discussing a claim that both groups undoubtedly made: that God was their father and that they were children of God. The author began by attempting to demonstrate that only those who act justly can be said to be begotten of God. Thus, even though the opponents claim to be begotten of God, they are not because they are sinners (something they would deny). But, in the author's eyes, the opponents do not love the brothers and so are sinners and, consequently, are children of the devil, not of God. So while he does not reject the possibility of such a claim, he rejects the opponents' right to make it.

But woven into this is a complex pattern of affirmations regarding Jesus that distinguish the author's views from those of his opponents. While these may seem ordinary to the modern reader, it is due, in large part, to the work of the author that these insights have been articulated and preserved within Johannine Christianity. Every statement the author makes about Jesus contradicts the views of the opponents.

First, he affirms that the believer needs to remain in Jesus. Jesus has a permanent role in salvation and, if the believer does not remain in Jesus, the believer will not be able to be confident on the day of his (second) coming. The opponents deny a permanent role for Jesus and deny any future judgment or even a Second Coming itself.

Second, although both groups claim a status as children of God, the author, while recognizing that this is a marvelous gift, asserts that the believers are not yet perfect (as the opponents claim for themselves) but rather must work in order to make themselves holy as Jesus is holy. Consequently, proper behavior is necessary in order to be "holy" at the time of Jesus' return.[16] The opponents contend that they have been so radically transformed by the eschatological Spirit that the effort to avoid sin is unnecessary as is any future judgment.

Not only will Jesus return in judgment and not only is he a model of holiness, but the author twice affirms that Jesus is the one who takes away sin and who does away with the works of the devil. Thus, the active and essential role of Jesus is again affirmed — contrary to the beliefs of the opponents.

---

16. It will be noted that the author does not use the term "judgment" although he implies the imminence of judgment when he speaks of having confidence and not shrinking from Jesus at his return.

And so, as he had shown previously (2:20-27) that one could not properly believe in God (as the opponents claimed to do) unless one believed in Jesus, neither can a person be a true child of God without acting justly. And at the end, the author prepares to specify just what acting justly must include when he appends his statement that the one who does not love one's brother is not acting justly.

Addendum: The Background of the Stereotyped Pattern of Argument in 2:28–3:10

The stereotyped argument used by the author in 2:28–3:10 is common in apocalyptic literature. This pattern of argumentation distinguishes between two groups as coming from either God or from the devil. The parentage of the groups is reflected in their actions, actions seen as either good or evil. This pattern, either in full or in part, is found not only in 1 John 2:28–3:10 but also in *1QS* 3:13–4:26; *TJud* 20:1-5; *TAsh* 1:3-9; and *TNaph* 2:6–3:1. It is also evident in John 8:38-47 and in 1 John 4:1-6.

The generalized form of such polemic consists of five elements, not all of which are always present. Put briefly, these elements are: (1) the contrasting principles (God/Satan) are introduced and characterized (e.g., the Father is just [2:29a]; the devil sins from the beginning [3:8b]); (2) persons are allied with either God or Satan (e.g., "to be begotten of" [2:29b; 3:9d]; "to be children of" [3:1b]; or simply to be "of" [3:10c] either God or Satan); (3) characteristics of each group are then described ("The one committing sin is of the devil" [3:8a]; "Everyone begotten of God does not commit sin" [3:9a]; "The believer is not able to sin" [3:9c]; "everyone not acting justly" [3:10c]); (4) specific characteristics of each group are described (only at the end is the specific act of "not loving the brothers" mentioned [3:10d] but the next section will be devoted to a fuller elaboration of this); (5) the polemic is expressed within the framework of apocalyptic dualism.[17]

The purpose of this form of argument is to lay out the options open to an individual or group in starkly contrasting alternatives depending upon their choices. This pattern of argument is sufficiently common and fixed that it appears in four distinct literary genres: instruction manual (the *Rule of the Community* from Qumran), testamentary literature (the *Testaments of the Twelve Patriarchs*), Gospel (the Gospel of John), and "tract" (1 John).[18] In addition to helping the interpreter understand the flow of the argument here (as well as the interruptions to it), the presence of an argument of this type in 1 John is another indication of the pervasive apocalyptic worldview of 1 John.

17. The pattern is discussed in more detail and in relation to its other manifestations in the SDQ, the *T12P*, the Gospel and in 1 John 4:1-6, in my article "Polemic."

18. In the Introduction, I noted that the genre of 1 John is the subject of considerable discussion. The term "tract" is here intended to be taken loosely, since 1 John also has elements of exhortation, diatribe and homily.

The Proclamation to Love One Another

+11 Because this is the proclamation that you heard from the beginning, that we should love one another.

> +12 Not as Cain was of the Evil One
> > +and slaughtered his brother.
> > +And why did he slaughter him?
> +Because his works were evil, but those of his brother just.

+13 And, Brothers, do not be surprised if the world hates you.

14 We know that we have crossed over from death into life
   because we love the brothers.

The one not loving, abides in death.
15 Everyone hating his brother is a murderer,
and you know that every murderer does not have
   eternal life abiding in himself.

16 In this we have known love
   inasmuch as that one [Jesus] has laid down his life for us.
And we ought to lay down our lives for the brothers.

17 Whoever has the life of the world
   and sees his brother in need
   and closes his heart from him,
      how does the love of God abide in him?

18 Dear Children, let us not love
   in word nor with the tongue,
   but in work and truth.

NOTES TO 3:11-18

V. 11 Because This links v. 11 to what has preceded and explains why the author has equated the one not acting justly with the one not loving his brother.

proclamation This is the second (and last) time this term appears in the Letter. It was used in 1:5 to introduce the affirmation that God is light.

that we heard from the beginning This is the seventh (and last) time this expression appears in the Letter. Throughout, it has been a constant reminder that the author claims his message is the true and original one, as opposed to that of the opponents. Just why it now ceases to be a theme is not evident.

that we love one another On mutual love, see at 1 John 2:10. Although elsewhere mutual love is generally spoken of as a commandment, here it is also described as one of the two primary objects of the author's proclamation.

V. 12 Not as Cain The Greek expression is *ou kathōs,* which appears elsewhere in the Johannine literature only in John 6:58, where it is also associated with a reference to Scripture. This reference to Cain is the only explicit Old Testament reference in the Letter. However, here the story of Cain and Abel is cast within a dualistic worldview not present in Genesis (see Strecker, *Epistles* 108-9). Such recasting of biblical events in a dualistic worldview was typical of apocalyptic literature.

was of The expression "was of" is intended to identify one's father (see at 3:8).

his brother Abel is not mentioned by name in the Letter. The description of Abel as "just" and Cain as "evil" occurs with some frequency. Josephus (*Ant.* 1.53) speaks of Abel as "just" *(dikaios)* and Cain as "evil" *(ponēros).* References occur elsewhere in the New Testament (Matt 23:35; Heb 11:4; Jude 11) and in non-canonical literature (see Strecker, *Epistles* 109).

Evil One This title as a designation of Satan first appeared in 2:13 and is discussed there.

V. 13 Brothers This is the only instance in the Letter where the author addresses his readers as brothers. His usual terms of address are "Dear Children" and "Beloved." If these other terms tend to emphasize the relation of the writer to readers as one of priority of some sort, the use of the term "brothers" here is very significant for it shows his awareness of an even more fundamental tie between the author and his readers, that of being children of the same father! It also emphasizes the relation of the members of the community to one another rather than their relation to the author.

do not be surprised if the world hates you The hatred of the world for the believer is regularly associated with statements about "evil deeds" and "the Evil One" (see at John 3:19 [3E]).

V. 14 crossed over Brown (*Epistles* 445) points out that this verb is a strong one that "sharpens the sense of a dualistic division between death and life."

from death into life "Death" is mentioned only six times in 1 John. Two instances are here and the other four are in connection with the "sin-unto-death" in 5:16-17.

In 1 John, eternal life is conceived of both as "realized" in the sense that the believer already has life in him/herself through birth from God and also as "future" in the sense that the believer must work to bring the life to perfection. This present statement is the clearest expression of the realized dimension of that eschatology. See also the discussion of the eschatology of 1 John in Volume 1, Part 4, Section 5.6.

abides in death The death spoken of here does not refer to physical death but to spiritual death, that is, the failure to possess eternal life. It was the Johannine conviction that all believers die physically but only those who possess eternal life live forever.

The notion of "abiding in death" may not be intended to have the deeper connotations usually associated with "abide" and may be more properly translated simply as "remain." Undoubtedly the author would say that it was only the miracle of the "passing over" made possible by Christ that prevented all of them from "remaining" in death. However, from the point of view of the situation of the opponents, their abiding in death would be all the more lamentable since they had been so close to gaining life themselves!

V. 17 life of the world The Greek here is *ton bion tou kosmou*. The translation given is literal but refers to material resources, those things necessary for support of physical existence.

closes his heart The Greek here literally means "entrails" *(splanchna)*. But the "entrails" are used to symbolize the source of compassion and mercy toward others. There is a close parallel to this in *TZeb* 7:3 ("If you do not have the means to give to the one in need [*tō chrēzonti*], have compassion with innermost feelings of mercy [*splanchna eleous*]") and 8:2 (". . . because in the last days God will send his innermost feelings [*splanchna*] upon the earth and where he finds feelings [*splanchna*] of mercy, there he will dwell").

how does This is an abrupt change of logic but not editorial. Rather, it reflects the style of the author who is given to interrupting himself in his eagerness to address all the aspects of an issue (see, e.g., 1:1-4; 2:25; 3:3a).

love of God The genitive here is ambiguous: is this love *from* God (subjective genitive) or love *for* God (objective genitive) or *divine* love (qualitative genitive)? This is the same phrase as appears in 2:5. There we were not able to determine the meaning with certainty.

All three meanings are possible in this context. It is Johannine theology that God cannot continue to love a person if that person does not return love. For example, John 15:10: "If you keep my commandments, you will abide in my love, just as I have kept the commandments of my Father and I abide in his love" (see also John 15:14). But there is nothing quite parallel to this in the First Letter.

It is also true of Johannine thought that a person cannot be said to love God if the person does not love his brother. This is exemplified in 1 John 4:20-21: "If someone says 'I love God' and hates his brother, the person is a liar. For the one not loving his brother, whom he has seen, is not able to love God whom he has not seen. And we have this commandment from him, that the one loving God should also love his brother" (cf. also 4:8, 12; 5:1bc). In 4:20-21, it is apparent that the opponents claim to "love" God, just as they claimed to "know" him and to "abide" in him. Here the sense could well be that the author rejects the claim (to love God) on the part of anyone (e.g., the opponents) who does not love the fellow community members.

Finally, it is also possible that the phrase be taken to mean "divine love" in the sense that one cannot be said to have a love like that which God has, if one does not help the one in need. However, there is less evidence of this meaning within the Johannine writings. In the light of the repeated statement of the *second* notion in the First Letter, I opt for that meaning here.

V. 18 let us not love Most commentators assume that the love spoken of here is love of one's fellow community members but this is not the only possibility. Since the author has spoken previously about whether a person can truly love God if the person does not love fellow community members, this could be a return to that and a statement that the believer is to show love for God not just with word but with deeds. In the light of the immediate context, the logical conclusion is that it does, in fact, refer to love for God (although this is manifest in love for one's fellow community member).

(not) in word nor with the tongue but in work and in truth *TGad* 6:1 has a somewhat similar expression, "loving one another in work and in word" *(agapōntes allēlous en ergō kai logō),* but in *TGad* the meaning is quite different. There, the idea is that love can be manifested in both word ("loving words") and deeds. That is, "loving words" are an example of proper deeds. In 1 John, the notion of loving "in word and with the tongue" suggests that such love is *only* words and insincere. To be true, love needs to be manifest in deeds.

Although "word" and "tongue" are synonymous here, work and truth are not. The latter are more properly an example of hendiadys (that is, works that are true). Does this mean that one expresses love by being "of the truth"? There is precedent for this in 2 John 4-6 where true love of the brothers is manifested by one's own walking in the truth. Or does it mean that the only "true" love is that which expresses itself in deeds? This also would fit the context although there is less discussion of this elsewhere in the Letter.

OVERVIEW OF 3:11-18

These verses begin the second major part of the Letter with the recollection of the second fundamental aspect of the community's proclamation: "that we love one another." The example of Cain who killed his brother is recalled. But we know we have gone over from death to life by the fact that we love the brothers. The one who does not love remains in death and is a murderer. The example Jesus showed when he laid down his life is the example the believer is to follow. And so the believer should lay down his life for the brothers by sharing material goods with those in need. Love should be shown in action and not just in word.

THE STRUCTURE OF 3:11-18

As just noted, within the structure of the Letter as a whole, these verses mark the beginning of the second half of the Letter.[1] This is indicated by the remarkable verbal parallels with 1:5, by the fact that this is the only other time when "proclamation" is used in the Letter, and by the fact that the statement serves to introduce the second of the main themes of the Letter.[2] Finally, this divides the Letter into roughly equal parts.

---

1. Brown (*Epistles* 467) begins a new section (the second half of the Letter) here. It extends to 3:24. Schnackenburg (*Epistles* 169, 177) sees vv. 11-20 as a subdivision of the larger section running from 3:4-24.

2. This will continue until the Epilogue (5:13-21).

The First Half of the Letter:
    1:5: (a) ". . . this is the proclamation . . .
           (b) that we heard from the beginning . . .
           (c) that God is light. . . ."
The Second Half of the Letter:
    3:11 "(a*) . . . this is the proclamation . . .
           (b*) that you heard from the beginning . . .
           (c*) that we love one another."[3]

We had seen earlier that v. 10d was chained to v. 11 by the reference to mutual love. We now see that, in addition, the earlier reference to "is not of God" in v. 10c is chained to "is of the Evil One" in v. 12a.

The section, which extends from 3:11 to 3:18, concludes with the statement that we are to love in "work" and in "truth." The reference to "works" in this statement not only concludes (for the time being) the discussion of love that had begun at v. 11 but also forms a kind of inclusion with the beginning of the section. This section had not only begun the discussion of loving one another[4] but had commenced with the example of the "works" of Cain. Verse 18 now also adds the words "and in truth." Though awkward here, these words provide a clear chaining to the *next* section, which describes how believers know they are "of the truth."

Within the section, there is remarkably little structure other than the repeated use of contrast (e.g., evil/just; death/life; love/hate) and parallelism (e.g., "that one laid down his life"/"we ought to lay down our lives").

This section is almost entirely paraenetic. There is only one (although it is an important one) reference to Christ (v. 16b) and only one reference to God (v. 17d).

THE INTERPRETATION OF 3:11-18

After the general discussion of how acting justly or unjustly reveals one's Father, the author now turns to a concentrated discussion of the topic of mutual love,

---

3. Some commentators (for example, Brown and Klauck) see an inclusion between 3:11 and 3:23. Both are parallel in structure:

    (3:11) because this is the proclamation . . .
               that we love one another
    (3:23) and this is the commandment
               that we believe in the name of his Son, Jesus Christ.

However this divides 3:23 into two parts and does not explain the second part of the verse. The verse is better interpreted as a whole and understood as a chiasm (see below).

4. This is the true discussion of mutual love whereas v. 10d had served simply as a catchword to prepare for 3:11-18.

which, as he has stated (v. 10d), is the primary indication that one is acting justly. Although the topic had arisen previously (2:9-11), this will be the fullest development so far.[5]

The author begins (v. 11) by asserting that mutual love, like the proclamation that God is light (1:5), is part of the proclamation that they heard "from the beginning." Throughout the previous section, the author employed the principle that the actions of the son reflect the character and actions of the father. Here he continues this theme. After the proclamation that believers are to love one another, the author returns (v. 12) to the very beginning of the Old Testament and recalls the failure of mutual love that marked the first brothers in history, Cain and Abel. The reason Cain failed is that he was "of the Evil One." He was "of" the Evil One; his works were evil and therefore he killed his brother.[6]

The author then (vv. 13-15) draws a conclusion from this for his own time: the world will hate the members of the author's community just as Cain hated Abel because the world is also of the Evil One and will do the works that are typical of the Evil One. For the author "the world" includes all who are hostile to the community but most particularly the opponents who fail in love.

The author then returns to an assertion of what the believer "knows": that the believer has gone over from death to life. He is affirming that this transformation has already taken place and is therefore "realized" rather than simply "future." But the author argues that such a claim is not an empty one that cannot be verified. The fact that the believer loves the brothers is a proof that he has indeed gone over from death to life. The author intends this only in the positive sense. The fact that one loves the brothers is not the *only* test of whether one has been transformed, but it is an essential part of such a test. However, when it is put in its negative form, it is completely true: the one who hates (that is, does not love) the brothers remains in death. That person does not have life and is a murderer; and it is certain that a murderer does not possess eternal life.

In v. 16, the author speaks of the model for the community's love. This will be the only direct reference to Jesus in the passage, yet its role is central. The meaning could not be clearer and the demand put forward for the believer

5. In the remainder of the Letter, mutual love will be introduced and/or discussed in eleven more verses: 3:23; 4:7 [twice], 8, 11, 12, 19 [implicit], 20, 21; 5:1, 2. Thus, it becomes a dominant theme of this half of the Letter.

6. So also Klauck, *Erste Johannesbrief* 203. Although the contrast here is between Cain and Abel, the more significant contrast is between Cain *and Christ,* who provides the perfect example of how to express love. It is often pointed out that this is the only explicit reference to the OT in 1 John. That is true but it does not mean that the author has no concern for the OT or the community's Jewish heritage. Rather, the interpretation of the OT, which had been such a matter of contention at the time of the second edition, was not disputed at the time of 1 John (so also Beutler, *Johannesbriefe* 94).

could not be greater: "That one" (Jesus) laid down his life for us — and we ought to do the same for the brothers." The ideal of Christian love, as the author views it, is not just to love as we love ourselves (as it was in Matt 7:12), but to love as Jesus loved us. We should love in the same extreme way as he did when he laid down his life for us.[7]

Then (v. 17) the author provides a concrete test for this love. If someone has sufficient material resources and sees his brother in need, and closes his heart to the person, how does the love of God remain in him?[8] Jesus literally laid down his life, and the believer must be willing to do the same. Here, the obligation is less ultimate but nevertheless real — and evidently not being fulfilled. The believer needs to share his material resources with those brothers (community members) in need. The one who keeps his resources to himself when he sees his brother in need cannot claim to love God truly. Thus, the author confronts yet another of the claims of the opponents: their claim to love God. As he will say even more clearly in 4:20-21, if a person does not love one's fellow believer, how can that person claim to love God?

The author then concludes his exhortation to love by pointing out (v. 18) that such love must not just be in words but must be actualized in deeds. This is the only place in the Letter where a contrast between pretending to love and actually doing it is an issue. Whether this is intended to contrast the true believer with the opponents is unclear.[9] Elsewhere, the opponents are simply said not to love (cf. 2:10-11; 3:14-15, 16-17; 4:7-8, 11-12; 4:20–5:2). In the light of the situation described in 3:17, it may be intended to emphasize the need to act on the brother's behalf.

The translation of v. 18c as "to love in work" is awkward (to love "in deed"

---

7. Schnackenburg (*Epistles* 182) contrasts this with the actions of Cain (v. 12) and comments: "Those who hate deprive others of life. Those who love sacrifice their lives for others."

8. Some scholars have attempted to see in this statement a reference to specific events in the community. For example, Brown (*Epistles* 475) has speculated that when the secessionists left the community, they depleted the financial resources of the community either by theft or because they were the ones who were more financially secure. While this is certainly possible, it is not obvious from the text. There could have been many possible causes of the community's need without it being caused by the opponents. Strecker (*Epistles* 118) goes to the other extreme and suggests that the injunction to mutual love in this section is not at all directed at the opponents and in fact has nothing at all to do with them but is simply a general ethical exhortation. I do not find this convincing either. The best approach seems to be a "middle" one in which the exhortation is seen to refer to the opponents but not to a specific set of circumstances. Their error is in thinking that no ethical directives are necessary.

9. Brown (*Epistles* 476-77) sees this not as a charge of hypocrisy but as an affirmation of the necessity of good deeds in contrast to the view of the opponents who claimed that they already had eternal life and so no good deeds were necessary. While I agree with this view of the opponents, I do not see how Brown's understanding can be read from the verses. The verses clearly contrast those who only talk about loving and those who put their love into deeds.

would be smoother) but has been done to show the verbal similarity between this and 3:8, 12. In either case, the meaning is clear.

However, the meaning of "to love . . . in work and truth" is less clear. There are two related explanations of this phrasing. First, "work(s)" appears only three times in the Letter: here and earlier in 3:8, 12. In the first of those instances, it was said that Jesus was revealed to do away with the works of the devil. In the second, it was said that the works of Cain were evil. In light of the use of the term twice in the recent context, it is likely that the linking of "work" and "truth" is meant to be hendiadys: should be made manifest in works that are in accord with the truth rather than in accord with the devil or similar to those of Cain.

But there is also another factor. As awkward as it is theologically, the phrase's presence here conforms to the pattern whereby the author appends a word or phrase at the end of a section that establishes a catchword connection with the following section.[10] The introduction of the theme of "truth" here prepares for v. 19 in the next section, which explains how the believer can know whether one is "of the truth." This is probably the primary reason for the phrase's presence here.

---

10. This technique is discussed in more detail and other examples given in the Introduction, Section 7.2.

3:19-24

The Commandment to Correct Belief
and the Commandment to Mutual Love

19[And] in this we shall know that we are of the truth,
and before him [God] we will convince our heart,
   20with respect to what the heart accuses us of,
      that God is greater than our heart
      and knows all things.
21Beloved, if the heart does not accuse us,
   we have confidence before God,

    22and whatever we may ask for, we receive it from him [God]
    +because we keep his [God's] commandments and we do what is pleasing
    before him [God].
      +23And this is his [God's] commandment,
        +that we believe in the name of his Son Jesus Christ
        and
        +that we love one another,
      +just as he [God] gave us commandment.
    +24And the one keeping his [God's] commandments abides in him [God]
    and he [God] in him.

And in this we know that he [God] abides in us,
   from the Spirit of which he [God] gave us.

NOTES TO 3:19-24

V. 19 [And] in this The textual evidence is slightly greater for the inclusion of "and" but the UBS committee brackets it to indicate the mixed attestation.

we shall know This is the future. The parallel expression in v. 24b uses the present.

that we are of the truth "Of the truth" here is another instance of a dualistic expression marking allegiance. The same phrase had appeared earlier in 2:21. It can be compared to being "of God" and "of the devil" (cf. 3:8-9).

and before him The pronoun here refers to God (cf. v. 20).

Vv. 19-20 that . . . to what . . . that There are both textual and grammatical problems associated with these verses. The textual problems are undoubtedly due to scribal attempts to improve the awkwardness of the original text. But the best Greek manuscripts attest *hoti* three times: v. 19a, v. 20a and v. 20b.

In the first instance, the word means "that." In the second, it probably means "because." But, if that is so, then the third instance is superfluous. This has led scholars to suggest that even the best texts have been corrupted and that the second *hoti* (followed by *ean*) should be read *ho ti an* and translated "with respect to whatever." This is the view followed by Smalley, Schnackenburg and many others. Brown (*Epistles* 456) objects to this on the grounds that such a combination does not appear anywhere else in the New Testament, that soon after the author uses *ho ean* (not *ho ti ean*), and that the verbal parallelism between 20a and 21b suggests that *ean* means "if" in both. Yet in Brown's own translation the double "that" is not evident and just how Brown understands the verse as he proposes the grammar is not clear. As a result, the alternate view seems the only plausible one.

we will convince our heart "Convince" (Gk: *peithō*) appears only here in the Johannine literature although the word occurs frequently in the remainder of the New Testament.

V. 20 the heart This is the only occurrence of "heart" in the Johannine Letters. The heart was considered the center of physical life and also of moral decisions (cf. 1 Sam 24:5; Acts 2:37).

accuses us In the Greek, the word translated "accuses" (*kataginōskō*) is a cognate of "know" (*ginōskō*) and means literally "to know something against," but it generally is used in a legal context and so is best translated "accuse."

The word translated "us" *(hēmōn)* is in the genitive and could grammatically mean "our heart" or it could be the object of *kataginōskō*, which takes the genitive. The use of the verb without an object would be awkward and so I have chosen to understand it as object. The heart that is spoken of is the person's own heart, and so the clause really means "if *our* heart accuses *us*."

V. 21 we have confidence "Confidence" *(parrēsia)* is used here of the attitude necessary to make requests of God. The same linking of confidence and making requests is found in 5:14-15. The two other times the word appears, it describes the attitude the believer may assume at the Day of Judgment (2:28; 4:17).

V. 22 from him The pronoun here refers to God. This is clear from the fact that God had been mentioned at the end of v. 21 as well as from the consistent use through the remainder of vv. 22-24.

his commandments Throughout the Letters, the commandments are God's rather than Jesus', as they will be in the third edition of the Gospel. See further at 2:3.

V. 23 his commandment Again, this refers to *God's* commandment.

that we believe The form here is aorist subjunctive, indicating, as Brooke (*Epistles* 104) points out, that "it lays stress, not on the initial act of faith . . . , but on the whole process conceived as an unity." This is the first appearance of the verb "believe" *(pisteuō)* in 1 John. In spite of its prominence in the Gospel, the term appears only here and eight other times: 4:1, 16; 5:1, 5, 10 [three times], 13 (it does not appear in 2 or 3 John). This is probably to be explained by the fact that, in the Gospel, the issue was one of belief versus unbelief whereas, in the Letters, the matter was conceived of as a correct articulation of belief.

In 1 John, the Greek verb *pisteuō* occurs with four constructions: three are followed by the dative (3:23; 4:1; 5:10b); two are followed by a *hoti*-clause (5:1, 5); one is followed by the accusative (4:16); three are followed by *eis* with the accusative (5:10a, 10c, 13). Many have attempted to see a distinction in these various uses. Of the four, the meaning of the use with the accusative and with *hoti*-clauses is clear.

The verb *pisteuō* with *eis* and the accusative seems to be interchangeable with the same verb and the dative case. This is certainly true of the use in the Gospel, where *pisteuō* occurs with *eis* in 3:36 but with the dative in 5:24 with no difference in meaning. In John 2:23, it appears with *eis* in a context where the belief is insufficient. So also in John 4:39. As Schnackenburg (*Epis-*

tles 189) says: "Here [1 John 3:23] it can only mean the same thing as 'in the name' *(eis to onoma)*, that is, faith in Jesus Christ who is Son of God in an ontological sense."

Schnackenburg also comments that many have been offended that faith is made the object of a commandment. Such a reaction manifests a failure to understand the true Johannine intent, which is to say that faith should be of a particular type: "in the name of his Son Jesus Christ."

in the name of Here "name" appears in the dative case after "believe" whereas in 1 John 5:13 it is in the accusative after the preposition *eis* ("into"). As was explained above, there is no evidence of a difference in the two uses.

For the Semitic sense of "name," see at 2:12. There is no difference intended between "believing in the Son of God" (1 John 5:10) and "believing in the name of the Son of God" (1 John 5:13). Yet the specific character of the faith that is commanded is that it is in Jesus as Son and as Christ, the two claims disputed by the opponents.

V. 24 Throughout this verse, "he" refers to God, except for the last word in v. 24a. This is evident from the context in v. 21 onward where the pronouns have consistently referred to God. Moreover, in 4:1, the Spirit will be explicitly said to be "from God."

abides in him and he in him This is the first instance in the Letter of the author speaking of a mutual abiding of the believer and God. In the Note on 2:6, I discussed the variety of uses of the verb "to abide" *(menō)*, reserving for this verse the discussion of those instances where a *mutual* abiding is spoken of.

Such mutual abiding is introduced here in v. 24a. In v. 24b, it is said that the Spirit attests to the fact that God abides in the believer. The topic will not be introduced again until 4:12-16, where it will appear three times in close succession, each time being related to an important element of the believer's faith.

In the various texts where the concept appears, the order of the statements varies and the order does not seem to be significant. In 3:24a, 4:13bc, 16de, the abiding of the believer is mentioned first. In 4:15bc the abiding of God is mentioned first. (In 3:24b and 4:12, the abiding of God is mentioned alone but the context accounts for this seeming anomaly.)

Because the believer had been said to abide in God before (2:6, 24), the new element is the mention that God abides in the believer. Brown (*Epistles* 260) comments succinctly: "['Abide'] . . . communicates two important points: first, that the Christian's relationship to God is not just a series of encounters but a stable way of life; second, that the stability does not imply inertia but a vitality visible in the way one walks."

There is a background for the development of such a concept in Old Testament and late Second Temple Judaism. For example, Yahweh was said to dwell in his Temple and among his people (2 Chr 6:18). This would continue in the end-times (Ezek 48:35; Zech 2:14-15 [10-11]; cf. *Jub.* 1:17, 26). In a non-cultic sense, Wisdom is said to dwell among people (Sir 24:1-8), but the closest example is the description of Wisdom "passing into holy souls" (Wis 7:27). Nevertheless, the Johannine notion portrays this abiding in a more intimate and mutual way than any Jewish text.

from the Spirit "From" (Gk: *ek*) indicates how we know that he abides in us. It is not a partitive genitive as it is in 4:13. Apart from this difference, 4:13 is almost identical with this verse.

This is the first mention of Spirit in the Letter. It will appear a total of twelve times in 1 John (3:24; 4:1 [twice], 2 [twice], 3, 6 [twice], 13; 5:6 [twice], 8) but not in 2 or 3 John. It can be used in a general sense to refer to either good or evil spirits (4:1, 2). In the good sense, it is identified as "the Spirit" (3:24; 5:6, 8); the Spirit of God (4:2); his Spirit (4:13); the Spirit of Truth (4:6); and the Spirit *is* the truth (5:6). But it can also be used of the Spirit of Deception (4:3, 6). Unlike the Gospel, the Letter never refers to the Spirit as "Paraclete" nor as the "Holy" Spirit.

of which he gave us. The words "of which" in this clause translate the single word *hou* in Greek and this word is in the genitive case. It is often thought that the genitive here is a result of assimilation (also referred to as "attraction") to the genitive of "Spirit" and that properly it would be in the accusative. However, this is unlikely in the present case. As we shall see in 4:13d, there is another instance of God giving the Spirit and the grammar there is clear that God is giving "of" the Spirit to the believer. In that instance, it is unambiguous that the genitive is a partitive genitive, stating that God bestows a portion of the Spirit upon the individual. It is only upon Jesus that it can be said that God bestows the Spirit "without measure." In the light of this important theological distinction elsewhere, it seems certain that the genitive here should also be construed as partitive rather than as a genitive of attraction.

OVERVIEW OF 3:19-24

The author now returns to the theme of confidence before God and attempts to assure the reader that God is greater than our hearts, and that what we ask for, we will receive because we keep his commandments by believing in the name of his Son Jesus Christ and by loving one another.

He then awkwardly appends the reminder that the one keeping the commandments remains in God and "we know God remains from the presence of the Spirit that he gave us."

THE STRUCTURE OF 3:19-24

This section is chained to the previous one by the phrase "of the truth" (v. 19) that resumes "in truth" from v. 18c. At the end of the section, in v. 24c, the theme of the Spirit is introduced awkwardly as a manifestation of "remaining" and that reference chains this section to the one that follows, in which the Spirit will be discussed at length.

The section is structured internally by a variety of rhetorical devices. First, the section as a whole is bound together by an inclusion in v. 19a and v. 24b: v. 19a ("[And] in this we shall know that . . ."); v. 24b ("And in this we know that . . .").

Verses 19-20 are interwoven with catchwords, some verbal, some thematic. In v. 19, "heart" is introduced and becomes the topic in vv. 20-21. The guiltless heart in v. 21 becomes the grounds for boldness, which is then understood as a ground for making requests of God in v. 22a. Then in v. 22bc, keeping the commandments is introduced and this forms the first element of a chiasm that structures vv. 22bc-24.

Of these features only the chiasm needs further comment. The existence of a chiasm in vv. 22-24 is important because it confirms from a structural and stylistic point of view the understanding of the commandments, which had been previously confirmed on the grounds of content.[1] The chiasm begins and ends with a general reference to keeping the commandments. In the second and second-to-last elements, attention is focused on a single commandment. In the third and third-to-last elements, the content of the commandment is defined. The entire chiasm can then be said to hinge on the single word "and" at the very center.[2]

Two elements of this chiasm are particularly striking. First, in each half of the chiasm we find the pattern of (a) general exhortation to keep the commandments, (b) introduction of a reference to commandment in the singular,

---

1. As far as I am able to tell, this has not been noticed before. It is not referred to in the major commentaries although Smalley (*Epistles* 209) does speak of an inclusion between v. 23a and v. 23e.

2. It could also be said that the chiasm has a double focus on the content of each of the two commandments and that the word "and" is not significant for the arrangement. In either case, the parallelism and the focus on the content of two distinct commandments are obvious. The arrangement is illustrated in the translation above.

(c) definition of the content of the commandment.[3] This is the same pattern that appears in all instances where commandments are discussed. Here, because it is a chiasm, the pattern appears twice but, in the second, the order is reversed. Second, the chiastic arrangement confirms the existence of two commandments and, by the position they occupy, the content of each is identified and emphasized at the heart of the arrangement.

THE INTERPRETATION OF 3:19-24

The logical progression of this section is very difficult to map. Brown finds these, as do many other commentators, some of the most obscure verses in the Letter. He comments: "We have already seen that the epistolary author is singularly inept in constructing clear sentences, but in these verses he is at his worst. . . . At the least, it offers the Prologue competition for the prize in grammatical obscurity."[4] Brown then goes on to list what he refers to as "the nine most disputed points of interpretation." Here we are not able to address these all at length but have attempted to give some sense of the alternatives available and to suggest a reasonable interpretation.

The author begins (v. 19a) by explaining that it is "in this" that one can know whether one is "of the truth." But just what "in this" refers to is not immediately clear. One would expect it to refer to something yet to be mentioned, but there is nothing in the next verses that indicates this is so. Consequently, it is most likely that the author is using the phrase to refer back to the fact that the believer loves "in work."[5] If this is so, then we know we are of the truth when we demonstrate our love in actions rather than just in words. That is certainly in conformity with the emphasis elsewhere in the Letter on the necessity of backing up claims with one's actions.

In v. 19b, the author uses the conviction that the one who loves in work is "of the truth" as a foundation for confidence when the believer stands before God. Although it is not said specifically, the author seems to have the image of apocalyptic judgment in mind again (cf. 2:28; 3:2c). Previously, the author had spoken of having confidence and not shrinking from Jesus at his coming and had expressed the hope that the believer "will be like him" (3:2e). The author now begins to speak of the proper attitude of the believer "before God" and three times speaks of the believer's "heart" in relation to God.

3. On the existence of this pattern, see Appendix 5 (The Johannine Commandments) in this volume and also von Wahlde, *Commandments* 22-31, 52-54, 60, 62-63.

4. Brown, *Epistles* 453.

5. So most other commentators, for example, Schnackenburg, *Epistles* 184; Strecker, *Epistles* 121; Klauck, *Erste Johannesbrief* 215; Smalley, *Epistles* 200.

If we analyze the statement logically, the first element is found in v. 20a where the author speaks of the believer's heart accusing him/her. This means that the believer's heart accuses the believer of sin, that is to say, the believer recognizes, due to what we might call "conscience," that he/she is a sinful person.[6] But if this is so, the believer should persuade his/her heart that God is greater than his/her heart and that God knows all things. If the believer recognizes this, the end result will be (v. 21b) that the believer's heart will no longer accuse him/her and the believer will have confidence before God (v. 21c).[7]

But what precisely does it mean to say that God is greater than one's heart and that God knows all things? The expression "God is greater than our heart" appears only here in the literature and so a study of parallels is not possible. That God/Jesus "knows all things" appears nowhere else in the Letters. In the Gospel (where it appears twice) once (2:24) such knowledge is reason for severity and the other time (21:17) it is the basis for leniency. It is not surprising then that the history of interpretation reflects both types of opinion regarding the phrases. In the one, the fact that God is "greater than one's heart" is understood to mean that the judgment of God will be more severe than our own heart's evaluation of our conduct since God is greater than our heart. In this interpretation, the fact that God "knows all things" confirms this by being understood to mean that nothing escapes the knowledge of God and so his judgment will be thorough.

In the second interpretation, the statement that "God is greater than our heart" is taken to mean that God is greater and more merciful and forgiving than our heart is and that, because he knows all things, he is able to judge intentions fully and be merciful.[8] This is most likely to be the correct understanding of the verse when viewed in the context of the Letter.[9] That is, the section had begun positively with the reminder that believers knew they were of the truth by the fact that they put love into action *and so* they were able to convince their hearts before God. Now such confidence is bolstered by the fact that God is greater than our heart and knows all things and as a result is merciful.

6. This would not be an inappropriate response in light of the author's comments in 2:8-10.

7. It is possible that the presence of the believer "before God" is meant to refer to the scene of final judgment. Two other instances of "confidence" refer to the Second Coming of Jesus (1 John 2:28) and the final judgment (1 John 4:17). However, the fact that the scene goes on to talk about prayers of petition suggests that this is a more general reference.

8. See, for example, Hos 11:8; Heb 10:16-19; Jas 2:1-6, 13; and 1QH 4:34-36.

9. Both R. E. Brown and Schnackenburg conclude that a decision on the basis of grammar is not possible and that the decision needs to be made on the basis of similar attitudes elsewhere in the Letter. They find no passages that speak of severity toward the believer but point to two earlier passages where the author speaks of encouragement. Brown points out that 2:1-2 speaks of a Paraclete for those who sin and 2:28 speaks of abiding in Christ to have confidence at the Second Coming.

Next (v. 22) we hear that, if our heart does not accuse us, we will have confidence; and, with this confidence, the believer will receive what he/she asks for from God. This is the first of two passages in the Letter that deal with the theme of asking and receiving (see also 5:14-16). In both cases the ability to make such requests is based on "confidence." The asking here is unqualified, but in 5:14 the author says that if we ask "for anything according to his will," God hears us. Also in the next verse the author speaks of "whatever we ask for" but goes on to say that we should not ask regarding "sin-unto-death." So the best that can be said is that, within the Letter, such asking is qualified.

Here two reasons are given for the believer's ability to receive what is asked for. First, it is because the believer has confidence before God but, second, because the believer keeps God's commandments.[10] Thus, as Smalley says, there is nothing ". . . mechanical or magical about prayer. For it to be effective, the will of the intercessor needs to be in line with the will of God; and such a conformity of wills is brought about only as the believer lives in Christ."[11]

Although v. 22b continues the sentence begun in v. 22a, the second part is treated separately here since, on the basis of content, it begins the chiasm that extends through to v. 24a. Verse 22b explains that "we" keep the commandments and do what is pleasing before "him" (God).[12]

After this reference to the commandments in general, the author then proceeds to specify the commandment (singular) as is the common pattern in such exhortation. The content of the commandment is then given: to believe in the name of God's Son, Jesus Christ.[13] We had seen this "first" commandment earlier, where (2:5) correct belief had been referred to as "keeping the word of

---

10. This does not imply a legalistic piety but does seem to imply that there are certain necessary conditions for being able to make petitions of God. Within the third edition of the Gospel, the author regularly uses the conditional categories of Deuteronomic theology. This is true even of Jesus (cf. John 15:10) where Jesus says: ". . . I have kept the commandments of my Father and I remain in his love." So Jesus says of the disciples: "You are my friends if you do the things that I command you" (15:14). See also 10:17-18; 14:21. For a further discussion see von Wahlde, *Commandments* 226-33.

11. Smalley, *Epistles* 205. In the Gospel, the theme of making requests of God appears four times (14:13-14; 15:16; 16:23c-24, 26). As is indicated in the Commentary on those verses, in every case there is evidence that those verses belong to the third edition. As is the case here in the Letter, the requests are said to be made to God the Father, but here there is no mention of making the requests in Jesus' name, whereas in the Gospel such is explicit in every instance.

12. In the Gospel, Jesus does both (cf. 8:29; 14:31; 15:10).

13. Rather than see this as part of a chiasm, Brown (*Epistles* 480) treats this as an inclusion with "This is the proclamation . . ." of 3:11. The appearance of the pattern common to all commandment citations (that is, a statement about the commandments in the plural, a shift to the singular of commandment, and the definition of a specific commandment) in both halves of the chiasm speaks strongly for its function in relation to the remainder of the chiasm rather than in relation to 3:11.

God" and later (2:7) simply as "the word that you heard." What is particularly noteworthy here is the phrasing of the commandment: belief is to be "in the name of Jesus." Thus, belief, which is ultimately in God,[14] is to be such as to acknowledge Jesus who is specifically identified as "God's Son" and "Christ."

The importance of acknowledging the role of Jesus in salvation and that he is "God's Son" and "the Christ" is evident from the numerous statements of 1 John in which it is precisely these titles that are at stake: 2:22 ("Who is the Liar if not the one denying that Jesus is the Christ?"); 2:23 ("Everyone denying the Son does not have the Father"); 4:2-3 ("Every spirit that confesses Jesus come in the flesh is of God, and every spirit that does away with Jesus is not of God"); 4:15 ("Whoever confesses that Jesus is the Son of God"); 5:1 ("Everyone believing that Jesus is the Christ"); 5:5 ("The one believing that Jesus is the Son of God"); 5:10 ("The one believing in the Son of God"); 5:12 ("The one who has the Son has life; the one not having the Son of God does not have life").

In light of this massive emphasis on the proper confession of Jesus as Son and as the Christ, the commandment to believe "the name of God's Son, Jesus Christ" becomes the focus for correct belief and the very antithesis of the position of the opponents![15]

The chiasm hinges on the "and" (v. 23c), which binds the two commandments together, except that now the elements of the second half are in reverse order. The *content* of the second commandment is given first: it is also necessary "to love one another." Then the reader is reminded to do this, "just as he gave a commandment to us."[16] Although love of the brothers and of one another has been spoken of several times already, this is the first time that it is defined as a commandment. The members of the community are to show loving

---

14. See at 5:10b. One cannot have God without having Jesus (cf. 1:3; 2:23), but it is clear that belief is ultimately in the Father.

15. It is also the set of titles that is used to describe belief in the first ending to the Gospel (20:31). Brooke calls it "a compressed creed." However, that does not mean, of itself, that the usage in 20:31 is the work of the third author. We have noted repeatedly that the titles "Son" and "Christ" were the primary confessional titles of early Christianity and were understood within the context of both high and low Christology. Consequently, it is sometimes difficult to know when they should be understood to have a very specific content as they do here in 1 John and when they are being used in a more general sense.

16. Klauck (*Erste Johannesbrief* 224) prefers to speak of this as a "double commandment." It is true that, in the theoretical order, correct action follows from correct belief. But in the perspective of the author, the reverse is also possible. See, for example, 2 John 4-6 where the issue is correct belief and the author says that we demonstrate love of the brothers by believing correctly. Furthermore, even in cases such as this, the distinction between two commandments is clear. In the end, reducing the commandments to a "double commandment" collapses the distinctiveness of each commandment and does not do justice to the literary facts. That is, this view does not account for the fact that there is a pattern in the presentation of the commandments and that, at different times, each commandment is spoken of individually.

regard for one another in addition to their correct belief. By labeling these two obligations "commandments," the author has identified them as the two central obligations of the believer: proper belief, which is belief in Jesus as the Christ and the Son, and proper action, defined as love for one another based on the model of Jesus' love for the believer.[17]

The author then concludes his chiastic arrangement by another general reference to keeping the commandments, asserting that keeping the commandments will bring about the abiding of the person in God and God in the person. Thus, the author's summary of the commandments ends with the affirmation that keeping the commandments will bring about the abiding that both the author and his opponents have claimed as a prerogative.[18]

Although the words "in this" in v. 19a had referred back to what preceded them, here (v. 24b) they refer to what immediately follows: We will know that God abides in us by our experience of the Spirit that God gave us.[19] This is the first mention of the Spirit in 1 John. From a literary point of view it forms a catchword connection between what is concluding here and what will follow in 4:1-6. However, the author would not link these two ideas *only* for stylistic reasons; there had to be a theological reason also.

As a result, the particular question to be answered here is just how the presence of the Spirit was seen to be evidence of this abiding. It is not impossible that the Johannine community had a palpable experience of the Spirit that served as "evidence." However, it is more likely that the abiding was attested by the presence of a Spirit that led to the correct confession of Jesus, as will be the focus of the following section. The correct confession would indicate the presence of the correct Spirit that then could in turn be said to indicate that God was abiding in the believer (and the believer in God).[20] This will be the topic of the following section.

Addendum: The Johannine Understanding of Mutual Love

The identification of mutual love as the second commandment within the Johannine tradition takes place in 3:23de for the first time in 1 John, and so it will be useful to give some more detail about the meaning and context of this commandment. What will emerge from this discussion is that, although the content of the second

---

17. Because of its importance, we will return below to a more detailed discussion of the meaning of this love as it is understood by the Johannine writer.

18. For example, 2:6, 24. It will be noticed that elsewhere in the Letter the claim to "abide" is linked both to proper belief (2:6, 24, 27; 4:15) and to the practice of mutual love (3:17; 4:12, 16)

19. There is an almost exact verbal parallel to v. 24 in 4:13.

20. So also Brown, *Epistles* 483.

commandment differs from that of the first, in many other ways the two commandments parallel one another very closely.

As is the case with the first commandment within 1 John, the formulation of the second commandment is somewhat fluid. Here and in 2 John 5 it is defined as: "That we love one another." In 4:21, it is defined as: "That the one loving God should also love his brother."

Also similar to the first commandment is the fact that the content of the second commandment is referred to often in the Letter without specific reference to it as a "commandment." In these cases there is even more variety, for example, 2:10 ("The one who loves his brother . . ."); 3:10 ("the one not loving his brother"), 11 (". . . this is the proclamation . . . that we love one another"), 14 ("we love the brothers"), 3:16c ("we ought to lay down our lives for our brothers"); 4:7 (". . . let us love one another . . ."), 8 ("The one not loving . . ."), 11 (". . . we too should love one another").

As was the case with the first commandment, the commandment to practice mutual love is paralleled in the third edition of the Gospel by a commandment given to Jesus. Thus, the Father's commandment to Jesus to lay down his life out of love (10:15b-18) is paralleled by Jesus' commandment to the disciples to love one another as he has loved them (13:34-35; 15:10-17). In 1 John, mutual love also becomes the object of a commandment except that here the author attributes the commandment to God rather than to Jesus because the author seeks to show that the claims of the opponents regarding their relationship with God are untenable because they have distorted and minimized the role of Jesus.

The Content of Mutual Love

According to 1 John, loving one another is the object of both a proclamation (3:11) and of a commandment (3:23; 4:21).

In the first discussion of mutual love, such love is linked to the claim to be in the light. Thus, "being in the light," which the author uses as a symbolic presentation of having proper belief, is said not to be possible without mutual love. Thus, from the beginning, the author seeks to show that the two commandments are closely related: in essence one cannot have the one without the other. To claim to be in the light but to hate one's brother means that one is in fact still in darkness. The one who hates his brother is in darkness and has been blinded by the darkness. Thus, love is not something that covers up reality but is precisely that which takes away darkness, brings light, and allows the person to see things as they are (2:11).

In his second treatment of mutual love (3:10-18), not loving one's brother is shown to be equivalent to not acting justly and is evidence that one is not "of God" (3:10). Since to be "of God" means to be "begotten from God," loving identifies one as being begotten of God. Mutual love is also the evidence that one has crossed over from death to life, whereas the one who hates his brother is a murderer and does not have eternal life remaining in himself (3:14-15).

This mutual love is to express itself in deeds and not just in words (3:18). If a person has sufficient means of livelihood and sees a brother in need and closes his heart to him, the love of God will not remain in that person (3:17). Love is to go so far as to be willing to lay down one's life for the brothers just as Jesus laid down his life for them (3:16). Thus, mutual love has a new and perfect model: the love that Jesus showed for them. Because of this there can be times when mutual love may call the believer to heroic love, even to laying down one's life for the brothers.

A Love That Is Restricted to the Community

In spite of the remarkable dimensions of mutual love as the Johannine community saw it, the community understood this love as to be extended only to other members of the community. In this sense, it does not envisage a context in which love is to be extended even to one's enemies as in Matt 5:43-48.

However, this type of "restricted" love is paralleled in the *T12P* and in the SDQ and, as we have seen,[21] was formulated to reflect the circumstances of a community in which to love and help one's enemies was tantamount to taking part in their evil deeds. Within the Johannine context, such love would never be commanded by God. Consequently, any interpretation of the Johannine commandment of mutual love must take these circumstances into account in order to do it full justice.[22]

21. See the discussion in Appendix 5 (The Johannine Commandments) in this volume.
22. For additional discussion of mutual love, see Vol. 1, Part 4, Section 8.3 and 8.4.

4:1-6

The Spirit of Truth and the Spirit of Deception

1 Beloved,
  do not believe every spirit,
  but test the spirits
    to see if they are from God,

  +because many false prophets have gone out into the world.
    +2 In this you know the Spirit of God:
      +every spirit that confesses Jesus Christ come in the flesh is of God,
      +3 and every spirit that does away with Jesus is not of God.
    +And this is the (spirit) of the Antichrist, which you have heard is coming,
    +and is now already in the world.

4 You are of God, Dear Children,
and you have conquered them,
  because he who is in you is greater than he who is in the world.

5 They are of the world,
  because of this they speak out of the world
  and the world listens to them.

6 We are of God.
  The one knowing God hears us;
  the one who is not of God does not hear us.

From this we know the Spirit of Truth and the Spirit of Deception.

NOTES TO 4:1-6

V. 1 believe every spirit The word "believe" is followed by the dative here and indicates that one should not accept the prompting of every spirit. Thus, the author recognizes the possibility of evil spirits as well as the Spirit of Truth. The reader will recall that in the second edition of the Gospel, there was no suggestion that the author conceived of the possibility of more than one spirit. Such a plurality is a clear indication of apocalyptic dualism. See also at 5:10b. Distinguishing between good and evil spirits was a problem in Pauline communities also (see, for example, 2 Thess 2:2).

test (Gk: *dokimazō*) Appears only here in the Johannine literature but is used by Paul in a variety of contexts. It means "put to the test" or "examine."

if they are from God The Greek can mean either "it is from . . ." or "they are from . . ." since the neuter plural is expressed with a singular verb. However, the context suggests that the plural is intended simply as a consequence of the plurality of spirits mentioned previously. But it does not thereby imply a belief on the part of the author in the existence of multiple "holy spirits."

The issue here is not the discernment of charisms spoken of by Paul in 1 Cor 12:11. Second Corinthians 11:4, which speaks of being preached to about a "different Jesus" and of receiving a "different spirit," is closer. Among the Pastoral Epistles, 1 Tim 4:1 describes a similar situation when it says: ". . . in the last times some will leave the faith, paying attention to deceitful spirits and the teachings of demons."

false prophets (Gk: *pseudoprophētai*) This is the only appearance of this term in the Johannine literature although it appears in the Synoptics (Mark 13:22; Matt 7:15; 24:11, 24; Luke 6:26), in Acts 13:6; in 2 Pet 2:1; in Rev 16:13; 19:20; 20:10 and in the SDQ (1QH 4:7, 12-13). The author asserts that the presence of both the false prophets and the Antichrist is an indication that the end of the age is "already" (cf. v. 3) present.

Hengel (*Question* 55) sees this as a reference to false prophets elsewhere in early Christianity and not necessarily only ones from the Johannine community. For further discussion of the Old Testament and New Testament background of the notion of false prophets, see Klauck, *Erste Johannesbrief* 231-32.

V. 2 you know The verb form here *(ginōskete)* may be either imperative or indicative. In the context it is more likely to be indicative.

Jesus Christ come in the flesh There are two major schools of thought regarding the meaning of this confessional statement. In the first, the intention is anti-docetic (Marshall, *Epistles* 205; Strecker, *Epistles* 134). According to this view, the author affirms that Jesus Christ was essentially "fleshly" ("incarnate") in his earthly existence and his flesh was not merely an accidental feature of his existence. Others (e.g., Brown, *Epistles* 505; de Boer, "Death" 336-37; Klauck, *Erste Johannesbrief* 234; Schnackenburg, *Epistles* 201) argue that "coming" refers not to Jesus' earthly existence as such but to the significance of his actions while in the flesh. That is, it affirms that what he did while in the flesh is significant salvifically.

There are two important elements to understanding this expression.

First, it is important to recognize that, in a number of texts in 1 John, and particularly here, the verb *erchomai* ("come") is used in a quasi-technical sense. Here and in 2 John 7, we read of Jesus "coming in the flesh." In 1 John 5:6, we read of him "coming in water" and "coming in water and blood." In these instances, the verb does not have its normal meaning of "moving toward a point near the speaker." Rather, it identifies the means by which the effect of Jesus' ministry is achieved. That is, in the case of "coming in the flesh," the statement means that the flesh of Jesus is an integral part of the process by which the effect of Jesus' ministry is achieved. The same would be true of the expressions "coming in water" and "coming in blood."

Secondly, it is important to recognize the importance of "the flesh" for the author of 1 John. The author of the second edition of the Gospel had stressed the importance of the Spirit, over against "the flesh." Within the second edition, such a statement sought to assert the importance of the Spirit and "flesh" would have referred to the state of human existence without the gift of the Spirit. The second author's most striking statement in this regard was in John 6:63 ("The Spirit is what gives life; the flesh is useless"). But this statement could easily be understood as also implying that the realm of the material was irrelevant to salvation. In John 4:19-24, Jesus had said that true worship would take place neither in Jerusalem nor on Gerizim but "in Spirit and truth." Again, the statement originally asserted the necessity of having the Spirit; but, by the time of 1 John, the author's opponents interpret statements such as John 4:19-24 and John 6:63 in the more radical sense to mean that nothing on the physical level can be of use salvifically. In response, the author of 1 John asserts the importance of the actions of Jesus done "in the flesh." Here in 4:2, he means specifically that the death of Jesus was itself of soteriological value.

From the phrasing of the expression as a whole here and from the fact that it appears in a very similar form in 2 John 7, it seems that this was a slogan used in the debate between the two groups.

Later (5:6), we will see another parallel set of terms that reflect the same contrast. There the author contrasts "coming in water" with "coming in blood," the first referring (in the same theological jargon) to the fact that Jesus came to give the living water of the Spirit and the second referring to the fact that Jesus came to die an atoning death in blood. Thus, "coming in the flesh" seems intended to contrast with "coming in the Spirit" (a slogan that does not appear in the Letter) just as "coming in water" contrasts with "coming in blood."

At its very least, this present expression is a variant expression for the author's conviction that the death of Jesus was of soteriological significance. The author is convinced that Jesus cleansed people from sin *by his physical death* (explicit in 3:16; implicit in 4:10; 2 John 7). Thus, the expression underlines the physical aspect of his atonement for sin (2:2; 4:10d; cf. 3:5, 8cd; 4:14c).

It may also be, however, that the expression had a wider importance for the author. As was pointed out above, in the second edition, all aspects of the realm of "flesh" were seen as irrelevant. The statement that Jesus has come in the flesh can be understood as affirming that the flesh itself is good. Although this is less clear in 1 John than in the third edition, where ritual as such (in the realm of the flesh) and bodily resurrection are affirmed, certainly such a statement paved the way for a clearer statement about the realm of the material and physical aspects in general. In all of this, the realm of the "flesh" had an importance. It was a balance against an overemphasis on the spiritual.

V. 3 does away with There is a difficult textual problem in this verse. The UBS and Nestle texts prefer the reading *mē homologei* ("does not confess"), which is attested by ℵ A B and a considerable number of minuscules and early versions. The other major variant is *lyei* ("does away with"), which is attested only in a marginal note to one Greek manuscript (MS 1739) but found in a number of early Greek and Latin fathers (Irenaeus, Origen and Clement of Alexandria, Tertullian). It is also found in a number of Old Latin manuscripts and in the Vulgate. In spite of minor attestation, the second reading is preferred by scholars such as Bultmann, Schnackenburg, R. E. Brown, Hengel (*Question* 57), and Painter. The arguments for *lyei* are varied. It is the *lectio difficilior* and the majority reading is easily explainable as a deliberate change in imitation of 2 John 7. The attestation of *lyei* is early and present in both the Latin and Greek tradition. It should also be noted that it is unusual for Greek to use *mē* (not) with the indicative verb (where normally it would be *ou*). Finally, *lyei* makes better sense with the single name "Jesus," which is not a confessional statement in itself.

I am inclined to follow the reasoning of the scholars who opt for *lyei*. However, if the reading *mē homologei* is accepted the difference in meaning is not as great as some would argue. See also the Note immediately below.

Jesus Also of concern is the text of the words constituting the object of the verb in this sentence. At issue is whether the text reads simply "does away with Jesus" or whether some form of the longer statement in v. 2 is repeated here. The reading "Jesus" is the shortest and also the best attested (A, B, several minuscules, versions and Fathers). As the UBS committee suggests, the variety of combinations in the longer readings suggests they are secondary improvements.

If the shorter reading is accepted, then the question arises whether it is intended to be an elliptical form of the statement in v. 2b or is to stand on its own as a total rejection of Jesus.

I suggest that it is not simply elliptical but a statement that articulates a complete rejection of Jesus. It is not a rejection of this or that aspect of Jesus' role (that is, as Christ, as Son, as come in the flesh) but a denial of any permanent role for him. In that case, the statement is quite similar to those statements that speak in an unqualified way of "not having the son" (2:23; 5:12; 2 John 9).

this is the (spirit) of the Antichrist The word "spirit" does not actually appear in the Greek, only the neuter pronominalized adjective. The meaning could also be rendered "this is the one of the Antichrist."

which you have heard In Greek, the word translated "which" is neuter and so refers grammatically to the neuter pronominalized adjective (understood to refer to "the spirit" of the Antichrist) rather than to the word Antichrist itself (which is masculine).

Does this mean that the expectation was not of the Antichrist himself but of the *spirit* of the Antichrist? Law (*Tests* 297) proposes that the use of the neuter indicates that the author thought of the Antichrist as a force rather than a person. Or is this simply another instance of grammatical imprecision on the part of the author? I am inclined to think this latter proposal is the explanation — especially in the light of the further peculiarities that follow in v. 4 and v. 5.

V. 4 of God See at 2:19.

you have conquered them "Them" refers to the opponents. For the believer in 1 John, the actual expression "conquering the world," applied to the community, appears twice in 1 John 5:4-5, where it is said that the "conquest" is our faith and that the one who conquers the world is the one who believes that Jesus is the Son of God (See also at 2:13-14, where it was said that the "young people" had conquered evil).

he who is in you is greater The gender of adjectives continues to be a problem here. In the Greek, *meizōn* is masculine, which gives rise to the question who is referred to as being greater: God? Jesus? or the Spirit?

Smalley (*Epistles* 227) sees "an allusion to God as Father, Son *and* Spirit." Such an attempt at harmonization seems unlikely. The majority of scholars think that God is the intended antecedent. This fits the grammar well since *meizōn* (greater) is in the masculine (thus referring to God). Moreover, there is a parallel in 3:20 where God is referred to as greater than our hearts. But at the same time this is problematic since God is never referred to as being "in" the believer in the Johannine literature even though he is said to "abide" within the believer. Some claim *meizōn* refers to Jesus, but this is not convincing since, within the surrounding context, Jesus is not an active agent.

R. E. Brown and a few others think that it refers to the Spirit both because of the surrounding context where the contrast is between spirits and also because in John 14:16-17 the Spirit of Truth is said to be "in" the disciples. However, Brown does not attempt to explain the presence of the awkward masculine gender rather than the expected neuter, which would agree with the neuter *pneuma*.

In v. 2 and v. 3 the Spirit of God and the spirit of the Antichrist are contrasted. If we judge from the context (and I think Brown is correct here), the author of 1 John seeks to affirm that it is the Spirit of God that is greater than the spirit of the Antichrist. But in so doing, the author accidentally confuses the gender of the adjective and substitutes the masculine *meizōn* (referring to *theos*) for the more accurate *meizon* (neuter referring to *pneuma*). Thus, "grammatically" the author affirms that *God* is greater than *the Antichrist*, whereas from the context we would be expecting him to affirm that the *spirit* of God is greater than the *spirit* of the Antichrist.

Both statements are theologically true: God *is* greater than the Antichrist; the Spirit of God *is* greater than the spirit of the Antichrist. It is only a matter of which the author intended. The overall context, where the single issue is the comparison, suggests that he intended to refer to the *spirit* and so the fact that *meizōn* appears suggests the author made a minor slip. The fact that a very similar statement in 3:20 used the masculine (referring to God) could have been yet another contributing factor.

than he who is in the world The world is here defined as the totality of those influenced by the Spirit of Deception.

V. 5 they are of the world The opponents belong to the group the author has just defined as "the world," and they speak in a way that is typical of the world and so the world finds attractive what they say.

V. 6 Spirit of Truth . . . Spirit of Deception While it is literally true that this is the only time the term Spirit of Deception appears in the New Testament, the verb *planaō* (to deceive) appears three times and *planos* (deceiver) appears twice in the Johannine Letters. Thus, it is a common accusation that the opponents are deceivers. That they are enlivened by the Spirit of Deception is a minor step beyond that.

OVERVIEW OF 4:1-6

Thematically the author now turns to the issue of distinguishing the Spirit of Truth from the Spirit of Deception and so develops the theme of the Spirit introduced at the end of the previous section (in 3:24c). There are false prophets in the world and it is possible to identify them by what they confess. The Spirit of God confesses that Jesus Christ has come in the flesh; the one who dismisses the role of Jesus is not of God but is dominated by the Spirit of the Antichrist. The author reminds his readers that they are of God and have conquered the false prophets because of the Spirit that abides in them. But the opponents are of the world. Those who are of God listen to the author and those who do not are not of God.[1]

THE STRUCTURE OF 4:1-6[2]

The verses as a unit are attached to the previous section by the catchword use of "spirit" in 3:24c. The unit itself is bounded by a neat inclusion between the beginning (v. 1bc), which introduces the notion of a plurality of spirits and the need to differentiate the good from the evil, and the final verse (v. 6d), which states with assurance that what has preceded is the certain way to distinguish between the spirits. Within the first member of this inclusion there is an instance of antithetical parallelism consisting of v. 1b ("do not believe") and v. 1c ("but test").

More significantly, vv. 2-3b constitute a brief chiasm as is illustrated in the Translation.[3] In the first and last elements of the chiasm the presence of evil "in

1. As many have pointed out (for example, Brown, *Epistles* 501-2; Klauck, *Erste Johannesbrief* 227), there are a number of similarities between 4:1-6 and 2:18-27: (1) dominance of the theme of the Spirit; (2) the central role of proper confession; (3) the arrival of the Antichrist; (4) terms such as "truth" and "deception"; (5) the departure of the opponents.

2. Both Klauck (*Erste Johannesbrief* 226) and Schnackenburg (*Epistles* 196) consider 4:1–5:12 to constitute a major division although they differ somewhat with respect to subdivisions within the material. Brown (*Epistles* 556) proposes that 3:23-24 describes the "twofold commandment" and acts as a transition to the two sections it prepares for. Thus, 4:1-6 deals with proper faith and 4:7–5:4a deals with proper love.

3. So also Smalley, *Epistles* 216; Brown, *Epistles* 502. Some include the parallel statements

the world" is spoken of. In the second and second-last elements, opposing Spirits are mentioned: the Spirit of God and the spirit of the Antichrist. In the third and third-to-last elements, the specific contrasting confessions are given. The chiasm then hinges on the word "and."

There is an instance of a triple parallelism in the beginning words of vv. 4, 5, 6: "You are of God," "They are of the world," and "We are of God."[4]

The author also uses minor parallelism and contrast throughout vv. 4-6. Thus, in v. 4 there is a contrast between "he who is in you" and "he who is in the world." Although this can be distinguished in English translation, the contrast is even more striking in the Greek.

In v. 5, there is a complementary parallelism between "they speak out of the world" and "the world listens to them." This description of the opponents is then contrasted in v. 6ab with the author and his followers: "the one knowing God hears us." And then this is reversed in v. 6c: "The one who is not of God does not hear us."

The section then ends with the inclusion as mentioned above. Together these features serve to structure and unite the material of the section and serve as a guide to the author's thought.

THE INTERPRETATION OF 4:1-6

Once again the author sets out to provide a distinction between truth and falsehood. Here his focus is on identifying the spirits that exist within people. There are two spirits, the Spirit of Truth and the Spirit of Deception, and these are the powers leading to truth and falsehood. Those who have the Spirit of Truth are "of God" and the others are "of the world." And there are two ways of distinguishing between these spirits: (1) by the confession one makes regarding Jesus and (2) by whether the person listens to "us."

Thematically these verses have many parallels in 2:18-27. Both sections discuss correct confession of Jesus, both make reference to the Antichrist, both speak of truth and deception, both speak of community members departing and finally 2:18-27 speaks of the "anointing" (by the Spirit) that the believer has received from God and 4:1-6 speaks of the Spirit, which is the effect of that anointing.[5]

---

from v. 3a ("many false prophets have gone out into the world") and v. 3cd ("that you have heard is coming and is now already in the world"). While these are synonymous and form a kind of inclusion, they are not properly part of the chiasm because they both refer to those who have the evil spirit, while the first part of the chiasm proper refers to those who have the Spirit of God.

4. So also Klauck, *Erste Johannesbrief* 238.

5. See also Klauck, *Erste Johannesbrief* 227.

Vv. 1-3

After addressing his readers as "Beloved" (v. 1) the author immediately turns to the topic of the Spirit and the spirits. Although the Spirit had been introduced briefly in the previous verse, this is the first time in the Letter the Spirit and the spirits are brought forward for explicit discussion.[6]

The reader is warned not to believe "every spirit" and — for the first time in the Johannine tradition — the author situates his understanding of the (Holy) Spirit within the context of a plurality of spirits typical of the modified dualism found in apocalyptic. Immediately it becomes clear that the claim to be spirit-filled is not enough, one may well have a spirit, but that spirit may not be "of God." This passage is also important for the way it makes clear that the author is confronting a situation in which both parties claim to possess the Spirit.[7] Thus, both groups believe that the eschatological outpouring of the Spirit has taken place, and in this sense can be called "believers." At the same time, both groups have come to different beliefs about the implications of their possession of the Spirit. This made the argument all the more difficult. This is not a situation like that of the Gospel where the opponents do not believe that the eschatological outpouring is about to take place (or has taken place). At the time of 1 John, both groups claim such an outpouring but understand it differently.

At this point the author's argument becomes elliptical. He immediately interjects that many false prophets have gone out into the world. Although they are identified by apocalyptic language, these are persons who had been members of the community but have now seceded. Although the term "false prophet" appears in six other books of the New Testament, this is the only appearance of the term in the Johannine literature. The author suggests that the presence of both the false prophets and the Antichrist is an indication that the end of the age is "already" (cf. v. 3) present.

Characteristic of a prophet was the claim to possess the Spirit (e.g., 1 Sam 19:20, 23; 2 Chr 15:1; Ezek 2:2; Mic 3:8; Zech 7:12), and so these make that claim also. But the author argues that the spirit these false prophets possess is not that of God. Their prophetic activity would have been what the author describes in 2 John 9 as "going beyond and not remaining in the teaching of the Christ." In v. 3, he will be more specific about exactly how this manifests itself. Taking their clue from v. 4d, some scholars (e.g., Klauck and Culpepper) tend to see this sec-

---

6. However, as we saw in the previous note, in 2:20 the author speaks of the anointing from the Holy One that the believer possesses. This refers to the possession of the Holy Spirit although the term "Spirit" itself is not used.

7. Undoubtedly the opponents would understand this outpouring of the Spirit to be an eschatological event. Without such an understanding, none of their other claims would be intelligible (the claim to "know" God; the claim to "abide" in him; the claim to be "sinless").

tion primarily in terms of distinguishing true from false prophets. In spite of the obvious association of "spirit" and "prophecy," I do not see a special significance in the appearance of the term "false prophets." The term appears only here in the Johannine literature and even here is paralleled with "Antichrist." We have seen that in 1 John words associated with falsehood are common (see at 1:6) since they represent the opposite of truth, which is the quality associated with God. Together these factors indicate that the term "false prophets" in its usual sense is not the issue. Rather, the author employs it here simply as a stereotyped term referring to deceivers associated with the end of the age.

The *central* issue here (and throughout) is what is necessary for anyone who claims to possess the eschatological Spirit.[8] If the opponents claim to have the Spirit, the author now explains (v. 2) how to know the Spirit of God: every spirit that confesses Jesus (to be) the Christ, come in the flesh, is of God. Conversely, every spirit that does away with Jesus is not of God.[9] Thus, the author proposes an objective criterion by which one can test the claim to have the spirit: what confession does the spirit make about Jesus?

Conversely the author (v. 3) identifies the (spirit) that does not confess properly as the spirit of the "Antichrist," which he identifies with the formulaic "that you have heard is coming."[10] As was argued above (see the Note to 2:18), for the Johannine community the title of Antichrist was probably intended as a generic title for a representative of Satan who would appear at the end of the world and would confront Christ in the final eschatological battle.[11]

Vv. 4-6

In the remainder of the verses, the author shifts his focus from the two Spirits to the two groups that are affected by the Spirits. In v. 4, the author, addressing his readers as "Dear Children," reminds them that they are "of God" and that they have conquered their opponents. In 2:13-14, the believers were said to have conquered the Evil One, *the very principle* of evil. Here, the believer's victory is described in terms of the *people* who are conquered.[12] Although some

---

8. Schnackenburg (*Epistles* 199) begins by pointing to the false prophets but then rightly sees the issue as larger than this and identifies the opponents as "seducers" who "falsely claim to be filled with the Spirit."

9. There is a parallel here with 1 Cor 12:3 ("No one speaking in the Spirit says, 'Cursed be Jesus,' and no one is able to say 'Jesus is Lord' except in the Holy Spirit"). But the text in 1 Cor is not concerned to set up a test of Spirits.

10. See the verbal similarity to the description in 2:18c.

11. In the Greek, "already" is at the end of the sentence and that position implies some shock or surprise on the part of the author that this has happened so soon.

12. Thus, in the first text (2:13-14), the principle of evil is described as conquered; here the

scholars propose that the author has a concrete event or experience in mind that could be called a victory,[13] I think that he is speaking of the relationship between the two groups in terms of the apocalyptic battle that was taking place and his conviction that the true believer is victorious over the opponents. For the author that which is in the believer is greater than "that" which is in the opponents. As was explained in the Note, the author is expressing his conviction that the Spirit of God that is in the believer is greater than the spirit of the Antichrist that is in the world. Thus, the author encourages his listeners to believe that they are superior to "the world," whatever their present experience might suggest.[14]

The opponents, the false prophets and Antichrists, are said (v. 5) to be "of the world" and to speak in a way typical of the world — and the world hears them. As Smalley points out,[15] both the idea and the wording here are very close to that of John 3:31 ("The one who is of the earth [*ho ōn ek tēs gēs*] is of the earth [*ek tēs gēs estin*] and speaks in an earthly way [*kai ek tēs gēs lalei*]"). Some think that this verse is an indication of the popularity of the opponents' position. This is possible but certainly the main intention is to identify those who would find the message of the opponents appealing.

But (v. 6) the believers, who are of God (cf. also 4:1d), know God and hear the author. Brown and Klauck see the present scene against the backdrop of Deut 13:2-6; 18:15-22, where the true prophet was to be listened to and the false prophet was to be "purged from the midst of the people."[16] Although there is certainly an echo of the Deuteronomic text, the parallel is hardly exact. In the Deuteronomic text, the false prophet is to be put to death (which is a specific form of "purging" not suggested in the Johannine text). Moreover, in 1 John

---

very persons are mentioned; and in the third (5:4-5), it is "the world" that is said to be conquered. In John 16:33, Jesus says "I have conquered the world" (3E).

13. Brooke (*Epistles* 114) sees the victory as coming from the new birth through Baptism. Klauck (*Erste Johannesbrief* 239) sees the victory in their conquering of the danger to their faith posed by the opponents' Christology and their remaining faithful in the crisis.

14. Schnackenburg (*Epistles* 204) calls attention to a similar exhortation to the members of the community at Qumran and to the assurance that they will be victorious over the sons of darkness (1QS 4:22-23).

15. Smalley, *Epistles* 228.

16. Brown, *Epistles* 488; Klauck, *Erste Johannesbrief* 231-32. The notion of "testing" prophecy is found in the OT (for example, Deut 13:2-6; 18:20; 1 Kings 22:22-23; Jer 23:16, 21, 25). Klauck points to this as the primary background of the current passage. However, such testing does not involve the overall worldview of modified dualism as is present here. Consequently, the use of the term "false prophet" should not be the primary determinant of the background. The issue in vv. 1-6 is most properly testing *spirits*. While there is a relationship between the two, the worldview and discussion should be seen against the background of dualism throughout rather than only at the end, as Klauck seems to hold.

there is no indication that the false prophets have been banished; rather they have gone out of their own accord.

What is particularly important about v. 6b is the reference to those who "know" God. Thus, the author recalls the promise made to the Israelites that in the last days they would "know God," which has been fulfilled. All those who have received the eschatological outpouring of the Spirit truly know God. Consequently, the use of "know" carries with it the conviction that only the faithful truly know God because only they have received the Spirit of God.

The readers "hear us" in the sense that they agree with the words of the author.[17] And so this becomes a second test for determining whether one has the Spirit of Truth. As an argument it has only rhetorical, and not objective, force; for the argument presumes that the author has the truth on his side.

In this section, we have seen that for the author there is a clear method for testing the spirits: (1) one can determine what they confess about Jesus; (2) one can determine whether they listen to and agree with us. This is how one is able to identify and distinguish between the Spirit of Truth and the Spirit of Deception.[18]

17. In the Gospel, Jesus had said (8:47 [3E]): "the one who is of God listens to the words of God."

18. In 1 Cor 12, Paul lists as one of the gifts of the Spirit the ability to discern spirits (v. 10) but this is not the process that is talked about in the Johannine text. For Paul, discernment of spirits has to do with the proper uttering of good prophecies, not the distinguishing between prophecies of good and evil spirits (see also 1 Cor 14). The same is true of 1 Thess 5:19-22.

God's Love and Love of One Another

7 Beloved, let us love one another,
+because love is of God
+and everyone loving has been begotten of God and knows God.
+8 The one not loving did not know God
+because God is love.

9 In this was the love of God revealed in us,
that he has sent his unique Son into the world
so that we may live through him.

10 In this is the love,
not that we have loved God,
but that he loved us and sent his Son
as an atonement for our sins.

11 Beloved,
if God so loved us,
we too should love one another.

12 No one ever has seen God.
If we love one another,
God abides in us
and his love is brought to perfection in us.

NOTES TO 4:7-12

V. 7c everyone loving No object is expressed here. However, in v. 7a the topic was specified as "loving one another."

has been begotten of God In 5:1, it will be said that everyone believing that Jesus is the Christ is "begotten of God." It should be pointed out that what appears to be the universality of this statement was not intended in the way that many moderns read it. The author is speaking within the context of his own community situation and contrasting the believer with his opponents, who, on principle, say that love (ethical conduct) is unnecessary.

and knows God The claim to know God (Jesus, the Spirit) has been repeatedly addressed from various angles in the Letter. In 2:3-4, it is said that the one who knows God keeps his commandments. In 2:12-14, the author says that the Fathers have known God from the beginning. In 3:1, it is said that the world does not know the Father. In 3:6, the one sinning has not known Jesus; in 4:2, a person knows the Spirit of God by whether the person confesses Jesus Christ come in the flesh. In 4:6, the one knowing God hears the author and his followers.

V. 8 God is love This is one of the most often quoted statements from 1 John and stands, in its brevity, as one of the most exalted formulations of Christian belief in the New Testament.

As Brooke (*Epistles* 118) says, "Love is not merely an attribute of God, it is His very Nature and Being. . . ." Smalley (*Epistles* 239) comments that this affirms "not simply that love is *one* of [God's] activities, but that all his activity is loving. . . ." It parallels the statement in 1:5 that God is light.

V. 9 love of God Although this phrase is sometimes ambiguous (cf. 2:5), it is God's love for the person that is intended here. John 3:16, composed later by the author of the third edition, reflects very closely the thought of v. 9.

in us This is an unusual expression. We would perhaps expect "toward" (*eis*, literally "into") rather than *en* ("in"). The phrase refers to the love of God towards us.

he has sent . . . so that we might live The sending here includes the atoning death of Jesus but the present expression does not limit the purpose of the sending to that death. The entire ministry of Jesus was connected with that purpose (see also the parallel statement below in v. 10cd).

his unique Son This is the first instance of the term in the Johannine tradition. It is also the only instance of the term in 1 John.

Monogenēs is often translated "only begotten" or "only," both of which are inaccurate. It is not derived from *gennaō* ("to be begotten"). Rather, it means "unique," "only one of its kind" (from *monos* and *genos*). See Büchsel, *TDNT* 4:737-41. It makes the point that the sonship of Jesus was unique and was intended to disallow the claim to a sonship equal to that of Jesus on the part of the opponents.

into the world "World" here is used in the "neutral" sense.

so that we may live This is the only instance of the verb "to live" in 1 John but this fact is not of special significance. Elsewhere 1 John speaks of the "entity" as a noun. Both are used in the Gospel. The "living" that the author speaks of is "eternal" life.

V. 10 not that we have loved . . . but that he loved The first verb is in the perfect tense indicating the present results of a past action. But the second is in the aorist and focuses on the past event of the love that motivated the decision to send the Son. There are some more significant textual variants discussed in R. E. Brown and others, but they can be said to have been resolved by the UBS/Nestle editions.

sent his Son as an atonement for our sins This is parallel to v. 9bc above but focuses here on God's desire that the death of his Son be an atonement for sin.

V. 11 Beloved This form of address appears here for the sixth and last time in the Letter.

V. 12 No one ever has seen God This notion will appear again in 4:20. In the Gospel it is mentioned both in the second edition (5:37; 6:46) and in the third edition (1:18). The author is making the point that the believer cannot expect to have a proper relationship with the "distant" (unseen) God if he/she is not able to have a proper relationship with the one who is close by and seen.

However, the author of the third edition does not use the fact of the "unseen" God in relation to loving one's brother (as does the author of 1 John) but rather in relation to the importance of Jesus, his unique son, who makes him known and is therefore the only means of access to God.

In the Jewish tradition there was debate about whether anyone, even Moses or Elijah, had ever seen God.

in us Although this is the same expression as in v. 9a, the meaning here is "in" (in the sense of "within") us. That is, the results of this love are evident in the believers.

OVERVIEW OF 4:7-12

Thematically the entire section deals with "love," just as the previous section had dealt with "faith." However, although v. 7 introduces the exhortation to love one another, the constant theme of vv. 7-10 is really a demonstration of God's love for us. Verse 11 summarizes this love and joins it again to the exhortation to mutual love. Then v. 12 introduces two benefits that accrue to the believer from mutual love.

The verses, which constitute one of the clearest and most straightforward sections of the Letter, are a powerful exhortation to the believer to love.

But even these verses do not fail to contribute to the author's contrast between the true believer and the opponents in their description of one who loves (and has been begotten of God and knows God) and one who does not (v. 8).

THE STRUCTURE OF 4:7-12

The chaining to the previous section is less obvious here but Haas et al. (*Handbook* 105) are probably correct to see a chaining between "knowing God" and "knowing the Spirit of Truth" in v. 6 and "knowing God" in v. 7c.

There is considerable discussion about where this section ends and the next begins.[1] The decision one reaches on this issue has considerable impact on one's interpretation of the material that follows. My own view is that the present section ends after v. 12. At the end (v. 12cd) the author makes two claims: (1) God abides in us; (2) his love is brought to perfection in us. The mention of these two themes in v. 12 then prepares the reader for the extended discussion of them in the following section (4:13-18). This decision will be justified at greater length in the discussion of the Structure of the next section.[2]

The section itself is punctuated by two moments of direct address as "Beloved" (4:7 and 4:11). There is a small chiasm in vv. 7b-8.[3] Two sentences begin:

1. See the extended discussion in Brown, *Epistles* 542-47.
2. This is proposed by Haas, et al. (*Handbook* 105) and is now followed also by Smalley, *Epistles* 249.
3. Brown (*Epistles* 548) suggests a chiastic arrangement that Strecker (*Epistles* 144 and n. 14 there) rightly rejects. However, the one proposed here has greater symmetry and encompasses more of the text than that proposed by Brown. It also accounts for the problems noticed by Strecker.

155

"In this . . ." Finally, there are paired conditional sentences supposing that "if God loved us . . ." and "if we love one another. . . ."

THE INTERPRETATION OF 4:7-12

With this verse, the author begins an extended discussion of love. The primary topic is the love that God manifests (vv. 7, 8, 9, 10) and then the need to love one another if God loves us (vv. 11, 12).[4] The final verse introduces the themes of the next section.

Vv. 7-8

These two verses constitute the beginning of the section and in them the author continues (from 4:4-6) his project of contrasting those who believe and behave correctly with those who do not. Here (vv. 7-8) the point of comparison is the fact that the one begotten of God loves his brother, and the one not loving does not "know" God.

He begins with an exhortation to mutual love and gives as the basis for his exhortation the fact that love is of God (v. 7b) and that "God is love" (v. 8b). Both of these statements form the parallel outer members of a brief chiasm.

In this he affirms one of the most remarkable aspects of Christian theology. Although hardly exclusive to the Johannine, or even the Christian, tradition, the centrality of love to the identity of God is articulated in a unique way by the Johannine tradition, and within that tradition, by the First Letter.

Between these two anchor points (the outer parallel members of the chiasm in v. 7b and v. 8b), the author puts two other parallel statements (the one positive [v. 7c] and the other negative [v. 8a]) explaining that "being begotten of God" and "knowing God" depend on whether a person is loving.

When the author (v. 7c) says that the one who loves is begotten of God, he does not mean to say that the act of loving is what causes the birth but only that one can tell one is begotten of God by whether or not one loves. Similarly, he had said in 2:29 that everyone acting justly has been begotten of God and will say (5:1) that everyone believing that Jesus is the Christ is begotten of God.

Although this is expressed as a universal statement, it is certainly not intended in an unqualified way but rather to be understood within the con-

---

4. In this section, there is no mention of Jesus nor is there mention of the need for the believer to love God.

text of the community situation, namely that those who love with Christian love are those who are begotten of God and who know God — in contrast to the opponents who do not love and who are not begotten of God and do not know him.

Vv. 9-10

Just as the two halves of the chiasm had expressed the same ideas, one positively and the other negatively, these two verses (vv. 9-10) express ideas almost identical to each other except that they are in the form of *parallel* statements. The point of both is how the love of God is manifest in the sending of Jesus. Each statement in vv. 9-10 is comprised of three elements except that v. 10 adds a parenthetical remark. Both verses begin (1) with statements that what follows will manifest the love of God. Both then (2) say that this love was manifested in that God sent his Son, except that the second will interject the comment that we did not love *first* but God did. Finally, (3) the purpose of the sending will be expressed. Verse 9 expresses what is *given* as a result of the sending: "so that we may live through him"; v. 10 expresses what is *taken away* so that we might live: he was "an atonement for our sins."

This parallelism of expression is instructive for understanding the author's point of view regarding the relation between attaining eternal life and the forgiveness of sin. It seems that the relation between getting rid of sin and the attainment of life was something over which there was some dispute within the Johannine community. Life comes through the possession of the Spirit, yet what the relative roles of Jesus and the Spirit were in the forgiveness of sin was not clear. There was Old Testament (and other) precedent for seeing the infusion of the Spirit as cleansing one from sin. But at the same time, at least some elements within the Johannine tradition (as well as within most of the other currents within early Christianity) saw the death of Jesus as a sacrificial atonement for sin. It is the position of the author of 1 John that (the death of) Jesus was such an atonement.

Because of the desire to understand the overriding consistency of thought, it is easy to pass over the intrinsic profundity for Christian belief of the statement in v. 10a-c: "In this is the love, not that we have loved God, but that he loved us and sent his Son. . . ." For the Christian there can be fewer more powerful statements! But the following verse spells out the consequences that are equally powerful: ". . . if God so loved us, we too should love one another. . . ."

Vv. 11-12

In the remaining verses, the author exhorts his readers to love one another. In v. 11, the author urges his readers to imitate, by loving one another, the love God has showed us.[5]

He then (v. 12) contrasts the visible and the invisible realities. The author affirms that they have not seen God; but, if they love one another, two things will happen (v. 12c, v. 12d). First, God will remain in them (v. 12c). In 4:20, the author will again make reference to God "whom he has not seen" and say that the believers cannot love the unseen God if the believers cannot love the brother whom they see. But for the present, the comparison between the seen and the unseen is a positive one. If believers love one another, then God abides in them. Brown comments that the author "does not mean that when we begin to love one another, then God comes to dwell in us; rather our love is the evidence of God's abiding."[6] While I agree with the first part of Brown's comment, I do not agree with the second. The author is not speaking about the *evidence* of God's abiding but about the *condition* for it: "If we love . . . God abides."

Second, the author introduces a final benefit or result of the believers' mutual love (v. 12d): if the believers love one another, God's love will be brought to perfection in them. Thus, by the fact that Christians love one another, the love that God has for humanity has reached its perfection (that is, has achieved its full effect). It has reached perfection because that love has been recognized and imitated (as God had hoped it would be).

*   *   *

These verses deal with and reject the views of the opponents in a variety of ways. In vv. 7-8, he had made loving (which the opponents do not do) the ground for the claims to be begotten of God and to know God. Second, he argued that God's love was revealed in the sending of his son (something with which the opponents would agree), but then added that this son is "unique," that the sonship of Jesus is not the same as the filial relation of the believer. In v. 10, the author's conviction that Jesus was an atonement for sin would have also contradicted the views of the opponents. Finally, in vv. 11-12, the author returns to his exhortation to mutual love, something the opponents did not practice. Although it is aimed at his followers, this exhortation is also by its very nature a refutation of the opponents.

---

5. In John 3:16, the love of Jesus in laying down his life "for us" will be given as an example of how the believer is to lay down his life for the brothers.

6. Brown, *Epistles* 555 n. 37.

And he argues that God does not abide unless one loves and, unless one loves, the love of God is not brought to perfection. As is his custom, the author has been arguing that the claims of believers (that God abides in them and that God's love is brought to perfection in them) are true only if they are attested by correct action (that is to say, by mutual love). Much earlier in the Letter (2:5), he had said the same about correct belief: "The one who keeps his word — in this person the love of God is truly brought to perfection. In this we know that we are 'in him.'" Consequently, the author has now brought forward the same prerequisites for both proper belief and proper action.[7]

7. This is one other example of the remarkably consistent way in which the major claims of the community and its opponents are linked to both correct belief and correct action. For a complete listing, see Chart E-6, pp. 367-369.

The Spirit and Abiding

₁₃In this we know
  that we abide in him [God]
  and he [God] in us,
    because he [God] has given of his Spirit to us.
₁₄And we have seen and we witness
  that the Father has sent the Son as Savior of the world.

₁₅Whoever confesses that Jesus is the Son of God,
  God abides in that person
  and that person in God.

₁₆And we have known and have believed
  the love that God has for us.
God is love,
  and the one abiding in love abides in God
  and God abides in that person.

+₁₇In this, love has been brought to perfection among us,
  +that we have confidence on the Day of Judgment (because just as that one
  [Jesus] is, so are we, in this world).
    +₁₈There is no fear
      +in love,
        +but
      +perfect love
    +casts out fear
  +because fear has punishment,
+and the one fearing has not been brought to perfection in love.

+19 Let us
  +love because
    +he [God]
    +first
  +loved
+us.

NOTES TO 4:13-19

V. 13 In this we know This verse is an almost exact repetition of 3:24bc.

we abide in him . . . and he in us The antecedent and referent of "him" in this clause is ambiguous. In my view, it refers to God the Father. First, in the latter part of the verse, the one who gives the Spirit, gives of "his" Spirit and surely it is God's Spirit that is given. Second, the abiding spoken of is a mutual abiding with God the Father. "He" then must also refer to God.

Up to this point in the Letter, there have been repeated assertions that the believer does and should "abide" (e.g., "in God" 2:6; 3:24; 4:13, 15, 16; "in the light" 2:10; "in the Father and in the Son" 2:24; "in Jesus" 2:28) and that other things do and should abide in the believer (e.g., "the word of God" 2:14; "what you heard from the beginning" 2:24; "the anointing" 2:27; "God's seed" 3:9; "the love of God" 3:17). And God abides (e.g., "in the one who keeps the commandments" 3:24; "in those who love one another" 4:12; "the believer" 4:13; "in whoever confesses that Jesus is Son of God" 4:15; "in the one abiding in love" 4:16). The opponents also make the claim to remain in God, yet this must be tested. Those "not loving" abide in death (3:14)!

It is clear that God makes possible a mutual abiding between himself and the believer, yet this abiding is also able to include an abiding in Jesus. But this abiding is always conditioned by the actions and beliefs of the individual.

because This is the second occurrence of *hoti* in the verse. The first was translated "that" and gave the content of the knowledge (of mutual abiding). Here the author gives the foundation of the knowledge.

of his Spirit This is the partitive genitive and indicates that God has bestowed the Spirit on the believer in a partial way. That is, the believer does not receive the Spirit totally as a literal reading of eschatological hopes might indicate. The way in which the believer possesses the Spirit is made explicit here. The way in which Jesus possesses the Spirit is not made explicit until the third edition, where, in John 3:34 and with reference to Jesus' reception of the

Spirit, the author says: "For he [God] does not bestow his Spirit [upon Jesus] in a limited way."

V. 14 we have seen The Greek verb here is *theaomai* rather than *horaō*. Some propose that the present verb signals appreciative contemplation and recognition rather than simple seeing. I am inclined to think this is overly precise.

Savior of the World This title appears only here and in John 4:42 within the entire New Testament. The shortened title "Savior" was applied to God in the Old Testament (LXX) (e.g., Deut 32:15; Ps 24:5; Isa 12:2). It appears in the authentic Pauline writings only at Phil 3:20. It appears somewhat more frequently in Luke-Acts, the Pastorals, and 1 and 2 Peter. It was used frequently in pagan religions, particularly the healing cults. It is also found in inscriptions as a title for Hadrian.

Rather than comparing it with the verbally similar title in pagan religions and in the emperor cult, I understand it in connection with other universal statements in the Johannine tradition. For example, in 2:2, it is stated that Jesus was an atonement for the sins "of the whole world." Given this interest on the part of the author, the similarity to the imperial title appears to be simply accidental.

V. 15 Jesus is the Son of God Although there are many statements within 1 John that involve the designation of Jesus as "son," there are three places (4:15; 5:5, 10) where the statement "Jesus is the Son of God" appears as a fixed confessional statement. This formula, like the formula that "Jesus is the Christ," is denied by the opponents but affirmed by the author of 1 John.

There are several similarities between this formula and that which confesses "Jesus as the Christ." First, both incorporate the most common and, at the same time, perhaps the most foundational titles applied to Jesus in the Gospel(s). They are the two titles that appear in the first conclusion to the Gospel in 20:31 and that comprise the entire object of belief there.

Second, like the statement that "Jesus is the Christ," this second formula cannot be intended in its simple, literal form since, in that form, it would apply to someone who was not a believer rather than to someone who had become a believer but had come to deny this of Jesus.

Third, like the prerogative of being "anointed," the prerogative of being "son" is something that could be applied to both Jesus and the believer. Jesus is repeatedly called "the Son" in 1 John just as the believers are repeatedly called "children of God" (3:1, 2, 10; 4:4; 5:2)[1] and are referred to as "begotten of God"

---

1. In all cases, the reference is explicitly to children *of God*. The author also referred to be-

(2:29; 3:9 [twice]; 4:7; 5:1 [twice], 4, 18 [twice]). It is a major claim of the community that believers have been begotten of God and are now children of God. Thus, the tradition affirms something of the believer that is very close to what the tradition affirms of Jesus himself. Given this fact, it would be very easy for the opponents to draw the conclusion that there was no significant distinction between the sonship of the believer and that of Jesus. The opponents cannot be denying that Jesus was in any sense "son" or in any sense "anointed" since they claimed this even for themselves. The only possible meaning is that, when the opponents deny that Jesus is the Son of God, they are in fact denying that Jesus has a unique role as "son" and so does not merit the title "Son of God" in any unique sense.

But, as was the case with *christos*, the author of 1 John argues that the sonship of Jesus is different from the "childhood" of the believer. The author declares that the sonship of Jesus is unique (*monogenēs*; 1 John 4:9). He makes it clear that the sonship of Jesus is unique in two ways: First, Jesus is preexistent but the believer is not. Jesus is never said to be begotten but "revealed" (1:2 [twice]; 3:5, 8) and he was in the presence of the Father before his earthly existence (1:2). See also the discussion of Christology in 1 John in Volume 1, Part 4, Section 1.3. Second, he has received the Spirit without measure (John 3:34-35) whereas the believer has received only a "portion" of the Spirit (1 John 4:13).

This explains how a group that believed that the outpouring of the Spirit had taken place, and that had believed that this outpouring resulted in both an anointing and in a rebirth could, upon later reflection, derive conclusions from those prerogatives that challenged the conviction of a unique role for Jesus.

V. 16 and the one abiding in love This is the only text that speaks of abiding in love. It seems to be intended not to make a distinction between God's love for the believer and the believer's love for God or even the believer's love for his/her brother. Rather, failure in *any* of these forms of love is an indication of a failure to abide in love. The various dimensions of the Johannine understanding of love are so interrelated that one cannot separate the one from the other. There was no dispute about God's love for the believer, nor was there a dispute about the claims to love God. But the author makes it explicit that we cannot be said to love God if we do not love our neighbor (4:20-21).

V. 17 just as that one is, so are we in this world The antecedent of "that one" is Christ. See Smalley, *Epistles* 258.

In what respect are we "just as that one is . . . in this world"? This is a repe-

---

lievers as "my" children (1 John 2:1, 12, 28; 3:7, 18; 5:21) or "children" (of another community: 2 John 1, 4, 13; 3 John 4).

tition of the idea contained 3:2 where the author said: "Now we are children of God, and it has not yet been revealed what we will be." As was pointed out in the discussion of 3:2, that the believer could be called a "child of God" already indicated a status close to that of Jesus who was God's "Son." In 3:2-3, the author said this of the believer when comparing the present state of the believer with a future state in which another dimension of "what we will be" would be revealed, so here the author uses the already-present similarity as a basis for confidence on the Day of Judgment.

V. 18 perfect love It is unlikely that this refers to the believer's perfect living out of love for God and love for his/her brother although it would not exclude such love. Rather, it refers to the believer's awareness of God's perfect love. If the believer is fully aware of that love, the believer will have no fear.

This view is also supported by the fact that the statements immediately before (16abc) and immediately after (v. 19) speak predominantly of God's love for the believer.

fear has punishment The expression is unusual. Smalley (*Epistles* 260) translates it as: "Fear has to do with punishment."

V. 19 Let us love Just who is loved is not stated in this verse. However, the thrust of the argument that follows in vv. 19-21 focuses on the authenticity of claims by the one who claims to love God.

he first loved The antecedent here is ambiguous and could possibly refer to either God or Jesus. However, as is explained in the discussion of the Structure, this verse seems to provide the typical ending for a section by looking back at what is concluding and also looking forward to what is coming. What is coming is a discussion of love for the fellow believer, and it is based on the love that "he" showed first to the believer. But that is the love that has been spoken of in v. 16 and that is in the background throughout vv. 17-18. Indeed throughout the remainder of the section, Jesus is not mentioned and only love for God (4:20b, f; 21b; 5:1b; 2b, 3a) and God's love for the believer (v. 19cdef) are spoken of.

OVERVIEW OF 4:13-19

The section has two overriding themes: mutual abiding between God and the believer and love of God brought to perfection. These were introduced in v. 12cd as benefits of mutual love. Here they are described at length. In vv. 13-16, the author describes three ways the believer can know of mutual abiding, signaled structurally by the repeated statements regarding mutual abiding.[2] In vv. 17-18, within an extended chiasm, the author explains the second benefit of love: the believer will have confidence that will drive out fear on the Day of Judgment. Then, in the final verse, having shown evidence of how God loves us first, the author reintroduces the theme of loving one another (which he will fully develop in the next section).

THE STRUCTURE OF 4:13-19

This section is chained to the end of v. 12 by the double themes that: (1) God abides in us and (2) his love is brought to perfection in us. Thus, "abiding in God" is developed in 4:13-16 and "love being brought to perfection" is developed in 4:17-18. Chapter 4:19 then functions as a conclusion and an introduction. It concludes the present section by summarizing the theme of the love of God that has dominated the discussion since 4:7, but it reintroduces the theme of love for one another that had also appeared in vv. 7-12 (i.e., vv. 7a, c, 8a, 11c, 12b) and by reintroducing it prepares for the section that follows.

Within the first unit (vv. 13-16), the actuality of the mutual abiding of God and the believer is attested three ways: (1) interiorly, it is attested to by the Spirit; (2) externally, it is attested, first, by correct confession; (3) and, second, by the fact that the believer loves. Each attestation of abiding is also marked by the repetition of the refrain (with only minor variation): "We abide in him and he in us" (v. 13bc, 15bc, 16de). This parallelism helps confirm that the author indeed intended to relate these statements about the Spirit, correct confession and correct love to mutual abiding.[3]

The second unit (vv. 17-18) is identified as such by the presence of a chiasm that organizes (and indicates the limits of) the material of the verses. Thus, in the first (v. 17a) and last (v. 18g) elements, there is a contrast between love being, and not being, brought to perfection.[4] In the second (v. 17bc) and second-last (v. 18h) elements there is a contrast between the confidence on the Day of Judgment of the one who loves perfectly and the fear of punishment in the one who does not love perfectly. In the third element (v. 18a) there is men-

---

2. Smalley (*Epistles* 249, 250) is one of the few to recognize fully the parallelism here.

3. Brown (*Epistles* 545-47) proposes a break after v. 16c. However, it is more likely, in my view, that v. 12cd introduces the two themes around which vv. 13-18 are organized and that these are developed in vv. 13-16 and vv. 17-18 respectively and that vv. 17-18 are a chiasm.

4. As Klauck (*Erste Johannesbrief* 269) points out, it is love that is spoken of in v. 17a, and it is the person in whom love is not brought to perfection that is spoken of in v. 18i. But the striking parallel remains. Klauck sees these two elements as framing the material but he does not see the remainder of the parallels.

tion of (no) fear and in the third-to-last element (v. 18e) there is mention of casting out fear.[5] In the fourth (v. 18b) and fourth-last (v. 18d) elements, there is mention of love. In addition, the notion of "perfection in love" appears here near the center and reflects the same theme in the outermost elements. Finally, the chiasm can be said to hinge on the conjunction "but."[6] Thus, the verses constitute a well-balanced chiasm that is disturbed only by the contents of the parenthesis in v. 17bc.

Although the parenthesis in v. 17bc is, in some sense, a disruption of the balance of the chiasm, it is surely part of the original. We have already seen another instance where a statement was interjected in a similar way into a chiasm (2:25). In that instance, the comment had the rhetorical effect of calling attention to itself by the way it interrupted the balance.[7] Here the interjection introduces the one reference to Jesus within the chiasm. Both here and in 2:25 the interjections allow the author to make important "footnote" observations that are theologically pertinent to the topic being discussed.

Finally, in v. 19, the author returns to the theme of our manifestation of love as related to the love that God manifests. By doing this, the author recapitulates 4:11, where almost the same words appeared. This, in turn, forms an inclusion that brackets off all of vv. 12-18 and demonstrates formally how this material speaks not primarily of love but of the benefits of love. This verse also is arranged in a brief chiasm as is indicated by the arrangement in the Translation.

In addition to the careful internal structure of the two units that make up this section, a chaining of ideas unites the section internally. It is because of the Spirit (v. 13) that the believer witnesses (v. 14), and what the believer witnesses to (v. 14a) [namely, that the Father sends the Son as Savior] is linked to the confessional statement regarding Jesus (v. 15a), which is then shown to be a condition for abiding (v. 15bc). Verse 16 continues the theme of faith but switches to the notion of "believing" (v. 16a) the love that God has for us (v. 16b). And then it is said that the one who abides in love (v. 16b) also abides in God (v. 16b) and God abides in that person (v. 16c).

Continuing to the next unit within the section, the love spoken of in v. 16 is chained to the notion of perfection of that love (v. 17a), and that is viewed in relation to confidence on the Day of Judgment (v. 17b) and is shown to be a source of confidence that casts out fear (v. 18). He then concludes with a final reference to the love that God has for us and that we are to give to one another.

5. The description here reflects the arrangement in the English text. Although the parallelism and arrangement can be approximated in the English translation, a greater similarity exists in the Greek, where the word order is significant.
6. In a more substantive way, the chiasm hinges on the double-central element that speaks of the importance of love.
7. See at 2:25.

The result is a section of the Letter that exhibits a remarkably intricate literary structure but one that is also important theologically.[8]

THE INTERPRETATION OF 4:13-19

Although most scholars see this section as a continuation of the theme of love, that is only partially true. Properly speaking, the section is concerned with a description of *the two benefits* of mutual love as they had been described in v. 12.[9] Thus, once again, the catchword appended to the previous section introduces the topic of the present one.

Vv. 13-16

In v. 12, the author had recalled for the reader the conviction that God abides in the one who practices mutual love. In vv. 13-16, the author will now speak of this mutual abiding at length. In doing so, he will introduce three discrete units, each of which is identifiable by the repetition of the statement about mutual abiding. The first of the benefits of mutual *love* is mutual *abiding* of God and the believer (vv. 13-16). The themes of the Spirit (v. 13), proper confession (v. 15) and love (v. 16) are introduced as a means of knowing and certifying the mutual abiding. This will be the overarching perspective that governs the comments that follow.

In v. 13 the author begins to speak of this abiding at length. This mutual intimate abiding was one of the most exalted privileges of the believer's relation with God. It speaks of a unique privilege given to the believer, and it assures the reader that the believer will be aware of this abiding by means of the Spirit. Although the author makes reference to the Spirit here in a positive sense and in positive context, the nuance he gives his expression is hardly casual. It is clear from the author's words that the believer does not receive the Spirit fully.

8. The material of 4:13-18 deals with much the same content as 3:19-24 but in somewhat reverse order. Thus, 3:19-21 speaks of the confidence the believer should have before God; this is also the theme in 4:17-18. In 3:22-23b, the theme is belief as a commandment; in 4:14-15, the theme is belief. In 3:23de, the theme is mutual love as a commandment; in 4:16, the theme is loving. In 3:24a, the theme is (for the first time in the Letter) the mutual indwelling of the believer and God; in 4:13bc, 15bc, 16de, the theme of mutual indwelling is also developed (the only other place in the Letter where such mutual indwelling is addressed). In 3:24bc, the theme is the gift of the Spirit; in 4:13, the theme is the gift of the Spirit.

9. The theme of love does not reappear until v. 16, where it is not the primary focus but rather introduced as part of the series of comments dealing with mutual indwelling. In vv. 17-18, the focus is not primarily on love but on the confidence that should come from love.

Rather, God has given the believer "of" his Spirit. That is, the believer is given *a share* in the Spirit. Such a view would be a direct contradiction of the view of the opponents who understood the eschatological outpouring to be complete and unqualified. But for the author of 1 John and for the author of the third edition, it was only Jesus who had the Spirit in a complete and unqualified way, something stated explicitly by the third author in John 3:34. In this sense, the author's understanding is similar to that expressed by Paul when he refers to the believer's possession of the Spirit as "the first installment" (*arrabōn tou pneumatos;* 2 Cor 1:22; 5:5).

But how will the Spirit be a way of knowing the reality of this mutual abiding? An examination of vv. 13-14 in connection with the earlier occurrence of this concept (3:24) is very helpful. In 3:24, the author had told the reader that the Spirit was a means of determining the reality of the abiding, but it was there that the author immediately instructed the reader to test the spirits because not all were from God. The test there was proper confession of Jesus. Here we see the same argument being put forward but expressed more elliptically. In v. 13, we hear of the Spirit and mutual abiding and then immediately in v. 14, the author indicates that this enables the believer to "see" and to witness that the Father has sent the Son as Savior of the World.[10] Although the primary topic here is the presence of the Spirit as proof of mutual abiding, the presence of the Spirit is confirmed by correct confession. The focus is not on proper confession in itself although that is important.[11] Rather, the focus is on the presence of the Spirit as the necessary basis for mutual abiding. This is the interior criterion for such abiding. However, although the mutual abiding of God and the believer is signaled by the presence of the Spirit, the presence of the Spirit is signaled by correct confession. This is confirmed and elaborated by the following verse.

In v. 15 the author affirms that the one who confesses Jesus is the Son of God abides in God and God in that person. Here the criterion for determining the reality of mutual abiding switches from the internal criterion of the presence of the Spirit to the external criterion of proper confession of Jesus. We meet proper confession just as we had in v. 14. However, the difference here is that in this verse (which is a unit discrete from vv. 13-14 that precede it and from v. 16 that follows it) the focus is on the proper confession of Jesus. This is an external means of determining the reality of the mutual abiding.

---

10. Schnackenburg (*Epistles* 219), who sees the theme of these verses as focusing on love, says that the two verses are "clearly a digression. Only in v. 16a does the author return to his theme, the theme of love." However, recognizing the continuing theme here as "abiding" and as supported by three kinds of evidence and as related to the double statement in v. 12 solves the problem of the alleged digression completely.

11. In order to explain the primary argument as clearly as possible, I will continue with that and return to a discussion of the content of the confession.

Finally, in v. 16, the author turns to the third of the units and speaks (by way of introduction) about the love God has for the believer and says that the one who "abides in love" can also be known to experience mutual abiding. Thus, the one who loves (and the object is left open and can refer to either God and/or one's brother) will experience mutual abiding. Thus, in three verses the author provides three "tests" for mutual abiding. One is internal (the presence of the Spirit)[12] and two are external (proper confession of Jesus and proper love).[13]

Vv. 17-18

The author now begins to describe how love can be known to have been brought to perfection within the believer. The material of these two verses is arranged as a chiasm, an arrangement that helps not only to recognize the extent of the development of this theme but also to understand the interrelation of the various observations the author makes about it.

The author's conviction is that it is possible to know that love has been brought to perfection within the believer by the fact that the believer has confidence on the Day of Judgment. Here the primary focus is on the effect of love on the believer. Thus, this is the second of the benefits accruing to be believer, as had been said in v. 12d. The love that the author speaks of here is probably meant to be the love in which the believer abides (cf. v. 16d). In other words, the one who truly abides in love and therefore experiences mutual abiding is the one who should have confidence.

In v. 18a-f (all the elements of the chiasm except the two outer ones) the author moves on to contrast fear and love and tells his reader that there is no fear in love; they are incompatible with one another. Perfect love casts out fear. This is also evident from the way the two words are contrasted with each other within the framework of the chiasm. If the person abides in love and experiences love, that experience should cast out the fear that would normally be associated with the Day of Judgment. Fear has to do with punishment and the one who abides in love should have confidence. Then in the final element of the chiasm, the author returns to the negative of the first element and explains that the one who still fears indicates that he/she has not been brought to perfection in love.

12. From a strictly logical point of view, the first one is indirectly external also since the (internal) presence of the Spirit is ultimately confirmed by the (external) witness and confession of Jesus as Savior of the World.

13. The pattern of argument in this threefold test of mutual indwelling is similar in structure to that of 5:6-8 where the witness of the Spirit is internal and the witness of the water and blood is in some sense external.

When we began, I commented that the primary theme was not love but the benefits that accrue from love. That should be particularly apparent in vv. 17-18. The benefit is confidence on the Day of Judgment, a state of affairs that makes fear an inappropriate response. If one fears, then love has not been brought to perfection in that person.

V. 19

The author then ends (v. 19) with a short comment arranged chiastically that encourages the reader to love and to do so because of the love that God first showed the believer. As is often recognized, v. 19 is very close in both wording and ideas to 4:11 ("If God so loved us, we too should love one another"). The only difference between the two is that in the present verse there is a reminder that God *first* loved us. This then forms a kind of inclusion with v. 11 and so marks off the intervening material as a single unit describing the two benefits — and that is precisely what has happened. At the same time, by returning to the theme of the love that the believer manifests, the author prepares the reader for what is to come in the next section and so provides a chain linking the sections.

* * *

Within the context of the community's theological crisis, vv. 13-16 are of particular importance. First, as is clear from v. 13d, the author's view is that God has given the believer *a share* in his Spirit. As we saw above, such a statement would have been unacceptable to the opponents who believed they had been given the Spirit in a complete and unqualified way. The author's view is of considerable significance both for the community's understanding of anthropology and also of Christology. For the author of 1 John and the author of the third edition, the way Jesus possessed the Spirit is different from the way the believer does. Thus, another criterion is presented for distinguishing the status of Jesus from the status of the believer, a distinction that the opponents had failed to make.

Second, the fact that the believer has only a share in the Spirit means that the believer cannot claim to be totally perfect. Rather, the believer has the roots of perfection but is still capable of sin. As a result, "Everyone having this hope in him [Jesus] makes himself holy as that one is holy" (3:3). That is, the believer must work to attempt to "be like him [Jesus]" at the time when Jesus is revealed (3:2). Consequently, the believer has need of ethical exhortation and instruction.

Moreover, from both v. 14b and 15a, it becomes clear that the opponents could not witness that God had sent the Son as "Savior of the World" or that he is "Son of God" and so could not claim either to have the Spirit abiding in them or to abide mutually with God the Father.

In vv. 17-19, the author deals with the possibility of fear in the face of judgment day. Those faithful who recognized the continuing possibility of sin and the reality of a final judgment could become fearful and lack confidence when comparing their own perspective with that of the opponents. The opponents would certainly have no fear because they were convinced that they had been so totally transformed by the Spirit that they would never sin. Such a view would inevitably be an attractive possibility. Moreover, if (as is likely) the opponents continued to hold to a non-apocalyptic worldview, they would have also been convinced that they would not "come into judgment" but had already "crossed over from death to life" (John 5:24 [2E]). When compared with such a view, the possibility of continuing sin and a future judgment could be disturbing. To counter this, the author of 1 John argues that perfect love drives out fear and brings about confidence on the Day of Judgment. Thus, these verses become not only a powerful argument against the opponents but also an encouragement to the faithful.

Loving God and Loving One Another;
Loving God and Correct Belief

+20 If someone says
 +"I love
  +God"
   +and
  +( ) his brother
 +(he hates)
+the person is a liar.

+For the one not loving
 +his brother, whom he has seen,
 +God, whom he has not seen,
+(he) is not able to love.

21 And we have this commandment from him [God],
 that the one loving God
 should also love his brother.

+5:1 Everyone believing that Jesus is the Christ
 +has been begotten of God, and everyone loving the begetter loves the one begotten of him. 2 In this we know that we love the children of God,
  +whenever we love God and obey his commandments.
   +3 For this is the love of God
  +that we keep his commandments. And his commandments are not burdensome,
  +4 because everything begotten of God conquers the world. And this is the conquest that conquered the world — our faith. 5 Who is the one conquering

172

the world if not
+the one believing that Jesus is the Son of God?

NOTES TO 4:20–5:5

V. 20 If someone says . . . This has often been used by the author to introduce claims (1:6, 8, 10; 2:4, 6, 9). It is certainly intended to refer to the opponents. Thus, they claim to love God (as do the author and his followers), but the author argues, by means of *a minore ad majus* argument, that their claim can be tested by whether they love the brothers.

( ) In order to indicate the chiastic order of the verse in Greek, the words in parentheses have been moved from their English word order. Their proper location in English is indicated by the empty parentheses.

hates This is the final occurrence of this verb in 1 John. It has always been used either of hating one's brother or the world hating the author's followers. See at 2:9. This is a Johannine reflection on the two great commandments of the Synoptic tradition in that it reflects the obligation both to love God and also to love one's neighbor. In the Johannine view the first is not possible without the second.

liar See at 1:6.

V. 21 from him "Him" refers to God as the one who, throughout 1 John, gives the commandments.

that the one loving God This is not presented here as a separate commandment but only to indicate that the one who claims to love God should obey the commandment to love his brother.

5:1 that Jesus is the Christ It was already said in 2:22 that the opponents reject this confession just as they reject the confession that Jesus is the Son of God. It was argued earlier that both of these confessional statements were understood in a particular way at the time of 1 John. Rather than denying that Jesus was in any sense Christ or Son of God, the opponents rejected such a statement because it implied a unique status for Jesus. It was essentially this unique status that they denied. See also the Note on 2:22; 4:15.

V. 2 love the children of God This is the only time that the object of love is said to be "the children of God." This term is chosen to reflect the language in the previous verse where the one to be loved was identified as the one who confessed Jesus as the Christ and was *begotten of God.*

whenever we love God This clause is epexegetical of the phrase "In this . . ." at the beginning of the sentence. R. E. Brown finds great difficulty with this sentence and comments: "[L]ove for God becomes the criterion for knowing that we love God's children, whereas a few verses earlier (4:20) the reverse was true: Love of one's brother was the criterion for genuinely loving God." Brown then refers to Bultmann as saying that "the normal interpretation would then produce a circular paradox comprehensible only to the Johannine insider. . . ." While Brown sees this as a problem to be solved, I see it as typical of the author's rhetoric intended to show the unity of these obligations. This is not unlike the structuring of arguments from multiple perspectives in 2:28–3:10.

obey his commandments The Greek here has "do" *(poiōmen),* an expression that appears only here in the New Testament. There is no significant difference in meaning.

V. 3 love of God Although this phrase is ambiguous at times (cf. 2:5), here it is the person's love for God that is intended.

burdensome This is an unusual term, appearing only here in the Johannine literature and elsewhere in the New Testament only at Matt 23:4, 23; Acts 20:29; 25:7; 2 Cor 10:10. Schrenk (*"Barys," TDNT* 1:557-58) suggests that it reflects the theme of liberation from the Law. There was also a rabbinic distinction between "heavy" and "light" in the Law but the Law is not at issue in 1 John. Matt 11:30 ("For my yoke is easy and my load [*phortion*] light") is closer to the point of the Johannine text. Schnackenburg (*Epistles* 229) suggests that the statement is an assurance to those who may feel inadequate or weak in the face of the requirement to love.

V. 4 Everything The shift to the neuter gender here is awkward. Smalley (*Epistles* 270) suggests that it may be a way of universalizing the reference. Marshall (*Epistles* 228, n. 37) thinks it may refer to *teknon* ("child"), which is neuter. I do not find these views convincing but recognize that such a switch is not unusual for the author of the second (e.g., John 6:37, 39) or third (17:2) editions of the Gospel, although it appears only here in 1 John.

conquest The Greek word *nikē* could be translated "victory," but I have translated it "conquest" in order to show that the word is from the same root as the Greek verb *nikaō* ("conquer").

conquered Although "conquer/conquest" is used here more frequently than elsewhere in the Letter, the notion had appeared earlier to describe the young members of the community who were said to have conquered "the Evil One" (2:13, 14). It was also used of the members in general who followed and possessed the Spirit of Truth who were said to have conquered "them" (4:4; the adversaries). Here it is used of all those begotten of God who are also said to have conquered "the world."

our faith. This is the only time the noun faith *(pistis)* appears in the Johannine writings. Elsewhere the verb form is used.

V. 5 Jesus is the Son of God This confessional formula has appeared earlier in 2:23; 4:15.

OVERVIEW OF 4:20–5:5

This section is structured in a way very similar to the one before it. In vv. 20–21, the author argues that one cannot love God without loving one's neighbor and does so in another instance of triple repetition. He follows this with another extended chiasm in 5:1–5 in which the author calls attention to correct belief (Jesus is the Christ and is the Son of God) and links this proper faith with love of both God and one's brother. As a result, the theme of loving both God and one another permeates and intertwines throughout the entire section but, at the same time, *focuses on mutual love in the first half and on correct faith in the second half of the section.*

THE STRUCTURE OF 4:20–5:5

This section is chained to the previous one by a continuation of the theme of love, which had appeared in v. 18 and appears again in v. 19 and throughout the section. The section ends with the confessional statement that Jesus is the Son of God. The following section will then be chained to the present one by a further discussion of "Jesus Christ," which appears in the emphatic position at the end of v. 6a.

The structure within the section is remarkable for its variety and intricacy. Within the section, there are three chiasms. Two are brief (4:20a–e; 4:20f–i). Yet each, by the way elements are compared and contrasted, exhibits what the author wishes to emphasize throughout the section.

The first chiasm is more apparent, and easier to diagram in Greek than in

English. This is due to the fact that in the Greek the personal subjects "I" and "he" are communicated by the verb form whereas in English a pronoun is needed in addition to the verb. Moreover in Greek the order of "his brother" and "he hates" is easily reversed, although this cannot be done in English. We may explain the parallel elements as follows. The person spoken of in the first element is said, in the last, to be a liar if the conditions in the intervening elements are fulfilled. In the second and second-to-last elements "love" is contrasted with "hate." In the third and third-to-last elements, the two personal objects are paralleled and contrasted: "God" and "his brother." Finally, the hinge word of the chiasm is "and."

Thus, in both the first (v. 20a-e) and second (v. 20f-i) chiasms, there is a juxtaposition of love of God and love of one's brother at the center, stressing that one cannot have the one without the other.

In the following verse (v. 21), there is also a close parallelism (although not a chiasm), juxtaposing, for a third time, love of God with love of one's brother and indicating that the one is necessary for the other.

Then in the remaining verses (5:1-5), there is a third and much more extended chiasm.[1] The chiasm begins (5:1a) with a statement about the identity of one believing that "Jesus is the Christ." This is paralleled in the last element (v. 5b) with an almost identical statement about the one believing that "Jesus is the Son of God." These two parallel confessional statements are the two central Christological statements rejected by the opponents and affirmed by the author.

The second element (vv. 1b-2a) introduces and focuses on the theme of "birth." It identifies the one believing by saying that the person is "begotten of God" and that "everyone" (masculine) loving the begetter also loves one begotten of him. This element then continues by saying that we know we love the children of God (and the conclusion will occur in the next element). The second-last element of the chiasm (vv. 4-5a) returns once more to speak of the one "begotten of God" but then, in turn, introduces and focuses on the theme of "conquest" and says that what is begotten of God conquers the world. The "conquest" is, in turn, defined as "our faith." Then the author poses a question involving, for a final time, the theme of conquest of the world that will be answered by the faith confession of the final element. Moreover, there is an extensive word play that appears in the second and second-to-last elements of the chiasm. In the second element there is the repetition three times of words asso-

---

1. Smalley (*Epistles* 265-66) proposes a "near-chiastic" pattern different from the one proposed here but ends it in v. 4. That pattern proposed is loose and refers only to the most general of themes. Culpepper ("Pivot" 26) proposes that 1 John 5:1-5 is "a tightly constructed paragraph . . . in which there is an interesting *inclusio*." Contrary to Smalley, Culpepper includes v. 5 and this *inclusio* is in fact the outer elements of the chiasm, as I propose it.

ciated with being begotten *(gegennētai, gennēsanta, gegennēmenon)* and in the second-to-last element there is the fourfold play on the notion of conquest and victory *(nika, nikē, nikēsasa, nikōn).* Clearly the author sought to embellish his argument with such details of style.

The third element (v. 2bc) then identifies how we love the children of God: by loving God and obeying his commandments.[2] The third-to-last element (v. 3bc) provides the definition of the love of God (now reversing the order of the previous statement in v. 3c) by saying that the love of which he speaks is manifest in our keeping his commandments — and his commandments are not burdensome. Thus, both elements speak of keeping the commandments and each is filled out by an additional comment appropriate to the context. And then the chiasm comes to a climax and hinges on the statement of v. 3a where the definition of the love of God is initiated.

Thus, the chiasm begins and ends with the two central and disputed affirmations regarding Jesus.[3] The second and second-to-last focus, respectively, on "birth" and "conquest of the world." But in doing so the second enlists "love" as an argument and the second-to-last enlists "faith" as its argument. In both the third and third-to-last elements (and only here within the chiasm), there are introduction and discussion of the commandments. In the hinge element is the topic of love of God, which is central to the entire argument. These chiasms (together with the isolated but significant v. 21) account for the overall structure of the section.

Beyond this, however, there are a number of minor techniques such as the use of generalization ("everyone who . . ." and "everything that . . ."); the use of definition ("this is the love . . ." [v. 3a]; "this is the victor . . ." [v. 4b]) and the use of logical implication ("if . . . , then").

By using the variety of techniques mentioned above and especially the various chiasms, the author emphasizes what he sees as the logic of his argument.

---

2. The two comments that make up the third element should not be considered distinct elements of the chiasm but as an example of hendiadys. The believer demonstrates love of the children of God by loving God and this is the same as obeying his commandments. Likewise, the two statements in the third-last element, about keeping the commandments and the commandments not being burdensome, are also examples of complementary statements rather than distinct elements.

3. From this, it will be clear why I do not see the section ending at 5:4a as do some other scholars. For example, Brown (*Epistles* 545) proposes that the unit ends at 5:4a. He points to two inclusions that bind 5:1 with 4:7 and 5:3 with 4:10. The problem is, however, that the proposed similarities between 4:7 and 5:1 do not constitute a true inclusion because they do not occur at the very beginning and end of the respective sections (as do the two statements I propose for the limits of the chiasm in 5:1 and 5:5c). Second, the similarities between 4:10 and 5:3 are general but the grammar is different and the second is a true definition while the first is not.

THE INTERPRETATION OF 4:20–5:5

Vv. 20-21

The thought of these verses is generally quite straightforward. In another example of an attempt to make his point by demonstrating the logic of his argument, the author insists on the necessity of love for one's brother if one claims to love God.

The author begins by arguing (v. 20a-e) that, if someone claims to love God without loving one's brother, that person is a liar. And then (v. 20f-i) he says that the reason for this is that, if one cannot love the one he/she sees (brother), the person cannot love the one that is not seen (God). The fact that both of these statements are chiastic confirms structurally the similarities and contrasts intended throughout.

Finally (v. 21), the author explains that the source of this relationship between loving God and loving one's brother is a commandment. That commandment is that the one who loves God should also love his/her brother. This is expressed in a parallelism that again points to the relationship between the two.

The theological point here is quite clear and forceful. Beginning with the claim that a person loves God, the author argues that it is possible to test whether one truly loves God by determining whether that individual loves his brother since they have received the commandment that the one who loves God must also love his brother.[4]

5:1-5

Then in a remarkable development of the argument, the author seems to change the subject radically when he states that the one believing that Jesus is the Christ is begotten of God. However, the fact that vv. 1-5 are organized in the form of a chiasm again helps both to identify the extent of the subunit and also to show the relation of the various elements of the argument to one another. The result is a complex, but clear, progression of the Johannine logic. Within the chiasm, the author's typical chaining of terminology and use of definitions are employed to lead beyond the immediate meaning of terms to other logical, but perhaps unforeseen, conclusions.

The argument proceeds step by step. At the beginning (v. 1a-b), the au-

---

4. In saying this, the author is taking a position quite similar to one he had adopted in 2:4. There we had heard that, if a person said he "knew" God but did not keep his commandments, that person was a liar. Here the claim and the test are different but the consequence is the same: the one who fails the test is a liar. Here the test is loving one's brother; in 2:3-11 the test was keeping the commandments. After an explanation of why love of one's brother is important, he goes on to say that the commandment in focus is that the one who loves God should also love his brother. In 2:5, 7, the commandment referred to was specified as keeping the word of God.

thor affirms that the one who believes that "Jesus is the Christ" is begotten of God. Thus, the one who confesses belief as the tradition properly understands it, is defined as the one "begotten of God." Then in step two (v. 1b), the author, after presuming (from the prior context) the conviction that the believer loves God (the begetter),[5] goes on to say that everyone loving the begetter loves the one begotten from him.[6] Thus, the writer says (v. 1cd) that one cannot truly love God without loving one's fellow believer.

But just when we expect the author to say more about mutual love, he (v. 2ab) reverses the direction of his argument and, in the third step of the argument, says that true love of a fellow believer is demonstrated in the act *of loving God* and keeping his commandments! Thus, while the reader's attention had seemed to be directed at love *of one's fellow believer,* now suddenly it is turned back to the notion *of correct love of God!* The Johannine notion of love works both ways: love of God demands love of the brothers; love of brothers demands love of God. But he also makes it clear that correct love implies performance of the commandments.

The author now comes to the center of his chiasm (v. 3) by subtly adding a fourth step to the chain of his argument. He now builds on what was stated in v. 2b ("Whenever we love God and keep his commandments") and creates the first of his "definitions": "This is the love of God . . ."). But the actual definition of this love (v. 3bc) constitutes the next element of the chiasm: "That we keep his commandments and his commandments are not burdensome"). So he has moved from the specifics of mutual love to the more general commandment "love of God" and "keeping his commandments." But in v. 3 he appears to move from the general back to the specific when he provides the definition of "love of God," a definition we would expect to be specific. But instead, the specific definition of love of God repeats the general to keep the commandments, adding that they are not burdensome.

Then in a fifth step (v. 4a), the author returns to speak of the one "begotten of God" (cf. vv. 1b-2a)[7] and explains that "everything"[8] begotten of God conquers the world.[9] Then comes the sixth step (v. 4bc), the author defines the

5. It will be noticed that this step in the argument is not stated explicitly but is presumed by what follows.

6. Thus, this argument reverses the logic of 4:20abc and 4:21, where it was said that the one who loves God should love one's brother.

7. It will be noted that this second reference to the one born of God parallels the first within the structure of the chiasm.

8. See the Notes for discussion of the neuter gender here.

9. From the grammar, it is evident that the author understands that this conquest of the world helps explain that God's commandments are not burdensome, but just *why* this is so is not immediately clear.

"conquest that conquered" the world as "our faith."[10] In the final (seventh) step of his argument (v. 5), the author poses the question about the identity of the one who conquers the world and (in v. 5b) he will answer this in the concluding statement of the chiasm. The author now completes the final step, as was mentioned above, and that is to identify the one who conquers with the one who believes that "Jesus is the Son of God." This then introduces the second of the controverted confessions regarding Jesus and binds the entire chiasm together. Thus, when we look back at the chiasm we see how the structure confirms the organization of the thought throughout these verses.

In 2:28–3:10, the author had spoken extensively of being "begotten of God" and being "children of God" and having "God as Father." Here, he has returned to speak of the one "begotten of God." His affirmation at both ends of the chiasm is that the one begotten of God makes the correct confession of faith. But in the middle he has shown that this correct confession is an example of keeping the commandments and that keeping the commandments demonstrates love of God and is not burdensome.

Thus, the author ends by affirming the second major Christological confession of the Letter ("Jesus is the Son of God"). In addition to this, in the first half, he has spoken of the relation between mutual love and love of God; and, in the second half, has shown that faith is the means by which the world is conquered.

*   *   *

Once again, the primary topics of the section are love of one's brother and correct faith. In vv. 20-21, the author confronts the opponents with his conviction repeated four times (including the statement in 5:1b) that one cannot claim to love God without loving one's brother.

But the one to be loved is defined in 5:1 as the one who has correct faith. Thus, a concrete criterion is provided for the identification of the brother. In 5:1, this correct faith is evident in the one who makes the correct confession,

---

10. Verse 4b occupies a curious place within the argument of the chiasm. The sense and sequence of vv. 4-5 would be fine without it. Moreover, it awkwardly interrupts the chaining process by transposing the *verb* of "conquering" from v. 4a and v. 5a and the *verb* of "believing" from v. 5b into *nouns* in v. 4b ("conquest" and "faith."). Thus, the author introduces the second of his "definitions." With v. 4b in place, the author stresses his conviction that the *conquest* of v. 4a is the believer's *faith.* Then v. 5, somewhat repetitiously, asks the identity of the one who conquers and answers that it is the believer, but now v. 5 takes the argument to its final form by specifying the content of the faith mentioned in v. 4b as belief "that Jesus is the Son of God." The repetition of words dealing with "conquest" is the first of three such pleonastic expressions that manifest a (less than sophisticated) rhetorical effect.

that Jesus is the Christ. Then in 5:4-5 the author returns to a specific identification of the faith that conquers the world, and it is said to be the confession of Jesus as Son of God. Thus, in 5:1-5, the author has shown that you cannot have love without proper faith. And he gives the precise content of proper confession in terms of the two primary confessional statements of the community. Moreover, he affirms that correct faith means that one is begotten of God (5:1ab) and correct faith means that one has conquered the world (5:5).

While the repeated exhortations to love one's brother (and to confess one's faith in Jesus) continue to have a relevance for the Christian community in the modern world, the full appreciation of the meaning of this love and this faith requires an understanding of the particular circumstances of the Johannine community at the time of the Letter's composition. For while such love of one's brother is often difficult in any circumstance, at the time of the Letter the author was confronting a group of opponents for whom such conduct was considered theoretically unnecessary because they considered themselves "perfect" through their reception of the eschatological Spirit. As he has often done before, the author makes it clear that the various claims made by the opponents in the light of their possession of the Spirit are simply lies if they are not linked with proper love of the brothers and proper confession of faith.

Having the Son and Having Life

6 This is the one coming through water and blood, Jesus Christ.
  Not in the water only but
    in the water
    and the blood.

And the Spirit is the one bearing witness
  because the Spirit is the Truth.

  7 Because there are three witnessing:
    8 the Spirit
    and the water
    and the blood,
      and these three are as one.

9 If we accept the witness of humans,
  the witness of God is greater
    because this is the witness of God
      that he has witnessed about his Son.

10 The one believing in the Son of God has the witness in himself.
The one not believing God has made him [God] a liar
  because he has not believed in the witness
    that God has witnessed about his Son.

11 And this is the witness,
  that God gave us eternal life,
  and this life is in his Son.

12 The one who has the Son has life;
the one not having the Son of God does not have life.

NOTES TO 5:6-12

V. 6 coming The Greek here is an aorist participle indicating an action in the past. Scholars in general understand this to refer to elements of the historical ministry. In vv. 7-8, the witnessing is in the present tense and so thought to refer to something other than the historical events.

It is also important to recognize that here and in 1 John 4:2 "coming" has the connotation of "acting salvifically." It does not simply refer to the appearance of Jesus but connotes that salvation will be brought about by the specific manner of that coming. Schnackenburg (*Epistles* 232) comments: "The aorist 'came' forces us to envision certain salvation events that took place with Jesus' once-for-all coming into the world." Brown (*Epistles* 576) says: "'Coming' in this [the most common] theory is not simply entrance into the world but salvific mission. . . ."

The means by which this salvation will be effected are then described by the preposition with its object ("in water" or "in water and in blood"). See also the discussion referred to at 4:2.

through water and blood It is remarkable that there are no references to "water" in 1 John, other than the one here and in v. 7. "Blood" *(haima)* appears in 1:7. For a discussion of the meaning of the terms, see the following Note.

not in water only but in water and in blood There is some variation in the grammar of "water and blood" that should be noted. In v. 6a, the preposition "through" *(dia)* is used, but only before the first noun, and no article is used with either water or blood. In v. 6bcd, the preposition "in" *(en)* appears before each noun along with the article "the" *(tō)* before each noun. Some have thought there is a deliberate nuance intended by the shifts. However, in both instances, the author makes a statement of his own position and in both he uses different expressions. If he had used one for the opponents' view and the other for his own, there would be some reason to suspect a distinction. As it is, the shift is almost surely simple stylistic variation.

But what is the meaning of "not in the water only, but in the water and in the blood"? These two are almost certainly elliptical expressions that would have been readily understood by both parties to the dispute. But because they are so brief, their meaning is debated today.

Previous scholarship regarding the meaning of the phrase "in the water" and "in the water and in the blood" has been thoroughly documented by Brown in his commentary (*Epistles* 573-78) and by de Boer (*Perspectives* 254-57). Here I will discuss only the position of Brown and major theories since Brown.

Most recent scholars see the two references as pointing respectively to events at both the beginning and the end of the ministry of Jesus. There is general agreement that the mention of coming "in blood" is a reference to the atoning death of Jesus. Most scholars see the reference to coming "in water" as referring somehow to the baptism of Jesus, but there is considerable variation in details.

For example, Brown (*Epistles* 596-97) proposes that the opponents' reference to Jesus as coming "in water" refers to their claim that "Jesus was the Christ, the Son of God, at his baptism, through his coming in water, as revealed by the Spirit." However, for the author "in water" referred to the giving of the Spirit at the moment of his death and "in blood" referred to the sacrificial aspect of that death.

According to this view, the author and the opponents understood "coming in water" differently. Not only do they associate it with different moments of the ministry; but, in each, the one whom the water affects is different (Jesus, the believer). Yet there is no indication in 1 John 5:6-8 that the two groups understood this term differently. Rather, the text indicates that the author *affirms* a "coming in water" as the opponents propose it, but sees the need to complement it with "coming in blood."

Schnackenburg (*Epistles* 233-34) sees the reference to "come in water and in blood" to combine the understanding of the opponents (that the coming of the Spirit on Jesus at his baptism was salvific) with the author's own conviction that the death of Jesus was an atoning sacrifice for sin ("coming through . . . blood" 5:6). However, according to 1 John 5:6, Jesus himself is said to "come" in water. This indicates that it is an action that Jesus performs rather than something that is done to Jesus.

Smalley (*Epistles* 277-80) sees the water and blood as referring to the two terminal points of the life of Jesus and as affirming their importance in the face of a docetism that claimed the Christ withdrew from Jesus before his death. Thus, the author stresses (against his Greek opponents) that Jesus was truly man and so baptized and crucified and also truly divine and so "already Messiah on both occasions." "The true identity of Jesus . . . is only to be discovered by looking at the whole of his life, including its end. . . . He came not only with baptismal water, the timeless symbol of cleansing, but also in the actual, historical means for achieving this. . . ."

Strecker's view (*Epistles* 182-83) is similar. He proposes that "the author is thinking of the two Christological 'saving realities,' the baptism and sacrificial death of Jesus Christ." While Strecker grants that Jesus' baptism is not specifically described in the Fourth Gospel, he argues that "it is presupposed, in accord with the Synoptic tradition, that Jesus was baptized by John the Baptizer." "If an opposing, docetic teaching is in view, the reference back to the baptism and death of Jesus, the beginning and end of Jesus' life, emphasizes that these are to be understood as real, historical events, and that eschatological salvation cannot be separated from the empirical person of the earthly Jesus." While Strecker's association of "water" with the baptism carries with it the same problem as Brown's, Strecker avoids understanding "water" differently when it is associated with blood. But, for Strecker's view, there is the additional question whether the problem being confronted is really docetism.

Klauck (*Erste Johannesbrief* 293-94) also sees docetism "in the widest sense of the term" as the position being confronted by the author. Klauck proposes that the image of Jesus receiving the Spirit at his baptism becomes the soteriological model for the believer. According to this model, by means of Baptism, the believer receives the Holy Spirit and because of that the earthly existence of the believer is changed into a new, "pneumatic" existence that is no longer subject to the conditions of worldliness. As a result, the life-giving activity of Jesus' death loses its significance.

However, Klauck intermingles the experience of the believer with the events of Jesus' ministry. What is talked about in 5:6 is only the actions of Jesus. While it may be true that, *in the later community*, the believer received the Spirit at Baptism or at some other initiation rite, *on the level of the ministry itself* it is clear in the second edition that Jesus himself promises the gift of the Spirit to those who believe. The importance of the Spirit is not simply based on Jesus' baptism as a model for the believer.

Yet other proposals suggest that "water" in v. 8 is a symbol of the Spirit and that "coming in the water" refers to the giving of the Spirit. Among those who propose this view are Thüsing (*Erhöhung* 165-74) and Grayston (*Epistles* 19). However, neither Thüsing nor Grayston associates the giving of the Spirit with the death but rather imply that the giving of the Spirit involved a rejection of any meaning for the death of Jesus. According to Grayston (*Epistles* 137), the author argues that "the benefits symbolized by water cannot be had apart from the sufferings symbolized by blood." Yet this does not ascribe any soteriological value to the death itself, but sees it only as a necessary occasion for the giving of the Spirit.

More recently, de Boer (*Perspectives* 253-307) has proposed a somewhat similar view in which he sees the water as referring to the Baptismal rite of the community (a rite performed by Jesus himself during his ministry [303]) through which the believer was cleansed from sin by the Spirit. De Boer says (*Perspectives* 267), "For the secessionists, the claim that Jesus Christ is 'the one who came in water *only*' effectively signifies that baptismal initiation is sufficient for salvation." This view presumes that Jesus baptized with the Spirit before his glorification. Clearly, it was the desire of the later tradition of the Gospel to deny that Jesus baptized at all and, according to 7:37-39, the Spirit was given only at the glorification of Jesus (so also Painter, *Epistles*

304). This also presumes an interest in ritual in the secessionists that I find not to be the case.

According to de Boer, the author of 1 John counters this view by arguing that blood also cleanses from sin. Because the reference to the blood of Jesus cleansing us from all sin (1:7) occurs in a context where perfectionism is discussed, de Boer proposes that the "coming in blood" refers to "especially, though probably not exclusively, post-baptismal sin" (*Perspectives* 303, see also 281). Thus, for de Boer the atoning death of Jesus is important but the quasi-restriction of the effects of Jesus' blood to post-baptismal sins is puzzling and unique in the literature.

The Role of John 19:34 in the Interpretation of vv. 6-8

In all of this, scholars are divided about the role of John 19:34. Many scholars seek to interpret 1 John 5:6 in the light of John 19:34. Then, the interpreter must determine what is actually emphasized in 19:34. Is the phrase "blood and water" a double symbol that attests true death (that is, the blood and water have separated), or are blood and water individual symbols, the first a symbol of atoning death and the second a symbol of the effusion of the Spirit? If it were not for John 19:34, there would be no reason to think of water and blood as a double symbol. In fact, there would be no precedent for the use of these as symbols at all!

On the other hand, if 1 John was written *before* John 19:34 (as I argue), then we must attempt to understand 1 John 5:6 within the context of 1 John itself and John 19:34 does not play a primary role in the determination of the meaning of 1 John 5:6. In 1 John 1:7, the author had explained that what "cleanses us from all sin" is the blood of Christ. The author of 1 John is at pains to emphasize the fact that the salvific effect of the death of Jesus occurs by the death of Jesus in blood. It is only in 5:6 that we find out that the author of 1 John agrees that Jesus comes in both water and in blood. Moreover, we find out that he is confronting some who claim that he came only in water. Thus, on the basis of 1 John, we see that the expression in v. 6 cannot be a double symbol but must contain two distinct ones.[1]

---

1. However, if it is true, as is argued in this Commentary, that John 19:34 was written *after* 1 John 5:6, then we also gain a clearer light on John 19:34 since it then becomes clear that John 19:34 is to be understood as a corroboration of 1 John 5:6 rather than the reverse. Therefore, blood and water in 19:34 must be intended as two symbols rather than one. John 19:34 is not intended to be an attestation of the reality of Jesus' death (symbolized by the separation of blood from water) but to have the same symbolism as 1 John 5:6, that Jesus has come to die an atoning death and also to give forth the Spirit.

My View

First, there is no evidence that "coming in water" meant one thing to the opponents and something else to the author (contra Brown). Rather, the author agrees that Jesus "came in water" but argues that he also "came in blood."

But what does "coming in water" mean? Discovering the meaning of the phrase is complicated by the fact that the term appears only here and in v. 8 in the Letter. Consequently, we are obligated to go outside the Letter in search of its symbolic meaning.

In the second edition of the Gospel, the primary gift of Jesus is the Spirit, and, in the second edition, (living) water plays a prominent role as a symbol of this Spirit. This occurs first in 4:10-15 where Jesus offers the Samaritan woman living water. In John 7:37-39, at the feast of Tabernacles, Jesus invites those who believe in him to come and drink of the living waters that will flow from his belly. The second author then explains that this is a reference to "the Spirit that those who believed in him were to receive. For the Spirit was not yet because Jesus was not yet glorified." Thus, in the second edition, Jesus offers the Spirit under the imagery of living water at the time of his glorification (that is, his Crucifixion) to those who believe in him. In 13:4-11, the second author portrays Jesus' symbolic prefigurement of his washing them with the Spirit in his washing of their feet with water. These are not the only passages of the second edition that deal with the gift of the Spirit, but, from these, it becomes clear that *(living) water was the primary symbol for the Spirit that Jesus will give.* Moreover, Jesus' offering the Spirit is *not a minor motif* of the Gospel; it is the central soteriological event of the second edition! Both adjectives here are crucial: it is *central* to the second edition and it is *soteriological.* We have seen that the offering of the Spirit is central to the second edition; it is soteriological because it was this gift that accomplished salvation as the community understood it. Thus, when we interpret "coming in water" in light of the second edition, we find a clear and unequivocal answer: when the second author speaks of Jesus as "coming in water," he is speaking of the effect of Jesus' death as the giving of the Spirit. This is the view of the opponents.

However, the view of the author of 1 John was more complex. The author agrees that Jesus had "come in water." That is, he agrees with his opponents that Jesus came to give the Spirit. That this view continued to be held by the author's followers is clear first of all from 1 John 5:6 itself, which affirms that Jesus "came in water." But it is also evident from the repeated statements to this effect as late as the third edition. In John 14:15-17, 26-27; 15:26-27; 16:7-11, 12-15, Jesus, in the Farewell Discourses, affirms again and again that he will send the Spirit when he returns to the Father at his death. Thus, belief that Jesus had "come in water" was not confined to the time of the second edition but continued to be a significant element of belief as late as the time of the third edition.

However, the difference comes in the fact that the author of 1 John (as well as the author of the third edition after him) testifies that Jesus also came "in blood." That is, his death was an atoning sacrifice. In 1 John, the role of the blood of Jesus had already been explained as "cleansing us from all sin" (1 John 1:7). In 2:2 and 4:10, we heard that Jesus was an atonement for the sins of the whole world. In 2:12, it is said that the sins of the community are forgiven through his name. All of these are various ways of expressing the role of Jesus in the forgiveness of sin. Here the reference to "coming in blood" is an alternate way of indicating that his blood has a salvific, cleansing effect.

Thus, it can be seen that the discussion echoed in 1 John 5:6 centers, not on the relation of the baptism of Jesus to his death, but rather on two interpretations of his death. For the author of 1 John, the "coming in water" occurred at the death of Jesus as did his "coming in blood." It was a matter of complementing the view of the opponents rather than denying it. His argument, then, is a kind of shorthand that expresses the conviction that the death of Jesus resulted in the gift of the Spirit and also resulted in an atoning sacrifice for sin.

It should be obvious that this explanation has a much firmer foundation in the Gospel than previous explanations, primarily because of the clarity gained regarding the composition of the Gospel and the relation of 1 John to the understanding of the second edition. But this is not its only value. The verse, as we understand it here, shows that the opponents attributed some positive role to Jesus and it also shows what that role was. The opponents did not reject Jesus totally; they only rejected the claim that he came "in blood." This is in complete agreement with the charge by the author of 1 John that the opponents denied that Jesus "came in the flesh." That is, the physical aspects of his ministry were not of significance, something that is emphatically denied by the author of 1 John.

And the Spirit is the one bearing witness The Greek here is a present participle "the one bearing witness."

because the Spirit is the Truth This is another instance of poetic identification. In 4:6, the Spirit is said to be "the Spirit *of* Truth." The point is that the Spirit is (the source of and guarantees) Truth. The technique appears also in 5:20: "This (Jesus Christ) is the true God and eternal life." This type of expression also appears regularly in the Gospel. See particularly John 4:24; 6:63.

V. 7 Because there are three witnessing The Greek word for "three" is in the masculine although all three Greek words to which it refers (water, blood, Spirit) are neuter. Schnackenburg (*Gospel* 3:235-37) sees this as an indication that the author is now referring to sacraments. While the masculine is puzzling, it is not at all clear that this indicates a reference to sacraments. Schnackenburg suggests that the emphasis on the presence of "three" witnesses may be a reference to the proper number of witnesses as explained by Deut 19:15 where it is said that valid witness should be given by two or more witnesses.

More important is just how the water, the blood and the Spirit are to be understood as three distinct witnesses. The problem is caused in part by the fact that the author is moving from correcting the opponents to affirmations of his own position. In v. 6, the author is correcting the opponents and stating the truth. The fact that Jesus "came in water" witnesses to Jesus in the sense that this is part of why it is true that Jesus is the Christ. Moreover, *the fact* that Jesus "came in blood" also witnesses to Jesus in the sense that *the fact* that his death was salvific also witnesses to (explains why) Jesus is the Son of God. But the Spirit also witnesses independently to the correctness of all this. The water and blood witness to the identity of Jesus, and the Spirit witnesses to the correctness of these affirmations. As was the case in the Gospel, such a listing of and understanding of "witness" is credible only to a believer (and the author recognizes this when he says [v. 10] that the believer "has the witness in himself").

V. 8 and these three are as one Up to this point the author has spoken of three witnesses. Now he adds that all three of these witnesses are "as one." That is, they agree in their testimony.

V. 9 because this is the witness of God that he has witnessed This is the first of four cognate accusatives that the author will use in the next seven verses. Two of them involve the noun *martyria* and the verb *martyreō*: ". . . this is the witness of God that he witnessed about his Son." The third, in v. 15, involves "requests" *(aitēmata)* that we have requested *(ētēkamen)*. In the present verse, the focus begins to shift from the one doing the witnessing to the content of the witness although the actual content of the witness will not be given until v. 11a.

V. 10 in the Son of God Here the preposition "in" appears before "Son of God."

believing God "God" is in the dative case. The issue is not whether one has faith in God but whether one believes what God has said, which, on the face of it, would appear to be absurd. To the author of 1 John, however, failure to accept Jesus is failure to believe the witness that God has given regarding him, and so the person, in effect, does not believe God and thus makes God a liar. See also at 4:1.

liar Once before (1:10) the author has accused those who deny that they have sinned of making God a liar. For both groups, such a charge would be the greatest horror. However, by speaking of the effect such a statement would have on the opponents, I do not imply that 1 John was actually written to be circulated among the opponents. Rather, the statement here (as in 1:10) is a rhetorical ploy designed to show the enormity of the implications of the opponents' beliefs and to prevent the author's followers from adopting such a belief.

the witness that God has witnessed This is the second of the three cognate accusatives in the immediate context. (See also v. 15 ["the requests that we have requested"] and v. 16 ["sinning a sin"].) Typically such expressions reflect a Semitic influence. (Cf. "sinning a sin" in Lev 5:6; Ezek 18:24 [LXX].)

V. 11 And this is the witness "Witness" here refers to the *content* of the witness, namely "that God has given. . . ."

OVERVIEW OF 5:6-12

The overriding purpose of this section is to show the reader that both the Spirit and the Father witness to the identity of the Son. The point to be clarified is the correct understanding of the Son. This understanding concerns the "coming" of Jesus, whether he came "in water only" or "in water and blood."

In vv. 6-8, the author shows that the Spirit (in whom the opponents believe and which they claim to possess) witnesses to a proper understanding (and confession) of Jesus.

In vv. 9-12 the author turns to the second witness: God the Father (whom the opponents also believe in and claim to know). In these verses the author shows the specific witness the Father provides, namely that the Father's gift of eternal life is not possible without the Son.

THE STRUCTURE OF 5:6-12

The fundamental division of this section is into two units, as was mentioned above. Each unit deals with the witness of a different person. In the first unit (vv. 6-8), the basic theme is the witness of the Spirit to Jesus and, in the second unit (vv. 9-12), the witness of God to Jesus.

The other rhetorical features of this section are not complex and contribute to its overall presentation. There is rough parallelism between the statement that the Spirit witnesses (v. 6e) and that God witnesses (v. 9cd). There is a contrast in v. 10ab between the one believing and the one not believing. There is a certain parallelism between the two pleonastic expressions that speak of "the witness that God witnessed."

In addition to these more extensive rhetorical features, there is the use of definition (v. 11); chaining (v. 11bc); and contrasting parallelism (v. 12). Finally, there is the repetition involving "about his Son" (vv. 9, 10) and "in his Son" (v. 11), both of which occur in the emphatic position at the end of sentences.

THE INTERPRETATION OF 5:6-12

Vv. 6-8

With his mention of "this one" (v. 6a), the author hearkens back to the end of v. 5 with its mention of belief that Jesus Christ is the Son of God. He explains that this one (Jesus Christ) has come "through water and blood." This is the author's firm conviction and he contrasts it with the view of his opponents who hold that Jesus came "in water only."

As we have seen in the Note, the meaning of these terms and their immediate context have occasioned wide disagreement among scholars. According to Brown, this passage illustrates both the strengths and the weaknesses of 1 John. On the one hand, it illustrates "the burning conviction of the author, the oratorical power of his short phrases, the vividness of the imagery. . . ." On the other hand: "The weakness . . . is the utter obscurity of what he is talking about. . . . If one counts the discussions of the Johannine Comma . . . , more ink has been applied to paper in discussing these verses than in discussing any other comparable section of 1 John."[2]

In his commentary, Brown reviewed past scholarship on this topic and in the Note to the verse, we have reviewed the major scholarship since Brown. In that Note, it was also argued in detail that "coming in water" was a slogan derived from the theology of the second edition that referred to the conviction that the purpose of Jesus' ministry was the bestowal of the Spirit (symbolized in the Gospel as "living water"). It was also argued that "coming in blood" was a slogan utilized by the author of 1 John that referred to the conviction that the death of Jesus was an atoning sacrifice that cleansed the believer from sin. Within the Johannine tradition as we have understood it, this verse in particular (and also vv. 7-8) is the community's first attempt to articulate the full understanding of the soteriological effect of Jesus' death. It is the view that will later be articulated in John 19:34.

Thus, at the time of the writing of 1 John, the author knew the community's Gospel in the form of the second edition.[3] In that edition, Jesus had

---

2. Brown, *Epistles* 595.

3. It is particularly important to recall that, at the time of the second edition, the author of 1 John could not appeal to John 19:34 to refute the opponents since that verse was not added to the Gospel until the third edition.

promised the outpouring of the Spirit upon all who believed in him. That Spirit was to be the principle of eternal life for the believer. However, while the author of 1 John affirmed this giving of the Spirit and while he recognized that the opponents also affirmed this, for the author this was not enough: Jesus came not only in water but he also came in blood.[4] Thus, the author affirms (in v. 6) that the purpose of Jesus' coming was double: it released the Spirit and it was a sacrifice for the removal of sin.

In support of his position, the author then (v. 6ef) reminds the reader that the Spirit is the one witnessing to this and the Spirit is the Truth. It may be somewhat surprising to find the author being so explicit in his reference to the Spirit here after the symbolic reference to him in v. 6bc. There are a number of possible reasons for this. First is the likelihood that the terms "in water" and "in blood" were jargon used for the key terms in the community debate and so they were readily understood by the readers in that context. Second, if the author suddenly becomes explicit, it may be because by referring to the Spirit under another title, he is able to distinguish the *giving* of the Spirit as *object of belief* from the *action* of the Spirit as *interior witness to* the proper content of belief. This distinction will be important for him in vv. 7-8 and he is preparing for that here. Third, he distinguishes because he wishes to refute the opponents by clarifying what the Spirit *really* witnesses to. As we have seen, the opponents were firmly convinced that they had received the Spirit and that the Spirit inspired them with what to believe about Jesus. But the author of 1 John explains that the Spirit really witnesses to the fact that Jesus Christ came both in water and in blood.[5]

What would have been perhaps equally surprising to the Johannine reader who knew only the second edition was the fact that the author of 1 John refers to the Spirit as a "witness." In the second edition, the author was at constant pains to show that there were four witnesses to Jesus: John the Baptist, the words of Jesus, his works, and the Scriptures (cf. esp. 5:31-40). Of these, only the final three were essential. Yet the author of 1 John understood that the Spirit also witnessed to Jesus and so could the members of the community (e.g., 1:2). The present text together with the earlier references to the witness of the members of the community is the first attestation of these further witnesses. As we shall see in the third edition of the Gospel, in the Farewell Discourses, when Jesus is preparing his followers for the future, after referring to the three witnesses of the ministry for a final time in the second edition (15:22-25), the third

---

4. If we cannot find any texts in the second edition of the Gospel that speak so clearly about "blood" as they do about "water," this should not be surprising since the Gospel in its second edition had spoken only of the giving of the Spirit.

5. As Schnackenburg (*Epistles* 234) says: "The little clause [v. 6ef] leads to the next verses which are intended to strengthen the basis of faith after referring to its content."

author will formally add to this list these two additional witnesses that will be operative in the time *after* his earthly ministry (15:26-27).

But the complications of the text are not yet totally resolved. In vv. 7-8, the author makes another puzzling comment and explains that there are actually three witnessing: the Spirit, the water and the blood. In explaining this, the tendency among scholars has been to attempt to explain how each of these is a distinct witness and then to relate that answer to the context. In my view this is the wrong way to proceed. The problem is that, if the verse is read this way, it neglects the fact that, in the next verse, the author is going to speak about yet another witness: the witness of God. It is surely the case that the author does not then mean to imply that the author is speaking in the present context of a total of four witnesses.

Rather, the key lies in a proper understanding of what these three witnesses are witnessing *to*. They witness *not* to the issue of "water and/or blood" but rather to the reality and importance of Jesus Christ as the Son of God as the author understands him. Belief that Jesus was the Son of God was the topic in v. 5 ("the one believing that Jesus Christ is the Son of God") and it will be the topic of vv. 9-12 with its numerous references to his Son (vv. 9, 10a, 10d, 11c, 12a, 12b). Consequently, what the author says in vv. 6-8 should be understood in relation to that larger topic. These three are witnesses to these elements that are part of true belief. That Jesus came in water (that is, that he bestowed the Spirit) and that he came in blood (that is, the fact that his death was a sacrifice and atonement) are both elements of a proper understanding of what it means to say that Jesus is the Christ.

Then the author turns to the witness of the Spirit. Earlier he had spoken of the conviction that the Spirit was given at the time of Jesus' glorification when he referred to Jesus as "coming in water." Now the author speaks of the Spirit in its present role as active within the believer and points out that the Spirit now testifies to the fact that Jesus came in water and in blood and that this is true of Jesus as the Son of God.

It is important to see that, in this verse, the Spirit is *both the active agent* of witnessing *and also the object of* the witness. The Spirit *(active agent)* residing within the individual witnesses to the fact that Jesus came "in water," that is, to give the Spirit *(object of witness)* . . . and also that Jesus came in blood.

Thus, all three together point to the same thing: the correct identity of Jesus. As the author says "and these three are as one" *(kai hoi treis eis to hen eisin)*, a statement that, as was explained in the Notes, means that all three of these agree and point to the correct understanding of Jesus as Son of God. Thus, the author argues (but always in a way and with a logic and presuppositions that are apparent only to the believer) that Jesus is the Christ, the Son of God.

It will be noted that now, at the end of v. 8, the author has finished his discussion of the witness of the Spirit and will now turn abruptly to a discussion of the witness of God the Father. Thus, he will eventually show the reader that *both* the Spirit *and* the Father witness to the correct identity of the Son.

Vv. 9-12

We now come to the second subsection of this unit. This subsection will deal with the witness of the Father. In v. 9, the author comments on the relative value of human and divine witness. There are two possible explanations of what this refers to. First, it could well be intended to affirm what will be obvious to both the followers of the author and to the opponents: that the witness of God is greater than that of humans; and, if we accept that of humans, then we should all the more accept the witness of God. It could also be that the author is alluding to the listing of proper witnesses in John 5:31-40 (which comes from the second edition). Thus, the witness of humans would be that of John the Baptist. But the witness of God is the witness that he had given through the works of Jesus (John 5:36), the words of Jesus (John 5:37-38) and the witness of Scripture (John 5:39-40), all of which had their origin in God.

In any event, the author has begun another of his arguments set up on successive logical steps. The assertion of the trustworthiness of God's witness sets the stage for the assertion (which he will make in v. 10) that if one does not have correct belief in Jesus, then that person (that is, the opponents) is making God a liar and rejecting his witness. The author then prepares the reader for the witness of God and does so in an awkward and pleonastic way: ". . . this is the witness of God that he has witnessed about his Son."[6]

At this point, it is important to notice that the author does not actually give the witness of the Father. When he says (v. 9c) that "this is the witness," he is referring to the witness that will not be actually specified until v. 11, where he says again: "And this is the witness."

Before the author states the actual content of God's witness (v. 11), he contrasts (v. 10) the one believing (v. 10a) with the one not believing (v. 10bcd). The one who believes in the Son of God "has the witness in himself." Just what this means becomes evident after we understand v. 10bcd. In the second part of the verse (v. 10bcd), the author talks about the one who does not believe God (that is, the one who does not accept the witness of God about Jesus).[7] This person

---

6. We have seen such pleonasm before in 5:4-5, where the author uses four variants of words dealing with conquest. Throughout 5:9-11a, noun and verb forms dealing with witness will appear eight times!

7. Verse 10cd is a very close parallel to v. 9cd, including the pleonasm. The repetition and the pleonasm are evidently intended to emphasize the fact that this is God who is now witnessing and it is his witness that they are rejecting.

makes God a liar.[8] The meaning of this is obvious, but we must recall that the opponents claimed to believe in God the Father and that the author regularly seeks to argue from the premises he shares with the opponents — and to show that these premises themselves demand belief as the author himself understands it. Here, the author has reminded the reader that God the Father is trustworthy and there could be no reason not to believe him. Yet the Father has witnessed to Jesus and the opponents reject that witness. The author then claims that, by rejecting this witness, the opponents have done, in effect, what the opponents would never allow themselves to be accused of, namely claiming that God is a liar!

We may now return to v. 10a with an understanding of its immediate context. The author's main intention has been to reveal the effects of not accepting the witness of God. But before doing this, he spoke about the one who had accepted the witness of the Father. That person "has the witness in himself," that is, the person has accepted the witness of the Father. The author does not intend the reader to infer by his words (v. 10a) about "having the witness in himself" that there is some special *manner* by which the witness is accepted but simply says that the believer accepts the witness of God and "has" it within. And then he proceeds to contrast the believer with the opponent who does not accept God's witness about the Son.

Up to this point, the author has been carefully building his argument step by step. We have heard that the witness of God is greater than the witness of humans and that God has borne witness about his Son. We then read a comparison between the one who accepts the witness and the one who does not.

In vv. 11-12, we come to the climax of the second part of the author's argument and learn the precise content of the witness that God has borne. We will examine each aspect of it individually and then summarize.

"And this is the witness" (v. 11a). Here the author prepares to explain the content of God's witness. The two clauses that follow will be in apposition to this and will contain the actual witness.

"[T]hat God gave us eternal life" (v. 11b). This is the first part of God's witness. This was the central element of the community's belief and it had been what drew them together initially as a community. They had all come to realize that the eschatological events had transpired in the ministry of Jesus. This element of belief was not disputed; both the author and his opponents agreed that they had been given eternal life by God.

---

8. Certainly this statement is intended to be shocking and to confront the one who rejects the witness of the Father with the charge of blasphemously making God a liar! Presumably, because the opponents had put all their belief in God, this charge would be intended to call into question the authenticity of their most basic conviction.

"[A]nd this life is in his Son" (v. 11c). This is the second part of God's witness and it is this element that the opponents reject. Here the author is very careful in what he says and what he does not say. The intent of the author is to call attention to the importance of the Son in the giving of life, and so he does not say that life consists in having the Spirit although that is a central conviction of both groups. If there is some ambiguity remaining at the end of this statement, it seems deliberate and will be cleared up in the next aspect of the witness.

In v. 12 the author explains, by means of another set of contrasting parallels, that "the one 'having' (that is, 'believing in,' 'accepting the role of') the Son has life." "The one not 'having' the Son of God does not have life." Thus, the author comes to the most disputed point. While the opponents say that Jesus was important as proclaimer of the Spirit's outpouring and therefore the outpouring of eternal life, they would not agree that they have to believe that the role of the Son is permanent. But the author makes it clear that the opponents are wrong. Thus, the author ends the major part of his argument in the Letter with two of his strongest comments about the opponents: (1) by not having proper belief in the Son, the opponents reject the witness of God the Father, in whom they claim to believe, and in so doing they make God a liar, and (2) by failure to believe in the Son the opponents do not, in fact, have life. Although they claim to have eternal life, because they reject the Son, they do not. Thus, they have lost the claim to the two central elements of their own religious convictions!

Looking back over this section, we see that the author has adduced two witnesses that show the opponents are wrong. Both of these are witnesses that the opponents would recognize as valid and reliable witnesses: the Spirit and God the Father. The opponents have constantly acknowledged both the Spirit and the Father, and yet they reject what the Spirit and the Father have to witness about Jesus. In the next section, the author will continue the theme of this section and will add additional important reflections, but at the same time he will begin to indicate that he is approaching the end of his Letter.

Addendum: Are There Sacramental References in 5:6-8?

Some modern scholars (among them, Schnackenburg, Smith, and Strecker) see a sacramental reference in 5:6-8, in the expression regarding coming in water and in blood. However, the majority of scholars reject this view (among these, R. E. Brown, Culpepper, Grayston, Klauck, Smalley, Painter). Schnackenburg has put forward the sacramental theory with the greatest detail and so it is on his arguments that I will focus.[9] Schnackenburg holds that the first reference to water and

9. Schnackenburg, *Epistles* 235-37.

blood (in v. 6) refers to the historical events of the baptism and death of Jesus. However, in v. 7 these same symbols are considered "not as events but as elements."[10] Water refers to the discussion of Baptism in chapter 3 of the Gospel; and blood refers to the discussion of the Eucharist in chapter 6. And both derive their life-giving power from the Spirit and prolong the saving message within the community. For Schnackenburg, what signals this change in meaning is the fact that when water and blood are spoken of as witnesses, they together with the reference to the Spirit are introduced in the masculine gender, even though the words themselves are all neuter. Second, he argues that the fact that water and blood are said to *witness* suggests that this is a function the water and blood have within the community rather than within the ministry and that the author has the sacramental actions of Baptism and Eucharist in mind.

Strecker, like Schnackenburg, argues that the reference in v. 6a ("through water and blood") is not a reference to sacraments but is an anti-docetic expression affirming that Jesus' ministry was important from the time of his baptism to the time of his death.[11] It is only with the unexpected change of preposition from "through" *(dia)* to "in" *(en)* in v. 6bcd that a sacramental reference is introduced.[12] Strecker agrees that v. 6a refers to events in the ministry of Jesus and that the switch of the preposition from "through" *(dia)* to "in" *(en)* signals the shift to sacramental references.

Schnackenburg goes on to note that, while John 19:34 has spoken of "blood and water," 1 John now reverses the order to "water and blood" in order to reflect the order of reception of the sacraments within the community. Thus, in this reading, the opponents accept Baptism but reject the Eucharist. Schnackenburg and Strecker also point to what they see as parallels in the views of known docetic opponents in the early second century, most notably Ignatius of Antioch. According to Ignatius, his own opponents abstained from the Eucharist "because they do not consider the Eucharist to be the flesh of Jesus who suffered for our sins."[13]

However, other scholars point out a number of difficulties with seeing references to sacraments in these verses. Chief among their objections is their rejection of the possibility that the words "water" and "blood" could refer to different entities in v. 6a and in v. 6bcd. The order of the two nouns is also a very weak basis on which to argue for a sacramental interpretation.[14] Elsewhere in the New Testament "bread" is used as a reference to the Eucharist but never the term "blood" alone. When the Johannine tradition speaks of the Eucharist, it uses the combined term "flesh and blood," not just "blood."[15] Strecker finds little problem with this and pro-

---

10. Schnackenburg, *Epistles* 236.

11. Strecker, *Epistles* 183-86, here 186.

12. Strecker, *Epistles* 183.

13. Ignatius, *Smyrneans* 7.1.

14. Painter (*Epistles* 306) proposes that the order of the words is determined by the fact that the opponents mention water and so the author takes that up first.

15. Brown, *Epistles* 582-83; Smalley, *Epistles* 277.

poses that, in the Gospel, when the reference to "blood" is combined with "flesh," one finds the Eucharistic language of John 6:51-58. But this does not take account of the fact that the word *sarx* appears nowhere in the present context.[16]

While a comparison of the Johannine opponents with the opponents of Ignatius can at times be fruitful, as employed here, such a comparison entails two problems. First, the terminology used in 1 John is not that of the docetic opponents of Ignatius who speak of the "flesh" *(sarx)* of Jesus rather than his "blood." Second, if Baptism and Eucharist are thought to be discussed in 1 John 5:7 because they were challenged by the opponents, why is there no mention of problems regarding Baptism in Ignatius?

Finally, in the Gospel, the references to sacramental actions are quite clear, particularly in 3:3-5 (Baptism); 6:51-58 (Eucharist); and 20:22 (forgiveness of sin). In other words, the tradition knew how to speak of sacraments explicitly. This makes it more difficult to think that the author of 1 John would resort to such oblique references if he intended to introduce them at all. In the light of these factors, I do not think that there is sufficient evidence to find references to ritual sacraments in these verses.

Addendum: Chrismation in 5:8?

W. Nauck,[17] followed by de la Potterie,[18] has argued that the reference to the Spirit in 5:8 is a symbolic reference to a ritual act of anointing. Both trace this ritual through the Syrian church and argue for references to it in 1 John. This proposal has not gained wide acceptance. A major problem is that the Spirit is said to witness to the water and blood and, if "water" and "blood" (vv. 6-7) are symbols of Baptism and Eucharist, the Spirit should not be witnessing to but should be conceived of as alongside water and blood as symbols.[19]

Addendum: A Brief Note on the Johannine Comma

The "Johannine Comma" is a term used to refer to a lengthy addition appearing after v. 7a and before v. 8 in many later manuscripts.[20] In English translation, vv. 7-8 together with the addition (indicated by italics in the following) read: "For there are three that are witnessing *in heaven, the Father, the Word, and the Holy Spirit; and*

---

16. Strecker, *Epistles* 184.

17. W. Nauck, *Tradition* 147-82.

18. De la Potterie, *Vie* 107-67, esp. 153.

19. For a critique of this theory, see Schnackenburg's review of Nauck's book in *BZ* 4 (1960) 297.

20. For extensive discussion of the Comma and bibliography, see Brown, *Epistles* 775-87.

these three are one. And there are three that bear witness in earth, the Spirit, and the water, and the blood, and these three are as one." The Comma first appears, not in a manuscript of the New Testament, but in the *Liber Apologeticus* 1.4 of Priscillian (d. A.D. 385). Apparently it was first introduced into margins of biblical manuscripts as a reflection on the Trinity. It does not appear in any Greek manuscript before the fourteenth century and even then it is added primarily as a gloss to earlier manuscripts. It does not appear in manuscripts of the Old Latin until the seventh century or in manuscripts of the Vulgate until the eighth century. Until the year A.D. 1000, it appeared almost exclusively in Latin manuscripts of Spanish origin. Since it is not part of the original text of the Letter, it does not concern us here.

Prayer for Sin and Conclusion

13I wrote these things to you
    in order that you might know
        that you have eternal life,
        believing in the name of the Son of God.

14And this is the confidence that we have before him [God],
    that if we ask for anything according to his [God's] will
        he [God] hears us.

15And if we know
    that he [God] hears us regarding whatever we ask for,

we know
    that we have the requests
        that we have requested from him [God].

16If anyone sees his brother
    +sinning a sin not unto death,
        +he [the believer] will ask,
            +and
        +he [God] will give life to him [the sinner],
    +to those [sinners] not sinning unto death.

    There is a sin-unto-death.
    I do not say that a person should make a request about that.

+17Every injustice
    +sin
        +(is)
            +and

+there is
+a sin
+not unto death.

18 We know
that everyone begotten of God does not sin,
but the one begotten of God protects himself
and the Evil One does not touch him.

19 We know
that we are of God
and the whole world lies in the grasp of the Evil One.

20 We know
that the Son of God has come,
and he has given us insight
so that we know the True One.
And we are
in the True One,
in his Son, Jesus Christ.
This is the True God
and eternal life.

21 Dear Children, guard yourselves from idols.

NOTES TO 5:13-21

V. 13 believing The Greek participle is in the dative case, agreeing grammatically with the more distant dative of "you" in the first clause rather than agreeing, as would be expected, with the nominative subject of "might know." It is one of many unusual grammatical and stylistic features of this unit.

V. 14 the confidence This is the fourth occurrence of this term (Gk: *parrēsia*) in 1 John and in each case it appears in a context that is meant to give true confidence to the believer. In 2:28, it is confidence at the Parousia of Christ; in 3:21, it is confidence with respect to forgiveness of sin; in 4:17, it is confidence on the Day of Judgment. Here it is confidence in prayer.

before him — according to his will — he hears us The antecedents to these three pronouns are ambiguous. However, the same person is being referred to in all three cases and there are three factors that point to the antecedent being God. First, the last person mentioned was the Son of God, but one could argue that the author is actually thinking of "God" as the antecedent since that was literally the last person mentioned. Second, the only other mention of doing something according to someone's "will" is in the phrase "will of God" in 2:17. That would also support seeing "God" as the antecedent here. Finally, in material that comes from the third edition of the Gospel, there is no doubt that petition is made directly to God (but in the name of Jesus — cf. 14:13; 16:23b-24, 26-27). Consequently, the evidence that God is the antecedent is consistent and probably correct.

V. 15 that he hears us regarding whatever we ask for The grammar here is somewhat awkward. After "hearing," there is a double object: *whom* he hears ("us") (in the genitive case as is normal) and *what* he hears (in the accusative). I have inserted the word "regarding" to clarify the relationship. The antecedent of the subject pronoun is "God."

V. 16 sinning a sin This is the third cognate accusative the author has used in the last seven verses.

he will ask The "he" here refers to the person who prays for his brother.

and he There are several possibilities for this clause. The one who does the giving could be understood as either God, Jesus, or the petitioner (who through his/her prayer could be said to give life). The person to whom life is given is almost surely the sinner although some have argued that life is given to the petitioner because of his love for his/her brother.

A number of scholars (among them R. E. Brown, Schnackenburg, Klauck) lean in the direction of considering the believer to be the subject of the verb. One main argument in favor of this view is that the subject of both clauses is the same. However, to have different subjects for both clauses is not a problem. It would be the equivalent of saying "I will ask and he will do it." In this case, "he" would refer to God. Since the one being petitioned throughout is God, it is logical to conclude that the one giving life will also be God. To say that the fellow believer gives the life would be unique in the Johannine writings. As we will see in the following Note, it is also almost certain that the final "him" is the sinner.

One might well ask why the sinner would need life to be given to him/her if the sin is not "unto death." Ordinarily one would think that the more serious sin-unto-death would be the type of sin that requires "giving life" again, but that is ruled out by the author's words. It is likely that the words should not be taken so literally. The problem as a whole cannot be resolved until the notion of sin-unto-death is understood. Here I will presume the conclusions of the following Note and suggest that "giving life" means that God will strengthen the person with life so that the person can resist sin.

to him, to those The singular and the plural here refer to the same person. That is, life could be given to anyone (or many) sinning a sin not unto death.

This combination is noteworthy for the obvious lack of grammatical agreement in the shift from the singular to the plural in a statement where the object is the same in both cases. The parallelism rules out any possibility that the antecedent of "him" is the petitioner. This lack of proper grammatical agreement is also an indication that we cannot be certain to find careful nuancing or subtle expression in the surrounding verses either!

not sinning unto death The distinction between the two kinds of sin in this verse appears nowhere else in the Johannine tradition. This observation, coupled with the fact that the distinction is of immense importance since one should not even pray about forgiveness from sin-unto-death, has led to great discussion.

The meaning of "sin not unto death" can best be understood from an analysis of the brief chiasm in v. 17. This chiasm forces the reader to ask what the relationship is between the first and last elements of the arrangement: "every injustice" and "sin not unto death." Does v. 17 intend to identify the two or to distinguish them? Since it is clear from the overall context that the author is dividing all sin into two classes, then "every injustice" must be one or the other. Yet it is difficult to believe that the author is saying that "every injustice" is sin-unto-death! Consequently, it seems reasonable to conclude that the author understands "every injustice" to refer to the wide variety of less serious moral infractions. In that case, "sin not unto death" is almost surely a term that is applied to "ordinary" acts of "injustice." This is confirmed by looking back to 1:9 where it was said (in the only other use of *adikia*) that "He cleanses us from all injustice *(apo pasēs adikias)*."

There is a sin-unto-death The meaning of sin-unto-death is more difficult to determine. A related question is why the author says that he is not saying they should pray about that. Because both issues are related they will be treated together in the following Note.

I do not say that a person should make a request Although the Greek word *hina* usually expressed the purpose of an action and is translated "in order that," here the combination *legō hina* reflects a weakened use of the term and should be translated: ". . . say that." Such a combination often appears after verbs of request (cf. BDAG 476 [*hina*, section 2, g]). The word order of the Greek is also important here. Literally, these words would be translated: "Not about that do I say that a person should pray." The author is attempting to focus his readers' attention on their response to sin that is *not* unto death. The author is not addressing the necessity of praying for those who have sinned a "sin-unto-death," but neither does he explicitly forbid it. At the same time, the author mentions sin-unto-death four times in vv. 16-17, and he takes such pains to distinguish it from "sin-not-unto-death" that it is clear that, for the author, sin-unto-death is a completely other class of offense.

As was indicated above, there are various explanations put forward about why a request should not be made regarding sin-unto-death, and these are related to the various proposals regarding the meaning of this type of sin.

Some have argued that the verse intends to say that the believer does not have to pray about the most serious of sins but should trust the resolution of those to God. This possibility is favored by Schnackenburg (*Epistles* 251).

A theory that avoids the issue altogether makes a distinction between the use of *aiteō* (to request) and *erōtaō* (to ask questions) and argues that the believer should pray but should not ask questions about it. This is unlikely. Others propose that *aiteō* is used of requests from a superior while *erōtaō* is used of requests from equals and that therefore it is a matter of *how* to ask. But this distinction between verbs is not consistent in the Johannine literature (e.g., John 4:40, 47; 19:31).

Some understand sin-unto-death in relation to Old Testament texts that speak of sins leading to death (e.g., Num 18:22; Deut 22:26, etc.). However, these are sins that lead to *physical* death while it is evident that the author of 1 John is speaking of *spiritual* death. Others have thought it refers to what was later called mortal and venial sin. Another view holds that prayer is only to be directed at a brother or sister who sins, and those outside the community are not to be prayed for. Some have thought that it refers to the distinction between unintentional and intentional sin as is found in the Old Testament (e.g., Lev 4; Num 15:27-31; Deut 17:12). Such "intentional sin" was thought to be unforgivable and so it would be inappropriate to pray for it. Others compare it to the unforgivable sin of Mark 3:29 or to the similar sin mentioned in 1 Cor 5:5 and Heb 6:4-8 and 10:26-31.

However, recent commentators (e.g., R. E. Brown, Smalley, Strecker, Klauck, Painter, Beutler) have come to a considerable consensus that the sin-unto-death is the sin of secession. Thus, the author's opponents are the ones who have committed this sin. I agree with this view and will discuss it more in the Interpretation, where I will also discuss my own view as to why this sort of sin is excluded from prayer.

V. 18 everyone begotten of God does not sin This is almost a verbal repetition of 3:9 where the same idea was expressed chiastically. Again the author argues from the action that is seen (avoidance of sin) to the spiritual reality (this person is truly begotten of God) that is unseen.

but the one begotten of God protects himself There are several problems associated with determining the meaning of this statement. The first is a textual problem near the beginning of v. 18c, which reads "begetting" rather than "begotten." In the past, a few scholars have argued that this is the correct reading and that it is this "begetting" that protects the individual. This is the reading that was adopted by Jerome's Vulgate but appears in only two Greek minuscules and in a few other late sources. This is not a serious option today. A second question is whether "the one begotten of God" (in v. 18c) refers to the believer or to Jesus. Nowhere else in the Johannine literature is it said that Jesus is "begotten" of God, yet this is often said of the believer. Consequently, this second is the more likely explanation. In addition, it would be extraordinary to have practically the same expression in both v. 18b and v. 18c refer to the believer in the first case and to Jesus in the second. Those who favor this position argue that Jesus is the expected opponent of the Evil One, but it is clear from 2:13, 14 that members of the community are said to conquer the Evil One, so this is not a problem.

The third problem is the meaning of the Greek verb *tēreō*, which is regularly translated "keep." The verb *tēreō* is often used with "commandments" and "words" (for its usage, see at John 8:51 and 1 John 2:3). The closest parallels to the present usage are in John 17:11, 12, 15, where Jesus says that he has kept the disciples in the Father's name (17:12) and where he prays that the Father keep them in his own name and where he says: "I do not pray that you take them out of the world but that you keep them from the Evil One" (*. . . all' hina tērēsēs autous ek tou ponērou*). Here the verb "keep" is best translated "guard" or "protect." The meaning of *tēreō* in v. 18c is surely to be understood in the same way as in John 17:11, 12, 15, except that in those instances this "guarding" was done by the Father and the Son. But the parallel in John 17:15 is particularly close in that the protection is said to be from "the Evil One," as in 1 John 5:18d. If we recall that those instances (which come from the third edition of the Gospel) were written after 1 John, we have another example of how the thought of 1 John is developed by the later author.

The fourth problem is who the object of "protecting" is intended to be. This last problem is complicated somewhat by the presence of textual variants for the pronoun and so it could read either "him" or "himself." The textual evidence favors "him," and the variant can easily be explained as an attempt to make it clearer that the one begotten of God is to protect himself. However, it is commonly noted by scholars that reading *auton* ("him") in v. 18c is not a problem (in spite of what the scribes thought who changed it to *heauton*) and because it can be used reflexively (BDF §283). Some understand "him" to refer to God and so the believer "keeps" God. However, this would mean that "him" in v. 18b and in v. 18c would refer to different individuals.

We have seen above that, in 1 John, the believer is thought of as being able to protect him/herself from the Evil One. This is evident from 2:13, 14, where it is said that the "Young People" (that is, believers) have "conquered the Evil One." Moreover, if John 17:11-15 comes from the third edition, it was composed after 1 John and it would not be appropriate to use it as a model for the usage in 1 John. In any event, in Johannine thought there is regularly a reciprocity between the effort of Jesus/the Father and the effort that the believer himself/herself must exert and it would be inappropriate to rule out one or the other element.

The author of 1 John is referring (in both v. 18b and v. 18c) to the need for the believer to take an active role and to exert effort on his/her own behalf. In v. 18b, he speaks of the effort necessary not to sin; and, in v. 18c, he speaks of the effort to guard himself. If he does exert this necessary effort, the Evil One will not take hold of him.

Brown (*Epistles* 621) argues that the main objection to this proposal is that, of the 25 times the verb *tēreō* appears in the Johannine literature, this is the only instance where it is used with a reflexive pronoun. However, this view of the statistics distorts the picture since, of those 25 instances, only this and the three instances of John 17 have the meaning "protect." Moreover, if the three instances in John 17 belong to the third edition of the Gospel (as I have argued) and were composed after 1 John, there would be no pattern of contrary usage since this present instance would be the first occurrence of the verb with this meaning.

The second problem listed by Brown regarding this view is the awkward repetition of "the one begotten of God" in v. 18b and v. 18c. However, the repetition of "the one begotten of God" in v. 18b and v. 18c is undoubtedly intended to emphasize that the author is speaking of what is characteristic of "the one who is begotten of God." First, the one (truly) begotten of God does not sin and, secondly, the one who is (truly) begotten of God guards himself, and the Evil One does not take him into his grasp. As we shall see in the Interpretation, this view also fits well within the immediate context.

V. 19 and the whole world lies in the grasp of the Evil One This is the fifth and last time the author will make reference to "the Evil One" in his Letter (cf. 2:13, 14; 3:12; 5:18, 19). This accounts for all but one of the instances of the word *ponēros* ("evil") in 1 John, and that one instance is a reference to the "works" of Cain that were evil because Cain himself was "of the Evil One." In retrospect, it is apparent that, for the author of 1 John, this was a favorite designation of the personal source of evil opposed to God and Jesus.

The verse expresses well the apocalyptic viewpoint that the world is under the control of Satan. For an explanation of the full paradigm underlying this statement, see at John 3:19 and at 1 John 2:13.

V. 20 he has given "He" here is Jesus, the Son of God.

insight (Gk: *dianoia*) This is the only Johannine use of the term.

the True One "True" as an adjective *(alēthinos, alēthēs)* appears seldom in 1 John and does not have a special meaning. Chapter 2:8 says that the author's statement that the commandment about which he is writing is new is "true" because (2:8) the "true" light is already shining. In 2:27, the anointing that the believer receives is said to be true. However, the overall concept of truth has played a large role in the Gospel and it is in this context that the reference to God as the True One should be viewed.

The "True One" is God as can be seen from the fact that the Son of God has given insight and this insight is oriented toward knowing another: God. Moreover, in vv. 20-21, the True One is distinguished from his Son. In John 17:3 (from the third edition), God the Father will be identified with this same title.

V. 21 guard yourselves In v. 18c, it was said that the one begotten of God "guards himself" *(tērei auton)*. Although the Greek verb here *(phylassō)* is different, the meaning is much the same. It is an exhortation to the members of the author's community to put forth the effort to prevent succumbing to the temptation of idols. It is noteworthy that in the third edition of the Gospel (17:12) the term is used alongside *tēreō* with no difference in meaning.

from idols. Although the term "idols" could refer to the gods of the various pagan religions at the time, it is unlikely that the author would introduce such a radically different topic here. For Painter (*Epistles* 80, 330), the presence of this term is an indication that the social context of the Johannine community was to a large extent non-Jewish. However, there has been no indication of such a makeup to this point in the Letter and to draw such a conclusion solely from the use of this word is not warranted.

Smith (*Epistles* 137) suggests that the reason for the reference to idols here is probably due to a desire to create a contrast with the statements of v. 20 about "true" God. The author of 1 John has spoken of sin and failure to believe properly. These failures are characteristic of the opponents; their ideas are false and their beliefs are false, so their "god" is false and all that is connected with it can be summarized as an "idol." Throughout the Old Testament, idols were gods that were in opposition to the true God and it is likely that it is in this sense that the term should be understood here. The SDQ seem to reflect a similar understanding. For example, 1QS 2:11-12 says: "Cursed be the man who enters this Covenant while walking among the idols of his heart, who sets up before himself his stumbling-block of sin so that he may backslide." See also 1QS 2:17; 1QH 4:9-11, 15; CD 20:8-10. Idols thus become the symbol for all that is false.

OVERVIEW OF 5:13-21

In this final section of the Letter, the author continues his discussion of belief in the Son of God in relation to eternal life. The author reminds his readers that he has written to assure them that they do in fact have eternal life since they have correct belief in the Son of God.

But now he also speaks about those who have sinned and are in need of having eternal life restored. He speaks of ordinary transgressions and contrasts these with the sin-unto-death. The sin-unto-death, as we shall see, is the sin that results from holding the viewpoint of the opponents. This type of sin cannot be prayed for. But the believer is able to pray to God for his/her fellow believer who has sinned and God will give that person life.

One final time the author sets forth the alternatives in stark dualistic contrast, with the assurance that the member of the author's community is "of God." The author then issues a final reminder that there will be a future coming of the Son of God (in judgment), but the Son of God has given them "awareness" so they have eternal life. He ends by encapsulating his message in a single sentence, exhorting his readers to guard themselves from "idols."

THE STRUCTURE OF 5:13-21[1]

The most pervasive structural element of these verses is the repetitive parallelism of "we know." It appears first in double parallelism in v. 15a and 15c and

---

1. Klauck (*Erste Johannesbrief* 23, 318-20) considers v. 13 the conclusion of the Letter proper and vv. 14-21 as an Epilogue and the work of someone other than the author. This is the only editorial addition Klauck would see in the Letter. Smith (*Epistles* 121-22) also considers this a possibility and suggests that the remaining verses are added to address issues that arose after the original Letter was written. Brown (*Epistles* 631-33) argues that the evidence for the verses being the work of the author is stronger than the evidence for a different hand. I would agree (as does Strecker, *Epistles* 198-99).

Although there are terms that appear only here in the Letter (for example, *dianoia*, *tērein auton*), vocabulary not found in the Gospel also appears once or seldom in other parts of the Letter (for example, *koinōnia* [1:3, 6], *hilasmos* [2:2], *pistos* [1:9], *elpis* [3:3]). Although the introduction of the themes of petition and forgiveness of sin as well as the mention of "idols" in the

again in triple parallelism in vv. 18, 19, 20. Among the minor rhetorical devices used by the author are definition (v. 14a), pleonasm (v. 15) and repetition (vv. 14b-15). Finally, brief chiasms in v. 16 and v. 17 are helpful in determining the meaning of "sin-not-unto-death."

THE INTERPRETATION OF 5:13-21

The author had discussed eternal life most recently in 5:11. It continues to be the overriding theme as the author begins (v. 13) the conclusion to his Letter. He now reviews briefly the reasons he has had for writing to them and, in doing so, he echoes his statement in 1:4 at the beginning of the Letter. The author of 1 John is convinced that eternal life is a present possession and he is writing to assure his readers of this reality.[2] He wants them to know that they have eternal life *because* they believe in the name of the Son of God.[3] It is those who have rejected proper belief in Jesus that do not have life.

Although the Letter is almost over, or perhaps because of this fact, the author now (vv. 14-15) becomes particularly abrupt in the way he introduces the following topics. Without preparation, he/she begins speaking of the confidence that the believer has before God, a confidence that is the basis for making petitions of God and for the assurance of their being granted.[4] In spite of the abrupt way this is introduced, the confidence the believer should have in prayer is detailed at some length. This, then, constitutes the first reference to the community's understanding of petitionary prayer.[5]

---

final verse are quite awkward and abrupt, such abruptness is also found elsewhere in the Letter (1:1-4; 2:1, 25; 2:28-3:10). The grammatical ambiguities that characterized the Letter are also evident here as is the parallelism of "we know"; and the use of chiasms is typical.

2. For a final time, the author emphasizes the "realized" aspect of eternal life. He also recognizes a future dimension to this eternal life. This dimension is determined by one's actions, as we have seen throughout (esp. 2:28-3:10) and so it is possible to lose this life (v. 16).

3. The word order of the Greek in this verse is designed to have a special effect but it is difficult to capture that effect in an English translation. The author begins by saying "These things I wrote to you, in order that you may know that you have life that is eternal." And then he ends the sentence with a participial phrase agreeing grammatically with "you" in the first part of the verse: "[I wrote to you . . .] the ones believing in the name of the Son of God." The effect is to call attention to the fact that it is precisely *because* they believe in the name of the Son of God that they have eternal life.

4. That the author intends to begin with an emphasis on confidence is evident from the way he puts this word at the beginning of its sentence. But the topic then shifts to that of making petitions.

5. Although petitionary prayer had been mentioned briefly in 3:22a, this is the first significant development of the topic. It will be taken up again in the third edition of the Gospel (cf. John 16:23b-24, 26-28).

The believer is to have confidence that, if he asks for anything according to the will of God, God will hear the individual. The author then goes on to draw out the logical conclusion of this. But, in doing so, he first repeats much of his previous statement and then presents, as the conclusion, his conviction that God has answered "the requests that we have requested from him." The overall effect of the wording is labored.

In v. 16, the reader learns the reason for introducing the topic of prayer. This is not a discussion of general petitionary prayer. Rather, the author introduces the topic so that the believer can pray for the fellow-believer who has sinned and God will grant the person life. And the believer will do so in confidence that God will hear his/her petition (cf. v. 15).

The author then speaks about "sin-unto-death." He explains that he is not suggesting that they make a request about that. As was explained in the Note, the notion of sin-unto-death appears only here in the Johannine literature. Although the term itself has mysterious connotations and has been the object of protracted discussion by scholars, recently there has been a growing consensus that it refers simply to the sin of the opponents, a sin that is founded on false belief and on wrong behavior and so leads to spiritual death.

This is also confirmed by the larger context of the Gospel and Letter. The central claim for both groups within the community was that they had passed over from death to life because of their belief. In the second edition, Jesus had said (John 5:24) that the one believing "has crossed over from death to life" *(metabebēken ek tou thanatou eis tēn zōēn)*. The author of 1 John agrees and provides a test for having passed over when he says (1 John 3:14): "We know that we have crossed over from death to life" *(hoti metabebēkamen ek tou thanatou eis tēn zōēn)* ("because we love the brothers").

When we take into account the immediate context of the references to "sin-unto-death," we find confirmation of this view. At the end of the previous section (5:11-12), the author has said "that God has given us life and that this life is in his Son. The one who has the Son has life; the one not having the Son of God does not have life." At the beginning of the present section (5:13), he confirmed "that you have eternal life, believing in the name of the Son of God." Thus, the context stresses twice that life comes through the Son and the one not having the Son does not have life. Thus, for the author of 1 John, the true sin "unto death" would be the sin that denies Jesus, the very source of the power to cross over from death to life!

If this is, in fact, the meaning of the sin-unto-death, why was it that the author did not encourage praying for it? The various suggestions by scholars have been reviewed in the Note. Those that have gained most favor focus on the notion of unforgivable sin in various religious currents about the time of Jesus.

Within the Old Testament, several texts speak of a distinction between intentional and unintentional sin (Lev 4; Num 15:22-31; Ps 19:12-13). While unintentional sins could be atoned for, intentional sins could not. For example, in Num 15:22-31 the author says that the one who commits intentional sin is to be "utterly cut off; his iniquity shall be upon him." The same notion is evident in the writings of the Qumran community, where a person who committed an unintentional sin could be restored to the community after two years but the one who sinned intentionally would be banished forever.[6]

In the New Testament, we meet the notion of an unforgivable sin in Mark 3:29 (cf. Matt 12:32). In this instance, the issue is not intentional versus unintentional sin, but blasphemy against the Holy Spirit by attributing the power of Jesus to Satan. The one who commits this sin "can never have forgiveness but is guilty of an eternal sin." This sin is enormous precisely because it counters the very heart of Christian belief. The same could be said of the sin of the secessionists in John because they reject the role of Jesus in salvation.

It is also noteworthy that the text from Qumran as well as the Marcan and the Johannine texts are couched in an apocalyptic worldview. The language of dualism is by definition a language of extremes. The opposing parties are seen as under the influence of good and evil spirits. In such literature, there is little hope of change from one viewpoint to the other.[7] As the author says in v. 19: "we are of God and the whole world lies in the grasp of the Evil One!"

While these provide useful examples of decisions elsewhere in the religious thought of the time to classify some sins as outside the possibility of forgiveness, it is possible that we are able to get a glimpse of the specifically Johannine reasoning behind 1 John 5:16gh in the third edition of the Gospel. If we judge from the perspective of the community at the time of the third edition, not only are there clear references to the present possession of life that is "complemented" by a future perfection of that life at the coming of Jesus, but there is also a present judgment (John 3:18) that is complemented by a future judgment (John 5:27-29; 12:48) at the coming of Jesus.

As we have seen, in the context of 1 John, it would appear that it was the

---

6. Brown (*Epistles* 617) calls attention to the Hebrew text of *Jub.* 21:22, which cautions against sinning "a sin-unto-death before the Most High God; or He will hide His face from you . . . and root you out of the land and your seed from under heaven." Brown goes on to comment: "In John 3:18-21 the judgment of all human beings is based on whether they believe in the name of God's only Son and come to the light, or refuse to believe and prefer the darkness." (These verses come from what I would designate as the third edition and are undoubtedly intended to incorporate this viewpoint in the Gospel.)

7. The author of 2 John can urge his readers not to accept opponents into their houses: "For the one who gives him a greeting also takes part in his evil deeds" (2 John 11). Praying for those who sinned unto death would probably be seen (within a dualistic worldview) as somehow beyond the possibility of prayer, even though, under other circumstances, one would surely affirm the mercy that God extended to all sinners.

sin of the secessionists, the failure to believe properly, that was considered the "sin-unto-death." This was the sin that truly and definitively cut one off from the source of life. From the perspective of John 3:18 (from the third edition), the person who did not believe "in the name of the unique Son of God" had already been judged. Two things are noteworthy about the expression of belief here. First, John 3:18 (to believe "in the name of the unique Son of God") is carefully formulated in order to exclude the belief of the opponents as they appeared at the time of 1 John.[8] Second, we can appreciate even more fully the appropriateness of John 3:18 for the context of 1 John 5:16-18, when we note that the wording of John 3:18 is almost exactly the same as that of the statement in 1 John 5:13, where it was said that if a person believes "in the name of the Son of God" that person has life.[9]

Thus, 1 John says that those who believe "in the name of the Son of God" have life, and the third edition says that those who do not believe "in the name of the unique Son of God" are already judged. It may be here that we see the reason why the sin of non-belief or incorrect belief is called "sin-unto-death." The person who does not believe has committed the sin-unto-death and has already undergone judgment. As a result, there is no place for prayer on that person's behalf.

This view of the unforgivability of the sin of the secessionists is a view that conforms, in general lines, to the "unforgivable" sins of Qumran and of Mark's Gospel. They are all sins that strike at the heart of belief in God or Jesus. Yet at the same time, in the third edition of the Gospel, we see a rationale for the unforgivability of the sin that is articulated within the distinctive framework of Johannine theology.

Finally, I close with an observation on 5:16-17. It is noteworthy that the language used here does not speak in terms of atonement or sacrifice for sin but in terms that are quintessentially Johannine. When one sins, one loses life. One type of sin is so great that it is sin-unto-death and from that there is no rescue. But even lesser sin (every injustice, sin "not unto death") requires that life be given to the person, so that sin and freedom from sin can be said to be understood entirely in terms of life and death. Sin is essentially conceived of as taking away the life that had been given to the believer through rebirth in the Spirit of God!

The author now goes on (v. 17) to speak of lesser forms of sin. "Every in-

8. It will be recalled that the opponents would not agree that Jesus was the "unique" Son of God since they claimed that the status given the believer through being begotten of God raised them to a status equal to Jesus. For details, see Vol. 1, Part 4, Section 1 (Christology) and Section 9 (Anthropology).

9. For another echo of 5:13-18, see the references to "evil" and "the Evil One" in vv. 18-19 below.

justice" *(pasa adikia)* is sin, but these injustices are not "sins unto death." "Injustice" is not a common word in the Johannine vocabulary but it had appeared in 1:9, where it was said that if we confess our sins, "He forgives our sins and cleanses us from all injustice *(apo pasēs adikias).*" The parallelism between "sin" and "injustice" in 1:9 shows that sins that can be forgiven are referred to as acts of "injustice."[10] In 1:9, the author affirmed that the believer him/herself can obtain forgiveness for sins "if we confess our sins." Here, the author speaks of the role of the fellow community member in the process of forgiveness and the restoration of life. Yet there is no indication here of any sort of interaction between the two believers. Rather, the one is to pray to God that he may give life to the one sinning. It need not involve any external, ritual action.

In vv. 18-19, the author continues the theme of sin, but now speaks of the avoidance of sin and returns to the theme of perfectionism as he understands it. He affirms that "everyone born of God does not sin." But this perfectionism must be understood as the author has meant it, namely, that sinlessness is *characteristic* of the one begotten of God. Yet, the author has just spoken of the brother who has sinned and how prayer to God can result in life being restored to the person. Thus, the author does not deny that sin is possible for the believer but, at the same time, he makes it clear that it is typical of the one begotten of God *not* to sin.

The author's point throughout the Letter has been that one's status (e.g., "being born of God") is not simply a once-and-for-all state but is also determined by one's actions. This was particularly clear in his discussion of who is a child of God and who is a child of the devil in 2:28–3:10. There, the one acting justly "has been born from him [the Father]" (2:29b), but one's status of having been born from the Father can be determined by one's actions. Further, it is made clear in the same passage that *effort* is needed to reach the full stature of a child of God (3:3). Finally, it is there that we hear the words very similar to those of v. 18b: "Everyone abiding in him [Jesus] does not sin" (3:6). This statement, which is quite close to 5:18c, does not say that freedom from sin is automatic, but rather that it is characteristic of one who abides in Jesus not to sin. Thus, both in 2:28–3:10 and in 5:18, the author reminds the reader that, if he/she wants to claim genuinely to "abide in Jesus" and/or to be "begotten of God," that person must not sin since not sinning is characteristic of the one who truly abides in Jesus and of the one who is begotten of God. Thus, in the present verse, the author is *as much exhorting* his reader *as reminding* him/her that one who is (truly) begotten of God does not sin.

But the author now balances his first statement that the one begotten of

---

10. It should be recalled that this interpretation is supported and confirmed by the chiastic arrangement referred to earlier.

God does not sin, with a *positive* statement explaining (and exhorting) that the person must protect himself because, if he does guard himself, the Evil One will not seize control of him.[11] Thus, the effort the believer exerts will be successful in warding off the influence of the Evil One and so in avoiding sin. Then (v. 19), as if to summarize, the author reminds the readers of the most important distinction in their lives as believers: "We are of God and the whole world lies in the grasp of the Evil One."

Much earlier (2:13-14) the author had reminded the community (especially the Young People) that they had conquered the Evil One. Later he had contrasted Abel with Cain, who belonged to the Evil One and who acted as he did because his actions were "evil." Now, a final time, the author refers to the Evil One and portrays the opposition between the community and the Evil One in its starkest, dualistic form.[12]

In v. 20, the author reminds the reader that "the Son of God is coming." This is a point that had been denied by the opponents but was crucial for the believer. The Son of God will return in judgment and the believer's actions will be judged at that return.

In this, his final affirmation of the Letter, and in cryptic terms familiar to the community, he states the essentials of their belief: the Son of God has given the believer "insight" and this insight leads to knowledge of God the Father (the "True One"), and the believer has union with the True One and with his Son, Jesus Christ. And this is the True God and the source of eternal life.

While most of this statement would not be new for the believer, what is significant is that here that insight is said to come from Jesus rather than from the Spirit. In 2:20, it was said that the believer has an anointing from the Holy One and "knows all." Here "insight" comes from Jesus (compare also 2:27; 4:2-3a). Although his primary purpose is assurance, the way the author phrases his assurance reflects his intention to counter the views of the opponents. For the author of 1 John, it is important to show that Jesus does everything that the Spirit does.

11. In this respect, 5:18 also echoes the thought of 2:28–3:10 in that both speak of the effort needed to be sinless.

12. When we look ahead to the third edition of the Gospel, we see that the author will take over this term and make use of it three times (3:19; 7:7; and 17:15). In each case, we can see how closely the third author echoes the thought and apocalyptic worldview of the Letter. In John 3:19, the author comments through the words of Jesus that "the light has come into the world but people loved the darkness more than the light, for their works were evil" *(ēn gar autōn ponēra ta erga)*. In John 7:7, Jesus will say: "The world . . . hates me because I bear witness about it that its works are evil" *(hoti ta erga autou ponēra estin)*. In John 17:15, Jesus will pray that the Father not "take them [the disciples] out of the world, but that you [the Father] keep *[tērēsēs]* them from the Evil One *[ek tou Ponērou]*."

In v. 21, in a final and most abrupt comment, the author issues a last warning: "Children, guard yourselves from idols." Abrupt as this may sound to the modern reader, as we have seen in the Notes, "idols" was a term common to the religious literature of the time and was a symbol of all that was false. Its sudden introduction here is intended to summarize and encapsulate the entire enterprise of the opponents. Their teaching is false and to follow it would be to follow an idol. Consequently, the author's entire message can be summarized in these few words. With this sudden, final appeal, utilizing a symbol of such historical association and emotional impact, the author concludes his Letter.

THE SECOND LETTER OF JOHN

Introduction to 2 John

A. THE GENRE OF 2 JOHN

The Second Letter of John is a true letter to a Johannine community at some distance from that of the author.[1] This distinguishes it from 1 John, which is not a true letter, but also from 3 John, which is a letter to an individual rather than to a community.

Second John has the elements typical of an ancient letter, including the name of the sender and the addressee, a greeting, the expression of joy and then the formal request introduced by direct address. It ends with an expression of hope for a visit and greetings from others.[2]

Although it seems to be a letter intended for a single community, it is not impossible that it was intended to be circulated to a number of groups. There is nothing in the content of the Letter that would prevent it from having a broad application. In favor of seeing it as addressed to a single community, however, is the reference in v. 13 to the greetings "from your elect sister." Those who see it as a circular letter argue in response that this greeting is simply part of the letter convention.

---

1. Among modern scholars, a few continue to hold that 2 John is not a true letter. For example, Bultmann (*Epistles* 107-9) thinks that it was not addressed to a particular community but was "catholic" in nature, composed from 1 John and 3 John and given to communities as the need arose. Schmithals (*Johannesevangelium und Johannesbriefe* 285-86) holds a somewhat similar view.

2. A more detailed discussion of the form of ancient letters can be found in Appendix 6 (Formal Elements in Greek Letter Writing) in this volume.

B. WORLDVIEW

Although it is generally recognized that 1 John is written against the background of apocalyptic dualism, some scholars have suggested that 2 John is not. Strecker has argued that the apocalyptic worldview is present in 2 and 3 John but only in "rudimentary form" in contrast to 1 John. He sees this as an indication that they were written before the Gospel and before 1 John.[3]

J. Lieu represents a more radical view. She speaks repeatedly of the "loss of the dualist context" in 2 John.[4] From a review of her references to the lack of dualism, it becomes clear that, for Lieu, both members of a dualistic pair must be present for there to be evidence of dualism.[5] According to Lieu, to speak of "truth" (even in a context that contains other features normally associated with dualism) without explicit reference to "falsehood" cannot be said to be dualistic. This is an excessively high standard and one that fails to take account of the genre of 2 John. While 1 John was a theological tract, 2 John is an occasional letter. In 1 John, there is a formal description of the views of both the opponents and the author, and both views are associated with the opposed dualistic perspectives. The Second Letter of John is written not for the purposes of describing both groups and the features that mark them as belonging to one or the other. Rather, 2 John addresses specific problems, presumes the framework of apocalyptic and simply makes use of elements of the worldview as necessary.

Moreover, there are statements in 2 John that can only be understood fully in an apocalyptic framework. First, the statement in v. 7 ("many deceivers have gone out into the world") is almost identical verbally to the comments about false prophets going out into the world in 1 John 4:1. In 1 John 4:1-6, the mention of the world is then developed in a dualistic sense. Second, the references to "deceivers" and to "the Deceiver" in 2 John 7 echo apocalyptic dualism and the reference to the Spirit of "Deception" in 1 John 4:6. Finally, the author uses "Antichrist" as the embodiment of evil in 2 John 7; this is a figure associated with the apocalyptic hour as is evident from 1 John 2:18.

Thus, 2 John 7 reflects three central elements of 1 John 4:1-6, one of the most clearly dualistic sections of 1 John. It is much more likely that 2 John 7 represents a less developed form of the argument found in 1 John 4:1-6 than that

---

3. Strecker, *Epistles* 4, 226.

4. Lieu, *Second and Third* 69, 84, 87, 175. In this she builds on the earlier work of Bergmeier, "Verfasserproblem" 95-100. (The term "dualist" is hers.)

5. See especially Lieu, *Second and Third* 84, but also 87. Her position is confirmed by the way she speaks of the "Spirit of Truth" in the Gospel. Because this term does not appear in explicit contrast with the "Spirit of Deception," as it does in 1 John, Lieu claims that it cannot be understood dualistically (175).

1 John 4:1-6 is an expansion of 2 John 7. The statement in 2 John 7 is simply a condensation appropriate for such a short letter.

A second example is the statement in 2 John 8 that speaks of not losing "those things that you have worked for but that you receive a full recompense." While there is no direct discussion of a final judgment, this verse implies one at which the believer will receive either reward or punishment. This is also typical of apocalyptic. Yet another example of the way the apocalyptic worldview is implicit throughout the Letter is the notion of love that is restricted to members of the community. This is a concept that also derives from the dualistic mentality, as we have seen in the discussion of mutual love in 1 John.[6]

Therefore, while it is true that categories of the apocalyptic worldview are developed less extensively than in 1 John, this does not mean that 2 John is any less influenced by that worldview in general.

C. THE STRUCTURE

In keeping with the letter format, the structure of 2 John in its simplest form consists of three parts: (1) opening matters (vv. 1-3); (2) body of the Letter (vv. 4-11); (3) closing conventions (vv. 12-13). Other elements of the Letter are subsidiary to these, and divisions of the body of the Letter within the Interpretation will reflect those subdivisions.

D. THE CIRCUMSTANCES OF THE COMMUNITY

This Letter is written to a satellite Johannine community at some distance from that of the Elder. The Elder had written 1 John to deal with a division within the community. While it was a division evident within his own community, it had a larger dimension since it was, in fact, an interpretation that concerned the tradition as a whole. That "Letter" had been concerned to explain the errors of the opponents and to exhort the community to avoid them while remaining faithful to the tradition they had had "from the beginning."

An older view, that still has supporters, was proposed by Houlden, who argues that 2 John was a Letter written after the Gospel and that the reference to having much to write (v. 12) was a reference to the matters written of in 1 John.

---

6. See also Vol. 1, Part 4, Section 8.3. Lieu herself recognizes this but evidently does not see its implications for the overall worldview when she says (*Second and Third* 73) that such love "is reflected elsewhere in early Christian literature, largely from a theologically dualist and sectarian context like the Gospel of Thomas." See also her footnote 67 there, which gives dualistic parallels in the SDQ.

Houlden argues that 2 John was written, hoping that the visit would soon take place, but when it did not eventuate, 1 John was composed to put those matters in writing and to make up for the visit that had not taken place.[7]

Painter argues that 2 John was the accompanying Letter for 1 John and conveyed the personal greetings and communication absent from 1 John.[8] Yet 2 John has a specific, self-contained purpose (see below) that does not include any reference to another document it was accompanying.

In 2 John, the specific occasion for writing seems to be to warn the community about the possibility of proponents of false teaching coming to the community as visitors.[9] These visiting missionaries would be intending to win over "the Elect Lady" to their point of view. Does this mean that the community had not previously encountered such teachers? It is difficult to tell. Because the exhortation of 2 John focuses so intensely and so exclusively on the matter of truth and of correct teaching and because of v. 4, which speaks of "some of your children walking in the truth," it seems that although the community had already experienced some influence from false teaching, the two groups had become even more clearly distinguished from one another, and so it was now all the more necessary to reject the false teachers' request for any sort of reception by the community.

E. LITERARY TECHNIQUES

The Second Letter of John is a brief document, and so we cannot expect the number of literary techniques that we found in 1 John. In the light of that fact, it is remarkable that we find a majority of the techniques characteristic of 1 John. As we will also see, the use of these techniques is concentrated in vv. 4-6, which represents the heart of the author's theological argument and sets forth the principles that undergird the advice given in the remainder of the Letter.

1. Catchword (or "Chaining") Technique

In 2 John, there is one extended example of chaining, and that appears in 2 John 4-6, which constitute the heart of the Elder's argument. The chaining there consists of "commandment" (v. 4b) with "commandment" (v. 5a); "love" (v. 5c) with "love" (v. 6a); and then a return to "commandment" (v. 6b), which links to "commandment" (v. 6b also). This extensive chaining will be discussed further in the Commentary.

7. Houlden, *Epistles* 31-32.
8. Painter, *Epistles* 356.
9. So also Culpepper, *Gospel and Epistles* 278.

2. Chiasm

There is one major chiasm in 2 John and it appears in vv. 4-6. There are also minor chiasms in v. 7 and in v. 10c-d.

3. Definition

We saw the extensive use of "definition" in 1 John. The same technique appears in 2 John 4-6. In v. 6a, we see "and this is the love," which defines the love spoken of in the love commandment; and in v. 6b the commandment that had been mentioned earlier is now defined and is introduced by the words "this is the commandment."

4. Reciprocity and Interrelatedness of Topics

In 2 John 4-6, the author makes various elements of the two Johannine commandments serve one another. Thus, he begins by arguing that they have a commandment and this commandment is that they love one another and this love is that we walk in the commandments. Then he moves again from the general definition of commandment to the specific requirement: ". . . that we walk in it." While this type of argument would seem somewhat trite to many, its theological purpose is clear. And so the author shows that the commandment to love one another supports the commandment to believe properly because we show love by exhibiting proper belief!

5. Parallelism

There are also a number of instances in which the author uses a kind of parallelism of thought. These are generally brief and of relatively little significance unlike the major instances apparent in 1 John. One example appears in v. 3, where the verse begins with three wishes (grace, mercy, and peace) that are followed by the two "sources" (from God . . . from Jesus) and then the parallel of "in truth" and "in love." Some minor parallelism is also evident in v. 9 and in v. 10.

6. Demonstration of Logical Argument

In addition to the presence of definitions themselves, there is also a chaining of these definitions. This is demonstrated in 2 John 6 ("this is the love that we walk according to his commandments; and this is the commandment . . . that we walk in it"). Together these are intended to create the impression of a careful logical sequence that cannot be refuted.

F. THE AUTHOR OF 2 JOHN

The view proposed here is that the author of 2 John is the same as that of 3 John and 1 John. The evidence for this is presented in the General Introduction to the Letters. The question whether the Elder, as the author of 2 and 3 John identifies himself, is to be identified with any of the classes of "elders" in early Christianity or with John the Elder is a complicated one and is discussed in detail in Appendix 8 (The Elder and the Elders) in this volume. The question of the relation between the Elder of 2 and 3 John and the Beloved Disciple is also complex and is discussed in detail in Appendix 9 (The Beloved Disciple) in this volume. The conclusion reached in those appendices is that "Elder" is the self-designation of the author of 2 and 3 John. He is the primary "witness" behind the tradition preserved in the Johannine literature, and it is primarily his witness that is preserved in the third edition of the Gospel. It is this same individual who is later referred to in the third edition of the Gospel as "the disciple whom Jesus loved."

G. THE DATE OF COMPOSITION

The Second Letter of John was probably written between the composition of the second and third editions of the Gospel. The evidence for this has been presented above and will not be discussed again here.[10]

H. THE PLACE OF COMPOSITION

This was discussed in the General Introduction to the Letters, where it was suggested that the meager information we have suggests that all the Letters were written in Ephesus or in the area around Ephesus.

---

10. The evidence that 1 John was composed before the third edition of the Gospel is presented in Vol. 1, in the discussion of the date of the third edition of the Gospel. The evidence indicating that 2 and 3 John were written after 1 John but before the third edition of the Gospel is presented in the General Introduction to the Letters.

Commentary and Notes on 2 John

1 The Elder to the Elect Lady and her children,
  whom I love in truth,
  and not I alone
    but all those who know the truth —
      2 through the truth abiding in us —
      and it will be with us forever.

3 May grace,
mercy and
peace
    from God the Father and
    from Jesus Christ, the son of the Father,
      be with you,
        in truth and
        in love.

*   *   *

4 I rejoiced greatly to find
  +some of your children walking in truth,
    +just as we received a commandment from the Father. 5 And now I ask
    you, Lady, (not as one writing a new commandment to you but one that
    we have had from the beginning)
      +that we love one another.
      +6 And this is the love,
    +that you walk according to his commandments; this is the

commandment, as you heard it from the beginning,
+that we walk in it.

+7 Because many deceivers have gone out into the world,
+persons not confessing Jesus Christ as coming in the flesh.
+This one is the Deceiver and the Antichrist.

8 Watch yourselves, in order that
you not lose those things for which you have worked but that
you receive a full recompense.
9 Everyone who is "progressive" and
who does not remain in the teaching of the Christ,
does not possess God;
the one who remains in the teaching has both the Father and the Son.

10 If someone approaches you and does not bring this teaching,
+do not receive
+him
+into your house
and
+greetings
+to him
+do not give.

11 For the one
who gives him a greeting also
takes part in his evil deeds.

12 Although I have many things to write to you,
I did not want to,
by paper and ink;
but I hope to be with you and
to speak face to face,
so that our joy may be the fullest.

13 The children of your elect sister greet you.

NOTES TO 2 JOHN

V. 1 The Elder The author identifies himself as "the Elder." Although the Greek is a comparative form, this is probably an indication that the individual is older than most of those to whom he is writing. See the discussion of Authorship above and Appendix 8 (The Elder and the Elders) below.

Elect Lady There are two problems here. The first is the meaning of the title and the second is to whom it refers. The resolution of the second helps in the resolution of the first.

Although some have proposed that an individual person is intended by this title, the more common view is that the Elect Lady is not an individual but an honorific title for the community to which the author is writing. Such personification has parallels in the Old Testament and in pagan religions (Lieu, *Second and Third* 65-66). There is some variation between the singular and plural in direct address in 2 John and this is compatible with a view of a community that could be conceived of at times collectively (and so as the "Lady") and at times individually (and so as composed of "children"). See further v. 5 below.

It is not a title bestowed only on that specific community, however, as is indicated by the fact that in v. 13, the Elder will also refer to his own community as "elect." In the Gospel (John 6:70; 13:18; 15:16, 19), the disciples are said not to have chosen Jesus but to have been chosen by him. In light of this usage, it would be particularly appropriate for members of the community to refer to themselves as "elect." Nevertheless, it is not unusual for the wider circle of early Christians to refer to themselves or others as "chosen" *(eklektos)*. Similar usage is found in 1 Pet 5:13 and in the salutation of Ignatius, *Trall.* Consequently, although I am inclined to think that the choice of the title is based on the Johannine usage, it cannot be proved that the derivation is particularly "Johannine."

I have translated *eklekta kyria* as "elect lady." This assumes that *kyria* is a noun ("lady"). *Kyria* can also be taken in an adjectival sense and so mean "noble." There does not seem to be much difference between the two meanings. It is not possible to say whether designating the addressee as *kyria* indicates some preeminence in relation to the author's own community.

and her children The Greek for "children" here is *teknon*. The term is used to refer to the relation of the members ("children") to the community rather than as a description of their relation to God, which was gained through birth from the Spirit. For more detail, see at John 1:12 and 3E-5.

whom I love in truth This is similar to the expression in 1 John 3:18, "Let us . . . love . . . in truth" (see also 3 John 1). Although the phrase can be used adverbially, the present context indicates that it refers to the truth that is in dispute within the community. At the very least, the expression means that the love is to issue into action as would be indicated by the parallel with 1 John 3:18. However, the context of 2 John that follows makes it very likely that the author means that his love is coupled with and the expression of correct belief.

and not I alone but all those who know the truth The other members of the author's community also love the sister church and do so from their rootedness in truth.

V. 2 through the truth abiding in us — and it will be with us forever. The author emphasizes the fact that he and his followers know the truth through the truth abiding in them. It is possible that the phrase "the truth abiding in us" refers to the presence of the Spirit within them giving them such knowledge. A similar expression occurs in 3 John 12c, where "the truth" is said to witness to Demetrius. It is the Elder's conviction that the truth will be with them forever.

V. 3 May grace, mercy and peace The Greek verb here is the future indicative with the force of a wish. It is not simply a prediction of what will happen. This is part of the greeting of the Letter. It is similar to the common Pauline blessing ("Grace and peace"; see 1 Cor 1:3; 2 Cor 1:2; Gal 1:3; etc.) and could be seen as having elements of both the common Hebrew greeting ("Peace" or "Peace and mercy") and the common secular Greek greeting ("Rejoice"). Elsewhere in the Johannine writings, "grace" *(charis)* appears only in the Prologue of the Gospel (John 1:14, 16, 17), which became part of the Gospel in its final edition. "Mercy" *(eleos)* appears nowhere else in the Johannine tradition, a fact that suggests it was included here simply as part of a stereotyped expression.

"Peace" *(eirēnē)* appears in the Farewell Discourses of the Gospel where Jesus wishes the disciples peace (14:27; 16:33) and in his two appearances to the disciples after the Resurrection, where he begins by wishing them peace (20:19, 21, 26). It could be understood as simply the traditional greeting.

from God the Father Although God is regularly referred to as "Father" in the Johannine literature, this is the only instance of the combination "God the Father" *(para theou patros)*.

from Jesus Christ The conjunction of the name and title of Jesus appears here and in v. 7.

in truth and love This is a model of the succinct summation of the two essential elements of the believer's life as it was understood in the Johannine tradition. The errors of the opponents in 1 John could be summarized as violations of truth and love. These are also the essential objects of the two Johannine commandments (see Appendix 5 [The Johannine Commandments] in this volume).

V. 4 I rejoiced greatly "Joy" is a mark of correct belief according to the author. In v. 12, he wishes them "complete" joy. See also 1 John 1:4; 3 John 4, and the comment at John 3:29. Although joy is commonly part of the greeting in a letter, the expression here is not simply stereotyped but genuine and due to the fact that the addressees are "walking in truth."

In 3 John, the author takes the same approach, expressing joy at the fact that Gaius and others are "walking in truth." Given the struggle of the community over "the truth," such a concern was not simply a literary convention but a heartfelt conviction.

some of your children The author qualifies his statement by indicating that "some" of your children "walk in truth." This need not mean that others have gone over to the side of the opponents. Rather, as is evident from the exhortation that follows in the remainder of the Letter, the author feels that some need further strengthening in the truth. In 3 John 4, the statement is not so qualified: "that I hear my children are walking in the truth."

walking in truth The use of "walking" here is metaphorical. In the Gospel and in 1 John, it is used of walking in darkness *(peripatein en skotei* John 8:12 [3E] [see also 11:10 (3E)]; 12:35 [3E]; 1 John 1:6; 2:11), walking in light *(peripatein en tō phōti* [see John 11:9 (3E); 12:35 (3E)] 1 John 1:7), walking "according to the commandments" *(peripatein kata tas entolas* 2 John 6).

However, the expression "walking in truth" *(peripatein en tē alētheia)* appears only in 2 John 4 and in 3 John 3, 4. *Peripatein* does not appear with either the dative of love *(agapē)* or commandment *(entolē)* in any of the Johannine writings, nor in the remainder of the New Testament. In the Gospel and in 1 John, we find the similar "doing the truth" *(poiein tēn alētheian)* (John 3:21 [3E]; 1 John 1:6).

just as we received a commandment from the Father This identifies "walking in truth" as an object of a commandment. The same conjunction and almost identical wording ("just as he has given us a commandment") are used in 1 John 3:23 to define the commandment of love. The peculiar phrasing is to be accounted for in both instances by the fact that the identification as a commandment appears *after* the specification of the content of the commandment.

V. 5 I ask you . . . a new commandment to you The pronoun in both of these instances is singular and is probably due to the fact that he is addressing the community collectively. However, he returns to the plural in the next verse (v. 6c). The singular does not appear again until the conclusion (v. 13).

Lady The direct address here, without some word such as "My" or "Dear" before it, is awkward in English; but, in fact, the Greek has none and the translation here attempts to mirror that.

V. 6 And this is the love There are two meanings for "love" here that fit the grammar. The first is that the love referred to is love for God. Thus, love for God is manifest in keeping the commandments. The second is that it refers to love for the brothers, which had been mentioned in v. 5. Remarkably, there is a precedent for both of these meanings in 1 John 5:2-3. In v. 2, we read: "In this we know that we love the children of God, whenever we love God and obey his commandments." This would support the view that obeying the commandments is evidence that one loves the children of God. However, in v. 3 we read: ". . . this is the love of God that we keep his commandments." As a result of this parallelism, it becomes clear that either meaning would have precedent within the Johannine Letters and both would make sense within the context. What is equally remarkable is that, like the present passage, 1 John 5:1-5 as a whole constitutes a chiasm. It deals with and interrelates the commandment to love one another with the commandment to be faithful to the word of Jesus (belief). At the same time, it focuses on the idea of correct belief in the outer (the first and last) elements!

In spite of precedent within 1 John for either meaning, I think it is possible to distinguish which was intended by the Elder in v. 6. In 1 John 5:1-5, v. 3a ("For this is the love of God") constitutes the central element of the chiasm. It is also clear that, in 1 John 5:3a, "love of God" refers back to the same phrase immediately before it, in v. 2b.

When we turn to 2 John 4-6, we see what appears to be the same technique at work. Not only is the overall passage a chiasm as was 1 John 5:1-5, but the reference to love in v. 6a, if it parallels the technique in 1 John 5:3a, would refer back to the use of love immediately before it. That instance was "love of one another." Second, in the chiasm of 2 John 4-6, the central element is double. Given this fact, it is likely that the love spoken of in both parts of the central element is the same. On these grounds also, the love referred to would be "love of one another." Since both indications lead to the same conclusion, it is most likely that "love" in v. 6a refers to love of one another and that is the view that will be adopted here.

in it (Gk: *autē*) There is much discussion of the antecedent of this pronoun. For a summary of that discussion, see von Wahlde, "Argument" 209-11. The feminine nominalized adjective could refer to "love" *(agapē)*, "commandment" *(entolē)*, or "truth" *(alētheia)*.

However, there are several cogent reasons for concluding that it refers to truth. First although the Greek words for both "love" *(agapē)* and "commandment" *(entolē)* are feminine in gender and could grammatically agree with *autē*, there is no instance where *peripateō* occurs with "love" (that is, "walking in love"). When *peripateō* is used with *entolē* (2 John 6), *entolē* appears in the accusative with the preposition *kata*. Thus, it is unlikely that *autē* in v. 6 refers to "commandment" here.

Second, that *autē* refers to "truth" is confirmed structurally by the fact that, as is typical in a chiasm, the two outermost elements of the chiasm reflect the same notion. In this case, the parallel element speaks of "walking in truth."

Third, the sole topic of the Letter is "truth" and perseverance in the proper teaching. This makes it even more likely that the antecedent here is "truth." Of particular importance is the fact that immediately after v. 6, the author discusses the failure in matters of correct belief that is evident in those who do not confess Jesus Christ come in the flesh. These persons are described as "deceivers" (those who do not speak the truth!). In v. 9, the essential (and only) point concerns remaining in the teaching of the Christ, which is again an issue of the "truth." Finally, vv. 10-11, the last verses of the argument (body) of the Letter, exhort the reader about how to deal with one who does not bring this teaching. Thus, from beginning to end the issue is the truth of correct teaching and of correct belief. The way this proceeds from the exhortation to "walk in it" leaves no room for understanding the antecedent as referring to anything other than "the truth."

V. 7 persons not confessing Jesus Christ as coming in the flesh This statement is very close to that of 1 John 4:2. As was the case in 1 John 4:2, the author seems to take for granted that his readers understand the meaning of "coming in the flesh" because he does not explain it. Its short and cryptic formulation suggests that it was a slogan in the debate between the Elder and his opponents.

The only difference between this verse and the statement in 1 John 4:2 is the aspect of the participle. While 1 John 4:2 has the perfect participle, here we find the present. There are two major views of this shift. In the first view, the text in 2 John 7 refers to the future coming of Jesus in the flesh rather than to his "first" coming in his atoning death. This argument is made in the light of the fact that in Greek the present participle frequently has a future aspect to it. Thus, the difference is intentional and refers not to the value of the death of Jesus but to the nature of his Second Coming. In this sense, the statement affirms that, when Jesus returns in his future coming, he will come in the flesh.

Strecker (*Epistles* 232-36), who considers 2 John to have been composed prior to 1 John and by a different person, modifies this theory, arguing that the Johannine conception of the Parousia was not a simple one but rather an early three-stage expectation involving: (1) the Resurrection; (2) the Parousia and a 1,000-year earthly reign of Jesus; and then (3) the end of the world and final judgment. Thus, Strecker associates the Parousia with the beginning of the 1,000-year reign and claims that the opponents of 2 John deny that Jesus is going to return in the flesh at the time of the establishment of the 1,000-year reign. His evidence for this view is found in the *Epistle of Barnabas* (6.9; 7.9; 15.4-5), which speaks of such a "fleshly" inauguration of the millennium. While a *certain* indication that "come" had a future aspect in v. 7 would make the Johannine view compatible with that in *Barnabas,* the lack of certainty about the participle makes the likelihood of a three-stage expectation untenable.

The second view suggests that the difference is insignificant and that the author is referring to the importance of the atoning death of Jesus in both instances. Brown (*Epistles* 669-70) takes this position and in doing so points to yet a third text (1 John 5:6) where in a similar expression the author uses an aorist — again without apparent difference in meaning.

In the Note to 1 John 4:2, I argued that the slogan's essential meaning needed to be understood against the background of the second edition's emphasis on the Spirit. The opponents understood the emphasis on the Spirit to make the flesh (and the realm of the material in general) irrelevant to salvation. To counter this, the Elder now stressed that the flesh does have a role in salvation and that Jesus had come "in the flesh."

But this does not solve the problem of the aspect of the participle. If Jesus' "fleshly" death was disputed within the community, then, conceivably, the nature of his return could also be a matter of contention. At the same time, this is unlikely. Throughout, the opponents have been portrayed as implicitly denying any form of future judgment. They did not debate the *nature* of his return but denied *its very occurrence* (see also Vol. 1, Part 4, Sections 5.2 and 5.3). Further, it seems clear that the present expression (as well as the formulation in 1 John 4:2 and 5:6) served as a slogan in the debate between the author and his opponents. If this was so, it seems very unlikely that two slogans would be distinguished by such a slight nuance. When these factors are coupled with the fact that yet a third form of the participle appears in 1 John 5:6, it seems unlikely that the aspect was intended to have any significance.

the Deceiver (Gk: *planos*) This is used as a title only here but, in 1 John 4:6, there is mention of a Spirit of Deceit *(pneuma tēs planēs).* In Rev 20:7-8, Satan is set loose to deceive *(planēsai)* after the thousand-year reign of Christ.

Antichrist On this, see at 1 John 2:18.

V. 8 recompense Literally "wage."

V. 9 "progressive" The Greek term is *proagō,* meaning "to lead forward." It refers to those who claim authorization for their beliefs in the inspiration of the Spirit and do not require that these beliefs need to be consistent with the teaching of the historical Jesus. They brought in beliefs that were innovations and not part of what the community had believed and witnessed to "from the beginning."

the teaching of the Christ I take this as a subjective genitive (the teaching that the Christ brings). Against the view that it is objective (that is, the teaching about the Christ) is the fact that in the Johannine tradition there are no human teachers; Christ and the Spirit are the ones who teach. See also the next Note.

The use of "the Christ" as a designation for Jesus is striking but is probably a reflection of the confessional statement of the community that Jesus is "the Christ." In time "the Christ" becomes a title for Jesus and reflects the conviction that the author and his community thought of Jesus as the only "Christ."

V. 10 this teaching The "teaching" here refers not to the exhortation of the author but the teaching of the Christ. The author has said that there is only one teacher and that is Jesus. The author himself only "witnesses" to what he has heard, and seen and touched (1 John 1:1-4).

do not receive (Gk: *lambanein*) *Note on the translation:* The English word order here has been modified in order to give the reader a sense of the chiastic arrangement evident in the Greek. The result is some awkwardness in the English. However, the meaning should be clear.

This verb was part of the community's quasi-technical language for the process of accepting fellow believers from other Johannine communities who were on a journey for some religiously motivated reason (Malherbe, "Inhospitality" 223 and literature referred to there).

In addition to the important practice of Christian hospitality, there was the matter of refusing it to those who brought false teaching. That this is a problem is reflected particularly in sub-apostolic times (*Did.* 11:1-2; Ignatius, *Smyrn.* 4:1; *Eph.* 7:1; 9:1). Irenaeus (*Adv. Haer.* 1.16.3) refers to 2 John in his admonition not even to greet gnostics whom Christians would meet.

house The advice here reflects the practice of extending hospitality to fellow Christians, particularly traveling missionaries. The same practice is reflected throughout 3 John, which is set against a series of visits between two communities and the acceptance or rejection given to those visitors. Such traveling missionaries or emissaries would expect to be able to receive assistance from the Christian community in the town through which they were passing. It was looked upon as a failure in Christian love not to receive such travelers, thus forcing them to seek lodging among non-Christians (cf. 3 John 7). Travelers were to be given, first, a Christian welcome (2 John 10), second, support in the form of food and lodging (2 John 10), and finally support necessary for the travelers to continue their journey (3 John 5). The religious justification for extending hospitality to such travelers was first of all that it was an expression of Christian love (cf. 3 John 6a) but also that, by doing so, they would become co-workers with the missionaries (3 John 8). As we will see in v. 11 below, the rejection of such hospitality to the opponents was also a duty — for the same reason.

That this practice had been common among early followers of Jesus is evident from 1 Cor 9:5-8 where Paul speaks of the practice in some detail. According to Paul's account, it was acceptable, if not customary, for a married person to travel with one's spouse and for both to be supported within the community they were visiting. It was evident in Paul's case that such visits were sometimes lengthy. In order to avoid any hint of self-seeking, Paul gave up such privilege and took on a job to support himself. For further discussion of, and literature on, Christian hospitality, see the Introduction to 3 John and the Interpretation of 3 John 7-8.

greet More is intended than a simple verbal greeting. The believer is not to communicate with or cooperate with the opponent in any way that would indicate approval or acceptance of what he or she stood for.

V. 11 takes part in The verb here is *koiōneō* and is related to the fellowship *(koinōnia)* spoken of at the beginning of 1 John (v. 3). To be in fellowship was an indication of agreement on matters of belief and practice. To accept those who brought deceitful teaching was to be in fellowship with their evil work.

evil deeds Evidently this is a reference to the attempts of the opponents to preach this progressive doctrine. The use of the word *ponēros* in the Gospel and Letters was discussed in the Note on John 3:19. Here this is the Elder's ordinary term for describing not just evil actions but "the Evil One," the personal source of evil opposed to God. Thus, these constitute the evil side of the dualistic (apocalyptic) paradigm of good and evil. The paradigm is most evident in 1 John 3:12 where Cain is said to be "of the Evil One" and therefore to do evil deeds. Those who are bringing false doctrine are understood to be on the side of the Evil One. In 3 John 10, Diotrephes is said to slander the Elder "with evil words."

V. 12 Although I have many things to write to you . . . paper and ink Literally, "Having many things to write, I did not want to by papyrus and ink." The statement is elliptical. Although he has many things to write about, he does not want [to communicate them] by paper and ink.

The Greek word *chartēs* referred specifically to writing material made from papyrus. The word for ink is a substantive form of the neuter of *melas* ("black"). Ink was made in a variety of ways in the ancient world, often involving lampblack mixed with gum arabic, sometimes thinned with water or other liquid. Ink is mentioned in the New Testament three times: 2 Cor 3:3, here, and in 3 John 13.

face to face Literally, the Greek reads "mouth to mouth" *(stoma pros stoma)*.

our joy Schnackenburg (*Epistles* 288-89) suggests that the reference to "our" is not meant to be inclusive but epistolary and so to refer only to the joy of the author. This would be consistent with the authorial "we."

may be the fullest This is a typical Johannine expression. True joy is that which is complete and this seems to have an eschatological element to it.

V. 13 elect sister This is the only instance of this precise expression in the New Testament. The community had been referred to as "elect" in v. 1.

you Throughout the body of the Letter the author has addressed the community in the plural. However, here he uses the singular form, evidently treating the community as a unit.

THE INTERPRETATION OF 2 JOHN

VV. 1-3 (THE OPENING OF THE LETTER)

The Structure and Literary Features of Vv. 1-3

The first three verses constitute the opening of the Letter *(praescriptio)* and consist of the identification of the sender, recipient, greeting and remembrance or health wish.

The Interpretation of Vv. 1-3

Vv. 1-2

Second John is a true letter and as such begins with the identification of the writer and the addressee. As I have argued above in the discussion of the identity of the author, 2 John is written by "the Elder," the same individual as the one identified in the third edition of the Gospel as "the disciple whom Jesus loved."

It is addressed to a community that is at some distance from that of the Elder and that is identified as "the Elect Lady and her children."

Even before he gives the greeting customary at the beginning of a letter, he recalls what he values most in his relation to the community and in so doing reveals what is most on his mind: his concern for the truth. The author states that he loves this community "in truth," meaning that his love is rooted in the truth. This is the truth that his community confesses and that is shared by the Elect Lady and her children. Those who know the truth (the other members of his own community) also love the Elect Lady and her children and do so through the truth abiding in them.

Some argue that the understanding of truth in 2 John is not the dualistic use of truth as found in 1 John and indeed that 2 John does not exhibit any sense of dualism.[1] However, it is important to recognize the difference in the literary genres of the two documents. The First Letter of John was a formal exposition of the positions of the opponents and the author's refutation of those views. In such an exposition we can expect a more explicit and detailed presentation of the worldview. However, 2 and 3 John are occasional letters, which focus on particular issues and, in so doing, presume such distinctions rather than elaborate them. Yet if we examine the broader presentation of 2 John, it is evident that, while the opposite (falsehood, lying) is not mentioned explicitly, it is certainly implicit. For example, in texts such as 2 John 4, the author expresses joy to hear that the members are walking in truth; this implies that not walking in truth is a real danger. The opposition is also evident in the description of those who have gone out (v. 7) and those who do not remain in the teaching of the Christ (v. 9). Moreover, the expression of love is the dualistic Johannine sense, which forbids love to those who are opposed to the truth (v. 10).

V. 3

Verse 3 constitutes the greeting of the letter. In his greeting, the author wishes his readers "grace, mercy and peace." Of these, the last should perhaps be understood, as it is intended in the Farewell Discourses, as a deliberate wish for peace in a troubling time. Such a wish would also be worthwhile in the time of the community crisis evident in the Letters.

If the greeting shows some signs of being stereotyped, there are two elements that are not stereotyped and that reflect the particular crisis dividing the community. First, the blessings he wishes come not just from the Father but from the Father and from Jesus. Thus, Jesus is paralleled with the Father, emphasizing the role of Jesus and the need of "having" both the Father and the

---

1. See the discussion in the Introduction.

Son, something he will reinforce explicitly in v. 9. This was one of the central issues in the crisis confronting the community and opposed by the author of 1 John. Moreover, Jesus is identified as both Christ and as the Son of the Father, the two titles of Jesus rejected by the opponents. Thus, this aspect of the greeting in 2 John is hardly stereotyped but intended to confirm one of the essentials of their faith in a way that the opponents could not do. It is very close to the statement at the beginning of 1 John where the author states that "our fellowship is with the Father and with his Son, Jesus Christ" (1 John 1:3b).

Second, the final element of the greeting also reflects the doctrinal crisis of the community when the author expresses his hope that these blessings be with the members of the community "in truth and love." Thus, the two issues (correct belief and correct action) that were central to 1 John appear again here as hopes for the community. It should also be noted that, from the way the issues of truth and love are introduced here, it would seem that the author expects the recipients to be familiar with his understanding of the terms and so suggests that 2 John was not the first writing to address this issue. This is confirmed by what follows in v. 4.

VV. 4-11 (THE BODY OF THE LETTER)

The body of the Letter consists of vv. 4-11. Within these verses there are three units (vv. 4-7, 8-9, 10-11), each containing an exhortation (request). The first of these units begins with the expression of joy that commonly functions as a transition to the body of the Letter. This is then followed by direct address to the reader together with the presentation of the author's first request. In the present instance, vv. 4-6 also consist of a chiasm that is then followed by the single v. 7 that provides a final explanation of the request.

The overall purpose of vv. 4-6 is to commend *some* for walking in the truth but also to provide a general exhortation to *all* (the readers) to do the same. The general exhortation in these verses will be complemented by more specific discussion of what constitutes correct belief and what poses a particular threat to it in the remainder of the Letter.

V. 4 (THE TRANSITION AND EXPRESSION OF JOY) AND VV. 5-7 (THE FIRST REQUEST)

The Structure and Literary Features of Vv. 4-7

Although these verses make up three elements of the letter (transition, expression of joy and the first request), they are all joined together by the major structural feature of these verses, a chiasm encompassing almost all of vv. 4-6. However, the author also uses his technique of "definition" and "chaining" throughout. Twice he provides definitions: "And this is the love . . ." (v. 6a) and "This is the commandment . . ." (v. 6c). He then chains these together to achieve his woodenly logical conclusion that, if they love one another, this also demands that they walk in the truth.

I. de la Potterie was the first to propose that the structure of these verses is chiastic.[2] I would agree but would suggest alterations that I believe show the symmetry more clearly. The chiasm is somewhat rough and lacks perfect balance, but the intent to compose a chiasm is evident and the major elements are unambiguous.

The chiasm begins in v. 4b. The two outermost elements of the chiasm (v. 4bc; v. 6d) speak about "walking in truth" (correct belief).

The second (v. 5ab) and second-last (v. 6bc) elements then identify walking in the truth as a commandment. In addition, both of these elements speak of commandments that they have received "from the beginning." In the first instance, the author is introducing the commandment of mutual love "that we have had from the beginning" and the second speaks of the commandment to walk in the truth "as you heard from the beginning."

The third (v. 5c) and third-to-last (v. 6a) elements of the chiasm constitute the double central element of the chiasm.[3] It is here (and only here) that love is spoken of. In the first part of this central member, the commandment, which had been introduced in the previous element, is now defined as "loving one another." Then in the other part of the chiasm's central member, the definition of this love is given.[4]

2. De la Potterie, *Vérité* 2:652.

3. This element is almost identical to that of 1 John 5:1-5 inasmuch as both speak of love and both contain a definition of what makes up that love. However, in 1 John 5:2, the love is love of God, while in 2 John 5, the love is mutual community love.

4. This is the third such chiasm that attempts to define and/or interrelate the two commandments of the Johannine tradition. The first was 1 John 3:22-24; the second was 1 John 5:1-5.

The second of these (1 John 5:1-5) bears the most remarkable similarity to the present one in that the first and the last elements of the chiasm deal with correct belief. In 1 John 5:1-5, the first element speaks of believing "that Jesus is the Christ"; the last speaks of believing "that Jesus is Son of God." In 2 John 4-6, the first and last elements both speak of the need "to walk in truth" (that is, in correct belief).

In 1 John 5:1-5, the second element focuses on mutual love and second-last element focuses on faith. In 2 John 4-6, the remainder of the first half focuses on mutual love and the second half leads up to the final statement on correct faith.

In 1 John 5:1-5, the central element is love. In 2 John 4-6, the central element is love. Moreover, both chiasms move (each in its own way) from urging obedience to a specific commandment to urging obedience to the commandments in general and then from there to obedience to the other commandment.

Verse 7 constitutes a minor chiasm and gives the specific truth the opponents deny: that Jesus has come in the flesh.

The Interpretation of Vv. 4-7

V. 4ab (Expression of Joy)

As we have seen in the Notes, there are a number of issues connected with the meaning of the individual words in these verses, particularly the pronouns. The interpretation here presumes the conclusions arrived at in the Notes. There is also further discussion of these verses in Appendix 5 (The Johannine Commandments) in this volume.

The author begins (v. 4) the transition to the body of the Letter with an expression of joy.[5] This joy is caused by the Elder's experience of some of the members of the community "walking in truth." Although such expressions of joy were typically expressed at the beginning of a letter,[6] this present one is no perfunctory comment. To walk in truth undoubtedly meant that those to whom he was referring were in agreement with the Elder about the interpretation of the tradition.[7] In 3 John, the Elder does not speak of the entire congregation but only about Gaius, whom the Elder knows also walks in truth. It is probably significant that, in the community of the Elect Lady, not all were adhering to the tradition as the Elder understood it.

V. 4c (Transition)

Above, we saw that this forms the transition to the body of the Letter and that it is clear from its formulation that it was not simply a stereotyped wish. Here, we call attention to the end of the verse where the author reminds his readers that by their walking in truth they were acting "just as we received a commandment from the Father." Thus, to walk in truth was the object of a commandment given by God. This is one of the clearer instances of the "first" of the Johannine commandments, the commandment about proper belief, to "walk in truth." This is already

5. This expression of joy will be paralleled in 3 John in vv. 3-4. That "our" joy may reach its fullness is hoped for in v. 12e. However, in 2 John, the Elder ends his Letter with a hope for further joy (v. 12f), an expression not paralleled in 3 John.

6. See Appendix 6 (Formal Elements in Greek Letter Writing) in this volume and the literature referred to there.

7. Thus, I disagree with Lieu (*Second and Third* 71), who comments: "This [v. 4] may well tell us little about the church situation envisaged but merely provides a courteous way of leading into what follows." This is not simple courtesy. Walking in the truth is the very heart of the Elder's concern.

the fifth time that "truth" has been mentioned in the first four verses, and here he identifies it as the object of one of the two Johannine commandments. In fact, truth is the central concern of the Letter and, in v. 6, he will make his formal request that the church continue walking in the truth. In v. 7, he will speak of deceivers who do not confess correctly. In v. 9, he will speak of those whose teaching is "progressive" and who do not remain in the teaching of the Christ. In v. 10, he will speak about how to handle false teachers (those who do not bring the truth). And here at the beginning, the Elder's joy is great at finding that "some of your children" are walking in truth, as we have "received a commandment."

Vv. 5-6 (The First Request)

The Elder now (v. 5) addresses his correspondent ("the Elect Lady and her children") directly as is common at this point in such a letter.[8] Apparently moving on to a new topic, he makes his formal request of the community. The Elder explains that the commandment he is writing about is not a new one but one that "we" have had from the beginning: that we love one another. The author is interested ultimately in the commandment to walk in the truth. But his argument will take several steps in order to get there. Already in v. 4ab, the author had taken step #1 although it was not yet apparent that this was part of an extended argument. Here (in step #2) he begins by speaking of the love commandment. As is almost always the case, the Elder introduces topics and perspectives that would be unacceptable to his opponents but that are central to the tradition he upholds. The love commandment is not a "new" commandment but one they have had "from the beginning."[9] The Elder reminds his readers that they have had the love commandment "from the beginning" and that it could not be rejected as unnecessary, as the opponents did in their misguided understanding of perfectionism. In this respect, the love commandment could not be part of the "new" teaching of those who are "progressive" and who do not "remain in the teaching of the Christ" (v. 9).[10]

---

8. For the similar arrangement of request and direct address, see 3 John 5.

9. The notions of "new" and "old" also appear side by side in 1 John 2:7-8. The terms have two frames of reference in the Johannine Letters. The "old" commandment is one that they have had "from the beginning" of their tradition, as it was given to them by Jesus. It is not "new" in the sense of being the work of those who go beyond the teaching of the Christ (2 John 9). However, when viewed within the history of salvation, the commandment is new because the ministry of Jesus is "new" (in the sense of "recent") and the darkness that was "of old" is now being taken away. See also at 1 John 2:7-8.

10. It is also true that the opponents even rejected the necessity of the kind of ethical behavior indicated by the love commandment itself. But the Elder reminds his readers that they had had the love commandment "from the beginning."

Then in v. 6, in a clear instance of his technique of demonstrating reciprocity and interrelatedness, the author moves (in step #3) from the specificity of the love commandment to a more general conclusion, namely, that the love (of which he had just spoken) is manifested in the general keeping of the commandments! While this hardly seems to represent any progress in terms of the argument, there is a logic that is leading him on. However, before moving to the next stage of the argument, we need to ask how love of the brothers is manifested in the keeping of the commandments. To fully appreciate the Elder's purpose here, we must remember that the Johannine commandments were formulated to express the necessity of both correct belief and correct behavior. These were the two central elements of the tradition that the opponents rejected. However, if the faithful members of the community kept both of those commandments, they would demonstrate an example that would not only be supportive of their brothers in general but would also show specific support of each other (in keeping with the purpose of the "second" commandment).

Then (in step #4) he introduces another stage of his argument, this time in the opposite direction, from obedience to the commandments in general to obedience to a specific commandment. And, once again, we find that the Elder speaks about a commandment "as you heard it from the beginning." And so, once again, he implicitly refutes his opponents who did not hold to the commandments that had been the property of the community "from the beginning." But this time, the specific commandment he speaks of is "walking in it [the truth]." And so the Elder returns to the theme with which he began: the commandment to walk in the truth.

Thus, by means of definition and logical deduction, the Elder has shown not only that the commandment to walk in the truth is a commandment in its own right but also that the commandment to love requires that they keep all the commandments and therefore that the commandment to love also requires that they walk in truth. And so, the Elder shows that the love commandment and the commandment of correct belief are interrelated; one leads to obedience to the other.[11] True love of one another will also lead the person to walk in the truth. It is a sort of rhetorical argument that may be awkward and unappealing to many modern readers but its intent is clear.[12] And the technique is one that was common within the Johannine Letter tradition.[13]

11. So also Beutler, *Johannesbriefe* 156; Klauck, *Zweite und Dritte* 49.

12. Brown (*Epistles* 665) speaks of "the obscure logic of the whole section." I would argue that there is a clear logic but that it is wooden and awkward — and determined by the author's conviction that truth is reciprocal and interrelated. Thus, each commandment not only has its own validity but supports and demands the other.

13. We have seen this technique previously in 1 John 2:7-11, where the author argues that obeying the commandment regarding the word (the first commandment) is to be "in the light,"

V. 7

This verse has a close connection to what precedes it as is indicated by the fact that v. 7 begins with "because" *(hoti)*. In a verse with many parallels to 1 John 4:1-3, the author reminds his readers that many persons who were formerly members of the community "have gone out into the world." "Going into the world" is a theological evaluation of the opponents. In 1 John 4:2d, he had applied it to the opponents, described there as false prophets. Here, too, the opponents, in true apocalyptic fashion, are now said to be "of the world" rather than "of God."

Throughout, the author's concern has been on "truth" and "walking in truth." Here (also in close parallelism with 1 John 4:1-4), he calls attention to the fact that these deceivers who have gone out into the world deny that the physical death of Jesus had any salvific significance (cf. 1 John 4:2b). The issue at stake was soteriology. Was eternal life given only through the Spirit ("in water") or was it also through the atoning death of Jesus ("in blood")? The Elder had argued throughout 1 John that "the blood of Jesus cleanses us from sin" (1:7c); that Jesus was "an atonement for our sins" (2:2a). In 5:6a, he had explained precisely that Jesus was "the one coming through water and blood. . . . Not in water only but in the water and the blood." In 1 John 4:2-3, the Elder had said that the Spirit that confesses "Jesus Christ come in the flesh" is "of God" whereas the one who "does away" with Jesus is not of God and is, in fact, the Spirit of the Antichrist. Here, he returns to that language and refers to the person who would hold such a belief as "the Deceiver" and "the Antichrist." Thus, the Elder makes it clear that failure to confess properly was one of the characteristics of the deceivers and this was one other manifestation of their failure to "walk in truth." Moreover, he has done so within the worldview of apocalyptic throughout as is clear from both the theology and the terminology.[14]

---

but that the one claiming to be "in the light" must love his brother (the second commandment). It is also present in the chiasm of 5:1-5, where the commandment to love is shown to support the commandment of correct confession of Jesus.

14. A lingering question posed by this passage is why the Elder has singled out the false understanding of the death of Jesus as the error to be confronted here. Why did he not choose to comment on belief in Jesus as "the Christ" or as "the Son of God" as he regularly did in 1 John? We simply do not know. His Letter was a brief one. Clearly, he could not be exhaustive in his treatment of any topic. It may be that this was a particularly sensitive issue at the time of his writing. But, in the end, we do not know.

VV. 8-9 (THE SECOND REQUEST)

The Structure and Literary Features of Vv. 8-9

Verses 4-6 had provided the theological foundation of the author's argument for the Letter. Verse 7 explained one of the implications of failure to walk in truth. The author will now go on to explicate further the central issue of the Letter: correct faith. In the verses that follow, the author specifies what constitutes correct and incorrect belief. However, the structure is much less developed than in the previous section.

The Interpretation of Vv. 8-9

The Elder has just spoken of those who were deceivers and had gone out into the world. Now (v. 8) he turns to the members of his community and reminds them that they must take care lest they, too, fall prey to the temptations of the Deceiver and the Antichrist. They must be careful not to put in jeopardy "those things for which you have worked." The members of the community have done well and achieved much up to this point, but they have not yet attained the complete realization of eternal life and have not received "the full recompense" that will become a reality only at the final judgment. The present time is not a state of complete enjoyment of the eschatological gifts. Moreover, the future holds the possibility of their loss as well as the hope of their total realization (see 1 John 3:2-3). In keeping with his understanding of perfectionism, and recognizing that sin is still possible, he reminds the readers that they, too, could succumb to the deception of those who have gone out into the world and that they must continually strive to attain what they hope for.[15]

Verse 9 now returns to speak of the opponents, and the Elder becomes more specific about their faults. They are persons who are "progressive" and who have not remained "in the teaching of the Christ." Thus, we read in the clearest of terms one aspect of the opponents' fault: they have gone beyond the teaching of the Christ. They do not give special honor or a unique authority to the word that they heard "from the beginning."[16] Several aspects of this expression are important.

This is the first time we find a reference by the Elder (or by the author of any of the editions of the Gospel) to the word of Jesus being called "the teach-

---

15. Culpepper (*Gospel and Epistles* 277) suggests that the verse could refer to the effort necessary for the growth of the church of the Elect Lady. While this is possible, the entire context of 2 John (as well as of 1 John and 3 John) is concerned directly with the beliefs and practices that are part of a correct interpretation of the tradition.

16. So also Brown, *Epistles* 97; Hengel, *Question* 42.

ing." The noun is used in the Gospel (7:16, 17; 18:19) but primarily on the lips of unbelievers and there it did not have any special connotation. The more common noun for the content of Jesus' teaching is "the word of God" (as it was in 1 John) or "the word of Jesus" — "my [Jesus'] word" (as it was in the Gospel).

In the Gospel, the verb "to teach" is used of Jesus who was said to teach (e.g., 6:59; 7:14; 8:20, etc.) but neither he nor the Evangelist refers to what he said as "teaching," except in 7:16 where Jesus briefly adopts the terminology used by "the Jews." In 1 John 2:27, the author makes clear that there are to be no human teachers; only "his anointing" (that is, the anointing in the Spirit) is said to teach about all things.

However, here in 2 John, the noun appears in v. 9 and again in v. 10. This seems to indicate that the author assumes a certain fixity to the message of Jesus. However, it may also be that we are dealing once again with a form of jargon used to refer briefly to what was called elsewhere "the word of Jesus." Certainly the current expression is no briefer, but it could be said to be clearer.

In addition, there is a significant difference in the designation of the origin of content here. In 1 John, the content of faith ("the word") had been designated as of *God* (1 John 2:5, 7, 14, etc.); here it is linked to the Christ. In 1 John, the author attributes various features to God that will be attributed to Jesus in the third edition of the Gospel. In our discussion of this feature in the Introduction to 1 John, we speculated that the Elder did this in order to achieve a common ground with his opponents, since the understanding of the role of Jesus was in dispute but not that of God. Here, the author is speaking to members of the community and is able to speak of the teaching as being "of the Christ" since the members of the community recognize that the word of God is also the word of Jesus.

Third, this is the only use in the Johannine literature of the term "the Christ" as a third-person reference to Jesus other than as a predicate or apposition in a confessional title. The normal reference in the Letters is "Jesus Christ" and in the Gospel it is "Jesus." Yet, this instance is enough to show us that at times the community referred to Jesus simply as "the Christ." Thus, it is an indication that although they believed that every believer had an anointing (just as Jesus did) only one was called "the Christ." Thus, we see how the confession that "Jesus is the Christ" could be used and understood within a community that held that, in a real sense, they all had been anointed and, to an extent, could be called "christ-ed." But here the use of the term is also probably intended to be ironic. The opponents who claim to have a *chrisma* (anointing) (cf. 1 John 2:20, 27) go beyond and do not remain in the teaching of the one who is truly and most fully *christos*!

The author then argues that the one who does not remain in this teaching "does not possess God." The opponents had argued that they believed in God but not in Jesus. But, once again, the author argues, as he had done three times already in 1 John (1:3b; 2:22-23, 24): One cannot be said to believe in ("have") God if one does not also believe in ("have") the Son since true belief in God includes belief in the Son. Here, he modifies that somewhat by saying that one cannot have God if one does not remain in the teaching that the Christ had brought.

VV. 10-11 (THE THIRD REQUEST)

The Structure and Literary Features of Vv. 10-11

The structure and argument of these verses are simple and straightforward. The only feature to be noted is a minor chiasm in v. 10c-d that appears to be done simply for stylistic reasons.[17] That chiasm is diagrammed in the Translation, although reproducing the Greek word order results in quite awkward English. Nevertheless, the meaning should be clear.

The Interpretation of Vv. 10-11

In v. 10, the Elder gives advice about persons who approach the community but do not bring "this" teaching. They are not to receive the individuals into their house or to give them "greetings" (that is, any sort of positive welcome and acceptance). In spite of what was the common practice of providing a welcome and necessary support to Christian believers who visited the community, the members of the community were not to do so for those who brought false teaching.

The Elder then goes on (v. 11) to explain the reason for this order. For a member of the author's sister community to give the customary acceptance to someone not bringing the correct teaching would be to cooperate with the evil that the person is doing. Agreement with his/her false views would in fact be furthering the work of the Spirit of Deceit.

From these verses, we get a glimpse of the practice of Christian hospitality. It is evident that it was common for members of the various Johannine communities to travel between communities for the purpose of missionary work, for mutual support or, as in this case, for the purpose of bringing some special teaching.[18] Because they were undertaking their travels in Jesus' name, the trav-

---

17. So Klauck, *Zweite und Dritte* 64.

18. For further detail on the practice of such Christian hospitality, see Malherbe, "Inhospitality"; Malina, "Received"; Klauck, *Zweite und Dritte* 95-96.

elers should seek nothing from non-believers. As a result, the brothers, who also believe in the Name, should receive them as Christian guests. Not only was this an opportunity to extend Christian love to the brothers; but, by doing so, they would be coworkers with the travelers in their work for the truth. Just as the travelers acted out of religious motives in their travels, so those along the way should act out of religious motives and give them any support they needed.[19]

In addition to the glimpse this passage gives us of the practice of Christians regarding fellow Christian travelers, we also see an example of what the author and his community saw as the limits of the mutual love so characteristic of the Johannine tradition.[20] In the dualistic worldview held by the community, to extend love to those who were doing the work of the Spirit of Deceit would be to take part in that evil work and actually to support and further those evil deeds. Clearly that would be an inappropriate form of love as the community understood it and indicates that the mutual love enjoined upon the community was in no way a naïve love![21]

VV. 12-13 (CONCLUSION TO THE LETTER)

The Structure and Literary Features of Vv. 12-13

From a form-critical point of view, these verses contain features typical of an ancient letter as we will see below.[22] The verses are essentially devoid of literary devices although there is a minor parallelism between the "paper and ink," which the author does not want to employ, and the "face to face," which he does.

19. In 3 John, the giving (and non-giving) of such hospitality will be even more central to the Letter. Here, the author urges the community not to accept persons who may want such hospitality if they do not bring the proper teaching. In 3 John, he will admonish Diotrephes for *not* accepting those with proper teaching and at the same time praises Gaius who does accept emissaries from the Elder's community and encourages the future reception of Demetrius, another such traveler.

20. Hengel (*Question* 42-45) makes this point well and gives examples of such exclusion from love elsewhere in early Christianity (for example, 1 Cor 5:9, 11; Matt 7:15; *Did.* 12.1).

21. Schnackenburg (*Epistles* 287) makes this point clear: ". . . the enemies of the faith are more insidious than personal opponents. That is why the need for forgiveness (Matt. 5:23-25) and love of the enemy (Matt. 5:44-48) must not be played off against it." In such circumstances, there was no hope of converting the opponents, and it is very likely that they were looked upon as having committed the "sin-unto-death" and thus having already been judged by God.

22. There is some disagreement whether v. 12 is part of the closing of the body of the Letter or conclusion of the Letter. R. E. Brown sees it as the closing of the body of the Letter while Funk takes it as part of the conclusion of the Letter as a whole. The view taken does not affect the interpretation of the text since the sentiments in vv. 12-13 typically occur in this sequence at the end of such letters.

The Interpretation of Vv. 12-13

Much of what appears in vv. 12-13 is conventional.[23] The Elder begins with the statement that there is much more to be said but he will not do it at present. He does not wish to write "by paper and ink." He also expresses the hope that he will be able to visit the recipients in the near future. At that time, communication by "paper and ink" will be replaced by communication "face to face."

Finally, he sends greetings to the Letter's recipients from the members of the author's own community. The equality and intimacy of the two communities are indicated by the way the author refers to his own community as a "sister" of the recipients' community.

Although vv. 12-13 are quite similar to those of the conclusion in 3 John, there are differences. In 2 John, there is an expression of hope that the anticipated meeting between the Elder and the community will be an occasion of joy, while in 3 John there is no such statement.

At the same time, the greeting in 2 John is briefer than that in 3 John. Consequently, by comparison, that of 3 John seems more heartfelt and personal. As a result, it does not seem possible to say that the differences reflect differences in the author's relation with either the direct recipient or the circumstances.

The author now describes his own community as "the children of your elect sister" just as he had described the recipients' community as "elect" in v. 1. This confirms the view that the title of "elect" was not something bestowed only on the particular community to which the Elder had been writing.

In the Note to v. 1, it was proposed that although the title was used elsewhere in early Christianity, the use of the title "elect" in this Letter may have been intended to reflect the Johannine conviction that the believers were "chosen" by Jesus. We will see that in the conclusion to 3 John, the Elder asks Gaius to address the members "by name." While this expression may be intended simply to refer to the author's concern for each individual in the community, it is also possible that it was intended as an allusion to the parable of the good shepherd in which Jesus calls his sheep "by name." If this is correct, we have subtle allusions to the special status of the Johannine believer in the conclusions to both Letters.

---

23. For parallels, see Appendix 6 (Formal Elements in Greek Letter Writing) in this volume.

THE THIRD LETTER OF JOHN

Introduction to 3 John

The Third Letter of John is the shortest work in the New Testament. It is 15 verses long and has only 219 words.[1] The Letter has the distinction of being the only document in the New Testament that does not contain either the name "Jesus" or "the Christ."[2] In addition, it contains a significant number of ecclesiastical terms not found elsewhere in the Johannine writings: "assembly" *(ekklēsia)* (vv. 6, 9, 10), "the name" *(onoma)* (v. 7); "coworkers" *(synergoi)* (v. 8), etc.

We also find in it the first reference to someone exercising, or attempting to exercise, leadership within the Johannine community other than the Elder. This suggests that it represents a stage of ecclesiastical development later than the first and second editions of the Gospel and possibly later than 1 (and 2?) John. Only the third edition of the Gospel manifests an awareness, and acknowledgment, of a structured office of leadership beyond that which seems to emerge in 3 John.

A. THE GENRE OF 3 JOHN

As was the case with 2 John, this is a true letter and reflects the standard format of an ancient letter more than any other letter in the New Testament.[3] Indeed,

---

1. Roller (*Formular* 38) lists the number of words as 185 but this is clearly incorrect. The number 219 is my count of the text in the Nestle[27].

2. While this is literally true, in v. 7 members of the community are said to have gone out "for the sake of the Name." That is almost certainly a reference to the name of Jesus, as we shall see below.

3. This format is discussed in more detail in Appendix 6 (Formal Elements in Greek Letter Writing) in this volume.

its brevity is typical of such ancient letter writing. It would have taken up a single sheet of papyrus, which was typically about 8 inches by 10 inches.

B. WORLDVIEW

The Third Letter of John is, like the other two Johannine Letters, written against the background of apocalyptic dualism. However, like 2 John, the schema is not developed as explicitly as it is in 1 John. This is due, first, to the brevity of the Letter, which allows for little development of any topic. Secondly, as will be seen, the Letter focuses almost entirely on the issue of Christian hospitality and so there is no need for anything more than minor allusions to the apocalyptic framework. Although "truth" is not explicitly contrasted with falsehood, the constant emphasis on truth and its importance certainly implies the possibility of falsehood and that these are the two options open to Gaius. Further, the Elder speaks of Diotrephes using evil words *(logoi ponēroi)*. Throughout the Johannine tradition (see Note below and on John 3:19), deeds that are *ponēroi* are typical of the Evil One *(ho Ponēros)*. Again the dualistic worldview is implied. Finally, in v. 11, the Elder alludes more clearly to apocalyptic dualism. There he compares those doing good with those doing evil and says that only the former are "of God." Not only the comparison in general, but especially the expression "of God," speaks of one half of the apocalyptic schema, belonging to God, which is implicitly contrasted with being "of the Evil One" (cf. 1 John 4:2b-3a). Indeed, 1 John 4:6bc is identical to v. 11cd except for the change of one verb.[4]

C. THE CIRCUMSTANCES OF THE COMMUNITY

The Third Letter of John deals with the world of Christian "travelers." Such individuals or groups would undertake travels for various religious purposes, and it was the practice (and for the Johannine community, an obligation) for communities along the way to provide lodging and support for such travelers. If we are to judge by 3 John, the community of the Elder and outlying communities associated with his experienced a substantial amount of such traffic. The author, in his Letter to Gaius, refers to reports he has received from travelers coming from Gaius' community. The Elder also speaks of another group of travelers who had come to the community where Diotrephes was a member. This second group of travelers seems to have come from the community of the Elder with a

---

4. On the apocalyptic background of this phrasing, see 3E-11.

letter of recommendation written by the Elder. But Diotrephes did not accept the recommendation and so rejected the travelers. Finally, in the present Letter, the Elder recommends Demetrius, who is yet another traveler, to Gaius and assures him that Demetrius should be shown full Christian hospitality.

One of the chief difficulties confronting the interpreter of 3 John is determining, in detail, the background of the events mentioned in the Letter. Why did Diotrephes reject the Elder's emissaries? Was Diotrephes a secessionist or someone with secessionist tendencies? Or was he so cautious that he would accept no travelers at all? What precisely was Diotrephes' status in the community? Was he the owner of the house where the community met? Did he simply put himself forward by strength of personality or did he claim some authoritative office? Were Diotrephes and Gaius members of the same community? There is little agreement, and little hope for agreement, about these matters simply because so little information is provided. The Third Letter of John is an occasional letter. It is brief and presumes that the reader knows the circumstances that form the background of the problem he is addressing. Therefore, much of the information we would like to have is simply not provided. At the same time, while it can be useful to discover as much as possible about the historical circumstances surrounding the writing of the Letter, it is not necessary to have definitive answers to all these questions in order to understand the theological message of the Letter. With this in mind, in our examination of the Letter, we will focus on the message of the Letter and will discuss the historical background to the extent it is necessary to understand the message. Discussion of nonessential historical elements will be confined to the Notes and to the footnotes.

D. LITERARY TECHNIQUES

In the Introductions to both 1 and 2 John, we have seen that the author has used a considerable number of literary and rhetorical techniques in his composition. The author of 3 John also manifests the use of similar techniques.

1. Chiasm

We have seen that the Elder regularly uses chiasms to structure his thought. In 3 John, the use of chiasms increases considerably and is the main literary device used by the author. While such minor and sometimes artificial-seeming devices were popular in the literature of the ancient world, they do not always coincide with our own sensibilities. Nevertheless, in many cases, these chiasms are not simply stylistic devices but are intended to call attention to certain words and ideas that the author considers important. Such chiasms are quite helpful in revealing aspects of the author's intentions in a way that the words alone do not.[5] This is particularly true of the chiasm in v. 2, which helps explain the meaning and the peculiar placement of the phrase "in all things" *(peri pantōn)* in v. 2a. A second example is in vv. 5-6 where the recognition of the chiasm gives an added measure of certainty to the explanation of the meaning and the function of "you [will] act faithfully" *(piston poieis)*. These are clear instances of how what appear to be a grammatical (or, perhaps, textual) problem can be resolved by an awareness of the author's intention as revealed by the structural arrangement of the material.

In addition to these chiasms, which account for elements of the Letter that had previously been particularly problematic, there are others that compare and contrast ideas in useful ways but are not as significant as the prior ones. These appear in vv. 7-8 and in v. 11 and are discussed in the Commentary.

2. Parallelism

There is also some evidence of deliberate parallelism on the part of the author. The most obvious appears in vv. 3-4 where the author expresses his joy twice in a parallelism that repeats previous ideas but also provides new information. It could also be said that v. 12 is made up of two elements that parallel one another, although not as extensively or as clearly as vv. 3-4.

3. Poetic Identification

In 3 John 12c, the Elder says that Demetrius is witnessed to "by the truth itself." This is a form of poetic identification because, in fact, "the truth" cannot testify apart from the individuals who do so. This is best described as poetic identification.

4. Overall Structure of the Letter

So much of 3 John is arranged chiastically that the absence of it in the discussion of Diotrephes seems almost deliberate. Apart from the Opening (v. 1) and the Conclusion (vv. 13-15), the body of the Letter consists of brief chiasms and parallelism, except for vv. 9-10, which deal with Diotrephes: v. 2 (chiasm); vv. 3-4 (parallelism); vv. 5-6 (chiasm); vv. 7-8 (chiasm); vv. 9-10 (Diotrephes); v. 11 (chiasm); v. 12 (parallelism). Perhaps the disruption of the rhythm of the Letter is intended to reflect the disruption caused by Diotrephes.

---

5. Except where noted (that is, v. 11), the several chiasms (and other instances of parallelism) have not been pointed out previously.

In addition to these subunits, there is also a certain overall arrangement evident in the Letter. The Elder has organized the body of his Letter around references to three individual believers. At the beginning, Gaius is the center of attention. In the middle, it is Diotrephes who is in the spotlight. And, at the end, Demetrius is focused on.

There is also a certain balance to the body of the Letter in the treatment given to each individual. In each case, we get a theological assessment of the character of these individuals in distinctively Johannine terms. Both Gaius (vv. 1, 3-4) and Demetrius (v. 12) are "witnessed to" by the brothers and praised for their adherence to "the truth." Diotrephes is criticized by the Elder as having been shown to be in league with "the Evil One."

Likewise, near the beginning (vv. 5-7) Gaius is given a general exhortation to do "what he can" when travelers come to the community. Near the end (vv. 11-12), Gaius is again exhorted (implicitly) to care for the brothers who come to his community. This time the exhortation is by way of contrast with Diotrephes, who does not do so. With the mention of Demetrius, the specific occasion of the request is revealed: Demetrius is coming and Gaius should give him lodging and support.

Finally, as has been pointed out, 3 John is a genuine Letter and so is structured according to the conventions of letter writing in the first century. The Interpretation will follow and reflect the various constituent elements of the Letter form as it was employed by the author.

E. THE AUTHOR OF 3 JOHN

The view proposed here is that the author of 3 John is the same as that of 2 John and 1 John. The evidence for this is presented in the General Introduction to the Letters.

F. THE DATE OF COMPOSITION

The dating of 3 John relative to the other Letters was discussed in the General Introduction. Here I will call attention to a particular feature unique to 3 John that suggests it was written prior to the third edition of the Gospel. In 3 John 12, the Elder makes reference to those who bear witness and whose witness Gaius knows is true. He testifies to his own trustworthiness with the words "and we bear witness and you know that our witness is true." In the third edition of the Gospel (John 21:24), almost identical words are used to describe the witness of the BD ("and we know that his witness is true"). It is very unlikely that the Elder would take words that had been written about another figure known to the community as "the Beloved Disciple" and apply them to himself. This would be utter arrogance. It is most likely that the words are those of the Elder himself and that the author of the third edition later applied them to the figure now known as the BD — and who was in fact the one who identified himself as "the Elder."

G. THE PLACE OF COMPOSITION

This was discussed in the General Introduction to the Letters.

Commentary and Notes on 3 John

1 The Elder
   to Beloved Gaius,
      whom I love in truth.

2 Beloved, I pray that,
   +in all things,
        +you are doing well
          and
        +that you are in good health
      +just as () is doing well
   +(your soul).

  3 For I rejoiced greatly
     when the brothers came and bore witness to your truth,
       how you walk in truth.

  4 I have no greater joy than these,
  that I hear my children
    are walking in the truth.

5 Beloved,
     +you (will) act faithfully in whatever you may do
       +for the brothers
       +and this for strangers. (6 They witnessed to your love before the
        assembly!)
     +and you will act well, having sent them on in a way worthy of God.

  +7 For, for the sake of the name, they went out,
    +accepting nothing

+from the nations.

+8 Therefore, we

+ought to accept such as these

+so that we may become coworkers for the truth.

9I wrote something to the assembly.
But Diotrephes, the one who loves to act as leader among them,
does not receive us.

10Because of this, if I come,
I will bring up the things he is doing,
bringing unjustified charges against us with evil words
and, not being satisfied with this, he does not receive the brothers himself
and prevents those who wish to
and ejects them from the assembly.

11Beloved,

+do not imitate evil but

+good.

+The one doing good is of God.

+The one doing evil has not seen God.

12Demetrius has been witnessed to
by all and
by the truth itself.
And we bear witness also and
you know that our witness is true.

13I had many things to write to you, but
I do not wish to write by ink and pen.
14But I hope to see you very soon, and
we will speak face to face.

15Peace to you.
The friends here greet you.
Greet the friends there by name.

NOTES TO 3 JOHN

V. 1 the Elder The author used the same self-designation at the beginning of 2 John.

Beloved This term is probably not a mere formality since, in what follows, the

Elder repeats the expression of his love and links it to the fact that Gaius is "in the truth" (see below).

Gaius Gaius was a common name in the ancient world. Paul mentions a Gaius who was his host in Corinth (Rom 16:23; cf. 1 Cor 1:14). Acts 19:29 mentions a Gaius with Paul in Ephesus, and Acts 20:4 mentions yet another "of Derbe."

Third John is the only one of the Johannine Letters to mention individuals, and Gaius is the first of three individuals mentioned (see also Diotrephes, v. 9, and Demetrius, v. 12). These are Greco-Roman names and may indicate the presence of Gentiles in the community. However, to judge ethnicity by the background of the name is risky since, according to the Gospel, some of the first disciples of Jesus also had non-Jewish names (e.g., Philip, Andrew).

whom I love in truth This is also said to the community addressed in 2 John. Bultmann (*Epistles* 96, n. 6) argues that "in truth" is simply an affirmation of the truth of what had been said (I genuinely love Gaius). However, given the role of truth in the remainder of the Letter (as well as in 2 John and the remainder of the Johannine tradition), it is virtually impossible that this is its primary meaning here.

Rather, the point is that the Elder's love for Gaius is religiously motivated. The Elder's love is based on the fact that Gaius adheres to the truth at a time when many were not doing so. Given the appearance of this expression in both Letters, it would seem that it was crucial for the Elder to assert at the very beginning that the most important thing about both addressees is their loyalty to the truth. In the eyes of the Elder, this distinguished his addressees from others who did not keep to the truth and were his opponents in the community crisis.

V. 2 Beloved This is the second occurrence of "beloved" and the third reference to the "love" that the Elder has toward Gaius.

I pray This word is related to the verb for prayer *(proseuchomai)* but does not necessarily imply that the wish is directed to God. The more conventional meaning "I wish" is also possible. There are no other references to prayer in the Letters.

in all things The word order of the translation here is somewhat awkward but is intended to reflect the word order of the Greek. The present wording is unattested in ancient letters (details in Lieu, *Second and Third* 44 and notes there). In what is perhaps the most thorough study of the issue, Lieu (*Second and Third* 44) points out that the normal wording is "before all" *(pro pantos* or *pro pantōn),* that is, in either a temporal or a local sense — or possibly as "above all," in the sense that what the writer is about to say is most important.

Attempts to deal with the text have been remarkable by their ingenuity. Turner (*Style* 270) translated it as "above all." Harris ("Study" 167) amends the text to *pro pantōn,* as does Funk ("Form" 425, n. 7). Lieu suggests that "We may have here a rare, personal or regional variation. . . ." However, the present wording is almost surely correct, and both its meaning and its placement can be easily explained by the author's arrangement of the material chiastically, as we shall see in the Interpretation.

you are in good health (Gk: *hygiainein*) This is a standard wish in ancient letters, as is also often the case in modern letters.

soul *Note on the word order of the translation:* In order to reflect the chiastic arrangement of the Greek, I have moved the words "your soul" from their normal English word order to a place at the end of the sentence to reflect the word order of the Greek. Parentheses have been placed in the appropriate place in the text to indicate where the words in parentheses would appear in the normal English word order.

In the Johannine writings, *psychē* typically refers to the physical life of the individual (e.g., John 10:11, 15, 17, 24; 12:25; 13:37, 38; 15:13; 1 John 3:16). Only in John 12:27 and here does it have a different meaning. In John 12:27, Jesus speaks of his soul being in turmoil at the approach of the hour (*nyn hē psychē mou tetaraktai*) but this could also be understood simply as a way of referring to the self. However, here the sense cannot be construed as a simple wish for well-being since that has already been given in the initial clause. Thus, it must refer specifically to the "soul."

V. 3 witness to your truth In v. 6, it will be said that the brothers have also witnessed to his love. Such witness was a common feature of Johannine theology and was a solemn attestation of truthfulness regarding some matter. Here, the brothers are witnessing to the fact that Gaius himself is loyal to the truth as the community understood it.

how you walk in truth (Gk: *kathōs*) This clause is in apposition to what precedes it and explains "your truth."

V. 4 than these Literally "than these things." The plural is presumably used to refer to the report about several of the author's children walking in truth.

my children are walking in the truth In 2 John 4, the Elder had spoken of "some of your children" walking in truth. Here there is no such qualification although we might expect it, given the actions of Diotrephes.

V. 5 you (will) act faithfully *Piston* ("faithfully") is the neuter of a substantized adjective used as an adverb (Zerwick, *Biblical Greek* §74 [53]; BDF §160; cf. Strecker, *Epistles* 258, n. 2; Lieu, *Second and Third* 105-6). This is not recognized by R. E. Brown, but it is an important element in the understanding of vv. 5-6. In the Interpretation below, we will see that there are compelling reasons for seeing v. 5b and v. 6b as parallels to one another and as elements of a brief chiasm.

The full meaning of *piston* here is not communicated well by the English word "faithfully," a word that suggests simple fidelity or loyalty. Gaius will be demonstrating fidelity by such action; but, more precisely, the Elder indicates that Gaius will be acting in a way that is informed *by his religious faith and in keeping with his faith,* if he welcomes the visitors.

Yet another parallel feature in the two expressions is evident from an analysis of their role within the letter form. In Greco-Roman letters, the opening of the body of the letter contained an expression of joy (which we have seen above) and a polite petition. A common introduction to the polite petition is the clause "you will do well to. . . ." Such a petition in precisely this form appears in v. 6b below. However, for Christians "doing well" had a distinctly religious frame of reference, and so the expression here: "You act in keeping with your faith," should be understood as a Christian variant of this typical formula and is intended to specify that "doing well" for a Christian meant "acting in a faith-filled way" (so also Funk, "Form" 427, without noticing the chiastic arrangement).

in whatever This clause is in apposition to *piston* from the previous clause and explains what it is that leads the Elder to conclude that Gaius is acting in keeping with his faith.

and this for strangers In the Greek, this is elliptical, consisting of only three words *kai touto xenous* ("and [you do] this [for people who are] strangers [to you]"). The reference to the visitors as "strangers" *(xenoi)* could be taken as a play on the etymology of the Greek word for hospitality *(philoxenia)*, which means literally "love of strangers." However, in the present instance, the Elder seems to want to call attention to the fact that the visitors were genuine strangers.

V. 6 They witnessed The relation between the tense of this verb and that of the next *(poiēseis)* is inconsistent. From the present verb, it would seem that the brothers who had been treated well by Gaius had returned to the Elder and had witnessed to him about the love shown them by Gaius. However, the second verb ("you will do") seems to imply that they are still with Gaius and in need of assistance (see further below).

to your love This refers to the love manifest in the aid extended to these emissaries on their travels.

before the assembly The term *(ekklēsia)* appears here for the first time in the Johannine literature. It will also appear in vv. 9, 10. There is no article before "assembly" in the Greek but in spite of attempts to find a difference in meaning, it is likely that no difference is intended. It refers to the assembly with which the Elder is associated.

The question whether the appearance of this term reflects a distinct stage in the conceptualization of the community experience is debated. Brown (*Epistles* 709-10) tends to downplay the significance of the term here. He uses comparisons with the Synoptics to argue that the absence of the term in the Gospel is not significant (since it does not appear in Mark or Luke either) and comparisons with 2 Tim and Titus (which together are about the same length as 1 John) to argue that its absence from 1 John is also not significant.

On the other hand, Lieu (*Second and Third* 105) speaks of the term as "one of a number of significant 'ecclesiastical' terms that 3 John shared with other New Testament writings but not with the Gospel or other Letters with their lack of 'institutional' language."

The term itself regularly appears in Paul's Letters, and so its use is hardly a late development. Yet even here, the choice of the term *ekklēsia* (which is derived from the verb "to choose") may be intended to recall that the community is "chosen," as was indicated by the author's addressing the community in 2 John 1 as "the Elect Lady," which was in turn likely to be related to the description of the disciples in the Gospel as "chosen." See John 6:70; 13:18; 15:16, 19. If this is the case, then it is possible that its use here is "non-technical" (contra Lieu, *Second and Third* 105, n. 134).

If it is "late," it is late in relation to earlier conceptualizations of the community experience *within the Johannine tradition.*

and you will act well The use of "act" in the translation here is somewhat awkward but is intended to reflect the parallelism with v. 5b where the same Greek verb *(poieō)* is used. In English, one would typically say "and you will *do* well. . . ." The verb here is in the future and seems to exhort Gaius to future conduct with the same emissaries who had (seemingly) already returned to the community *(ekklēsia)* of the Elder. Brown (*Epistles* 710-11) points out that this clause occurs frequently in secular letters and introduces the main purpose of the Letter.

having sent them on Once again the grammar is awkward. Literally, the clause reads: ". . . whom, you will do well, having sent on, worthily of God." Because the verbal form here is a participle, it indicates a point of time prior to the time of the main verb ("you will do well").

This verb *(propempō)* becomes almost a technical term in Christian circles for the aid rendered to fellow believers who were on a journey for religious purposes. It appears with this meaning in Acts 15:3; Rom 15:24; 1 Cor 16:6, 11; 2 Cor 1:16; and Titus 3:13. See also Polycarp *Phil.* 1:1.

in a way worthy of God This seems to refer primarily to the actions of Gaius although it can also refer to the actions of the emissaries.

V. 7 For The verse begins with the conjunction "for" *(gar)*, as did v. 3, and provides the reason why they should be treated in this way. Our English translation is somewhat awkward because of the repetition of "for." However, it is important that "for the sake of the Name" appear near the beginning of the clause since it appears there in the Greek and its position is balanced by "in order . . . the truth" at the end.

for the sake of the Name Scholars have made a variety of suggestions about the intended references of "the name." It has been proposed in the past that "the Name" was the name by which the Johannine believers as a community are known, or by which Christians in general are identified (in this case the name would be *"Christianoi"*). Today some hold that the name is that of God. Lieu *(Second and Third* 107-8) argues that this is evident from the fact that it parallels the earlier "worthy of God" in v. 5d. The more popular view is that it refers to Jesus' name (Smalley, Strecker, Painter, Culpepper, Klauck). However, R. E. Brown and Beutler are uncertain.

Some point out that in the Gospel (17:6) Jesus had said that he reveals the divine name to those the Father had given him. Brown speculates *(Gospel* 2:755-56) that the name he revealed is "I AM." He also suggests that "the Name" referred to here is I AM. However, several factors militate against this view. First, "I AM" is not used by others as a title in either the Gospel or the Letters. Second, it is unlikely that reverence for the divine name would have allowed the community to make a reference to it a common name for their community. Third, as we will see immediately below, elsewhere in the Johannine literature, the focus is on the name of Jesus. And it is much more likely that the reference is to the importance of acting in the name of Jesus.

If we focus our inquiry on the Johannine literature, it becomes clear that "name" appears in a variety of combinations: "in *his* name" (John 1:12; 2:23; 20:31); "in the name of the unique son of God" (John 3:18); "in my name" (John 14:13, 14, 26; 15:16; 16:23, 24, 26); "in the name of my Father" (5:43; 10:25); "your name" (17:6, 26); "in your name" (17:11, 12). In John 15:21, it is predicted that believers will be persecuted "because of my name." In 1 John, sins are forgiven "because of his name" (2:12); people are to "believe in the name of his Son" (3:23) and "in the name of the Son of God" (5:13).

Thus, the members of the community, like "the Jews" and like those who had seceded, claim to believe in God the Father; but, unlike "the Jews" and the secessionists, the members of the Johannine community believed in God the Father *in the name of* Jesus. It was this particular configuration of their faith that made their belief in God distinctive. Consequently, to say that they went out "for the sake of the Name" would be a natural description of the purposes for which they labored. Even more immediately pertinent is the fact that, throughout the Letters, the author sees the opponents as not believing in Jesus.

None of the texts elsewhere in the Johannine tradition is an exact equivalent of 3 John 7, since in 3 John 7 "the name" is used without explaining whose name is being referred to. And so 3 John 7 can be said to represent a new mode of expression. While there cannot be certain proof, because this is the only instance of the usage in the Johannine literature, it is very likely that this usage is simply another instance of the community's theological "jargon" used to refer succinctly to this idea that is expressed elsewhere in more developed form.

That this is possible is confirmed by a survey of the rest of the New Testament, where we see evidence of a usage very close, but not identical, to this usage. For example, Acts 4:12 ("There is no other name under heaven given to humanity by which we are to be saved") speaks of "the Name," but the usage is clearer because Jesus is mentioned in v. 10. In Acts 4:17 ("to speak to no one 'in this name' again"), it is clear from the general and immediate context (cf. v. 13) that the reference is to Jesus. Finally, in 1 Pet 4:16 ("If one of you is made to suffer as a Christian . . . let that person glorify God 'in this name'"), there is mention of Christ in vv. 13, 14.

In the later (sub-apostolic) literature, we have instances of what can be called the genuinely "absolute" use. For example, *Epistle of Barnabas* 16:8 ("Having received the remission of sins, and having put our hope on the Name . . ."); Ignatius, *Eph.* 3:1 ("I am prisoner for the Name"); *Phil.* 10:1 ("to appoint a deacon . . . to glorify the Name"). Thus, the use in 3 John 7 seems to reflect a usage later than that evident in Acts and 1 Peter (where "name" was used "absolutely" but with some explicit reference to the fact that it was the name of Jesus that was being referred to) and closer to the later usage evident most clearly in *Barnabas* and Ignatius, where there was no need to make this identification explicit.

they went out The same verb (Gk: *exēlthon*) was used in 1 John 2:19; 4:1; 2 John 7 to refer to the opponents who left the community. In 2 John 7, the Elder said: "Many deceivers have gone out into the world." This would seem to indicate that the opponents had not only left the Elder's community but that they were a danger to the faithful, perhaps because they were engaged in proselytizing. While these members of the Elder's community had "gone out for the sake of the name," of itself the expression only indicates that they had gone out for religious purposes. However, if we interpret it within the context of 2 John 7, we may be correct in thinking that their purpose was to counteract the effects of the opponents' missionaries.

accepting (Gk: *lambanō*) This is the first of three verbs having the general meaning "accept, receive" (cf. also *hypolambanō*, v. 8, and *epidechomai*, vv. 9, 10). I will translate the first two by "accept" and the last by "receive."

nothing from the nations The word *ethnikos* itself is a nominalized adjective meaning "belonging to a nation," with the connotation that it is a foreign nation. The word is related to *ethnos*, which in the singular could refer to the Jewish nation (cf. John 11:48) but which, in common Jewish usage in the plural, referred to non-Jews.

Christian emissaries were to be supported by the communities in which they resided. This is reflected in 1 Cor 9:1-18, where Paul presumably could have expected to be supported by the Corinthian community. However, Paul continued a gainful occupation when he resided among the Corinthians in order not to be accused of taking advantage of this privilege for selfish reasons.

V. 8 Therefore This is the only instance of the Greek particle *oun* in the Letters, although it appears almost 200 times in the Gospel. The pronoun "we" is in the emphatic position and is meant to contrast with what non-believers do. This contrast is borne out by its central place within the chiasm of vv. 7-8.

to accept (Gk: *hypolambanein*) See "accepting" above in v. 7.

coworkers for the truth "Coworkers" *(synergoi)* occurs with the dative case here but never in the LXX nor elsewhere in the New Testament. Although the cognate verb occurs with the dative, the noun normally occurs with either the genitive or with *eis* and the accusative. The common explanation is that this is a dative of advantage, a noun in the dative that presents that on behalf of which the action is undertaken. More likely, it should be understood as a dative of respect (Zerwick, *Biblical Greek* §53 [38]; BDF §197).

With whom are the supporters coworkers? With the emissaries or with the truth? Brown (*Epistles* 714) takes the view that these will be coworkers with the truth and so understands the force of the dative to indicate "in cooperation with" rather than "in service of" the truth. Brown points out that, although the cognate verb (e.g., *synergeō*) regularly has a person as object, this is not a problem since truth is sometimes personified in the Johannine tradition. However, this argument is not completely convincing since the parallels adduced by Brown are instances of the dative after the cognate *verb* (which we see regularly takes the dative). In v. 8c, it is the *noun* that appears, and we have seen that there is no precedent for a dative occurring naturally with the noun. It is more likely that the dative is the more general dative of respect. In that case, v. 8c is probably elliptical and would, in its full expression, be something like: "In order that we may be coworkers [with the brothers who work] for the truth." This is confirmed by the structure of the chiasm, in which the supporters (v. 8c) are paralleled with the emissaries (v. 7a).

According to 2 John 10-11, the one who supports false teachers takes part in their evil deeds. Thus, those who support the missionaries will be coworkers with those missionaries — (in their witness) to the truth.

V. 9 I wrote something Some interpreters are offended by the thought that a Letter by the Elder would have been rejected and have made various attempts to change the plain sense of the statement. Some early scribes introduced the particle *an,* making the statement hypothetical. Others made "Gaius" the subject of the verb. Still others think it is an "epistolary aorist" and refers to the present Letter, but that makes the text excessively awkward. As a result, most agree that it refers to a different letter.

Any decision about the nature of the previous writing must depend to a considerable extent on one's judgment of other issues in connection with the conflict between the Elder and Diotrephes. As a result, my own view will be postponed until the more detailed discussion in the Addendum below.

to the assembly This is the second reference to the community as an *ekklēsia.* It is probably not significant that it was written to the assembly rather than to Diotrephes himself. Certainly Paul did the same (e.g., 1 Thess 5:12), and no distinction is intended there.

Diotrephes A Greek name meaning "Nurtured by Zeus." It is also attested in secular literature. He is known only from this reference and from what is said about him in this and the following verse.

loves to act as leader (Gk: *philoprōteuō*) The literal meaning of this word is "to love to be first." It appears nowhere else in the extant Greek literature although some cognate forms do occur. Bultmann (*Epistles* 101) argued that the author used it to avoid recognizing Diotrephes' actual title of bishop. If taken alone, the title could be used to emphasize the fact that Diotrephes has no official standing but simply puts himself forward by force of personality. This is certainly possible, but the actions Diotrephes performs also seem to be functions of one in recognized authority: he rejects the Letter of the Elder; he excludes visiting missionaries; he expels individuals who attempt to accept the missionaries. I do not think there is enough evidence to decide with certainty one way or the other.

receive (Gk: *epidechomai*) This term appears again in v. 10 and refers to the lack of acceptance extended to the Elder (here) and to the brothers (v. 10). In the present instance, Diotrephes has not received (that is, accepted) what the Elder had written. In v. 10, it is the brothers themselves who were not received when they visited Diotrephes' community. From the word itself, we cannot tell the reason for the rejection (see Mitchell, "Diotrephes").

us There is some discussion whether the pronoun here is the authorial plural or whether it is meant to refer to the group of tradition-bearers, the Johannine school. The Elder had begun the sentence writing as "I." In the coming verses there is an alternation between the first-person singular and plural ("if I come" [v. 10a]; "I will bring up" [v. 10b]; "we bear witness" [v. 12d]; "our witness" [v. 12e]; "I had many things" [v. 13a]; "I do not wish to write" [13b]; "I hope to see" [v. 14a]). Some of these are necessarily in the singular since the Elder is speaking of his own personal actions and intentions. The instance most likely to be an authorial "we" is the present one, where the lack of reception granted "us" (v. 9c) refers to the rejection of what "I" had written.

Throughout 2 and 3 John, when the Elder exhorts or expresses an important viewpoint, he writes on the basis of his own "witness." If he were writing on behalf of a "school," we would expect the Elder to make reference to the fact that such was the group's perspective in many places where he expresses what is clearly his own view (e.g., 2 John 1cd, 4a, 12a, 12de; 3 John 3a; 4ab [where the brothers are referred to as "my" children], 9a). Moreover, with some consistency, the author distinguishes himself from the others in the community and never suggests that they are anything other than members or brothers or "my children" (e.g., 2 John 1cd, 13; 3 John 3b, 12b, 15b). As a result, I would see the plural here as an authorial "we."

V. 10 If I come This is the subjunctive in Greek and indicates that the Elder is not certain that he will actually come to the community. We do not know the eventual outcome.

I will bring up While the action indicated by this verb would seem to be weak in the light of the actions of Diotrephes, this is the verb that will be used later, in

John 14:26 (3E), where the Paraclete is said to bring up to the disciples all that Jesus said. It may well be that the verb had a quasi-technical sense in the community indicating that this was considered the proper manner for addressing erroneous belief or behavior.

If the implications of this terminology are correct, then the verse probably reflects a situation in which the Elder does not claim for himself a special power to teach or to exercise authority. On the other hand, by designating Diotrephes as one who "loves to be first," it may well be that the Elder is indicating that Diotrephes is acting with a kind of self-appointed importance. In keeping with his understanding of the tradition, the Elder can only "witness" and "remind."

bringing unjustified charges against us The Greek verb *phlyareō* ("to indulge in utterance that makes no sense, talk nonsense about," BDAG 1060) appears only here in the New Testament, although the cognate adjective *phlyaros* is used of "gossipy" widows in 1 Tim 5:13. As can be seen, the verb has a wide range of meaning. It can refer to speech that is untrue but annoying but also to speech that is untrue but that is deliberate, formal and public. Which of these meanings one chooses here affects the meaning of the overall statement considerably. In the present instance, the fact that this speech involves "evil words" and the fact that terminology such as this reflects, within the categories of apocalyptic dualism, activity in league with the Evil One (see the following Note) indicates that the speech of Diotrephes is seriously evil. This is not "gossip" or "foolish talk" as would be ascribed to the widows of 1 Tim 5:13 who are said to be *phlyaroi*. The speech in the present instance is more serious and more evil. Consequently, R. E. Brown's translation "spreading evil nonsense" does not capture the full seriousness of what Diotrephes is doing.

"Us" in the phrase is the authorial plural (see the Note on v. 9).

with evil words The seriousness of Diotrephes' actions would seem to be indicated by this phrase. He does not utter idle chatter but deliberate falsehood. The overall use of the word *ponēros* in the Johannine tradition is discussed in the Note to John 3:19. Given the fact that this term reflects the apocalyptic worldview throughout the Johannine writings, it should be clear that the words of the Elder here are to be understood as indicating that what Diotrephes is doing is seriously evil. He is acting as one who belongs to the side of the Evil One, along with the opponents of 1 John and those who spread false teaching in 2 John. What he is doing is not a minor matter.

not being satisfied with this A precise understanding of the grammar here is important for a correct understanding of the verse. This is a participial phrase and the second one to appear in the sentence. Brown (*Epistles* 719) argues that it is in parallel with the previous participial phrase ("slandering us") (cf. Note on v. 10c). This is incorrect. While both are participial phrases, the first participle is in apposition to "what he is doing." However, the second is not. Rather, it modifies the implied subject of *epidechetai*. If one takes Brown's reading of the grammar, both phrases are in apposition to "what he is doing," namely, "slandering us" and "not being satisfied." In reality, the things Diotrephes is doing are "slandering us" and "not receiving the brothers and preventing . . . ejecting." However, in order to achieve this, the Elder shifts the grammar, using a participial phrase to describe Diotrephes' first action and a series of indicative verbs in independent clauses to indicate what he does with respect to the brothers.

I would argue that both the meaning Brown attributes to *phlyarōn* and his reading of the grammar in v. 10b-e lead him to misread v. 10 as a whole. In the mind of the Elder, as it can be discerned from his grammar, Diotrephes is doing two things that are distinct from one another. The reason Diotrephes slanders the Elder is the same as his reason for not receiving the brothers, but the Elder conceives of the one being possible without the other.

he does not receive the brothers himself As was implied in 2 John 10-11, the Johannine commandment of mutual love required that believers should welcome into their home fellow believers who were travelling for religious purposes. In the instance described in 2 John 10, those who might come to the community and bring false teaching were to be treated in precisely the opposite way: "Do not greet him" and "Do not accept him into your house." This is what Diotrephes is doing to the emissaries of the Elder's community, and the Elder sees it as a violation of the commandment of mutual love.

he prevents those who wish to This implies that Diotrephes had considerable power within the community. It is thought that, in most cases, house churches met in the home of a wealthier member of the community and that it was this person who would generally be the one to give hospitality to travelers (see Malherbe, "Inhospitality" 223-26). It is clear from this verse, however, that hospitality could be extended by any of a number within the community. Presumably, Diotrephes prevented community members from accepting the travelers by threatening them with expulsion (see immediately below).

ejects them from the assembly This was some form of disciplinary exclusion of the believer from the assembly. As is explained in the Note on John 9:34, the word itself has a neutral meaning. From the expression, we cannot know whether it was a formal and permanent process or simply a momentary response. However, the fact that Diotrephes could do this indicates a degree of power and *de facto* authority that could be seen as going beyond the level of simple force of personality.

V. 11 Beloved This is the third time the Elder has addressed Gaius with this title. Each time, the Elder begins a new exhortation.

The one doing good ... The one doing evil The parallel between these two statements is even closer in the Greek *(ho agathopoiōn ... ho kakopoiōn)*. The language, particularly in the first statement, is not found elsewhere in the Johannine literature but is nevertheless typical of apocalyptic dualism. The expression "is of God," which identifies one's allegiance as being with God rather than Satan, appears in John 8:47 (3E); 1 John 3:10; 4:4, 6 [twice]; 5:19. This statement is so general that it has been taken in an unqualified sense to mean that *all* good deeds reveal that the person is close to God. But it was hardly the intention of the author to either affirm or deny such a broad statement. His intention was much more focused and "doing good" was certainly understood in terms of the Johannine commandments.

The second statement is curious. The Elder claims that the one doing evil "has not seen God." What is being referred to here is unclear. It was the constant view of the Gospel that *no one* had seen God (John 1:18; 6:46; 1 John 4:12); yet there were some partial qualifications of this. In John 5:37-38, it was said that no one had heard the voice of God nor seen his face but that they had his word because it was spoken by Jesus. In John 14:9, Jesus said that "the one who has seen me has seen the Father." The formulation closest to the present one is found in 1 John 3:6, where it is said that "everyone sinning has neither seen him [Jesus] nor known him." The verbal formulation is so close to the present one that it seems likely that this is what is being referred to. Yet in 1 John 3:6, it is *Jesus* who has not been seen. It may be that the author of 3 John thought of Jesus in terms similar to those of John 14:7, 9 and so felt justified in making the statement.

The radicality of these statements is one more indication that the Elder considered the actions of Diotrephes not to be some minor infraction but a serious breach of the conduct that was expected of a member of the community.

V. 12 Demetrius There have been various attempts to identify Demetrius with persons of the same or similar name elsewhere in the New Testament. One theory is that he is Demetrius the silversmith, who lived in Ephesus (Acts 19:24), and that he had been converted and was a member of the Johannine community. He is also associated with Demas (as a shortened form of Demetrius) who had been a companion to Paul but who had deserted him (2 Tim 4:10). The Apostolic Constitutions (4th century) state that Demetrius was made bishop of Philadelphia by the apostle John.

has been witnessed to As always is the case, the "witness" of community members was the primary form of commendation.

by all The "all" here are other members of the community rather than simply the members of the "school." If the Elder were writing as a member of a school, we would expect some other designation here.

by the truth itself The meaning of this phrase is the object of much discussion. To some it appears that truth is personified in such a way as to refer to Jesus (14:6 "I am the Truth") while others think it refers to the Spirit (1 John 5:6 "The Spirit is the Truth"). Brown (*Epistles* 723) argues that, while the Spirit witnesses to Jesus (John 15:26; 1 John 5:7-8), it is not said to witness to humans. While Jesus witnesses to "what he has seen and heard" (John 3:32), to the rejection of the prophet (John 4:44), to the fact that the world is evil (John 7:7), and to his coming betrayal (13:21), none of these is similar to the witnessing here. It would also be unusual to have the testimony of Jesus or the Spirit between two references to human witnessing.

I am inclined to agree with Dodd (*Epistles* 167), who suggests that it is a way of affirming that Demetrius' character is not witnessed to only by humans (who may be in error) but by the truth itself. Thus, it becomes a poetic personification of the truth. A similar idea is expressed in 2 John 2ab.

And we bear witness also Scholars are divided whether this is the authorial "we" or whether it refers to the Johannine school. Among more recent scholars, Beutler, Brown, and Smalley think it refers to the "we" of the Johannine school. Strecker, Schnackenburg, and Klauck think it is the authorial "we."

When the Elder writes, he consistently refers to himself in the singular. When he exhorts, he speaks in the singular. Here, he has already spoken of the "all" who witness to Demetrius. In that context, it seems that the "we" is really an "I" and should be termed the authorial "we" (see also the Note on v. 9 above).

Regarding the use of "witness" here, Painter comments (*Epistles* 378): "The use of the language of witness to refer to Demetrius, not to Jesus as in the Gospel, is un-Johannine. It [the true Johannine witness] is a threefold witness (see 1 John 5:7), though there is no reference to the threefold nature here." Painter is correct that, in the Gospel, the witnesses witness to Jesus and that here the witnessing is done to community members. However, the very act of witnessing is what is so Johannine, because the members rely on their experience of the truth rather than on any set doctrine or authoritative teaching office. Within the life of the community, it becomes necessary to bear witness to the truth and the love of community members as a way of discerning and acknowledging that they possess the Spirit of Truth rather than the Spirit of Deceit. In 1 John 5:7, however, the witness to Jesus was threefold: the Spirit was the individual doing the witnessing and the other witnesses were "water" and "blood," which referred to the *content* of the witness rather than the *agent*.

and you know that our witness is true Something almost identical is said of the Beloved Disciple in the Gospel (19:35; 21:24). Here the Elder appeals to his own character as a reference to the accuracy of his witness. Although it is possible that the Elder is referring to the Johannine "school" here, the overall context of 2 and 3 John suggests that this is not the case (for the notion of a "school," see the Addendum below).

V. 13 I had many things to write to you This is a part of the standard closing of the ancient letter and may (or may not) imply that there are a number of other pressing issues that the author would like to discuss with the recipient.

by pen and ink See on 2 John 12 and Appendix 6 (Formal Elements in Greek Letter Writing) in this volume.

V. 14 I hope . . . face to face This would be a part of the standard closing of a letter (see on 2 John 12 and Appendix 6 [Formal Elements in Greek Letter Writing] in this volume).

V. 15 friends (Gk: *philoi*, literally "friends") This is to be distinguished from "brothers" *(adelphoi),* which was the term used elsewhere for the community members in their role as community members. Here it is their friendship that is stressed. The Greek text does not contain the words "here" and "there" but the English sense requires them.

THE INTERPRETATION OF 3 JOHN

V. 1 (THE OPENING)

The Structure and Literary Techniques of V. 1

The Letter opens with a salutation identifying the author (the Elder) and the addressee, but unlike most secular letters it contains no greeting.[1] As was the

1. In this respect it is more like an official letter than a personal one. This could simply re-

case in 2 John, the author does not identify himself by a proper name but only by title. However, unlike 2 John, the recipient is a single individual and is identified by name.

The Interpretation of V. 1

Already in the salutation (v. 1), the Elder makes clear his affection for Gaius. Although "beloved" could be construed as a conventional term in the opening of a letter, the fact that the Elder goes on to speak of the basis of his affection suggests that the use here is intended to be more than conventional. The Elder loves Gaius "in truth." Again, we meet a term that could simply mean "truly" (see Notes). However, this mention of truth is almost surely a reference to the truth of the Johannine tradition as the Elder understands it. In the Johannine tradition, love can be given only to one who walks in truth and in love.

Consequently, right from the beginning, the Elder alludes to his own religious perspective in writing — and to the circumstances of the community at the time of writing. The community as a whole (that is, those sharing the Johannine tradition) has been divided over the interpretation of the tradition. In 1 John the author had detailed the correct interpretation of the tradition over against that of the opponents. That understanding was said to have two basic dimensions: correct belief and correct behavior.[2] The author refers to these symbolically as matters dealing with "truth" and with "love," since correct belief was "true" belief and since correct behavior was based on "love." It was also these two summary categories that had been formulated in the two commandments: to keep the word of Jesus (the truth of what he taught) and to love one another.

In 1 and 2 John, there had been more extensive discussions of truth. But here also the Elder will frame his words within the categories of truth (vv. 1, 3-4,

---

flect the personal preference of the Elder, or it could indicate that he seeks to create an official tone or a certain formality in the Letter because he does not know Gaius well. Neither of the latter alternatives seems to fit the remainder of the Letter and so it seems best not to attach any importance to this feature. For a summary discussion of the overall structure of the ancient letter, see White, "Epistolary"; Brown, *Epistles* Appendix V 788-95; Lieu, *Second and Third* 37-51 and the more specialized treatments referred to in those studies. On the Structure of 2 and 3 John in relation to such letters, see also Funk, "Form."

2. R. E. Brown regularly refers to the two main issues as Christology and ethics; but, as we have seen, in the area of belief, the author and his opponents disagree about much more than simply Christology. Consequently, it is more adequate to speak of the first category as "belief" (of which one important element is Christology) and the second as "ethics." For the Elder, correct belief is equated with the truth and correct ethics are expressed in love.

8, 12) and love (vv. 5-6 and the references to hospitality that was to be grounded in love). In fact, it will be in terms of these two categories that Gaius will be assessed (and praised) by the Elder when he reports that the brothers have witnessed to Gaius' truth (v. 3b) and his love (v. 6a).[3] Although much of this is yet to come in the Letter, being aware of this fact makes it clearer that the words to Gaius here are not conventional. They reveal the mind-set of the Elder.

V. 2 (THE WISH FOR WELL-BEING)

The Structure and Literary Techniques of V. 2

Now for the first of three times, the Elder addresses Gaius directly as "Beloved." This is significant for the structure of the Letter in that each time it appears it introduces an important new part of the Letter. Here it introduces the health wish and, in v. 5 and v. 11, it introduces the Elder's petitions to Gaius.[4] The Elder structures the verse itself by means of a brief chiasm. Although it is brief, the chiasm provides new and clearer light on the meaning and purpose of the verse.

The Interpretation of V. 2

As was just mentioned, the Elder begins his health wish (v. 2) by addressing Gaius as "Beloved." By doing so, he begins what, to all appearances, is simply a conventional expression at this point in ancient letters.[5] However, the Elder makes use of this convention to praise Gaius in a way that goes beyond simple convention.

The Elder's wish is expressed in the form of a brief chiasm that has apparently gone unnoticed before. The first element of the chiasm parallels the expression "in all things" with "your soul" in the last. The second and second-last elements speak of "doing well." Thus, together the first and second elements constitute the general wish that Gaius do well "in all things," and the last two elements provide a point of comparison by means of a reference to the fact that Gaius is "doing well" spiritually. The central element, then, expresses the specification of the more general wish, namely that Gaius will be in good physical health. So it is here in the central element that the conventional element of the health wish appears. But the Elder contextualizes this by making Gaius' spiri-

---

3. There is reference to the crisis itself in the Letter, although the topic is not developed. In 3 John, the focus is on providing hospitality for travelers.

4. Lieu, *Second and Third* 40.

5. Although the health wish was a conventional element of ancient letters, it does not often appear in Letters in the NT and so its appearance here is striking.

tual health the standard against which he puts his hopes for Gaius' well-being in all other things.

In the Note to v. 2, we pointed out that the appearance of the phrase that I have translated as "in all things" is awkward and without parallel at this point in any ancient letter. Its presence has provoked various attempts at explanation. However, when viewed in the light of the chiastic structure, a clear explanation emerges. The phrase "in all things" is located where it is precisely in order to parallel it literarily with the reference to "your soul" at the very end. It is the parallelism (more natural in the Greek than in an English translation) of these two elements that shows that the first element ("in all things") is simply a hope that his physical health will be equal to what is his obvious spiritual health. What is remarkable, however, is that the Elder views even the conventional health wish within a spiritual context and so praises his spiritual health while hoping Gaius' more general health is as good as his spiritual health.

VV. 3-12 (THE BODY OF THE LETTER)

VV. 3-4 (THE TRANSITION AND AN EXPRESSION OF JOY)

The Structure and Literary Techniques of Vv. 3-4

The Elder now begins the transition to the body of the Letter. Verse 3 begins with "for," a feature that, at first, creates some awkwardness. But what follows is closely linked to what was just said because, in it, the author will explain how he knows about the well-being of Gaius' soul.

Once again, we see that the author has used a very modest amount of literary organization and composed the two verses so that they closely parallel one another in a way that is repetitive but that also provides two perspectives on the content.

Both begin with expressions of joy ("I rejoiced greatly"; "I have no greater joy"). Next is the cause of the joy. In v. 3, the cause is the witnessing of the brothers; in v. 4, the cause of the joy is what the Elder hears. Finally, there is the content of the witness, which is described in identical terms in each case. In v. 3, what is witnessed to is described as: "how you walk in the truth" and, in v. 4, what the Elder hears is described as: "that my children walk in the truth." However, the perspective and emphasis in each are somewhat different, as we shall see.

The Interpretation of Vv. 3-4

In v. 3 we learn that some of "the brothers," members of the community, have arrived at the Elder's community and (in terminology distinctive of the Johannine tradition) have "witnessed" to Gaius' "truth," saying that he "walks in truth." All of this brings great joy to the Elder. At this point the Elder does not specify how Gaius' adherence to the truth had been manifested, but he is assured that such is the case by the witness of those who had recently arrived from Gaius' locale.

While v. 4 would seem to be largely repetitive of v. 3, in fact, in v. 4 we learn three things we had not known before. First, the Elder makes a point of saying that *nothing gives him greater joy* than that he hears of them walking in truth. This is the culmination of the Elder's considerable focus on truth. Four times the Elder has called attention to the "truth" of Gaius. He loves Gaius "in truth." The brothers witness to Gaius' "truth" and to the fact that Gaius "walks in the truth." And now he adds his own final attestation to the joy it brings that Gaius "walks in truth." Within the context of the crisis that has divided the community, this emphasis on truth indicates in the clearest way possible that Gaius is one who agrees with the Elder as to how the tradition is to be understood.[6]

Second, in v. 4 the Elder reveals more about his relation to Gaius when he refers to him as being among his "children." Gaius is evidently not someone unknown to the Elder but one over whom the Elder has some sort of present or past responsibility. The fact that he refers to Gaius as his "child" suggests that the Elder is the one responsible for Gaius' conversion and Gaius' very life as a believer. Understandably, the Elder is deeply happy to hear that Gaius has remained faithful to the truth.[7]

Third, from the way the Elder writes, it is clear he holds a position of preeminence in relation to others. Not only is he speaking to the others as to his children, the Elder is taking *de facto* responsibility to speak for the tradition

---

6. Brown (*Epistles* 740) claims that "the Presbyter's joy over Gaius' truth and walking in truth is associated entirely with the love he has manifested in showing hospitality to the brothers." Although truth and love are closely related throughout the Johannine tradition (see particularly 2 John 4-6, where love is said to be evidenced by walking in truth), here (in 3 John 3-4), the Elder speaks entirely of Gaius' following the truth. Then, in vv. 5-8, he turns to a discussion of Gaius' love. That these are distinguished is evident also from the separate statements that the brothers witness to Gaius' truth (v. 3) and that they also witness to his love (v. 6).

7. If we take this expression literally, it would seem that Gaius had been converted by the Elder and so was personally known by the Elder. It is also possible that the Elder thought of Gaius as his "child" in the larger sense that Gaius was a member of a community founded by the Elder and the community of which the Elder was the preeminent witness. If this was the case, then what the Elder has mentioned to this point has been due to the witness of those who had been with Gaius.

and to say what should bring joy and what constitutes the truth. But, at the same time, there is no indication that it is a preeminence based on some authoritative role but rather on some personal qualities as well as his relation to their lives as believers. He is "the Elder." They are his "children."[8]

Verses 3 and 4 are also the first reference to the fact that members of these communities engage in travels between one another bringing reports of events. Already in 2 John we have seen a reference to the community of "the Elect Lady." It seems unlikely that Gaius belongs to that community. If this is correct, then we have evidence of at least three communities (that of the Elder, that of the Elect Lady, and that of Gaius) at some distance from one another but all joined in relation to one another and particularly in relation to the Elder.

VV. 5-6 (THE FIRST REQUEST)

The Structure and Literary Techniques of Vv. 5-6

With v. 5, the body of the Letter proper begins and the Elder signals a new point and seeks to reawaken Gaius' attention with his second address to Gaius as "Beloved." Once again the author composes his thoughts in a brief chiasm that extends through vv. 5-6. Because the details of the chiasm are so intimately related to the thought of the verses, it seems more appropriate to explain the details of the chiasm in the Interpretation to avoid excessive repetition. However, it will be noted that once again recognizing the presence of a chiasm in the verses brings considerably greater clarity to the meaning of the verses and explains well the problems regularly puzzled over by scholars.

The Interpretation of Vv. 5-6

The parallelism between the first (v. 5b) and last (v. 6b) elements is extensive. First, there is the important parallelism between *piston poieis* (v. 5b) and *kalōs poiēseis* (v. 6b). Each of these expressions consists of an adverbial form together with the verb *poieō*.[9] Moreover, both are intended to be understood (see Note

---

8. Lieu (*Second and Third* 106) thinks "that the Elder is advancing his case with great caution...." I am inclined to disagree. Rather, the overall tone is set by the Elder's words about how much joy it brings to him to hear of Gaius walking in the truth (vv. 3-4) and to hear that his love is also attested (v. 6a). I do not take this as flattery, nor as simply one of the conventions of such letters, but as genuine joy. The Elder seems to have no reservations about Gaius.

9. Lieu (*Second and Third* 105-6) recognizes the adverbial usage of *piston*, something not noticed by R. E. Brown. However, Lieu fails to notice that *piston poieis* probably is intended to have a future force and that it is a Christian variant of the common secular formula *kalōs*

above) in a future sense and so speak of actions the Elder recommends to Gaius.[10] Also, these two expressions have significant (and identical) functions within the typical letter format. The expression *kalōs poiein* (v. 6b) was a common way of introducing the main request of an ancient letter. Yet, the author holds this expression for last and begins with *piston poieis* (v. 5b), a Christian variant of the more common formula, a variant that expresses the conviction that, if Gaius does as the Elder suggests, he will not just be "acting well" *(kalōs poiēseis),* but he will in fact be "acting in accord with his faith" *(piston poieis).*

The remaining parts of the first and last elements of the chiasm are also parallel. Each element (v. 5b and v. 6b) speaks of the action that is being encouraged. However, in the first, the action is described in the general: "Whatever you do for the brothers." In the second, it is the more specific: "Having sent them on in a way worthy of God."

This is considerable parallelism — but it is obscured by the material in v. 5c and v. 6a. Not only does the material of v. 6a not have a parallel within the unit, but the tense of the verb is out of keeping with that of the surrounding verbs.[11] In order to understand v. 6a properly, we need to retrieve something of the larger context in which the verses appear. We recall that, in v. 3, some of the brothers had come to the Elder's community and had witnessed to Gaius' *truth* (cf. v. 3cd). Here, in v. 6a, the Elder makes a statement almost identical to that in v. 3cd, except that this time he says that the visitors have witnessed, not to Gaius' *truth,* but to his *love.* But the Elder's recollection of this witness appears in an exclamatory interjection that interrupts the sequence of v. 5 and of v. 6b. It is identical to the way, in 1 John 1:2, the Elder had interrupted the flow of his thought with an interjection about the extraordinary reality of the life that had been revealed in Jesus. Thus, the Elder breaks off his exhortation in order to recall how Gaius' love had been publicly witnessed to also. The Elder uses this recollection as the basis for his own confidence that Gaius will show his love again by "whatever you may do for the brothers" who will now be visiting, and specifically by "sending them on in a way worthy of God."

If the words of v. 6a are an exclamatory interjection, then we should not expect them to have a formal place within the structure of the chiasm even though they are related to it in *content.* Once the nature of v. 6a is understood in

---

poiēseis, which she does notice (see Funk, "Form" 427). However, it is only when these insights are combined that we are able to notice the extent of the parallels between v. 5b and v. 6b and fully understand the force of the verses.

10. The use of the present with future force (see the Note) enables the Elder both to make reference to what Gaius is already doing for the brothers (as witnessed to by the visitors) and also to express the hope that Gaius will continue to do this for visitors.

11. In the other verbs, the tense is actual (v. 6b) or implied (v. 5b) future. In v. 6a, the verb is aorist. This has led to various theories that attempt to explain the awkwardness.

this manner, we can account not only for the way the words interrupt the flow of thought but also for the seemingly awkward shift in tenses of the verbs. The words of v. 6a are a recollection of the brothers' *past* witness to Gaius' *past* love that provides hope for similar actions by Gaius *in the future.*

Once we have accounted for the awkwardness of v. 6a, it becomes clear that the central structural element of the chiasm consists of the words "and this toward strangers." As is the case in any chiasm, the central element is intended to be the focal point. Here, the point is that the community's love is to be shown to these brothers *even though they are strangers.*[12] The point is that it might be easier to extend love to one who is known by the host, but love modeled on the example of Jesus should be extended even to strangers. At the same time, given the crisis the community was undergoing, to accept strangers was undoubtedly more difficult. And so the Elder is sending this Letter.

When the Elder speaks of "sending the emissaries on their way," it appears that he is referring to a practice that was well established within early Christianity. In Rom 15:24, Paul speaks of his hope to visit the community in Rome and "to be sent on my way [to Spain] by you." Here the dual notions of reception and "sending on the way" are the same as in 3 John and, indeed, even the Greek verb used to describe the "sending" *(propempō)* is the same.[13] This suggests that the process of sending involved supplying the visitor with the (perhaps substantial) material resources necessary for the next stage of the trip.

The Elder speaks here of the brothers in the plural and this is, to all appearances, simply a general exhortation. However, it is likely that the Elder is preparing the way for his recommendation of Demetrius, who was apparently bringing this Letter to Gaius and for whom the Elder was seeking Christian hospitality. But, for the present, the Elder exhorts Gaius to extend such Christian love to strangers and then to provide the support necessary to send them further on their way in a way worthy of God.

We noted that v. 6a interrupts the otherwise orderly structure of vv. 5-6. However, the placement of v. 6a suggests that Gaius' love had been demonstrated precisely in offering hospitality to "Johannine visitors" on another occasion. So now the Elder writes to ask him to receive and support yet another group of the

---

12. See Malina ("Received" 182-87) for a description of "hospitality" in first-century Mediterranean culture. Although Malina criticizes Malherbe's methodology, it is not immediately clear how Malina's description advances the understanding of the situation beyond that provided by Malherbe. Malina in turn mistakes the genre of 3 John in calling it a letter of recommendation (187-88).

13. See also Acts 15:3; 1 Cor 16:6, 11; 2 Cor 1:16; Titus 3:13. The similarity of vocabulary in these texts has led scholars to conclude that an almost technical vocabulary developed to describe the various aspects of this practice. See Malherbe, "Inhospitality" 223, and the literature referred to there.

brothers, persons who are travelling "for the sake of the Name" and who are undoubtedly bringing the current Letter. This is the heart of the Elder's request, expressed within the conventions of the ancient letter (using the typical expression "you will do well to . . ."), but, at the same time, supplementing that conventional expression (by using the Christian formula: "You will act faithfully") and so casting the request within a decidedly Christian framework.[14]

VV. 7-8 (BACKGROUND TO THE REQUEST)

The Structure and Literary Techniques of Vv. 7-8

In the previous two verses, the Elder had urged Gaius' support for the missionaries. Now he describes what the missionaries themselves have done and the need to cooperate with their work. Structurally vv. 7-8 make up yet another brief chiasm as we shall see.

The Interpretation of Vv. 7-8

From vv. 7-8, we get a clear picture of Christian hospitality as it was practiced in the Johannine tradition. We know that, at the time, public lodging was not plentiful and the inns were often dangerous places, frequented by thieves. But it would be wrong to think that the welcome and hospitality to be extended to fellow believers was just a matter of avoiding such public lodging. Rather, it was something that was offered as a mark of Christian love.

When the brothers went on a journey on behalf of the community, they would not seek lodging among the nations (that is, non-Christians). While it is true that public lodging in the ancient world presented a number of dangers, as is clear from 3 John, lodging among fellow Christians was not just for the purpose of avoiding such danger.[15] From vv. 5c-6a, it is evident that offering such hospitality was understood as an expression of Christian love and was to be extended even to strangers. In Johannine terms, this would be an important example of how the commandment of mutual love was to be fulfilled. Secondly, as

14. This is the third "conventional" element of the Letter of which the Elder has made use while, at the same time, subtly infusing each one with a distinctively Christian (and Johannine) perspective. He had done so with his address of Gaius as "Beloved," followed by his explanation of why he was so beloved in a Christian sense. He had done the same in the health wish by means of his reference to Gaius' spiritual health, and now he introduces a religious perspective when he supplements "you will do well" with "you will act faithfully."

15. For historical and social science analyses of hospitality, see the articles of Malherbe ("Inhospitality") and Malina ("Received") already referred to.

is clear from v. 8c, helping the brothers in their travels was to become, in effect, a coworker with the brother and a coworker for the truth. Thus, those who supported the emissaries would be considered to have a part in the success of the activity the travelers were engaged in.

Although we do not know the specific purpose of the travels mentioned in v. 7, they were religiously motivated and so concerned with some type of ongoing need of the communities. If we are to judge from 2 John, the emissaries were probably engaged in teaching work (cf. v. 10). If there was a crisis of teaching within the community as a whole, undoubtedly, individuals and groups would circulate among the communities attempting to win over individuals to their own interpretation.

When we look at the New Testament as a whole, we see that it contains examples of Christians engaged in such travels for a variety of reasons. One of these purposes was certainly evangelistic. It was by means of such missionaries that Christianity spread so rapidly. While the missionary was in a city, it was expected that he would be given lodging by the community (e.g., Acts 21:4, 7, 16-17; Rom 12:13; 1 Tim 5:10; Heb 13:2; 1 Pet 4:9; cf. also Matt 10:11-14). Paul was the recipient of such hospitality (Rom 15:29; 16:23; Phlm 22) and urged it for others (Rom 16:1-2; 1 Cor 16:10-11; Phil 2:29). Yet, at times, he rejected such support to make it even clearer that he was acting simply for their good and not for anything he could get in return (1 Cor 9:3-18).

Such travelers were also at times engaged in seeking support for a community in need. The poverty of the Jerusalem community led Paul to take up a collection among Gentile communities for their support (Rom 15:25-32; 1 Cor 16:1-4; 2 Cor 8–9; cf. Acts 24:17). Not only would such a collection show the concern and the love of Gentile Christians for their Jewish-Christian brothers and sisters, but it would be another form of the support for one another that Christian love required.

Within the Johannine communities, sometimes visitors came to a community either directly or indirectly for the purpose of teaching. The Johannine community had undergone, and was still undergoing, a crisis of interpretation of the tradition. Because of this, there would have been the need for ongoing instruction and clarification regarding what the Elder and those with him understood to be the truth about Jesus. First John itself was a document forged to clarify the interpretation of the tradition and may well have been circulated among the related communities by such emissaries. Likewise, in 2 John 10-11, we hear of an admonition by the Elder not to accept those who bring false teaching. They are not to be accepted for the same reason that those who bring truth should be, namely, that providing support and lodging was to take part in their deeds and to further their aims and goals.

In these verses, the Elder speaks of the motives of the emissaries as well as the motives appropriate for those receiving them. He expresses this chiastically. In the first element of the chiasm, the Elder recalls the motives and actions of the emissaries. They have gone out "for the sake of the Name." That is, they have undertaken travels that are intended to contribute to the welfare and increase of belief in Jesus. In the last element, the Elder expresses the need for the members of the community to become coworkers in the same activity. In the second and second-last elements of the chiasm, the obligation of the missionaries "not to accept" (help from unbelievers) is paralleled with the obligation of the members of the community being approached "to accept" (those traveling for the sake of the Name).

Then, in the two central elements, the two respective groups are identified and contrasted: the non-believers and the Christian community.[16] The travelers would reject the thought of accepting hospitality from non-Christians, and this, in turn, increases the responsibility of "the brothers" to offer them such hospitality and support. Taken together, vv. 7-8 remind Gaius that receiving such visitors is not only a matter of Christian love but also a matter of actually cooperating in the work of the emissaries and so becoming partly responsible for the success of their work.

VV. 9-10 (THE ACTIONS OF DIOTREPHES)

The Structure and Literary Techniques of Vv. 9-10

For the first time since the Salutation element of the Letter, the Elder has not chosen to employ any rhetorical device to carry his thought. Given the fact that the Elder will return to a chiastic arrangement again in v. 11, it may be that the lack of balance and order here is intended to communicate stylistically the disruption of order created by Diotrephes himself.

The Interpretation of Vv. 9-10

In v. 9, we hear that the Elder had written something to the assembly. Most scholars think this was a letter of recommendation given to emissaries from the Elder's community.[17] But one of the members of the community, a man by the

---

16. The parallelism of the two central elements is not perfect. In the first of the two central elements, the pagans are grammatically part of a prepositional phrase while "we" (the members of the community) are the subject of the coming verb. Nevertheless, the impact created by contrasting the pagans with the members of the community is effective.

17. This presupposes that the failure to receive what the Elder wrote is to be linked with the failure to receive the brothers (cf. v. 10e), a reasonable assumption.

name of Diotrephes, refused to be receptive to the Elder. When he narrates this to Gaius in his Letter, the Elder says that if he comes to the community of which Diotrephes is a member, he will bring up what he is doing. The Elder then explains that in addition to not accepting him, Diotrephes also is slandering the Elder with lies. Finally, not only does Diotrephes not accept the visiting brothers, but he prevents other members who want to accept them and expels them from the assembly. This, in short, is the situation. But it is a situation that calls forth many questions. In order to deal with them adequately, they will be treated in the Addendum that follows.

Addendum: The Context within Which 3 John Is Written and the Status of Diotrephes

The conflict between the Elder and Diotrephes appears in only two verses within 3 John and so inevitably we do not have as many details regarding the situation as we would like. As a result, any conclusions must be based on brief hints within the text. Specifically, there are four aspects of the context within which 3 John was written and with regard to which it would be useful to have greater clarity. The first is the nature of the Elder's previous writing, mentioned in v. 9a. The second is the status of Diotrephes within his own assembly. The third is the nature of the disagreement between Diotrephes and the Elder and the fourth is the relationship between Gaius and Diotrephes. Although these problems can be distinguished from one another for the sake of discussion, the evidence for the one inevitably impacts the understanding of the other. Consequently, at times we will have to anticipate conclusions that will be supported only later in the Addendum.

(1) The Nature of the Previous Letter Rejected by Diotrephes

There are a variety of theories about the nature of the document the Elder had written to the assembly earlier and to which he refers in v. 9a. Although a few have proposed that it was the document now known as 1 John, this view is not in favor among recent scholars.[18]

However, a growing number (Grayston, Thyen ["Entwicklungen" 298-99], Strecker, Painter) have proposed that it is 2 John. Those in favor of this view point to the fact that 2 John was written to an assembly and not to an individual. It is also

---

18. It would be puzzling if the Elder referred to his writing of the tract of 1 John simply as "something." If 1 John lays out the essential differences between the Elder's and his opponents' understanding of the tradition, the document would seem to be too important to be referred to in this way.

argued that the urging in 2 John 10-11 not to extend hospitality to those not bearing the proper teaching has been reversed and used by Diotrephes against the Elder's emissaries. If we must select among extant writings, 2 John would be the choice, but I do not find the internal evidence sufficiently convincing to make the claim — and it is possible that it refers to a writing now lost.

Most scholars do indeed propose that the reference is to a document other than 1 or 2 John. Among those who hold this view, the majority (Schnackenburg, Malherbe, R. E. Brown, Lieu, Smalley, Klauck) think that the Elder is referring to a letter recommending the emissaries to this community. Kim has demonstrated in detail both the existence and the form of the type of letter intended as a recommendation for an emissary.[19] The purpose of such a letter was to identify the bearer(s) as certified by the sender. In this case, the Letter would have identified the bearers as coming from the community of the Elder and therefore worthy of acceptance and support. It is very likely that 3 John itself was just such a letter.

While I agree that 3 John is almost certainly a letter of recommendation for Demetrius, I do not think that the document referred to in v. 9a is such a letter. As we will see in more detail below, the reaction of Diotrephes and the Elder's reaction to Diotrephes would scarcely have been so vehement if it were simply a matter of failure to extend hospitality to a particular group of brothers. Extension of hospitality was a common matter unless there was some other reason for the rejection. Other reasons (that is, failure to bring the correct teaching) are suggested in 2 John 10, but, if we judge from his words in 3 John, the Elder did not expect to be rejected when he sent the first document to the assembly. Consequently, it would appear that the Elder's prior writing had revealed circumstances of which the Elder was unaware. While scholars have proposed various theories about what the circumstances were, it will be argued below that the prior writing uncovered the existence of (incipient) doctrinal differences in Diotrephes' community and that Diotrephes was the leader of the opposition.

If the document written by the Elder was not a letter of recommendation, what was it? Perhaps the most that can be said is that it was a document that laid out beliefs in a way objectionable to Diotrephes. Only this can satisfactorily account for the vehemence of the reaction on both sides.

(2) The Status of Diotrephes within the Assembly

The second question concerns the status of Diotrephes within his community.[20] The Elder describes him as "loving to be first." But, because this is the only instance of the word in ancient literature, we must estimate the meaning from its etymology

19. C. Kim, *Form.*
20. For a brief, but helpful, summary of the full range of views, see Smalley, *Epistles* 354-57.

and from what little the context tells us.[21] Was Diotrephes the authoritative leader of the community? Some scholars think that Diotrephes held a form of "hierarchical office" such as that of bishop. The classic presentation of this view was by Harnack, who saw Diotrephes as a monarchical bishop "whose name we know."[22] A variant of this view is that the Elder represents the end of a line of disciples whose authority was based on that of an eyewitness, while Diotrephes represented an early example of those whose authority was based on some other claim.

Some think that he was one who had no official status but ruled by force of personality.[23] A variant of this view is that Diotrephes was a wealthy homeowner at whose house the assembly gathered, and that because of this he possessed the *de facto* power to include or exclude as he wished.[24]

The Elder says that his earlier writing was to the assembly, not directly to Diotrephes. Yet Diotrephes was the one who prevented its implementation. Does this mean that Diotrephes was the individual who received the document and was, therefore, the head of the assembly? Or did Diotrephes intervene at some other stage to block the document's reception and the reception of the brothers who brought it? We cannot be sure. We can say with certainty that Diotrephes is acting in a way that reveals, if not authority, certainly power. He does what people in authority do. He personally prevents visitors from being received into the community, and he expels from the assembly those who want to receive them.[25] Yet there is no indication that Diotrephes has any official authority.

In the community at the time of the second edition of the Gospel, "power" would have been determined entirely by recourse to the Spirit. Even at the time of 1 John this was the primary determinant, although, in 1 John, the author puts reliance not just on what the Spirit says but on the congruence between this and what had been heard "from the beginning." There is no evidence of acknowledgment of

---

21. Bultmann (*Epistles* 100) claimed that it was intended to refer to a monarchical bishop but the Elder did not want to use the term and so used this. There is certainly no dearth of proposals. Brown (*Epistles* 733-36) discusses six of the major ones.

22. Harnack, "Über" 21.

23. Brown should probably be grouped with this view. He argues (*Epistles* 738) that Diotrephes is an individual who is turning away from the Johannine model of the Paraclete as teacher and moving toward the role of a presbyter-bishop as in the Pastorals or of a monarchical bishop as is represented by Ignatius.

24. See Painter (*Epistles* 363). Malherbe ("Inhospitality" 224) examines the role of the head of house churches in Paul and concludes they did not have a particular power because of that. However, they did have distinct responsibilities and these may have led to the tendency to act with authority.

25. It must be said that we cannot be sure of the nature of this expulsion either. Was it a formal and permanent excommunication? Was it simply a temporary refusal based on the force of his personality — or on the basis of some other community rule? Was it simply because the assembly met at his house and he claims authority over those present? We do not know.

any human authority within the Johannine tradition until the time of the third edition, and then the only recognition was that extended to the role of Peter. If the historical development in other sectors of early Christianity at the time was in the direction of an emerging hierarchical organization, this was not the case in the Johannine community. If Diotrephes is a secessionist or, at least, has secessionist leanings, Diotrephes' claim to authority, like that of the secessionists, would be based on a claim to possess, and to be led by, the eschatological Spirit rather than on any claim to ecclesiastical authority. If the community around him was convinced that he possessed such a Spirit-based "teaching," they would inevitably be willing to listen to him even if he did not have stature as an eyewitness to Jesus or as an appointed official.[26] This very well may be why the Elder refers to Diotrephes as desiring "to be first."[27]

(3) The Nature of the Disagreement between Diotrephes and the Elder

Why did Diotrephes reject what the Elder wrote?[28] Malherbe thinks the struggle is personal rather than theological.[29] Diotrephes is one who seeks to rival the Elder, and his power resides in the fact that he is the owner of the house where the assembly meets and that he exercises his prerogative to exclude those he will.[30] However, that the issue is larger than willful use of power is indicated by the Elder's complaint that Diotrephes is "bringing false charges against us with evil words."[31]

Others (e.g., R. E. Brown, Klauck) have thought that his rejection of the Elder and of the visitors was based on advice such as that of the Elder himself in 2 John 10-11, forbidding acceptance of persons bringing false teaching. Rather than risk accepting a false teacher, Diotrephes had rejected all visitors. In this view, there is no significant ideological difference between the Elder and Diotrephes other than this overly cautious attitude. Yet this seems unlikely to be the case, given the harsh words that Diotrephes has directed at the Elder. If he were simply being cautious, there would be no reason for Diotrephes to have spoken so harshly of the Elder. His

---

26. Mention should also be made of the proposal by Käsemann ("Ketzer") who argued that the Elder was looked upon as a heretic and as holding gnostic views. As a result, he has been expelled by Diotrephes and is now attempting to regain followers. This view is generally rejected.

27. A common categorizing of the Elder and Diotrephes is to see one as representing a hierarchical authority and the other as representing a Spirit-given authority. However, which represents which is disputed. In any event, the dispute in 1 John and in 2 John is between what might be called a "moderate Spirit-given authority" represented by the Elder and an "extreme Spirit-given authority" represented by Diotrephes.

28. For a particularly helpful survey of earlier literature, see Strecker, *Epistles* 261-63.

29. Malherbe, "Inhospitality" 227-29.

30. Malherbe gathers his information about the nature of such house communities from the Pauline examples. To what extent they are the same cannot be determined.

31. Malherbe does not address any of the content of v. 10c in his essay.

position is not born of ignorance but of conviction. Moreover, it is difficult to think that the Elder, in turn, would have described Diotrephes in language that links him with the work of Satan, if Diotrephes were simply being over-cautious. The difference seems to go deeper.

From v. 9, it would seem that *Diotrephes takes issue* with certain of the Elder's *beliefs*. The first evidence of this is in v. 9c, where Diotrephes is said not to "receive us." This does not refer to a rejection of hospitality to the Elder but a rejection of the views put forward in his Letter. In addition, Diotrephes brings up charges against the Elder and evidently does so vehemently (that is, with evil words). It is hard to think of this either as being caused by ignorance of the Elder or as relating to the Elder's personality. It must concern the Elder's teaching.[32] Diotrephes is convinced that the situation was sufficiently serious that he rejects the Elder's emissaries, prevents others who wish to receive them, and even ejects such members from the assembly! Thus, from the perspective of Diotrephes, the situation is a serious one and seems to deal with everything represented by the Elder.

When we read the evidence *attempting to determine the attitude of the Elder* to Diotrephes, we see much the same thing. The Elder says that Diotrephes is bringing *false* charges against the Elder *with evil words*. The language used by the Elder to describe Diotrephes' actions here is the same language the Elder had used in 1 and 2 John to describe the secessionists. According to the Elder (v. 10), Diotrephes' words are *ponēroi* ("evil"). This is the word used to describe the actions typical of one who, in apocalyptic language, is "of the Evil One" *(ek tou Ponērou)*. The next verse (v. 11) makes clear that Gaius should not imitate evil (that is, not imitate the actions of Diotrephes). Rather, if he does the right thing, he will be "of God" (implying that Diotrephes is not). Moreover, by implication (cf. v. 11), because Diotrephes does not do good, he "has not seen God." Thus, from the perspective of the Elder also, the situation is a serious one, and, by his rejection of the message of the Elder, Diotrephes fails in the matter of correct belief.

But, in the eyes of the Elder, this is not all Diotrephes does. In v. 10d-f, the Elder explains that Diotrephes does not extend hospitality to the brothers. This constitutes an additional two-pronged failing on Diotrephes' part. We know both from 2 John 10-11 and from 3 John 8 that to accept Christian envoys and to give them hospitality was to take part in their works. Clearly Diotrephes does not want to take part in the works of the brothers and so fails in the matter of being a coworker for the truth. But, in the eyes of the Elder, Diotrephes' failure to extend hospitality is also a failure in terms of the commandment of mutual love. The emissaries are brothers, and Jesus had commanded his disciples to love one another. Thus, in the eyes of the Elder, Diotrephes is failing in the two fundamental categories by which believers are to be judged and the secessionists identified. He rejects the belief of

---

32. Painter (*Epistles* 364-65) thinks that the difference was theological and that the key lies in the description of Diotrephes as using "evil words." Painter sees these as essentially the same as the evil works referred to in 2 John 11.

the Elder and is not a coworker for the truth, and, in addition, he does not extend love to the brothers.[33]

Although the Elder never compares Gaius and Diotrephes directly, there are several implicit comparisons. They tell us much about the Elder's evaluation of them both. Gaius is said to "walk in the truth" (v. 3); the implication is that Diotrephes does not.[34] Gaius demonstrates love for the brothers (v. 6); Diotrephes does not. Moreover, Diotrephes does not show love for the Elder since he "brings false charges against the Elder with evil words." In addition, the Elder's exhortation to Gaius not to imitate evil appears to be an implicit reference to the evil being done by Diotrephes. Finally, the Elder, speaking in the categories of apocalyptic dualism, says that the one doing good is "of God" while the one doing evil has not seen God. Again, the implication is that Diotrephes must be categorized with those who are not "of God."

Rejecting the teaching of the Elder and rejecting his emissaries would seem to indicate that Diotrephes was willing to break, and in fact had broken, *koinōnia* with the Elder and his followers. Yet, the Elder does not simply break off contact with him. Rather, he will come and bring up to Diotrephes what he is doing, a fact that would seem to indicate that the division was just beginning and the Elder thought Diotrephes could be won back.

From this, it seems correct to conclude that the issue between Diotrephes and the Elder is a theological one and that Diotrephes is manifesting secessionist tendencies. I said above that there is no indication, at the time of his earlier writing, that the Elder expected such a rejection by Diotrephes. This would suggest that the rejection of the Elder's emissaries was the first indication of Diotrephes' leanings and so he was still a member of the assembly, although he had begun to take authoritative steps to move the assembly in the direction of secessionist thought.

In spite of these factors suggesting that Diotrephes was a secessionist or one who favored their views, there are other factors that appear to be inconsistent with this picture and should be examined. First, if Diotrephes was a secessionist, how could it be that he was still a member of the assembly and had not been excluded (or simply departed)? There are a number of indications that 3 John reflects the very early stages of the division within the community so that Diotrephes has not yet "gone out" from the community himself. As was said above, there is no indication that, when the Elder wrote his earlier Letter to the assembly, he expected such a

---

33. Schnackenburg (*Epistles* 298) thinks there are two distinct problems, that caused by the Letter and that caused by the rejection of the emissaries. I would suggest that there is essentially only one and that the two problems are differentiated only because the Elder wishes to show that the first is a rejection of the message of the Elder (and so an offense against Truth) and the second is an offense against mutual love. But the content of the earlier writing led to the rejection of the emissaries.

34. The implication seems fully justified by the fact that Diotrephes brings false charges against the Elder.

reaction from Diotrephes. This would seem to indicate that Diotrephes' stance is new.

Second, the Elder's description of his own planned response to Diotrephes ("I will bring up the things he is doing") seems less forceful than one would expect if Diotrephes were a secessionist. Two comments are in order about this. First, the Elder has already described Diotrephes in terms and categories that associate him with evil. We could not expect language any stronger or more condemnatory than the various references to doing evil and not being "of God." Second, it may be that the Elder felt that the only proper "Johannine" way of responding to Diotrephes was to "remind" him of what he had done. This is the first instance of the verb "remind" (*hypomimnēskō*) in the Johannine tradition, but it is also the verb that will be used by the third author to describe the action of the Paraclete with respect to all that Jesus had said. Such may well have been the normal way of dealing with matters of truth and love in the community. Before the time of an established human authority, the only theological recourse open to the community was to recall what had been "from the beginning" and to listen to the witness of the Elder.

Third, how are we to account for the description of Diotrephes as "wishing to be first"? This term seems to reflect his personal desire for prominence within the community and so to be a matter of simple status rather than theological difference, and in any case it is not as forceful a term as one might expect if he were a secessionist. Again, it must be remembered that we do not know the precise meaning of the word *philoprōteuō* since it appears only here in ancient literature. It is also possible that Diotrephes' "love of being first" reflects his desire to impose his own convictions on others. It may be the Elder's way of describing one who claims the inspiration of the Spirit as the foundation for his power.

For Brown and for Smalley, the primary argument against the idea that the conflict is over doctrine is the fact that there is no mention of doctrinal matters in 3 John.[35] However, as we have seen, there is repeated praise of Gaius in terms of correct belief and mutual love. These are certainly "doctrinally" related. Moreover, there are clear allusions to Diotrephes' failure in this regard. Finally, it should be recalled that 3 John is not intended to deal with doctrinal matters. As we have seen, its primary purpose is to be a Letter to Gaius recommending Demetrius as an emissary worthy of Christian hospitality. Verses 1-8 and 11 deal exclusively with praise for Gaius, for his past demonstrations of love for the brothers and with the hope that he will extend the same love to the brothers in the future. Verse 12 speaks of Demetrius, whom the Elder recommends for acceptance as a visitor. Verses 13-15 are simply the conventional elements associated with the closing of a letter. The only remaining verses are 9-10, which deal with Diotrephes. As such, the Letter is not intent on a discussion of doctrinal matters even if it necessarily includes allusions to them.

---

35. See Brown, *Epistles* 736-37; Smalley, *Epistles* 355-56.

Rejecting the teaching of the Elder and rejecting his emissaries would seem to indicate that Diotrephes was willing to break *koinōnia* with the Elder and his followers. Yet, the Elder does not simply break off contact with him. Rather, he will come and bring up to Diotrephes what he is doing, a fact that would seem to indicate that the division was just beginning and that the Elder thought Diotrephes could be won back.

(4) The Relation between Gaius and Diotrephes

Finally, we need to ask about the relationship between Gaius and Diotrephes.

Some have thought that Gaius and Diotrephes were members of the same church, but this is unlikely since Gaius does not appear to know about the Elder's earlier document to the assembly. In addition, Gaius has offered hospitality to the brothers (apparently the group that was rebuffed by Diotrephes), and he could not have done so without serious repercussions if he were a member of Diotrephes' church. It is more likely that Gaius is a member of another house-church in the area and had been able to render hospitality to the brothers rejected by Diotrephes.

Because of the report of the brothers (vv. 3, 6a), the Elder considers Gaius someone who could be counted on to assist the brothers in their travels. As a result, the Elder now writes to him rather than to the assembly of which Diotrephes is a part.[36] Whether the Elder had known Gaius before is unclear. Certainly the conclusion of the Letter speaks of an exchange of greetings between the "friends" of the Elder and those associated with Gaius "by name," but this could be a formality.

(5) Conclusions

If these four questions pique our curiosity, their importance should not be exaggerated. In the last analysis, they are tangential to understanding the basic message of 3 John. The Elder's primary purpose in writing was not to speak with Gaius about the rift with Diotrephes. The Elder's primary concern is to secure acceptance and support for members of the community who would be traveling "for the sake of the Name" and who would be passing through the place where Gaius (and Diotrephes) lived. We have seen earlier (vv. 5-8) that the Elder exhorted Gaius to be of help to such travelers in the future, just as he had done in the past. We see now (vv. 9-10) that Diotrephes has not extended hospitality to recent travelers and would not in the future. The Elder then exhorts Gaius again not to imitate evil but good (v. 11). And then finally (v. 12), the Elder will become concrete in his wish, hoping that Ga-

---

36. Malherbe ("Inhospitality") has suggested that Gaius was a wealthy individual and the head of another house-church in the area. While a wealthy person would be more able to provide such support, there is nothing in the Letter to indicate that this was the case.

ius will accept Demetrius, who will be traveling through the area soon and who may indeed be the bearer of 3 John. The primary purpose of the Letter is to assure Christian hospitality, and it is on this that the primary focus should remain.

VV. 11-12 (THE SECOND REQUEST)

The Structure and Literary Techniques of Vv. 11-12

In v. 11, the body of the Letter continues and, with these verses, comes to a conclusion. The Elder now addresses Gaius for the third time by the title of Beloved. By doing so, the Elder once again follows the conventions of the ancient letter and introduces the second of his requests. The Elder exhorts Gaius to action, using a final, brief, and much less artful chiasm in which the first and last elements speak of evil and the two central elements speak of doing good.[37]

The Interpretation of Vv. 11-12

Once again the basic thought is simple and clear. In v. 11, the Elder makes the most general of exhortations. Gaius should not imitate evil, but good. In defense of this, he reminds Gaius that the one who does good is "of God." That is, from the perspective of the apocalyptic worldview, this person has made the right choice and shows his allegiance to God rather than to the Evil One. The one who does evil has not seen God. In the Notes, we pointed out that this statement is awkward in that it was the Jewish belief that no one ever saw God face to face. But this phrasing may be due to the context of the theological crisis. It is a striking characteristic of 1 John (and one regularly pointed out by commentators) that features attributed to Jesus in the Gospel are attributed to God the Father in 1 John. We saw that this was due to the fact that, in 1 John, it was the role of Jesus that was being disputed, and therefore the author of 1 John took a step back, as it were, to argue with the opponents on the basis of convictions they held in common, namely the belief of both groups in God the Father. Although it is less obvious in 3 John (at least in part because of the Letter's brevity), the same thing seems to be true here. In v. 6b, the Elder had spoken of sending the guests on their way in a manner worthy "of God." Here he speaks of the one doing good as being "of God" and of the one doing evil as having never

---

37. This is pointed out by Brown, *Epistles* 720-21; Smalley, *Epistles* 359. To my knowledge these are the only places where this chiasm is noted in the literature prior to the present Commentary. I would describe it as "less artful" primarily because of the considerable imbalance between the first and second halves of the arrangement.

"seen God." From the Jewish tradition alone, it would be correct to say that no one could see God, and the author recalls this in 1 John 4:12, but in the Johannine tradition, because they believed that the one who saw Jesus saw the Father (John 14:9), such a statement would not have the same meaning as it would for a non-Christian Jew. But the final point is clear: the person doing evil does not have the proper relationship with God.

Although the Elder is now engaged in a request to Gaius, he reveals more of his own attitude toward the actions of Diotrephes. In the alternatives put before Gaius, the Elder uses the same language and categories as he used for the opponents in 1 John. We saw in the Note on v. 10 that the word *ponēros*, which the Elder uses for the words of Diotrephes, is the same word that is used throughout the Johannine tradition to describe the actions typical of Satan (*ho Ponēros*, "the Evil One"). In 1 John 3:12, the Elder used Cain as the paradigm of the one whose works were evil, saying that he was "of the Evil One." By applying this language to Diotrephes, the Elder declares that Diotrephes is in league with the Evil One. He does not do good and is not "of God." He has never seen God. Certainly the Elder views the actions of Diotrephes in the most serious light.

Verse 12 begins in a peculiar way, and it is important to notice what the verse does *not* say. Demetrius, who has not been spoken of to this point and who is evidently unknown to Gaius, is named and is said to be one who is witnessed to by "all, by the truth, and by the Elder." This is the extent of his statement. Immediately following this, the Elder begins the conclusion of the Letter.

In spite of this curious verse, most commentators assume that, by the juxtaposition of v. 12 to v. 11, the Elder is putting forward a concrete example of how Gaius will be able to imitate good *(mimou . . . to agathon)* and be one who "does good" *(agathopoiōn)*. We may assume that Demetrius is coming to Gaius' assembly and will be the bearer of the present Letter. Presumably Gaius is being encouraged to receive him (although Demetrius is a stranger — v. 5c) and to give his support (v. 8ab) so that Gaius can show himself to be a coworker with Demetrius (v. 8c). Since he is a stranger, Demetrius must bear a letter of attestation and recommendation so that Gaius can be sure of his character. The Elder describes Demetrius as witnessed to by all and by the truth itself. Thus, Demetrius receives the ultimate mark of praise from the Elder. It is, in fact, the same mark of praise that the Elder had used to describe Gaius himself at the beginning of the Letter. Thus, implicitly, the Elder is saying that Demetrius is of the same character as Gaius, a fact that should help Gaius view Demetrius as the Elder would. Moreover, the Elder, the witness par excellence, is also witnessing to him, and there can be no doubt about the Elder's witness.

I have said that most commentators see Demetrius as a visitor and perhaps one bearing the present Letter. Another view is presented by Lieu, who suggests that Demetrius is not a missionary nor the bearer of the Letter but simply one who is being held up as a model of the good to be imitated.[38] The Letter does not say that explicitly either. Nothing is said *explicitly* about why Demetrius is mentioned. But, if we look at both the overall and the immediate context of the Letter, the most natural conclusion is that the mention of Demetrius has to do with the fact that he is a Christian emissary and the Elder hopes Gaius will receive Demetrius as a Christian guest and give him the lodging and support appropriate for such a traveler. Throughout the Letter, the witness of the brothers is to certify the character of an individual to someone else at a distance. Thus, the brothers had witnessed to the truth and love of Gaius before the assembly of which the Elder was a part (v. 3). Now (v. 12) the Elder and all who are with him are witnessing to the goodness of Demetrius before Gaius. This would imply that Demetrius is coming to Gaius' community and is in need of similar witness. All of this is done in a Letter that is concerned throughout with the giving (and rejection) of hospitality. In vv. 5-7, the Elder had spoken in general terms of the need to love the brothers and to show this by providing lodging and support for visitors. Moreover, in vv. 9-11, he had spoken of the evil Diotrephes did in not extending hospitality to visitors. Then Gaius is encouraged to imitate good (and not to imitate Diotrephes). This can only mean that the Elder is recommending Demetrius as a visitor and one to be accepted with full Christian hospitality.[39]

The third of the witnesses here is said to be that which "we" bear. Scholars are divided whether this is meant to be simply the authorial "we" or whether it is meant to represent the "we" of the Johannine school. Whichever is intended, it is certain that the Elder is the central and authoritative voice within this "we." From the Elder's words, it is apparent that this witness is to be distinguished from that of all the other human witnesses. This witness is unique, and the Elder calls upon Gaius to confirm that this witness, based on the witness of the Elder (and those with him?), cannot be other than true.

It would seem also that the wording of this statement tells us something about the relationship of the Elder to the figure known as the Beloved Disciple. In 3 John 12, the Elder witnesses and says: "And you know that our witness is true." These are the words of an individual who claims a unique truthfulness and also claims that that unique truthfulness will be recognized by Gaius.[40]

38. Lieu, *Second and Third* 117-19.

39. As was said above, the Letter as a whole is not a letter of recommendation as that genre was understood in the ancient world. Such a letter would have a different format as Lieu (*Second and Third* 119) points out. The form of the Letter is that of a request to Gaius regarding hospitality, but it does contain a request/recommendation regarding Demetrius.

40. He does so either alone or as part of a group (the "we" of v. 12). If he does intend to present himself as part of a group, it is clear from everything else in the three Letters that he is, at the very least, the central figure of this group.

This is the same claim that is made for the BD in the Gospel by others who do not claim this prerogative for themselves. In John 19:35, we read: "And the one who saw has borne witness and his witness is true and that one knows that he speaks the truth. . . ." And in John 21:24 we read: "This is the disciple who bears witness . . . and we know that his witness is true." If 3 John is written after these passages, where the BD appears, the Elder would be claiming something that earlier figures did not dare claim for themselves and that was something attributed only to the BD! This is difficult to imagine.

Furthermore, it is curious, as Culpepper has pointed out, that, if the BD was the authoritative source to whom the community appealed at the time of the writing of the Gospel, there is no appeal to the BD at the time of the Letters (presuming they were written after the Gospel).[41] Instead, we find a figure who claims for himself the witness-value that was attributed to the BD in the Gospel. This is another indication that the traditional view of the sequence in which the material is written is probably not the correct one.

At the same time, if 3 John 12 is the earlier document, then the unique authoritative witness that the Elder claims for himself is understood as his own claim, a claim for which he alone is responsible but which he is confident that all the others will recognize as valid. In this case, the statements of John 19:35 and 21:24 can be understood as the attempt by members of the community to record the witness of that one who knew his witness was truthful — and whose truthfulness they were all ready to attest to, just as all would attest to the truthfulness of the Elder at the time of 3 John.

VV. 13-15 (CONCLUSION)

The Structure and Literary Techniques of Vv. 13-15

The Elder now brings his Letter to a close. In doing so he follows closely the conventions of his day.

The Interpretation of Vv. 13-15

In such a short letter, the Elder could touch on only a few matters and then only briefly. He has spoken mainly by allusion. For the one who would know more

---

41. Culpepper, *School* 281-82. Culpepper speculates that perhaps the opponents were claiming the authority of the BD for themselves, but it must be realized that this is mere speculation. There is no hint that the BD was taken as an authority by the opponents. At the same time, the Elder of 3 John claims precisely this authority.

about the history of the community at the time, that brevity is all too obvious. He has much to say but would prefer not to do it through ink and paper. Rather, he hopes to come soon and to say it face to face.

He wishes Gaius peace and sends greetings from the friends in the Elder's community, and the Elder also wishes that Gaius greet the friends "by name." The expression "by name" appears as a stock phrase in the conclusion of other ancient letters. The only other time this expression occurs in the Johannine writings is in John 10:3, where it is said that the good shepherd calls each of the sheep "by name." It is possible that the use of such a phrase here in the conclusion to the Letter would have recalled, for the recipients, that they were members of Jesus' flock that he called "by name" and so were known by name not only to the Elder but also to Jesus.[42] It is also noteworthy that, in 2 John, the use of "elect" in the first and last verses of the Letter could well be designed to recall the fact that the members had been "chosen" by Jesus. While it is not possible to prove that these allusions were intended, the fact that similar themes seem to appear in the conclusion of both Letters certainly makes it more likely.

*   *   *

We contended above that the focus of the Letter is not on what Diotrephes has done wrong, but on what can be done to secure lodging and support for the travelers. Here at the end, we are perhaps in a position to see that more clearly. This was not a general treatise on Christian hospitality; it was couched in the difficult circumstances of a particular community at a particular time. It was occasioned by the actions of one of the members of the community, actions that the Elder sees as violating both the norms of love and the norms of truth. It was a serious, and in some ways tragic, event. What the precise reason for the event was, we cannot be sure; nor can we know the further consequences. What is evident is that Gaius and the Elder took action to be sure that the community's practice of extending love to the brothers was not diminished. And that was the primary purpose of the Letter.

Addendum: The Johannine School

Alan Culpepper has studied the "schools" associated with important teaching figures in the ancient world and has compared them with features of the Johannine community as it appears within the Johannine literature. He concludes that "school" was an appropriate word to describe the entirety of the Johannine commu-

---

42. So Smalley, *Epistles* 364.

nity. Just as Jesus was the founder of the tradition, the BD was the founder of the school. The BD possessed several characteristics that qualified him to be viewed this way. He stood in relation to Jesus as Jesus stood in relation to the Father. In his witnessing, he manifested qualities that were to be those of the Paraclete. The Gospel reflects his witness and concerns primarily the crisis created by the community's expulsion from the synagogue. The Letters reflect a period after the composition of the Gospel and address a series of internal problems. All three Letters were written about the same time and address the same general class of problems. "Probably one ought to think of a central community in which the BD and later the presbyter taught (cf. the use of the plural in John 21:24; 1 John 5:18-20; 3 John 12) and satellite communities that shared its influence, tradition, and doctrine."[43]

This view of a Johannine school was later taken over by Brown and played an influential role in his understanding of the Letters particularly.[44] Brown differed from Culpepper in arguing that the notion of the Johannine "school" should probably not be used of the entire Johannine community but reserved for those members of the community who were looked upon as tradition bearers. Thus, the Elder uses "we" at times to refer to the entire community, and at other times he distinguishes a smaller group as "we" over against the "you" of the remainder of the community. Brown comments:

> . . . I use it [the term "school"] for those who felt so close to the Beloved Disciple that they sought to pass on his tradition through written interpretation. These include the evangelist, the redactor of the Gospel (and any other writers involved in it), the author of the Epistles, and the tradition-bearers with whom they associated themselves in their writing — in short, the "we" of John 21:24 . . . and of 1 John 1:1-2. . . . It is as a long-lived representative of such a Johannine school that 'the presbyter' speaks.[45]

Yet, how one understands the notion of a "Johannine school" will be determined by the understanding one has of the history of the composition of the Johannine literature as a whole. A somewhat more homogeneous notion emerges if one sees 1 John as being composed *after* the Gospel. In that view, one could speak of a sequence: the BD, the Elder, together with a "we" of Gospel passages such as 21:24 and the "we" of the three Letters.

If one views the Letters as being written *before* the final edition of the Gospel, it is still possible to speak of a school, in that there were separate authors for the first and second editions and then a voice for the three Letters and another for the third edition of the Gospel. However, the notion of a school implies a certain harmony of

---

43. Culpepper, *School* 286.
44. Brown first explored the notion of a Johannine school in *Community* 99-103 and later throughout his *Epistles* (see esp. 94-97).
45. Brown, *Community* 102.

views, and the second edition is such a radical revision of the theology of the first that it is difficult to know whether the first edition could properly be called a product of the same Johannine "school." While we can identify the material of the edition from its literary, ideological, and theological characteristics, we have no external information about its origin or its history prior to its becoming the foundational document upon which the remainder of the Johannine Gospel was built.

The second edition contained a theology that was related to that of the Letters and to the third edition, but its perspective was modified substantially by those of the Letters and the third edition. When it is looked upon from the perspective of the later tradition, we can see both continuity and discontinuity. The continuity with the later tradition suggests that it could well be said to be the product of "the Johannine school." Yet it is equally clear that, by the time of 1 John, there were what could be called two Johannine "schools." The one is represented by the author of the Johannine Letters and by the author of the Gospel's third edition. The second is represented by the opponents. They both claimed to be legitimate interpreters of the tradition, but, in the end, only the interpretation represented by the Elder and his followers was accepted as canonical.

There was a growth in the theology of the tradition throughout the four stages represented in the canonical Johannine literature, and so it is not simply a matter of a single perspective being represented by a variety of individuals. If we include the second edition as a product of the Johannine school, then we must speak of three stages of development within the school.[46] Moreover, the growth reflected in these three stages is substantive. Is it possible to use the term "school" for such a development? I would say yes with two precautions. One must really speak of a second Johannine school (the secessionists), even though this second group was not accepted as a legitimate interpretation by the first. The second group did indeed base its belief upon principles from the second edition of the Gospel. The first group, however, adopted the second edition of the Gospel only in a modified form but it became the branch of the school that was accepted within the circles of what became canonical Christianity. The second caution I would propose is that, while it is important to study parallel examples of "schools" in the ancient world, it is also important to recognize that the Johannine school was indeed unique and needs to be understood primarily in terms of the features uncovered by our analysis rather than by imposing too rigorously the features of other schools.

46. The literature as a whole reflects four stages of development, since it includes the first edition of the Gospel.

Quotations of the Old Testament and Their Introductory Formulae in the Gospel

The use of the Jewish Scriptures in the Gospel of John has occasioned considerable study over the past forty years.[1] Of particular concern is the source of the quotations used in the gospel. While some are taken from the LXX, others appear to come from the Hebrew version. At times there appears to be no precise parallel either in the LXX or in the Hebrew. Study of these passages has led to a categorization of the similarities and differences between the Johannine text and that of the Hebrew and Greek Bibles. Of additional concern are the formulas used to introduce these quotations.[2]

Here I will briefly survey opinion on the matter while also asking about the distribution of these quotations and references to Scripture within the three editions of the Gospel. In order to review them easily and within a brief space, I have grouped them according to the way they are distributed within the three editions.[3] They are reviewed with particular attention to the source of the quotations and to the particular form of the introductory formulas employed. Of particular interest are: (1) the light cast upon puzzling elements of the quotations themselves by the compositional process proposed in this commentary, and (2) the light cast upon the variations in introductory formulas when viewed in the light of the Gospel's compositional process.

---

1. The major studies are those of Freed *(Quotations)*, Reim *(Hintergrund)*, Schuchard *(Scripture)* and Menken *(Quotations)*. Other significant studies are referred to in the bibliographies of these books.

2. See, in particular, Carson, "Written: John"; Evans, "Formulas"; Fitzmyer, "Quotations"; Reim, *Hintergrund*.

3. It should be noted that the distribution of the quotations was determined *after* the material containing the quotations had been identified using the criteria listed in Vol. 1. Thus, the consistency that is revealed by the analysis in this appendix is properly called a "feature" rather than a "criterion."

There has been some disagreement about exactly which texts should be included in a study of John's use of the Old Testament.[4] The basis of this disagreement is primarily whether one judges the proper object to be direct quotations only or whether allusions and references should be included. Here I will include (1) those texts that are, or claim to be, direct quotations of the Old Testament (1:23; 2:17; 6:31, 45; 7:38; 10:34; 12:13, 15, 38, 40; 13:18; 15:25; 19:24, 28, 36, 37); as well as (2) those texts that contain allusions or references to biblical texts and (3) those also with some reference to the fact that it is Scripture that is being referred to (primarily through the presence of an introductory formula) (7:42; 8:17; 12:34; 17:12).[5] The resulting list is somewhat larger than the typical one. The reason for this more inclusive approach will become apparent at the end when we examine these texts in the light of the editions in which they appear.

A. TEXTS IN THE FIRST EDITION

1. 1:23 "I am the voice of one in the desert crying, 'Make straight the way for the Lord.'" *(Egō phōnē boōntos en tē erēmō, Euthynate tēn hodon kyriou.)*

This quotation is generally recognized as coming from Isa 40:3. There is also general agreement that John is dependent upon the LXX for this text.[6] The Johannine version differs from the original only with the addition of *Egō* at the

---

4. Sometimes this is determined by the purpose of the study. The range of such perspective is indicated by the following. Menken *(Quotations)* studied only eleven texts because these differ from the Hebrew or LXX and so some possible intention in the changes may be discerned. Freed *(Quotations)* studied only the fifteen explicit quotations and did not include allusions or references. Reim *(Hintergrund)* studied all variety of texts and allusions, including the slightest verbal similarities, as part of his overall study of all aspects of the OT background of the Gospel. See also Carson, "Written: John," who gives one of the most inclusive listings.

5. Freed *(Quotations)* excludes 8:17 and 12:34. Menken *(Quotations* 12) excludes 17:12 and 19:28 from detailed study because, although there is an introductory formula, there is no quotation. He also excludes 10:34; 12:38; 19:24, which he judges to be derived verbatim from the LXX and not in need of study (14-15). Further, he excludes 7:42; 8:17; and 12:34 because they are too general to make an identification of a specific text-source possible and 12:13 because he sees this as an allusion to Scripture rather than a quotation (15-18). Schuchard *(Scripture* xiii) excludes 7:38, 42; 12:13; 17:12; 19:28.

I will not discuss 20:9. Although the verse indicates that the Resurrection was predicted in Scripture, there is no reference whatsoever to a specific verse, nor is there any introductory formula.

6. For example, Barrett, Menken, and Reim. Freed *(Quotations* 5) goes against this when he concludes that "John, a Jew thoroughly trained in the Hebrew and Greek Scriptures, drew from his memory of various texts, or combination of texts and sources, a quotation to suit his purposes." Freed also suggests that John may not be using the OT directly at all but interpreting the Synoptics *(Quotations* 7).

beginning and the change from *etoimasate* ("prepare") of the LXX to *euthynate* ("make straight").

The "introductory" formula (which in this case actually follows the quotation) is: ". . . as Isaiah the prophet said" *(. . . kathōs eipen Ēsaias ho prophētēs).*

2. 7:42 "Does the Scripture not say that the Christ comes 'from the seed of David' and 'from Bethlehem,' the village where David was?" *(Ouch hē graphē eipen hoti ek tou spermatos Dauid kai apo Bēthleem tēs kōmēs hopou ēn Dauid erchetai ho Christos;)*

This statement is not a quotation from Scripture and so a precise source cannot be determined. For the same reason it cannot be determined whether John was dependent upon a Hebrew or a LXX text. It is possible however to suggest more general sources for the convictions registered in 7:42. For example, the text that most clearly indicates that the future ruler will come from Bethlehem is Mic 5:2. A number of texts allude to the fact that the messiah will be from the seed of David (2 Sam 7:12-14; Ps 88(89):3-4, 35-37; Isa 11:1, 10). That Bethlehem is the city of David can be found in 1 Sam 16:1, 4; 20:6.

Whether this statement can be said to have an introductory formula is uncertain. The words *ouch hē graphē eipen hoti* . . . ("Does not Scripture say that . . .") function more as a reference to Scripture rather than to introduce a particular passage. Nevertheless, for the sake of this completeness, the words will be treated as a formula.

B. TEXTS IN THE SECOND EDITION

3. 2:17 "Zeal for your house will consume me." *(Ho zēlos tou oikou sou kataphagetai me.)*

Scholars are in general agreement that the source of this quotation is Ps 68(69):9 (Ps 69:10 [MT]) and that it is from the LXX. The only change from the LXX is that John has changed the past tense of the verb *(katephagen)* to the future *(kataphagetai).* This shift to the future is intended to show that the original statement was a foreshadowing of the eschatological reality in the ministry of Jesus.[7]

The introductory formula is: "His disciples remembered that it was written . . ." *(Emnēsthēsan hoi mathētai autou hoti gegrammenon estin . . .).*

4. 6:31 "He gave them bread from heaven to eat." *(Arton ek tou ouranou edōken autois phagein.)*

---

7. We will see that the change of verb tense has this same purpose in the Scripture citations in 6:32 and in 7:38.

There is considerable disagreement about the precise source of this quotation. There are no exact parallels but the closest texts are generally thought to be Exod 16:4, 15; Neh 9:15; and/or Ps 77(78):24.[8]

Borgen has argued that the text is a combination of Ps 77(78):24 with the two Exodus texts. He argues that the presence of the Exodus texts is appropriate to the homiletic format where typically a Pentateuchal text (John 6:31) is followed by a text from the prophets (6:45). In addition, this combination makes the most sense of the Johannine context (including the reference to murmuring in v. 41).[9]

Menken takes another tack and argues that, if one examines the LXX of Ps 77(78):24 in its context, one could easily suppose that variations were supplied from the verses immediately surrounding it, according to accepted Jewish exegetical principles.[10] If this is the case, then Ps 77(78):24 is the best single candidate as the source for John's quotation.[11] While the Hebrew and Greek versions are similar in this instance, verbal similarities with the LXX version suggest that the source was the LXX rather than the Hebrew.[12] While none of the proposals is completely satisfying, I am inclined to think that Menken's explanation, which sees the Johannine text as to a certain extent already exegeted, is the more likely.

The introductory formula is: ". . . as it is written . . ." (. . . *kathōs estin gegrammenon . . .*).

5. 6:45 "And all will be taught by God." *(Kai esontai pantes didaktoi theou.)*

There is considerable (but not universal) agreement that the text quoted is Isa 54:13a and that it is taken from the LXX.[13] The primary difference from both the Hebrew and the Greek is the fact that the Johannine text is an independent clause rather than a verbal phrase. As Menken shows, however, it is

8. According to Freed (*Quotations* 15), the Johannine quotation appears to be a combination of the two Exodus texts and "contains elements from both the Heb. and Gr. texts." Reim (*Hintergrund* 15) opts for Exod 16:4, 15 as the source and sees it as coming from the Hebrew. Barrett (*Gospel* 289) suggests that Ps 78:24 is probably the closest to the Johannine version, but he speculates that "John may well have known and combined all these passages" (that is, Neh. 9:15; Exod 16:15 as well as Ps 78:24).

9. Borgen, *Bread*, passim.

10. Menken, *Quotations* 52-53. Menken refers to studies of such exegetical techniques in the Qumran scrolls and elsewhere.

11. It should be noted that, in all of the proposed texts, the subject of the verb is never Moses, as is implied in the Johannine exegesis of the text.

12. So also Menken, *Quotations* 52-54, 65.

13. Burney (*Aramaic*) (quoted in Freed, *Quotations* 18) contends that the text comes from the Hebrew but was influenced by the LXX. So also Reim. Freed (*Quotations* 20) concluded that the source cannot be determined.

common in quotations of Scripture in the first century for the writer to supply a form of the verb "to be" if it is needed for situating the citation within a given grammatical context.[14]

The introductory formula is: "It is written in the prophet . . ." *(estin gegrammenon en tois prophētais . . .).*[15]

6. 7:38 "The one who believes in me — as the Scripture says, 'rivers of living water will flow from his belly.'" *(Ho pisteuōn eis eme, kathōs eipen hē graphē Potamoi ek tēs koilias autou rheusousin hydatos zōntos.)*

This text has been a perennial problem for interpreters. It is complicated by matters of punctuation and grammar. In the Note on 7:37-38, we discussed these matters and concluded that the first six words ("The one who believes in me") are probably intended to begin a new sentence and to function as a "hanging nominative," which is later taken up by the similar words in v. 39.

Here we will focus on the question of the Old Testament text being quoted. The most commonly suggested parallels are various passages dealing with Moses drawing water from the rock in the desert, for example, Ps 104:41 (LXX) "he struck the rock and waters flowed out, rivers went forth in the waterless land" or the possible conflation of v. 16 and v. 20 from Ps 77 (LXX) (v. 16) "and he led forth water from the rock and led down waters like rivers"; (v. 20) "since he struck the rock and waters flowed and torrents flooded forth."

A third possibility is Isa 48:21: "If they thirst, he will lead them through the desert, he will draw out water from the rock for them. The rock will be split and water will flow out and my people will drink."[16] All of these speak of water being given by God in time of need during the Exodus.

Yet another possible candidate related to the general theme of water in the desert is Isa 44:3 (LXX): "because I will give water in time of thirst to those journeying in a waterless place, I will place my Spirit upon your seed."[17] This text is striking because of the way it associates the giving of water with the giving of the Spirit. While this text does not appear to be the source of the actual quotation, it is useful because it shows that the gift of water could be understood to refer to the gift of the Spirit.

Still other texts speak of water flowing from the city of Jerusalem in eschatological times. See, for example, Joel 3:18; Zech 14:8; Ezek 47:1-9; Ps 46:4. Of

---

14. Menken, *Quotations* 73-75.

15. There is also some discussion about the use of the plural of "prophet" here rather than the singular. However, the issue is not significant for our purposes. See Menken, *Quotations* 68-71.

16. See also Ps 114:8; Isa 43:19, 44:3, 55:1, 58:11. Freed (*Quotations* 23) lists other suggestions.

17. Suggested by Freed, *Quotations* 21. That these two lines are meant to be understood in association with one another is evident from the wider context of the psalm.

these, Zech 14:8 ("And on that day living water will flow from Jerusalem") is the most commonly cited.[18] According to Jer 17:13, it is Yahweh himself who is the source of living waters.

Scholars have put forward a wide variety of opinions regarding which of these texts is the source of the quotation but none has gained complete acceptance.[19] In my view, there can be no doubt that the quotation is meant to refer to the gift of water from the rock at the hand of Moses in the desert. Just as water flowed from the rock in the desert, so living water will flow from Jesus.[20]

Isaiah 44:3, with its mention of Yahweh giving water to those who thirst and the paralleling of this with the giving of the Spirit, provides the overall context for 7:37-39. This verse states that Yahweh will give water and this is parallel to the notion in 7:37 that Jesus will be the source of the water. Also, in the Isaiah text, this giving of water is paralleled with the giving of the Spirit. In John 7:39, the author makes it clear that the giving of water refers to the giving of the Spirit. However, these elements of the Johannine passage are not found in the

18. The LXX text is close enough to the Hebrew so that one cannot tell if this is LXX or Hebrew.

19. Freed (*Quotations* 35-38) after reviewing a number of previous proposals concludes that a definitive solution to the problem is not possible but proposes that a partial background is to be found in Prov 18:4. This is from the Wisdom literature, where the majority of references to something similar to the "interiority" spoken of by *ek tēs koilias* appear. Moreover there are frequent references to *hē pēgē tēs zōēs* ("the spring of life") in Proverbs, but Prov 18:4 itself is the only passage in the Hebrew or Greek OT where a combination of the words "water," "river," and "life" occurs. In addition, Freed points out, that verse speaks of *en kardia*, which is close to the meaning of *koilia*. It must be said that Freed's view has not gained wide acceptance, primarily, it would seem, because the associations are too general.

Reim (*Hintergrund* 71) makes a proposal very different from most scholars. He claims that others have misunderstood the actual quotation and argues that the quotation is comprised of only the words "the one believing in me" and that these words come from Isa 28:16. The remainder of the words are Johannine and are not put forward as Scripture. Menken (*Quotations* 199-201) proposes that the closest parallel is a text that combines Ps 77:16, 20 (LXX) together with the designation of "living water" from Zech 14:8. He also argues that the presence of *ek tēs koilias* is due to a complex exegetical process in which the parallelism of "rock" and "spring" in Ps 114:8 allows for the exegetical substitution of the Hebrew for "spring" for "rock" in similar passages. Menken then argues that the Hebrew of "spring" could be given a different pointing, which would then result in its being translated "from inside" rather than "from the rock." While this sequence is possible, it involves a number of suppositions that, when taken together, seem unlikely. Witherington (*Gospel* 173-74) proposes that it comes from "a now-lost sapiential saying" that is related to Sir 24:30-32. This is of course impossible to prove or disprove.

20. When one reviews the pertinent passages from the OT together with the ways these were understood elsewhere in the NT (for example, 1 Cor 10:4), it is difficult not to conclude that the Johannine text (which, we must recall, does not verbally match any single OT text) was an attempt to link (as had others before him) the tradition of the water from the rock in the desert with the eschatological water that would flow from Jerusalem.

quotation but rather in something just as important — the interpretative context for the quotation.

I am inclined to think that Ps 104:41 and Ps 77:16, 20 are the texts closest to that of John 7:38. In Ps 104, the significant words "waters," "flowing," "like rivers" appear in the same verse. In my view, this gives the edge to Ps 104 rather than Ps 77, where the significant words are spread over four verses.

However, if we take Ps 104:41 as the original source of the Scripture, how can we account for the changes? I would propose that the process that accounts for the text in 7:38 is the same process of exegetical paraphrase that is more detailed and more explicit in 6:31-33. In the exegesis performed in 6:31-33, a Scripture passage is quoted, modified, and then shown to apply in a deeper sense to a new (eschatological) reality, namely the events of the ministry of Jesus.[21]

In 6:31-33, the original text is given and then the interpretive changes are made by Jesus. Here in 7:38, only the modified text is given and the reader is intended to understand that this is the "already interpreted" Scripture.[22]

Thus the aorist *(erryēsan)* of the verb "to flow" in Ps 104:41 is changed to the future *(reusousin)* in order to show that what happened in the past is a foreshadowing of the eschatological event that will take place in the future.[23] And the waters mentioned in Ps 104:41 are now understood to be the "living waters" of the Spirit and they are understood to flow, not "from the rock," but "from Jesus."

For the believer, to say that rivers of living water came forth from Jesus, just as ordinary water came forth from the rock like rivers at the time of Moses, would function very much as the interpretation of Scripture in chapter 6, where the Father gives Jesus as the true "bread from heaven" just as Moses had origi-

---

21. This form of interpretation is known as *pesher* ("interpretation") exegesis. This is a type of interpretive exegesis that presumes the primary meaning of a text was not to be found in the context of the original writer but in the future eschatological age. It also presumes that the interpreter is living in the eschatological age and should apply the text to his own age. This type of exegesis is known to us from the commentaries at Qumran.

22. The text is not fully explicated as is done in 6:34-50, but the narrator's explanation in v. 39 serves essentially the same function. And most importantly it will be noted that the central message of both is the same although the second focuses more on the time when the life will be given. In 6:32-33, we learn that the Father gives the true bread from heaven and this is the bread that gives life to the world. In 7:38-39, we learn that Jesus will give living water from his own belly to those who believe and this living water is the Spirit (the principle of eternal life) that will be given when Jesus is glorified.

J. Marcus ("Rivers") has proposed something similar using the text of Isa 12:3, which was also associated with Tabernacles. However, even when the possibility of the text being paraphrased in order to reinterpret it is taken into account, the similarity is not, in my opinion, sufficient to suggest that it was a primary referent.

23. The shift of verb tense is a common technique in the Gospel to show that the text is now fulfilled eschatologically. See the other examples in 2:17 and 6:32.

nally given the manna in the desert. In both cases, the Scripture has reached its eschatological fulfillment in Jesus.

The process as described above has all come from the author of the second edition. However, there is quite substantial evidence that this is not the only editing that the text has undergone. In none of the proposed texts is there a reference to water coming from "the belly."[24] Consequently, the presence of those words in the citation must be due to some other factor than a quotation of Scripture. That "other factor" would seem to be that these words also constitute an addition intended to exegete the deeper meaning of the original text.

Jesus' promise that living water will come from his "belly" finds its fulfillment in 19:33-34, a text that describes the piercing of the side of Jesus and the flowing of blood and water.[25] *Without 19:33-34, there would be no fulfillment of the detail regarding living water flowing from the belly of Jesus.* And, just as important: without 19:33-34, there would be *no need* for a reference to the belly of Jesus in 7:38. However, as can be seen in detail in the discussion of the Composition of 19:31-37, these verses are the work of the third author and were not part of the Gospel at the time of the second edition. Consequently, when the third author inserted 19:31-37, it is very likely that he also inserted the reference to the "belly" of Jesus in 7:38 as an interpretation of the source of the waters, thus rendering the correspondence between the Scripture and the fulfillment even more extensive.

At the time of the second edition, the text had already been paraphrased in order to show that what had happened in the time of Moses happened again in the time of Jesus although in a fuller, eschatological, sense. The third author then simply continued this interpretation by showing that, at the time of Moses, water came forth from the rock and, at the time of Jesus, living water came forth from the belly of Jesus himself.

If we examine the Greek original (given at the beginning of the discussion of this citation), we see that the words in question, together with a literal translation, are: *ek* (out) *tēs koilias* (of the belly) *autou* (of him). Although we cannot

24. Again, scholars regularly presume that these words are part of the original quotation of Scripture. Yet efforts to relate the words to Scripture have not been convincing. Some have argued that "belly" functions here as a synonym for "heart." Others have suggested that it is an overly literal translation from Aramaic and should be rendered simply as "from him." For a critique of earlier views, see Brown, *Gospel* 1:323-24; Menken *Quotations* 187-203. Menken himself has argued (*Quotations* 199-201) that the insertion of the words *ek tēs koilias* was justified by means of an exegetical tradition in which the "rock" in the desert could be interpreted as a "spring" and in which the Hebrew for spring, in its unpointed form, could be read "intestines." However, while such an exegesis is possible, the protracted series of steps it requires makes it difficult to establish with any certainty.

25. It is quite clear that the third author held the conviction that Jesus gave not only water but also blood from his side at his death, but this would not prevent him from affirming the giving of the Spirit as in 7:37-39, which he would view as true, but not complete.

know with certainty, it is likely that the third author added only the words *tēs koilias* and that at the time of the second edition the text read: *ek* (out) *autou* (of him). This would be completely consistent with the promise of the Spirit at the time of the glorification of Jesus. Of course, at the time of the second edition, the reference to water flowing "from Jesus" would have been metaphorical, just as all references to the Spirit under the image of water had been throughout the second edition. The second author manifests a disdain for the purely physical throughout his additions but regularly uses symbols and metaphors. But, when the third author modified the Scripture citation by the reference to the belly and added the account of the piercing of the side of Jesus, he intended the reference to the flow of water (and blood) to be both literal and symbolic!

As is explained in the Interpretation of 7:37-38, this enables the third author to affirm the giving of the Spirit but, at the same time, to link it inextricably with the flow of blood. This reference to the flow of blood signified, in the symbolic language of the community, that the death of Jesus itself was efficacious as atonement for sin, a topic essential to the third author's refutation of his opponents.

The introductory formula here is: ". . . as the Scripture says . . ." *(kathōs eipen hē graphē . . .).*

7. 8:17 "And in your Law it is written that the witness of two persons is true." *(Kai en tō nomō de tō hymeterō gegraptai hoti duo anthrōpōn hē martyria alēthēs estin.)*

There is general agreement that this statement refers to Deut 19:15 (cf. Deut 17:6). But it is not possible to tell whether the source is in the Hebrew or the Greek because there is no attempt at a direct quotation but only a reference.[26]

The introductory formula here is: ". . . in your Law it is written . . ." *(en tō nomō de tō hymeterō gegraptai hoti . . .).*

8. 10:34 "I said, You are gods." *(Egō eipa, theoi este.)*

Once again there is general agreement that the source of the quotation here is Ps 81(82):6. Some would say that it is not possible to tell if John has used the Hebrew or the LXX since both agree.[27] However, those who attempt to distinguish the two argue that the text betrays the LXX.[28]

---

26. So also Barrett, Reim, and Menken. Freed does not treat the passage. Menken (*Quotations* 16) does not study the text in detail but does point out that only the numeral *duo* and the root *martyr-* appear in both the Johannine text and in either the Hebrew or Greek. It should also be noted that the Hebrew and Greek of Deut 19:15 are in substantial agreement.

27. So, for example, Barrett, *Gospel* 28.

28. Reim (*Hintergrund* 23-26) argues that John has derived his translation from the LXX because of the use of *eipa,* which appears here and in the LXX text but nowhere else in John. So also Menken, *Quotations* 14-15.

Jesus begins his statement with the rhetorical question: "Is it not written in your Law . . ." *(Ouk estin gegrammenon en tō nomō hymōn hoti).* While this is not precisely an introductory formula in the same sense as the other texts, its function is to introduce Scripture and to show its applicability. Because of this and because of its similarity to the other formulae, it is included here.

9. 12:13 "Hosanna! Blessed is the one coming in the name of the Lord." *(Hōsanna, eulogēmenos ho erchomenos en onomati kyriou.)*

This quotation is generally thought to come from Ps 117(118):26 with the addition of *Hōsanna* from v. 25 of the same psalm. Without the initial word, the text is a verbatim quote from the LXX of Ps 117(118):26. If the initial word were taken directly from the LXX, we would expect it to have been *translated* as is done elsewhere in the Old Testament rather than being transliterated (as is done here — and in the Synoptics). However, even the presence of the transliterated form does not mean that the author worked directly from a Hebrew text since even when working from the Hebrew, there would be no reason to transliterate it rather than translate it.

The verse has not often been the object of detailed study. Menken refers to the citation without attention to the initial exclamation and states simply that it is a verbatim quotation from the LXX.[29] Schuchard excludes it from his list, saying, "This passage represents not a reference to the Old Testament *per se*, but simply a rendering of a popular Jewish festal greeting derived from Ps 118 (117)."[30] This is also indicated, according to Schuchard, by the fact that it has no introductory formula.[31]

Freed argues that the fact that the same transliterated form *Hōsanna* appears with the wording of Ps 117(118):26 in both Mark 11:9 and a very similar form in Matt 21:9 indicates that the immediate source of the quotation was the Synoptics and not the Old Testament.[32] Before Freed, Lohse had argued that the exclamation was used as a liturgical formula in Judaism before the time of the New Testament.[33] As a result it could well be that (particularly Jewish-) Christian communities were familiar with it and took it over in transliterated form.

---

29. Menken, *Quotations* 15. Menken does not discuss the quotation in detail but refers to it as an "allusion." Presumably this is because it does not have an introductory formula immediately connected with it. However in v. 16, the statement is referred to as Scripture with the same formulaic expression as is used in other quotations of Scripture. In his brief remark on 12:13, he indicates that the author drew from the LXX of Ps 117(118):26 but does not make reference to the presence of *Hōsanna* with the obvious significance of this term for the origin of the quotation.

30. Schuchard, *Scripture* 13.

31. Schuchard, *Scripture* 13, n. 14.

32. Freed, *Quotations* 68-73.

33. Lohse, "Hosianna."

Both the presence of the "liturgical" form of *Hōsanna* and the similarity to Mark and Matthew suggest that John was familiar with a wider tradition of the entry in which both of those elements were found. As a result, I am inclined to accept this as the proper explanation rather than the use of either the Hebrew Old Testament or the LXX directly. However, I would agree with Reim (against Freed) in that it does not appear that John has borrowed directly from the Synoptics but rather that John reveals his knowledge of a common tradition.[34] As we will see below, the wider context in Matt 21 (vv. 2-11) also contains a form of the quotation found in John 12:15. This suggests that John 12:12-15 reflects knowledge of a wider testimonial tradition regarding the entry of Jesus into Jerusalem. In spite of this knowledge of a similar tradition, it is evident that John has understood the tradition in a way quite different from that in Matthew or (to the extent they are parallel) in the other Synoptics.

It is regularly pointed out that there is no introductory formula for v. 13 and that this is the only quotation in the Gospel that is not accompanied by such a formula. However, to say only this is to give a misleading impression of the context, for the quotation is referred to in 12:16 and here we find the following: "His disciples did not know these things at first, but after Jesus was glorified then they remembered that these things were written about him . . ." *(tauta ouk egnōsan autou hoi mathētai to prōton, all' hote edoxasthē Iēsous tote emnēsthēsan hoti tauta ēn ep' autō gegrammena . . .).*[35] Thus, the author understood the statement of the crowd to be a quotation from Scripture and it is clear that the wording used to refer to the passage is the same as is used in the other more readily recognizable formulas.

10. 12:15 "Do not fear, Daughter of Zion. Behold your king comes sitting on the foal of a donkey." *(Mē phobou, Thygatēr Siōn. Idou ho basileus sou erchetai, kathēmenos epi pōlon onou.)*

This text is complicated and requires more extended discussion. There is general agreement that the text is taken from Zech 9:9; however, there are substantial differences that need to be accounted for. These are perhaps best explained by reference to the LXX text that runs as follows: ***Chaire sphodra,*** *Thygatēr Siōn.* ***Kērysse, Thygatēr Hierousalēm.*** *Idou ho basileus sou erchetai* **soi** **dikaios kai sōzōn autos, praüs kai** *epibebēkōs epi* **hypozygion kai** *pōlon* **neon.** *(The boldface indicates words not in the Johannine text.)*

The Johannine version represents a text that has been considerably short-

---

34. See Reim, *Hintergrund* 28.

35. *Tauta* is plural and refers to the quotations in both v. 13 and v. 15. If there is any doubt that the plural has this meaning, it should be noted that this is the only "formula" in the Gospel that is plural.

ened. Changes include *mē phobou* in John whereas both the Hebrew and the LXX have expressions that would be translated "Rejoice greatly." John uses the nominative of *Thygatēr* rather than the vocative *Thygater* as in the LXX. The Johannine version also omits the second direct address as well as the words from *soi* to *epibebēkōs* (which is changed to *kathēmenos)*. Also the conclusion of the quotation in John differs from both the Hebrew and the Greek. The Hebrew has "riding upon an ass, indeed upon a colt, the foal of an ass." The LXX has "mounted on a beast of burden and a colt."

If we look for parallels in other texts, we find that the first two words *(mē phobou)* occur in Isa 40:9 but without *Thygatēr Sion*. The Hebrew combination represented by *Mē phobou, Thygatēr Siōn* appears in the Hebrew of Zeph 3:14-17 but it does not appear in the LXX translation of those verses. In addition to the shortening of the quotation, the second author also uses *kathēmenos* (seated) rather than the *epibebēkōs* of the LXX, and the identification of the animal on which Jesus was riding is changed to *pōlos onou.*

Scholars are very much divided whether the source of the quotation is the Hebrew or the LXX text.[36] Freed comments that in 12:15 "The main part of the quotation is an abbreviated form of Zech 9:9, conflated with a preceding line from an unknown source."[37] Further, Freed takes the words "Do not fear" as being synonymous with "Rejoice" (cf. *Chaire sphodra* of Zech 9:9 LXX) and thus complementing the acclamation of the crowd. With regard to the shortened form of Zech 9:9, Freed concludes that the quotation "is a free artistic composition on the basis of Mt to give added strength to the writer's theme of Jesus as king."[38] He argues that the Zech quotation is closer to the Synoptics than to either the Hebrew or the LXX.[39]

Barrett notes the "striking differences from both the Hebrew and the Greek."[40] He suggests that John quoted loosely from memory and that his changes at the end of the citation were intended to clarify the ambiguity of the Hebrew parallelism. He suggests that here John is reproducing a traditional *testimonium*.[41]

Menken also struggles with identification of the source of the quotation. The clearest parallels are to the LXX but the LXX follows the Hebrew closely. But Menken thinks some of the other elements *(kathēmenos, pōlos onou)* are closer

---

36. Menken (*Quotations* 81, nn. 9, 10, 11) surveys past opinion and finds eight scholars who see the source as the Hebrew and two who see the source as the LXX and three who argue that the Synoptics are the immediate source of the quotation.

37. Freed, *Quotations* 77.

38. Freed, *Quotations* 80.

39. Freed, *Quotations* 81.

40. Barrett, *Gospel* 29.

41. Barrett, *Gospel* 418-19.

to the LXX than to the MT.[42] Menken's conclusion is: "We can only establish that John mostly quotes from the LXX, and suspect on this basis that, as far as he is responsible for the final form of the quotation, he has done so here as well."[43]

In my own view the Johannine author changes the initial exhortation from the LXX form by using an expression about "not fearing," which he would have been familiar with from elsewhere in the Scriptures. He used it in the singular to agree with the singular "Daughter Zion" and intended it as a way of expressing a reaction to the previous acclamation of the crowd and of proclaiming that Jesus comes *not* as a king in the sense that would cause fear among the populace.[44]

It is obvious that the Johannine author has truncated the Zech text and (as Freed points out) "included only the essentials." What remains of the central element is in verbal agreement with the LXX. In contrast to Menken, I do not think it is necessary to find a parallel elsewhere in Scripture for every detail of the changes (e.g., omission of *soi*, the use of *kathēmenos, pōlos onou*).[45] These changes in vocabulary are due to the adaptation and, when the author shortened the citation, he also reduced to a single statement the poetic parallelism in the description of the animal Jesus chose. If this is correct, then it would also be correct to conclude that the Johannine text, which is an adaptation in any case, is an adaptation of the LXX rather than the Hebrew.[46]

In the discussion of John 12:13, it was pointed out that Matt 21:1-11 is quite similar in several respects to this Johannine scene. Specifically, both Gospels contain versions of the quotations in John 12:13, 15; and both use them in relation to the scene of the public acclamation during Jesus' entry into Jerusalem. The form of Ps 117(118):26 is exactly the same in both John and Matthew. Both

42. Menken argues that the closest verbal parallel to *pōlos onou* in the LXX is in Gen 49:11. However, I would argue that, if the Johannine author shortened the text himself (which would seem likely — Matt also shortens the text but not to the same form as John), he probably rephrased the final words himself, retaining the same meaning as the original.

43. Menken, *Quotations* 96.

44. Menken (*Quotations* 85-88) argues that the change is deliberate, the work of Johannine editing, intended to calm the fears aroused by the power of Jesus' miracle. The choice of the Zechariah passage and the entire point of the choice of a donkey are meant to correct the views of the crowd with their false understanding of kingship echoing 6:15 and in their choice of palm fronds for the acclamation.

45. While the text of Gen 49:10-11 could well be associated with Zech 9:9, I see no reason to argue that it has influenced the Johannine text verbally. The appearance of a reference to "the foal of his ass" *(ton pōlon tēs onou autou)* in Gen 49:11 is sufficiently different in form and in the role it plays there to indicate a likely influence on the Johannine text.

46. Whether John knew a shortened form from the Synoptics is difficult to say. The similarity to Matthew is striking, but at the same time it is not perfect. In any event, it would seem that the present form is due to John.

John and Matthew use the same text as a basis of their other quotation also, but the form is considerably different. Also significant is that the order of the quotations in John is reversed from the order in Matthew. Finally, the interpretation of the scene in John is considerably different from that in Matthew. Nevertheless, it would seem that the similarities are so great that it is difficult to conclude that both Matthew and John did not work from the same general tradition. But the shortening of the text in John could not have been simply a shortening of Matthew but had to be a shortening based on the original text, which was probably the LXX. Thus, it would seem that the author gives evidence of knowing and using (but adapting) some common testimonial tradition here rather than either the LXX or the Hebrew.

The introductory formula here is: ". . . as it is written . . ." *(. . . kathōs estin gegrammenon . . .).*

11. 15:25 "They hated me without cause." *(Emisēsan me dōrean.)*

There are two identical Old Testament (LXX) texts that are quite close to the Johannine citation: Ps 34(35):19; 68(69):4. The only difference between the text of the Psalms and that of the Gospel is that what is expressed in participial form in the LXX is expressed as a finite (aorist) verb in the Gospel. As is often suggested by scholars, this change is probably due to the author for whom the participial form would simply be awkward in the Gospel context.

The introductory formula here is: "But in order that the word written in their Law might be fulfilled . . ." *(All' hina plērōthē ho logos ho en tō nomō autōn gegrammenos hoti . . .).*

C. TEXTS IN THE THIRD EDITION

12. 12:34 "We heard in the Law that the Christ remains forever . . ." *(Hēmeis ēkousamen ek tou nomou hoti ho Christos menei eis ton aiōna).*

Because this text refers to Scripture rather than quoting it, we are able to ask about the text it refers to but are not able to determine the version of the Scriptures that was used. A search for such a statement in the Jewish Scriptures has led scholars to a number of texts, all of which speak in some way or another about the perpetuity of the line of David. Texts such as Isa 9:6; Ps 61:8;[47] 72:17; 110:4 bear some similarity to the Johannine text and have been proposed as sources. Also the Targum on Isa 9:5 has been proposed but has not been widely accepted.[48]

---

47. Bampfylde ("Light") has proposed this as the source but the proposal has not been widely accepted.

48. McNeil, *Quotation.* But see the critique by Chilton, "John xii 34."

However, van Unnik has argued convincingly that Ps 89:37 is the most apt background since it speaks of the "seed" of David "remaining forever" and this descendant is then referred to later (v. 51) as "anointed."[49] However, as it evident, even the resemblance of this citation to the Johannine text is quite general and indeed more general than most of the other texts referred to in the Gospel.

In 12:34, the quotation is introduced by *Hēmeis ēkousamen ek tou nomou hoti.* . . . This is not a true introductory formula, but in a way similar to the case with the "formula" in 10:34, the statement functions to introduce a reference to Scripture and so is included here. Thus, this is the most vague of the instances we have studied. This is also the only quotation in the third edition where the speaker is not either Jesus or the narrator. Rather, the speakers are referring to what they understand as a scripturally warranted aspect of the coming messiah. As was said above, the text cannot be identified with any certainty and it is introduced by words that do not constitute a true formula.

13. 12:38 "Lord, who believed our voice? And to whom was the arm of the Lord revealed?" *(Kyrie, tis episteusen tē akoē hēmōn; kai ho brachiōn kyriou tini apekalyphthē;)*

This quotation is from Isa 53:1. There is general agreement that John follows the LXX here. The Hebrew and Greek texts agree with the exception that the LXX and John begin the quotation with *Kyrie*. Menken argues that the fact that John and the LXX begin with *Kyrie* (and the Hebrew does not) and the fact that John uses *apokalyptō* (in agreement with the LXX) rather than his more common *phaneroō* indicate his dependence upon the LXX.[50] However, it would be wrong to think that *apokalyptō* and *phaneroō* are simply synonyms and the choice of *apokalyptō,* which has the connotation of "take the cover away from" rather than simply "manifest," is perhaps more appropriate for the context. While these may indicate dependence on the LXX, it must be said that this evidence is not compelling.

The introductory formula here is: . . . *hina ho logos Ēsaiou tou prophētou plērōthē.* . . .[51]

14. 12:40 "He blinded their eyes and hardened their hearts, lest they might see with their eyes and know in their hearts and turn and I will heal them." *(Tetyphlōken autōn tous ophthalmous kai epōrōsen autōn tēn kardian, hina mē*

---

49. van Unnik, "Quotation" 174-79. This view is now followed by, among others, Barrett, Menken, Reim, and de Jonge (*Stranger* 94-96).

50. Menken, *Quotations* 14-15.

51. Faure ("Zitate" 99-121) notes that, beginning with this verse, citations of Scripture are introduced by the formula "that the Scripture may be fulfilled." Faure saw this as an indication that a different author was responsible for the text from here to the end of the Gospel.

idōsin tois ophthalmois kai noēsōsin tē kardia kai straphōsin, kai iasomai autous.)

Scholars are in general agreement that this citation is taken from Isa 6:10. There is also general agreement that the Johannine version reflects influence of both the Hebrew and the LXX.[52] This particular state of the quotation is attributed variously to quoting loosely from memory (Barrett) or to the intention of the author (Hoskyns, Menken).

This quotation is the second in a series (the first was in 12:38). The introductory formula here reflects that fact and is in a form that will be found again in 19:37. It reads: ". . . because again Isaiah said" *(. . . hoti palin eipen Ēsaias . . .).*

15. 13:18 "The one eating my bread raised his heel against me." *(Ho trōgōn mou ton arton epēren ep' eme tēn pternan autou.)*

It is generally recognized that the Johannine text here is a rendering of Ps 40(41):9. However, the Johannine version is substantially different from both the LXX and the Hebrew. The Johannine text differs from the LXX *(ho esthiōn artous mou, emegalynen ep' eme pternismon)* ("the one eating my bread [pl.] made great deceit against me") as can be seen by comparing it with the text above. But the LXX also differs from the Hebrew. While the first part of the LXX translation is a reasonable translation of the Hebrew, the LXX use of *pternismon* ("guile") rather than *pternan* ("heel") to translate the Hebrew for "heel" is not.

The judgment of the majority of scholars has been that the text is closer to the Hebrew than to the LXX.[53] This line of thought has been continued more recently by Menken who proposes that in the first century the psalm in question (Ps 40[41]:9) was often understood in the context of the betrayal of David by Ahithophel in 2 Samuel and that this was seen as a parallel to the betrayal of Jesus by Judas.[54] Specifically, Menken argues that the wording of 2 Sam 17:2-3 (Hebrew) has influenced the Johannine translation and has given

52. Barrett (*Gospel* 29) comments that "John, the Hebrew and the Greek are all different, but John is perhaps a little nearer the Hebrew than the LXX." Reim (*Hintergrund* 37-39) also argues that the text comes from Isa 6:10 and is closer to the Hebrew than the Greek. Menken (*Quotations* 121) argues that the peculiar form of the quotation is due to Johannine redaction and that perhaps he had a form of the Greek text unknown to us.

53. Schuchard (*Scripture* 109, n. 9) lists twenty scholars who see the Hebrew as the source. Conviction regarding this ranges from that of Freed (*Quotations* 91) who is more skeptical and does not reach a certain conclusion but suggests there may be some slightly greater similarity to the Hebrew than to the LXX to that of Reim (*Hintergrund* 40) for whom there is no doubt that it comes from the Hebrew although it is not an exact translation.

54. For a detailed comparison of the parallels between the portrayal of Judas in the NT and Ahithophel in 2 Samuel, see Menken (*Quotations* 135). These parallels have been noticed repeatedly in the literature.

rise to the Johannine version. I would agree with Menken that the quotation shows influence of 2 Samuel and of John's own free translation. Thus, I would side with the majority of scholars that the Hebrew has influenced the Johannine translation.

The introductory formula here is: ". . . but in order that the Scripture might be fulfilled . . ." *(. . . all' hina hē graphē plērōthē . . .).*

16. 17:12 ". . . and none of them was destroyed except the son of destruction . . ." *(kai oudeis ex autōn apōleto ei mē ho huios tēs apōleias).*

Once again we meet a reference to a text from the Old Testament rather than an actual quotation. In such instances, it is generally not possible to ask about the version the citation comes from since it is in fact not a full quotation. Scholars point to a number of passages in the Old Testament where phrases similar to *ho huios tēs apōleias* ("the son of destruction") appears. Among those cited are, for example, Isa 57:4 *tekna apōleias* ("children of destruction"); Isa 34:5 *ton laon tēs apōleias* ("the people of destruction"). The phrase *huios tēs apōleias* appears elsewhere in the New Testament notably in 2 Thess 2:3 where it denotes an eschatological figure associated with the Second Coming of Christ.

However, most commentators do not look to these texts for parallels but are content to look for a more general background. Barrett suggests that the author is referring to Judas and that the Scripture is the one quoted in 13:18 (Ps 40[41]:9) rather than a new one.[55] This is the view followed by most commentators.[56]

Freed makes two proposals regarding the verse. First, he proposes that 17:12 is to be read in sequence with 6:70-71 and 18:9 and so refers actually to the fulfillment of the word of Jesus rather than to Scripture. As a result he does not "consider Jn 17:12 a quotation in the usual sense."[57] However, this is unlikely. The Gospel always distinguishes between the word of Jesus and Scripture, even though both have their origin in God. Here the reference is to the fulfillment of Scripture, whereas in 18:9 the reference is to the fulfillment *of the word of Jesus.* Thus, while 18:9 may refer back to 6:70-71, 17:12 stands on its own, and it is proper to look for a similar text in the Old Testament.[58]

Second, in spite of this prior opinion, Freed proposes a Scripture text as possible referent in 17:12. He also speculated that the reference could be to Prov 24:22a *(logon phylassomenos huios apōleias ektos estai)* ("the Son keeping

---

55. Barrett, *Gospel* 509.
56. Freed (*Quotations* 96-98) is an exception, as we will see below.
57. Freed, *Quotations* 96.
58. So also Brown, *Gospel* 2:760.

the word will be outside destruction").[59] It is curious that this verse, which does not appear in the Hebrew text but only in the LXX, contains three of the more significant words of John 17:12 *(phylassomenos, huios,* and *apōleias).* Nevertheless, this proposal has been rejected by most scholars. Schnackenburg rejects it, speculating that Freed has misunderstood the quotation and taken *huios apōleias* as joined together rather that *apōleias* as the genitive with *ektos.*[60]

However, there are substantial reasons for thinking that the Proverbs verse mentioned by Freed is the correct one but for very different reasons than those proposed by Freed.[61] The key to the solution of the problem is that scholars have regularly misconstrued the relationship of this citation to the Johannine context in which it appears. There can be no doubt that in the overall context of John 17:6-19 the focus is on Jesus' prayer for the disciples.[62] Verses 11-12 focus on Jesus' prayer to the Father to "keep them in your name." In v. 12, Jesus recalls for the Father that he himself has "kept them in your name and I guarded them and none of them was destroyed." This speaks of the faithful disciples who have guarded and protected. It has regularly been assumed that the fulfillment of Scripture had to do primarily with Judas. But the context indicates it has to do primarily with the fact that Jesus has not lost any of those he had chosen. And Prov 24:22a speaks precisely of the son who keeps the word of God and so avoids destruction, i.e., is saved.[63]

As Schnackenburg points out, in Prov 24:22a, *apōleias* is not to be taken with *huios.* Prov 24:22a speaks primarily of the son that keeps the word of God and so is "outside perdition." This fits the Johannine context well.

In 17:12bc, we read *egō etēroun autous en tō onomati sou hō dedōkas moi kai epylaxa, kai oudeis. . . .* The repetition of words for "guarding," "keeping" *(tēreō, phylassō)* is peculiar. Especially peculiar is the use of *phylassō.* Not only is it used alone without an object or other modifier, but the word itself is rare in

59. Freed, *Quotations* 95-98.

60. Schnackenburg, *Gospel* 3:436-37, n. 49.

61. This position is argued at greater length in my article "Judas."

62. It is commonly recognized that this section, which focuses on the disciples, appears after vv. 1-5 which pray for the glorification of the Son, and before vv. 20-21, which pray for those believing through the word of the disciples.

63. It is also quite plausible that Prov 24:22a was not only the text referred to in John 17:12 but was also the impetus for the formation of the phrase *huios apōleias* itself. Implicitly, the son who keeps the word of God — and so is *ektos apōleias* ("outside destruction," that is, preserved from destruction) is contrasted with the son who does not keep the word of God and who will therefore be subject to perdition. That will be the *huios apōleias* ("the son of perdition"). Although the term *huios apōleias* had not appeared in the OT literature previously, similar forms had (cf. Isa 34:5; 57:4) and it is on the model of these (and in the context of Prov 24:22a) that *huios apōleias* was apparently formed.

John and appears elsewhere only in 12:25, 47. Yet the word appears in the Proverbs text and so its use here serves as another verbal echo of that verse.

In the Proverbs text, it is the "son" who does the guarding (in the sense of obeying) the word of God. In 17:6, the same thing is said of the disciples; they had kept the word of the Father *(kai ton logon sou tetērēkan)* ("and they have kept your word"). This is precisely what is said to be what kept the "son" from perdition in Prov 24:22a. But the Johannine author also now applies the word *phylassō* ("guard") to Jesus, and so it may be his intention to show that (through a kind of exegesis) it was really Jesus who preserved *(ephylaxa)* the disciples, whom he had chosen.

The sole exception to this preservation of the disciples is Judas. Judas did not keep the word of God and so was not protected from destruction. He was not *huios apōleias ektos* ("a son outside destruction") but rather *huios apōleias* ("a son of destruction").[64] Thus, there can be little doubt that the Proverbs text is the one being referred to. Although the text from Prov 24:22a is referred to rather than quoted, we can nevertheless conclude that the author used the LXX as the source of the quotation since, as was mentioned above, the verse does not appear in the Hebrew text but only in the LXX.

There is an introductory formula here and it takes the form ". . . in order that the Scripture might be fulfilled . . ." *(. . . hina hē graphē plērōthē).*

17. 19:24 "They divided my outer garment among themselves and for my clothing they cast lots." *(Diemerisanto ta himatia mou heautois kai epi ton himatismon mou ebalon klēron.)*

There is little dispute about this quotation. The citation is taken from Ps 21(22):18. Because the LXX and the Hebrew texts agree, we cannot tell which the author has used as the source for his quotation.[65] Menken argues that the scale is tipped in favor of John's use of the LXX by the fact that his translation agrees with the LXX verbatim in spite of the fact that there were a number of synonyms the author could have used had he not been following the LXX.[66]

The introductory formula here is: ". . . so that the Scripture might be fulfilled that said . . ." *(. . . hina hē graphē plērōthē [hē legousa] . . .).*

18. 19:28 ". . . in order that the Scripture might be completed, he said 'I thirst'" *(. . . hina teleiōthē hē graphē legei, Dipsō).*

---

64. The presence of the definite articles in the Johannine text does not alter the meaning of the phrase.

65. Barrett, *Gospel* 28; Reim, *Hintergrund* 47-48; Freed, *Quotations* 100; Menken, *Quotations* 15.

66. Menken, *Quotations* 15. Menken does not discuss the passage in detail in his book.

This is not a true quotation of Scripture but rather a reference to it. It is one of the texts that is often not treated by scholars in detail. In the citation, the fulfillment of Scripture is accomplished entirely in the word of Jesus "I thirst."[67] In spite of this briefest of references, there is no text that matches the Johannine term identically. However, Ps 21(22):15 ("My strength is dried up like a potsherd and my tongue sticks to my throat") is close in thought if not in wording.[68]

Even if this is the meaning taken in the narrowest context, the larger surrounding context provides a different perspective and suggests a different text. Verse 29, which describes the actions of the crowd in giving Jesus vinegar to drink, is significant because it also appears (with minor variations) in Mark 15:36; Matt 27:48 and Luke 23:36. Although the Synoptics do not make reference to this event as being the fulfillment of Scripture, there can be no doubt that all four accounts reflect the same, or very similar, tradition. If, we understand the giving of vinegar as part of a tradition associated with the Crucifixion, then the proper source would seem to be Ps 68(69):21 ("they have given me poison for my food and for my thirst gave me vinegar to drink"). Thus, the reference to thirst in Ps 68(69):21 would be sufficient to account for Jesus' word.

The problem seems to be best solved by asking which action is understood to be the fulfillment of Scripture: the words of Jesus or the offering of wine. In the Gospel of John, the fulfillment resides in the words of Jesus rather than in the action of offering wine. As a result, I would suggest that the text referred to is that of Ps 21(22):15.

The introductory formula here is: "... in order that the Scripture might be completed ..." (... *hina teleiōthē hē graphē* ...). The use of the verb *teleioun* here in such an introductory formula is unique in the entire New Testament and is probably due to assimilation to *tetelestai* earlier in v. 28. In any event, the overall formulation has its closest parallels in the other formulas with *hina* and the subjunctive of *pleroō*.

19. 19:36 "No bone of his will be broken." *(Ostoun ou syntribēsetai autou.)*

Most scholars think that the phrase is intended to refer to the instructions accompanying the treatment of the Paschal lamb. Both Exod 12:10 and 46 read: "You will not break the bones of it" *(ostoun ou syntripsete ap' autou)*. Numbers 9:12 reads: "They will not break the bones of it" *(ostoun ou syntripsousin ap' autou)*. As can be seen, the differences are minor, but real.

---

67. In the Greek "I thirst" is rendered by the single word *dipsō*.
68. The UBS/Nestle text gives Ps 22:15 as a parallel to v. 28 and Ps 69:21 as the parallel to v. 29.

However, a very similar expression is used to describe the suffering of the just man in Ps 33(34):20 (LXX) ("the Lord guards all his bones; not one of them will be broken" [*kyrios phylassei panta ta osta autōn, hen ex autōn ou syntribēsetai*]). Here the word *ostoun* ("bone") does not appear in the same clause but the verb is third-person singular future passive — as is the Johannine text.

More recently, Menken has proposed that the Psalm text served as the basic text and the Pentateuchal texts supplied the material for the changes in it. Menken further proposes that the quotation probably comes from the LXX, arguing that *syntribēsetai* points in this direction, as does the circumstance that John usually quotes from the LXX.[69] Moreover, the connection of Ps 33(34):20 with the regulations concerning the paschal lamb have their antecedents in early Jewish and early Christian literature (see esp. *Jub.* 49:13).[70]

However, the *only word actually shared* by the Psalm text and John 19:36 is the form of the verb. But Exod 12 and Num 9 both have all the words (including the verb) and the only difference is in the *form* of the verb. Menken argues that it was considered a legitimate hermeneutical maneuver to combine texts in such quotations provided the texts had at least one word in common.[71] However, particularly when only one or two words are shared, it becomes more difficult to prove that one is actually witnessing a combination of texts rather than the simple alteration of words from a single text.

A reference to the Passover lamb would find precedent in John. In 1:29, 36 Jesus is referred to as "the Lamb of God" by John the Baptist. The fact that it was preparation day for Passover had also been mentioned in 18:28. The mention of the specific hour of Passover eve has been noted in 19:14 and that was the hour for the slaughtering of the Passover lambs.

The suffering just man has been alluded to by the reference to Ps 21:18 (LXX) in 19:24, 28 and by the reference to Ps 68:21 (LXX) in 19:29. And so it is not impossible that such a reference appears again here. However, given the overall context of Passover eve and the very slight verbal similarity of the text from Ps 33, it seems much more likely that the allusion in v. 36 is intended to refer to the Paschal lamb.

Because there are no significant differences between the LXX and the He-

69. Menken, *Quotations* 147-66; here, 165. I have difficulty with Menken's argument, which is based on what the author "usually" does, since there is considerable variety in what the author actually does in terms of quoting (sometimes using the LXX, sometimes the Hebrew, sometimes other forms known only from the testimonial tradition). Stating his tendency is helpful in knowing where to look, but it cannot be used to prove an argument.

70. Menken, *Quotations* 159-64.

71. Menken, *Quotations* 52-53, 169-70. The Psalm text and the Exodus-Numbers texts share the verb *(syntribō)* and the noun *(ostoun)*. Menken refers to the studies of this practice by Brooke *(Exegesis)* and Koet ("Today").

brew renderings of the Exod and Num texts, it cannot be determined whether John's version is taken from the LXX or the Hebrew.

The introductory formula for this quotation is ". . . in order that the Scripture might be fulfilled . . ." (. . . *hina hē graphē plērōthē . . .*).

20. 19:37 "They will look at the one they pierced." (*Opsontai eis hon exeken-tēsan.*)

There is general agreement that the Johannine text is a form of Zech 12:10. This text was a popular testimonial text in early Christianity (Matt 24:30; Rev 1:7; *Epistle of Barnabas* 7:9; Justin, *Apol.* 1.52.10-12; *Dial.* 14.8; 32.2; 64:7; 118.1). It is also generally recognized that while the textual form in these instances is not exactly that of either the LXX or the Hebrew, the texts presupposed in these other instances are remarkably similar not only to each other but to the form employed in the Johannine text.[72] This has led to the recognition that the Johannine version is taken from a Christian testimonial tradition.[73]

But this is not the only peculiarity associated with this text. Elsewhere in early Christianity the text was interpreted as referring to the eschatological "seeing" of Jesus at the end of time. That is, those who were guilty of putting Jesus to death ("piercing" him, through his hands and feet) would see him coming in glory and realize their guilt. This is almost surely not the meaning intended here. In the Johannine context, the quotation is joined with that in the previous verse and is meant to be associated with it. Thus, the first speaks of not breaking Jesus' bones and the second speaks of the piercing. The reference to "they will look on" in this context would refer to the attendants present at the Crucifixion. Thus, both the failure to break the legs of Jesus and the piercing of his side were done in fulfillment of Scripture.

The introductory formula here is: "And again another Scripture says . . ." (*kai palin hetera graphē legei . . .*).

D. OBSERVATIONS ON THE USE OF SCRIPTURE IN THE GOSPEL

If we examine the quotations from the point of view of the editions proposed here, we can make the following observations.

---

72. The texts and a detailed discussion are given in Menken, *Quotations* 168-70.

73. Menken (*Quotations* 171, n. 10) lists Dodd (*Scriptures*), Lindars (*Apologetic*), Freed (*Quotations*), Schnackenburg (*Gospel*) among the considerable number of scholars who hold this general view.

1. Regarding the Source of the Quotations

In the First Edition

There is one quotation within the first edition (1:23). In addition, there is one reference to Scripture (7:42), but the precise text to which reference is made cannot be determined. Both of the actual quotations are from Isaiah and are very close to, or identical with, the LXX form. Because only two quotations remain from this edition, it would be wrong to draw the conclusion that, for example, the first author uses only Isaiah. On the other hand, both seem drawn from the LXX and neither bears a similarity to the Heb text. That could well be more significant.

In the Second Edition

We have considered nine texts that appear in the second edition. Of these, one (8:17) is an allusion to Scripture and, while the text can be identified, it is not possible to determine which version the author had as source since the text is not quoted. The remaining eight are quotations: 2:17; 6:31, 45; 7:38; 10:34; 12:13, 15; 15:25. Here we notice that all but two are either identical with, or very close to, the LXX. The two most problematic texts (7:38; 12:15) also seem to be drawn from the LXX although this conviction is less certain than is the case with the other texts.

In the Third Edition

Nine Scripture texts appear in the third edition. Of these, three (12:34; 17:12; 19:28) are references rather than direct quotations. In these instances, we are able to determine a possible text being referred to, but it is not possible to determine whether the author was referring to the Hebrew or the LXX — except in the case of 17:12 where the text referred to (Prov 24:22a) appears only in the LXX.

The remaining six texts are quotations (12:38; 12:40; 13:18; 19:24, 36, 37). Of these one (19:24) is identical in the LXX and the Hebrew and so the Johannine version could have been taken from either. In the case of one other (12:38) the Hebrew and LXX versions are very similar with only a slight edge given to the possibility of the text coming from the LXX. The remaining four texts can with greatest likelihood be said to be based on the Hebrew rather than the LXX (12:38; 12:40; 13:18; 19:37[74]).[75] Thus, although it seems certain that the third au-

---

74. This is based on a generalized Christian testimonium.

75. It should be noted that Menken proposes that the reason "John" uses the Hebrew in these instances is that the LXX would not support his interpretation. This explanation is partic-

thor knew and used the LXX, it is also clear that he knew and made use of the Hebrew, something not evident in the work of the second author.

2. Regarding the Introductory Formulas

It is the presumption of this study that there is no *a priori* reason why all the introductory formulae in the Gospel (or in a given edition) should necessarily be the same. It is within this context that the following observations are made.

In the First Edition

The formula of introduction in 1:23 is similar in some respects to the formula used in 7:38, except that in the first edition the source is identified as "Isaiah" while in the second, the source is identified as "Scripture" *(graphē)*.

The reference in 7:42 is introduced in a way generally similar to that in 1:23 and 7:38 (with some form of the verb *eipon*). No general conclusion can be drawn from this. (See further the chart below.)

In the Second Edition

There are nine instances of introductory formulae in the second edition. Where there is a formula of introduction for the quotation, this is either *kathōs estin gegrammenon* (6:31; 12:15) or some variant form of it (2:17; 6:45; 8:17; 10:34; 15:25). In the one instance where there is no "introductory" formula (12:13), we find something particularly striking: when 12:13 is referred to in 12:16, it is said that *tauta ēn ep' autō gegrammena*. . . . The same formula appears — but three verses later. The only exception to this pattern is 7:38 where the formula is *kathōs eipen hē graphē*.[76]

Chapter 15:25 contains the only introductory formula in the second edition containing a form of *pleroō*. This formula is similar to that typical of the third edition. It begins with *hina* and also contains the aorist passive subjunctive of *pleroō*. However, in spite of these similarities, it is significant that the formula also contains the perfect passive participle of *graphō*, something found in all the formulas characteristic of the second edition. Thus, it cannot be said that the formula is totally characteristic of either edition. More significant is the fact that there are other characteristics of the second edition that permeate 15:22-26

---

ularly appropriate if one holds a view that all the quotations come from the same author. However, if more than one author is responsible for the introduction of quotations, then it is perhaps more appropriate simply to say that this author saw an appropriate meaning within the Hebrew text and so applied it to Jesus. That is, one need not speak of a "rejection" of the LXX in this case.

76. But I would argue that this exception does not refute the notion of a "pattern" in the use of such formulae but is simply an exception to it.

and indicate that those verses come from the second edition.[77] I would consider these other theological features as determinative of the identity of the material and would judge the formula in the light of that.[78] Consequently, I would suggest that the formula in 15:25 was probably first expressed in the manner typical of the second edition and was modified by the introduction of the fulfillment motif in the third edition at the time vv. 26-27 were added. (See further the chart below.)

In the Third Edition

As was said above, there are five quotations within the third edition (12:40; 13:18; 19:24, 36, 37). If we ask about the *introductory formulae* used in this edition, the number increases by two (17:12; 19:28) because of instances where an introductory formula appears without a specific quotation. In the first of these additional instances an introductory formula appears but the text can best be said to "allude to" or "refer to" a Scripture text rather than to quote it. In the second instance the author speaks of the general fulfillment of Scripture, using an introductory formula even though a specific text is neither given nor even alluded to. One text (12:34) is neither introduced by a true formula nor is the text a true quotation. That will not be considered in what follows.

In two instances, the third author has appended a second quotation to a first (12:40; 19:37). In both of these cases, the author uses an introduction for the second quotation, expressed as *"hoti palin eipen Ēsaias . . ."* (12:40) or *"Kai palin hetera graphē legei . . ."* (19:37). The remaining (five) instances constitute "normal" introductory formulae (13:18; 17:12; 19:24, 28,[79] 36). Of these all use the same formula *(. . . all' hina hē graphē plērōthē . . .)* except 19:28, which uses the formula *. . . hina teleiōthē hē graphē. . . .* However, the formula in 19:28 would appear to be simply a variation of that used by the third author elsewhere. The use of the verb *teleioun* (for such a formula) is unique in the entire New Testament. Moreover, it is a synonym for *plēroō* and is very likely due to assimilation to *tetelestai*, which appears two words earlier. In any event, the overall formulation has its closest parallels in the formula used elsewhere by the third author.

---

77. See the discussion of the Composition.

78. That is to say, the weightier evidence is the portrayal of the three witnesses in 15:22-26 (from the second edition) and the way the third author expands the list to include two other witnesses for the time after the ministry in 15:26-27. The introductory formula is a "feature," an element that emerges *from* the analysis, rather than a "criterion" that *determines* the analysis. Moreover, once the consistency of the formulae in the other eight instances within the second edition is recognized, the ambiguity of 15:25 should be explained in the light of the pattern rather than seen as a refutation of it.

79. Allowing for the variation noted above.

Thus, the third author has a preferred formula of introduction not found in the earlier editions.[80] He uses it with only minor variation to begin all of his quotations, allusions, and references to Scripture except where he is appending a second quote to a previous one. (See further the chart below.)[81]

It is also noteworthy and further evidence of the consistency of the third author's usage that twice the third author uses the same formula in relation to the fulfillment of the word of Jesus (18:9, 32).

Finally, it is important to note that the form of introduction used in the second edition was *a classical rabbinic formula* indicating that something was in accord with the canonical Jewish Scriptures. It appears regularly in rabbinic texts of the first century and later. As such, it is one more indication of the extent the second edition reflects a thoroughly *Jewish*-Christian exegesis of Scripture. On the other hand, the introductory formula used in the third edition is a typically Christian expression used to express the eschatological "fulfillment" of Scripture.[82] Thus the two types of formulae reflect the same conviction (the described action is in accord with Scripture) but each does it with a formula distinctive of different cultural and religious *milieux*.

3. General Conclusions

From the conclusions just presented, we see a two-fold consistency in presentation of the Old Testament quotations in the Gospel. Both the source of the quo-

---

80. This appears in a slightly different form in 19:28 *(hina teleiōthē hē graphē)*. While it may be simply intended to provide variety, as Moule has suggested ("Fulfillment-Words" 318), Moloney ("Scripture" 459) has suggested that the author deliberately made the change to indicate that, in this last act of Jesus, the Scriptures were now truly "brought to perfection." However, the use of the verb "bring to perfection" *(teleioō)* is more frequently and more naturally associated with "bringing to perfection the work of the Father" (4:34; 5:36; 17:4). It is more likely that no particular nuance is intended and the change is simply due to assimilation to *tetelestai*, which appears two words earlier.

81. Moloney ("Scripture") proposes another view of the shift in introductory formulae. He argues that the first appearance of the formula "in order that the Scripture might be fulfilled" "is a first hint of a relationship that might exist between the fulfillment of Scripture and the cross of Jesus" (459). "From 12:38 onward, every citation from the Scriptures is associated with Jesus' death, and they all claim that in his death *the Scriptures are fulfilled*" (459, italics in the original). Yet, certainly the Scripture passages introduced by the formula "as it is written" also indicate that there is a "fulfillment" in the related action of Jesus, even if the word "fulfill" *(pleroō)* is not used. Moreover, in 2:22, the "earlier" formula is used but the reference to being consumed by zeal for the Lord's house (2:17, 22; cf. Ps 69) refers to the death of Jesus as being a fulfillment of Scripture.

82. For example, it appears regularly in the Gospel of Matthew (most commonly referring to the fulfillment of the word of the prophets; but see Matt 26:54, 56) and less frequently Mark (14:49) and Luke (4:21; 24:44).

tations and the introductory formulae have a consistent but distinctive form in the second and third editions. On the one hand, this consistency is striking; but on the other hand, it seems to serve no specific theological purpose. Thus, it is all the more striking that there is such consistency. This consistency would seem to be an additional confirmation of the correctness of the history of composition presented here.

However, these conclusions regarding the source of the quotations and regarding the use of introductory formulae are not of equal certainty. The conclusions expressed above regarding the sources of the quotations are still disputed by some scholars, and the conclusions cannot be said to be universally accepted. One might well dispute one or another judgment regarding them. If the view presented above regarding the version from which one or another citation was drawn was to prove wrong, this would, at the worst, negate the consistency *regarding the source of the quotations.*

But the study of introductory formulae is more patent and straightforward. Conclusions regarding these would be unaffected by conclusions regarding the source of the quotations. The consistency here is also striking and, as was shown above, corresponds well with the view of the composition of the Gospel presented here. Some scholars would see the shift in formulae as theologically motivated. For example, Evans has argued that all the formulae are the work of the same individual and that the formulas appearing in the public ministry (prior to chapter 12) establish that Jesus is the messiah, but those from the close of the ministry to the end of the Gospel are designed to show that the rejection of this messiah by Israel was not an accident but a result of divine design.[83] Earlier, Faure had suggested that the shift in formulae indicates a distinct literary source used in the Passion.[84]

The present investigation indicates that neither of these observations is completely correct. The difference in formulae is obvious. The correlation of this shift with the authorship is also quite consistent.[85] It is possible that the third author intended to introduce a particular emphasis in his portrayal of the

---

83. See Evans, "Formulas" 82-83.

84. Faure, "Zitate." More recently Reim (*Hintergrund*, esp. 88-89) has proposed that some of the introductory formulae come from the Evangelist while others are traditional. But Reim finds no consistency in the usage. Fitzmyer ("Quotations" 299-305) studies introductory formulae in the Qumran literature and compares them with the usage in the NT. The Qumran documents do not use a single formula and the ones they use tend to overlap with usage in the OT and with usage elsewhere in the NT. There is however no precise parallel to the "fulfillment" formula as found throughout the NT ("Quotations" 303). In the Gospel of John, these formulae are found only in the third edition. See further below.

85. Carson ("Written: John" 247-48) speaks of the "enormous diversity" of the formulae. This is true only if one expects perfect identity in both wording and order.

Passion with his distinctive formulae; it is also possible that the theological distinctions are of our own creation and that the shift is simply due to distinctive authorship. They may be formulae with which the author was more familiar or comfortable. The usage is consistent but it is not exclusive. This should not be a surprise. Again, this is not a question of a "code" used by one author to distinguish his work from that of the other. Rather, these are differences that indicate a pattern of usage. While we cannot always identify the purpose of the pattern, it is quite easy to recognize it.

Finally, we may ask whether the use of the LXX or the Hebrew tells us anything about the circumstances of the community at the time. While the use of the LXX within the first and second editions is not unusual, it is perhaps of interest to note that, at the time of the third edition, the community does not seem to be losing contact with the Hebrew roots of its tradition but is fully capable of drawing upon the Hebrew as well as the LXX text to portray Jesus as the fulfillment of the Scriptures.

A LISTING OF THE INTRODUCTORY FORMULAE IN THE GOSPEL GROUPED ACCORDING TO THE EDITIONS FROM WHICH THEY COME

(1E) 1:23 . . . *kathōs eipen Ēsaias ho prophētēs.*

(1E) 7:42 *ouch hē graphē eipen hoti . . .*

* * *

(2E) 2:17 *Emnēsthēsan hoi mathētai autou hoti gegrammenon estin . . .*

(2E) 6:31 . . . *kathōs estin gegrammenon . . .*

(2E) 6:45 *estin gegrammenon en tois prophētais . . .*

(2E) 7:38 *kathōs eipen hē graphē*

(2E) 8:17 *en tō nomō de tō hymeterō gegraptai hoti . . .*

(2E) 10:34 *Ouk estin gegrammenon en tō nomō hymōn hoti*

(2E) 12:13 See 12:16: *emnēsthēs an hoti tauta ēn ep' autō gegrammena . . .*

(2E) 12:15 . . . *kathōs estin gegrammenon . . .*

(2E) 15:25 *All' hina plērōthē ho logos ho en tō nomō autōn gegrammenos hoti . . .*

* * *

(3E) 12:34 *Hēmeis ēkousamen ek tou nomou hoti . . .*

(3E) 12:38 *. . . hina ho logos Ēsaiou tou prophētou plērōthē . . .*

(3E) 12:40 *. . . hoti palin eipen Ēsaias . . .*

(3E) 13:18 *. . . all' hina hē graphē plērōthē . . .*

(3E) 17:12 *. . . hina hē graphē plērōthē.*

(3E) 19:24 *. . . hina he graphē plērōthē [hē legousa] . . .*

(3E) 19:28 *. . . hina teleiōthē hē graphē . . .*

(3E) 19:36 *. . . hina hē graphē plērōthē . . .*

(3E) 19:37 *kai palin hetera graphē legei . . .*

APPENDIX 2

The "I Am" Statements in the Gospel

There are a variety of statements in the Gospel that hinge on the words: "I am" *(egō eimi)* as spoken by Jesus.[1] These statements are the focus of this brief appendix. The purpose of the appendix is to show that these statements can be more adequately understood when they are viewed in the context of the compositional process proposed in this Commentary. First, we will review the various types of statements and then comment on their meaning and on their background. Finally, the role of these various statements in the developing Johannine tradition will be noted.

A. THE FOUR TYPES OF "I AM" STATEMENTS IN THE GOSPEL

The first of these statements is the ordinary, secular use of "I am" as a means of self-identification (4:26; 6:20; and 18:5), similar to the English: "It is I."[2] It can also have the related meaning of identifying a person with something. For example, in 4:26 it indicates that Jesus identifies himself with the title the woman is discussing (that is, "I am the one you are talking about"). In 18:5, Jesus responds "I am (he)" when the arresting party says that they are seeking Jesus of Nazareth.

---

1. This appendix is meant as only a brief introduction to a topic that has occasioned a considerable body of literature. For such bibliography, see Ruck-Schröder, *Name*; Williams, *"I Am He."*

2. In the past, scholars have categorized the statements in a variety of ways. The reader is referred to the survey by Ball *("I Am")* and the Appendix in Brown, *Gospel* 1:533-38. The first two of the categories that I would propose are generally accepted. Many would group together the texts in my third and fourth categories. But see the remarks of Ashton cited below.

The second and a more significant type are the so-called "absolute" I AM statements. These statements are often printed with the "I AM" in upper case letters to indicate that they are intended to replicate those statements in the Old Testament that use these words to identify Yahweh. Thus, when Jesus uses this expression, he is appropriating the highest possible Christology. Its clearest instance appears in 18:6, where the power present in the pronunciation of the divine I AM causes the arresting troops to fall to the ground. This exalted usage appears concentrated in 8:24, 28, 58 and later in 13:19 (and 18:6, 8).

The third type of "I am" statement is exemplified in those texts where the words are used with a predicate in a metaphorical sense. Thus, Jesus, using these words, identifies himself as the bread of life/living bread (6:35, 48, 51); the light of the world (8:12; 9:5); the gate for the sheep (10:7, 9); the model shepherd (10:11, 14); and the true vine (15:1, 5). In these cases, the predicate is used metaphorically to refer to some quality of Jesus, that is, that he nourishes; that he illumines; that he is the sole access point for salvation; that he is a model leader; that he is the source of life.

The fourth type of "I am" statement is exemplified in two texts where the words are used with a predicate but the statement is *elliptical* but not *metaphorical*.[3] In these statements, the predicate is part of the larger expression, most of which is presumed but not expressed.[4] The two texts of this type are: "I am the Resurrection and the Life" (11:25) and "I am the Way, the Truth and the Life" (14:6). Thus, the first of these statements: "I am the Resurrection and the Life" is undoubtedly intended to be understood in a way similar to the following: "(You should believe in me because) I am (the guarantor of) resurrection (and the means by which you may gain eternal) life." The statement: "I am the Way, the Truth and the Life" could be expanded as follows: "I am (the one who is) the way (to salvation); (I am one who speaks) the truth; (I am the one in whom you must believe in order to receive the Spirit and so gain) life."[5] Such statements

---

3. C. Koester (*Symbolism* 6-7) distinguished the statements of 11:25 and 14:6 from the other "I am" statements but would refer to them as metaphors of a less tangible type. But these predicates are different *in kind*. In no sense does Jesus claim to be "the Resurrection" in the same sense that he claims to be "the bread of life." In his description of 11:25 (p. 108), Koester seems to be saying the same thing I am saying but without labeling the expression "elliptical."

4. Ashton (*Understanding* 186) speaks of 11:25 and 14:6 as being the "supreme examples of . . . compression." Yet Ashton himself does not see these as constituting a distinct category. Bultmann (*Gospel* 225, n. 3) also sees 11:25 and 14:6 as constituting a separate category but not on the basis of their elliptical character.

5. Whether the use of "way" here is considered a true metaphor can be debated. Certainly, the image of a *hodos* ("road, path, way") can be considered a metaphor (see Lindars, *Gospel* 472), but its use is so common, especially in the Old Testament, that its metaphorical function is greatly diminished. In any event, the fact that 14:6 is elliptical and is intended to emphasize the third author's understanding of the role of Jesus over against the understanding

are part of a larger class of elliptical statements in which Jesus is not always the subject of the verb, for example, 6:63: "My words are Spirit and life." This must be understood as a compressed form of a statement that might be rendered more fully as: "(If you believe) my words (you will receive the) Spirit and (the Spirit is the source of eternal) life." The same is true of "His commandment is eternal life" (12:50a), which should be understood as something like: "(Obeying) his commandment is (what will lead to) eternal life."

It is important to distinguish these four types of statements for reasons that will be seen below. However, there is inevitably some ambiguity between the types.[6] Part of the problem is undoubtedly due to the editing that the Gospel has undergone. For example, in 18:5-8, the "I am," which was an instance of ordinary self-identification in the first edition (18:5), was taken over by the author of the third edition and made into an instance of what is clearly the "divine" use (18:6).

The instances that I would list as simple self-identification (4:26; 6:20 and 18:5) have been proposed at times by various other scholars to be instances of the divine "I AM."[7] The fact of this disagreement indicates the solution is not an easy one. However, in my view, to attribute 4:26; 6:20 and 18:5 to the divine use over-theologizes the language of the Gospel. If the Gospel contained none of the statements that are clearly the divine use, there would be no reason to think that 4:26 and 6:20 were instances of it.

Moreover, if we compare the uses in 4:26 and 6:20 with that in 18:6, we see that all occur in a narrative setting. Yet the meaning of the instance in 18:6 is absolutely clear and its utterance physically affects those who hear it. There is none of this in 4:26 or 6:20. Are we to imagine that Jesus utters the divine I AM to the Samaritan woman and there is no effect whatsoever and that he utters it to the disciples and there is no effect on them? Yet when he utters it to the soldiers who have come to arrest him, they are thrown to the ground. That seems implausible.

The presence of the third type of statement is not disputed. It is easily recognized. Yet this is not the same as the fourth type and, when the two types of statements are confused, faulty interpretation results. The third type is meta-

---

of the opponents is not diminished by the possibility that the first element of it is metaphorical. The third author also showed himself capable of metaphor in his use of "light" in 8:12 and 9:5 as well as in his use of "gate" in 10:7, 9.

6. Brown (*Gospel* 1:533-34) excludes the simple secular usage from his listing but then sees a "use where a predicate may be understood even though it is not expressed." The only texts assigned to this category are two of the ambiguous instances of the secular use (6:20 and 18:5). I see no reason to assign these instances to a distinct category. They are simply ambiguous instances of the secular usage.

7. Moloney is a recent example of a scholar who would see the divine use in all of these instances. On 4:26, see Moloney, *Gospel* 130, 134; on 6:20, see *Gospel* 203, 204; on 18:5, see *Gospel* 483, 485. However, Barrett (*Essays* 13, 17) would see all of these texts as simple identification.

phorical; the fourth is not metaphorical but only elliptical. This is certainly true of 11:25. Again the case is a bit more complex in 14:6 where one might argue that for Jesus to refer to himself as "the way" is metaphorical. At the same time, the other two terms ("truth" and "life") are clearly not metaphors. In these cases, the fullest meaning of the terms can only be achieved by supplying the words left out in the ellipsis.

B. THE SEARCH FOR THE BACKGROUND OF THE "I AM" STATEMENTS

Throughout the twentieth century there was much discussion of the background of these various types of "I am" sayings in the Gospel. Scholars proposed parallels in Egyptian religion, in the Hermetic writings, in Gnosticism, and in Hellenistic religion.[8] However, in recent years, scholars have tended to see the Jewish religion as providing the most likely background. However, even this has not been fully satisfying. For example, Ashton points out that there is no Old Testament parallel for the image of Jesus as "the gate."[9] Moreover, as Brown points out, the image of "the vine" in chapter 15 does not find close parallels in the Old Testament although there are numerous images of Israel as a vineyard.

However, when we view the third and fourth categories of "I am" statements from the perspective of the composition process put forward in this Commentary, we are able to see them in a new light and to discover that there is a consistency not previously noticed. As we will see below, those metaphors that derive *from the second author* find close parallels in and are best understood against the background of the Old Testament. However, the texts where these images undergo a secondary development and the texts in which the "I am" statements are elliptical rather than metaphorical: (1) are in all cases the work *of the author of the third edition;* (2) and do not have specific parallels in the Old Testament; and (3) at the same time address issues directly related to the internal crisis of the community. We will see this in more detail in what follows.

C. THE "I AM" SAYINGS, THEIR BACKGROUND, AND THE COMPOSITION OF THE GOSPEL

In order to put the various types of usage in context, we will examine the statements as they appear in the chronological order of the three editions together with their background.

8. Ball, *"I Am"* 24-45.
9. Ashton, *Understanding* 187.

Appendix 2

In the First Edition

In the first edition, we find all of the instances of the ordinary, secular use for self-identification, together with the sub-category in which Jesus identifies himself with a figure suggested by another. Thus, in 4:26, Jesus identifies himself with the figure of the Messiah, about whom the Samaritan woman had been speaking. In 6:20, we find the purest form of simple self-identification. Jesus identifies himself, as if by the sound of his voice, as the one they know and whom they should not fear. In 18:5, Jesus identifies himself, by means of this ordinary, secular usage, as the one the arresting party is seeking.

Of course, the background of this usage does not require discussion since this is common secular Greek usage.

In the Second Edition

In the second edition, the author introduces the use of "I am" with various metaphors. Thus, Jesus is the true bread from heaven, the good shepherd, and the true vine. These are images with rich biblical background.

The image of Jesus as the bread come down from heaven (John 6:35, 48, 51) evokes the entire Old Testament tradition of the giving of the manna to the Israelites in the desert (Exod 16:13-26).

The image of the "shepherd" also has an extensive Old Testament background. In the Old Testament, God is described as "shepherding" his people (Gen 49:24; Pss 23; 78:52; Mic 2:12). The leaders of Israel were also regularly referred to as shepherds (e.g., Num 27:16-17). Evil kings were described as "wicked shepherds" (1 Kings 22:17; Jer 10:21; 23:1-2; Ezek 34). In this context, the metaphor of Jesus as the good shepherd is completely at home.

When we come to the image of Jesus as the true vine, we must focus on the original parable and its explanation (15:1-2a, 3, 8) before turning our attention to the secondary development of the parable (15:2b, 4-7). If we look for a parallel to the original parable and the development as it appeared *in the second edition,* we find a close parallel in Isa 27:2-6. In this passage, God is the "keeper of his vineyard," who waters it and guards it.[10] If the vineyard gives forth thorns and briers, he will "march to battle against it" or "will let it cling to me for protection." But "[i]n days to come, Jacob will take root; Israel will blossom and put forth shoots and fill the whole world with fruit." If, in the original parable, Israel and Jacob are conceived of as a vineyard, it is reasonable to conceive of Jesus as a single vine and his Father as the vinedresser. Just as the vineyard of Isaiah gives forth shoots "in days to come," so the vine that is Jesus has branches and

---

10. For an expanded treatment of this image with other possible background texts, see Borig, *Weinstock* 247-52; C. Koester, *Symbolism* 244-47.

the keeper of the vineyard will "do battle with whatever does not bear fruit." But the disciples will go forth as branches and bear much fruit. This development is in close harmony with the original parable in Isaiah.

In the Third Edition

While the three images introduced by the author of the second edition are rich in their own right, each has been amplified in some way by the author of the third edition. Thus, for the second author, Jesus is the bread that is better than that given by Moses, but, for the third author, he is also the Eucharistic bread that is necessary for life.

For the third author, the original parable of the shepherd comes in for extensive expansion. For the third author, in addition to being the good shepherd, Jesus is also "the gate," through which all must enter in order to find life (10:7c, 9). In addition, Jesus is the shepherd "who dies for the sheep" in contrast with the hireling who runs away (10:11b-14a). And, finally, he is the shepherd who seeks to bring all the sheep together into unity (10:16).

And just as, in the second edition, Jesus is the vine, whose branches will be pruned by the Father, in the secondary development by the author of the third edition (15:4-7), the image of the vine is described as the sole source of life for the branches, a development that does not find close parallels in the Old Testament but like the other images employed by the author of the third edition, applies the original image to the circumstances of the community in such a way as it make it meaningful and appropriate for the community at the time of the crisis.

The third author undoubtedly formed these "I am" statements on the pattern established by the second author. Although he was capable of using Old Testament images as metaphors (cf. "I am the light of the world" in 8:12; 9:5),[11] the third author was less intent on demonstrating that Jesus was the fulfillment of such metaphors and more intent on asserting the unique, essential, and permanent role of Jesus in salvation.[12] Thus, in addition to being the "bread of life" in the metaphorical sense, Jesus was the bread of the Eucharist and such sacramental bread was essential to have life (6:51-58).[13] Because Jesus was "the gate"

11. Yet, even here, it could be argued that the image of "light" in 8:12 and 9:5 is due more to the imagery of apocalyptic dualism than to the non-apocalyptic heritage of Judaism that forms the background of the second edition.

12. Bultmann (*Gospel* 226) comments that the statements are polemical in intent so as to refute the claims of other revelatory figures. I would agree that the "I am" statements-with-a-predicate are polemical, but not against claimants from other religions but against the claims of the opponents from within the author's own community.

13. While sacraments as such were not an element of the community crisis, the attitude toward the material that it reflects was a concern at the time of the crisis. See Vol. 1, Part 4, Section 11.

Appendix 2

for the sheep, it was necessary to go through Jesus to achieve life. He also "laid down his life" for his sheep and that death was an atonement that gained life for them.[14] Finally, just as a branch needed to remain attached to the vine in order to live, so those who believed in Jesus needed to remain in unity with "the vine" because without him, they would die. Thus, once we understand the genesis of these secondary elaborations of biblical images, we are able to see that it is only a half-truth to say that these texts do not have parallels in the Old Testament. While this statement is literally true, the texts are rooted in biblical images and simply represent secondary developments of them, intended for a different *Sitz im Leben* of the community.

The third author also introduces two elliptical statements concerning Jesus as the Resurrection and the Life (11:25) and Jesus as the Way, the Truth and the Life (14:6). Once again, we see that these statements have no close parallels in the Old Testament, yet each has an important role in the clarification of the Gospel tradition over against the views of the opponents of 1 John. Jesus is the means by which Resurrection and Life can be attained (11:25). He is also the (only) Way to Truth and to Life (14:6).

Finally, the third author introduced a third type of "I am" statement: the "absolute" ("divine") use. As the author sought to clarify the Christology of the tradition, he sought various ways of expressing the identity of Jesus with God the Father and ultimately chose the very self-designation of God himself. He did this both by incorporating texts where Jesus proclaimed himself unambiguously as "I AM" (8:24, 28, 58 and 13:19) but also by reinterpreting texts where "I am" had the ordinary secular use in such a way as to have it be understood that they had the divine meaning (18:5-9). Thus, the third author took over the simple self-identification by Jesus in 18:5 and reinterpreted it in 18:6-9 in such a way that it was now understood to have the divine sense.[15]

The instances of this final category (the divine use) are solidly based on Old Testament usage, where the LXX regularly uses *egō eimi* as a translation of the Hebrew *'nî yhwh* ("I am Yahweh") and *'nî-hû'* ("I am"). This usage occurs particularly in the LXX of Deutero-Isaiah. See, for example, Isa 43:25; 45:18; 52:6.[16] In the third edition, Jesus' pronunciation (and appropriation) of the di-

---

14. Likewise, he brought together the scattered children of God into one (10:16). Although this expansion is also the work of the third author and was part of his theological agenda, it was not directly associated with the community crisis as reflected in 1 John. See further Vol. 1, Part 4, Section 10.

15. I would understand the instance of "I am" in 18:8 to be a resumption of the secular use although in this context, it certainly continues to carry the connotation of the absolute use.

16. For a fuller discussion, see Dodd, *Interpretation* 93-96 and Brown, *Gospel* 1:536-37. Moreover, this usage continues to be evident in rabbinic texts of the second century. Dodd (*Interpretation* 93-94) cites various instances.

vine name was undoubtedly understood as the fulfillment of the hope that in the age to come, the name of God would be revealed.[17]

However, scholars today would not understand Jesus' appropriation of this title to mean that he is simply to be identified with the God of the Old Testament although this was the way it was apparently heard by "the Jews" who accuse Jesus of blasphemy. Jesus continues to be Son in relation to the Father; but to see him as Son is to see the Father (14:9). As Barrett explains, Jesus' appropriation of this title does not mean: "'Look at me because I am identical with the Father,' but 'Look at me for I am the one by looking at whom you will see the Father (14:9), since I make him known' (1:18)."[18] Moloney puts it well when he says: "The difference is slight but important, as in the former Jesus is metaphysically associated with the divinity, while in the latter it is his one with God that makes him the consummate revelation of God."[19] Yet it was, in Schnackenburg's words, "an unprecedented status," unprecedented in Judaism of the first century and unprecedented even in the New Testament apart from the Gospel of John.[20]

D. CONCLUSION

From our review we have gained some significant insight into the usage and background of the "I am" statements in the Gospel. First, the distinction between the metaphorical and the elliptical statements has proved useful in its own right. This distinction leads to a clearer understanding of the meaning of these statements. Second, we have noted that each of the primary images used in the metaphorical statements has been previously recognized to come from the Old Testament, except for the statement that Jesus is "the gate." However, when we look at this particular text in the light of the composition of the Gospel as a whole, it becomes clear that this statement is the work of the third author. Third, it also becomes clear that the third author has reinterpreted each of the major metaphors in the second edition for his own purposes. By doing so, the author brought these images to bear on the circumstances of the community at the time of the internal crisis.

Fourth, we notice that the two statements that constitute the fourth class

17. The hope that the name of God would be revealed in the age to come is found in a statement by Pinchas ben Jair (A.D. 130-160), cited by Dodd, *Interpretation* 93-94. This view is corroborated by John 17:6 (3E) where Jesus says: "I have revealed your name to those whom you have given me out of the world. . . ."

18. Barrett, *Essays* 13.

19. Moloney, *Gospel* 134.

20. Schnackenburg, *Gospel* 2:88.

both come from the third author. They are not metaphorical (with the possible exception of the use of "way" in 14:6) but are meant to emphasize that these various theological features are to be identified *exclusively* with Jesus. Thus, without Jesus, there is no resurrection and no life; without Jesus, there is no access to truth and life; he alone is the way to them.

Finally, from the consistency of the usage, particularly in the second and third editions, we gain additional, indirect confirmation that the analysis of the Johannine tradition presented here is correct.

APPENDIX 3

The Structure of Theological Argument
in the Three Discourses with "the Jews"
(6:30-50, 8:12-59, and 10:22-39)

We have seen that, following the architectonic discourse of chapter 5, there are three major discourses within the public ministry of Jesus in the second edition. We have also seen that each of these is addressed to a group identified as "the Jews." Moreover, we have seen that each of these discourses develops in a substantial way one of the essential witnesses to Jesus as outlined paradigmatically in 5:31-40. It is my intention to call attention here to one other common factor within these discourses *as they appeared in the second edition of the Gospel:* the remarkably similar structure of argument in the three discourses.[1] The similarity is such that one could suspect that it represented a kind of *topos* within the Johannine community for refutation of opponents and consolation of believers. Because the structure appears in all three discourses, it seems best to treat it here in an appendix rather than in connection with any one of the discourses.

A. THE ELEMENTS OF THE PATTERN

We will first describe and illustrate the constituent elements of the pattern of argument and then draw some conclusions.

(1) Each section begins with a demand on the part of "the Jews" regarding the identity of Jesus.

    6:30   "The Jews" (cf. 6:41, 52) ask: *"What sign do you perform so that we may see and believe in you?" (Tí oun poieis su sēmeion, hina idōmen kai pisteusōmen soi;)*

---

1. An earlier discussion of this feature appeared in von Wahlde, "Literary."

8:25 "The Jews" (cf. 8:22, 31, 48, 52, 57) ask Jesus: *"Who are you?" (Su tís ei;)*

10:24 Again "the Jews" (cf. 10:24, 31, 33) surround Jesus and ask: *"How long will you keep us in suspense? If you are the Christ, tell us openly." (Heōs pote tēn psychēn hēmōn haires; Ei su ei ho Christos, eipe hēmin parrēsia.)*

(2) Jesus then responds that he has told them and they do not believe:

6:36 Jesus responds: *"But I said to you that you have seen [me] and you do not believe." (Eipon hymin hoti kai heōrakate me kai ou pisteuete.)*

8:25 Again Jesus responds: *"What I have been telling you from the beginning." (Tēn archēn ho ti kai lalō hymin.)*

10:25 Jesus says: *"I told you and you do not believe." (Eipon hymin kai ou pisteuete.)*

(3) Following this, Jesus states the reason for their disbelief:

6:37 Immediately after telling "the Jews" that they do not believe, Jesus explains: *"Everything the Father gives me comes to me . . ." (Pan ho didōsin moi ho patēr pros eme hēxei . . .),* thus implying that "the Jews" have not been given.

8:47 **"This is why you do not listen, because you are not of God."** *(dia touto hymeis ouk akouete, hoti ek tou theou ouk este)* (also 8:43: **"Why do you not know my message? Because you are not able to hear my word."** [*dia tí tēn lalian tēn emēn ou ginōskete; hoti ou dynasthe akouein ton logon ton emon.*])[2]

10:26 Jesus states that "the Jews" do not believe *"because you are not of my sheep" (hoti ouk este ek tōn probatōn tōn emōn).*

(4) Jesus then speaks of those who do believe:

6:37 *"Everything the Father gives me comes to me . . ." (Pan ho didōsin moi ho patēr pros eme hēxei . . .)* (See above.)

8:47a **"The one who is of God listens to the words of God."** *(Ho ōn ek tou theou ta rhēmata tou theou akouei.)* (See also the description of the "son" as "remaining in the house.")

10:27 Here Jesus describes his sheep: *"My sheep hear my voice, and I know them and they follow me." (Ta probata ta ema tēs phōnēs mou akouousin, kagō ginōskō auta, kai akolouthousin moi.)*

2. Boldface indicates material from the third edition and below.

(5) Jesus then says that he does not lose any of those that are his:

6:37   *"and the one who comes to me I will not reject" (kai ton erchomenon pros eme ou mē ekbalō exō).*

8:51   **"Amen, amen, I say to you, if a person keeps my word, that person will not see death forever."** *(Ean tis ton emon logon tērēsē, thanaton ou mē theōrēsē eis ton aiōna.)* (8:52: *"that person will not taste death forever."* [. . . *ou mē geusētai thanatou.* . . .])

10:28b *"and no one will snatch them from my hand." (Kai ouch harpasei tis auta ek tēs cheiros mou . . .)* (10:29: "from the hand of the Father . . ." [. . . *ek tēs cheiros tou patros.* . . .])

(6) He then affirms that those who believe will have eternal life:

6:40   *"everyone who sees the Son and believes in him may have eternal life" (pas ho theōrōn ton huion kai pisteuōn eis auton echei zōēn aiōnion).*

8:35   *"the son remains (in the house) forever" (Ho huios menei [en tē oikia] eis ton aiōna).*

10:28a *"and I give them eternal life, and they are not lost for eternity" (Kagō didōmi autois zōēn aiōnion kai ou mē apolōntai eis ton aiōna . . .).*

As can be seen from this diagram of the similarities, there are six topics that appear (although with different words) in each of the three discourses. We will first make some observations on the parallels themselves and then draw some conclusions regarding their function.

B. OBSERVATIONS ON THE PATTERN

It is evident that the structure referred to here does not organize each discourse in exactly the same way. This is more a series of "topics" to be addressed than simply a "structure" that is repeated unimaginatively in each discourse. The topics are developed in different ways and at varying length in the various discourses.

In chapter 6 the first element is separated from the remainder of the topics by several verses. While this may be striking at first, two factors account for it. First, the author has chosen to also incorporate a "misunderstanding" verbally similar to that of 4:15; second, the third author has made some additions within the intervening verses. When both of these features are taken into account, the gap in the structure is not excessive.

The fifth element in chapter six also requires comment. Here we see that when Jesus speaks of the will of his Father, there are two statements that are similar to one another structurally. As is explained in the discussion of the Composition of those verses, it is apparent that the heart of both verses comes from the second edition. This is confirmed by the function of the verses within the overall structure of the argument. That is, v. 39ab speaks to the topic of "not losing" and v. 40ab speaks to the topic of "eternal life" for those who see and believe.

In the discourse of chapter 8, the third element ("you are not of God" 8:47) is part of a much longer development that is cast in terms of the apocalyptic worldview of the third author. We can see much of the way the third author works by examining this element of the structure. First, as has been pointed out in the discussion of the Composition, these verses address the topic of why "the Jews" do not believe in Jesus *but do so from the viewpoint of the third author,* which is that of apocalyptic dualism. This is most apparent in vv. 38-49 where the author uses the stereotyped polemic worldview not evident before v. 38, or after v. 49. Yet, in an extended way, the author explains why "the Jews" do not believe in him. He does so in terms of fatherhood, understood apocalyptically, and also does so in terms of their response to his word, which is the (second and) particular form of witness being addressed throughout the discourse (in the material of both the second and the third authors).

Thus, it seems apparent that the third author recognized the pattern of argument since his additions have kept to the pattern, although he used his distinctive terminology and worldview in doing so.[3]

The pattern of argument in chapter 10 represents the "parade example" of the structure, that is, the occurrence of the pattern in chapter 10 appears in its simplest, clearest and most compact form. The various elements occur neatly in successive verses and the flow of the argument is clearest. All of the elements occur in material of the second edition.

C. THE SIGNIFICANCE OF THE PARALLELS

The recognition of this pattern of argument in the three discourses is significant for a number of reasons. From the comments that have already been made, it is evident that the pattern was introduced at the time of the second edition and was part of the original plan of the discourses.

---

3. At least at times, the third author was aware of the structure of the material he was modifying. For example, in his modification of the bread of life discourse, the third author shows his awareness of the homiletic format of the second edition material and extends it by means of his exegesis of "to eat" and by repeating the summarizing reinterpretation of Scripture in the conclusion. In 15:26-27, the third author recognized that vv. 22-25 were a summation of the three witnesses to Jesus even though the word witness did not appear in the verses. This is evident from the fact that the third author extends the list and in doing so, he makes it explicit that the Paraclete and the disciples are "witnesses" just as the previous three.

But the most significant conclusions deal with the material itself and the purpose of the material. First, the demand for proof of who Jesus is, is in each case seemingly unwarranted in the context. In chapter 6, the demand for a sign is strange after the multiplication of the loaves. In chapter 8, the question "who are you?" is strange after Jesus' various statements in vv. 12-24. In chapter 10, the surly question to tell them plainly if he is the Christ, again occurs in a context where Jesus' claims should be apparent already. This would now seem to be not a result of awkward editing but a literary device — designed to indicate a willful blindness of "the Jews" even when they should be able to answer their own questions and requests. In this sense, it functions much as the frequent "misunderstandings" in the second edition.

Second, in the light of the parallel between 8:25 and 6:36 and 10:25, the proposal that 8:25 should be translated "What I have been telling you from the beginning" receives additional support since this has a function within the pattern.

Third, there are the seemingly obscure references to "having told them" already. In each case there is no such statement in the immediate context. However, the parallelism seems to suggest that the author did not intend for there to be something in the context but that the statements were intended to be more general references.

D. THE FUNCTION OF THE PATTERN

When the pattern is looked at as a whole, it is evident that the author had intended to portray the experience of Jesus in the ministry in a way that reflected the experience of the community at the time of the author:

1. The appearance of willful rejection of Jesus by their fellow Jews. Jesus had provided all the proof that should be necessary but "the Jews" still did not see and so were led to request even more. Jesus does not give more at that point but only reminds them that they already have enough.

2. The reasons for their blindness. They have not been given by the Father; they are not "of God," they are not of Jesus' sheep.

3. The promise to the believers that they will be safeguarded. He will not reject them; they will not taste or see death; no one will take them from his (or the Father's) hands.

4. A description of the believers' reward. They will have eternal life; they will remain in the house forever; they will not suffer eternal destruction. In short, this would seem to be the essential message given to the Johannine believer who had been a member of the synagogue and who was faced with expulsion for his/her belief. It explained that the person's fellow Jews had had every opportunity to believe, but they were simply not "given" by God. On the other

hand, the believer is given by God, will be protected and will not be lost and will have eternal life! This is the heart of what was seen as the basic promise to the Johannine believer.

The fact that the pattern of argument appears three times is an indication of its importance and confirms all the more the common parallel function of these discourses. If the three discourses are already the three major discourses with "the Jews," and if they already function to show how each of the essential witnesses to Jesus functions to establish his identity, the further pattern of argument embedded in each discourse also serves to remind the reader that some will not accept this but that for those who do, eternal life awaits them.

APPENDIX 4

The Crisis That Divided the Johannine Community at the Time of 1 John

A. THE CRISIS: SOME PAST APPROACHES

The most important general issue confronting the reader of the Johannine Letters is the nature of the theological crisis that split the community at the time of 1 John. All scholars recognize that the community has been split by a crisis. However, there is considerable disagreement about the nature of that crisis.

R. E. Brown (1982) sees the opponents and the author of 1 John differing regarding the interpretation of the Johannine tradition.[1] Brown proposes that there are two major problems: Christology and ethics. The Christology of the Gospel was so high that the opponents concluded that the ministry of Jesus simply revealed the glory of the Father but did not achieve anything salvifically important. The opponents acknowledged the reality of Jesus' humanity (and so were not docetic) but "refused to acknowledge that his being in the flesh was essential to the picture of Jesus *as the Christ, the Son of God*."[2] *The sending of Jesus made it possible to get salvation in the sense that they could know God and possess eternal life.*

---

1. Brown (*Epistles* 69) comments: "Before the writing of I John a schism had taken place. The resultant two groups, consisting of the epistolary author's adherents and his adversaries, both accepted the proclamation of Christianity known to us through GJohn, but they interpreted it differently." According to Brown (*Epistles* 72) "There is no indication that the false views of the secessionists are derived from anything other than the tradition itself. I shall try to show that *every idea of the secessionists (as reconstructed from the polemic of I and II John) can be plausibly explained as derivative from the Johannine tradition as preserved for us in GJohn*" (italics his).

Vielhauer (*Geschichte*) was apparently the first to suggest that the schism could be understood as a disagreement over the interpretation of the Johannine tradition. Since that time Bonnard (*Épîtres*); Müller (*Geschichte*); Theobald (*Fleischwerdung*) have made similar proposals but vary in their understanding of the issues at stake.

2. Brown, *Epistles* 77; italics his.

With regard to ethics, Brown argues "that the secessionists were not libertines notorious for scandalous behavior but were indifferentists who attributed no salvific importance to moral behavior by believers."[3] The Johannine tradition spoke of mutual love too frequently for the secessionists simply to be able to deny it. However, he argues that perhaps the secessionists did not think that the members of the author's community were to be considered "brothers" and therefore were not to be loved.

There are many fruitful insights to be found in Brown's work. Among these is the fact that he has explored so fully the theory that the opponents and the author disagreed about the interpretation of the Johannine tradition. His commentary has been very influential in turning scholarship away from earlier proposals that the crisis was primarily concerned with confronting opponents who were either Docetic or gnostic.

However, one of the more substantial methodological problems with Brown's position is that since he argues that both groups are interpreting the entire Gospel in its present form, he is hard put to deal with texts in the Gospel that are incompatible with the views of the opponents. To counter this, he argues that the opponents based themselves on what he calls more dominant themes of the tradition. By doing so he finds support for the opponents' positions. But such an approach necessarily makes subjective decisions about what is dominant and what is not.

At other times, it is difficult to understand the logic of Brown's argument. For example, Brown proposes that the high Christology of the Gospel makes it possible to argue that the humanity of Jesus could be seen as not accomplishing anything that was significant soteriologically since the full significance of his life could be understood to be achieved by his incarnation, by which he brought eternal life into the world. Brown comments that the opponents "might interpret this to mean that the real purpose of Jesus' earthly life was simply to reveal God's glory in human terms . . . but not do anything new that changed the relationship between God and human beings."[4] But this does not adequately explain how the opponents would then claim to actually pass over from spiritual death to spiritual life. How is "salvation" actually achieved if it is not achieved in some way by the appearance of Jesus?

Brown claims the opponents have distinctive attitudes toward moral behavior, sin, and brotherly love.[5] He rightly calls attention to the "ethical silence" of the Gospel of John but does not explain its origin. Rather, he simply asserts that the Gospel focuses on Christology. Brown says, "No specific sins of behav-

---

3. Brown, *Epistles* 80.
4. Brown, *Epistles* 75.
5. Brown, *Epistles* 79-86.

ior are mentioned in GJohn, only the great sin that is to refuse to believe in Jesus."[6] Again he does not explain why this is so, nor does he relate statements
such as this to the commandment to mutual love, which is certainly an ethical
directive. When he speaks of perfectionism, he argues that perhaps the opponents thought that, through Baptism, they had become like Jesus who was sinless. But here Brown does not seem to see the implications of such a view elsewhere in the Letter.[7] When he speaks of the commandment to mutual love, he
argues only that the opponents probably did not consider the followers of the
author of 1 John as "brothers" and so did not acknowledge a need to love them.
Yet if the opponents did love their own fellow opponents, how could they be
said to be moral indifferentists or perfectionists? The end result is the sense that
Brown's view is forced and improbable.

S. Smalley (1984) holds that the author addresses two groups still within
the community but who have various views in need of correction.[8] The first is a
group of Jewish Christians who continue to have difficulty accepting the
messiahship of Jesus. A second group is composed of Hellenistic Christians, influenced by dualistic thought, who continued to have difficulty with the humanity of Jesus and so are close to what was later termed docetism. Thus, both
of these groups within the community need to have their Christological views
nuanced. The one group needs to emphasize the divinity of Jesus and the other
needs to focus on the humanity.

According to Smalley, both groups also need to have their views of ethics
corrected. The first group, which has a Jewish Christian background, needs to
move beyond their focus on the Jewish Law.[9] The second group needs to focus
on mutual love as a reaction to moral indifferentism.[10]

Finally, a third group consists of more radical members of either or both
of the first two groups. These more radical members had departed from the
community and are now the secessionists referred to in 1 John 2:18-19. Like
Brown, Smalley agrees that the views of the opponents are based on a reading of
the Gospel, but he is the only scholar reviewed here who sees more than one
group of opponents.

R. Schnackenburg (1984; ET 1992) holds the view that the opponents are
of gnostic leaning and from a predominantly Gentile group.[11] They attempt an

6. Brown, *Epistles* 81.

7. He does not see how the opponents' understanding of their new status is a threat to the
status of Jesus in other respects also (for example, "sonship").

8. Smalley, *Epistles* xxiii-xxxii.

9. In Smalley's view, this polemic against the old Law is evident primarily in the discussion of the new and old commandment in 2:7-8.

10. Smalley refers to 1 John 3:10-11 as the major text dealing with this issue.

11. Schnackenburg, *Epistles* 18. The views of the opponents can be gathered from the spe-

interpretation of the Johannine tradition with which the author disagrees. Schnackenburg focuses on seven statements that he feels are central to the position of the opponents. However, in addition to these statements, Schnackenburg also notes a number of "positive statements of Christological faith." He comments: "Even if these are not directed emphatically against the heretics, they do, taken as a whole, create a picture of the faith in its light and shade which ought to protect the church against these dangerous influences."[12] These statements include emphasis on what was "from the beginning," incarnation, atoning death, unique sonship and divinity of Jesus. The primary difficulty concerns Schnackenburg's view that the group has gnostic tendencies. The dualism of the Letter is the modified, ethical dualism of apocalyptic rather than the absolute dualism of Gnosticism and so there is little likelihood that the group is gnostic. Moreover, that the community is largely Gentile is unconvincing.

G. Strecker (1989; ET 1995) has proposed that the opponents in 1 John are to be identified as docetists.[13] Their beliefs are to be discerned from 1 John itself but the entire Letter is not concerned with the crisis. Rather, the crisis is mirrored only in 1 John 2:22-23; 4:1-6 and 5:6-8.[14] After a survey of early Docetic views, Strecker concludes that the closest parallels to the opponents of 1 John are the groups opposed by Ignatius of Antioch.

Strecker finds similarities to Ignatius' opponents in the denial that Jesus is the Christ and Son of God and the denial that Jesus Christ came in the flesh. He also suggests that the opponents devalued the Eucharist. He argues this on the grounds that the Gospel puts much value on the Eucharist and so was probably attempting to counter opponents.[15] He claims that nothing can be known about the anthropology or ethics of the opponents.[16]

---

cific confessional statements about Jesus as the Christ, as the Son of God, as coming in the flesh and as coming in water and blood. According to Schnackenburg, that the opponents are predominantly Gentiles is indicated primarily by the lack of argument from Scripture offered in 1 John and by the author's preference for "Son of God" as a title for Jesus.

12. Schnackenburg, *Epistles* 19.

13. Strecker, *Epistles* 69-76.

14. See especially Strecker, *Epistles* 70, n. 55.

15. I do not find Strecker clear on this point. In 1 John itself, I find no reference by either the author or the opponents regarding the Eucharist. If its neglect has been a problem the author opposed, surely there would be some mention of it. To argue from the traditions in the Gospel is tenuous, given the fact that Strecker holds 1 John and the Gospel to be independent compositions of a fairly large Johannine "school." See Strecker, *Epistles* 74. However, I would agree with Strecker that the Eucharist became a topic of concern in the final stage of the community's development and it may be that this conflict (from a period later than that of 1 John) is what is echoed in Ignatius's letter. More will be said of this below.

16. Strecker, *Epistles* 74. Thus, he would hold a view opposite to that of Beutler (see below). Also most scholars find a considerable emphasis on ethics throughout the Letter.

Perhaps the most significant problem with the approach taken by Strecker is that by limiting so severely statements dealing with the crisis, he does not seem to take adequate account of a large number of other statements with which the author of 1 John clearly disagrees and which he seeks to refute. Strecker also does not account for the fact that the views of the author and those of the opponents are so similar in many respects.[17]

H.-J. Klauck (1991), basing his views on what he sees as the essential ambiguity of the data in the Letters, rather than attempting to provide a definitive picture of the opponents, looks for the element in the Johannine tradition that has given rise to the problem. For Klauck, this element is the baptism of Jesus. This could be interpreted as the melding of Jesus and the Christ in a docetic way, but whether the Spirit departs from Jesus before his death or simply does not suffer is not answered by the Gospel. Klauck sees the baptism of the believer as the point of the reception of the Spirit and argues that a number of the elements of the opponents' beliefs reflect a radicalizing of various elements of the Johannine tradition connected with the Spirit.[18] For example, he understands the opponents to be transformed by their reception of the Spirit into a "pneumatic existence" that is no longer subject to the conditions of the material world. They have knowledge of God and fellowship with God; they have a purely present eschatology; the complete freedom from sin of children of God. They no longer have need of forgiveness. For them the gift of life and atoning death of Jesus lose their soteriological meaning.[19]

Although he associates the various claims of the opponents with a radicalized pneumatology, he does not ground this claim sufficiently but instead chooses to focus on the similarities with Docetic trends elsewhere in early Christianity.

Other Recent Views

Other recent commentators have forged positions that reflect varying modifications of the positions evident in the major commentaries; but, because of the limits of format, they have not been able to argue these theories so extensively.

17. Strecker (*Epistles* xl): "No sufficient evidence can be presented to show that the author of the Johannine Letters used the Fourth Gospel, as I will demonstrate below." So also Schnelle, *Antidocetic* 70, n. 169: "the derivation of their [the opponents'] theology from the Gospel of John must be called pure speculation, especially since there is no passage in 1 John regarding the opponents that can be regarded as even a remote reference to the Gospel." In this respect, both Strecker and Schnelle are at odds with the majority of modern scholars.

18. Klauck, *Erste Johannesbrief* 41, 295.

19. Klauck, *Erste Johannesbrief* 41, 295. In this respect, Klauck's view is close to mine. He in fact spells out a number of prerogatives of the outpouring of the Spirit that would account for elements of the opponents' position, as I do.

Because commentators will at times see a mixture of influences, it is often difficult to know which group to assign a commentator to.

Among those seeing an exaggerated pneumatology as the primary factor in the position of the opponents is **K. Grayston** (1984), who was among the first of this group to make such a proposal.[20] **J. Lieu** (1986), in her commentary on 2 and 3 John, also raises in an extended way the question of the role of the Spirit in the controversy. Lieu does so in the context of the repeated assertions of the author regarding the importance of the tradition *vis-à-vis* the role of the Spirit. In her view the problem of the relation of Spirit to tradition is "met . . . by understanding both tradition and Spirit Christocentrically."[21] **J. Beutler** (2000) sees the focus of disagreement as being rooted in anthropology rather than in Christology or ethics.[22] The opponents are "Pneumatiker," persons filled with the Spirit, and are defined by their attitudes toward community with God, sinlessness, knowledge of God, abiding in him, being in the light, having an anointing, etc. They claim that these characteristics are a result of the anointing they have from the Spirit and these do away with the need for Jesus as "anointed," as "son of God" and as a bringer of salvation. The author resists this by distinguishing a true possession of the Spirit from the false one asserted by the opponents. Thus, Beutler continues the direction of recent scholarship that focuses on the understanding and role of the Spirit as essential.

Taking his cue from Schnackenburg, **J. Painter** (2002) focuses his understanding on seven statements that are thought to reflect the view of the opponents.[23] He argues that the conflict evident in 1 John is based on divergent interpretations of the tradition and that it centers on issues of Christology and ethics. The conflict has been created, however, by the influx of considerable numbers of converts that are not of Jewish background and so attempt to interpret the tradition without respect to its Jewish background.[24] Painter concludes that the position of the opponents is not a single logical whole and so there are inevitably "loose ends" that cannot be fully understood within the context of the Letter.

Among those seeing the opponents as docetic is **D. M. Smith** (1991).[25] He

20. D. M. Smith (*Epistles* 106) also proposes that at the time of 1 John the community was in the process of working out "criteria by which genuine and false claims to Spirit inspiration had to be worked out."

21. Lieu, *Second and Third* 171-80, quote 177. Lieu articulates well the tensions between Spirit and "tradition" and between Spirit and Jesus.

22. Beutler, *Johannesbriefe* 20-24. In his emphasis on anthropology, he is diametrically opposed to the views of Strecker.

23. Painter, *Epistles* 79-94. Earlier versions of Painter's view had been worked out in his *John* 115-25 and "Opponents."

24. Painter, *Epistles* 80, 330; "Opponents" 50-51.

25. D. M. Smith, *Epistles* 130-32.

believes that ". . . 1 John presupposes familiarity with the Christian message and tradition as it is known from the Gospel of John or something substantially like it."[26] In the view of **R. A. Culpepper** (1998), the opponents have many traits of Docetists and may have later developed into Valentinian Gnosticism. The opponents held an even higher Christology than the author but one that removed Jesus from any connection with the flesh.[27]

B. THE VIEW PRESENTED IN THIS COMMENTARY

As we begin a discussion of the crisis that divided the Johannine community at the time of 1 John, it is helpful to recall the words of Brown about the attitude with which one should approach such a task: "In seeking to relate these reconstructed views to GJohn, one must approach them sympathetically. It is not a matter of whether one likes such views or judges them as a tolerable Christian variant; the real issue is the inner logic of secessionist thought."[28]

While some of the views of the opponents (secessionists) may seem improbable from our perspective, it is important to remember that this community of Christian-Jewish believers in Jesus were convinced that something radically new had taken place through the ministry of Jesus, and they sought to interpret that according to their Scriptures. But two views of the significance of what Jesus had done began to emerge, and both of these were based on the community's Gospel as it appeared in what I have termed its "second edition."

One group consisted of former members of the author's community, who came to believe that God had accomplished the eschatological outpouring of the Spirit through the ministry of Jesus and that they now possessed the prerogatives of this outpouring as these had been described in their Scriptures. They believed that this outpouring had been announced by Jesus and that Jesus was not only God's envoy for the announcing of this outpouring but that he himself embodied these promises. Yet Jesus' role was only temporary since, once the Spirit was bestowed upon the community, it was the Spirit that was necessary and sufficient.

The other group is represented by the author of 1 John. While this other group also believed that the outpouring of the Spirit had been accomplished through the ministry of Jesus, they did not agree that the role of Jesus was only temporary. Rather, his role was permanent and essential and inextricably linked to the role of the Spirit. Consequently, the job of the author of 1 John is to

26. D. M. Smith, *Epistles* 28.
27. Culpepper, *Gospel and Epistles* 48-54.
28. Brown, *Epistles* 72.

continue to affirm the proper role of the Spirit but to assert the various essential elements of the role of Jesus.

The author's task is a complicated one because (as we shall see below in detail) there are many points on which the author and the opponents agreed. Thus, his task of correction is made all the more difficult by the need to both agree with the opponents and to nuance and/or correct their views. For example, according to the Old Testament, after the outpouring of the Spirit, the people would have no need to be taught by anyone because they will "know" God. While the author of 1 John affirms this belief in general, he also holds that, because of the opponents' erroneous beliefs, they cannot be said to, in fact, truly know God. Yet, when he corrects his opponents, he does not do so by "teaching" since he agrees with the opponents that once the Spirit has been given they do not need a teacher. So his correction must be in the form of "witness" to "what was from the beginning," to what he and the others "have seen, heard, touched." We will also see that the same is true regarding topics such as "perfectionism," where both the author and his opponents hold a view of perfectionism but disagree about its meaning. It is because of the similarity (and yet the dissimilarity) of the views of the two groups that it has been so difficult to understand their respective positions. The role of the author in 1 John is essentially to correct the views of the opponents, agreeing where he must but changing what is erroneous.

C. ESTABLISHING THE CORRECTNESS OF THIS THEORY

In order to establish the correctness of this view in detail, I will attempt to show that the views of the opponents as I describe them (1) represent a reasonable reading of the position of the opponents as it can be discovered from 1 John; and (2) that their views are a reasonable reading of the theology of the second edition of the Gospel; and (3) that their views also reflect accurately the Old Testament background of the eschatological outpouring of the Spirit.

Moreover, I will attempt to show that the position described above (4) is a reasonable reading of the position of the author of 1 John and (5) that the background of 1 John is that of apocalyptic Judaism as it is evident in various noncanonical, apocalyptic documents influential in certain segments of first-century Judaism.[29]

The evidence for such a position is inevitably complex. In order to proceed as simply as possible and to avoid excessive duplication with presentations elsewhere in the Commentary, I will proceed as follows. I will examine, first,

---

29. In the more detailed discussion in Vol. 1, Part 4, the way in which the author's views are reflected in the third edition of the Gospel is also presented.

the various statements from 1 John that reveal the nature of the conflict in 1 John. Those statements are identified and the general conclusions drawn.

In the following section, we will see, in summary, how the views of the opponents and of the author are manifested in the eleven areas of theology that we first identified in the discussion of the theology of the second edition. By using these same eleven categories, it will be possible for the reader to see how the views of the opponents do in fact reflect the theology of the second edition. At the same time, it will be possible to see just how the author of 1 John agrees with, and differs from, his opponents on each of these issues.

As was indicated above, in order to avoid excessive duplication, here in Appendix 4 I will give only an outline of the views of the opponents and of the author regarding each of these topics. In Volume 1, Part 4, each of the elements is discussed in more detail, together with the history of religions background against which they are conceived. In that way, not only will the views of the opponents and the author be related to their appropriate history of religions background, but the crisis can be related to the appropriate stages of the development of the Johannine tradition.

As will become apparent in the discussion below and in the Commentary as a whole, the theory regarding the understanding of the crisis presented here is given considerable support, not only by the analysis of 1 John, but also by the fact that it is based on a literary analysis of the Gospel. For, with an increased clarity about the nature and extent of the tradition at the time of the second edition, we are able to see that the crisis at the time of 1 John was precisely a crisis of interpretation of the tradition *as it appeared in the second edition of the Gospel.*[30]

If the above seems complex, it may be reassuring to know that, although the differences between the author and his opponents had far-reaching consequences for all areas of theology, the author of 1 John himself ultimately understood the various points of disagreement to circulate around two basic issues: correct belief and correct behavior. In various sections of 1 John, he first explains what "correct belief" and "correct behavior" consist of and then he uses these, in a remarkably extensive and consistent way, as tests to determine whether a person can legitimately make any of the claims associated with the eschatological outpouring of the Spirit. We will see this in detail in the Commentary on 1 John, but how the various claims of the two groups are tested in terms of correct belief and correct behavior is summarized in Chart E-6 (pp. 367-69) and a review of that Chart may help to outline the issues dealt with.

---

30. That the crisis is related to the interpretation of the Gospel has been argued by a number of scholars, as we have seen. However, basing one's views on a complete analysis of the editorial history enables us to do this with more precision than previously possible. Now such a theory could be said to be established on the basis of evidence rather than by general surmise.

D. THE STATEMENTS FROM 1 JOHN RELATED TO THE THEOLOGICAL CONVICTIONS OF THE AUTHOR AND HIS OPPONENTS

There are a number of statements in 1 John that help clarify the nature of the crisis. Our primary sources for the views of both the author and his opponents are all three of the Johannine Letters, but because of the brevity of 2 and 3 John we must in fact rely almost entirely on 1 John for determining this information.

There are five topics central to understanding the views of both the author and his opponents. These topics are: (1) how the two groups understood their status and prerogatives as believers; (2) how the two groups understood the Spirit; (3) how they understood their relationship with the Father (and with Jesus); (4) how they understood belief in Jesus; and (5) how the two groups understood matters dealing with ethics, freedom from sin, and judgment.

1. How the Two Groups Understood Their Status and Prerogatives as Believers

From an examination of 1 John, we are able to make a list of statements regarding the claims made by the two groups. A listing of these claims is given in Chart E-1 (p. 343). From an analysis of that list, we can make the following four important conclusions.

First, there is a remarkable similarity in the claims of the two groups. The two groups share a total of eleven claims regarding their status. We know from the Letter itself that the opponents were once members of the community (4:1). If the author did not tell us, we would know it anyway from the nature of their claims. In the light of this fact, it seems unlikely that the problem that divides the community is something introduced from outside as some earlier scholars have claimed.

Second, these claims in 1 John are based on convictions that are central to the second edition of the Gospel. Most importantly, both groups claim to possess the Spirit — and it was the Spirit that was the central promise of Jesus to those who believe in him (1-1). The possession of this Spirit resulted in the possession of eternal life (1-2).

Third, these claims are also based on convictions that are central to the Old Testament understanding of the eschatological outpouring of the Spirit. As is shown in detail in the discussion of the pneumatology of the second edition,[31] the central claims of the community are identical with the prerogatives of the eschatological Spirit as these are described in the Old Testa-

---

31. In Vol. 1, Part 4, Section 3 (Pneumatology).

ment (1-2, 1-8, 1-9, 1-10). The other claims are derivative of this central claim. Thus, the notion of "birth" (1-4) and the believers' status as "children" (1-5) are related to the conviction that they possess the "life" of God through the Spirit. The notion of the believers' "fellowship" with God (1-3) and their "abiding" in him (1-11) are also related to their possession of the Spirit, as is the fact that they now "know" and "love" God spontaneously.

Fourth, in spite of these similarities, there are some differences that are traceable, in part, to the introduction of an apocalyptic viewpoint by the author of 1 John, a worldview that was not present in the second edition of the Gospel.

Although the essential claims of the author reflect an interpretation of the second edition of the Gospel, the author makes a major change in his understanding of the tradition when he speaks from within the framework of apocalyptic dualism. We will see elements of this throughout 1 John and in the discussion of the views of the author and his opponents, but the first vestiges of it appear in this chart.

Thus, the author speaks of being "of" God (or "of" the devil) (1-6) and he speaks of being "in the light" (or "in darkness") (1-7). When he speaks of "knowing the truth," he contrasts this with knowing and speaking falsehood and lies (1-8). All of this is typical of apocalyptic dualism.

We can also see how the views regarding the eschatological Spirit are woven into an apocalyptic worldview. For example, it is only at the time of 1 John that the community begins to speak of believers as "children of God." The introduction of this term shows that the community had understood the notion of being born of the Spirit from the second edition of the Gospel (3:3-8) as central to their new status. The author of 1 John takes over this conviction but now nuances it by speaking of birth *from God* (2:29; 3:9 [twice]; 4:7; 5:1, 4, 18 [twice]) rather than *from the Spirit*. These two views are not incompatible with one another but reflect different perspectives. The Spirit is the principle of new life in the second edition but ultimately it is God the Father who bestows the Spirit. Thus, just as the author regularly attributes to God the Father features that, in the Gospel, are attributed to the Son, so he attributes to the Father this feature that in the second edition had been attributed to the Spirit.[32] At the same time, the author now views the Spirit in an apocalyptic context when he contrasts the "Spirit of Truth" with the "Spirit of Deception." The implications of such dualism are also evident in the author's references to believers who are "children of God" and to the opponents who are "children of the devil" (3:10).

---

32. This is also true of the identity of the one who forgives sin in 1:9 ("God is faithful and just and so forgives our sins and cleanses us from all injustice") and also of the one who gives life in 5:11b ("God gave us eternal life").

When we ask how the community had received this Spirit, we find one clear statement. In 1 John 5:6, we get a brief, but remarkable, picture of how the author and his opponents agreed and disagreed about the role of Jesus. In doing so, the author gives us the only statement about what the opponents believed *about Jesus in his relation to the Spirit.* And it is precisely what we would expect: that Jesus had come "in water." As we will see in the Commentary itself, this statement, which has been a perennial puzzle to exegetes, takes on a whole new meaning in the light of the view of the crisis proposed here. It is clear from 1 John 5:6 that both the author and his opponents believed that Jesus had "come in water." That is, he had come to give "living water," the second edition's symbolic description of the Spirit! Thus, we know from this statement that (1) the opponents did believe that Jesus had a role of some sort; (2) that this had to do with the giving of the Spirit; (3) that the author of 1 John argued that the role of Jesus was more extensive than that. Both groups agreed that Jesus had come "in water"! But the author of 1 John went further and said that Jesus came "not in water alone, but in water and blood."

It is apparent that the statements in this chart are of great importance for understanding the crisis and that both groups claimed to have received the Spirit in its eschatological fullness and both understood their new status and prerogatives to be based on the reception of that Spirit.

CHART E-1
Convictions Shared by the Two Groups
Regarding Their Status as Believers

1-1. Both groups claim **possession of the Spirit**: the faithful (2:20; 4:1-6) and the opponents (implicit throughout 4:1-6).

1-2. Both groups claim **to possess eternal life**: the faithful (explicit in 2:25; 3:14; 5:11-15, 20; implicit in 1:2) and the opponents (explicit in 3:15; 5:12; implicit in 2:25; 5:11-13, 20).

1-3. Both groups claim **fellowship with God**: the faithful (1:3) and the opponents (1:6).

1-4. Both groups claim **a birth (rebirth)** (from God). This is evident from the author's statements regarding the faithful (4:7; 5:1). That the opponents claimed the same is implicit in the way such rebirth — and the conditions necessary for it — are described. It is also evident in the author's description of both groups as children of either God or the devil (see the following claim).

1-5. Both groups claim **to be children of God**: the faithful (3:1, 2, 10) and the opponents (3:8, 10).

1-6. Both groups claim **to be "of" God**: the faithful are (explicit in 4:4; implicit in 3:10) and the opponents are not (3:10; 4:5, 6).

1-7. Both groups claim **to be in the light**: the faithful (1:7; 2:9-10) and the opponents (2:9-11).

1-8. Both groups claim **to know the truth** as is clear from the discussion in 2:21-22 where a criterion for determining who does and who does not know the truth is found.

1-9. Both groups claim **to know God**: the faithful (2:3-4, 13-14; 4:6-7) and the opponents (2:3-4; 4:8a).

1-10. Both groups claim **to love God**: the faithful (implicit in 4:20) and the opponents (4:20).

1-11. Both groups claim **to abide in God**: the faithful (2:5-6, 24, 28; 3:6, 24; 4:12, 13, 15, 16) and the opponents (2:6 and implicitly in several of the above texts).

2. How the Two Groups Understood the Spirit

We now turn to an examination of the statements of 1 John regarding the Spirit. These are given in Chart E-2. As we have seen above, both the author and his opponents claimed to possess the Spirit. However, in keeping with his apocalyptic viewpoint, the author of 1 John argues that the spirit that the opponents have is not "the Spirit of Truth" but "the Spirit of Deception" (2-1, 2-2). The Spirit ("of Truth") gives them an anointing (2-3) that remains with them (2-4). It is true and not false (2-5). It is a witness (2-7) and enables them to know all (2-8) so that they have no need for anyone to teach them (2-9), and it enables believers to know that God remains within them (2-10).

For the author, the Spirit also has a role *vis-à-vis* Jesus. It confesses that he has come in the flesh (2-11), that he is the Son (2-12). It is also clear that Jesus is the one who gives the Spirit, and both the author and the opponents agree on this (2-6), but the Spirit teaches that the believer is to remain in Jesus (2-13).

This possession of the Spirit was understood against the Old Testament background of the hopes surrounding the eschatological outpouring of the Spirit. Elements of this are even more apparent in 1 John than in the second edition. For example, the repeated (2:20-27) references to an "anointing" in 1 John reflect the Old Testament association of anointing and bestowal of the Spirit in a way that is not apparent in the second edition of the Gospel.

The fact that, in 1 John, the Spirit teaches the believer all things and makes other teachers unnecessary is also clear in the Old Testament but not explicit in the second edition. Yet looking back at the second edition with this information in mind, we are able to see much more clearly why it is that the disciples are said to "witness" rather than "teach" and why it is that the Gospel itself could be said to present "a revealer without a revelation." Simply put: at the time of the second edition, there was an overriding conviction that the Spirit would supply the teaching and so a record of the teaching of Jesus was unnecessary — except insofar as it pertained to his offer of eternal life and the promise of the Spirit.

Yet the presentation of the Spirit in 1 John is different from that in the second edition in several ways. First, we notice that there is an emphasis on the fact that the Spirit of Truth leads one to various convictions *regarding Jesus*. It *confesses* Jesus Christ come in the flesh (4:2) and it *witnesses* that he came in water and blood (5:6-7). It *teaches* the believer to remain in Jesus (2:27). There is no mention of this in the second edition.[33]

Second, the Spirit in 1 John is portrayed within the framework and

---

33. The Paraclete sayings from the third edition will remedy this, but they belong to a later stage of the community's theology.

worldview of apocalyptic. No longer is it a question of whether one has the Spirit or not (as was the case in the Gospel) but rather whether one has the Spirit of Truth (as do the author and his followers) or the Spirit of Deception (as do the opponents).

Third, in 1 John (eternal) life is nowhere explicitly associated with the Spirit. While the association of the Spirit with life is not denied, explicit statements always associate life with the Son. The author speaks of the word of life (1:1) and says that life was "in the presence of the Father and was revealed to us" (1:2). Toward the end of the Letter, in his longest statement regarding eternal life, the author describes it as a gift of God, saying that "this life is in his Son. The one who has the Son has life; the one not having the Son of God does not have life" (5:11-12). Next, the author explains that he has written "that you might know that you have eternal life, believing in the name of the Son of God" (5:13; cf. 5:20). In all of this, the author stresses the essential role of Jesus in the gift of eternal life and the necessity of proper belief in him in order to receive it.

Appendix 4

CHART E-2
Views of the Two Groups Regarding the Spirit

2-1. The faithful have **the Spirit of God** (4:2). This is more precisely described as having received **"of" the Spirit of God** (4:13). The opponents have the spirit of the Antichrist (4:3b) and a spirit that is not "of God" (4:3).

2-2. The faithful have **the Spirit of Truth** (4:1-6, esp. v. 6; 5:6); the opponents have the Spirit of Deception (4:1-6, esp. v. 6).

2-3. The faithful have an anointing that **they received "from him"** (2:27). This can also be said to be **an anointing from the holy one** (2:20). The view of the opponents is unclear although they probably claim something similar.

2-4. The faithful have an anointing and **it remains in them** (2:27a).

2-5. The faithful have an anointing and **it is true and not false** (2:27b); implicit in this is that the spirit of the opponents is not true and is false (2:27b). This is confirmed by what follows below.

2-6. The Spirit **is given by Jesus**. This is expressed by the term "Jesus came in water" (5:6). Both the faithful and the opponents would agree to this. However, the author also argues that Jesus came "in blood," that is, his death was an atonement for sin.

2-7. The Spirit is **the witness of God** (5:9). The opponents would have undoubtedly said the same.

Functions of the Spirit

2-8. The faithful have an anointing that **enables them to know all** (2:20). Since the opponents claimed to know God, presumably they would have claimed it on the basis of their possession of the Spirit.

2-9. The faithful have an anointing and **have no need for anyone to teach them** (2:27a, 27b). The opponents surely would have agreed with the faithful, at least in theory.

2-10. The Spirit enables the faithful to **know that God remains in the believer** (3:24; 4:13).

The Spirit and Jesus

2-11. The faithful have a spirit that **confesses Jesus Christ come in the flesh** (4:2). The opponents have a spirit that does away with Jesus (4:3). The opponents are false prophets (4:1), that is, persons who claim to speak in the voice of the Spirit.

2-12. The Spirit witnesses **to the Son** (5:9). The opponents would not agree that the Spirit witnesses to the Son.

2-13. The Spirit **teaches them to remain in Jesus** (2:27). The opponents go beyond and do not remain in the teaching of the Christ (2 John 9).

3. Views of the Two Groups Regarding Their Perceived Relationship with the Father (and with Jesus)

We now turn to a review of the claims of both groups with respect to God the Father. These are presented on Chart E-3. We will also make reference to some of their different claims regarding Jesus because they are conjoined with texts about the Father. However, we will discuss the claims regarding Jesus in more detail in the section that follows this.

From the three sets of statements in Chart E-3, two things become eminently clear. First, **both the author and the opponents claim a relationship with the Father**. This belief was common to both groups (3-1, 3-2, 3-3, 3-4). In a group that inherited traditional Jewish beliefs, the Father was central to that belief. It was because of this common belief in the God of the Old Testament that the author of 1 John describes *the Father as the foundation of so much of what is said to be founded on Jesus* in the Gospel. By taking a step backward to the point of shared belief, the author of 1 John hoped to establish a common ground with his opponents and then to demonstrate, from that common ground, that belief in the Father (a belief that both groups claimed) required belief in Jesus.

In every case, the author makes it clear that **his disagreement with the opponents regards their rejection of a proper role for Jesus**. For his part, the author of 1 John claims to have fellowship with both the Father and the Son (3-1), to possess both the Father and the Son (3-2), to abide in both the Father and the Son (3-3). Finally, from 3-4 it is apparent, in a number of other statements, that the opponents make a claim to God but the author denies the possibility of the claim because they do not have the right relation with the Son.

Combining the results of our investigation of Chart E-3 with the results of the two previous charts, the outline of the opponents' belief becomes clear: *the opponents believed in the Father and in the Spirit and, while they believed that Jesus "came in water" (1 John 5:6), they rejected the belief that he "came in blood" and rejected the need for any permanent, enduring relationship with Jesus.*

CHART E-3
Views of the Two Groups Regarding Their
Perceived Relationship with the Father (and the Son)

3-1. The opponents claim **to have fellowship** with the Father (1:6); the faithful claim to have fellowship with the Father and the Son (1:3).

3-2. The opponents claim **to possess** the Father (explicit in 2:23; implicit in 5:12); the faithful claim to possess both the Father and the Son (2:23b; implicit in 5:12).

3-3. The opponents claim **to abide** in God (2:6); the faithful claim **to abide in the Son and the Father** (2:24) and to abide in Jesus (2:27, 28; 3:6; 4:13, 15, 16). From the nature of the exhortation in 2:24, 28, it is evident that this is a disputed issue and that only the author's followers claim to abide in both the Son and the Father (cf. 2:24).

3-4. In addition to these claims regarding the Father, that the opponents claim to believe in God the Father is evident from a number of statements in which the author says that by their false belief and improper behavior they offend God (whom they would not want to offend).

Thus, in a statement calculated to cause concern for one who believed in God, the author says that "the one not believing God has made him [God] a liar because he has not believed in the witness that God witnessed about his Son" (5:10). The author puts this most serious of charges (that God is a liar) forward as the implication of their rejection of the Son. In a similar statement the author says that, if a person denies the Son, the person does not have the Father either. But "the one confessing the Son has the Father also" (2:23).

In addition to differences regarding matters of belief, the two groups also disagree regarding behavior, and the author asserts that "If a person loves the world, the love of the Father is not in the person" (2:15). Thus, the opponents cannot claim to have the Father and fail in proper conduct.

4. Views of the Two Groups Regarding Belief in Jesus

In the fourth group of statements (Chart E-4), we focus on the beliefs of the two groups about Jesus. In all cases, these statements deal with aspects of the role of Jesus in salvation.

From an examination of these statements and the texts that contain them, we can see that there is almost no agreement about the identity or role of Jesus. The author and his followers believe that Jesus is the Son of God (4-2) and confess him as Son (4-3) and as Christ (4-5). The opponents do not. The author holds that Jesus has "come in the flesh," has "come in water and blood," and is an atonement for sins (4-6). His opponents do not. Moreover, the author and his followers consider the word of Jesus (which they had heard from the beginning) to be essential for proper belief (4-8); implicitly, the opponents do not.

As we have seen, of all the statements dealing with Jesus, there is only one in which the author indicates that the opponents held any positive convictions about Jesus: that he had "come in water." That is, Jesus had come to announce the outpouring of the Spirit after his departure to the Father.[34] Yet, while the author agreed that Jesus had come in water, he claims that the opponents did not go far enough and that they do not confess that Jesus also came "in blood."

Thus, Chart E-4 confirms in more detail what had begun to be apparent from the study of the previous three charts: in spite of consistent agreement regarding the Spirit and the Father, the two groups disagree almost completely about the status and role of Jesus.[35]

What are we to make of this radical disagreement? How could a community that was ostensibly composed of "believers" and that had undergone expulsion from the synagogue together come to disagree so radically about Jesus? In our discussion of the theology of the second edition, we saw that all the major elements of the second edition's theology could be understood in the light of the Old Testament hopes regarding the eschatological outpouring of the Spirit. For a group that was Jewish in origin and that for a considerable time during its early history had even continued to worship in the synagogue, such an understanding of the outpouring of the Spirit and its benefits would be no surprise. Their Scriptures repeatedly promised that one day the Father would send the Spirit in a final and definitive form.

However, in this Old Testament view, there is no need for an agent such as Jesus, at least as the author of 1 John understood him. Thus, while Jesus was ev-

---

34. The grounds for this understanding of 1 John 5:6-7 are argued in detail in the Interpretation of those verses.

35. The author disagrees with certain aspects of the opponents' understanding of the Spirit, but there is nevertheless much more agreement than there is regarding the role of Jesus.

erything he said he was and while he announced that God would send the Spirit in its eschatological fullness on all who believed in Jesus, once Jesus had performed this task, his role was viewed by the opponents as complete. This was the view that the opponents had taken so seriously and had followed out to conclusions that the author of 1 John considered to be inappropriate.

The author of 1 John considers this to be a one-sided view of what has actually taken place in and through the ministry of Jesus, and so in his tract he sets out to correct these views of the opponents. He does this by addressing and correcting the opponents' understanding of the various implications of their possession of the Spirit. Although these implications are never discussed in a systematic way, the author is remarkably thorough in the way he addresses each of them, as we shall see in our discussion of Chart E-6.

CHART E-4
Differences between the Two Groups
Regarding the Role of Jesus

4-1. The faithful **believe in the name of Jesus** (3:23); the opponents do not (implicit in 3:23).

4-2. The faithful **believe that Jesus is the Son of God** (1:3, 7; 2:23-24; 3:8, 23; 4:9, 10, 14, 15; 5:9-13, 20; 2 John 3, 9); the opponents do not (explicit in 2:23; 5:12; implicit in 5:10).

4-3. The faithful **confess the Son** (2:23; 4:15); the opponents deny the Son (2:22, 23; 4:1-3; 5:10-12).

4-4. The faithful **believe that Jesus is the Christ** (especially 5:1; but also 1:3; 2:1; 3:23; 4:2; 5:6, 20; 2 John 3, 7, 9); the opponents do not (especially 2:22; by implication 4:2 and in the above texts referring to the belief of the faithful).

4-5. The faithful **confess Jesus Christ come in the flesh** (4:2; 2 John 7); the opponents do not (2 John 7).

4-6. The faithful **consider Jesus an atonement for sins** (1:7, 9; 2:1-2, 12; 3:5; 4:14); but the opponents do not (see 1:10).

4-7. The faithful **believe that Jesus has come in blood** (5:6, 7) and that **his blood cleanses the believer from sin** (1:7); the opponents do not (5:5-7).

4-8. The faithful **are rooted in the word/teaching of Jesus that they have heard from the beginning** (1:1-3; 2:7, 24; 3:6, 11; 2 John 8, 9); the opponents are not (explicit in 2 John 9; implicit in the above texts).

4-9. The faithful **have life** because they have the Son (5:12); the opponents do not have the Son of God and so do not have life (5:12).

4-10. The opponents are against Jesus as can be seen by the author's reference to them as the **"Antichrist,"** a term that he apparently coins for the occasion, yet another indication that the opponents resist any role for Jesus.

4-11. In 5:6-7, the author speaks of Jesus as coming "not in water alone but in water and blood." From this, we can see that the author holds that **Jesus "came in water and blood."** The author is correcting his opponents who claim that Jesus came only in water. This is the only instance of the author indicating that the opponents have any place for Jesus at all.

The one thing that the opponents would confess is that **Jesus "came in water."** As is argued at length in the Notes to 1 John 5:6-7, the opponents hold that Jesus came only "in water," that is to give the living water that is identified with the Spirit and that flowed from his side at the moment of his death.

5. The Views of the Two Groups Regarding Sin, Ethics, and Eschatology

Up to this point, we have examined attitudes of both groups regarding their claims as believers (Chart E-1) as well as their convictions about the identity and function of the Spirit (Chart E-2), the Father (Chart E-3), and Jesus (Chart E-4). We now come to the last set of issues dividing the two groups.[36] These issues center on the notion of sin. Specifically, the issues deal with how sin is removed (soteriology), whether future sin is possible (perfectionism), what specific sorts of action are appropriate for a believer (ethics, that is, "non-sinful" action), as well as the future consequences of sin (judgment).

From the statements on Chart E-5, it becomes clear that the opponents believed that, because they now possessed eternal life in its fullness, they were radically sinless (5-1). This view is the view of a totally "realized eschatology," the present possession of life and the avoidance of the judgment that is spoken of in John 5:24-25 (2E). Because the opponents believe that sin is no longer possible (5-1), they hold that there is no need for ethics.[37] Although the absence of a need for ethical direction is never stated explicitly in the second edition, once we understand the opponents' claim to perfectionism, we understand the reason for this lack of reference to ethical directives (within the second edition).

The situation is almost the reverse regarding the opponents' conviction about a final judgment on the last day.[38] The second edition is quite explicit that the believer will not undergo judgment (5:24-25). However, in 1 John, while

---

36. It is not claimed that only the issues on these five charts were divisive for the community. There were a number of other issues related to these that are discussed in the Commentary but are not essential for determining the nature of the crisis.

37. There are two reasons why the opponents would see no need for ethical teaching. First, they possessed direct knowledge of the will of God because of their possession of the Spirit and so would not need instruction even if ethics were necessary; but, more directly, they did not need ethics because they were now "perfect."

38. Brown (*Epistles* 476) says: "[The opponents] taught that *actions or deeds were not salvifically important since one already possessed eternal life* through faith in Christ" (italics mine). I would agree with the italicized section since this is realized eschatology and the opponents have no need of ethics. The author would say this was true but the person could also sin. As Brown says (*Epistles* 478): "[According to the secessionists,] [o]ne is begotten by God through faith in Jesus, and deeds cannot change that." Again I would agree.

In describing the sinlessness of the believer, Brown (*Epistles* 477) comments: "Previously, in 3:6, 9 the author made statements about impeccability and perfection, namely, that the Christian does not sin and cannot sin. But in 1:8–2:2 he insisted that Christians must acknowledge that they have sinned and are not free from the guilt of sin. While these ideas seem contradictory, apparently the author has reconciled them, probably in terms both of *an internal principle of sanctity that produces sinlessness as it permeates Christian life,* and of a factual failure to live that life perfectly" (italics mine). I would agree completely with the italic section but add only that this is due to the believer's possession of the Holy Spirit.

the opponents' denial of judgment is never explicitly addressed by the author, the author repeatedly makes reference to a judgment on the last day (5-2).

When we turn to the views of the author and his followers regarding sin, ethics and eschatology, we see that they also hold to a theory of perfectionism (5-1) but their understanding is different from that of the opponents. In the view of the author, the believer is incipiently perfect but is still capable of sin. Consequently, it is important for the believer to continue to exert the effort necessary to become fully like Jesus (5-3) and to avoid the things of this world (5-7). In short, the believer must work to avoid sin and be ready for the judgment that will take place at the end of time.[39]

The author then exhorts his readers to keep the commandments (5-5) and particularly the commandment of mutual love (5-6) as the basic principle of ethical behavior and the commandment that encapsulates all ethical demands.[40]

But how is sin taken away? The author of 1 John makes it clear that forgiveness of sin takes place through the atoning death of Jesus (5-8, 4-6) and through his blood (4-7) but the opponents deny this. They deny that Jesus came in the flesh (4-5) and they deny that he came in blood (4-7). At the same time, they do believe that Jesus came and bestowed the Spirit (2-6, cf. 4-11). This points to the conclusion that the opponents saw forgiveness of sin as taking place through the cleansing action of the Spirit, the Spirit that was bestowed by Jesus.[41] This was certainly a common view in both canonical and non-canonical Judaism of the time.[42] Thus, while Jesus was important for a time, his actions "in the flesh" do not remove sin; it is the cleansing action of the Spirit that does.

---

39. In *The Johannine Commandments,* I presumed that belief in the Second Coming of Jesus and in a final judgment entailed a belief in final bodily resurrection. I now recognize that there is no discussion or acknowledgment of a belief in bodily resurrection in 1 John. While it is always important to be cautious about arguing from silence, in 1 John, where the purpose of the document is to confront the differences of belief directly, the fact that there is no mention of bodily resurrection convinces me that either it was not a belief of the community at the time of 1 John or that it was not yet considered to be an *essential* belief.

40. The author also expects that the believer will show love of God (cf. 2:5, 15; 4:8, 12; 5:1bc, 20-21) but his focus is not on that since both groups would claim to do that and there is no dispute about the need for it, only whether the opponents exhibit genuine love. Thus, the author holds to the "Great Commandment(s)" of love of God and love of neighbor although he does not label them as such and redefines neighbor to include only one's coreligionist.

41. The forgiveness of sin in the *third* edition is closely connected with (located immediately after) the statement of the *second* edition about the bestowal of the Spirit (20:22). This may also reflect such a conviction. See the Commentary on John 20:22-23.

42. See the detailed listing of texts from canonical and non-canonical Judaism in the discussion of the development of pneumatology in Vol. 1, Part 4, Section 3.

CHART E-5
Differences between the Two Groups
Regarding Sin, Ethics, and Eschatology

5-1.   The faithful **claim a perfectionism** (3:6, 7, 9; 5:18) but admit that they have sinned (1:7, 9; 2:1-2, 12; 3:5; 4:10; 5:16-17). The opponents hold a more radical form of perfectionism that does not acknowledge the possibility of sin (1:8, 10).

5-2.   The faithful **expect a final judgment of their actions** that will occur at the final coming of Jesus (2:18-19; 4:17); the opponents do not (implicit in the above and unnecessary in the light of their convictions regarding perfectionism).

5-3.   The faithful **acknowledge the need for effort** in order to be holy: to "walk as Jesus walked" (2:6); to do the will of God (2:17); to act justly (2:29; 3:7, 10, 12); and to work in order to make themselves holy as Jesus is holy (3:3). The opponents see themselves as already perfect (1:8, 10).

5-4.   The faithful **act justly** (2:29; 3:7; implicit in 3:12); the opponents act sinfully (3:4, 9, 10).

5-5.   The faithful **keep the commandments** (explicit in 2:3-8; 3:22, 24; 4:21; 5:2, 3); the opponents do not (2:4; implicit in 3:22, 24; 4:20; and in 5:1-5).

5-6.   The faithful **love the brothers** (2:10; 3:14, 16, 17, 18, 23; 4:7-12, 19-21; 5:1); the opponents do not (especially 3:17-18; also 3:10, 14-15; 4:19-21).

5-7.   The faithful **must not love the things of this world** (2:15-16).

5-8.   The faithful **claim that Jesus has freed them from sin** (1:9; 2:2; 3:5, 8; 4:9-10) especially by his death (1:7; 3:16). The opponents see no role for Jesus in the forgiveness of sin (explicit in the discussion of the role of Jesus [Chart E-4 above] and implicit in 1:7, 9; 2:2; 3:5, 8, 16; 4:9-10).

Summary

From our examination of these statements, we notice, first, that both the author and his opponents agree about the possibility of certain claims accruing to the believer but disagree about whether the opponents have a legitimate right to these claims. Second, we notice that the author and his opponents share a belief in God the Father and both claim to have the Spirit but disagree radically about the role of Jesus. Finally, we see that the author and his opponents disagree about various aspects of sinfulness: how it is forgiven, whether the believer is capable of future sin, whether ethical directives are necessary and whether there is a future judgment. This analysis then provides the foundation for understanding the nature of the heresy and it is to this that we now turn.

E. AN OVERVIEW OF THE HERESY

In order to provide a consistent presentation and a means of comparison, I will discuss the "heresy" in terms of the same eleven theological categories that are discussed in Volume 1, Part 4. This will provide a clear sense of how the differences between the author and his opponents affected each of these central areas of theology. What is provided here in extended summary is discussed in full in Volume 1, Part 4.

1. Christology

The Position of the Opponents

In 1 John, there is little that is said *positively* about how the opponents understood Jesus. From various statements in 1 John, it is evident that they believed they had received the Spirit and that they had various prerogatives associated with the reception of the Spirit, prerogatives such as eternal life, direct knowledge of God, perfectionism, and that they were children of God.

Because the opponents had been members of the Johannine community, they would have believed in Jesus at one time but now they denied various convictions held by the other group about Jesus. One of these differences was that the opponents challenged the *permanence* of the role of Jesus. The opponents apparently reasoned that since the Spirit is the principle of life, once they had the Spirit, the importance of Jesus receded. While the opponents held the high Christology of the second edition and agreed that Jesus was who he said he was (that is, the herald of the outpouring of the Spirit), once the Spirit was given, it was the Spirit that became the effective means of salvation and the central focus of attention.

The prerogatives of the Spirit also had implications for Christology. For example, because the prerogatives of the eschatological Spirit were so exalted, the opponents' understanding of anthropology became a threat to the distinctiveness of Jesus. Although Jesus was "Christ," there was no indication that he was unique in any sense, for the believer also had an anointing and so could be said to be *"christos."* We will see more of this below. The opponents' understanding of soteriology also had implications for Christology. In the opponents' view, the death of Jesus resulted in his departure to the Father and the bestowal of the Spirit, but it did not take away sin. This is the view of the second edition also.

The Position of the Author

From the way the author of 1 John develops his own view of Christology, it becomes clear that in spite of the fact that the opponents held to the high Christology of the second edition, he felt their Christology was inadequate.

In order to clarify the distinction between Jesus and the believer, the author of 1 John does not lower the status of the believer but articulates a Christology that is even higher than that of the second edition. Thus, he makes it clear that this Jesus was fully equal to God. He does this by means of two affirmations: (1) he was preexistent and (2) he was the *unique (monogenēs)* son of God. Thus, the author affirms that the identity of Jesus is not the same as that of the believer and explains how this is so.

In order to clarify the role of Jesus *vis-à-vis* that of the Spirit, the author affirms the effective role of the death of Jesus in salvation, as we shall see. He also affirms the role of Jesus as the giver of life.

2. Belief

The Position of the Opponents

It is obvious that the opponents once believed in Jesus. The opponents believed that Jesus came to give the Spirit. This is particularly evident in 1 John 5:6. They also believed that they had received the Spirit, as is evident from the way they emphasize the gifts of the Spirit as prerogatives they now possess. However, the fact that the author of 1 John spends so much effort correcting their belief indicates how different his views are from theirs.

The Position of the Author

For the author of 1 John, the fact that the opponents had believed is not enough — because they had believed incorrectly. The author spends considerable effort throughout the Letter attempting to clarify the correct content of belief, that is, Christology, pneumatology, soteriology, anthropology, ethics, etc. But it must be said that he focuses his attack on the failure of the opponents to confess properly the two main elements of the community's confession: that Jesus is the Christ and that he is the Son of God. As we shall see below, the opponents' anthropology was the chief threat to these convictions.

3. Pneumatology

The Position of the Opponents

The opponents believed that they had received the eschatological Spirit. In 1 John, this is expressed as "coming in water" (1 John 5:6), the symbolic language typical of the second edition of the Gospel (cf. 4:10-15; 7:37-39). In this sense, the opponents were in complete agreement with the theology of the second edition. But, also, in accord with one understanding of the second edition, the opponents argued that Jesus did not do anything himself that was of intrinsic salvific importance, such as dying an atoning death. His death, as is evident in the second edition of the Gospel, was simply a departure to the Father.

The Position of the Author

The author of 1 John would agree with the opponents that Jesus had bestowed the Spirit upon the disciples and upon all who believed in him (1 John 4:13; 5:6). However, the author would have disagreed with the opponents regarding three related matters. First, Jesus did not come just to give the Spirit, he also came "in blood"; that is, his death was salvific. Secondly, the author would deny that the opponents had actually received the Spirit of God, which he understood to be the Spirit of Truth. Rather, they had received the Spirit of Deception and did not know the truth. This was evident from their actions. Thirdly, he held the conviction that the believer did not, and could not, receive the Spirit in the same fullness that Jesus did.

He also disagreed with his opponents about various prerogatives associated with the reception of the eschatological Spirit. These differences will be discussed in what follows.

4. Eternal Life

The Position of the Opponents

It is clear from numerous references in 1 John that the opponents claim to be born of God (cf. 2:29; 3:9) and to be children of God (3:1-2, 10) and to possess eternal life (cf. 2:25; 3:14-15; 5:12). In this they are also in agreement with the theology of the second edition.

The Position of the Author

The author of 1 John also makes all of these claims (2:25). However, he would disagree with his opponents about the precise way that life was possessed and what was necessary in order to possess it. Thus, he argues that eternal life is not an absolute possession: it can be lost through sin — and most especially through "sin-unto-death" (5:16-17). Moreover, he argues that one cannot have life without "having" the Son (5:11-12) and without loving one's brothers (3:14-15). Thus, proper belief in Jesus is necessary for possession of eternal life.

5. Eschatology

The Position of the Opponents

The opponents understand their possession of the Spirit to be perfect and complete in the present. It is this that explains their beliefs in ethical perfectionism and in their avoidance of any judgment. This is built on the theology of the second edition and is a logical reading of the Old Testament prerogatives of the Spirit.

That the opponents held to a view of perfectionism is shown in sections 7 and 8 below. That the opponents denied a future eschatology is not stated explicitly but is evident in the second edition especially in statements such as 5:24. Moreover, their view can be implied from the frequent references to "the last day," to future judgment, and to the need for proper behavior in the thought of the author of 1 John.[43]

The Position of the Author

The author of 1 John argues for a more nuanced position. He affirms that the believer has crossed over from death to life (3:14) and so he does hold a "realized" eschatology. But he also affirms that even though the believer has life, the person is still capable of losing that life by various means (2:24-27).[44] Each believer will undergo judgment at the Second Coming of Jesus (2:28). Consequently, it is necessary for the believer to continue to work in order to grow to

43. See also Chart E-5 above.
44. Here the author speaks of the necessity of proper conduct and belief in order to continue "abiding." Thus, the fruits of belief can be lost through improper conduct and improper belief.

be like Jesus, so that at his coming the believer may appear to be as he (Jesus) is (3:2-3). The final and eternal possession of this life is dependent upon the judgment that will occur when Jesus is revealed again (4:17-18).

6. Knowledge of God

The Position of the Opponents

It is clear from 1 John that the opponents claimed to "know" God (cf. 1 John 2:4, 20-21). Whether one did or did not "know" God was also a major theme of the second edition of the Gospel. However, the opponents claim that their knowledge of God is direct and they have no need of any teacher (including Jesus himself and including his previous teaching). The Spirit alone is necessary since he will be the source of knowledge, in accord with the Old Testament teaching in this regard.

The Position of the Author

The author of 1 John argues that one who claims to know God but does not keep his commandments is a liar (2:3-4). Second, even though, by saying this, he adopts a position that is perilously close to that of the opponents, he agrees that possession of the Spirit gives direct knowledge of God and that the believer has no need of teachers (2:27). In this regard, the author sees himself only as a "witness" (1:2; 4:13). But, for the author, this is not all. In spite of this direct knowledge of God, the words of Jesus have a permanent validity and believers must keep what they have heard "from the beginning" (1 John 1:1-4; 2:7, 13, 14, 24; cf. also 2:27). Those who go beyond and do not remain in the teaching of the Christ (2 John 9) are in error.

7. Soteriology

The Position of the Opponents

As we have already seen, in 1 John, the clearest comparison of the soteriology of the opponents with that of the author of 1 John is in 5:6, where the author explains that Jesus did not come "in water" only, but "in water and blood." This view of the opponents is consistent with the view of both the Old Testament and the SDQ that the Spirit of God cleansed persons from sin. These various texts have been presented in detail in the discussion of the soteriology of the second edition in Volume 1, Part 4, and need not be repeated here. There can be no doubt that this was the common view in first-century Judaism. At the same time, the soteriology of the second edition of the Gospel consistently reflects this view. The most important passage in this respect is John 13:4-11. As is explained in the Commentary, the symbolic meaning of Jesus' washing of the disciples' feet at the Last Supper (in the "original" interpretation within the second edition) was that it was necessary for the disciples to be "washed" by Jesus if they were to have an inheritance with him. This necessary washing was the washing by the Spirit. At the same time, in the second edition of the Gospel, there is a notable absence of any references to the death of Jesus as salvific. It is consistently presented as a "departure" to the Father.

Finally, we may note that the active role of Jesus in the removal of sin is stated so often and so emphatically in 1 John and in the third edition of the Gospel that it is difficult to conclude that the author was not reacting to a contrary view. This view is that stated by the author in 1 John 5:6: Jesus came not only in water but in water and blood.

The Position of the Author

There is no need for detailed argument here regarding the author's view. As was indicated above, the author repeatedly stresses the fact that it was the death of Jesus that took away sin (e.g., 1:7; 2:2, 12; 3:5, 16; 4:10, 14; 5:6-8). He never suggests that sin is forgiven any other way.

8. Ethics

The Position of the Opponents

The author of 1 John says (1:8) that the opponents hold a view of perfectionism and that their view is incorrect (1:8-10). At the same time, it should be recalled that, in the second edition, there is no discussion of ethical directives, a fact that reflects the opponents' position and that is in accord with one understanding of the prerogatives of the eschatological Spirit.

The Position of the Author

Once again the author brings forth a nuanced position. The author agrees that the believer is sinless (2:1; 3:6, 8, 9) and will (that is, "should") sin no more. But he balances the view of the sinlessness of the believer with the recognition that sin is still possible (2:1-2). Because sin is still possible, there is a need for ethical directives, and the author asserts the role of mutual love as the proper basis for all conduct (e.g., 2:9-11; 4:11-13). To live out a life of love will require effort (3:18) in order to become fully what believers are capable of in their imitation of Jesus (3:3-6).

9. Anthropology

The Position of the Opponents

Nowhere, as we have indicated, does the author of the second edition state explicitly that Jesus, although truly Son of God and truly *"Christos,"* was to have no permanent role in salvation. But we have seen above how the various prerogatives of the believer could easily be understood as a threat to the unique role of Jesus. A combination of these factors undoubtedly led to conclusions that blurred and eventually did away with the distinction between the status of Jesus and the status of the believer. If Jesus was not thought of as preexistent but rather as one upon whom the Spirit had come in a definitive way and was "son" and *"christos,"* it would be easy to argue that, although he was truly "son" and "sent by the Father," once the believer had received the Spirit and had become a child of God, living with the same life as the Father (and Jesus), the status of the believer could well challenge any belief that the status of Jesus was unique.

That the status of the believer could challenge the role of Jesus as *"christos"* is evident from the repeated references of the author of 1 John to the fact that the believer received an anointing (2:20, 27 [twice]). Although the author never speaks of the believer as *"christos"* (as is understandable), his use of such similar language at a time when it could be misleading to do so indicates just how distinctive such language was of the tradition. Jesus was in human form (just as they were) and had received the Spirit (just as was now said of the believer). That some would confuse the role of the believer and Jesus is understandable, given the lack of clear articulation of the ways in which Jesus was unique.

If there could be confusion of the status of Jesus and the believer regarding *"christos,"* it was also possible regarding "sonship." Both the author and the opponents regularly refer to the believer as "born" of God (cf. 2:29; 3:9). And even the author of 1 John refers to believers as "children of God" (3:1-2, 10). If the identity of Jesus and the believer were being blurred by the opponents, it would have been risky for the author of 1 John to use such language *unless* it was in fact so rooted in the tradition that it was not a matter of neglecting it but of clarifying it.[45]

The Position of the Author

Once again the author sets forth a nuanced position regarding these matters. However, throughout his tract, the author of 1 John is at pains to nuance not only

---

45. It is particularly important to recall the words of R. E. Brown at the beginning of Section B of this appendix that, as improbable as such a view may be to our understanding of Jesus, "the real issue is the inner logic of secessionist thought."

his understanding of Christology but also his understanding of anthropology. In spite of the exalted status of the believer, a status that was so exalted that it could be seen to rival that of Jesus, the author makes it clear that there were essential differences between Jesus and the believer: Jesus was preexistent; he was the unique son of God; his words had a permanent value; he had a permanent and essential role in salvation; he came "in blood"; and "life" was possible only through him.

The author also distinguishes Jesus' possession of the Spirit from the way the believer possesses the Spirit. According to the author, the believer received "of" the Spirit (3:24; 4:13). While these statements of possession of the Spirit express a conviction that the believer receives a share of the Spirit, such a partitive genitive is never used in the second edition. Moreover, while this nuance is sufficiently significant for the author of 1 John to state it twice, it is not until the third edition of the Gospel that the contrast with Jesus' possession of the Spirit is made explicit. There it is said that Jesus received the Spirit "without measure" (John 3:34).

In addition, the believer was still capable of sin and would undergo judgment, as we have seen above. This was not true of Jesus. Thus, in spite of the exalted prerogatives of the Johannine believer, that status is not to be confused with that of Jesus. Anthropology cannot be a threat to Christology.

10. Ecclesiology

The Position of the Opponents

The position of the opponents regarding ecclesiology is difficult to determine. There is no reference to their beliefs in this regard, but if we speculate on the basis of their other beliefs, it would seem that they were bound only by their common beliefs, and that there was no hierarchical structure. If the opponents' attitude toward mutual love can be an indicator, we see that the author believed that the opponents did not exhibit love toward the brothers. This was a major criticism of them. But whether the opponents failed in this regard only toward the members of the author's community or whether it was true even of the members of their own group is not clear.

The Position of the Author

In 1 John, we see references to a self-awareness of the group as a "community." Thus, the author speaks of others having *koinōnia* (1:3 [twice], 6, 7) with himself and those with him. In addition, the members are to show love for one another (e.g., 2:10, etc.) and address one another as "brother" (e.g., 4:21; cf. 3:23), thus showing their conviction of the community as such.

Yet, if there was a sense of community among the members and although the author speaks from a position of prominence and authority, there is no indication that his is an officially recognized appointment. The author is a "witness" (1:2). Consequently, we can say that at the time of 1 John there was no evidence of a hierarchical structure in the author's community.

In 2 and 3 John, we see the use of terminology to reflect this *koinōnia,* but there is no evidence of hierarchy there either, and when Diotrephes asserts himself (3 John 9) he is chastised by the author as "loving to act as leader." Yet, it is probably significant that individuals were beginning to emerge who in fact were attempting to exercise an individual authority.

11. The Religious Significance of Material Reality

The Position of the Opponents

In the second edition of the Gospel, there had been a clear repudiation of the fleshly (material, physical, earthly) dimensions of religion as being salvifically important. This carries over into the failure of the opponents to confess Jesus as "come in the flesh" (1 John 4:2; 2 John 7). This is also consistent with the view of the second edition, which makes no reference to the death of Jesus as salvific and describes it only in terms of his going to the Father, the action necessary for him to give the Spirit. But it almost surely reflects the continuing belief that it was the action of the Spirit rather than any bodily or physical action of Jesus, such as his shedding of blood or his sacrificial death, that brought eternal life.

The Position of the Author

For the author of 1 John, the "fleshly" death of Jesus was of crucial importance. Not only does he reject a belief that does not confess that Jesus has "come in the flesh," but he emphasizes the believer's cleansing by the blood of Jesus (1 John 1:7).

But what of the other material aspects of religion? At the time of 1 John, the issue of ritual does not seem to be a serious concern. It certainly does not appear to be an issue of debate between the author and his opponents. Some scholars would find evidence of a baptismal ritual underlying the wording of parts of 1 John, and this may be correct, but there is no concerted argument regarding this aspect of belief.

However, there is a renewed emphasis in 1 John on the importance of the temporal and historical, in the sense that the author appeals to what his readers have "heard," "looked at," "seen" and to what "their hands touched." In short, the author affirms the importance of what happened in history and agrees that religious life without that historical and sensory experience is insufficient.

12. Conclusions

We have addressed the various controverted aspects of the theology of the opponents and that of the author of 1 John according to a series of eleven theological topics at the heart of Johannine theology. However, it should be clear that, in 1 John itself, the author did not choose to proceed in such an orderly fashion. Rather, he chose, at times, to contrast views of the opponents with his own. At other times, he chose to simply emphasize certain points and to leave the view of the opponents unarticulated. At still other times, he exhorted his listeners without reference to a specific point of controversy. However, from an analysis of the viewpoints as well as from attention to his striking silence on other points, it becomes clear that the controversy concerned the interpretation of the tradition at the time of the second edition.

When we come to the discussion of the third edition of the Gospel, we will see yet another stage in the development of the tradition. In the introduction to the Analysis of the third edition, it will become clear that many of the views of the author of the third edition of the Gospel will echo and reinforce the views of the author of 1 John. By doing this, the third author will incorporate these views within the community's actual narrative of the ministry of Jesus, thus reflecting the conviction that these were, indeed, the views of Jesus himself.

F. UNRESOLVED QUESTIONS ABOUT THE THEOLOGY OF 1 JOHN IN RELATION TO THE THEOLOGY OF THE SECOND EDITION

Although the views of the opponents and those of the author of 1 John are able to be identified from the pages of 1 John, and although how the author sought to correct and/or nuance the views of those opponents is also evident, it is not always clear exactly *how* the author of 1 John (and after him the author of the third edition) understood the way the views of the two groups were to be integrated. For example, it is difficult to know how the author understood the relation between his own apocalyptic viewpoint and the more traditional worldview of the second edition. Nor is it clear how the author understood the relationship between the life-giving properties of the Spirit and those of Jesus. In what specific way was Jesus said to give life? The same is true regarding the respective roles of Jesus and the Spirit in the forgiveness of sin. Was it a matter of sin being forgiven through Jesus and life being given through the Spirit? The author does not explain how the two are to be integrated. Although we cannot be sure, it would seem that these issues represent examples of what might be called the propensity of biblical authors simply to affirm two realities and assume that the reader would undertake the task of integrating them.

G. CORRECT BELIEF AND CORRECT CONDUCT AS THE TWO BASIC ISSUES IN THE DISPUTE

We have come to see the considerable number of the ways in which the author and his opponents differed. However, in spite of this, when they are reduced to their essential elements, there are two central issues in the crisis: correct belief and correct conduct. In the view of the author, correct belief involves a series of issues surrounding the person of Jesus: How does his sonship differ from ours? What is the role of his historical words as contrasted with the teaching of the Spirit? What is his role in the forgiveness of sin and the giving of life? The author can thus focus on the person of Jesus and affirm that he and his followers believe "in the name of Jesus." That is, they hold the person of Jesus to be central and permanent to their belief. It is a belief that is in harmony with everything that he said and stood for. The other way of expressing this is that they "kept the word of Jesus." By this they mean that his historical words are the empirical basis for their belief. Although they affirm the teaching of the Spirit, it is what they heard, saw, and touched "from the beginning" that was the basis of their faith.

The second central issue in the dispute was the nature and importance of ethics. The believers were not perfect in the sense that they needed no ethical direction. They were still capable of sin. Moreover, this ethical direction was essentially expressed not only in their love of God (which was not in dispute) but also in their love for one another. As the author says (1 John 4:20) "... the one not loving his brother, whom he has seen, is not able to love God whom he has not seen."

As part of his strategy in 1 John, the author seeks again and again to link the various prerogatives and claims of the believer to both of these concerns. That is, in his view, one cannot legitimately make these claims if one does not believe and act correctly. Although the distribution of these many statements throughout the Letter seems to be without pattern, the remarkable way in which so many claims are linked to both proper belief and action removes all doubt that such dual concerns were prominent in the mind of the author. In Chart E-6, I have gathered together twelve claims or prerogatives of the believer in order to show how the author links each to both correct belief and correct action. In most cases, the linkage is obvious and almost wooden; in some cases it is more implicit but still evident. All in all, the number of claims that are linked to these is remarkable and testifies to the importance that the author gave both to the claims and to the "tests" regarding whether a person had a legitimate right to those claims.

In addition to the focus on correct belief and correct action in the various aspects of the theology, there are additional ways in which the centrality of these categories is obvious. Within 1 John, we have seen (following the lead of Feuillet and R. E. Brown) that the two halves of the tract focus respectively on proclamation of God as light and the need to love. These are symbolic ways of representing the categories of correct belief and correct action.

Moreover, we can also notice that 2 and 3 John each have what can be called a primary focus. In 2 John, the focus is on walking in the truth and the importance of correct belief and remaining in the teaching of the Christ. In 3 John, the focus is on correct (loving) action as manifest in the acceptance of others in love.

Finally, the overriding thematic structure of the third edition takes up these categories and illustrates them in the public ministry through the stress on Jesus as "the light" (of correct belief, flowing from Jesus who is the light of the world), and in the Passion through the stress on the love that Jesus exhibits in his suffering and death.

CHART E-6

Correct Belief and Correct Behavior as the Two Central Issues in the Crisis Confronted by 1 John

1. Being "of God"

4:2: "Every spirit that confesses Jesus Christ come in the flesh is of God."

3:10: (put negatively) "Everyone not acting justly is not of God — and the one not loving his brother."

2. Being "of the truth"

2:21: (implicit in this negative statement) "I did not write to you that you do not know the truth, but that you know it and that every lie is not of the truth."

3:18-19: "Children, let us not love in word nor with the tongue, but in work and in truth. And in this we shall know that we are of the truth. . . ."

3. Born of God

5:1: "Everyone believing that Jesus is the Christ is born of God" (see also 5:4-5).

4:7: "Everyone loving has been born of God."

4. Knowing God

2:4-5: (implicit) "the one claiming 'I have come to know him' but not keeping his commandments is a liar. . . . But the one who keeps his word. . . ."

4:7-8: "Everyone loving . . . knows God. The one not loving did not know God because God is love."

5. Remaining ("Abiding")

4:15: "Whoever confesses that Jesus is the Son of God, God remains in that person and that person in God." (See also 2:24: "If it remains in you [what you heard from the beginning], you remain in the Son and in the Father"; see also 2:6.)

4:12: "If we love one another, God remains in us. . . ." (See also 4:16 ["the one remaining in love remains in God and God in that person."])

6. Being "in the Light"

1:7-8:   "If we walk in the light as he is in the light, . . . the blood of Jesus his Son cleanses us from all sin. If we say that we do not have sin, we deceive ourselves and the truth is not in us."

2:9-10:   "The one claiming to be in the light and hating his brother is still in darkness. The one who loves his brother remains in the light. . . ."

7. Knowing the Truth

2:21-22:   "I did not write to you that you do not know the truth but that you know it and that every lie is not of the truth. Who is the Liar if not the one denying that Jesus is the Christ?"

3:18:   ". . . let us not love in word nor with the tongue but in work and in truth."

8. Loving God

2:5:   "But the one who keeps his word, in this person truly the love of God is brought to perfection."

5:2-3a: "In this we know that we love the children of God, whenever we love God and obey his commandments. For this is the love of God that we keep his commandments. . . ."

9. Having Eternal Life

5:12:   (Throughout the Letter, the author insists that it is necessary to believe and confess Jesus properly. He refers to this as "having the Son"): "The one who has the Son has life; the one not having the Son of God does not have life."

3:15:   (negatively) "Everyone hating his brother is a murderer and you know that every murderer does not have eternal life remaining in himself."

10. "From the Beginning"

1:1-3   "That which was from the beginning . . . we proclaim to you. . . ." (See also 2:24: ". . . may what you heard from the beginning remain in you.")

3:11:   ". . . this is the proclamation that you heard from the beginning, that we love one another."

11. Two Commandments: Belief and Love

2 John 6: "This is the commandment as you heard it from the begin-

ning, that we walk in [the truth]." (See also 1 John 2:7 and below.)

2 John 5: "And now I ask you, Lady, not as one writing you a new commandment but one that we have had from the beginning: that we love one another." (See also 1 John 4:21 and below.)

In 3:23, the two commandments are described in sequence and arranged chiastically:

> "And this is his commandment,
> that we believe in the name of his Son Jesus Christ
> and
> that we love one another,
> as he has given us commandment."

12. These Commandments Are Both "From the Beginning"

2 John 6: "This is the commandment, as you heard it from the beginning, that we walk in [the truth]."

2 John 5: "And now I ask you, Lady, not as one writing a new commandment but one that we have had from the beginning: that we love one another."

H. HOW THESE DIVERGENT INTERPRETATIONS AROSE

R. E. Brown, in his commentary on the Letters, has argued that 1 John was written to confront a misreading of the tradition as it appeared in the Gospel. Arguing that the Gospel was forged in debate with the synagogue, Brown proposed that, as is often the case with polemic, by stressing some elements, other elements were neglected or were not addressed in a sufficiently nuanced way. As a result when the Gospel was read in different circumstances, that is, after the community had become independent of the synagogue and that crisis ceased to exist, the community read the Gospel in a way that was not intended. Brown then argued that the author of 1 John called attention to elements of the tradition that were minor themes in the Gospel due to the one-sidedness of the synagogue debate and brought them into balance with other elements of the tradition.[46]

However, if the crisis is understood against the background of the second edition (rather than against the background of the entire Gospel), it would be necessary to say that the views of the author of 1 John would represent those views that were absent (rather than de-emphasized) at the time of the second

---

46. Brown, *Community* 108; *Epistles* 97-100.

edition, possibly because of a one-sided focus on issues that were being debated within the synagogue.

At the same time, it will be obvious from what has been said above that many of the views of the author of 1 John are closely connected to the worldview of apocalyptic. It is difficult to conceive of the absence of an apocalyptic worldview in the earlier material as a "minor element that escaped emphasis in the second edition." Surely more is at work than this.

It is also noteworthy that the introduction of a belief in the death of Jesus as atoning is neither intrinsic to apocalypticism nor to the Old Testament background of the second edition. Just where these two elements of 1 John came from and what accounted for their incorporation into the tradition is in need of further exploration.

I. CONFRONTING THE CRISIS: THE JOHANNINE COMMANDMENTS

Throughout his Letter, the author of 1 John had argued that the two major issues involved in the crisis were correct belief and correct conduct. Although he argues that belief and conduct can be identified and can be tested in a variety of ways, the most prominent means is by making both issues the object of a commandment given by God. The commandments are articulated in the terms and worldview of 1 John. The first is variously expressed as to "keep the word of Jesus," to "believe in the name of Jesus Christ," and to "walk in the truth." But the essential focus is on correct belief. The second commandment is expressed variously as to "love the brothers" and to "love one another." The nature and function of these commandments will be discussed in greater detail in Appendix 5 (The Johannine Commandments) below.

J. VIEWS SIMILAR TO THOSE OF THE OPPONENTS ELSEWHERE IN EARLY CHRISTIANITY

Finally, we may ask whether there is evidence that the type of opinions we have attributed to the opponents can be found elsewhere in early Christianity. The answer is "yes," as we shall see.

1. General Similarities to the View of the Author and of the Opponents: The Outpouring of the Spirit

The conviction that the eschatological outpouring of the Spirit took place as a result of the ministry of Jesus is a basic tenet of all early Christianity. Most notably Paul speaks in detail of the outpouring of the Spirit and of its benefits. His presentation parallels that of the Johannine Gospel in a number of respects. A few examples, taken from Paul's Letter to the Romans, will suffice: (1) the Spirit is given by the Father and is the source of life (Rom 8:11); (2) the Spirit enables us to live not on the level of the flesh but on the level of the Spirit (Rom 8:4-9); (3) the Spirit makes us children of God (Rom 8:14-17) although we also wait for future adoption (Rom 8:23); (4) what we will be as children is not yet revealed (Rom 8:19); (5) the Spirit helps us to pray (Rom 8:26-27); (6) the Spirit gives knowledge (Rom 9:1); (7) love for others is a gift of the Spirit poured out by God into the believer (Rom 15:30). Paul can even speak of "being made holy in the Holy Spirit," a phrase that confirms the role of the Spirit in sanctification and would be close to the position taken one-sidedly by the opponents in 1 John.

The Acts of the Apostles also speaks eloquently of the role of the gift of the Spirit beginning with the scene in the Upper Room (Acts 2:1-13), when the Spirit is portrayed as descending upon them in tongues of fire. The radical change that takes place in the demeanor of the apostles as well as the repeated references to the role of the Spirit in the days following Pentecost attests to the importance of this gift.

However, when we look for more specific similarities to the crisis of 1 John, we find promising parallels in two documents from the early second century, Ignatius' *Letter to the Smyrneans* and Polycarp's *Letter to the Philippians*.

2. Ignatius' *Letter to the Smyrneans*

Ignatius (ca. A.D. 35-107) was bishop of Antioch in Syria and is said to have been put to death during the reign of Trajan. While under arrest and on his way to Rome, he wrote a number of letters, among them a letter to the community at Smyrna. In it, Ignatius encourages the community there to reject certain false teaching.[47] There are several topics addressed by Ignatius that would seem to have a bearing on the matter of the crisis he was confronting. A review of these shows substantial similarity to the crisis being confronted by the author of 1 John.[48]

---

47. Schnackenburg (*Epistles* 21-24) presents an analysis of the similarities between Ignatius' letter and 1 John that is similar in several respects to the one given here. However, my conclusions regarding the relation between 1 John and Ignatius' letter appear to account for the differences more adequately than does Schnackenburg.

48. A number of scholars confine their discussion of the views of Ignatius' opponents to the comments on "docetic" elements. However, the convictions of the opponents exhibit a wider range of features. When this wider range is taken into account, its similarity to the Johannine crisis becomes more apparent.

The first major issue confronted by Ignatius is a denial of the physical reality of Jesus. This doubt pertained to his life in general (1:1-2; 4:2; 5:2), but particularly to his Passion (1:2; 2:1) and then also to the physicality of his Resurrection (2:1; 3:1-2). Even before he makes mention of the opponents' views, Ignatius praises the faith of the Smyrneans and gives a brief account of it, making particular note of their belief in the physical and earthly aspects of Jesus, that is, that he was of the family of David "according to the flesh"; that he was born of a virgin, and truly nailed to a tree "in the flesh" (1:1-2). He also affirms that Jesus "truly suffered" and "truly raised himself" and that "he [Jesus] suffered all these things for us that we might gain salvation" (2:1).

Ignatius also refers to the fact that his opponents question whether Jesus was "in the flesh" after the Resurrection (3:1-3), a view that would suggest they believed his Resurrection was spiritual rather than truly physical. Ignatius refutes this by reminding his readers that Jesus showed "those with Peter" his resurrected body and said "Take, handle me and see that I am not a phantom without a body" (3:2).

In 5:2, Ignatius broadens his view to speak of those who deny generally that Jesus "was actually in the flesh" (*sarkophorōn*, literally "flesh-bearing"). In response, Ignatius affirms that all are to believe "on the blood of Christ" *(eis to haima Christou)* (6:1). It is in the Gospel that the Passion is revealed and the Resurrection is brought about (7:2). Finally, he reminds his readers: "I salute you all in the name of Jesus Christ, and in his flesh and blood, by his Passion and Resurrection both of flesh and spirit" (12:2).

If we ask where the opponents could have derived a belief that Jesus was not fully human but only "appeared" to be in the flesh, the most likely explanation would seem to be the Gospel of John. For it is there alone that we encounter a Christology capable of being interpreted as portraying a Jesus who is so superior to all aspects of human existence. Even his Passion, with its emphasis on glory, could be said to suggest no real suffering or anguish.

This is quite similar in several respects to the view of the opponents of 1 John who also deny the importance of material, physical reality in relation to the ministry of Jesus. In our discussion of soteriology above, we have seen that, in the second edition, there are indications that the eternal life of Jesus was understood in a way that made his life less than fully physical. In our discussion of 1 John, we have called attention to the author's emphasis on the saving reality of the physical death of Jesus. At the same time, for the author of the third edition, the physicality of the Resurrection was something that he emphasized as essential for belief. What we see in Ignatius' *Letter to the Smyrneans* is a situation that is quite similar to this.

The second topic of concern for Ignatius is the ethical attitudes of the opponents. Ignatius' discussion of this topic is not long but his picture of the opponents is clear. They reject all forms of love (6:2). They do not care for widows, nor orphans, nor the distressed or afflicted, nor for the prisoner or ex-prisoner, nor for the hungry or the thirsty (6:2). Ignatius reminds these opponents that love is necessary in order to gain resurrection (7:1). At the same time, he commends his readers for their demonstration of love (1:1). This aspect of the behavior of Ignatius' opponents is similar to the portrayal of the opponents in 1 John. There the author had repeatedly accused the opponents of not loving the brothers and of shutting their hearts off from those in need.

The third topic is that the opponents do not participate in the Eucharist and prayer *(Eucharistias kai proseuchēs apechontai . . .)* (7:1). Ignatius explains that they do this because they do not "confess that the Eucharist is the flesh of our savior, Jesus Christ, who suffered for our sins" (7:1). From what is said, it is evident that the opponents deny that the Eucharist is the flesh of Jesus. However, the precise foundation for the opponents' position is not clear. Working from what we are given, it is striking how the language of Ignatius quoted above reflects that of the third edition of the Gospel. First, there is the emphasis on the necessity of eating the flesh and drinking the blood to have eternal life in John 6:51-58.[49] Second, there is the reference to Jesus as "savior," which reflects the language of the third edition (John 4:42; cf. 3:17; 10:9; 12:47).[50] Third, there is the title "Jesus Christ," which also occurs only in the third edition of the Gospel (cf. 1:17; 17:3) and frequently in 1 John (1:3; 2:1; 3:23; 4:2; 5:1, 6) and twice in 2 John (vv. 3, 7).[51]

Ignatius also makes a brief reference to the opponents' rejection of participation in prayer. Again, it is impossible to determine specifically what is being referred to.[52] However, we can note that it is only in 1 John and later in the third edition that the Johannine tradition speaks of prayer. Was the introduction of these topics at a later point in the tradition intended to affirm their value over against opponents? From the Johannine tradition itself, it is difficult to tell. Yet the fact that Ignatius' opinion on this, which is seen as a problem in the community at Smyrna, once more echoes a topic that is found only in the later stages of the Johannine tradition suggests that Ignatius is confronting a situation similar to the crisis of 1 John.

Attention was called above to the similarity of Ignatius' language to that of the third edition. Such language is not unique within the New Testament;

---

49. For detail, see Vol. 1, Part 4, Section 11 (The Religious Significance of Material Reality).

50. That these are characteristic of 1 John and the third edition is discussed in detail in 3E-33. See also Vol. 1, Part 4, Section 7 (Soteriology).

51. For detailed discussion, see 3E-2.

52. In what follows, I presume *proseuchē* refers to personal prayer rather than prayer conceived of as a community ritual.

but, *within the Johannine tradition,* it is unique to the third edition. Given the other similarities to the Johannine tradition, it seems significant that Ignatius would echo this language so frequently. It is perhaps also the case that the situation in Ignatius' time reflects most especially a period subsequent not only to 1 John but also to the third edition of the Gospel. We have noted that in 1 John, there is no mention of the Eucharist in either a positive way or as the object of disagreement. Yet Ignatius indicates that the Eucharist was a central ritual for his community but not for his opponents.

In all of this it is apparent that the opponents were individuals who were once members of the community and who had been "believers" and still claimed to have the correct understanding of the "tradition." However, Ignatius' description of his opponents is not as detailed as that of the author of 1 John. As a result, we cannot tell the full contours of the belief of Ignatius' opponents and must be content with only a modest glimpse. Moreover, only in his discussion of the Passion can Ignatius be said to deal with a truly theological issue. Nevertheless, to a considerable degree, the opponents' beliefs fit the profile of the opponents as portrayed in 1 John, and thus the opponents of Ignatius may be evidence of a somewhat modified version of the beliefs held by the opponents of 1 John and so reflect their continuing presence in the region.

If there are similarities between the opponents of Ignatius and those of the author of 1 John, there are also differences. We have already called attention to what could appear to be a somewhat developed form of the opponents' attitudes toward the flesh of Jesus, but there are other differences. Rejection of the Eucharist was a problem for the community at Smyrna but there is no mention of this in 1 John. Ignatius speaks in detail of the celebration of the Eucharist, referring to it as the *agapē* and relating its proper celebration to the presence of a bishop. This is a development of church order not evident in 1 John. If we are correct in seeing in 3 John a criticism of incipient hierarchical authority on the part of Diotrephes, then the church situation reflected in Ignatius would be evidence of a more fully developed (and fully sanctioned) hierarchy in Smyrna. Thus, it would seem that we see evidence, both in the opponents of 1 John and in Ignatius, of a series of problems related to, and perhaps derivative of, the Johannine tradition.

However, if this is true, it is also true that Ignatius reflects a later stage in the development of these problems and a later, more developed, attitude toward church organization. If we were to attempt a trajectory of this development, it is most likely that 1 and 2 John reflect the first stage of this conflict and that a slightly later (second) stage is apparent in 3 John. The third edition of the Gospel, then, represents a third stage in the trajectory, while Ignatius reflects a somewhat later (fourth) period.

3. Polycarp's *Letter to the Philippians*[53]

Polycarp (ca. A.D. 69-155) was bishop of Smyrna and was said by Eusebius to have known "John" and others who had seen the Lord.[54] His letter was written to Philippi from Smyrna. Its date is uncertain. There are two statements that mention Ignatius. In 9:1, Polycarp lists Ignatius as among those who "ran not in vain." This would seem to imply that Ignatius is dead. However, in 13:2 Polycarp asks for information about "Ignatius himself and those who are with him." Of these two statements, it would seem that the one in 9:1 is more ambiguous: it could refer simply to the fact that Ignatius is under arrest and on his way to Rome. Thus, his "running of the race" would be over. In that case, 13:2 would refer to Polycarp's desire for information regarding Ignatius and the others who are under arrest and on their way to Rome. Consequently, I am inclined to put the letter of Polycarp before A.D. 107.

In the course of his exhortation to the community, Polycarp warns the members briefly of certain disorders. The caution begins in *Phil.* 6:3, where Polycarp urges the Philippians to strive after good, to avoid giving offense, and to stay away from "false brothers" *(pseudadelphoi)*[55] and from those who hypocritically bear the name of the Lord and who lead astray empty-minded persons. Then, in 7:1-2, Polycarp identifies the false ideas being promulgated by these hypocrites. All of these errors bear a close resemblance to errors we have identified with the opponents in 1 John and that are corrected by the author of 1 John and by the Gospel's third author.

He states (7:1) that anyone "who does not confess that Jesus Christ has come in the flesh is an Antichrist," quoting 1 John 4:2, 3. He continues by saying that anyone "who does not confess the testimony of the Cross is of the devil." This later term ("is of the devil") is strikingly reminiscent of the author of 1 John's term "is not of God" (1 John 4:3). In making these two statements,

---

53. See also Schnackenburg, "Ephesus" 41-64, esp. 56, 59.

54. The reference to Polycarp is from Irenaeus' Letter to Florinus, quoted in Eusebius *Hist.* 5.20.4-8: . . . *kai tēn meta Iōannou sunanastrophēn hōs apēngellen kai tēn meta tōn loipōn tōn heorakotōn ton kyrion. kai hōs apemnēmoneuen tous logous autōn* (". . . and how he reported his association with John and with the others who had seen the Lord. And how he remembered their words").

The meaning (that is, which John: the apostle or the elder?) and the accuracy (did he genuinely know eyewitnesses of Jesus' ministry?) of this statement have been debated. However, it is not impossible that the Elder had known John if this had taken place toward the final quarter of the first century.

55. The use of this term to describe those who do not confess Jesus as come in the flesh is striking in the light of the use in 1 John 4:1 of "false prophets" *(pseudoprophētai)* to describe those who make the same charge.

Polycarp is using hendiadys. That is, not confessing the witness of the cross is the same as denying that Jesus has come in the flesh.

Polycarp then goes on to argue that "Whoever perverts the sayings *(logia)* of the Lord to his own desires and says that there is neither a resurrection nor a judgment is the first-born of Satan" (7:1). The notion of "perverting the sayings of the Lord" is very similar, if not identical, to the charges leveled by the author of 1 John that the opponents "are progressive and do not remain in the teaching of the Christ." It is also consistent with the notion of not "keeping the word of Jesus" in the sense that they do not remain faithful to the (historical) words of Jesus.

Moreover, when we turn to the specific content of the perverted teaching of Polycarp's opponents, we see that they had a one-sided understanding of realized eschatology (as had the opponents in 1 John) claiming that there is no resurrection of the body and no final judgment. Such a claim is entirely consistent with a reading of John 5:24 without vv. 27-29. In fact, this interpretation of John 5:24 is all the more plausible when it is viewed in the light of the modification by the author of the third edition in John 5:27-29, where the entire purpose of the verses is to stress the reality of a physical resurrection from the tombs on the last day and the reality of a resurrection to life and *to judgment.*[56] Moreover, when Polycarp calls such a person the "first-born of Satan" *(prototokos tou Satana)* he echoes 1 John 3:10 and is close to the apocalyptic language of the third edition of the Gospel (John 8:44).

Polycarp then urges his readers at Philippi to "turn back to the word handed down to us from the beginning." Here he is once again very "Johannine" in his exhortation, for it is precisely the accusation of the author of 1 John that the opponents do not keep the word of Jesus — and it is also the position of the third author that the Spirit will not speak on his own but will take from what belongs to Jesus. Moreover, Polycarp urges his readers to look to what was "from the beginning" just as both the author of 1 John and the third Gospel author do.[57]

As was the case with Ignatius, Polycarp's references to the errors of the false teachers are brief and unsystematic. Also, when compared with the comments of Ignatius, we see that those of Polycarp do not describe the same range of problems as Ignatius confronted. However, although his account is brief,

---

56. In 1 John, there is no discussion of bodily resurrection. That is an element of the tradition that is first articulated in the third edition of the Gospel. By the time of Polycarp, the full extent of the disagreement was made clear and so the reference to belief in physical resurrection is appropriate.

57. Polycarp then turns to a series of exhortations made up of references to both Matthew and Paul regarding the need to watch in prayer and fasting lest the believer fall into temptation because the flesh is weak.

Polycarp speaks entirely of errors similar to those being faced by the Johannine community, even if they are articulated differently than was done by Ignatius. Moreover, Polycarp uses uniquely Johannine language in his discussion.

That Polycarp makes reference to the fact that the opponents do not believe in either resurrection or judgment indicates that at the time of his writing, such topics had become explicit issues. This reflects a period similar to that found in the third edition of the Gospel. Thus, Polycarp too would appear to reflect a period after that of 1 and 2 John. That he himself was a bishop also indicates a period later than that of 3 John and similar to that of Ignatius.

That Ignatius was writing *to* Smyrna and Polycarp was the bishop of Smyrna and was writing *from* Smyrna is curious. That Smyrna is so close to Ephesus, the traditional location of the Johannine community (in its later stages), is also striking. Yet Polycarp was writing to a community in Philippi, a considerable distance from Smyrna.

Reference was made earlier to the uncertainty regarding the date of Polycarp's letter. If it was written before the death of Ignatius, the two letters would have been written within perhaps a year of one another. Then Polycarp's letter could reflect yet a fifth stage in the trajectory of the theological crisis that is first addressed by 1 and 2 John. In any event, it seems reasonable to conclude that both authors confronted somewhat later manifestations of the positions held by the opponents of the author of 1 and 2 John.

APPENDIX 5

The Johannine Commandments in the Letters and in the Third Edition of the Gospel

A. INTRODUCTION

The theology of "commandment" is an important but an inadequately under-stood aspect of Johannine theology. Because of that, some summary observations may help us gain a fresh view of just what these commandments are and how they relate to the situation of the community at the time they were formulated.

The Johannine commandments first appear in the pages of 1 and 2 John. There they are spoken of as commandments *of God* given to the believer. The tradition is then taken over by the author of the third edition of the Gospel who expands the tradition by speaking first of two commandments given *to Jesus by the Father* and then of two commandments given *to the disciples by Jesus*. While scholarship has readily recognized the existence of the "second" Johannine commandment (the commandment of mutual love), there has been much greater reluctance to recognize what I would term the "first" commandment, the commandment that concerns proper belief.

In order to understand this element of the Johannine tradition ade-quately, I have chosen to treat the commandments in the Letters and in the third edition of the Gospel in a single appendix.[1]

*   *   *

In the Johannine tradition, "commandment(s)" never refers to the Decalogue, even though several aspects of its background appear to be shaped by the

---

1. The Love Commandment is also treated in Vol. 1, 3E-15. There the focus is on the con-ceptualization of "love" within the dualistic framework of apocalyptic. The background of that conception is also discussed there.

Deuteronomic tradition. The Johannine Jesus never refers to the Ten Commandments. Nor does he refer to what is known as "the Great Commandment" as such. While the Johannine Jesus speaks of loving God and of loving one's fellow human beings, the first of these is never identified as a commandment and the second is defined in a particularly Johannine way. For the Johannine tradition, "the commandments" take on a new meaning. They have a new content and a new frame of reference. Why this is so and how it could be will be explored below.

The most difficult aspect of the Johannine commandment tradition is the nature and formulation of the "first"[2] commandment. However, as we will see in this appendix, in spite of the peculiar variety of ways in which this first commandment is formulated, when the commandment tradition is viewed as a whole and when it is viewed within the overall context of 1 John and of the third edition, its existence and its identity cannot be denied even if the reasons for its puzzling formulation remain uncertain.

A detailed exegesis of the passages dealing with the commandments has been provided in the relevant passages of 1 John and of the third edition of the Gospel. Here we will draw together these observations as a way of clarifying the Johannine commandment tradition as a whole.

B. THE TWO JOHANNINE COMMANDMENTS IN THE LETTERS

The theology of the commandments in the Letters consists of several features that occur consistently whenever the commandments are discussed. First, throughout 1 John as well as 2 John, there is a clear indication that the author understands there to be a plurality of commandments. Second, each general exhortation to obey the commandments (plural) is followed by another exhortation in which attention is directed to one particular commandment. Third, this single commandment is then identified specifically either as dealing with correct belief or with correct behavior. Finally, the commandments are consistently identified as being "of God."

---

2. The designation of these commandments as "first" and "second" refers only to the order of their appearance in 1 John, where they are articulated initially.

C. THE COMMANDMENT TEXTS IN THE LETTERS

1. 1 John 2:3-11

This is the first of the passages dealing with the commandments in 1 John. It is a complicated passage made more difficult by the literary techniques of the author. The major problem is that the author interweaves his discussion of commandment with a discussion of three claims regarding the possession of eschatological gifts of the Spirit. Because of this, the phrasing is awkward and confusing and thus could make it appear that "word" is simply a synonym for "commandment" *(dabar)*. Some argue that the author is actually speaking only about the love commandment. We have discussed these problems in detail in the Commentary and will not repeat that discussion here. Rather, I will only summarize in order to show the pattern of usage that results from the interpretation arrived at in the Commentary.

The passage begins (v. 3) with the statement that we are sure we know God if we keep his commandments. But (v. 4) the one who claims to know God but does not keep his commandments is a liar. To this point, the focus has been on the first of the claims to eschatological gifts and on a way to test the truth of a person's claims. Thus, a person cannot claim to know God and yet not keep his commandments. Then, in v. 5, the author speaks of "the one who keeps his [God's] word." In this person, the love of God is brought to perfection. Keeping the word of God is a sure way to know if the person loves God.[3] And then the author suddenly adds: "In this we know that we are 'in him,'" thus introducing a second, distinct claim.

Now (in v. 6) the author addresses the matter of a second claim (to be "in him") and also introduces a test for the validity of this claim also. Again, the test is a matter of something external that can show that the claim is valid. Up to this point, the author has spoken of keeping *God's* word, not *Jesus'* word. At the time of 1 John, the opponents would have no problem thinking that they kept God's word; it was only the permanence of Jesus' word that they found problematic. Consequently, in v. 6, the author tests the validity of this second claim by acceptance of the activity of Jesus. He does so by saying that the person who makes this claim must walk as Jesus walked. That is to say, what God wants of humanity is demonstrated and defined in the life of Jesus. The author then returns to the notion of commandment (which he had introduced three verses earlier!) and explains that this commandment is one that they have had from the beginning. This is intended to anchor the commandment in the ministry of Jesus and to distinguish it from the "pneumatic" teaching put forward by the

---

3. Keeping the commandments is also a sure way to know that one is loved by God, but that aspect of the issue is not in focus here.

opponents. He then explains (elliptically) that "(t)his 'old' commandment is (to keep) the word that you heard." We have explained in the Commentary proper why "word" here cannot be a synonym for "commandment" but must be an elliptical reference to keeping the word of God in Jesus. Thus, no longer can one claim to keep the word of God without keeping the word of Jesus.

The author goes on to say that it is also possible to speak of the commandment as "new." It is not "new" in the sense that it goes beyond the word of Jesus, but in the sense that it has come to reality just recently in the ministry of Jesus. The taking away of the darkness began in Jesus and is being realized in those disciples who follow Jesus. The true light is already shining, but it shines only in Jesus. With these words, the author introduces the third eschatological claim, to be in the light.

Then in v. 9, the author addresses this third claim and again introduces a test for the claim. One can tell whether a person is "in the light" by whether the person loves one's brother. Failure to love one's brother indicates one is not truly in the light. This "second" commandment (although it is not identified as such here) is related to the first in that such loving behavior is a result of the knowledge and light that come from keeping the word of God. Thus, the author ends by using correct love as a test of correct belief.

As was said at the beginning, this is a complicated passage and made more complex by the fact that it seeks not only to speak of the commandment to keep the word of Jesus but also to address and test three distinct eschatological claims. Tracing the complete logic of the verses is difficult. Yet, from the focus on "keeping the word" of God, and the repeated references to the new/old commandment and to the identification of the word with commandment and with the embodiment of word in Jesus, the overall meaning of the commandment is discernible in spite of the complexities.

2. 1 John 3:21-24

In 1 John 3:22-23, we see one of the clearest references to the two commandments, together with a specification of each. However, it is not until one is aware of the chiastic arrangement of the material, that the consistency of the presentation can be fully appreciated. In keeping with the chiastic arrangement, we see, first, a general exhortation expressed in the plural. This is followed by a specification of the "first" commandment. This, in turn, is followed by the specification of a "second" commandment, and this, finally, is followed by a general exhortation in the plural. (The chiastic arrangement is diagrammed in the Translation of the verses in 3:19-24.)

In some ways, this passage is paradigmatic for the presentation of the commandments in the Letters. We see that the author first speaks of the commandments in the plural and then in the singular. When he speaks of commandment in the singular, he specifies a particular commandment. That this is a deliberate pattern is evident from the fact that, in the second half of the passage, the pattern is the same but the order is reversed since it appears in a chiasm. We also notice that there are references to two specific commandments: one dealing with proper belief and the other dealing with proper behavior. Finally, we notice that these are identified as commandments "of God," as is typical in the Letters. Here the theology of commandment is clear, as is the existence of *two* Johannine commandments. At the same time, the formulation of the first commandment is not precisely the same as in the first passage, yet both clearly deal with correct belief and that correct belief essentially involves Jesus (cf. 2:6, 8b in the passage above).

3. 1 John 4:21–5:5

In the two previous passages we have examined, we have seen that both the commandments of correct belief and correct love are mentioned together. In the first passage (2:3-11), correct love is a test of correct belief. In the second, the two are described individually but in parallel form to one another. Now, in the third passage, we will see that again the two commandments are theologically intertwined. We will also see that the author has arranged much of his argument chiastically (5:1-5).[4] This will help in understanding the argument.

As was the case with the previous passages, the details are given in the Notes and Interpretation, and here we will give only a summary. Chapter 4:21 is the last of three brief statements all of which reinforce the conviction that one cannot love God without loving one's brother. What makes 4:21 different is that loving one's brother is now identified as a commandment. This is an unequivocal statement of the "second" Johannine commandment. Then, using this principle as his base, the author begins a complicated argument that deals not directly with love of the brothers but with proper faith.

The author begins by bringing up the case of "everyone believing that Jesus is the Christ." While he will continue to speak of this person, it should be noticed how clearly this is paralleled by the last element of the chiasm ("the one believing that Jesus is the Son of God"). Thus, the two outermost elements deal with the issue of correct faith and indeed incorporate the two primary confessions of correct belief in the Letter and in the tradition as a whole.

In the second element of the chiasm (5:1b-2a), the author makes use of catchwords to further his argument. He begins by using the correct confession of Jesus as an indication that one is "begotten" *(gegennētai)* of God. He then reminds his reader that everyone who loves "the begetter" *(ton gennēsanta)* (that

---

4. The chiasm is illustrated in the text of the Translation.

is, God) should love "the begotten" *(ton gegennēmenon)* (that is, the "brother" who confesses properly). But then he reverses the logic of his argument and says that we know that we love the brothers when we love God — and keep his commandments.[5] Next, in the central element of the chiasm, the author again takes up the topic of what constitutes love of God, but he does not provide the actual definition until the following element of the chiasm. There the author continues his use of "definition" and "reverse logic" and takes this argument one step further by identifying "loving God" with keeping the commandments, "which are not burdensome."[6]

Then, in the second-to-last element of the chiasm, the author returns to a focus on the one begotten of God *(gegennēmenon)* and says that person conquers the world. He next defines this conquest by saying "and this is the conquest that conquered the world: our faith." And in the last element of the chiasm, he continues his definition of what "faith" consists in while at the same time returning to the topic at the very beginning of the chiasm: Who is the one conquering the world except the one believing that Jesus is the Son of God?

Thus, once again the author has provided an interplay between the necessity of proper belief and the necessity of mutual love. Yet it will be noticed that the author has not identified either proper belief or proper love specifically as a "commandment" within the chiasm itself.[7] Rather, he has kept the discussion of commandments general, but there can be no doubt that he intends to refer to both proper love and proper belief. By doing so in a context where the material is arranged chiastically, he has shown how the distribution of the material confirms the focus on the two discrete commandments and their distinct content but in the end how mutual love can serve the overall end of love of God and of correct faith.[8]

4. 2 John 4-6

In 2 John vv. 4-6, we meet yet another of the author's chiasms. This chiasm also is of considerable help in understanding the meaning of the passage.[9] Here the

---

5. In the barest of terms, the argument runs: "If we love God, we should love the brothers. And we can tell that we love the brothers if we love God."

6. Note that in v. 1b the author had said that the one who loves God should love the brothers; now he says that the one who loves God should keep his commandments.

7. He had identified mutual love as a commandment in 4:21.

8. Just as in 2:3-11 proper belief was identified as a commandment and proper love was spoken of but not specifically identified as a commandment, here the reverse is true. In 4:21, proper love is identified as a commandment but the proper belief spoken of throughout is not although its relation to proper love is essential and clear.

9. The passage is also discussed in von Wahlde, "Foundation." It is illustrated in the Translation of the verses within the Commentary proper.

author begins by expressing joy that he has found some of his readers "walking in truth," as they had received a commandment. This is the commandment to proper belief.[10] Then he begins to speak of mutual love, a commandment that they have had "from the beginning." Then in a clear (but stiff and awkward) chaining, the author explains that this love is manifest in walking in the commandments and then he defines the commandment as that they should walk "in it." Although "it" is grammatically ambiguous, the chiastic arrangement is one of several indications that "it" here refers to walking in the truth, as is explained in detail in the Commentary.[11]

Thus, we see a complex passage in which the author enlists the commandment of love as a support for the commandment to walk in the truth. This commandment to walk in the truth is then the foundation for the author's argument (in the remainder of the Letter) about proper confession of Jesus as "come in the flesh" and about avoidance of those who "go beyond" and do not remain in the teaching of the Christ (v. 9).

As was the case in the prior passage (1 John 5:1-5), the center of the chiasm hinges on a definition of love. In the prior chiasm the love mentioned was love *of God;* here the love referred to is *mutual* love. And also, as was the case in the prior chiasm, the author moves from the specifics of mutual love to the general exhortation to keep the commandments and then back again to the specifics of correct belief. Thus, he once again shows that it is not really possible for a person to love properly without believing properly.

Noteworthy as well is the fact that here we see yet a third phrasing of the author's convictions about correct belief: they are to "walk in truth."

10. Lieu (*Second and Third* 72) rejects the plain sense of the verse when she denies that the commandment is "to walk in truth." Instead, she claims "that it [presumably the commandment] epitomized the Johannine tradition to which they were faithful. She calls attention to a verbal echo of 10:18 although the commandment there is that Jesus will lay down his life out of love. But see her comments associating "keeping the word" with "keeping the commandments" (*Epistles* 178-79).

Brown (*Epistles* 682-83) is closer when he says: "Plausibly he is speaking of a general attitude, involving both belief and behavior. . . ." It is precisely belief and behavior that are the two objects of the two Johannine commandments. But they are not blended together. This is clear from the Gospel, where (in the third edition) Jesus is given two commandments by the Father: what to do (10:18) and what to say (12:50). The disciples then are to "walk in the truth" of what Jesus had said "from the beginning."

11. That "it" refers to the commandment to walk in truth is further indicated by the fact that he next addresses issues of false belief (that Jesus did not come in the flesh), and that the opponents are not remaining in the teaching of the Christ and that the remainder of the Letter continues to deal with issues of correct teaching.

5. Other References to the Two Commandments in the Letters

These four passages constitute the primary discussion of the commandments in the Letters. Yet, as is obvious even to the casual reader, there are numerous other references to proper belief beyond those few instances where it is spoken of as the object of a commandment. Thus, the other references to having the word in them (1:10; 2:14), to proper confession of Jesus (e.g., 2:22, 24; 4:2, 14, 15; 5:10), to the necessity of "having" Jesus (e.g., 2:23; 5:12; cf. 1:3), and to believing in the name of Jesus (e.g., 5:13) all speak of *the content* of the commandment without explicit references to *the term* "commandment" itself.

The same is true of the topic of mutual love. Although the author at times identifies mutual love as a commandment, he will make even more references to the importance of mutual love without specifically identifying such love as a "commandment." Such passages are numerous (e.g., 2:9-11; 3:14-17; 4:7, 11-12, 19-20; cf. 3 John 5-8). Thus, we see the centrality of these two topics not only in passages where they are labeled as the object of a commandment but also within the general content of the Letters.

6. Conclusions Regarding the Commandments in the Letters

We can now summarize our conclusions regarding the commandments in the Letters.

First, although initially puzzling, the use of the singular and plural of "commandment" is consistent. The plural is used in general exhortation and it is usually followed by a specification of the commandment that the author is thinking of, either the first or second of the Johannine commandments.

Second, there are two commandments in the tradition, and both of them are said to have been part of the tradition "from the beginning." The first commandment has to do with proper belief and the second has to do with proper behavior, behavior that is understood in the broadest of senses to be concerned with acting out of love.

Third, the content of each of the commandments is expressed in a variety of ways. Individual articulations of the first commandment may vary but all center on the notion of proper belief. The articulation of the first commandment in 2 John is perhaps the most general: the believer is to "walk in truth" (2 John 4ab, 6cd). In 1 John 3:23ab it is expressed as believing "in the name of his Son Jesus Christ." That is, their belief in God is to be that belief which is defined by the message "of his Son Jesus Christ." In 1 John 2:5-8, the commandment is defined most diffusely. In v. 5, the obligation is expressed as "keeping the word of God." In v. 7 (where the singular of the term commandment appears), it is simply defined as the word, but it is the word that has come to be realized in Jesus. Because of the orientation of 1 John to God (rather than to Jesus), it is specified here as keeping the word *of God* but it is the word manifest in *Jesus*.

Being faithful to the truth and keeping to the teaching of "the Christ" and the teaching that they have had from the beginning (as the remainder of 2 John explains) is the same as keeping the word that they have received from God through the Christ (1 John 2:3-11). Finally, in 3:21-24 we see this correct belief from another very specific perspective: that it should be in the name of Jesus Christ.

The second Johannine commandment is also expressed in a variety of ways. Thus, one is commanded to "love one's brother" (2:10; 3:10, 14; 4:20, 21), to "love one another" (1 John 3:11, 23; 4:7, 11, 12; 2 John 5), and to "love the children of God" (1 John 5:2). In the majority of cases, the exhortation is to mutual love, whereas in other cases the focus is primarily on the giving of love without concern for whether the love is returned. This variety is similar to, although certainly not as great as, the alternation found in the articulation of the first Johannine commandment. Yet it is sufficient that major commentators such as Brown, Schnackenburg, and Strecker have felt the need to affirm the identity explicitly.[12]

It is readily recognizable that the texts dealing with this first commandment are always put somewhat obliquely while the texts dealing with the love command are relatively straightforward. Two comments may help explain why this is so. First, although the articulation of the commandments is varied, the fact that the texts are dealing with various aspects of belief is patently clear. Second, if this is true, the problem may then lie in the author's attempts to develop a consistent way of expressing the content of this commandment with the precision demanded by the context. It may be that 1 John reveals the first attempt to articulate the content of the commandments. In doing so, both commandments are given alternate formulations. However, as we shall see below, by the time of the third edition, it would seem that the formulation had been settled and there is less variety.

We have repeatedly called attention to the fact that, although there are a variety of specific issues about which the author and his opponents disagree, they can be grouped — and in fact are grouped by the author — under the two major headings of "belief" and "behavior." In Chart E-6, I have summarized twelve ways in which the author makes both of these issues the basis for various claims and prerogatives. Here I point out that the two commandments constitute the eleventh and twelfth elements in this list. One commandment deals with belief and the second deals with correct behavior. Thus, there is also a correlation between the commandment tradition in the Letters and the primary,

---

12. Brown, *Epistles* 441; Schnackenburg, *Epistles* 178; Strecker, *Epistles* 107.

overarching themes of the Letter. This is an additional confirmation of the number and content of the two commandments, and it is an additional indication that the problem concerns not whether there is a commandment dealing with belief but our inability to know why the author chose to articulate it in the way he did.

D. THE TWO JOHANNINE COMMANDMENTS IN THE THIRD EDITION OF THE GOSPEL

The third edition of the Gospel takes up the commandment tradition from the Letters, but develops it somewhat and puts it in a larger framework. As we shall see, the third author speaks, for the first time, of two commandments given to Jesus by the Father. Moreover, the author also speaks of two commandments given to the disciples by Jesus. Finally, as we shall see, the commandments given to the disciples are directly related to and are correlates of the two commandments given to Jesus.

1. The Commandments Given to Jesus

a. The First Commandment: What to Say and What to Speak

In the third edition, there is a single text (12:46-50) that speaks of the first commandment given to Jesus by the Father, but the meaning of the text is quite clear.[13] At the close of his public ministry, for a final time Jesus describes his words in relation to the light, to judgment, and to their source in the Father. He ends by explaining (vv. 49-50): ". . . because I do not speak of myself, but the Father who sent me has himself given me a commandment what to say and what to speak. And I know that his commandment is eternal life. Therefore, those things that I say, I say just as the Father told me." The meaning of this text is patently clear: Jesus has received a commandment about "what to say and speak." As we can imagine, in the light of such a commandment what to say and speak, there is surely an obligation upon the disciples to hear and remain faithful to what Jesus says. That will be the third author's equivalent of the first Johannine commandment as it appeared in 1 John.

---

13. The fact that the discussion of this first commandment appears only once is an indication that it represents what Brown would call "a minor motif." This in itself is an indication that it may have been added by an editor. When the passage as a whole is analyzed in terms of the characteristics of the third edition, it becomes overwhelmingly clear that the material is that of the third author.

b. The Commandment of Love

In 10:15b-18, Jesus speaks of himself as the good shepherd who is willing to lay down his life for his sheep. No one takes his life from him; he lays it down of his own accord. In the end, Jesus explains: "I received this commandment from my Father" (v. 18). There is no explicit mention of love on the part of Jesus in this passage.[14]

However, that the laying down of Jesus' life is an act of love for his own is patently clear from 15:13 where Jesus says: "No one has greater love than this, that a person lay down his life for his friends." Moreover, later, when Jesus speaks of the commandment that the disciples love one another, he presents himself as the model of love for them when he says: "Just as I loved you, you should love one another" (13:34). Thus, the commandment that Jesus lay down his life is understood as a demonstration of his love for his own.

2. The Commandments Given to the Disciples

a. The Commandment to Keep the Word of Jesus (John 14:15, 21, 23-26)

In the Gospel, the commandments intended for the disciples are made explicit within the Farewell Discourses. This is appropriate since it is in keeping with the testamentary form as the place for Jesus' final, intimate instruction to the disciples. In content, the first commandment given to the disciples by Jesus parallels the first commandment given to Jesus by the Father: the disciples are to keep the word of Jesus, the word that Jesus was commanded to speak.

In a way similar to the presentation of the first commandment in 1 John, the presentation here is somewhat contorted. Yet when the discussion is done, it must be concluded that the problem is not that there is no commandment being discussed, but rather that the third author has interwoven the discussion of commandments with material from the second edition. However, when the material of the third edition is isolated, the direction of the discussion becomes clearer. First, there is the general statement (v. 15) that, if a disciple truly loves Jesus, he will keep Jesus' commandments. This is repeated in v. 21. Then in v. 23, the love of Jesus (which is already said to be shown in the keeping of the commandments) is now specified as "keeping my word." Thus, loving Jesus is expressed generally in keeping the commandments and specifically in keeping the word of Jesus. Next, Jesus asserts the negative of that statement: the one who

---

14. There is, however, an *implication* of love of the Father (as well as the Father's love of Jesus) in that Jesus' keeping of the commandments is a demonstration of his love for the Father. This is also clear from 14:31.

does not love me, does not keep my word. Then Jesus goes on to remind the disciple that the word that he speaks is not his own but the word of the Father who sent him (and the very word that Jesus had been commanded to speak [12:49]). Viewed in this light, the logic of the argument is manifest and the specification of the commandment as "to keep the word of Jesus" is also clear. As Lieu comments: "The call to discipleship therefore is a call to abide in Jesus' word, or to keep his word. In the Farewell Discourses 'keeping Jesus' word' (texts) is used in parallel to 'keeping Jesus' commands' . . . , but more than obedience to specific injunctions is in mind. . . ."[15]

b. The Commandment of Mutual Love

The second commandment given to the disciples receives two treatments in the Gospel, a first (brief) treatment in 13:34-35 and a more extensive one in 15:9-17.

In 13:34-35, the meaning is concise and clear: "A new commandment I give you, that, as I loved you, you also should love one another. In this, all will know that you are my disciples if you have love for one another." Although brief, this statement is clear and provides a detail that relates the statement to the statement in 1 John (2:7). In 1 John, the author was intent to show that the commandments were injunctions that they had from the beginning of the tradition and not something "new" that was a later addition to the community's tradition. However, here, the third author makes it clear that from the perspective of the ministry, the commandment *is* "new" because Jesus is just now giving it to them and because his giving of his life, which is the model of love for the disciples, is about to take place.

However, the second commandment receives its primary treatment two chapters later, in 15:9-17. As has been consistent throughout the Letters and the Gospel,[16] the third author begins his presentation (vv. 9-11) with a general exhortation to keep the commandments (plural). Then, in v. 12, he is explicit about the specific commandment he will address: "This is my commandment, that you love one another as I loved you." Jesus then goes on to elaborate various aspects of this commandment and then concludes in v. 17 by saying: "These things I command you: Love one another."

15. Lieu, *Second and Third* 178.
16. With the exception of the statement in 13:34-35 where the treatment appeared in truncated form.

E. SOME FINAL OBSERVATIONS REGARDING THE
JOHANNINE COMMANDMENT TRADITION

We may now briefly summarize, in a final way, the presentation of the commandments in the Letters and the third edition of the Gospel, calling attention to both the differences and to the similarities in their respective presentations. We will begin with the differences.

First, we have seen that the articulation of the first commandment (regarding correct belief) in the third edition of the Gospel is less varied than it is in the Letters. In the third edition, the first commandment is confined to speaking (on the part of Jesus) the word of God and to keeping Jesus' word (on the part of the disciples).

Likewise, the articulation of the second commandment in the third edition is described without the variant expressions found in 1 John. In the third edition, Jesus is said to lay down his life "for his own" and the disciples are commanded to "love one another." These expressions were found in 1 John, but the second commandment is not expressed as "loving one's brother" or "loving the children of God" as it is in 1 John.

Finally, in the third edition, the presentation is more complex inasmuch as there is discussion of both the commandments given to Jesus and the commandments given to the disciples. But at the same time the correlation between those given to Jesus and those given to the disciples indicates that there is no *essential* difference between the attribution of the commandments in the Letters and the Gospel. This is because both commandments ultimately go back to the Father.[17]

But if the differences are evident, the similarities are equally clear. First, there are two commandments in both the Letters and in the third edition of the Gospel. Second, it is also clear that the two commandments presented in the third edition of the Gospel are the same as those presented in the Letters, except that there is less fluidity of expression in the third edition. Third, both the Letters and the third edition of the Gospel exhibit the same pattern of the use of the plural in general exhortation and follow this with the discussion of a specific commandment.[18]

Finally, the purpose of the commandments is the same in both 1 John and

17. At this point, it is also easy to see that this theology of commandment was meant to be comprehensive in that it dealt with all areas of the believer's life, both belief and behavior. Once this is realized, it is clear how the description of the ministry of Jesus as a response to commandments given by the Father parallels and contains its own complex of ideas distinct from the complex of ideas that surround the theology of "work" that is used to characterize the ministry of Jesus in the second edition.

18. Again this is with the understandable exception of John 13:34-35.

in the third edition of the Gospel. They are to affirm the permanent validity of the words of Jesus and they are to affirm the importance of mutual love as the root of all proper conduct. Thus, we see that there is a development within the commandment tradition from its appearance in the Letters to its appearance in the Gospel. But this is a harmonious development rather than one in tension with that of the Letters. Indeed, it shows that the third author sought to base the community's understanding of the commandment tradition, not only on the word of Jesus, but on the actions of God toward Jesus, thus providing a broader and more fully developed background.

We have seen repeatedly that both of these commandments are directly related to the two central issues of the community's internal crisis and consequently take on an importance they would not otherwise have. Yet we have also seen that the first of these commandments is the more difficult to recognize. Part of this difficulty in seeing the specific meaning of the phrase "keep the word" (of God, of Jesus) is that, unless it is associated with the particular circumstances of the community at the time of its internal crisis, this terminology can easily be understood as only a general reference to the need for belief. However, when seen in the context of the community's internal crisis, it becomes clear that "to keep the word of Jesus" means to remain faithful to the belief that was expressed in and through Jesus. In this sense, it is a major issue of the community, expressed in a variety of ways but all centering on the essential importance of what Jesus said during his ministry.

Thus, it is a word that they have heard "from the beginning," a word associated with what they heard and saw and touched in the ministry (1 John 1:1-4). It is not a new message, claiming to be Spirit-inspired, yet differing from the original message of Jesus. The third author also makes it clear that what the Paraclete says will not be different from what Jesus said. The Paraclete will "remind you of all things that I have told you" (14:26). ". . . (He) will not speak on his own but will speak whatever he hears" (16:13). "That one [the Paraclete] will glorify me because he will take from what is mine and will proclaim it to you" (16:14). Thus, those who keep the word of Jesus will not be like those who are "progressive" and who do "not remain in the teaching of the Christ."

It is these two commandments, first articulated by the author of 1 John, that are incorporated into the third edition of the Gospel and given a broader foundation by associating them with the commandments given to Jesus. Thus, the foundation for the teaching regarding correct belief and correct love is built not only on Jesus but also on the very desires of God.

F. A PARALLEL TO THE JOHANNINE COMMANDMENTS IN THE "DOUBLE SCRUTINY" AT QUMRAN

In the light of our analysis of the Johannine commandments, it is evident that they are not simply a rephrasing of the two Great Commandments of the Old Testament and Synoptic traditions (Mark 12:28-34; Matt 22:34-40; Luke 10:25-29). It is true that the second Johannine commandment could be seen as a variant of the second Great Commandment, namely to love one's neighbor (as derived from Lev 19:18). But it is also clear that the "first" Johannine commandment, which is concerned with correct belief, is not at all a variant of the first of the two Great Commandments as derived from Deut 6:4-5. The first of the Great Commandments is to love God with all one's heart and is concerned with encapsulating all of the responsibilities due to God, just as the second Great Commandment encapsulates all of the responsibilities due to one's fellow human beings. However, the first of the Johannine commandments is concerned with proper belief.

Rather the Johannine commandments find their closest parallel in the "double scrutiny" from Qumran. This scrutiny, which appears several places in 1QS, is concerned precisely and explicitly with the areas of correct belief and correct behavior. We have also seen throughout our study that many of the concepts and the worldview of 1 John were closely paralleled in the SDQ as well as in the *T12P.* It should be no surprise, then, to find that the way the issues could be summarized in terms of correct belief and correct action would also find parallels in the SDQ, specifically in 1QS.

At Qumran, such an examination of one's understanding of the community's rules and of one's behavior was not only part of the initiation process of the community but was also an element in the annual review of the member.[19] The "double scrutiny" focuses on the same two types of issues as were raised throughout 1 John (Chart E-6) and which are symbolized by "light" and "love" in the structure of 1 John, and by the commandments in the Johannine tradition, namely correct belief (understanding) and correct action (deeds). In 1QS 5:20-24, we read:

> But when a man enters the Covenant to walk according to all these precepts that he may join the holy congregation, they shall examine his spirit in community with respect to his *understanding* and *practice* of the Law, under the authority of the sons of Aaron who have freely pledged themselves in the community to restore His Covenant and to heed all the precepts commanded by Him, and of the multitude of Israel who have freely pledged

---

19. For more on the double scrutiny at Qumran, see the Addendum to 1:5–2:2 in the Commentary on 1 John, regarding possible sacramental references in that section.

themselves in the Community to return to His Covenant. They shall inscribe them in the order, one after another, according to *their understanding* and *their deeds,* that every one may obey his companion, the man of lesser rank obeying his superior. And they shall examine *their spirit* and *deeds* yearly, so that each man may be advanced in accordance with *his understanding* and *perfection of way,* or moved down in accordance with the offenses committed by him. *(CDSSE)*

In 1QS 6:13-23, we also read about the examination of the one who would enter the community and also about the yearly review of the individual. As was described above, in both cases the individual is evaluated according to his understanding of the Law as interpreted by the community and also according to his behavior.

Every man, born of Israel, who freely pledges himself to join the Council of the Community, shall be examined by the Guardian at the head of the Congregation concerning *his understanding* and *his deeds.* If he is fitted to the discipline, he shall admit him into the Covenant that he may be converted to the truth and depart from all falsehood; and he shall instruct him in all the rules of the community. And later, when he comes to stand before the Congregation they shall all deliberate his case, and according to the decision of the Council of the Congregation he shall either enter or depart. After he has entered the council of the Community, he shall not touch the pure Meal of the Congregation until one full year is completed, and until he has been examined concerning *his spirit* and *deeds;* nor shall he have any share of the property of the Congregation. Then when he has completed one year within the Community, the Congregation shall deliberate his case with respect to his *understanding* and *observance* of the Law. And if it be in his destiny, according to the judgment of the Priests and the multitude of the men of their Covenant, to enter the company of the community, his property and earnings shall be handed over to the Bursar of the Congregation. . . . (1QS 6:13-20 [*CDSSE*])

The parallels between the two basic categories of concern for the author of 1 John and the two areas of scrutiny at Qumran are unmistakable, and, while this is not to say that the Johannine community borrowed this scrutiny from the Essenes, it does establish that such concerns for belief and practice were common in determining membership within Jewish groups in the first century.

Formal Elements in Greek Letter Writing and in 2 and 3 John

The Second and Third Letters of John are true letters. As such they exhibit elements common in secular letter writing of the ancient world. By comparing the Johannine Letters with secular examples, we are able to recognize the extent to which the Johannine Letters reflect those elements and so interpret the Letters more adequately.

There were a considerable variety of letter types in the ancient world but the one that most closely parallels the Johannine Letters is the so-called "documentary," or "personal" letter.[1] In recent decades, this form of letter has been the object of extensive study. The result has been an understanding of the formal characteristics typical of such letters. In the past, there has been something of a tendency for scholars to focus on the Pauline Letters and to treat the Johannine Letters as a development of the Pauline Letter tradition and so to explain the Johannine Letters by comparison with them.[2] While such a com-

---

1. A considerable number of letters have been preserved from the ancient world. Some come from Greco-Roman literature, others, the Oxyrhynchus papyri, were found in Egypt in the late 1800s. There are also letters preserved in the OT (esp. 1 and 2 Maccabees) and in the NT (not only the documents labeled as letters but also letters embedded in other documents (for example, in Acts 15:23-29; 23:26-30 and in Rev 2:1–3:22) and the correspondence of Simon bar-Kokhba from caves near the Dead Sea. Letters appear in a variety of forms in the ancient world. There are, for example, diplomatic, administrative, official, literary and the common letter tradition composed of business and personal letters. Here we are concerned only with the form of the personal letter. See White, "Epistolary" 1732-33.

2. This is something of the approach of White ("Epistolary"), whose primary focus is the Pauline Letter tradition. Although White does recognize the direct influence of the secular tradition on NT letters (1752, also 1755-56), he speaks of "Paul's influence upon NT epistolography" (1753, cf. 1752-55). It seems reasonable to suppose Pauline influence on the pseudo-Pauline Letters, but that there is an "influence" on the Johannine tradition would be difficult to establish, I think.

Brown, in his Excursus on Epistolary Format (*Epistles* 788-95), also tends to compare the

parison has its value, here we will study the form of the Johannine Letters on its own and in direct comparison with the form of the secular letter as it is known from extant examples. We do not know that the Johannine author was familiar with the Pauline Letter tradition or that he used it as a model. Moreover, as we shall see, the Johannine Letters manifest features that appear nowhere in the Pauline tradition but that are common in secular letters. Likewise, they lack features common to the Pauline tradition. This suggests that the Johannine Letter form came to be independently from that of the Pauline tradition.

A. LENGTH

The length of letters varied considerably in antiquity and so no standard length can be said to exist.[3] The length of the two Johannine Letters was probably determined by the size of a single sheet of papyrus. They are the shortest in the New Testament and contain only 245 and 219 words respectively.

B. THE OPENING FORMULA

The opening formula of an ancient letter typically contained three elements: the name of the sender, the name of the addressee (in the dative case) and a greeting. The opening formula in such matters was "'X' to 'Y', greetings."[4]

The opening formula in 2 John 1-2 reflects this form but is considerably expanded by the description added in vv. 1-2. The Third Letter of John does not have a word of greeting but simply: "The Elder to Gaius." Lieu points out that 3 John is the only New Testament letter, among those with prescripts, that does not have either a form of Pauline greeting or the simple "greetings" *(chairein).*[5]

Johannine Letters with the Pauline rather than directly with secular letters although examples from secular letters are also given. Lieu and Funk focus more directly on comparisons with the secular tradition.

3. The average length of the letters of Cicero, the Roman orator, is 331 words. For Pliny, the average is 175; for Seneca, 956. To some extent, length was determined by purpose. The letters of Seneca and Paul are primarily didactic and that accounts for the fact that they exceed the average (White, "Epistolary" 1739). At the same time, the length of Paul's Letters, which were also primarily didactic, varies from that of Romans (7101 words) to Philemon (335 words). The statistics are from Roller, *Formular.*

4. This does not appear in any of the letters of the NT except that of James and in two letters reported in Acts (cf. 15:23; 23:26). Paul normally uses "Paul to 'X', grace to you and peace. . . ."

5. So Lieu, *Second and Third* 46. See also Mullins, "Greeting."

In this respect it is closer in form to an official (rather than a personal) letter and the absence of a greeting may have been intended to indicate to the recipient that the Letter was something more than a familiar letter.

In letters of the time, the sender was normally identified by personal name. If a title was used, it was accompanied by a personal name. The Second and Third Letters of John deviate from this secular pattern and also are the only Christian letters of the time that give a title without a proper name. While this is unusual, it may be that such a use of titles in place of proper names reflects the practice elsewhere in the Johannine tradition of using a title for the person rather than proper names (see for example, the disciple identified only as "the disciple whom Jesus loved" and the use of "mother" rather than a proper name for Jesus' mother).

Likewise, the proper name of the addressee is commonly given in the secular letter. The Third Letter of John follows this with the identification of "Gaius." While 3 John does identify the addressee by name, it also expands the identification of the addressee by the words "the beloved, whom I love in truth."

In letters that are addressed to communities rather than to individuals (as is the case with 2 John), the location of the community is customarily given. The Second Letter of John is unique in not providing such an identification.[6]

In 3 John, the Elder addresses Gaius as "beloved." While this term was evidently a uniquely Christian designation, scholars commonly point out that the terms "most loved" *(philotatos)* and "most honored" *(timiōtatos)* were a conventional element in both familiar and in official letters and did not indicate a particularly affectionate relationship.[7] However, that the term had more than a conventional meaning in 3 John is indicated not only by the general emphasis on love in the Letter but also by the repeated use of the term itself throughout the Letter (vv. 1, 2, 5, 11) and by the use of the verb "love" *(agapaō)* in the same verse. Thus, it seems that the author has taken this formal element and imbued it with a particularly Christian meaning.

C. HEALTH WISH

Although secular letters regularly included a health wish, New Testament letters do not. The Second Letter of John does not have such a wish but 3 John does. In fact, 3 John is the only New Testament letter that contains a clear example of the traditional health wish, although even here the wish for physical

6. Brown, *Epistles* 789.
7. See, for example, Lieu (*Second and Third* 42), who gives secular parallels.

health is modeled on, and related to, the evident spiritual health that Gaius exhibits.[8] For the Johannine author, the primary focus was on spiritual health.

D. THANKSGIVING

There is no element of thanksgiving in either 2 or 3 John, although it could be said that the expression of joy functions implicitly as a thanksgiving. But there is no expression of thanksgiving similar to that found in Pauline or in secular letters.[9]

E. BODY OF THE LETTER[10]

Scholars have recognized that the body of the ancient letter also had certain formal characteristics associated particularly with the beginning and the end of the body.

Among the features found in the introduction to the body of the letter is an expression of joy. Koskenniemi proposed that such expressions of joy indicated (1) relief at the welfare of the addressee; (2) the importance of the letter for the sender.[11] Funk, referring to the work of Koskenniemi, Exler, and Schubert, provides examples from the papyri and from Polycarp and Philippians.[12] Both Johannine Letters have expressions of joy (2 John 4; 3 John 3, 4). In both instances, the joy is related to the spiritual welfare of the addressees inasmuch as it is caused by the report that members of the community are "walking in the truth."

It was common for the body of the ancient letter to contain a petition to the addressee. Usually the writer presented some background for the petition prior to the petition itself.[13] The Second and Third Letters of John contain petitions as part of the body of the Letter. Each is preceded by some element of background.[14] In 2 John, the background element is introduced by "I rejoiced

---

8. For examples of the health wish in secular letters of the first century, see Funk, "Form" 425-26.

9. For a study of the thanksgiving element in the Greek letter, see Schubert, *Form*.

10. On the analysis of the body of the ancient letter generally, see White, *Body*. As was mentioned above, White focuses on the study of the Pauline Letters but makes brief reference to the Johannine Letters in "Epistolary" 1753-55.

11. Koskenniemi, *Studien* 75-78. See also Funk, "Form" 425.

12. Schubert (*Form* 177) and Funk ("Form" 425-26) suggest that the expression of joy is the equivalent of the expression of thanks *(eucharisteō)* with which Paul regularly begins his Letters.

13. Mullins, "Petition"; Funk, "Form" 426.

14. Secular examples are given in White, *Body* 19-20.

greatly." The background itself is contained in the report that members are walking in the truth; and the petition is introduced by "I ask" *(erōtaō),* one of the most common verbs for this in secular letters.[15]

In 3 John, the petition is preceded by an expression of joy, as in the other Letter, but the petition itself is introduced by "You will act faithfully" *(piston poieis).* This expression is a Christian variant of "you will act well" *(kalōs poiēseis),* which is attested as a common form of more polite petition and which appears in v. 6.[16] Although this latter expression is common in secular litera-ture, 3 John contains the only instance of it in the New Testament.

In addition to the petition, other elements of the body of 2 and 3 John find parallels in the secular writing of the time. For example, it was not uncommon for the author to address the recipient directly when introducing a new topic or when beginning a petition.[17] We see this in 3 John with the thrice-repeated ad-dress to Gaius under the title of "Beloved" (vv. 2, 5, 11). Perhaps because 2 John is addressed to the entire congregation rather than to an individual, this per-sonal address is less frequent (although it appears in v. 5).

In secular letters it is not uncommon for there to be a recommendation for an individual in letters that deal primarily with other matters.[18] Such a com-mendation for Demetrius appears in 3 John 12. As was noted in the Interpreta-tion, this commendation is introduced quite abruptly and its relation to the surrounding context needs to be surmised.

It is also common for the author to make reference to previous letters. This appears in secular letters and is a conventional element. There is a refer-ence to a previous letter in 3 John 9. In this instance, however, it is part of the main body of the Letter and concerns the primary purpose for writing rather than being an example of the common and more perfunctory reference to past correspondence.[19]

The reference by the Elder in 3 John 10 to his possible visit to the locale where Gaius and Diotrephes reside is related to what has been described (with respect to the Pauline Letter tradition) as the "apostolic Parousia."[20] Although references to possible future visits were a standard part of the conclusion of the letter, this reference is more than that as can be determined in part by its place-ment here in the body of the Letter rather than in the conclusion.[21]

15. Secular examples can be found in Mullins, "Petition."
16. Funk, "Form" 427; Lieu, *Second and Third* 40. Examples in Koskenniemi, *Studien* 134.
17. See Lieu, *Second and Third* 40.
18. Funk, "Form" 428.
19. Lieu, *Second and Third* 40.
20. The term is that of Funk, "Apostolic."
21. This was also true of those instances in Pauline Letters where Paul felt that his pres-ence in a community was necessary to deal with a particular problem. Here the reference to the

The closing of the body of a letter is also marked by certain conventions. References to writing "with paper and ink" are examples of such conventions, and their mention in both 2 and 3 John is certainly to be understood in this way.[22] References to coming visits or to the hope for such visits are also common. However, this is to be distinguished from the so-called "apostolic Parousia" described above. The apostolic Parousia forms part of the body of the letter and when present is generally related to the actual purpose of the letter.

F. CONCLUSION

The conclusion of the letter also contained certain conventional elements. An exchange of greetings is typical in secular and other New Testament letters. The words in 3 John 15 ("The friends here greet you. Greet the friends there by name.") are quite close to the secular usage, and the expression "by name" and the general reference to "the friends" (both common in secular letters) appear only here in the New Testament.[23]

Normally Greek letters ended with some variation of "farewell." The Second Letter of John does not contain such a farewell. In 3 John, the closing is "Peace to you," an ending similar to that of 1 Peter.[24]

G. CONCLUSIONS FROM THIS REVIEW

The form-critical study of the Johannine Letters yields a number of helpful insights and it may be useful to gather them here. As we have seen, the health wish was a common element of the ancient letter. Although the Johannine author conforms to this pattern (most clearly in 3 John), he views it in relation to spiritual health, something he clearly values more.

The recognition of the conventional function of "you will act well" as the introduction to a petition, as well as the recognition of its appearance relatively late in the introduction of the petition gives a further confirmation that the expression "you (will) act faithfully" (which appears in the location where one

---

possible visit by the Elder corresponds to the Pauline *Parousia* in purpose but is much less developed than the Pauline form. On the development of this element of the Pauline Letter, see particularly Funk, "Apostolic."

22. Brown (*Epistles* 725) gives secular parallels.

23. Lieu, *Second and Third* 41-42. Lieu provides examples of secular usage.

24. Lieu (*Second and Third* 48) points out that this is identical to the form of greeting given by the risen Jesus (John 20:19, 21, 26).

would normally expect the other expression) is intended as a Christian variation of the more conventional expression.

Although the expression of a desire to visit was a common feature of the secular letter, as a conventional element it appeared in the conclusion of the letter. However, in 3 John, it appears in the body of the Letter and its placement provides further confirmation of the urgency of the desire to visit.

The genuineness of the Johannine Letters is also confirmed by features typical of the ancient letter that appear in them but nowhere else in the New Testament, features such as the health wish, the language of the polite petition and the distinctive wording of the conclusion, as noted above.

Finally, we have seen two instances where what would appear to be a conventional element of 3 John is modified and should be understood in a way other than the conventional one. The first is the use of "Beloved" as a form of address for Gaius, which could ordinarily be understood as a simple convention. Yet, given the emphasis on love in the Letter and the author's love for Gaius elsewhere, it becomes clear that the term takes on more than a conventional importance in this Letter.

The second instance occurs in v. 2, where the appearance of "in all things" would normally be understood to be related to "I pray that." This conventional association has led Lieu and others to question the peculiarity of the wording. However, once it is recognized that the material of v. 2b-e is arranged chiastically, then we are able to see that in fact the words "in all things" should be related to the words that follow ("you are doing well") rather than to those that precede as would be expected by the conventional form. This gives the verse a considerably different meaning.

Thus, we see that while attention to literary form can be of considerable help in interpretation, it is not an infallible guide and must be used critically.

John the Son of Zebedee and the Authorship of the Johannine Literature

A. INTRODUCTION

The authorship of the Gospel of John is discussed and contested more than that of any other New Testament work.[1] It is complicated not only by the variety and ambiguity of the external evidence but also by the fact that, in addition to the traditional attribution of the Gospel to John the son of Zebedee, the author is referred to in the Gospel as the Beloved Disciple and the author of two of the Letters is referred to as the Elder. Because the evidence to be evaluated is so considerable, I have chosen to divide the discussion into separate Appendices. This will inevitably lead to some repetition, but it will enable us to focus the discussion more closely and, hopefully, arrive at a clearer set of conclusions. The issue of attribution of the Gospel to John the son of Zebedee is discussed in this appendix. The identity of the Elder is addressed in Appendix 8, and the identity and function of the Beloved Disciple are discussed in Appendix 9.

The sources for our knowledge of the author of the Gospel can be divided into two classes: external evidence, that is, evidence from sources outside of the Gospel itself, and internal evidence, evidence about the author from within the Gospel. Our discussion will be divided accordingly.

---

1. *Guide to the various discussions of authorship:* What can be known of the authors of each of the three editions of the Gospel is given in the Introduction to each of the editions in Vol. 1. The discussion of the authorship of each of the Letters is given in the General Introduction to the Letters as well as in the Introductions to 2 and 3 John. John the son of Zebedee as well as the figures of the Beloved Disciple and the Elder are discussed in individual Appendices.

B. EXTERNAL INFORMATION ABOUT THE AUTHOR

We will begin with an examination of the evidence that John the son of Zebedee was the author of the Gospel and that he lived in Ephesus. In the New Testament itself, there is no evidence that John son of Zebedee was ever at Ephesus. Acts 3:1; 8:14 and Gal 2:9 show John, son of Zebedee, active in Jerusalem and Palestine until about the year A.D. 50. There is no mention of John in Paul's address to the elders of Ephesus in the year A.D. 58 (cf. Acts 20:18-20), nor in the Epistle to the Ephesians.

When we look at the earliest "sub-apostolic" literature we find the same. There is no mention of John in Ignatius' *Letter to the Ephesians* (ca. A.D. 110) although he describes Paul's presence and work in that city. Nor does Polycarp mention John in his own writings. Justin (*Dial.* 81.4) lived in Ephesus about A.D. 135 and mentions John, the author of Revelation, but does not use or mention a Gospel associated with John or with Ephesus.[2]

The earliest mention of the apostle John in the post–New Testament period is by Papias, who wrote five volumes entitled *Exposition of the Lord's Oracles* about A.D. 130. Papias makes reference to someone he calls "John the Elder." However, he makes no mention of either as being the author of a Gospel or of being from Ephesus.[3]

The first actual identification of John with the BD and with the authorship of the Gospel is from Irenaeus, who says (writing ca. A.D. 180-200): "John, the disciple of the Lord, who reclined at his breast, also published the Gospel while living at Ephesus in Asia" (*Adv. Haer.* 3.1:1-2). Later (*Adv. Haer.* 3.3.4) he says regarding the church at Ephesus, ". . . it was founded by Paul and John lived there until the time of Trajan."[4] Irenaeus explains in his *Letter to Florinus* (quoted by Eusebius, *Hist.* 5.20.4-8) that his information about John came from Polycarp, whom he had met in old age while he himself was a young man.[5]

However, from the time of Irenaeus on, there is a clear and consistent tradition of attributing the Gospel to John son of Zebedee and of locating it at Ephesus. Clement of Alexandria (ca. A.D. 150-215) claimed that John had gone to Ephesus after Domitian's death[6] and visited the churches there, appointing bishops and consolidating the churches (*Quis dives salvetur* 42:1-2).

Eusebius also lists Clement as describing John the apostle as the author

2. See Eusebius' reference to this incident (*Hist* 4.18.6-8).
3. We will examine the statement of Papias in detail in Appendix 8 (The Elder and the Elders).
4. Trajan was emperor A.D. 98-117. See also *Adv. Haer.* 2.22.5.
5. A second source of information is that of Eusebius (ca. A.D. 263-339) who also quotes the first passage above about Irenaeus' knowledge of John (*Hist.* 5.8.3-4).
6. Domitian died in A.D. 96.

and as associating him with Ephesus. "Last of all John, perceiving that the bodily facts had been made plain in the Gospel, being urged by his friends, and inspired by the Spirit, composed a spiritual gospel" (*Hist.* 6.14.7).

The so-called Muratorian Fragment, the earliest extant list of the works that make up the New Testament (composed ca. A.D. 170-200), recounts John as the author of the Gospel but describes him as the spokesperson for a number of the disciples who recalled "all things" to mind.[7] Eusebius (*Hist.* 3.31.3) also reports that Polycrates, bishop of Ephesus, in a letter to Pope Victor about the year A.D. 190, identifies John with the Beloved Disciple and associates him with Ephesus. He lists some of the more important early Christians buried at Ephesus and among these he lists "John, who reclined at the bosom of the Lord, who was a priest, wearing the mitre, and a witness *(martys)* and a teacher *(didaskalos)*; he sleeps at Ephesus." The possibility of this being a reference to John as the author of the Gospel hinges on the use of the term "witness" *(martys)*, the term used of the BD in John 21:24. Given the fondness of John's Gospel for the term "witness," it is thought by some that this is a way of referring to John as the author of the Gospel.

In the Anti-Marcionite Prologue to the Gospel of Luke (ca. A.D. 200), it is stated that John the Apostle wrote the Apocalypse on Patmos and afterwards wrote the Gospel.[8] The Anti-Marcionite Prologue to the Gospel of John[9] states: "According to the five exegetical books of Papias,[10] the dear disciple of John, this Gospel was published and sent to the churches of Asia by John himself during his lifetime." The Prologue also reports that the Gospel "was written down at John's dictation by Papias, a man from Hierapolis and one of John's near disciples." Yet this detail is almost certainly wrong since Papias himself gives another account, as we have seen.

1. Conclusions

From this survey of the external evidence, we can see that there is no mention of John as author of a Gospel nor in connection with Ephesus in other parts of the New Testament or in the earliest post–New Testament writings. When John is mentioned first (by Papias), there is no indication that Papias actually spoke with John himself, but only with the next generation of elders. Nor does Papias mention John as the author of a Gospel.

7. A photographic reproduction with translation is available in Leclercq, "Muratorianum" in *DACL* Vol. 12, Pt. 1, Cols. 543-60.

8. Marcion was an apostate who claimed that the only writer who truly understood the message of Jesus was Paul and so argued that the only authentic books should be ten Letters of Paul and a version of the Gospel of Luke with major sections excised.

9. The text of the Prologue to John survives "in a rather corrupt Latin version" (Carson, *Gospel* 27).

10. These books are titled *The Exegesis of the Dominical Logia*. They are no longer extant.

However, beginning about the middle of the second century there appear a considerable number of references identifying John as the author of a Gospel and as having lived at Ephesus. Irenaeus is the first to make mention of this and says his information came from Polycarp whom he had met in old age while he himself was a young man. Irenaeus also reports that Papias met John. But Papias himself says that he did not.

It is also significant that it was near the middle of the second century that the Gospel of John itself was coming into more frequent use in the churches, and the coincidence of this usage with the appearance of the Gospel's attribution to John at Ephesus has suggested to many that the close linkage of the Gospel with John the apostle was intended as an assurance of the Gospel's apostolic origin.

In all of this, the lack of early references to John as the author is more significant than the comments of Irenaeus since the accuracy of his report is in doubt. In short, there is no reliable information that John, the son of Zebedee, is the author of the Gospel in the first century after the composition of the Gospel.

C. INTERNAL EVIDENCE REGARDING JOHN THE SON OF ZEBEDEE

1. Internal Arguments in Favor of Identification of the Author with John, the Son of Zebedee

The most widely held and respected set of arguments for the traditional view of the internal evidence are those first formulated by Westcott.[11] His argument proceeds in five steps: (1) the author was a Jew; (2) a Palestinian; (3) an eyewitness; (4) an apostle; (5) the apostle John.

That the author was a Jew is generally accepted today. The discovery of many examples of Jewish forms of argument in the Gospel as well as similarities to the SDQ confirm this. That the author was a Palestinian is also generally accepted in the light of the detailed knowledge of Judea that is manifested in the Gospel. That he was an eyewitness is attested by both 19:35 and 21:24. However, some would argue that the BD, who is identified as the witness in these texts, is not a historical but a literary figure. For these, the notion that the author was an eyewitness is called into question.[12]

The view that the author was an apostle and one of the Twelve is generally based on the argument that, according to Mark 14:17, only the Twelve were at

11. Westcott, *Gospel* v-xxiv; *Essays* 41-42. See the continuing influence of his work in, for example, Bruce, *Gospel* 1-6; Carson, *Gospel* 70-72; Morris, *Studies* 139-92. For a recent review of their positions, see Culpepper, *Legend* 280-96, 313-21.

12. For a discussion of the BD as a literary fiction, see Charlesworth, *Beloved* 12-14.

the Last Supper, but the BD was at the Last Supper, and so therefore he must have been one of the Twelve. However, such an argument presumes that the same view of the Twelve is presented in both John and the Synoptics, something not borne out by a close analysis of this group in the two traditions. The Twelve held a very different place in the Johannine tradition than they did in the Synoptics. For example, the names of the Twelve are nowhere listed in John. Moreover, the Twelve are mentioned only four times (6:67, 70, 71; 20:24) and there is little attention paid to them as a group. Much more common is the title "disciple," and, although individual disciples are named, the names of the Twelve do not appear even scattered throughout the Gospel. In addition, there are disciples such as Nathanael, who are not mentioned by the Synoptics.

Finally, the argument that the BD is John, the son of Zebedee, can only be made on the basis of a particular understanding of chapter 21. In chapter 21, for the only time in the Gospel, the sons of Zebedee are mentioned together with two other unnamed disciples. The BD could not be James, it is reasoned, because James died very early and the BD was said to have lived long. So the BD could be any of the other three.

Some would argue that the fact that the Gospel mentions prominent disciples such as Peter and Andrew as well as lesser-known ones such as Philip and Judas (not the Iscariot) makes the absence of John very strange — unless he simply chose not to name himself. Some would argue that the fact that Peter and John are often linked elsewhere (e.g., Mark 5:37; 9:2; 14:33 and throughout Acts 3:1–4:23) parallels the pairing of Peter and the BD in the Fourth Gospel. Of these arguments, the pairing of Peter and John in the Synoptics and in Acts would at first appear to be of significance. However, a closer look shows that the association is not similar since the pairing of Peter and John in the Synoptic passages is actually not a pairing but a grouping of three, which includes James. In the portrayal of Peter and John in both the Synoptics and Acts, there is nothing of the comparison of their qualities, their destinies as well as their responsibilities.

Moreover, if John the son of Zebedee is to be equated with the BD, it would be John who gives himself the title "the disciple whom Jesus loved." But, as is regularly pointed out, that a disciple would give himself this title could only be seen as arrogance; it is almost surely a title conferred by the community.

2. Internal Arguments against Identification of the Author with John, the Son of Zebedee

It should be noted, first, that John is not mentioned by name in the Gospel (and "the sons of Zebedee" are mentioned only in chapter 21), so there is no internal testimony that would link the author directly with John, son of Zebedee.

Moreover, the author of the Gospel, as he can be discovered from information within the Gospel, is considerably different from John the son of Zebe-dee we know from elsewhere in the New Testament. Although not probative, it is curious that the author of the Gospel is evidently from Judea (given his famil-iarity with places there and the amount of emphasis given to it in the Gospel), but John the apostle is from Galilee.[13] It is argued also that the author is evi-dently well educated (on the basis of the style of the Gospel), but John, the son of Zebedee, is described in Acts 4:13 as ignorant and uneducated. This too may have a certain force but is not probative. The statement in Acts 4:13 could be taken to refer to John as uneducated much as this is said of Jesus in John 7:15.

The BD is known to the high priest (cf. 18:15), but the Synoptic John is a Galilean fisherman, unlikely to be known to the high priest in Judea. A rejoin-der to this is that John, who was a fisherman, according to the Synoptics, sup-plied fish to the high priest and so was known by him. While the fact that John was a fisherman is supplied from the Synoptics, the legend that he supplied fish to the high priest is just that, a legend from the *Gospel of the Nazarenes*.[14]

If we assume that the John of the Synoptics is the author of the Fourth Gospel, we find many features that are difficult to explain. For example, in Mark's Gospel, John is identified as being present at the raising of the daughter of Jairus, at the Transfiguration and at the agony in Gethsemane. Yet there is no report of any of these striking events in the Gospel of John. If John were the au-thor of the Fourth Gospel such an omission would be difficult to explain. The attitude toward Samaritans in the Gospel of John is positive, but in Luke (9:54) John and James want to call down divine punishment on a Samaritan town. The figure of the BD does not demonstrate any of the characteristics that would lead to his being called "son of thunder." In short, the BD does not appear at all like the figure of John, the son of Zebedee, as he is known from the Synoptics.

We have discussed above the various views that have been expressed re-garding the mention of "the sons of Zebedee" and the BD in chapter 21. While some would argue that John is the natural referent of the unnamed disciple, others argue that, if the BD were John, son of Zebedee, it would be extraordi-nary that the BD is mentioned five verses later and not associated with either of the sons.[15] On the basis of these factors, I would conclude that it is unlikely that, in chapter 21, the BD is to be identified with John, the son of Zebedee.

13. For an energetic defense of this view, see Hengel, *Question* 124. As Carson argues, by the time the Gospel was written John could well be said to have lived for a considerable period in Judea. Yet the Judean emphasis nevertheless suggests an orientation unusual for one from Galilee (especially given the Galilean emphasis of the Synoptics even regarding the Resurrec-tion appearances). While Carson's point is certainly possible, it seems less likely.

14. See *Gospel of the Nazarenes*, fragment 33.

15. However, it is argued also that out of modesty John, one of the sons of Zebedee, is present but does not want to refer to himself by name. See Bruce, *Gospel* 3.

3. Conclusions

We have seen a number of factors that both support and question the proposal that the Gospel bearing the name of John is authored by John, the son of Zebedee. The unanimity of attestation is remarkable beginning with Irenaeus. Yet the lack of earlier evidence is striking. The portrayal of the BD within the Gospel and the portrayal of the ministry by the Gospel appear quite different from what we would expect of John, son of Zebedee. At the same time, the Gospel claims to be the work of an eyewitness to the ministry, one present at the Last Supper and well known to Peter (with whom John is often associated in Acts). Complicating the issue is the fact that the Gospel in its final form is the result of editing and re-editing. As a result, I am inclined to suggest that while the evidence at our disposal cannot be said to prove that John was the author of the Gospel, at the same time this evidence cannot be said to disprove it either. We cannot rule out the possibility that one or another stage of the tradition that has come down to us comes from John.

Although by far the vast majority of scholars focus on the question whether the author is John, the son of Zebedee, others have argued that another John is being referred to. Two suggestions have been made for the identity of this other John: John Mark and John the Elder. The first of these is not widely held. There is no evidence for this internal to the Gospel. Elsewhere in the New Testament John Mark is associated with Jerusalem. It was said that he was the son of the Mary in whose house the Last Supper was celebrated and in which the earliest Christians gathered. Because of this he would be among the youngest and could have been at the side of Jesus. But the tradition about the upper room is uncertain, and it is fanciful that Jesus would reveal the identity of the betrayer to such a person. John Mark is associated with Paul and identified as a cousin of Barnabas (Col. 4:10). He may have had contact with the priestly class since his cousin Barnabas was a Levite (Col. 4:10; Acts 4:36). He is mentioned as being in Ephesus in 2 Tim 4:11. There was confusion in antiquity between these two Johns (cf. Chrysostom's Commentary on Acts 12:12). Yet John Mark is regularly identified not as the author of John's Gospel but of the other that bears the name "Mark."

The figure of John the Elder will be discussed in the appendix on the Elder (Appendix 8) and in that on the Beloved Disciple (Appendix 9).

APPENDIX 8

The Elder and the Elders

This appendix will survey what can be known about the use of the term "Elder(s)" in earliest Christianity and compare this to the use of the term by the author of 2 and 3 John.[1]

A. ELDERS IN EARLY CHRISTIANITY

The title "elder" in the early church grew out of its use in Judaism, where it referred to those older persons who were thought to be endowed with special wisdom and judgment.[2] In Mark, they are regularly portrayed as one of the three groups that made up the Sanhedrin (8:31; 11:27; 14:43, 53; 15:1).[3] Mark also speaks of them as persons who form the traditions (7:3, 5).

There are six significant periods and meanings associated with the term within early Christianity. An organizational "structure" involving such elders (#1) is portrayed in Acts as occurring in Jerusalem in the two decades after Jesus (11:30; 15:2, 23; 16:4) and in communities founded by Paul (14:23; 20:17). Such a structure is also (#2) evident in documents written in the latter part of the first century or the first part of the second century (cf. Jas 5:14; 1 Pet 5:1; 1 Tim 5:17; Titus 1:5).

A modified form of this government (#3) appears later, in the time of

---

1. *Guide to the various discussions of authorship:* What can be known of the authors of each of the three editions of the Gospel is given in the Analysis of each of the editions in Vol. 1. The discussion of the authorship of each of the letters is given in the General Introduction to the Letters as well as in the Introductions to 2 and 3 John. John, the son of Zebedee, as well as the figures of the Beloved Disciple and the Elder are discussed in individual appendices.

2. For further detail and discussion, see Bornkamm, *"Presbys," TDNT* 6, esp. 662-80; Brown, *Epistles* 647-51; Schnackenburg, *Epistles* 268-73; Lieu, *Second and Third* 52-64.

3. See also Acts 6:12.

Ignatius (last third of the second century), when it is evident that one of a group of such elders would be chosen to serve as *episkopos,* thus showing the emergence of an authoritative figure beyond that of the group itself.[4]

The title of "elder" was also used to refer to apostles (#4) and to a single individual called "John the Elder" (#5). Both of these uses appear in the work of Papias, bishop of Hierapolis (ca. A.D. 60-130). Finally, after the time of Papias, the term "elder" is used more generally to refer to third-generation witnesses, persons who heard the message of Christianity from those who spoke with the apostles (#6). This view is evident in Irenaeus, *Adv. Haer.* 4.27.1 when he says: "I heard it from a certain elder, who had heard it from those who had seen the apostles and from those who had taught."[5] Thus, Polycarp, who claimed to have listened to the apostles, would be an elder in this sense.[6] This process keeps alive the chain of witness but clearly does not refer to eyewitnesses. Consequently, if there is the possibility that "the Elder" of 2 and 3 John is mentioned elsewhere in early Christianity, it is in connection with #5 above ("John the Elder"). And so we must examine the quotation of Papias more closely.

As we saw above, Papias uses the term "elder" with reference to two groups. Both of these references appear in a passage from Papias in his multivolume work entitled *The Exposition of the Lord's Sayings (Logiōn Kyriakōn Exēgēsis).*[7] Papias, referring to the original twelve apostles, says:

> If, then, anyone came who had been a follower of the elders [*presbyteroi*], I inquired about the words of the elders, what Andrew, or what Peter said, or what Philip, or what Thomas or James, or what John or Matthew, or any of the other disciples of the Lord (said). . . .

4. Donfried ("Ecclesiastical") holds a similar view: ". . . at the end of the first century and in the early second the evidence is large that in many areas of the church *presbyteros* and *episkopos* are used interchangeably" (328). Independently, he points to parallels between the role of the Elder in 2 and 3 John and that of the Overseer *(mebaqqēr)* at Qumran. Interesting in this regard is the fact that the Overseer was the one charged with examining the entrants to the community with respect to their conduct (CD 13.11) and his beliefs and adherence to the truth (CD 13.12). These two functions correspond to the two basic elements on which the Johannine tradition sought to evaluate its members (that is, belief and ethics). On the "double scrutiny" at Qumran, see Appendix 5, Section F (pp. 392-94 above). On belief and ethics as the two main foci of the author's exhortation, see Appendix 4, Section G (pp. 365-69 above).

5. This position is developed particularly by van Unnik, "Authority." For other texts from Irenaeus, see van Unnick's article.

6. Van Unnik ("Authority" 256-58) argues that when Irenaeus attempted to refute the gnostics, he was simply using the form of authority that was common in his world, namely the sure link of witnesses, and in the case of Christianity, the elders had seen and heard of Christianity from the apostles themselves.

7. The works of Papias are no longer extant. However, fragments are quoted in Eusebius *Hist.* 3.39.4. All of the fragments of Papias are collected in Lightfoot, *Apostolic* 515-35.

In the same quotation from Papias, there is also a reference to a second group, composed of two individuals, one of whom is identified by proper name and known as "John the Elder" (#5). The reference to the second group follows the previous one immediately and reads as follows:

> ... and those things which Aristion and the elder [*presbyteros*] John, disciples of the Lord, say. For I was not of the opinion that those things in books would be as profitable to me as those from a living and surviving voice.[8]

There are two groups of disciples being referred to in this passage and there is a person named John in both groups. The members of the first group are all members of the Twelve. The second group is comprised of only two people, both called disciples. One is named Aristion, and the second is named John the Elder.[9] When speaking of the first group, Papias says that he speaks with *the followers* of those disciples and that he inquires about what *(ti)* the elders said *(eipen)* and then lists Andrew, Peter, Philip, Thomas, James, John, Matthew, "or any other of the disciples of the Lord."[10] He then speaks of the second group and elliptically refers to "those things" *(ha)* (not "what" [*ti*]) Aristion and John the Elder "are saying" *(legousin)*.

There are various opinions about the changes in the wording and verb tenses in this statement. Some scholars argue that those mentioned in the second group (Aristion and John the Elder) were first-generation disciples/apostles but are named separately because they were not members of the Twelve.[11] Moreover, it is argued that the change in pronouns and the change in the tense of the verbs are significant and indicate that the Twelve were no longer alive but that Aristion and John the Elder were. Other scholars argue that the tense of the two verbs is not significant and that both groups of disciples were still alive; they also argue that Papias talked to people who had talked with the Twelve, but

---

8. *Ei de pou kai parēkolouthēkōs tis tois presbyterois elthoi, tous tōn presbyterōn anekrinon logous, ti Andreas ē ti Petros eipen ē ti Philippos ē ti Thōmas ē Iakōbos ē ti Iōannēs ē Matthaios ē tis heteros tōn kyriou mathētōn, ha te Aristiōn kai ho presbyteros Iōannēs, hoi tou kyriou mathētai legousin. ou gar ta ek tōn bibliōn tosouton me ōphelein hypelambanon, hoson ta para zōsēs phōnēs kai menousēs* (text from Lightfoot, *Apostolic* 564).

9. Since Papias was writing about the year A.D. 130, some scholars object that none of the original generation could have been alive and therefore Papias may be referring to the disciples of the disciples (that is, the second generation). While *presbyter* can have this meaning, according to Brown (*Epistles* xci), it may simply be that Papias is reporting inquiries made years earlier.

10. It is often noted that the order of the first three apostles here is the order in which they are named in John 1:35-51. There is also some similarity in the remainder of the list to the order in John 21:2. See, e.g., Hengel, *Question* 17; Culpepper, *Gospel and Epistles* 111-12.

11. This view was argued by Munck, "Presbyters."

that he had talked directly with Aristion and John the Elder.[12] Still others argue that those in the second group were not apostles in any sense, a view that contradicts what is stated by the text.

It is my view that Papias is referring to two distinct groups and that this is indicated both by the change in relative pronoun and by the change in tense of the verb. As is recognized, the first group contains names of the Twelve while the second group does not. Nevertheless, Papias identifies both groups as disciples *(mathētai).* But the second group is distinguished by the fact that they were not members of the Twelve and by the fact that they are still alive.

Another significant element is that Papias concludes his statement by saying that it was better to learn from living and surviving voices than from books. In addition to the word "living," Papias uses the word *menousēs* (literally "remaining"). Thus, it was the living voice of witnesses that was important, and Aristion and John the Elder are among these and are still alive. This "John, the Elder" could be the Elder of 2 and 3 John. There is no other single individual called "John, the Elder" in early Christian literature. This would indicate that Papias spoke directly with John the Elder.

When Papias gives the names of those disciples who are among the Twelve (see the quote above), he lists them in an order that appears in none of the Synoptic traditions but only in John 1:35-51 and in John 21:2. In addition, the listing of disciples in John 21:2 distinguishes the BD from the sons of Zebedee. This is in accord with the listing provided by Papias, which puts John the Elder in a separate grouping from the Twelve.[13] All of this indicates that Papias knew the Johannine traditions.

B. THE ELDER OF 2 AND 3 JOHN

From 2 and 3 John, it is evident that the Elder exercised some sort of authority. This is evident, first, in the fact that he has taken the responsibility to write both Letters. Second, he gives praise, directions, and advice to the communities, as would one who expected his words to be acknowledged and respected. Third, he refers to members of the community as his "children," which suggests that he

---

12. Culpepper (*Legend* 110) quotes Barrett (*Gospel* 107) approvingly as understanding that Papias did not talk with Aristion and John the Elder directly but only with those who were their followers. In support of this is the last sentence of Eusebius, *Hist.* 3.39.7, which begins with the particle *goun* which Barrett understands to minimize the effect of the earlier statement about Papias speaking directly with John the Elder. Along with Hengel (*Question* 21), I think this is too strong a reading of the particle and the statement.

13. Hengel (*Question* 19) goes further and suggests that the two unnamed disciples in John 21 could well be Aristion and John the Elder.

saw himself as somehow responsible for their being believers. Fourth, he acts with authoritative stature when he indicates to Gaius that, if he comes, he will bring up to Diotrephes the evil that he is doing. Finally, it is likewise evident that the Elder makes no reference to any kind of authoritative power or office other than his ability to witness to the truth. As Brown says: "One gets the impression of prestige but not of juridical authority."[14]

C. THE ELDER OF 2 AND 3 JOHN
AND THE USES OF "ELDER" ELSEWHERE

If we compare the picture of the Elder as it appears in 2 and 3 John with the various usages of the term up to the second half of the second century, we can narrow down the options somewhat.

The term "Elder" as it is used in 2 and 3 John is not to be identified with (#1) or (#2) above (see p. 410). The Johannine use refers to an individual, and some other designation would be necessary if it were intended to refer to only one out of a larger governing group. Nor can the Johannine use be identified with that in Ignatius (#3). If the Elder was the leader of such a group, he would have undoubtedly chosen another title since the title of elder would not distinguish him from any of the others. Moreover, there is no evidence of the Elder of 2 or 3 John holding any conferred ecclesiastical office such as bishop. However, it is possible that the term refers to one of the last three possibilities: to an apostle (#4), to John the Elder (#5), or to a second-generation follower of an apostle (#6). Let us examine each more closely.

The usage in (#6) can also be eliminated. This is the usage that is apparent in Irenaeus. In this theory, the Elder was a disciple of the Beloved Disciple and thus one of the second-generation tradition-bearers of "the Johannine school."[15] This is the view of Brown, and it presupposes that the Gospel is written before the letters. Brown finds this to be consistent with the statement of John 21:24, which says that "we" know his [the BD's] testimony is true." Noting the parallel expression in 3 John 12 ("We bear witness also and you know that our witness is true"), Brown proposes that the "we" in John 21:24 and the "we" of 3 John 12 are the same group and that they are the ones who are responsible for the statement about the BD in John 21:24.[16] That is, the BD had been a true eyewitness and this other "we" knew the eyewitnesses. It is true that this view

14. Brown, *Epistles* 648.
15. Brown, *Epistles* 96, 651.
16. See, for example, Smalley (*Epistles* 317), who understands the elders of Papias to be the same second-generation hearers of the apostles as are spoken of by Irenaeus (see below).

can make sense of the sequence of composition as Brown sees it, but there is no positive evidence to suggest that it is actually the case. Moreover, two factors militate against his view.

First, the person who is the author of both 1 and 2 John makes it clear that he is an eyewitness and that he is speaking about things that he has personally witnessed. This is the same claim that is made for the Beloved Disciple in the Gospel (21:23-24). Brown would argue that the references to the "we" who have seen, heard, touched, etc. refers to the second generation of believers who were not actual eyewitnesses but who adopt this language on the grounds that they had heard and spoken with the eyewitnesses. In short, Brown is forced to claim that these "we" were not genuine eyewitnesses.

However, given the importance of eyewitness testimony in the Gospel and in 1 John, it is inconceivable for such references not to refer to actual eyewitness testimony. Again and again in both the Gospel and in 1 John, the author bases the authenticity of what is said on the fact that it is eyewitness testimony. The BD regularly witnesses to what he has seen and heard. The BD was said to be at the Farewell Dinner, to be at the foot of the cross, and to have entered the tomb. Similarly, the First Letter of John 1:1-4 repeatedly stresses that the witness contained in the "letter" is direct, sensory experience of Jesus. It is this direct experience that is the basis for being able to tell what was "from the beginning." This makes it highly unlikely that the Elder of 2 and 3 John would not truly be an eyewitness to the ministry.

Brown holds that 1 John was written after the entire Gospel; thus, in his view, the Elder cannot be the BD. But if the Johannine Letters were written before the final edition of the Gospel, then another, simpler, reading of the evidence is possible, a reading that does not force the evidence as much as Brown.

Let us look now at (#4). We saw that, in the quotation from Papias, the disciples/apostles are referred to as "elders." Something similar happens in 1 Peter, where Peter identifies himself as an apostle along with the term "co-elder" *(sympresbyteros)*. But the listing of disciples/apostles by Papias has more to teach us. In this text, two groups mentioned by Papias are both described as being "disciples" (a term synonymous with "apostle" for Papias). But Papias introduces a distinction not found elsewhere between the Twelve and two others who were disciples *but not members of the twelve.* These two others are Aristion and John the Elder. This would suggest that the Elder of 2 and 3 John could have been a disciple but not one of the Twelve. We know there were at least two such disciples and one had the title "The Elder," the same title as that of the author of 2 and 3 John. Thus the author of 2 and 3 John would be the "John the Elder" of (#5).

The distinguishing feature of this disciple is that, although he is not part of the Twelve, he is a disciple and he is singled out by name and given the title elder. This is the only figure known from the first two centuries singled out as "the Elder" and said to be a disciple and therefore an eyewitness and to be named John. In addition, he (along with Aristion) was a disciple who had outlived any of the Twelve. Therefore, within the known usage of the term "elder," this instance has a particular relevance.[17] There is nothing to rule out the possibility that "the Elder" of 2 and 3 John is the Elder of (#5).

A number of modern scholars argue that the Elder of 2 and 3 John cannot be identified with any of the groups listed above and that he is to be understood simply as the unnamed individual who was the tradition bearer for the Johannine community. He was the one responsible for both the Gospel and the Letters.[18] If the Letters were written before the final edition of the Gospel, then we are not forced into the position of claiming that the Elder was not an actual eyewitness but one who claimed to be, as it were, a "secondary eyewitness," on the grounds of having heard those who were actual eyewitnesses. Such an artificial explanation is no longer necessary.

Instead, the coalescence of evidence suggests that it was John the Elder, a living eyewitness to the ministry of Jesus, who wrote the three Letters. It is his witness that is later enshrined in the third edition of the Gospel. However, by the time of the third edition, the Elder had died and those who were responsible for the third edition had bestowed upon him the title of "the disciple whom Jesus loved."

However, we cannot fully understand the Johannine usage until we have reviewed the figure of the Beloved Disciple, and so any final conclusions regarding the identity of the Elder and his role within the overall Johannine tradition must be postponed until the end of that appendix.

17. Smalley (*Epistles* 317) dismisses the existence of John the Elder as one "whose hypothetical existence rests on a misinterpretation of the witness of Papias. . . ."

18. For a defense of this view see Lieu, *Second and Third* 52; Painter, *Epistles* 339-40. See also Dodd, *Epistles* lxxi.

The Beloved Disciple

A. THE BELOVED DISCIPLE TEXTS

In six texts within the Gospel (13:23-26; 19:26-27; 20:2-10; 21:7; 21:20-23; 21:24), there appears a disciple whose proper name is not given but who is identified as "the disciple whom Jesus loved."[1] These texts are the focus of our attention in this appendix. In a seventh text (19:35), a person witnesses to the flow of blood and water from the side of Jesus. This eyewitness is not specifically identified, but the only disciple said to be present is the BD. Moreover, the identification of his witness as being "true" is the same that is predicated of the BD in 21:24. As a result, I would understand that this is also a reference to the BD.

In addition to these seven, there are three other passages where an unnamed disciple (or disciples) appear(s): 1:35-40; 18:15-16; and 21:2. These passages are often thought to refer to the "Beloved Disciple" also. Although the ones referred to in these texts are somewhat more difficult to determine, substantial reasons can be given for seeing them as also referring to the BD.

Since such unnamed disciples appear in three passages, it is unlikely that these references are simply accidental. The role of the unnamed disciple is clearest in the last of the passages (21:2). Here it becomes apparent that, since all but two of the disciples are named and the BD himself is present but not named, he must be one of the two unnamed disciples. This gives us precedent for the author's including the BD among such a group.

If we look next at 18:15, we can see that there is substantial reason for thinking that the unnamed disciple here is the BD also. It is apparent from a

1. An extensive bibliography on the topic can be found in Charlesworth, *Beloved Disciple*. To that bibliography can be added: Bauckham, "Beloved Disciple"; J. Becker, *Evangelium* Exkurs 9, 2:434-39; de Jonge, "Beloved Disciple" 99-114; Kragerud, *Lieblingsjünger*; Kügler, *Jünger*.

careful reading of the seven certain BD passages, that there is a consistent contrast between Peter and the BD. In the verses that precede 18:15, Peter and another disciple are following Jesus. The other disciple enters the courtyard and
makes provision for Peter to enter also (not unlike the scene in which the BD
reaches the empty tomb before Peter). After entering the courtyard, Peter denies his association with Jesus, while we do not hear anything else of the other
disciple. Up to this point only two had been following Jesus; Peter now denies
him and runs away. But we will hear later that the BD was at the foot of the
cross. Thus, there are three factors that argue that this is a reference to the BD:
use of "unnamed disciple" as a reference for the BD elsewhere in the Gospel; the
implicit comparison with Peter in 18:15-17; and the logical conclusion that since
only one other disciple was following Jesus and since there is one disciple at the
foot of the cross and he is identified as the BD, then the second disciple of 18:15
must have been the BD.[2]

Finally, if we look at 1:35-40, we find the most ambiguous of the references. There are references to two of John's disciples standing with John when
Jesus approaches. At this point, there is no reason to expect the identification of
either one. However, in v. 40 we hear that Andrew was one of those who had
been with John, but no reference is made to the other. The material in 1:35-40
appears to come entirely from the first edition except for two brief modifications. There is no indication that the reference to the unnamed disciples is an
addition by the third author (and the failure to mention the second of the disciples may be due to omission by a later editor). Moreover, there is no comparison with Peter and no explicit mention of the BD in the context. As a result, I
am of the opinion that this text is not a reference to the BD. This is particularly
true if we meet the reference in the normal sequence of reading the narrative
(that is, without examining it in the context of 18:15 and 21:2). Consequently, in
what follows, I will treat only the references in 18:15 and 21:2 as valid references
to the BD.

Once we have clarified which passages within the Gospel can be said to
refer to the BD, we are in a position to ask what we know of his identity and his
function from within the text of the Gospel. We will answer these questions
first on the basis of the information provided in the Gospel, then we ask
whether the BD is a historical, or a literary, figure.

---

2. See particularly Neirynck ("'Other Disciple'") who argues in detail for the identification of this disciple with the BD. So also Thyen, "Entwicklungen" 281; de Jonge, "Beloved
Disciple" 103.

B. INTERNAL EVIDENCE REGARDING THE IDENTITY AND FUNCTION OF THE BD

The identity of the one we refer to as the "Beloved Disciple" is revealed not by a name but by his relationship to Jesus. It is not that he loved Jesus (although certainly he did) but rather that this person is "the disciple whom *Jesus* loved." This remarkable title does not reflect simple natural affection (although there must have been something of that also), nor can it be intended to refer to the love that the Father (3:16) has for the entire world because that was a love directed to all. This is a special love, a love that is defined by Johannine theology. But, according to the Gospel, whom does Jesus love?

Three times in the Gospel, Jesus says that he will love the one who obeys the commandments that he has given the disciples (14:21; 15:10, 14). Such obedience is necessary for a person to remain in Jesus' love. The commandments of Jesus in the Gospel of John are, like the figure of the BD himself, introduced by the third author in imitation of the theology worked out by the author of 1 John. These commandments are the two specific Johannine commandments: to remain faithful to the word of Jesus and to love one another.[3]

These two commandments were at the very heart of the struggle for the proper interpretation of the tradition over against the opponents at the time of 1 John. If, as we suggest below, the BD is the title *given by the community* to the disciple who is the founding witness of the community and who was also *the author of 1 John,* then this correlation is all the more significant, for he was the one who struggled to have the importance of the (historical) words of Jesus and the importance of mutual love recognized. The BD was the one who, par excellence, saw the importance of these commandments and obeyed them. Thus, he was loved by Jesus because he was so faithful in matters so essential.

Not only did the BD champion the importance of these commandments in his writing, but he also demonstrated his obedience to them by his conduct as presented in the Gospel. His faithfulness is affirmed by the way he does not desert Jesus, nor ever deny his allegiance to him, but remains with Jesus even to the cross. At the foot of the cross, he is entrusted with the care of Jesus' mother, a role that may reflect, at least in part, Jesus' recognition that the BD will *love* his mother. His role is unique; he is the only disciple who is so completely faithful.

The second major element of the BD's identity is that he has a degree of insight and understanding of Jesus that surpasses that of the other disciples. Not only does Jesus share information first with the BD at the Last Supper,

---

3. For a detailed discussion of the commandments, see Appendix 5 (The Johannine Commandments) above.

but the BD is always more perceptive in his understanding, and recognition, of Jesus.

The BD is always presented either explicitly or implicitly in comparison with Peter. In all cases, it is the BD who believes or who recognizes Jesus first. If, as we see in chapter 21, Peter is made the shepherd and the leader of believers, it is implicit that the BD is superior in matters of insight, belief, and love even to the one appointed leader by Jesus. Undoubtedly this superiority was understood in relation to the tradition enshrined in the Synoptics. It reflected the community's estimation of its own traditions within the compass of all other traditions about Jesus.

The third major element of the BD's identity is closely related to the second. Not only is the BD's insight superior to that of Peter and the other disciples, but the community knows that the witness he bears is true. We hear of this first when the disciple recounts his witness of blood and water flowing from the side of Jesus (19:35). But we also hear it in a more general statement at the end of the Gospel (21:24). Naturally, this assurance would be of general importance, but it would also give special assurance to the community that, because this disciple had such insight, his understanding of the tradition as put forward in 1 John would have been the correct one over against the opponents who championed another understanding of the tradition.

The fourth major element of the BD's identity is that he is not to be the shepherd. In chapter 21, the narrator explains that the role of shepherd is given to Peter. At the same time, it is clear from the Gospel that the community recognizes and affirms this role for Peter. The community also recognizes the importance of unity with other sectors of early Christianity and desires to have their relationship with those sectors identified.

Fifth, in 21:18-23, we learn that, while the ultimate destiny of Peter was to die for his beliefs, this was not to be the case with the BD. Both would serve Jesus in the way Jesus wanted. The BD was to be witness to his truth. By the time of the writing of 21:24, the BD had died. Moreover, his death had created a crisis for some because they had understood Jesus to say that the BD would remain until the return of Jesus. But the narrator makes it clear that this was a misunderstanding and that Jesus had only indicated that the destiny of the BD was something that was ultimately up to Jesus himself. The BD would not die for his beliefs; rather, he was to do what Jesus wanted for him.

Sixth, as is clear from what has been said up to this point, the BD was a historical person, not a literary fiction. The contrast with Peter and particularly the concern over his unanticipated death clearly indicate this.

Finally, if we include 18:15-16, we would also know that the BD was an acquaintance of the reigning high priest.

C. PAST PROPOSALS REGARDING
THE IDENTITY OF THE BELOVED DISCIPLE

Because of the uniqueness of the BD and because of his importance for the community, scholars have long sought to learn even more of the identity of this special figure. The traditional answer has been that the BD was to be identified with John, the son of Zebedee. However, there are serious questions about both the external and the internal evidence for this position.[4] The majority of modern scholars have come to conclude that the evidence does not support the view that John was the author.

But John is not the only figure proposed as the BD.[5] A frequent proposal is that the BD is Lazarus. Among the reasons for proposing Lazarus as the BD is the fact that the BD is introduced only late in the ministry, not long after Lazarus has been raised from the dead.[6] Moreover, Lazarus is the only other individual in the Gospel of whom it is said that Jesus loved him (11:5, cf. v. 36). Finally, since Lazarus had been brought back from the dead, it could be plausible to think that he would not die again as was thought of the BD (cf. 21:22-23). However, against this view is the fact that, in 11:5, the love expressed for Lazarus is also expressed for Martha and Mary and that as a whole this love seems to refer to natural affection rather than "religious" love. Without that element, the remaining factors appear to be a matter of coincidence rather than evidence.

A third person proposed as the BD with some frequency is Thomas the apostle. Perhaps the primary argument for seeing Thomas as the BD is that, when Thomas speaks (in 20:25) of wanting to place his hand in the side of Jesus, he seems to reveal a knowledge of this wound that would have been known only to the BD, who alone had been at the foot of the cross.[7] Thus, the BD becomes the one who witnesses to the death of Jesus and also the one who, par excellence, witnesses to his Resurrection. In keeping with this, it would then be the BD (Thomas), the one who has the greatest insight into Jesus, who makes the striking confession of Jesus as "My Lord and my God." Moreover, it is argued that Thomas and Judas are linked with one another, and this linkage makes sense only if Thomas is the BD. Thus, only Judas (6:71) and Thomas (20:24) are specifically identified as members of the Twelve. At the Last Supper, only Judas and Thomas (that is, the BD) know the identity of the betrayer. In keeping with the dualism of the Gospel, Judas is thought

---

4. See the discussion in Appendix 7 (John the Son of Zebedee) above.

5. Charlesworth, in his recent book-length treatment of the topic, lists more than a dozen additional figures who have been suggested by scholars as being the BD.

6. A helpful summary of scholarship proposing this view can be found in Charlesworth, *Beloved* 185-92. See also Culpepper, *Legend* 76-77.

7. The following discussion is summarized from Charlesworth, *Beloved* 225-87. Charlesworth proposes a total of twelve arguments that indicate the BD is Thomas.

to be portrayed as the betrayer and the ultimate unbeliever while Thomas, his opposite, is portrayed as the Beloved and the one who confesses most fully.

Other features that are said to argue for this identification include a proposed symbolism of Thomas as the perfect disciple because he is named *seventh* in the Gospel.[8] It is also argued that the BD (Thomas) had contracted ritual impurity by entering the grave of Jesus and went home to begin purifying himself ritually and it was because of this process that Thomas (the BD) was not with the remainder of the disciples until eight days later. In spite of later reports that Thomas died a martyr's death, the earliest traditions are that his death, like that of the BD, was a natural one.[9]

This accumulation of features is striking, but it has the marks of coincidence rather than of evidence. It is hard to imagine the circumstances under which the BD would at times be referred to by this anonymous title and at other times be referred to by his proper name. It is also reading too much into the account to conclude that the BD went home after seeing the empty tomb because he needed to begin ritual purification. There is simply nothing in the text that even hints at that — and, if he went home because of ritual purification, we would expect it also of Peter, but there is no indication that Peter was not with the disciples for eight days.

Still others have proposed that the BD is not to be understood as a historical figure at all but as a creation of the author.[10] Some would suggest that he is intended to represent the ideal disciple,[11] others that he represents the ideal author.[12] Still others have argued that he is a literary fiction that represents the Johannine community as a whole.[13]

8. Charlesworth, *Beloved* 248-53.

9. Details are given in Charlesworth, *Beloved* 239.

10. Without identifying the BD with a specific individual, Minear ("Beloved") argued that the BD was portrayed in ways that would reflect the description of Benjamin, of whom Moses said (Deut 33:12): "The beloved of the Lord rests in safety; the high God surrounds him all day long; the beloved rests between his shoulders." The similarity is thought to continue in the fact that Moses said this of Benjamin during Moses' farewell speech before his death and the BD appears for the first time in the Gospel during Jesus' farewell speech. Moreover, the BD is said to recline at the breast of Jesus.

11. Hengel (*Question* 78-80) argues that the BD is the ideal disciple but at the same time a historical figure. Bauckham ("Ideal" 34) argues that the BD cannot be the ideal disciple because the ideal disciple gives his life for the sheep as does Peter. There is clearly evidence in early Christianity for understanding martyrdom as the pinnacle of discipleship. However, martyrdom could not be sought out and so was not something that would befall every Christian. If the BD obeys the commandments and so "is loved" by Jesus, this would be a broader model for the ideal disciple within the Johannine community.

12. Bauckham ("Beloved" 24, 35-41) argues that the BD is the ideal witness to the meaning of Jesus' life and that this qualifies him to be the ideal author.

13. K. Quast, *Peter.*

D. IS THE BELOVED DISCIPLE
THE AUTHOR OF THE THIRD EDITION?

From the point of view of this Commentary, it would be reasonable to ask if the BD is the author of the third edition. However, there are three reasons for suggesting that he is not. First, his death is referred to in 21:23. Like Moses in Deuteronomy, he cannot have written the account of his own death. Second, and more importantly, it is inconceivable that the BD would refer to himself as "the disciple whom Jesus loved." To do so would be the utmost arrogance. Rather, it is a title that is applied to an individual by the community. Third, as I have pointed out in the discussion of 1 John and the third edition, the third edition does not simply and wholly represent the theological perspective of 1 John. There are a number of differences in the third edition that take the viewpoint of 1 John a step further. All of these factors suggest that the third edition of the Gospel is not the work of the BD.

At the same time, it seems clear that the third edition seeks to enshrine the witness of the BD within the framework of the Gospel. The third edition holds up the BD as the witness par excellence, and everything that was said earlier about the identity and function of the BD is the work of the author of the third edition.

E. THE BELOVED DISCIPLE AND
THE ELDER OF THE LETTERS

If it is true that 1 John was written *before* the third edition[14] and if it is true that the third edition of the Gospel was completed *after* the death of the BD,[15] then we are perhaps in a position to gain some further clarity about the identity of the BD. In the General Introduction to the Letters, I argued that all three Letters are the work of the same person. If that is the case, then *it may be that the person referred to as "the Elder" in 2 and 3 John and who is also the author of 1 John is the person who is referred to in the third edition as "the disciple whom Jesus loved."*[16]

14. See the discussion of the Date of the Third Edition in Relation to 1 John in the discussion of the Date of the Third Edition in Vol. 1.

15. See the discussion of John 21:23.

16. Others have made this claim (for example, Schnelle, *Antidocetic* 230-31) but the evidence on which the present claim is made is considerably different. See also Culpepper (*Gospel and Epistles* 83-84) who comments: "The suggestion that the Beloved Disciple is a literary representation of the elder has much to commend it. . . . The proposal does raise certain questions of chronology, however. It requires that 2 and 3 John were written before the final redaction of the

If the sequence of composition suggests this, we will see that there is also substantial internal evidence that this is so. We will look first at features of 1 John that confirm this hypothesis and then at those features in 3 John which do the same.

1. 1 John, the Elder, and the Beloved Disciple

It was argued above that the First Letter was written before the Gospel reached its final form. If this is true, we have the foundation for an explanation of the relationship between the BD of the Gospel and the author of the First Letter. The BD and the author of 1 John share three distinctive characteristics. (1) They both claim (or have it claimed for them) that they are *eye*witnesses. The author of 1 John claims this for himself (1 John 1:1-4), and in the third edition it is claimed for the BD (John 19:35; 21:24). (2) They both claim to be, and are recognized to be, witnesses to the community. They take their experience of the events and transmit it to the community. Moreover, these are the only ones who are identified as such. (3) A third feature, which is less crucial but nevertheless striking, is that both the BD and the author of 2 and 3 John are said to have lived to an old age. This is evident from the Gospel's statement about the possibility of the BD living until the return of Jesus, and it is evident from the self-designation of the author of 2 and 3 John as "the Elder."[17]

The most plausible explanation of these similarities is that the BD is, in fact, the Elder, who is the author of 1 John (although unnamed) and also the author of 2 and 3 John, and the one who is the source of the tradition, particularly the tradition as enshrined in the third edition. The one who most clearly defined the tradition over against those opponents and who called himself simply "the Elder" is recognized and honored in the final edition of the Gospel by the title "the disciple whom Jesus loved."

2. 3 John, the Elder, and the Beloved Disciple

If 3 John was written prior to the third edition of the Gospel, then the statement of the Elder in 3 John 12 ("And we bear witness also and you know that our witness is true") was written prior to the statements in John 19:35 ("And the one who saw has borne witness and his witness is true and that one knows that he speaks the truth, so that you also may believe") and John 21:24 ("This is the dis-

---

Gospel and that the elder died before the redactor of the Gospel inserted the references to the Beloved Disciple. This sequence of events is not impossible." The view proposed in this Commentary supports that view with more detailed evidence.

17. So also Smith, *Epistles* 18.

ciple who bears witness about these things and who has written these things, and we know that his witness is true").

It should be recalled that in 3 John 12, the Elder is making a claim for his witness, a claim for which he alone is responsible but which he is confident that Gaius will recognize as valid: "we bear witness also and you know that our witness is true." This is a claim that is made by no other individual in the Johannine tradition — except Jesus.[18] The Elder has asserted that his witness is true in a way that even the witness of "all" and of "the truth itself" cannot be. And he knows that Gaius will recognize that the Elder's witness is true.

At the same time, twice in the Gospel, the claim is made *for* the BD that his witness is true (John 19:35 and 21:24), and in 21:24 we find that the writer says the same thing that the Elder had expected of Gaius, namely the confirmation that "we know that his witness is true." Thus, the author of the third edition does for the BD what the Elder expects Gaius to do for him. The author of the third edition does not consider himself on a level with the BD but only one who confirms that the witness of the BD is true. However, the fact that the Elder had made this claim for himself indicates that the Elder spoke with an authority that the author of the third edition does not. The authority that the Elder claimed for himself in 3 John is the authority that is attributed to the BD by the author in the third edition of the Gospel. The most reasonable conclusion is that the one who calls himself the Elder in 2 and 3 John is the one who is called "the disciple whom Jesus loved" by others in the third edition of the Gospel.

In 3 John 12, the Elder does not speak as "I" but as "we." It was pointed out that the evidence is not clear whether this was an authorial "we" or indicated that the author spoke as a member of a group. Perhaps we are able to have a better perspective on that issue now that we have examined the text in a wider context. It would seem that the answer lies somewhere "between" the two alternatives given above. It does seem that in both cases there are those who accept the witness and an authoritative individual who gives it. Yet, when that individual writes, he wishes to assure his readers that he is not the only one who holds that position. He is part of a community, even if he is the central authoritative voice within that community. The "we" are the ones who hold the same views as the Elder, and these are opposed to the "they" who have gone out. The source of the witness is the Elder, but the community who recognizes and accepts that witness stands with him — and when he writes, he recalls that.

The major difficulty with this view, according to Brown, is that the Letters do not present the Elder as having the authority a first-generation disciple would

---

18. That the "we" in this verse does not refer to the Johannine school is discussed in the Note to 3 John 12.

have.[19] As evidence, Brown points to the Elder's ineffectiveness against the secessionists (in 1 John) and the Elder's lack of effective authority against Diotrephes (in 3 John). However, the presumption that an apostle would have been successful against a group such as the secessionists is just that — a presumption. We have seen throughout that the truth of the Johannine tradition rested on "witness." If witness is the chief means of establishing the truth, the author of 1 (and 2 and 3) John can only rest on "witness" against the opponents. In this sense, the author's argument could indeed seem weak; he can only argue that this witness is informed by the Spirit of Truth. The fact that the opponents also claim a spirit (as is evident from 1 John 4:1-4) necessarily means that his views would have less force than would those of one who appealed to either personal authority or that of some office. This lack of authority other than that of "witness" would be the case in the confrontation with the opponents of 1 John, but it would also be true of the confrontation with Diotrephes. Resorting to "witness" and confirmation by the Spirit was one of the great weaknesses of the Johannine tradition in time of crisis, as Brown himself later recognizes.[20]

If this view is confirmed by a convergence of evidence from a variety of features within the Johannine literature, it is also confirmed, I believe, by the unresolved difficulties in the commonly proposed view of the Johannine school, in which the Elder is one who represents the generation after that of the BD — and is therefore not the BD himself.

In the common understanding of the Johannine school, there is a line of authoritative "witnesses" stretching from the BD, through the "we" of John 21:24, to the Elder of 2 and 3 John, and also to the "we" of which he is a part.[21] But, if this is so, then there appears to be a "gap" in the line of authority between the BD (who has authority), the "we" of John 21:24 (who do not), the Elder of 3 John 12 (who has authority), and those like Gaius (who, like the "we" of John 21:24, recognizes and accepts the authority of another but who does not have authority himself). Does this describe a line of authorities? Certainly a distinction is being

19. Brown, *Epistles* 650.

20. Brown (*Churches* 121-23) sees this as the fourth and greatest of the weaknesses of the Johannine tradition. "In the divisive situation encountered in the Johannine epistle. . . . it is very clear that he [the author] is counting on the fact that his readers have been anointed with the Spirit and so can recognize the truth from him when they hear it. If the author were a presbyter-bishop in the model of the Pastorals, he could silence his adversaries by his own authority (Titus 1:11)" (122).

21. Brown's words (*Community* 102) are: ". . . I use it [the term 'school'] for those who felt so close to the Beloved Disciple that they sought to pass on his tradition through written interpretation. These include the Evangelist, the redactor of the Gospel (and any other writers involved in it), the author of the Epistles, and the tradition-bearers with whom they associated themselves in their writing — in short, the 'we' of John 21:24 . . . and of I John 1:1-2. . . . It is as a long-lived representative of such a Johannine school that 'the presbyter' speaks."

made between those who are authoritative witnesses and those who are not but who should accept that authority.[22] Thus, it would seem that this series is not an extended line of authoritative tradition-bearers but rather a series in which there are at most two individuals who claim (or have claimed for them) true authority as a witness. Further, the fact that the Elder *claims this for himself* makes his claim more radical than that *made by others for the BD,* since, like the title Beloved Disciple itself, it is not something that the BD claims for himself.[23]

In addition, it is curious, as Culpepper has pointed out,[24] that, if the BD was the authoritative source to whom the community appealed at the time of the writing of the Gospel, there is no appeal to the BD at the time of the Letters (presuming they were written after the Gospel). Instead of such an appeal, we find in 3 John a figure who claims for himself the witness value attributed to the BD in the Gospel.[25]

If what is proposed here is a simpler view of the relationship between these two figures, it is also a simpler view of the Johannine school.[26] It also brings together in a more plausible way a number of aspects of the relationship between the Letters and the Gospel.

3. Conclusion: The Elder of the Letters, the Beloved Disciple, and Papias' John the Elder

Finally, we may ask whether it is possible to go further and to identify the Elder of the Letters with John the Elder mentioned by Papias. The possibility of this identification, which has appeared from time to time in scholarship, has gained more popularity recently.[27]

22. It could be argued that there were tradition-bearers with various charisms, some who witnessed, some who wrote, etc. But there is simply not the slightest evidence for such a view.

23. In 3 John 12, the Elder witnesses to Demetrius. In 1 John, the Elder witnesses to the events of Jesus' ministry (1:1-4).

24. Culpepper, *School* 281-82. Culpepper speculates that perhaps the opponents were claiming the authority of the BD for themselves, but it must be realized that this is simple speculation. There is no hint that the BD was taken as an authority by the opponents. At the same time, the Elder of 3 John claims precisely this authority.

25. Like Culpepper, Brown (*Community* 103) also suggests that both sides were claiming the authority of the BD, but this is not the case. It is clear from 1 John that both sides in the crisis are claiming to have the Spirit (cf. esp. 1 John 4:1-6), not the BD. As was discussed above, it was precisely this reliance on inner guidance by the Spirit that made defining the parameters of the tradition so difficult. However, recourse to the figure of the BD represents a stage beyond that of recourse to the Spirit. The First Letter of John did not have recourse to an authoritative figure since the person who was later to become that authoritative figure was himself speaking in 1 John.

26. It would also call for a modification of what has become the common view of the Johannine school.

27. Most recently this position has been espoused at length by Hengel *(Question)* and

In favor of this identification is the fact that Papias' "John the Elder" is the only *individual figure* identified as "the Elder" in the first two centuries of the Christian era. In addition, this individual was said to be a disciple (and therefore an eyewitness to the ministry of Jesus) but not one of the Twelve. That the author of 2 and 3 John identified himself as "the Elder" would suggest that, in his case, this title was not an ecclesiastical title but a term that had a unique personal meaning. The fact that it was this title and not some other that "the Elder" adopted suggests that he was of advanced age. We have seen that this correlates well with John 21:22-23, which speaks about the apparently advanced age of the BD, something that is recognized by most scholars.[28] Thus, there are four respects in which the use of "the Elder" in 2 and 3 John is consistent with the identification of Papias' John as "the Elder." This must be said to be significant evidence! Consequently, although it probably cannot ever be proven, *there is, it seems, a very strong likelihood that the Elder of the Johannine tradition, the Beloved Disciple, and Papias' John the Elder are one and the same individual.*

Bauckham ("Papias") who claim that John the Elder is the same as the Elder of 2 and 3 John and also the Beloved Disciple of the Gospel. Bauckham ("Papias" 26) refers to six other scholars who, in the past, have proposed the threefold identification of BD, John the Elder (of Papias), and the Elder of the Johannine Letters: Delff, *Geschichte;* Sanday, *Criticism,* cf. 17-18, 98-99; Burney, *Aramaic,* cf. 133-49; Burkitt, *Gospel,* cf. 247-55; Colson, *L'énigme;* and Rigato, "Apostolico," cf. 451-83.

28. See Bauckham, "Papias" 27, n. 16.

Index of Authors

Index of Scripture and Other Ancient Literature